Dictionary of American Young Adult Fiction, 1997–2001

Dictionary of American Young Adult Fiction, 1997–2001

Books of Recognized Merit

Alethea K. Helbig
and
Agnes Regan Perkins

GREENWOOD PRESS
Westport, Connecticut • London

Library of Congress Cataloging-in-Publication Data

Helbig, Alethea.
    Dictionary of American young adult fiction, 1997–2001 : books of recognized merit /
Alethea K. Helbig and Agnes Regan Perkins.
        p. cm.
    Includes bibliographical references and index.
    ISBN 0-313-32430-1 (alk. paper)
    1. Young adult fiction, American—Bio-bibliography—Dictionaries. 2. American
fiction—20th century—Bio-bibliography—Dictionaries. 3. American fiction—20th
century—Dictionaries. 4. Young adult fiction, American—Dictionaries. 5. Young adult
libraries—Book lists. 6. Young adults—Books and reading. 7. Best books. I. Perkins,
Agnes. II. Title.
PS374.Y57H45   2004
813'.54099283'03—dc22   2003056804

British Library Cataloguing in Publication Data is available.

Library of Congress Catalog Card Number: 2003056804
ISBN: 0-313-32430-1

First published in 2004

Greenwood Press, 88 Post Road West, Westport, CT 06881
An imprint of Greenwood Publishing Group, Inc.
www.greenwood.com

Printed in the United States of America

The paper used in this book complies with the
Permanent Paper Standard issued by the National
Information Standards Organization (Z39.48-1984).

10   9   8   7   6   5   4   3   2   1

Contents

List of Entries

Preface

Dictionary of American Young Adult Fiction, 1997–2001: Books of Recognized Merit deals with books that eminent selection committees have singled out as appealing to and appropriate for young adults. It is a companion to our several dictionaries of children's fiction that cover books from 1859 to 1999, our critical references on multicultural literature for young readers, and our volume on myths and hero tales, all published by Greenwood Press. This *Dictionary* is intended, as are the previous references, for the use of librarians, teachers, literary scholars, researchers in comparative social history, parents, booksellers, publishers, editors—everyone who is concerned with young adult literature in any way. Its 741 entries treat such elements as titles, authors, characters, and settings based on 290 books by 242 authors.

As university teachers of literature for children and young adults for more than thirty years and as people trained in the study of literature as literature, we are convinced that books for young readers must be judged by the same criteria as those by which books for adults are judged, keeping in mind, of course, the intended audience. We also firmly believe that books for young people should be appreciated for themselves as examples of imaginative literature and not merely as tools for other disciplines, although, for example, they can enrich the social studies curriculum.

With these aspects in mind, we are gratified to note that many fine books are represented in this *Dictionary*. Some have been written specifically with a teenage audience in mind, while others are books published for adults that the selection committees deemed appealing to a younger audience and worthy of inclusion. Thus, the range in subject matter and reading skill is broad, spanning later middle school and junior high to well beyond high school. It is obvious that the selection committees are well aware that one size does not fit all young people. Teenagers have many interests and levels of ability in reading and understanding. The books examined here are intended to satisfy that range of interests and ability.

As in our previous books, the entries in *Dictionary of American Young Adult Fiction, 1997–2001: Books of Recognized Merit* are of several types, chiefly title, author, and character. A book's title entry gives a plot summary and a critical assessment from the literary standpoint. Other entries about a particular book provide additional information about that book. Taken together, and also considering the author entry, they form a short essay, complete in itself for classroom or library use, available to serve as a valuable starting point for research, discussion, and enjoyment.

Author entries focus on those aspects of the writers' lives most relevant to literature for young people and to the particular novels in this *Dictionary*. Several other published and online sources give biographical information about authors, but none considers all those whose books are in this reference. Having the information in the same volume is not only of convenience for researchers but also of special value to libraries on limited budgets.

Title entries consist of bibliographical information; the subgenre to which the book belongs; a plot summary incorporating the plot problem, if any, significant episodes, and the conclusion; a note about sequels, if any; critical comments; and awards and citations in abbreviated form. (A list of the complete names of the awards and citations, along with their abbreviations, follows this Preface.) Entries vary in length. Since some plots can be summarized more briefly and critical judgments stated more succinctly for some books than for others, the number of words in an entry does not indicate the importance or quality of the book.

A few books that appeared in one of our earlier dictionaries or critical references[1] have received additional awards during this period. The entries for these books are shorter and refer readers to the more complete evaluation in the earlier volumes.

While most readers will be familiar with the terms that we have used for subgenres, a few may need explanation. By *realistic fiction*, we mean books in which events could have happened some time in the world as we know it, as opposed to an imaginary or fantastic world, and not necessarily that the action is convincing or plausible. *Historical fiction* includes those books in which actual historical events or figures function in the plot, as in *The Secret Diary of Anne Boleyn* or *Shakespeare's Scribe*, or in which the specific period is essential to the action and in which the story could not have occurred in any other time, as in *Heroes*, *Alice's Tulips*, or *Nory Ryan's Song*. Books that are merely set in the past, like *Go and Come Back*, *Gold Dust*, *Gideon's People*, *The Boxer*, *The Chatham School Affair*, and *A Long Way from Chicago*, we call *period fiction*. Although all plots are driven by problems, we have used the term problem novel in the more recent sense to refer to those stories in which social, physical, or psychological concerns dominate, as in *Bad*, *Kissing Doorknobs*, *Silent to the Bone*, and *The Luckiest Girl in the World*.

Author entries contain dates and places of birth and death, if available; education and vocational background; major contribution to literature; significant facts of the author's life that might have a bearing on the work cited; titles that have won awards, if pertinent; frequently, titles of other publications, usually with brief information about them; and critical judgments where they can safely be made. Authors whose biographical entries have appeared in earlier volumes are again included, but usually with briefer sketches and references to the original entries.

Character entries include physical and personality traits for important, memorable, or particularly unusual characters who are not covered sufficiently in the plot summary. They focus on such aspects as how the characters function in the plot, how they relate to the protagonist, and whether the characterization is credible and skillful. Characters are classified by the name by which they are most often referred to or by the name by which the protagonist refers to them, for example, Grampa Freegy, Mr. Moreland, Uncle Zeno McBride, and Mitch. The name is also cross-referenced in the Index under the most likely possibilities. If the character's surname does not often appear in the story, it usually does not appear in the Index; when it is included, it is usually as a family name: Boleyn family, LaBauve family, and so on. If the plot summary gives all the significant information about characters, as with many protagonists, they are not discussed in separate character entries. All major characters, however, are listed in the Index.

Miscellaneous entries include particularly significant settings and elements that need explanation beyond mention in the title entry.

Every book has title and author entries, and all entries are in alphabetical order for convenience. Asterisks within entries indicate that the item has a separate entry elsewhere in the book. Entries are intended to supplement, not duplicate, one another, and when read together, provide a unified essay on the book.

As well as the list of awards and their abbreviations that follows this Preface, a list of books classified by awards is in the back of the volume. The Index includes all the items for which there are entries and such elements as cross-references, major characters for whom there are no separate

entries, specific place settings, settings by period, and such matters as themes and subjects, books of first-person narration, unusual narrative structures, significant tone, authors' pseudonyms, illustrators, and genres.

Of the 290 books examined here, about 80 were published for adults. The committees have chosen from well-known writers like Barbara Kingsolver and Martha Grimes. Many published for young people are similarly by well-known hands, among them Cynthia Voigt, Richard Peck, Chris Lynch, and Gary Paulsen. All these are writers who can be counted on to tell a good story well. There are newer writers, too, less well-known voices whose style and ideas open new vistas, like Adam Bagdasarian, Ernesto Quiñonez, Adrian Fogelin, Dianne Gray—all of whom are represented by first novels—Kristen D. Randle, Nancy Butts, Anne Isaacs, and Patrick O'Leary. Very few books appear on more than one award list, and there are 242 authors for the 290 books, two factors that may indicate, as we have noted with our other recent dictionaries, that critics do not agree about what the best books are. It may also indicate that publishers are welcoming fresh voices, a situation to be applauded.

As might be expected when books range from middle school to adult, subject matter is varied, as are the demands on reading ability, intellect, comprehension, and experiential response. The most difficult books, again as expected, are by and large those for adults, while the problem, family life, and adventure stories are generally the least demanding in terms of scope and vocabulary, but not necessarily in apprehension.

In many instances, however, it is the sheer length of the adult book rather than content or use of language that makes the adult book more demanding. Some adult books require generous amounts of persistence to complete because they are very long and the print is small, relatively speaking. One of these is Michael Crichton's *Timeline*, which offers substance for thought and excitement but requires sturdy perseverance to reach the end. Some books intended for teens, however, while not difficult in vocabulary or substance, like *The Girls* by Amy Goldman Koss, a problem novel in a school setting, require persistence simply because the subject matter and characters become repetitive and tiresome. While such a broad range places extra burdens on the adult who may be choosing for a young reader, the dividend is that the breadth opens exciting opportunities for readers and those who may be advising them.

Historical and period fiction, which have fallen behind among books intended for young readers, are represented by some skillfully fashioned books for both audiences. In fact, more than 50 of the total 290 fall into this subgenre. These range in setting from ancient times, like *Song of the Magdalene*, about Palestine in the time of Jesus, and *The Sand-Reckoner*, about the mathematician Archimedes who lived in the third century B.C., through the American Revolution with *Cast Two Shadows: The American Revolution in the South*; the yellow fever plague in Philadelphia in 1793 with *Fever 1793*; the times of Henry VIII with *The Secret Diary of Anne Boleyn* and *Mary, Bloody Mary*; slavery in the American South with *Stealing Freedom*; the American Civil War with *Soldier's Heart: A Novel of the Civil War*; the Great Depression with *Esperanza Rising* and *A Year Down Yonder* to World War II with *Last Days of Summer* and *Torn Thread*; and the activist days of the 1960s and 1970s with *Caucasia*. Many

of these are skillfully crafted, powerful stories that bring their periods alive.

Fantasy and science fiction are somewhat fewer in number, but are represented by strong books, most of which were intended for adults. A large number of these are futuristic and not only create convincing worlds and have a good measure of adventure and tension, but, as good fantasy usually does, they invite the reader to scrutinize today's world of reality. *The Last Day*, set mostly in Jerusalem and its environs at the end of the second millennium, features a young woman who calls herself Jeza. She takes to task such institutions as churches, for failing to assume their obligations to the unfortunate.

The fantasy *Heartlight* sweeps across most of the twentieth century, postulates an ongoing war between good and evil, suggests that the most devastating events of the time were those caused by evil, like World War II, the assassination of John F. Kennedy, and similar highly disrupting occasions, and intimates that good people have an obligation to align themselves on the side of good to prevent future such disasters. *Higher Education* strongly criticizes present-day schools, and *Night Flying* explores the limits and responsibilities of those in power.

Adventure and survival stories are fewer, but many are memorable. *Jason's Gold* follows a boy who sets out for the goldfields during the Klondike rush, and *Cloudy in the West* and *Dust Devils* are good old-fashioned westerns. Mystery-detective and thrillers are among the best for sheer reading pleasure. *Nathan's Run* and *At All Costs* concern innocent people fleeing from authorities; *Killer.app* and *Ordeal* involve terrorists; *People of the Mist*, a historical fiction, finds a Native American tribal leader solving a murder in the fashion of Hercule Poirot or Columbo; and

The Ghost in the Tokaido Inn overflows with gothic conventions as a mystery in Japanese samurai times is solved. Sports novels, chiefly about baseball and basketball, are not only filled with lively and authentic details about games, they also tackle interpersonal relationships and moral issues. *Choosing Up Sides*, for example, concerns a left-handed pitcher whose preacher father refuses to let him play because he believes the left side is the devil's side, creating moral, religious, and interpersonal dilemmas for the boy.

Problem novels, long a popular subgenre for young people, are, not unexpectedly, well represented, and most of them, also not unexpectedly, were written with a young adult audience in mind. Numerous issues are tackled, like gangs, incarcerated girls, interracial romance, unmarried mothers, parents obsessed with their deceased children, and pressures toward conformity. Mental illness appears in several novels, while other problems, in addition to the usual ones of romance and parent–child tension, include obsessive compulsive disorder, identifying one's gender orientation, obesity, and anorexia. Abuse, including rape, occurs with frequency in both domestic and romantic situations.

Few books fall into the humor category, unfortunately, although many have moments of levity that offset tension or seriousness. *I Want to Buy a Vowel* concerns a naive Guatemalan immigrant who has picked up phrases, without knowing their meaning, from American television. *Love Among the Walnuts* involves eccentric residents of a retirement home, *Never Trust a Dead Man* is a lighthearted ghost story, and in *The Princess Diaries*, a girl ironically resists becoming the heir of a European principality. *Sunshine Rider: The First Vegetarian Western* is an incident-

filled, tongue-in-cheek tale of a trail drive filled with a wild assortment of characters and raucous incidents.

Not unexpectedly, a good percentage of books focus on racial, ethnic, or religious minorities. *No Strange Fire* and *Gideon's People* deal thoughtfully with the pull the outside world has on young Amish men, the first in a mystery setting and the second in a family situation. *Bodega Dreams*, *Buried Onions*, and *Esperanza Rising* feature Hispanics, and *People of the Mist*, *Power*, and *The Window* (by Michael Dorris) involve Native Americans. Most of the novels in this category concern African Americans, like *Dangerous Skies*, about an unfair judicial system; *Crossing Jordan*, about interracial friendship; and *Imani All Mine*, about a single-parent, never-married mother and inner-city violence.

Realistic novels set outside the United States have become rare in books for young readers, except for World War II and Holocaust stories. Here memorable titles not only give a strong sense of setting in time and place but also address social and/or political issues as well. *Habibi* is set in present-day Jerusalem against the Israeli–Palestinian conflict. *Homeless Bird* tells of a widow's problems in India, *Torn Thread* and *Stones in the Water* deal with slave laborers during World War II in Europe, and *Forgotten Fire* takes place in Turkey during the Armenian Holocaust. *Adem's Cross* takes place in Kosovo; *Rebel: A Tibetan Odyssey* is set in Tibet; and *The Tree of Red Stars* revolves around political repression in modern Uruguay, while *Many Stones*, *The Poisonwood Bible*, and *No Condition Is Permanent* are set in recent Africa.

While variety is the key word in describing the books examined, not all of them are equally well written, of course.

First-person narration is all too frequent, appearing in about one-half of the books and in these too often the narrators are uninteresting in themselves as persons. What holds the interest is the setting or plot. Too many, particularly adult novels, ramble on, exhibiting their writers' tendency toward self-indulgence with words and subject. These novels could have benefited from more careful editing. Far too many novels written specifically for adolescents plow old fields, like teenage pregnancy, drugging-drinking parties, and dysfunctional families.

Equally as many, however, are to be applauded for innovation in concept or structure, like *The Gift*, in which interior stories are layered; *Exegesis*, about artificial intelligence; *The Rover*, which plays engagingly and deliberately with well-known fantasy elements; *Mind's Eye*, related entirely in dialogue; *King of Shadows*, in which a fantasy framework encloses a well-evoked historical fiction about William Shakespeare; and *Sirena*, a lyrical, engaging look at part of the Trojan War from the perspective of a siren. Among the most compelling is *Stuck in Neutral*, where events are seen through the eyes of a boy born with cerebral palsy, a story notable for the boy's view of self and handicap and also for his relationship with his father who, he fears, may be planning to end what the father thinks is the boy's misery by killing him. The book looks nondidactically at the handicap and nonjudgmentally at euthanasia.

While reading habits of teens are characterized by reading backward, taking up easier books that may seem enticing, and also by sampling harder ones that lie ahead, this selection of novels gives the age plenty of material to test the waters in both directions. The range of possibilities is wide. Young readers can be as eclectic as they like by choosing from the books examined in this *Dictionary*. They will find much good reading here.

As with our earlier dictionaries and their several companion volumes, we have read every book that is discussed in this *Dictionary* and have done the research and writing for it. We are fortunate, as in the past, to have had valuable assistance from a number of sources. Specifically, we thank Margaret Best and other staff members at the Eastern Michigan University Bruce T. Halle Library; the Ann Arbor, Michigan, District Library Youth Room and its branches; the Peters Branch of the Ypsilanti, Michigan, District Library; and the Venice and Winter Haven, Florida, public libraries. We thank them all, not only for their help in locating books and their valuable suggestions but also for their ongoing interest, support, and encouragement.

NOTE

1. Reference works (all by Helbig and Perkins and published by Greenwood Press) cited in some entries are:

Dictionary of American Children's Fiction, 1960–1984: Books of Recognized Merit (1986)

Dictionary of American Children's Fiction, 1985–1989: Books of Recognized Merit (1993)

Dictionary of American Children's Fiction, 1990–1994: Books of Recognized Merit (1996)

Dictionary of American Children's Fiction, 1995–1999: Books of Recognized Merit (2002)

This Land Is Our Land (1994)

Many Peoples, One Land (2001)

Key to Awards and Citations

Alex   Alex Award for Top Ten Adult Books for Young Adults

ALA/YA   American Library Association Best Books for Young Adults

Booklist   *Booklist* Adult Books for Young Adults

NYPL   New York Public Library Books for the Teen Age

Printz Honor   Michael L. Printz Award for Excellence in Young Adult Literature
                Honor Books

Printz Winner   Michael L. Printz Award for Excellence in Young Adult Literature
                Winner

A

ABELOVE, JOAN   Received her B.A. from Barnard College and her Ph.D. in cultural anthropology from City University of New York. Her experiences conducting doctoral research in the Amazon jungle in the early 1970s provided material for *Go and Come Back** (DK Ink, 1998), which was selected for young adults by the American Library Association. *Saying It Out Loud** (DK Ink, 1999), about a girl whose mother dies of a brain tumor, was also an ALA/YA choice. Abelove lives with her husband and son in New York City. For more information about Abelove and a title entry, see *Dictionary, 1995–1999* [*Go and Come Back*].

ABOGEE KIM (*Necessary Roughness**) Father of Chan, the narrator, and Young* and husband of O-Ma* Kim, Korean Americans, who settle in Iron River, Minnesota, where they encounter ethnic discrimination. Abogee is conscientious and loyal to his family to a fault. He works very hard in the family's convenience store, Froggie's 24-Hour Express, and insists that the children help out, but later he sees that football is an important aspect of his son's life and hires someone else to help him. It is possible, however, that it is less out of love for his son and more from the realization that Chan's skill at the game is gaining the family recognition and customers that he releases Chan from working in the store. Abogee loaned money to Bong, his brother, more than the family could afford, and now pays debts Bong has incurred, causing hardship for his wife and children. A small, thin man, a chemist by education, Abogee is often tense and irritable. He finds it hard to drop old Korean ways; for example, he belches at the table, an old-world way of showing appreciation, and places great store in getting good grades and being deferential to one's elders. He thinks Americans are crude and discourteous.

ABRAHAM (*Jim the Boy**)   Black field hand of the McBride family, who first appears in the story when Jim Glass is trying to help his uncles weed the corn. Abraham saves Jim, whom he always addresses as Mr. Glass, and Jim's pal, Penn

Carson, from the town toughs who claim as their own the Aliceville back alley into which the boys have blundered. He pulls a knife at the critical moment, and the toughs run. One tough soon returns with the town policeman, having told him that Abraham tried to knife him. When the policeman sees Abraham cutting up an apple and the graffiti that deface the walls, he gets the drift of what has been going on and hurries the tough away. During all this, Abraham has been softly reciting Psalm 23. The incident reflects attitudes toward and the position of blacks in the early-twentieth-century, pre–Civil Rights South.

ACHILLES (*Ender's Shadow**)   The bully whom Poke selects at Bean's suggestion to protect her little band on the Rotterdam streets. Because he has one damaged leg, he is not respected by the other big boys who dominate the streets, but he is smart enough to see the advantage of taking on Poke's crew and calling the affection-starved kids his "family." By badly beating one bully, with the help of stone-wielding little children, he establishes his place in the soup-kitchen line, intimidates the other big boys, and by smarmy politeness sucks up to the women running the kitchen and wins their favor. This brings him to the attention of Sister Carlotta, who is looking for highly intelligent and leader-type children for the Battle School of the International Space Fleet. Because he has been humiliated by Poke in her original approach to him, Achilles bides his time, tricks her into being alone with him at night on a dock, and kills her. Bean realizes that Achilles plans to kill him, too. Believing Bean's accusations, Sister Carlotta switches her support from Achilles, but he has already been scheduled for operations to repair his leg and his tests impress the hierarchy at the Battle School. Eventually, they send him to the orbiting Battle School over her protests, and Bean must work out an elaborate plan to save himself and get a tape-recorded confession to a series of murders by Achilles. Although he is returned to Earth and sent to a mental hospital, by the time Bean gets back to Earth, Achilles is again on the streets, and, since he is a psychopath and unforgiving, he once again is a threat.

AN ACQUAINTANCE WITH DARKNESS
(Rinaldi*, Ann, Gulliver, 1997)   Historical novel set in Washington, D.C., from the beginning of April to mid-July 1865, revolving around the end of the American Civil War, the assassination of President Lincoln, and the practice of body snatching to secure cadavers for medical research and instruction. Emily Bransby Pigbush, 14, the narrator, lives with her genteelly raised, Southern mother, Mary Louise, who is dying of the Wasting Disease (tuberculosis). Their house is next door to that of the Surratts, known to be Rebel sympathizers. Their daughter, Annie*, 17, and son, Johnny*, 20, are Emily's best friends. Since her mother and Uncle* Valentine Bransby, a respected doctor, medical scientist, and benefactor of the poor, are on the outs, Emily plans to go to live with the Surratts upon Mary Louise's death. Although warned against this by Marietta, a teacher one-eighth black and a good friend of Uncle Valentine; by Maude, his African American housekeeper; by Robert* deGraaf, his young assistant; and by Uncle Valentine, Emily refuses her uncle's offer to live with him in his elegant palatial house. After Lincoln is shot at Ford's Theater and police seek Johnny and John Wilkes Booth, who is a friend of the Surratts, Uncle

Valentine hurries Emily off for safety to his house. Soon after, he shows her papers indicating that he is her legal guardian. Although everyone speaks very highly of him and his patients love him, Emily suspects him of devious conniving and of grave robbing and body snatching. Even after the Surratts are arrested, briefly including Annie, and a price is posted for Johnny, Emily still suspects Uncle Valentine and thinks she may go to live with an aunt in Richmond, although she knows the city is starving. While Uncle Valentine is doing what he can to get lawyers for the Surratts and to help his good friend, Dr. Mudd, the historical physician who attended Booth, Emily spies on him and twists what she sees and hears to his disfavor. Finally, she packs her bags and sets off for the train to Richmond. She gets caught up in a veterans' parade and is brought home by Robert. He admits they do body-snatch but only because they need to learn more about human anatomy in order to help people. He explains that the laws specify that only the bodies of criminals may be used and the current supply is insufficient. After Annie, who loyally visits her mother in prison up until Mary is hanged, candidly tells Emily that she is selfish and simply does not know what suffering is, Emily sees things in a different light. She comforts Annie during the hanging, realizes that she loves Robert, apologizes to him for her uncharitable and often surly and juvenile behavior, and tells him she wants to become a nurse. Except for Emily, her mother, her uncle, and Robert, almost all the characters are historical, and most of the events that occur in the city actually happened. The novel is full and rich with details. Its weakest link, at first thought, appears to be the protagonist, headstrong, deceptive, not especially likable. It is these qualities, however, and her gradual understanding that there may be two sides to every question that inform the reader credibly about the era and issues, in particular the state of medical science. The night-blooming flowers that grow in Uncle Valentine's backyard and appear in the plot here and there provide metaphoric texture (good things do happen under cover of night, the time when the flowers bloom and the snatchings take place). The times—the general unrest, rumors, confusion, anger, the poverty and despair of the freed slaves—are so clearly depicted that one almost feels one is there. An extensive, valuable author's note giving background and a bibliography conclude the book. ALA/YA.

ADAH PRICE (*The Poisonwood Bible**) Birth-damaged daughter of Nathan, the fundamentalist Baptist preacher who takes his family to Africa to minister to the heathen. Adah is thought to have been starved for nourishment in the womb by her twin, so that half her brain does not develop, causing hemiplegia. Because she drags one foot, has one weak arm, and almost never talks, she is thought to be retarded until she starts school, where, along with her twin, Leah*, she is declared to be gifted. Mathematically, she is near genius level, but she also reads widely, loves poetry, especially that of Emily Dickinson, and views life from a cynical, sideways point of view. She can read as well backward as forward, and often thinks in palindromes: "Ada," "Damn mad!" or, longer, "Elapsed or esteemed, all Ade meets erodes pale!" In Kilanga she spies on the pilot, Eeben Axelroot, and knows he is a smuggler, has a radio, and is certainly a political agent and probably a double agent. Her great fear is being left behind. When the ants invade the village, her mother, Orleanna*, stares at her baby, Ruth* May, and crippled Adah, and takes Ruth May to save her. Adah saves herself by grabbing the leg of a husky man and being borne bumping along the road to the river. After they leave Kilanga, Orleanna manages to get herself and Adah back to Georgia, where Adah tells the head of admissions at Emory University that she must go to his school and then to medical school although she has had no formal education beyond part of elementary school. After she does astonishingly well on entrance exams, he finds funds for her tuition because her father was a veteran. In medical school, a neurologist questions whether her physical impairment is necessary, and in a long experiment trains her to cross-coordinate and walk straight. After medical school, however, she finds she cannot bear to save premature or damaged children when so many perfectly formed African youngsters die of disease or starvation. She switches to epidemiology and laboratory study of viruses.

ADAM KNOTT (*Up Jumps the Devil**) Older brother of Deborah Knott, the protagonist and narrator, and twin of Zach Knott. Adam unexpectedly returns from California, where he has been living in a big house with his wife and children, who attend exclusive prep schools. He has a Ph.D. in microelectronics, the only member of the Knott family except Deborah to have such advanced education. His way of life, with a big, well-appointed house, two Jaguars, a four-car garage, and a boat, is lavish, particularly by Colleton County, North Carolina, standards. It is learned that he has been downsized by his firm and has lost almost everything he has. Although the family and people in their community resist selling to a developer, Adam decides he must sell the few acres

he owns, even though the sale will give the developer an opening in the Knott region. Adam's circumstances make him a murder suspect.

ADEM'S CROSS (Mead*, Alice, Farrar, 1996)   Realistic novel of the desperately difficult lives of the people of Albanian descent in Kosovo, which used to be a province of Yugoslavia. Although they make up 85 percent of the population, they are dominated and oppressed by the Serbs who control the police and army and are determined to stamp out any movement toward independence in the area. The conflict is seen through the eyes of the narrator, Adem, 13, starting in 1992. At first his resentment centers mostly on his cousin Besim, 16, a lazy, vain boy who has come to live with them because his mother has just died and seems to be favored by Adem's father. There are harassments by the Serbs, including the periodic tear-gassing of the Albanian section of the school, where the children are segregated from their former friends and classmates, but they have learned to endure most of the hardships. The situation soon becomes more serious after Adem accompanies Besim and his sister, Fatmira, 16, to the nearby town of Prizren, where his sister has confided to him she and a number of other teenage girls will each read a poem from one of the ancient Ottoman bridges that the Serbs are planning to dynamite. Fatmira makes Adem promise not to tell of her plan, a promise he deeply regrets when a crowd gathers, chanting "De-moc-ra-cy!" and the police begin to disperse them with clubs. Then he hears a machine gun, and sees Fatmira fall. He throws himself on top of her and retrieves the poem, but she is taken to a hospital and the next morning the police bring her body to his home. An unprecedented number of people arrive for her funeral, and the Serbs respond with tanks and armored vehicles constantly patrolling their little village and parking near their house. In the middle of the night the special police arrive, trash the house, ostensibly looking for weapons, beat Adem's father, and drag him away. Two of the Democratic Alliance leaders come from Prizren and promise to try to help. The family also appeals to the local turncoat, who, for a bribe, eventually arranges for Adem's father to be released, but he is badly injured and no longer seems to know his family. Serb soldiers take over the little store that Adem's grandmother has run in the front room of their house, so there is only a thin wall separating the family from them. His parents counsel patience, infuriating Adem who wants to leave, to try to reach Albania or Macedonia. One day Besim disappears, and Adem realizes that his father has paid someone to smuggle him out before he could be drafted into the Serbian army. This further embitters the boy. When the soldiers in the house leave for a few days, Adem goes into the store and is caught when they return. Although they let him go, Adem is shaken. He finally confesses to his mother that he knew of Fatmira's plan and that he is responsible for her death, and his mother comforts him, saying none of them could have known what would happen. The next day Adem finds his way to a Gypsy village, where he knows a young man named Fikel and asks to be taken when the group leaves again. Fikel tells him to come back at the end of the month, bringing what money he can get. On his return to the village, Adem is accosted by three soldiers who demand to know where Besim is, accuse Adem of being a spy, and carve an Ortho-dox cross across his chest and stomach. His parents take him to the Democratic Alliance people in Prizren, who argue about the best course of action and take a photograph of his mutilation. A British journalist tries to interview him, but Adem does not trust anyone not to be a spy. When they leave him alone, thinking he is sleeping, he sneaks out the back, finds his way past guards, and eventually reaches the Gypsy camp. Fikel has a bear cub that he plans to take to a cousin on the Albanian border, who will smuggle it to Italy for a lot of money. Shocked by the sight of the cross, he makes a plan to get Adem out of the country, first putting him into the trunk of a car driven by a Serb, a man who assures Adem that they are not all like the soldiers. Then Adem, Fikel, and the bear hike a long way through mountains to a flint cave, where they sleep. Fikel tells Adem that they are at a lake on the border, where Albanians are selling gasoline to Serbs. The next night, as they creep around the lake, a border patrol shoots Fikel. Adem waits until they move off, then goes on with the bear, trying to find Fikel's cousin and eventually make his way to Elbasan in Albania, where he has relatives. The novel is clearly on the side of the Albanians of Kosovo, but it does a good job of showing the complicated loyalties, treacheries, and antagonisms of the Balkans and how the lives of ordinary people are ruined by super nationalists on both sides. The selflessness of some individuals offsets the brutality of others. Adem's fury and frustration are believable and well evoked, and while there is no assurance that he will survive, the novel ends with hope. An author's note at the beginning and a map of the area are very helpful, even for readers who have tried to follow the violent and confusing wars of the 1990s. ALA/YA.

THE ADVENTURES OF BLUE AVENGER (Howe*, Norma, Holt, 1999) Lighthearted chronicle of what happens to David Shumacher of Oakland, California, after he decides, on his sixteenth birthday, to change his name to Blue Avenger, the hero of a comic strip he has been drawing for several years. Since the death of his father, a police officer, three years earlier, David has worried about causes of events, whether human beings are responsible for their own actions, as his father thought, or whether actions are predetermined and free will is an illusion, as the new girl in his class, Omaha Nebraska Brown, says. Blue's first heroic action is to save the principal, Mrs. Manning, from a swarm of killer bees by sweeping her up off the outdoor judges' stand and jumping with her into the swimming pool. A sports photographer, there to film the award ceremony, catches a shot of the action and soon it is reprinted all over the country. A retired school principal from Austin, Texas, sends Blue a check for two thousand dollars. Since he thinks he should do good deeds secretly and without reward, Blue is troubled, but Omaha convinces him that he can do more good if he keeps the money. Blue makes a deal with a dermatologist to treat his friend, Mike Fennell, who has terrible acne and no medical insurance, the doctor pretending that he is just interested in the case and willing to treat it without charge, while actually sending the bill to Blue. The guidance counselor who agreed to change his name on school records calls in the favor by asking him to intercede with the staff of the school paper, who are running a three-part article on AIDS and want to accompany it with a very graphic set of drawings on condom use. The counselor has no objection to the story but knows that the sponsors who provide funds for the paper will cut off support if they see the illustrations. Blue buys a packet of condoms, attends the editorial board meeting of the paper, shows the printed instructions in the package, and persuades the kids that in the interest of continuing publication, they can simply add a caution, at the end of the article, to follow the directions in the condom package carefully. He saves an eighth birthday party for hellion African American twins by converting a long wait for the Fun-Time PartiBus that threatens to turn into a riot to a scavenger hunt for junk in the parking lot with cash prizes for the winning team, thereby cleaning up the place and delighting the twenty-five boys. His Uncle Ralphy teaches him to drive and gives him a decrepit sandwich wagon he has rebuilt. Just then Omaha gets a letter from her half brother, Travis, who is in prison in Walla Walla, Washington, and is being married, asking her to come and be a witness. Omaha's mother wants nothing more to do with Travis, but agrees they can go in the sandwich bus when Blue's mother gives permission, providing that there is no hanky-panky and that his younger brother, Josh, goes along as a chaperone. At the prison Blue meets the Winger brothers who have just perfected a new weapon with a tranquilizing bullet that works instantaneously, and later he persuades the Oakland City Council that their controversial proposal to outlaw guns should be changed to outlaw bullets, substituting the Winger-Stingers, and pleasing everyone, especially Omaha, who is very antigun. All this time Blue has been struggling to make his favorite lemon meringue pie without having the meringue weep. He figures out a way to add gelatin to the egg whites and sends his solution to "Auntie Annie," a syndicated newspaper column tackling the problem, and is the only winner out of 7,396 recipes sent in. The dermatologist decides to treat extreme acne sufferers, those with no insurance, free, so Blue still has his two thousand dollars. Whether he will use it to help Omaha find her father, who may be in Rome, remains an open question, depending on whether determinism or free will prevails. The bizarre incidents, which are treated with such deadpan seriousness that they become believable, are entertaining, but the strength of the book is in its many asides and editorial comments, from philosophical and scientific theories to pie recipes, that continually surprise and amuse. ALA/YA.

AIRFRAME (Crichton*, Michael, Knopf, 1996) Realistic contemporary mystery-detective novel published for adults and set for one week mostly at Norton Aircraft in Burbank, California, involving in-flight plane problems and corporate intrigue. The initial chapter is horrifyingly gripping: TransPacific Airlines Flight 545 from Hong Kong to Denver experiences such great turbulence that fifty-six people are injured, three killed, and the first officer very severely injured. Casey Singleton, vice president of quality assurance at Norton, heads the investigation, in which the videotape that a young father happened to make of his family during the incident provides the information Casey needs to solve the crucial case. Conflicting reports appear: in requesting permission to divert the flight to Los Angeles, the pilot reports turbulence; a passenger's story points to slats deployment, that is, a wing problem, which, however, does not square with the amount of harm to the passengers; and the pilot has received only glowing reports for competence, among other puz-

zling matters. Casey soon also finds herself in the midst of tension between union and management, since Norton hopes to sell a large number of planes to Beijing, China, along with a wing, technology that will enable China to manufacture their own planes, with a resulting large loss of American jobs. Casey's other problems include not being able to interview all the crew, who were immediately ordered home; lack of information from the flight recorder; a mysterious threatening phone call; several very unsettling stalkings; and the strange behavior of Bob Richman, a seemingly bumbling young company relative whom John Marder, Norton chief operating officer, has named as her assistant. Most troubling of all is the intrusion of the media in the person of young, aggressive Jennifer Malone of *Newsline*, an investigative television show. Jennifer is determined to persuade the world that Norton's N-22 plane is a death trap. She wishes to establish herself in her field and garner high viewer ratings. Although a few episodes revolve around other figures, most follow Casey as she sorts through information and seeks the truth about why a plane that tests out all right experienced such a terrible disaster. She is especially adamant about continuing her investigations when Marder instructs her to lie during the interview with Malone and say that the wing slats are defective when Norton's tests have proved exactly the opposite. Eventually it is learned, through persistent testing by dedicated technicians and Casey's clever deduction, that adverse publicity will kill the China sale and enable Marder to become president of Norton. He has secretly been negotiating with Korea for a large plane sale with Richman's help, a deal that will be tremendously lucrative for him but that will effectively destroy the company. Casey also learns that the highly praised TransPacific captain had left the cockpit and put the plane in the charge of his son, a very young man who was not qualified to fly an N-22 and whose misjudgment caused the injuries and deaths. Scenes have force, since they allow the reader to follow with Casey the work of the various technicians and read faxes, inside memos, and the like. The title has several meanings: the body of the aircraft; the attempt of TransPacific to protect the reputation of its pilots; and an attempt to set Casey up to take the blame. The novel provides grand reading for those who enjoy well-delineated insider technical information and also for those who simply like a carefully developed and sustained mystery. Booklist.

ALEXANDER, LLOYD (CHUDLEY) (1934–)   Born in Philadelphia, Pennsylvania; educated at West Chester State Teachers' College, Lafayette College, and the University of Paris (Sorbonne); translator and versatile, prolific author best known for his lively, amusing fantasies for middle graders and young adults, in particular, the five books in the Chronicles of Prydain, of which *The High King* (Holt, 1968) received the Newbery Award. He has also written novels of high and romantic adventure and political intrigue, one of which, *The Iron Ring** (Dutton, 1997), a mythological fantasy involving a journey-quest, was recommended by the American Library Association for young adults. He has recently published *The Gawgon and the Boy* (Dutton, 2001), about an ill boy in Depression-era Philadelphia, and *The Rope Trick* (Dutton, 2002), concerning a magician princess in Renaissance Italy. Alexander resides in Drexel, Pennsylvania. For more information about Alexander, titles, and title entries, see *Dictionary, 1960–1984* [*The Black Cauldron*; *The Book of Three*; *The Castle of Llyr*; *The Cat Who Wished to Be a Man*; *The First Two Lives of Lukas Kasha*; *The High King*; *The Kestrel*; *The Marvelous Misadventures of Sebastian*; *Taran Wanderer*; *Westmark*]; *Dictionary, 1985–1989* [*The Beggar Queen*; *The Illyrian Adventure*]; *Dictionary, 1990–1994* [*The Remarkable Journey of Prince Jen*]; and *Dictionary, 1995–1999* [*The Arkadians*; *The Iron Ring*].

ALFRED MAYES (*Only Twice I've Wished for Heaven**)   Handsome, charismatic preacher in the New Saved Church, collecting donations for good works that go almost entirely into his own pockets. He also owns and operates a brothel, deals drugs, and has a yen for prepubescent girls. After he has been arrested for the murder of Valerie Nicholae, Judd tells Miss* Jonetta Goode about his background. Judd's family came from Louisiana in 1904 with the Mayes family, and several years later both had sons, Judd, an ordinary-looking boy, and Alfred, a beautiful child whose parents protected him and made him into a model boy, whom everyone called Scooter. When Alfred is about twelve, his father dies, and Judd begins to feel sorry for him, getting him to play stickball and showing him the secret places around the street, including the fire escape in the whorehouse, where they peek into the windows. To his horror, Alfred sees his mother and a strange man having intercourse. After that, Judd says, he just went bad every way he could. Although both Miss Jonetta and Tempestt know he did not actually push Valerie over the railing, he admits that he did it, possibly because he knows that if he goes to trial all his other crimes will be exposed.

ALFREDO SANTAYANA (*I Want to Buy a Vowel**)   Guileless Guatamalan boy who has walked and hitchhiked to Waxahachie, Texas, where he stops simply because he is tired. He left his home and his eighteen brothers and sisters because he has seen *Wheel of Fortune* on American television and has an idea that if you buy a vowel, you are given a car. When he crosses the border in Laredo, he is disappointed not to see the *Statue of Liberty*. Because everyone in his family has had to work, he has never been to school. His last job was in a souvenir shop where they made and sold fake Mayan relics to tourists. His conversation in English consists almost entirely of phrases he has memorized from television but does not understand: "Hey Andy. Hey Barn"; "See your Ford dealer today"; "Proud to be your Bud. Weiser." When Eva* and Ava Galt first approach him and try, by signs, to find out whether he is hungry, he thinks they want something to eat and offers them his bag of Fritos, the only food he knows enough to buy. Alfredo's cheerful good humor disarms everyone he comes in contact with. Police Chief McLamore* says he will expedite contact with the immigration officials, but points out that he knows how to "expedite real slow." To get his congregation involved in finding Alfredo a job, David Galt, an Episcopal minister, gets permission to take him from jail to church, where, asked to speak, the boy strings together phrases he has memorized: "My broker is E. F. Hutton" and "The best part of waking up is Folgers in your cup." At first the congregation is baffled. Then, when they see that their minister is amused, they break into laughter, applause, and cheers. Alfredo acknowledges this by a return to the microphone: "For sinus, think Sinex." His comment, when he learns that his repugnant job is to scrape the remains of armadillos from the highway, is that he hopes he will be allowed to wear gloves.

ALICE'S TULIPS (Dallas*, Sandra, St. Martin's, 2000)   Epistolary novel set in Iowa during the American Civil War. The letters, starting in December 1862, and ending in May 1865, are all from Alice Keeler Bullock, 16, to her sister Lizzie, a couple of years older and married to feckless James. At first Alice, a lively, fun-loving girl, is thrilled that her husband, Charlie, has enlisted along with his friend, Harve Stout, but soon she is fretting about being left at Bramble Farm with Charlie's mother, a dour, disapproving woman who demands hard work from her daughter-in-law. The women in the nearest town, Slatyfork, organize a quilting group and name Alice, the best seamstress, head, and they turn out a large number of quilts to send to the men at the front. In the area some of the people are copperheads, Confederate sympathizers, including Frank Smead and his brother, Samuel, but Alice genuinely likes Frank's wife, Nealie, and is not above flirting with good-looking Samuel. Gradually, things get harder. Alice loses the baby she is carrying. Harve's spoiled, self-centered wife, Jennie Kate, who was once Charlie's girlfriend and is still sweet on him, has her baby, whom she calls Piecake, and insists that if she should die, Alice must take the baby as her remembrance to Charlie. The lazy hired man quits; the Negro, Lucky, disappears; the horse dies. One morning they find in the barn a ragged woman about Alice's age, Annie Tatum, and her blind daughter, Joybell, 7, and add them to the household, the first real help they have had, but cash is short, and they have a hard time scraping along. Heavyset Mrs. Kittie Wales, the wealthiest woman in town, who has outlived three husbands and is looking for a fourth, offers to pay Alice to accompany her to Hannibal, Missouri, where she has "business." It turns out that she is meeting Henry Howard, an ex-soldier willing to marry her for her money and has arranged with Samuel Snead to meet them "accidentally" and squire Alice about town. Although she is usually game for any adventure, Alice is shocked and, when Snead tries to force her to accompany him to Memphis, terrified, but escapes to the hotel and gets back to Slatyfork unharmed. Not through, however, Snead waylays Alice in the woods near Bramble Farm and rapes her. She tells no one, but some weeks later his body is found in the woods, and Alice is under suspicion, especially when Henry Howard tells that they were together in Hannibal. Women of the town cut her, the quilting group meets without her, and her only friends are Annie and Nealie, who by now is pregnant and admits to Alice that it is the result of rape by Samuel. To everyone's surprise, Jennie Kate, who whined and played sick often, dies, and Piecake is added to the household at Bramble Farm. All summer Mother Bullock's health has been failing. On her deathbed, she sends for the sheriff and confesses to murdering Samuel Snead to prevent him from burning down the farm. The day she dies, Nealie who has been staying with them, has her baby, a boy they name Thomas. When her husband comes to get her, Joybell, who is afraid of men, disappears, and they hunt through a blizzard for her. Alice finds her, burrowed into a haystack, and the blind girl leads her home, but Alice's foot is frozen, and her toes must be amputated, making it difficult for her to walk. In April, the war ends. Charlie, who has been in Andersonville prison camp, does not return, but

Harve does, and when he sees what a hard time the women are having, comes every day to help. After some weeks, he suggests to Alice that, since he needs a mother for Piecake, he could marry her if Charlie does not come home. Alice is touched, but declines and points to Annie, who is very fond of Piecake and would make a good wife. Harve proposes at once, but Annie is reluctant. Weeping, she confesses to Alice that she killed Samuel Snead when she found him raping Joybell in the barn. Alice advises her not to tell Harve or the sheriff, but to marry Harve and make a home for both their little girls. Some weeks later, when she has almost given him up, Charlie comes limping down the road, having walked from Georgia on a damaged leg. The novel is full of interesting period detail and the main characters are convincing, but it suffers from a frequent problem with epistolary novels. Too many things that the recipient, though not the reader, must already know are spelled out, and in particular, the long letter about Charlie's return is in narrative form and written before they have even gone to bed together, not the exuberant burst of joy one would naturally write hurriedly with details to follow later. The tulips in the title refer to bulbs Mother Bullock planted in the fall, knowing she would not be there to see them bloom and telling Annie that they are for Alice. An interesting addition is the paragraph heading each section telling about a different quilt pattern. Booklist.

ALLEN STANCIL (*Up Jumps the Devil**) Womanizing, smooth-talking, affable man of about forty, Mr.* Jap (Jasper) Stancil's nephew and heir, a prime suspect in the old man's murder, and former husband of Deborah Knott, the protagonist and narrator. Allen unexpectedly appears from Charlotte, North Carolina, returning to Colleton County after Mr. Jap's son, Dallas Stancil, is shot to death. Allen moves in with Mr. Jap and soon Mr. Jap is drinking again, sprucing up his repair shop so that Allen can fix cars, and planning with Allen to restore the many old cars that sit rusting in his yard. Allen and Deborah were married briefly when she was eighteen and at loose ends after her mother's death. Almost as soon as they married, Deborah realized the marriage was a mistake, and her father had it annulled. Although people in the novel seem to like him, the reader does not from the beginning, since he is seen through Deborah's eyes. The book's title may refer to him, but it also may pertain to the temptation of the money that selling the rural land to developers would bring.

ALL LOVES EXCELLING (Bunting*, Josiah, III, Bridge Works, 2001) Contemporary novel of the devastating effects the pressure to get into a high-prestige college, specifically Dartmouth, has on a bright, talented girl. Amanda Bahringer, 17, enters St. Matthew's school in the Fingerlake region of New York state as a postgraduate, having finished high school at Lawrence, Long Island, with mediocre grades and been turned down for entrance to Dartmouth, her first choice, and wait-listed by three other colleges. Conventional wisdom and her mother's ambition hold that a year at St. Matthew's can raise her grades and her SAT scores and make her an acceptable candidate for any prestigious college. St. Matthew's, long a school for boys, has a tradition of high academic standing and has now turned into a mill for grinding out just what college admission officers are looking for, students academically outstanding and tal-

ented athletically, musically, or any other way they can market. This means that all the students, but particularly the PGs (postgraduates), are under pressure to achieve and not let down their families, who are paying heavily for the opportunity. Amanda's father, Joey, is relaxed about her prospects, but her mother, Tess, who works in a high-powered public relations firm, is herself driven to achieve and is highly ambitious for her daughter. At St. Matthew's a few of the teachers and staff increase the pressure: Coach Kellam, who insists that losing a few pounds can translate into a few seconds better time for girl runners; Mr. Arnett, academic counselor, who stresses performance objectives; Miss Rodman, hall master at Morrison Residence Hall, who urges her to try harder; Roderick Steele, master of history, who prides himself on never giving higher than an A minus grade; and especially, Mr. Carnes, math teacher known as a "prime intimidator." The only class Amanda actually enjoys is Hopkins and Houseman, a seminar taught by Dr. Carlisle Passmore, the headmaster, a rather old-fashioned academic much admired by parents and some students but considered "past it," by the deans who actually run the school. He sees in Amanda one of his few students ever with a genuine understanding of poetry, especially Hopkins, whom few of them appreciate but whose abstemious lifestyle appeals to her. Amanda has no real friends, though Toby Carrington, from Virginia, an easygoing boy, tries to get to know her and worries when he sees that she eats almost nothing, and she practices for cross-country with Danielle Ben, a brilliant and athletically talented Native American girl, who consistently outruns her. After Christmas the pressure is ratcheted up by approaching SATs and semester finals, since college acceptances will not look at second-semester grades, and a growing number of SDs (systemic departures), students expelled or giving up, are announced daily over the public address system. By almost starving herself, Amanda loses weight in an effort to increase her three-kilometer time, actually becoming bulimic, and she practices obsessively on a showy Chopin ballade, of which they plan to make a video to send to Dartmouth, although she loves Schumann's music far more and plays it better. She drives herself relentlessly, using a variety of antianxiety drugs both prescribed and swiped from her mother's medicine cabinet, and prodded by frequent phone calls from Tess who, with barely veiled anger, assures her she can do better. Although Amanda does bring her SAT scores up considerably, her semester grades are not high enough to impress Dartmouth, and she is again rejected. With her systematic precision, she writes a farewell note to her parents, goes out into the forbidding winter night landscape to the Seneca River, fills her pockets with rocks from the edge, and walks out across the thin ice to the running water. At the St. Matthew's memorial service attended by her parents and conducted by Dr. Passmore, only he and Toby Carrington seem to realize how they have all failed Amanda. The novel has a sense of inevitable doom, deftly built as the bright autumn landscape sinks into gray, featureless winter, so that the final suicide comes as a deplorable result of the system and her mother's long-term directiveness but not as a surprise. The title is that of the St. Matthew's school hymn. Booklist.

AMONG THE HIDDEN (Haddix*, Margaret Peterson, Simon & Schuster, 1998) Futuristic novel set after overpopulation and government ineptitude have turned the country into a totalitarian dictatorship that forbids, among other things, any family from having more than two children. Luke Garner, 12, has spent all his life in hiding, seeing only his parents and his two older brothers, Mark, 14, and Matthew, 15. Because their farm has been isolated, this has not prevented him from enjoying the outdoors, helping in the garden, and roaming the barn and orchard. When the government suddenly demands that the farm woods be sold for the construction of expensive houses, his life changes dramatically. In fear, his parents restrict him to his attic bedroom and insist he eat not at the kitchen table with the rest of the family but sitting at the bottom of the stairs, where not even his shadow can be seen from outside and where he can retreat in a hurry should anyone come to the door who might report his existence to the dreaded Population Police. When the government also forbids their raising pigs, lest the odor offend the Barons, the higher-class new residents, and raises their taxes because the neighborhood is upgraded, Luke's mother gets a job outside the home to supplement their meager income, leaving Luke alone much of the day. He is not allowed to use the radio, television, or computer for fear his presence can be detected through these devices, and although he can read, they have few books. At first he is almost driven crazy by boredom. He discovers, however, that if he climbs on boxes he can see out the vents at each end of the attic without being seen from outside. He watches the building of the houses and the people who move in, and soon he knows the residents by sight, counts the children, always one or two, and learns their routines. His nearest neighbors, whom he calls the Sports Family, have two older boys and parents who both work, but after much careful watching he is sure someone else lives in the house. Sometimes wind stirs the heavy blinds, and he sees a light after the boys and parents have left. Sometimes a window shade moves; once he is even sure he sees a face. Finally, he screws up his courage and leaves his house, crawls, then sprints across the space to the Sports Family house—only to find the door locked. In frustration, he jams his hand through the screen, unlocks the door, and starts to explore. To his astonishment, he finds a girl about his age, who, after a brief tussle because she thinks he is a burglar, introduces herself as Jennifer Rose Talbot, called Jen, another third or shadow child, much more sophisticated and privileged than Luke. Jen is skilled in the use of the computer and has a network of shadow children she communicates with. They are planning a "rally," to march on the president's house and demand that they be recognized as legal. She is scornful of Luke's fears that the government can detect their presence through the computer or telephone, calling it propaganda, and casually describes her stepfather's high position and use of bribery. Although he is terrified, Luke returns again and again to her house, learning more about the outside world than he has ever guessed. As the date of the rally approaches, he is torn, but decides that in fairness to his family, who would be fined, imprisoned, and possibly even executed if his presence were known and who have no money or power to bribe officials, he cannot take part. Feeling he has betrayed Jen, he waits breathlessly for some news of the rally, but his parents say nothing and he hears nothing when his father turns on the radio news. Finally, in desperation, he dashes to Jen's house, searches unsuccess-

fully for her, then switches on the computer to the shadow-child chat room, typing frantically "Where's Jen? Is anybody there?" He is interrupted by a man pointing a gun at him and recognizes Jen's father. When he admits that he, too, is a shadow child, her father puts the gun down and tells him of her death, shot along with the other forty children who got to the rally, with all evidence destroyed. While they are talking, the Population Police arrive, alerted by the activity on the chat room, which they are now monitoring. Luke is hidden by Jen's father, who bribes the police with fur coats to do only a cursory search, and, after they are gone, offers to get Luke a fake ID. Realizing that it is his only chance to lead a normal and productive life, Luke accepts and a few days later leaves home forever and starts a terrifying and exciting life as Lee Grant, a boy recently killed in an accident but supposedly being sent to a boarding school as punishment for running away. While the solution is somewhat abrupt and too pat, Luke's character has been so well developed that it is acceptable, since he understands that he must seize the opportunity, that even though his family loves him, they will have an easier time with him gone, and that the only way he will ever get to help other shadow children and honor Jen's memory is to take this chance. Although the picture of the future is extremely pessimistic, the overall effect is hopeful, since there are still children like Luke and Jen whose spirits survive despite the oppression. ALA/YA.

AMOS GLASS (*Jim the Boy**) Grandfather of Jim Glass, whom Jim has never met because his widowed mother, Cissy, forbids it. Amos lives on Lynn's Mountain in a rundown, strangely designed house.

Although very old, Amos still has the reputation he had throughout his life, as a mean and nasty man. He once operated a successful moonshining business, so successful that his enterprise built up a wide trade and caught the attention of revenuers. He organized a group of local men to oppose the revenuers and even tried unsuccessfully to get his part of the mountain to secede from the Union. He was sentenced to nine years in prison. A hard man, he was prepared to murder his son, Jim's father, for attempting to keep him from the hands of the law when he decided to revive his business. As a result, Jim's father left Lynn's Mountain and moved to Aliceville, where he met and married Cissy McBride, Jim's mother. Amos got a glimpse of his grandson through the window of Uncle* Zeno McBride's house when Jim was a tiny baby, a scene described by Uncle Zeno that is a startling and poignant parallel to that in which Jim glimpses Amos on his deathbed.

AMY RUGGERIO (*Swallowing Stones**) Classmate of Michael MacKenzie, a girl who uses too much makeup and is generally considered an easy lay. Apparently almost friendless, she turns out to be the most compassionate young person in Briarwood, New Jersey, a girl who welcomes Michael to her home when she sees he is troubled and who not only helps Jenna Ward recover from a panic attack at a movie, but who writes her a note expressing sympathy for her father's death and explaining that she lost both her parents in an automobile accident. Later, she tells Jenna that the worst of that experience was her feeling of guilt for surviving the accident that took their lives. This revelation is instrumental in bringing to light Jenna's suppressed feeling of guilt for her

father's death. After Michael starts seeing Amy, Darcy Kelley, his old girlfriend, and her friends tell Amy that he is being nice to her on a bet that he can get her to sleep with him and the whole track team. She is badly hurt but forgives Michael when she sees how worried and afraid he is. She admits that at the party she saw him with the gun and knew he must have fired the fatal shot, but she did not tell.

ANDERSON, LAURIE HALSE (1961–) Born in Potsdam, New York, writer of novels and picture books. *Speak** (Farrar, 1999), her story of a young high school girl whose trauma after being raped at a party leaves her mute, was cited by the *School Library Journal* and the American Library Association. *Fever 1793** (Simon & Schuster, 2000) is a historical novel about the terrible yellow fever epidemic in Philadelphia. For earlier biographical information and a title entry, see *Dictionary, 1995–1999* [*Speak*].

ANNA DALASSENA (*Anna of Byzantium**) Imperious, conspiratorial grandmother of Anna Comnena, crown princess of Byzantium at the time of the First Crusade. Anna Dalassena is presented as cunning, scheming, manipulative, and very skillful (but not honest or fair) at statesmanship. She seems to have the best interests of her son, Emperor Alexius, at heart, provided his objectives do not conflict with hers. At first, Anna admires her grandmother's ability to turn situations to her advantage but later recognizes that the woman is selfish, scheming, and mean-spirited. Anna Dalassena tries to undermine Irene, Alexius's wife and queen, whenever she can. Within a few years after she conspires to place John, Anna's younger brother, on the throne, to Anna's surprise he turns against their grandmother's controlling ways and divests her of all power.

ANNA DONNELLY (*Nory Ryan's Song**) Little, very old woman who lives alone in a rude hut near the Ryan family, with whom Nory Ryan becomes close friends. The area's healer, Anna soon notes that Nory is quick, observant, and caring and teaches her how to use herbs for healing, an art she says will be an Irish gift to America later. She shares what little food she has with Nory and little Patch, especially milk, and she teaches Nory to gather and prepare nettles and other common greens. Learning how Anna's son, Tagus, died on the cliff overlooking the sea gives Nory the idea to hunt birds and birds' eggs by dangling over the cliff on a rope. Although Nory's father sends Nory two tickets to America and Patch has gone with the Mallons, Anna refuses to leave her home and her dog, Maeve. Anna will think of Nory in America singing as is her habit, happy and without hunger, and that is all Anna wants.

ANNA OF BYZANTIUM (Barrett*, Tracy, Delacorte, 1999)   Biographical novel of the childhood of historical Anna Comnena, crown princess of Byzantium (1083–1153), set mostly in Constantinople just before and during the First Crusade. Anna writes her story from a mountain convent to which she has been exiled for treason against the crown and the attempted murder of her younger brother by five years, John, now the emperor. Intelligent, educated beyond the norm, diligent, Anna relieves her boredom by copying manuscripts in the scriptorium; finishes the historical *Alexiad*, about the deeds of her father, Alexius, emperor of the Byzantines and conqueror of the Turks; and records her memories of her

own youth. She reflects on her betrothal at age five to handsome, golden-haired Constantine Ducas, a distant cousin on her mother's side, to unite the two main royal families of the empire; on her studies as the prize pupil of Simon*, the slave who is her cherished, wise tutor; and on the few times she is allowed to stand by the side of her beloved father's throne as his firstborn and heir apparent. When she is seven, her father's mother and chief adviser, Anna* Dalassena, begins to train Anna in statecraft, ways of acquiring and dispensing power, and imperial protocol. Anna's mother, Irene, a gentle, kind woman who takes her Christian religion seriously, complains bitterly to Alexius that his mother is making Anna hard and cruel, and demands that Anna Dalassena be dismissed from court, a request that Alexius refuses. For some time, Anna is full of her own importance. Proud of her learning, Anna also draws a sharp contrast between herself and her younger sister, Maria, a good student, too, and their brother, John, a whiny, spiteful, snoopy, lazy, almost illiterate child. When Anna is ten, she acquires a maid, Sophia, a young Turkish woman captured in war and enslaved. Anna comes to appreciate Sophia's loyalty, quick thinking, friendship, and valiant spirit. As Anna grows older, Anna Dalassena realizes that the girl will not be as easy to mold to her will as she had thought and turns her attention to John, promoting him at every turn. In what Anna thinks is a private conversation with Simon in the library over a shipment of new books, Anna mentions what steps she would take as empress, among them exiling John. The conversation is overheard by the sneaky, prying boy and reported, and Anna is immediately removed by her father as his heir and replaced by John. Heartsick at being rejected by her father,

Anna now devotes herself completely to her studies. She also shows true compassion to Sophia by bringing to the palace Sophia's betrothed, Malik, and secures a position for him as Simon's helper. Anna is betrothed to the eminent historian, scholar, and soldier, Nicephorus Bryennius, and passes the next years in near isolation while Alexius is away fighting the Turks to regain Jerusalem. He returns after two years, seriously ill, and soon dies. John is immediately crowned emperor, and when he tries to have Anna declared illegitimate, Anna and Irene conspire to poison him, but their plot is detected, and both are banished to convents. In addition to writing, Anna becomes the healer in the area. Sophia, to whom Anna had given her freedom, visits, along with Malik and their daughter, named Anna after the princess. An author's endnote adds details about Anna and the royal family, which come mainly from the extant, twelve-volume *Alexiad*. Surprisingly, John becomes a skillful and beloved ruler. Anna eventually marries Bryennius and has a family of her own. Most characters, excluding Simon and Sophia, are historical, and the novel is a vivid if limited re-creation of the opulent palace during the height of the Byzantine Empire as well as a good story about a brave if occasionally foolish young woman, who becomes a victim of her own passionate nature, circumstances, and palace political intrigue. Barrett also notes that Anna was probably only one of many learned women of the times. ALA/YA.

ANNE BOLEYN (*Mary, Bloody Mary**; *The Secret Diary of Anne Boleyn**) Beautiful raven-haired, French-reared courtier who becomes the wife of Henry* VIII of England and the queen of En-
gland, supplanting Catherine* of Aragon, and mother of Elizabeth I. She is the stepmother of Mary Tudor, who tells the story in *Mary* and later also becomes queen of England. To Mary, Anne is scheming, vicious, unscrupulous, bad tempered—utterly reprehensible, without any redeeming qualities. She sees Anne as ruthlessly working to get rid of Catherine and Mary herself so that she, Anne, can become queen and any issue she might have be declared heirs to the English throne. In *Secret Diary*, Anne is the pretty, fairly well-educated daughter of noble Thomas Boleyn, who uses her to advance his interests. Anne's beauty and coquetry attract Henry, whose passion she inflames by refusing to become his paramour. After she arouses his ire by not giving birth to a son, Anne schemes that Elizabeth be accorded what Anne feels is her rightful position in line for the throne. Throughout the novel, Anne relies for moral support on her brother, George. Both George and Anne are imprisoned in the Tower of London where they are beheaded.

ANNIE SURRATT (*An Acquaintance with Darkness**) Historical daughter of the Surratt family, who were accused of complicity in the assassination of President Lincoln. Annie is presented in the novel as the best friend from childhood of nonhistorical Emily Bransby Pigbush, the protagonist and narrator. Annie figures in several important scenes, among them that in which she accompanies Emily to visit her mother's grave and the two girls observe Mole and Spoon, historical dwarves who robbed graves for cadavers for physicians. Annie is briefly incarcerated along with others thought to be conspirators in Lincoln's assassination. She has a hard time thereafter, since she is aware of the deplorable living conditions her mother must endure in prison. Annie is also a witness to her mother's hanging and is responsible for Emily's seeing that she has been selfish, opinionated, and spoiled. No one-dimensional plaster figure, Annie is a competent foil for Emily.

ANOTHER KIND OF MONDAY (Coles*, William, Jr., Atheneum, 1996) Present-day mystery novel of a strange treasure hunt into which two high school seniors are drawn and from which they get not the expected riches but understanding, which may be more valuable in the long run. Having misplaced his copy of *Great Expectations*, required for his honors English class, Mark Bettors grabs the nearest one from his Moorland High School library and finds, folded inside, an envelope containing three new one-hundred-dollar bills and a note inviting him to join a "quest," the goal being a fortune. To achieve this great expectation, he must work in secrecy to solve a puzzling verse, which in turn gives him a further riddle. Each clue leads him to a part of Pittsburgh and a piece of local history he does not know. Following the first verse he goes to the decaying town of Braddock and the Edgar Thompson Works, an abandoned steel mill. The clue he finds there (with more money) leads him to Allegheny Observatory, built by John Brashear, a lens maker devoted to astronomy. The next clue changes the rules of the game. Mark is to find a partner, a girl who is not already a friend. He chooses Zeena Curry, a classmate he has long admired from a distance, the daughter of a black activist woman and a white professor, now divorced. Zeena is very intelligent, but prickly. They bicker and cooperate, alternately, through the next six discoveries, the first at the grave of the Biddle broth-

ers, arrested (probably framed) for murder, freed by the jailor's wife, and shot by a posse. Next they go to the Clayton House, a museum that was once the home of industrialist Henry Clay Frick, called the "Coke King," who was shot by an anarchist, Alexander Berkman. The clue they find there leads them to St. Anastasius Church, where a Hungarian refugee claimed sanctuary and painted a huge, surrealistic mural that so shocked the congregation that a riot broke out and the church was firebombed. As they leave the boarded-up church with a new clue, Mark is attacked and ends up in the hospital. Their next stop is at a nursing home to see the Pennyman, a street person from the previous generation, a mentally handicapped man who polished up and passed out pennies to school children and other acquaintances. Although he is disturbed by their visit, they learn that he raised a monument, a "church," to feral dogs he befriended that were shot by the police. Worming through the brush in a hollow behind Highland Park, they discover the remains of a structure of cobblestones, where they find a clue leading them to Brilliant Cut, a railroad cut that exposed fossils in Ames limestone. In their final assignment, they are sent to a fortune-teller with Tourette's syndrome. Up to this point, each clue has been accompanied by an increased amount of money, up to twenty-four one-hundred-dollar bills. The final note, which should contain their great expectations, contains only eighteen dollars and a rambling thank you for being part of a story imagined by the constructor of the treasure hunt and advising them to look at their own lives as stories. Although they have acquired no great fortune, they have learned much about the history of Pittsburgh. They have also come to terms with their anger toward their fathers, each of whom left his family. Mark has lost his longtime, rather shallow girlfriend, Merial, and Zeena has given up her infatuation with Silk, an older African American college man they both admire, but they have found each other, a real friendship that may become more. Although the underlying premise of an anonymous benefactor contributing wealth to their lives is far-fetched (as it is in the Dickens novel), each episode in the treasure hunt is exciting in itself and explores an unusual aspect of the city's history. That the clues, even well hidden and protected in packets wrapped in black plastic, could remain undisturbed for years, especially when they contain large sums of money, and then be found by Mark and Zeena is not entirely plausible, but interest stays high, and the two main characters are likable and well developed. The title comes from a poem Zeena writes, wanting a new start, "another kind of Monday," after the pain of her parents' divorce. ALA/YA.

ANOTHER WAY TO DANCE (Southgate*, Martha, Delacorte, 1996)   Girl's career and growing-up novel, set in New York City at the time of publication. African American Vicki Harris, 14, the narrator, has been the best in her school of ballet dancers in Montclair, New Jersey. She is extremely proud to have been chosen for the summer program at the School of American Ballet in New York City. Impressionable, she is ecstatic about working in the same neighborhood in which her idol and fantasy love, Mikhail (Misha) Baryshnikov, has performed, and yearns to catch a glimpse of him. She eases the hurt of her parents' recent divorce by dreaming of his arms about her. When practices at school go poorly and she overhears a comment from a class-

mate that she has been chosen only because of affirmative action, she fantasizes about how much Misha appreciates her work. Her Misha-bubble bursts when she cuts a class to attend his personal appearance at Macy's where he is promoting his line of dance wear. She thinks the merchandise is tawdry, realizes his face has deep age lines, and is keenly disappointed when the blue eyes she imagined would be strikingly personal remain veiled and distant, even while he presumably autographs a poster specifically for her. Throughout the summer she continues to hope that her parents will get together again, even though she knows that this, too, is just another daydream. This dream-bubble bursts at her fifteenth birthday party, when her parents greet each other kindly and kiss politely but obviously without their old affection. She makes two friends at school, Stacey Rogers, an African American girl her age from Chicago, who commiserates with Vicki about how hard the school is. Vicki's other friend is Debbie Turner, a white girl from Ann Arbor, Michigan, who is clearly one of the best of the summer students, pencil slim, limber, poised, and talented. Several times Vicki dates good-looking Michael, 15, a black youth who works at the nearby Wendy's. He takes her to the zoo, where he confides that he wants to become a veterinarian; to his church on Sunday morning, where the minister addresses discrimination against blacks; and to his home where she meets his lawyer mother. On a shopping excursion, they are denied entrance to a store because the salespeople evidently fear being held up, a matter that infuriates Michael because it is blatantly an instance of racial stereotyping. All three friends help Vicki to see that no one deserves ill treatment because of skin color. On the last day of classes, she bids her teachers and her friends good-bye. Neither she nor Stacey is asked back for the fall session. They both rejoice that Debbie has been selected for more training, since she so clearly is deserving. Although Vicki is disappointed, she knows she has done well and is a person of value. Characters are thinly created types: warm, wise, accomplished actress Aunt Hannah, Ma's friend with whom Vicki lives for the summer; sensible career woman Ma; Pa, a history professor at Rutgers, almost stridently proud of black culture; Michael, the nice-boy type, every mother's dream for her daughter; bratty Beth, the pesky little sister; understanding, ambitious Stacey Rogers, a true-blue friend and confidante; and Debbie Turner, the white girl who has everything going for her, including talent but is always kind and caring. Dialogue is often awkward or artificial. The plot seems constructed to thesis—African Americans must value themselves although others may not. The best part of the book lies in its convincing, if limited, view of the ballet training—the etiquette, the rigid routine, the complicated moves, the intimacy among the students, the urge to starve to stay extremely slim, the constant worry about appearance, the great love for the dance, and the keen competitive spirit among the dancers. ALA/YA.

ARA SARKISIAN (*Forgotten Fire**) Gentle giant of an old man, Armenian, with whom the protagonist, Vahan Kenderian, stays for a few days, until Ara finds a place for him temporarily at a Swiss orphanage for girls. Ara is the only resident left in the village where he works, and, although Armenian, he is unhurt by the Turks because being a blacksmith he is valuable to them. He has rescued a little boy with withered legs, whom he found in the street. He treats the boy like his son, carrying him wherever he must go, holding him close, and gently teasing and chiding him. When he sees how much Vahan wants a home and family again, he tells him to "build his home in his heart," where he will never be alone and will always be safe. He is one of the few attractive figures in the novel, an effective foil for cruel, callous Selim* Bey.

ARCHANGEL (Shinn*, Sharon, Ace, 1996)   Elaborate fantasy published for adults using Old Testament place-names and characters in a highly revisionist way to tell what is essentially a love story between Gabriel*, archangel designate, and Rachel*, the slave chosen by Jovah to be his bride and angelica. She is destined to sing beside him at the great Gloria festival, where he will replace the current archangel, Raphael*. Because the time approaches and he will soon need an angelica, Gabriel has visited the oracle, Josiah, who consults with Jovah and says the young woman is a hill farmer's daughter from Jordana, one of the three provinces that make up Samaria, the other two being Gaza and Bethel, and that the Kiss of the God, an amber stud embedded in his flesh when he was a few days old, will heat up and flare when he finds her. Gabriel discovers that the village where Rachel was born has been destroyed. He seems to have no way to trace her until he attends a wedding of a rich merchant's son in Semorrah and his Kiss begins to flare in the presence of a slave. Investigation shows that this is indeed Rachel, who, after the attack on the village, was found and adopted by the Edori, a nomadic people whose original home was Ysral, and later, after a raid by a Jansai war band, sold as a slave. To Gabriel's astonishment and chagrin, Rachel is not delighted to become angelica, hoping only to return to the Edori. She refuses to be flown to the Eyrie*, the mountaintop home of the angels of Bethel, because heights make her physically ill. After she travels by carriage from Semorrah to Velora at the base of the mountains, Gabriel seizes her in his arms and flies to the Eyrie. She faints and, waking, attacks him furiously. Their life together is a series of angry encounters, interrupted occasionally by episodes when they are clearly attracted to each other. Rachel has her own rooms. Unable to be flown down from the Eyrie, she spends much of her time in the recital chambers, where she listens to recordings of the various masses sung at the Glorias, especially those by Hagar, the first angelica, so difficult that no one else can sing them. She makes only a few friends, among them Matthew, an Edori leather worker; Hannah, the mortal stepmother of Gabriel; Nathan*, Gabriel's brother angel; and Obadiah, a young angel who is much attracted to her. Gabriel is gone most of the time, trying to remedy things that have been allowed to occur by Raphael during his tenure as archangel. On their wedding day, Gabriel gives Rachel, besides beautiful bracelets, which she refuses publicly, a way down from the Eyrie, a sort of elevator that runs in a shaft hewn from the stone of the mountain. In Velora she meets Peter, an ex-priest, who is attempting to start a shelter for street children, many of whom are the offspring of angels and humans, discarded because they did not turn out to be angels. With the help of Gabriel, she pours her energy into the project, expanding it into a school and an apprentice program. Although the time for the Gloria, which she must lead, approaches, she opts to go to the Edori annual gathering with Matthew, where she enjoys the old

life and stays with Naomi, her dear friend. On the way back, she is attacked by angels of Raphael, who take her to his hold, Windy Point, where she is imprisoned in a stone tower. She discovers that his plan now is to keep her until after the time for the Gloria. Gabriel cannot sing it with any but his angelica, and if it is not sung, Jovah will send a thunderbolt to Mount Galo; if it not sung in the next three days, he will destroy the world. Raphael, who does not believe in Jovah's power, knows that with Gabriel discredited, he can continue as archangel. To make it possible for Gabriel to choose a new angelica, Rachel squeezes out a narrow window, climbs to the top of the Windy Point hold, and steps off to certain death. Gabriel, however, having sensed where she is, flies up, catches her, and takes her back to the Eyrie. The day before the Gloria, Raphael and all his followers encamp in defiance at the top of Mount Galo, while all the faithful wait below. A great lightning bolt strikes and destroys the mountain. The Gloria, sung two days later, is the best in generations. After more partings, misunderstandings, and yearnings, Rachel and Gabriel, both setting aside their pride, eventually admit true love and lifelong devotion. The angels, though of great beauty and power, are very human in their emotions. Characters are well developed, and the action in this long book is mostly compelling, though the conflicts caused by the stubbornness of the main protagonists become tedious. Booklist.

ARCHIE (*Stargirl**) Archibald Hapwood Brubaker, retired paleontologist who loves to converse with schoolkids and lives in a house littered with fossil bones. Archie is beloved by the town kids for the "school" he conducts at his house on Saturdays, during which he entertainingly teaches "everything from toothpaste to tapeworms." He calls his school the Loyal Order of the Stone Bone and gives members pendants made of fossil bones strung on rawhide. Kevin Quinlan suggests that Leo and he consult Archie about Stargirl. Archie simply tells the boys that she is one of them, hardly the answer they expected. It is intended to provoke thought but is unfortunately unsuccessful. Archie functions as a sort of clan elder, a mystic who speaks in riddles and seems to see far more than anyone else.

ARIA OF THE SEA (Calhoun*, Dia, Winslow, 2000)   Charming fantasy of a girl who wants to devote her life to dancing, set in preindustrial times in an archipelago of Windward, very much like that in Ursula LeGuin's Earthsea books. With her father, a sailmaker, Cerinthe Gale, 13, comes from her home in Normost, in the Northern Reach, to Faranor, the capital, to try out for the School of Royal Dancers. Although he doubts the wisdom of the move, her father has brought her because it was his wife's last wish. He thinks Cerinthe should return with him and follow the path of Gwimma, the old local healer, who has been teaching the girl. Cerinthe herself shuns the idea of healing, since she thinks she caused her mother's death by using the wrong herbs during her illness. At the trial, fifteen girls are singled out to dance again, but Cerinthe is not among them. Discouraged and depressed, she decides she would rather stay in Faranor, even as a servant, so she can learn more by watching dancers. She leaves a note for her father, saying she has a job, and applies at the back door of the school, where she is taken on as a laundry maid. For a couple of days she toils in the damp, dark basement, until the woman in charge sends

her with bandages to the dispensary where she meets Mediri Grace, one of the great healers who are reported to have magic powers and are feared in the farther reaches. Losing her way in returning, she runs into the great entrance hall and finds her father, who has come seeking her, talking to some of the staff. They point out to her the list of students accepted by the school, where her name is on top, since all the judges agreed, and there was no need to see her dance again. Thereupon her life changes dramatically, although in some ways it is harder. The school is strict and the work arduous, but her chief problem is Elliana Nautilus, acknowledged as the best dancer among the younger girls, who takes every opportunity to belittle her, referring to her as "Smudge," the term used for the lowest servants, and playing mean tricks on her. More than once Cerinthe sneaks out to meet Thorndon of Tycliff, a young sailor she met on the trip to Faranor, who is now an apprentice shipbuilder. Cerinthe has one good friend, Tayla, a housemaid who befriended her when she was a laundry smudge. Elliana breaks a crystal seagull that is Cerinthe's only memento from her mother, and blames it on Tayla, who is demoted to the laundry. For a class assignment to design a dance in honor of the birthday of the princess, Cerinthe creates one on the birth of the Sea Maid, a goddess to whom she has always felt close, but Elliana catches her choreographing secretly in an attic practice room and insists that the dance is meant for her. Although Cerinthe hates to give up the dance, she admits that Elliana, though she is unable to create anything, performs it better than she can, and she helps her learn it to honor the goddess. Their rivalry continues until Elliana, who is extremely manipulative, challenges her to dance on the dangerous platform before Kasakol's gable, so called because of the legend that a girl who dances there will be as great as the dancer for whom the gable is named. Against her better judgment, Cerinthe agrees and, with all the girls watching, they dance until Elliana falls some six feet to another stretch of roof. Although she fears she might do the wrong thing, Cerinthe climbs down and staunches Elliana's bleeding and gives other first aid. Mediri Grace comes and with help takes Elliana to Healer's Hill, a hospital and training school run by the mediri. After a couple of days, Cerinthe gets permission to visit her, only to be insulted by the girl and blamed for her broken leg. Mediri Grace finds her weeping in the herb garden, assures her that she probably saved Elliana's life, and suggests that she may want to become a mediri. At the ballet, *Archipelago Princess*, composed and performed in honor of the birthday of Princess Zandora, Cerinthe dances the part of the young princess, while Sileree, an older girl who has been nice to her, takes that of the maturing princess. After a brilliant performance, they are received by the royal family. When the princess bestows diamond earrings upon both of them, Cerinthe asks that hers be sold and the proceeds used to get a healer or mediri for the school. The queen is horrified to learn that no such position exists and promises to remedy the situation. Tayla, who has developed pneumonia from working in the laundry, is sent to the country to recover. Thorndon, who plans to go to the new colony on some western islands, wants to marry Cerinthe, but realizes there will be no place for dancers there. Sileree, who had wanted to be a singer but was forced by her family to turn to higher-paid dancing, takes her own life. Torn, Cerinthe reviews

her options and realizes that the Sea Maid sings for her only if she is healing someone, and she goes up to Healer's Hill to become a mediri. All the main characters in the novel are well developed, even Elliana, who is essentially a neglected girl in a wealthy family. The fantasy world of Windward is very real, and Cerinthe is a sturdy, sensible, and appealing protagonist, able to face her problems and choices with courage. The whole school of dancing, with its pain, rivalries, hard work, and thrills is fascinating. ALA/YA.

ARIEL DEWITT (*The Door in the Lake**) College student who with Ethan* Glass helps Joey (Joseph Patrick) Finney discover what happened to him while he and his family were camping in the Allegheny Mountains. She is described as being tall and having corkscrewed auburn hair. A premed student, Ariel hopes some day to become a research physician. She works at the hospital where Joey is taken after he collapses at the Minit Mart. She helps to smuggle Joey out of the hospital so he can return to Smokewater Lake by pretending that she is transporting a body to the hospital morgue. Throughout, she reminds Ethan that while his assertion that Joey was abducted by space aliens may be correct, there may also be medical reasons for Joey's problems. She provides a healthy restraint for Ethan's exuberance.

ARMAGEDDON SUMMER (Yolen*, Jane, and Bruce Coville*, Harcourt, 1998) Novel of an apocalyptic cult based in Massachusetts whose leader believes the world as we know it will be destroyed by fire on July 27, 2000, except for 144 faithful, who will be saved to restart a new society, purer and more devout. Events of the summer leading up to the date of the predicted Armageddon are told in alternate chapters by two teenagers, Marina Marlow, whose fourteenth birthday will fall on the fatal day, and Jed* Hoskins, a little older, a well-organized thinker and skeptic. Marina, whose mother, Myrna, has discovered Reverend* Raymond Beelson's Church of the Believers, is strong in her faith, although she worries that her father, a nonbeliever, will burn in the fires to come. The faithful from Beelson's church in Mount Holyoke and some from another of his groups near Boston gather near the top of Mount Weeupcut, where in the three weeks before the fateful date they start transforming the campground into a fortress to keep out any latecomers after the foreordained 144 have arrived. Marina and four other teenage girls are known as "Cherubs" and are assigned to fetch and carry for the Lady Angels, or anyone else who asks them to. Jed is assigned to work with two middle-aged men, Hank and Alex, to fence the perimeter and string wire, later to be electrified. Because her mother is obviously in love with Beelson and so under the spell of his charisma that she ignores her daughter and her five young sons, it falls to Marina to care for little Leo, 3, who is unhappy and increasingly unwell. Although Beelson has planned ahead to stockpile enough supplies to last until the Believers can harvest their first crop and expects to allot the young women to the men as "Eves" to repopulate the world, Jed notices that he has neglected to save any animals, and the boy spots some other gaping holes in the preparations for the new Eden to come. Both Jed and Marina have noticed each other, but do not get together until Jed sneaks up the mountain with his laptop computer, which he has surreptitiously brought along, although such modern technology is banned from the group, so that he can listen to news of the outside world. She begins to question her strong belief when she discovers that the guards at the campground gate are armed and the electric fence has been turned on. As the appointed day arrives, so do several groups outside the gate: people clamoring to get in to be saved; parents and grandparents insisting on seeing their children; sheriff's deputies; state police; and reporters and television crews. On the night of July 26, the Believers gather in the dining area to be given white robes, in which they will greet the end. As the robes are distributed, gunshots break out, and suddenly the whole place is in an uproar, the gate having been breached and a horde swarming in. As some woman tries to pull Jed's robe from him, he turns to see his father, who as an Angel is armed, fire at her. Swept up by the crowd, he is unable to stay with his father, but he helps Marina round up the little children and head up the mountain to a cave they had spotted earlier. Turning back to find his father, he sees Beelson standing on the steps of the now burning building, praying and singing as the fire consumes him. Having retrieved his laptop, Jed heads up from the turmoil, hoping to send out a call for help, but he is hindered by Mrs. Marlow, who is injured, and another woman, mother of a small baby, who needs to be dragged away from the fire and persuaded that Marina has the baby at the cave. He is stopped by Hank, who turns out to be FBI Agent Hummiston and who commandeers the laptop to send his own call for reinforcements. Hank also lets Jed know that his father has been killed in the riot. When Jed and the two women reach the cave, they find Marina and her brother, Grahame, guarding the entrance, all the little children safe inside. The book ends with letters from Marina to Jed, telling about her family's new life in Boston, and from Jed to Marina, about his new life in Colorado, where his mother lives, and their tentative plans to get together at Christmastime. The novel is strongest in the growing sense of unreality in the religious group and the terror of the final night. Marina's great desire to believe is convincing, as is her gradual doubt. Beelson is portrayed not as a charlatan but as a sincere, if misguided, leader, intent on carrying out his interpretation of Biblical prophecies, and bravely facing his own end in the fire. ALA/YA.

AT ALL COSTS (Gilstrap*, John, Warner, 1998)   Adult mystery-thriller hefty in length at 452 pages and in substance involving a hazardous-materials disaster, murder, and political intrigue. It is set in the southeastern and midwestern United States and in Washington, D.C., for about one week near Halloween in 1997. The Brightons—Jake*, manager of a body shop; Carolyn, a department-store salesperson; and their son, Travis*, 13—have lived in a trailer park in Phoenix, South Carolina, for about five months. Everything changes early one morning when federal agents burst into Jake's shop looking for body-shop men involved in drugs. At first afraid they are robbers, Jake pulls a gun from his desk and then is arrested for resisting the orders of the lead officer, FBI Special Agent Irene* Rivers. A fingerprint check identifies him as Jake Donovan. Jake and Carolyn Donovan are high on the FBI's Ten Most Wanted list. Through wit and luck they escape, launching the reader into a fingernail-biting account of their efforts to remain free and prove that they are innocent of the charge of bombing a hazardous-materials depot in Newark, Arkansas, in 1983, which killed sixteen people. They collect Travis from school and head for a hideout

in the West Virginia hills. Along the way, they tell Travis (and the reader) their story. Not long out of college, part of an Enviro-Kleen task force, they are sent to Newark to inventory the contents of a U.S. Army warehouse sealed by the Environmental Protection Agency so that the hazardous materials inside can be disposed of appropriately. While they and their companions are inside, they hear gunfire, and suddenly the whole place explodes. By grit and wit they manage to escape the conflagration and flee into the hills to escape contamination and a mysterious gunman. Being the only survivors, they are soon blamed for the disaster as environmental radicals. Numerous characters appear before the Donovans are exonerated: Harry Sinclair of Chicago, Carolyn's wealthy tycoon uncle, who finances their several flights; Thorne, his right-hand man; Clayton Albricht, senator from Illinois and chair of the Senate Judiciary Committee; Peter Frankel, ambitious, ruthless deputy director of the FBI, who is determined to capture the notorious Donovans and thus become FBI director; Wiggins*, his psychotic hit man; Irene Rivers, the FBI special agent in charge of apprehending the pair, who comes to believe in their innocence; Nick* Thomas, the safety engineer at the hazardous-materials site at the time of the explosion, now with the Enviromental Protection Agency, who works with Jake to ferret out the truth; and many others who drop in and out of the long story that is filled with close encounters and daring escapes. The plot moves rapidly toward the conclusion after Jake brazenly breaks into Irene's apartment very late one night. He describes what happened to him and Carolyn at the depot, pointing out that it is curious that the explosion was so early attributed to them and that no systematic investigation of the incident was ever undertaken. Following his logic, Irene explores the archives and deduces that Frankel, in 1983 the agent in charge of investigating the explosion, had in fact been selling arms from the depot, was himself responsible for the explosion to cover up his criminal activity, and framed the Donovans, who conveniently for him, had fled the contaminated area for their safety. Jake and Carolyn are granted full pardons and a large financial settlement. Although filled with thriller conventions, the book is a super page turner from beginning to end. The reader is firmly on the Donovans' side all the way, so sympathetically are they presented. The narrative moves smoothly from one set of characters and one sector to another. Characters are well differentiated, and, although most have little depth, they play their parts appropriately. Some questions remain unanswered, but they matter little in the total context. Some scenes are deliberately melodramatic and sensationalized, but this, too, is conventional for the genre. Some social commentary appears; for example, in a nation of laws, what is more important, finding out the truth or just capturing the most likely suspects? The title has several applications, to do anything to gain or retain power, prestige, and wealth, as in the case of most of the cast, or to protect one's family, as in Jake's case. Alex.

ATKINS, CATHERINE   Radio news reporter and talk-show host, teacher of alternative education, writer. Her first book, *When Jeff Comes Home** (Putnam, 1999), concerns the return after several years of a boy who was abducted and sexually abused and of his difficulties in fitting into normal life again. A second novel is *Alt Ed* (Putnam, 2003).

AUSTIN   (*Ordeal**)   Steve Austin, African American former FBI agent who now runs Guaranteed Security Associates, providing bodyguards for high-profile public figures and trying to prevent assassinations. About sixteen years before the action in *Ordeal*, he was the FBI agent whom Wren Cameron, then Lizzie Montgomery, contacted about the environmental community that was robbing banks and growing increasingly violent. He promised her that when they raided the place, no one from the community would be injured, but things got out of hand and many were killed, even some children. His guilt about that has driven him to leave the FBI and gives him reason to aid Cam* when he asks for help, even keeping the abduction from authorities in the hope of rescuing Wren and her son, Daniel. Austin even goes against FBI orders and circulates a story that the Armageddon Army leader, Hunter, is homosexual, knowing that such a charge will enrage the man and may smoke him into the open. In the end, Austin figures out where Hunter may have taken Daniel and sends agents to the rescue, but they arrive after Wren has already killed Hunter.

AVI (AVI WORTIS) (1937–   )   Born in New York City; educated at the universities of Wisconsin and Columbia; resident of Providence, Rhode Island; versatile, highly productive, respected, and acclaimed writer of four dozen books for children and young people in several genres. Among many honors, he received the 2003 Newbery Medal for *Crispin: The Cross of Lead* (Hyperion, 2002), about a peasant boy in fourteenth-century England. *Beyond the Western Sea: Book One: The Escape from Home** and *Beyond the Western Sea: Book Two: Lord Kirkle's Money* (both Orchard, 1996) are substantial Dickensian period novels that begin in England and carry the characters to America in 1851. The first one is an American Library Association choice for young adults. Both are exciting, filled with adventure, intrigue, treachery, close encounters, and numerous colorful moments. For more information about Avi, titles, and title entries, see *Dictionary, 1960–1984* [*Emily Upham's Revenge*; *Encounter at Easton*; *No More Magic*; *Shadrach's Crossing*]; *Dictionary, 1985–1989* [*The Fighting Ground*; *Something Upstairs*]; *Dictionary, 1990–1994* [*The Man Who Was Poe*; *Nothing But the Truth*; *The True Confessions of Charlotte Doyle*; *"Who Was That Masked Man, Anyway?"*]; and *Dictionary, 1995–1999* [*The Barn*; *Beyond the Western Sea: Book One: The Escape from Home*; *Beyond the Western Sea: Book Two: Lord Kirkle's Money*; *Poppy*].

B

BAD (Ferris*, Jean, Farrar, 1998) Contemporary sociological-problem novel, set in a Girls' Rehabilitation Center. Dallas, 16, the narrator, resents her father's saying that she is "turning out just like her mother," Dixie Lee, who died while driving drunk when Dallas was four. Like Dixie Lee, Dallas loves excitement, the rush that life on the edge brings when she, Ray (her boyfriend), and friends Pam and Sonny "skate"—snatch purses, shoplift, or hot-wire a fancy car, just for the thrills, not for the stuff itself. She feels only slight hesitation when Pam hands her the shiny silver pistol Pam took from her father for Dallas to use when they stick up a Jiffy-Spot that night. While the other three get away, Dallas is apprehended by a night watchman, taken to Juvenile Hall, and sentenced to six months at the Girls' Rehabilitation Center when her stodgy (as she sees him) father refuses to take her home because he is fed up with her defiance and uncooperative behavior. Her roommate at the Center is black Shastasia, 17, who has a little girl, 1 1/2. The rules are numerous and oner-

ous, especially since Dallas has been used to making her own. The days are severely scheduled, with specific times for meals, work detail, classes, writing, and physical education—never any deviation, a regularity that she surprisingly comes to like. Discussion sessions on such topics as drugs, gangs, sex, contraceptives, and AIDS yield insights into the lives of the other "bad" girls, the counselors, and herself, although Dallas seldom speaks up, holding herself aloof. Like the other inmates, she feels she is in detention for nothing significant and puts the blame on her father. The girls, a large number, range widely in personality and offense. Big, brash, outspoken Dahlia forced a black woman at knifepoint to give up her seat on the bus. Black Damaris, severely beaten by her drug-dealing boyfriend, is in for dealing drugs. Shastasia is in for bus bombing. Thin, unhealthy-looking Toozdae, 14, has been sentenced for prostitution. Lolly, in for assault with a knife, appears bulimic. Of the counselors, or coaches as they are also called, Connie truly cares about the girls, as does Kate, a teacher, who gives Dallas books to read, like *The Member of the Wedding*. Nolan gives her a guide to Texas when she leaves, a humorous suggestion that she needs to find a better direction for her life. Mary Alice, whom the inmates hate and dub "Malice" for her spiteful ways and cruel tongue—she calls the girls names, like Dyke and Spic Whore—is lured into a shower stall and badly beaten. Dallas is closest to Shastasia, to whom upon release to a group home she promises verbal support. At book's end, since she feels no nearer to having a good relationship with her father, she chooses to go to a group home. She is not yet ready to admit culpability, accept her father as he is, and be self-directing in a positive way. Based on actual observations and conversations in a rehabilitation facility, the stories and dialogue are believable, with credible incidents and plenty of trash talk, some of it lurid. Although it is hard to keep track of the very large cast, Shastasia stands out, a good friend to Dallas, a leader in the center, and Dallas's foil. Ultimately, of course, the novel suggests that there are no easy answers to achieving good lives for girls such as these, whom society typically rejects as "bad," but are in most part the products of their environment. ALA/YA.

BAGDASARIAN, ADAM   Author of *Forgotten Fire** (Dorling Kindersley, 2000), a novel based on records left by his great-uncle about the great-uncle's experiences during the Armenian massacre by the Turks in 1915. The novel was cited by the American Library Association and the New York Public Library for young adults. This is Bagdasarian's first book; it elaborates on his short story, "The Survivor," which won *Yankee* magazine's Fiction Award. He has also published *First*

French Kiss and Other Traumas (Farrar, 2002), fictionalized personal experience. He lives in New York City.

BARRETT, TRACY (1955–   )   Born in Cleveland, Ohio; attended the Intercollegiate Center for Classical Studies in Rome and received her A.B. in classics from Brown University and her Ph.D. in Italian and French from the University of California–Berkeley. She lives in Ashville, Tennessee, where she teaches Italian at Vanderbilt University. A grant from the National Endowment for the Humanities supported her research for the biographical novel *Anna of Byzantium** (Delacorte, 1999), which was selected for young adults by the American Library Association. Barrett has also published short stories for children in the educational series "Reading Works," been an editorial assistant for professional journals, translated medieval poetry from Italian into English, and written several nonfiction books for young readers. These include *Nat Turner and the Slave Revolt* (Millbrook, 1993); *Harpers Ferry: The Story of John Brown's Raid* (Millbrook, 1994); *Growing Up in Colonial America* (Millbrook, 1995); and books about the states of Virginia, Tennessee, and Kentucky.

BARRON, T(HOMAS) A(RCHIBALD) (1952–   )   Born in Boston, Massachusetts, but grew up in the mountains of Colorado, where he now lives. He received his B.A. degree from Princeton University in 1974 and attended Oxford University as a Rhodes scholar, graduating in 1978. He later received M.B.A. and J.D. degrees from Harvard University. An environmentalist, he founded the Environmental Studies Program at Princeton, is a former trustee of Nature Conservancy of Colorado, and has led workshops for the Wilderness Society. *The Lost Years of Merlin** (Philomel, 1996) is the first of five novels in a series based loosely on the Arthurian enchanter. He is also known for his Heroic Kate trilogy: *Heartlight* (Philomel, 1990), *The Ancient One* (Philomel, 1992), and *The Merlin Effect* (Philomel, 1994), fantasies with a strong female protagonist. Barron has been a full-time writer since 1989.

BAT-AMI, MIRIAM (1950–) Born in Scranton, Pennsylvania; professor, writer. She received her B.A. degree from Hebrew University in Jerusalem in 1974; her M.A. from California State University–Los Angeles in 1980; and her Ph.D. from the University of Pittsburgh in 1989. The daughter of a rabbi, she has been concerned with questions of faith and the Jewish experience, as in *Dear Elijah* (Farrar, 1995), a novel for middle grades written as letters, and in *Two Suns in the Sky** (Front Street, 1999), in which a Catholic American girl and a Jewish boy in a New York state refugee camp during World War II struggle with the conflicts between their love and their religions. She has also written a picture book, *Sea, Salt, and Air* (Macmillan, 1994). Since 1989, she has taught at Western Michigan University, after briefer periods at the University of Pittsburgh and Southwest Missouri State University. She makes her home in Mattawan, Michigan.

BAUER, CAT Actress, writer. She grew up in a New Jersey suburb, but has lived in New York, Los Angeles, and currently in Venice, Italy. Her first novel, *Harley Like a Person** (Winslow, 1999), is about a high school girl in a town very like Bauer's childhood home who feels stifled by the conventionality of the place and the secrets in her family which nei-

ther of her parents is willing to face or discuss. Bauer has worked as a professional actress and has written plays.

BAUER, JOAN (1951–) Born in River Forest, Illinois; worker in both sales and advertising, writer of both fantasy and realistic fiction for young adults. Her two best-known novels are both stories about unglamorous but fulfilling careers. *Rules of the Road** (Putnam, 1998), about a girl who loves selling shoes and matures in her job to take charge of her own dysfunctional family, was cited as a Best Book by the *School Library Journal*, and has since been named to the American Library Association Young Adult list and as one of the best books of the year by the New York Public Library. *Hope Was Here** (Putnam, 2000) is set mostly in a Wisconsin diner, where a teenage girl waits tables and helps turn around the corrupt town political system. Bauer has recently lived in Brooklyn, New York. For earlier biographical information and a title entry, see *Dictionary, 1995–1999* [*Rules of the Road*].

THE BEETLE AND ME: A LOVE STORY (Young*, Karen Romano, HarperCollins, 1999) Contemporary novel of a girl's fascination with the ancient Volkswagen Beetle in the icehouse of their rural Connecticut home and her determination to repair it. Daisy Pandolfi, 15, the red-haired narrator, is in a family of car lovers. Almost any warm evening or weekend will find her father and his brother, Uncle Phil, a car racer who lives nearby, with their heads bent over the engine of one of their various automobiles. Phil's wife, Aunt Nicole, is a mechanic who runs her own garage. Daisy earns spending money not only baby-sitting Phil and Nicole's three-year-old, Arny, but also doing oil changes and minor repairs in Nicole's garage.

Daisy's mother, a nurse, knows more about automobiles than she lets on, and even Daisy's sister, Helen, and their cousin, Imogene, both of whom at sixteen are beautiful, popular, and have their own cars, know how to change tires and oil, and will get their hands dirty when necessary. The family's favorite entertainment is going to the Summer Cruise, a weekly car show and sale at The Landing, a place on the lakeshore, where owners display their vehicles, many of them restored vintage automobiles, and dicker with potential buyers. There she sees the car of her dreams, a royal blue 1957 Volkswagen Beetle, the same model as the car she knows is dead and stripped of many of its parts in the icehouse at their farm. When she offers her entire savings, four hundred seventy-five dollars, the owner smiles and gently tells her he's asking six thousand, bottom. This only whets her desire to get at the purple Beetle in the icehouse. With difficulty, she persuades her dad to let her look at it. Reluctantly, with the whole family gathered and staring at the Beetle, he agrees that if Daisy does all the work, pays for the parts, and gets it running, she can have it. All summer she works on the car, refusing help, with occasional detours to the lake. Helen, who is in love with Tom Bixby, and Imogene, who is in love with anyone handy, usually ignore Daisy, but one night when the boys are all busy, they ask her along on a girl picnic. She wanders off and follows the sound of a guitar to the dock, where she meets Daniel Schweitzer, new in town and by coincidence the son of the blue Beetle owner, and sings with him until the others join them. Imogene, with long-practiced skill, appropriates him, but not before Daisy, for the first time, has fallen in love. When school starts again, Daisy talks her way into auto shop class, where she often works with Ben Van

Buskirk, one of Imogene's boyfriends, and his buddy, Billy Hatcher, who drives a Thunderbird, owned two-thirds by his older brother. At the fall production of *The King and I*, Imogene and Daniel get the romantic roles, Helen leads the dances, and Daisy works on the lighting with Billy. When his brother, off at college, has the Thunderbird, Daisy volunteers her Beetle to borrow some equipment from St. Mary's school, with Billy driving, since at fifteen she still cannot get a license. Just as they get back to her yard, the engine makes a strange noise. When she gets up the nerve to look, the next day, she finds oil covering everything. Painstakingly, she cleans it up, studies every surface, and cannot discover what is wrong. Finally, unwilling to get help from her own family, she calls Billy who comes out. Together they slide under the car and discover that it has "sucked a valve." Her fierce independence undermined, she asks her father to help her get parts, and they go to Mr. Schweitzer, who knows the right suppliers. Daniel, who is there with Imogene, has no interest in or knowledge of cars, to his father's disappointment. Daisy vacillates emotionally between her infatuation with Daniel and her growing affection for Billy, but remains totally in love with her purple Beetle. After she repairs it, she makes a major decision. Billy has admitted that his brother has sold the Thunderbird, his absentee father has stopped sending any support because Billy is now eighteen, and he will have to earn money to help make payments for the mortgage and other expenses, with little prospect of college. After midnight mass, she gives him the keys to the Beetle, a long-term loan until she is old enough to drive it herself and a commitment to their friendship. The novel is often amusing and always refreshing in its picture of a high school girl with interests other than boys, with no obligatory big drinking-and-drugging party, and with family members supportive and generally understanding. Even Imogene, the utterly confident young beauty, is not deliberately mean. The purple 1957 Volkswagen Beetle becomes a main character, with a personality of its own. ALA/YA.

BELLE PRATER'S BOY (White*, Ruth, Farrar, 1996)   Novel of twelve-year-old cousins in the Virginia mountains in 1953 who both learn unsettling truths about their parents, but, helping each other, manage to survive and accept the willing help of their remaining families. For a longer entry, see *Dictionary, 1995–1999*. ALA/YA.

BENNETT, CHERIE (1960–)   Born in Buffalo, New York; received her B.A. from the University of Michigan. She has had a varied career: author, playwright, syndicated columnist of a teen advice column ("Hey, Cherie!"), actress, director, vocalist, and lecturer. She has written plays and screenplays, several of which have won awards, and nearly one hundred books mainly for young adults. Most of her novels appear in sets, among them Sunset Island, Club Sunset Island (for younger readers), Surviving Sixteen, Wild Hearts, Hope Hospital, Pageant, and, cowritten with her husband, Jeff Gottesfeld, a writer and producer, Teen Angels, Trash, Mirror Image, and University Hospital. Chosen by the American Library Association for young adults, *Life in the Fat Lane** (Delacorte, 1998) is a problem novel about weight gain. Other titles include *Haunted Heart* (Avon, 1999) and *Love Him Forever* (Avon, 1999). Bennett's books have been praised for their lively style and ability to address the interests

and concerns of teenage girls with sympathy but without sentimentality.

BEN QUEEN (*Hotel Paradise**)   Man about sixty who is still remembered with fluttering hearts by women in the Spirit Lake area, including Emma Graham's great aunt, Aurora Paradise. Originally from Flyback Hollow near Cold Flat Junction, he went west when he was a teenager and came back at twenty, so handsome that all the women, as Jude Stemple says, "followed him around like puppies." Then he "run off" with Rose Fern, youngest of the Devereau sisters, a woman far above him socially and so beautiful that Jude still gets starry-eyed when he talks about her. When she was found twenty years later murdered viciously in the barnyard, Ben was arrested, convicted, and sent to prison, though he never testified in his own defense. When he finds Emma at the Devereau house wearing Mary-Evelyn's dress that she has tried on, he says it is a mighty pretty color that matches her beautiful eyes. It is the first compliment she has ever received on her appearance, and it confuses and disarms her. He is surprised to learn that Aurora is still alive and tells Emma that she was wild in her youth, that when someone dared her, she stripped off her clothes and jumped buck naked into the lake in front of twenty people. He also talks to the girl seriously, saying he did not kill either his wife or his daughter, but he is tired of running. When they part, he tells her, "If it goes too hard on you, turn me in." This, as much as anything else, keeps Emma from telling the sheriff about what she knows.

BERG,   ELIZABETH   (1948–) Writer of novels for both adults and young people, as well as some nonfiction. She attended the University of Minnesota and St. Mary's College, and before becoming a full-time writer worked in a variety of jobs—waitress, chicken washer, singer, information clerk, registered nurse. *Joy School** (Random, 1997) is a sequel to *Durable Goods* (Random, 1993), both about Katie, the strong-spirited daughter of an abusive father. Among her other novels are *Until the Real Thing Comes Along* (Random, 1999), in which a girl falls in love with a gay boy; *Open House* (Random, 2000); and *Never Change* (Pocket Books, 2001). One of her novels for adults, *Talk Before You Sleep* (Random, 1993), is conversations with a friend dying of cancer. Berg also wrote several books in the Festivals of the World Series. She makes her home near Boston.

BEYOND THE WESTERN SEA: BOOK ONE: THE ESCAPE FROM HOME (Avi*, Orchard, 1996)   Lively, intricate, Dickensian period novel, with a very large cast and an abundance of action and incidents. The plot revolves around the efforts of two boys to leave Liverpool, England, in 1851 and sail to the United States. It ends with both on board a ship bound for Boston. The book is mostly plot and is a page turner from start to finish, with cliffhanger chapter endings, a good measure of villains and villainy, and plucky heroes. At the same time, it gives an interesting but limited view of the times in Ireland, where it starts, and in England. The story continues in *Beyond the Western Sea: Book Two: Lord Kirkle's Money*. Previously the book was cited by the American Library Association for younger readers. For a longer plot summary, see *Dictionary, 1995–1999*. ALA/YA.

BILLY COLLINS (*Bull Catcher**) Friend, classmate, and teammate of Bull Larsen, Jeff* Hanson, and Ngo Huynh Phuong* at Shipley (Wisconsin) High School. For years, Billy has hidden the beatings his father gives him, a fairly easy matter, because Billy's father is very careful not to beat his son in any visible place. The man usually pummels Billy's arms. When asked why he cannot, for example, handle a pencil in class or cannot throw the ball with his usual force, Billy lies, since he is afraid that his father will take his wrath out on Billy's sisters instead. The intervention that follows when cheerleader Sandi* Watkins asks Bull and Jeff for help gives Billy some relief, but the attacks resume. The summer before senior year begins, Billy is killed in an accident while driving after drinking. When he learns about Billy's death, which happens while he is at summer camp, Bull regrets not having helped Billy when, for a second time, Sandi asked Bull to help her intervene. Bull refused, since Bull was jealous because by that time Billy and Sandi were sweethearts.

BIRD, SARAH (1949–)   Born in Ann Arbor, Michigan; editor, writer of both novels and nonfiction. She received her B.A. degree in anthropology at the University of New Mexico in 1973 and her M.A. degree in journalism at the University of Texas in 1976. The child of an Air Force family, she was well acquainted with the difficulties and restrictions on the dependents of servicemen overseas that form the background for her scathing novel, *The Yokota Officers Club** (Knopf, 2000). Among her other novels are *The Alamo House* (Norton, 1980), a comic novel based on graduate students at the University of Texas; *The Boyfriend School* (Doubleday, 1989), about a romance writers' convention; *The Mommy Club* (Doubleday, 1991); and *Virgin at the Rodeo* (Doubleday, 1993). She also wrote five romance novels under the pseudonym, Tory Cates, and one as Sarah McCabe Bird.

BLACKWOOD, GARY (1945–) Born in Meadville, Pennsylvania; graduate of Grove City College; amateur actor; teacher of writing and playwriting at Missouri Southern State College and of writing-for-publication at Trinidad State Junior College; playwright; writer of fiction and nonfiction for middle graders and young adults. Among his novels is *The Shakespeare Stealer** (Dutton, 1998), an American Library Association choice for young adults about an orphan boy, Widge, in William Shakespeare's company of players. In its sequel, also an American Library Association choice for young adults, *Shakespeare's Scribe** (Dutton, 2000), Widge joins the company on the road and discovers a man who claims he is Widge's father. Blackwood and his wife live near Carthage, Missouri. For more information about Blackwood, additional titles, and a longer title entry, see *Dictionary, 1995–1999* [*The Shakespeare Stealer*].

BLANCA MERCADO (*Bodega Dreams**) Nancy Saldivia Mercado, wife of protagonist and narrator Julio Mercado. She has acquired the nickname Blanca because she is a good person and sincere in applying her religion to her everyday life. She tries to be patient with Julio, even when she knows he has not told her the whole truth. Scenes show her in her Pentecostal church, to which she is devoted, and a sharp contrast is drawn between her and her sister, Negra, a loose, foul-mouthed woman who is constantly in some kind of trouble. Realistic most of the time, at least more so than Julio, Blanca attempts to help Claudia, an immigrant from Colombia, acquire a husband so she can stay in

the United States. She promotes a match between Claudia, 27, and Roberto Vega, an evangelist ten years Claudia's junior. Roberto is an "anointed," a person who their church believes is one of the 144,000 who will go to heaven to be with Christ.

BLETSUNG MACLEOD (*The Last Sin Eater**) Woman who lives alone in a cabin on the mountainside in the secluded valley in which the family of Cadi Forbes also live. Bletsung is shunned because gossip has it that she killed her father and mother. Cadi watches her work with her bees, which she does with skill and gentleness so that she is never stung. Although Bletsung's existence is meager, she shares what she has with old Miz* Elda Kendric. Cadi also observes that Bletsung is friends with the sin eater. Later, Cadi learns that Bletsung's mother had committed suicide because Bletsung's father abused her verbally and physically and that the sin eater, Sim Gillivray, killed Bletsung's father to keep him from raping her. Bletsung and the sin eater have been in love for many years, and their relationship was one of the reasons that the Kai clan conspired to make Sim the sin eater. At the end of the novel, it is revealed that Sim and Bletsung married and had a son.

BLOOD AND CHOCOLATE (Klause*, Annette Curtis, Delacorte, 1997) Contemporary fantasy novel of magic, werewolves, and romance between a human and a werewolf. Exotically beautiful werewolf Vivian Gandillon, 16, yearns for love. She thinks she finds it with handsome human Aiden, knowingly violating the pack rule: "Don't date if you can't mate." She is aware that she may be endangering the pack, a clear hint of what eventually occurs. The many details of wolf life and culture are fascinating, the love scenes and sexually explicit dialogue give the book a highly erotic tone, the style is vigorous and compelling, and Vivian's problems and needs as an outsider are convincing and filled with tension. Previously, the book was cited by *School Library Journal*. For a longer entry, see *Dictionary, 1995–1999*. ALA/YA.

BLOOR, EDWARD (1950–)   Born in Trenton, New Jersey; novelist, teacher, editor. His novel, *Tangerine** (Harcourt, 1997), earlier named to the Fanfare list and as a Poe nominee, was more recently cited by the American Library Association to its young adult list. For earlier biographical information and a title entry, see *Dictionary, 1995–1999* [*Tangerine*].

BOBBY MOSES (*The Yokota Officers Club**)   Obese, sleazy entertainer who takes Bernie Root from Okinawa to Japan, ostensibly to dance as part of his program for armed services groups, but actually to act as Zelda, the dumb-blond straight man for his act. Although he tells Bernie's mother that he is gay, he makes a few easily rebuffed passes at Bernie and usually seems to be seeking some female-for-pay companionship. Early in their tour, Bernie realizes that his real money, which he throws around with abandon, comes from dealing in amphetamines. He insists that Bernie dye her hair blonde, use vivid makeup, and wear white go-go boots, even though he cannot find any big enough for her in Japan, so she is virtually unable to dance. At the same time, he is generous, sharing his sumptuous midnight meals with her and buying gifts for all her family. When she saves his show at the Yokota Officers Club from bombing, he does not acknowledge it, but he seems genuinely sorry to see her go and almost admits he is fond of her.

BODEGA DREAMS (Quiñonez*, Ernesto, Vintage, 2000)   Realistic adult novel set for a few weeks in Spanish Harlem, El Barrio, New York City, in probably the mid-1980s. Ecuadorian Puerto Rican American Julio Mercado (also called Chino because of his Oriental features), the earnest narrator of about twenty-one, and his pregnant wife, staunchly Pentecostal Nancy Saldivia Mercado, called Blanca* because she is good, kind, and hardworking, both attend Hunter College, hoping through education to attain the American dream of good jobs, a house, and a family. Blanca dislikes Julio's associating with street-smart, tough-guy Sapo, with whom he has been friends since fourth grade. She often takes Julio to task over it, especially when Sapo, who deals drugs for the El Barrio boss, Willie Bodega, persuades Julio to store them in their apartment for him. The real action starts when Sapo takes Julio to meet Bodega, at Bodega's orders. Bodega has a dream that Spanish Harlem can be a fine place for Latinos, and has set out to make that dream a reality. He has been buying up property to renovate and helping the people who live there in various ways, financing his efforts by selling drugs. The biggest drug dealer in the area, he is aided in this enterprise by Edward Nazario*, a clever, pragmatic lawyer. Bodega, whose real name is William Carlos Irizarry, wishes to enlist Julio in the cause because he wants to build a cadre of young professionals to serve as role models and create a solid middle class, and also because the woman he has long loved, Veronica, now known as Vera, is Blanca's aunt. Bodega lures Vera from Miami, but her very wealthy, elderly Cuban husband is a definite impediment. At the request of Bodega, Julio meets with Vera and Bodega when her husband, John Vidal, arrives.

Vera shoots John, but Bodega insists that, if questioned, Julio swear that Bodega shot the man. Then Bodega is also shot and killed, and Nazario insists that a rival drug lord perpetrated the crime. Although Blanca has left him because she is angry about his continued association with the Bodega bunch, she tells Julio that her mother says that Vera had never been in love with Bodega but rather with Nazario. Julio then realizes that Nazario has been behind an elaborate plot to get Vera, her husband's wealth, and Bodega's power for himself. Julio reports Nazario to the police, and after a well-attended funeral for Bodega, Nazario and Vera are arrested for murder. Sapo hopes to take over the drug trade, and in the book's last pages, Julio dreams that Bodega shows him a happier, prosperous Spanish Harlem, in which both English and Spanish languages blend in a new dialect the dream Bodega calls "Spanglish," apparently a sign that Julio may try to make Bodega's dream of an economically and socially improved El Barrio a reality. After a slow start, to establish characters, relationships, and setting, plot intensity builds and holds to the very last sentence. Bodega is a fascinating combination of romantic and idealist, and Nazario seems opportunistic and a likely villain from the outset. The book's greatest attribute is the setting, a graphically revealed region of burned-out buildings, prostitutes, "pissed up" elevators, junkies, tough-guy cops, vacant lots littered with stolen cars, frequent shootouts and holdups, and Latinos who know that one must always protect one's back, that one must never acquire too much material goods so that one can easily clear out, and, equally important, that one must never endanger one's self by knowing too much about what is going on. In contrast is the Pentecostal church to which Blanca belongs, which is a strong force for stability and morality. Style supports setting, with its mixture of trash and street talk in Spanish and English. NYPL.

THE BODY OF CHRISTOPHER CREED
(Plum-Ucci*, Carol, Harcourt, 2000) Mystery in which the disappearance of an unlikable high school boy deeply affects not just his peers but also a number of adults in his town. Although he has never cared for Christopher Creed, who clings like a leech to anyone even slightly nice to him, and even joined in tormenting the boy when they were younger, the narrator, Torey (Victor) Adams, 16, is very uncomfortable with the jokes that his schoolmates make about the possibility of suicide. When Christopher disappears, he and his friend, Alex Arrington, a computer whiz, retrieve an e-mail note to the principal, sent by Christopher from the school library, which complains of his own "personality defects," lists more fortunate boys, including Torey, and ends "I only wish to be gone." Soon everyone in their little conservative south New Jersey town of Steepleton is speculating about where the body might be. Torey questions the sincerity of Mrs. Creed, who makes appeals in church and at the school, saying things about Christopher he knows to be false. Some people think Chris might have been killed by one of the tough "boons," the young people from the rural areas nearby known as the boondocks. When Ali McDermott, who used to be Torey's girlfriend but who lately has gained a reputation for being easy and wild, urgently asks him to come over, he does reluctantly. She shows him that from her bedroom she can see right into the Creed house and tells him about how restrictive and domineering Mrs. Creed is. She also has seen Chris write in a diary

night after night, then hide it behind a picture on his wall. They watch as Mrs. Creed, whom Ali thinks might have killed Christopher and is trying to destroy evidence, systematically searches Chris's room, obviously hunting for the diary. To Torey's surprise and dismay, Ali's current boyfriend, Bo* Richardson, a big boon who has always seemed very threatening to Torey, arrives. Told by Torey and Ali their suspicions of Mrs. Creed, he volunteers to steal the diary. Thinking of movies he has seen, Torey says they need a diversion to get Mr. and Mrs. Creed away from the house and phones from a nearby park, offering information for a lot of money. He races away before the Creeds get there, but they all end up in the police station, where Torey at first is afraid to admit his part in the scheme, then is not believed when he does, since the police have their suspect in Bo, a boy who has previously been in trouble with the law. Torey's mother, a lawyer, takes Ali and Ali's little brother home with her and gets Bo out on bail. Although Bo did not actually break into the Creed house, he got the diary from Chris's younger brother. Torey and Ali read it with dismay. It details events from the summer before, when he worked for an uncle at a waterfront restaurant in Margate and had a touching affair with a shy girl named Isabella Karzden, a waitress there. Torey and Ali, finally contacting the right Karzden, go to Margate only to discover that the diary was fiction, that Isabella is not at all what Chris described, but a tough, experienced girl who tried to be nice to him at first but soon became fed up. She suggests, however, that they consult her Aunt Vera, who is psychic and might know Chris's whereabouts. Aunt Vera, an obese woman eating potato chips, seems like a fake, but she describes a place

Torey knows, an Indian graveyard with three big stones not far from his house, where she says he will find the body of one who shot himself. Against his inclination but unable to rest with that prediction, Torey goes to the graveyard and climbs on the stones as he and Alex often did as children. His weight, however, has increased enough to make one of the stones shift, fall on his leg, and open a cave beneath, where he sees some wrapped Indian bodies and one white corpse, which disintegrates as he watches it, literally burning up in front of him. When he regains consciousness in the hospital, he learns that the body was not Christopher's, but that of a man who disappeared nearly a generation earlier in an almost parallel situation, and that the cave, a limestone cavern, had been sealed airtight, thereby preserving the bodies until his moving the stone allowed oxygen to reach them and disintegrate them before his eyes, in a process almost like burning. Torey spends some time in a psychiatric hospital, then goes off to boarding school for his senior year. What has happened to Chris is never determined, though clues that Torey and Ali turn up seem to indicate that he had stashed away some money and simply left to escape his mother. What happens to the town is almost as important as Chris's story. Several prominent people are found to have skeletons in their closets. Torey's vivid imagination and sense of decency lead him to get involved in Chris's disappearance in the first place and account for his horror at what he sees in the Indian cemetery. Since all the action is seen through Torey's eyes, the tension and increasing terror make a compelling story even if, in retrospect, some of the elements seem far-fetched. ALA/YA; Printz Honor.

BOMBINGHAM: A NOVEL (Grooms*
Anthony, Free Press, 2001)   Historical
novel for adults of the civil rights movement set mainly in Birmingham, Alabama, in the year leading up to the
bombing of the Sixteenth Street Baptist
Church in 1963. The title alludes to the
many bombs and fires the city has been
experiencing, so many that it has been
nicknamed "Bombingham." The novel
might also be titled "Book of Battles,"
since it involves several other conflicts as
well, beginning with that of narrator and
protagonist African American Walter
Burke, who is in the U.S. Army in Vietnam in a rice-paddy battle, where he loses
his buddy, Haywood Jackson. As he ponders what he will write to Haywood's parents, his thoughts go back to when he was
eleven, and known as Waltie, he shared a
paper route with his best pal, Lamar Bur-
rell. Waltie has several battles of his own.
He struggles to sort out his relationship
with strong-minded, willful, and not always sensible Lamar, and look after his
little sister, Josie, 9, especially when his
father, Carl, tells him that his mother,
Clara, is dying of a brain tumor. He must
also cope with his worries over his
mother. A secretary for an insurance company, Clara battles with her illness, becoming weaker and weaker and unstable
of mind. She refuses to consider an operation, believing that, whatever the outcome, her illness and eventual death are
God's will. She is also conflicted about the
civil rights protests and prefers that her
family stay away from the activities of
Martin Luther King, Jr., and his associates. Carl, a high school science teacher,
also has his battles: with Clara over an operation, which he favors; with guilt because during an argument he struck her;
with his drinking; with not being with his
family because Clara has ordered him

out; and about participating in the movement. Although Waltie knows that Lamar
can be a bad influence and tends to gossip, he enjoys Lamar's company. Scenes
stand out: Waltie and Lamar discussing
the movement and Clara's illness, which
Lamar is sure is pregnancy; Waltie, Josie,
and Lamar sneaking into a Whites-only
park and being rudely ordered out; and
meeting Reverend Timmons, who is a
close friend of Lamar's mother, and participating in workshops he and other leaders present designed to teach children and
young people Black history and engage
them in demonstrations and protests.
They see Martin Luther King, Jr., hear
about sit-ins at local department stores,
and observe how people's lives are affected by bus strikes. Curiosity takes them
to marches in progress, and they see people arrested, dragged to paddy wagons,
and carted away, including King. They get
knocked about by police and experience
the terror of being set upon by snarling,
salivating police dogs. When Josie disappears during a protest, they learn that she
is being held at a 4-H dormitory at the
State Fairgrounds. Waltie tells the officer
in charge that his mother is dying and
needs her daughter, and Carl arrives with
release papers, but the officer hassles
them, insisting that what Blacks really
want is everything the Whites own. Another powerful scene occurs when
Waltie's mother's stepfather tells Waltie
how Waltie's grandfather died, in prison,
incarcerated for life because, although innocent, he was accused of murder and
rape. Waltie and Lamar decide to go to
the Sixteenth Street Baptist Church after
the bombing, just to look around. On the
way, Lamar is shot to death by a White
boy sitting in the back of a truck. After
Clara's death, Carl becomes irresponsible,
and Waltie drifts through school, until

Carl suggests he might as well join the army because he will only be drafted anyway. At book's end, Walter is still struggling with what to write to the Jacksons. The book never lags and is more powerful because of the restrained portrayal of the different battles, which are symbolic and at the same time very personal. So also is Waltie/Walter himself, both an individual and symbolic of Blacks of the times. Walter's Birmingham life and his Vietnam life are skillfully connected by the death of Haywood and the parallel one of Lamar. Booklist.

BO RICHARDSON (*The Body of Christopher Creed**)   Big, tough high school boy from a rural area near Steepleton, New Jersey, one of the "boons" (for boondocks) that Torey Adams and his friends fear and try to ignore. When Torey finds that Bo is Ali McDermott's current boyfriend, he is shocked, but he soon changes his mind. The first thing Bo does is stomp upstairs and tell the man that Ali's mother is sleeping with to get out, since he has been taunting and humiliating Ali and her younger brother by making sure they can hear the loud sounds of their sexual activity. Bo's size and determination are enough to scare the fellow away. Bo impulsively offers to steal the diary that Ali has seen Chris Creed hide, since they think that it may have clues to his disappearance and that Mrs. Creed may be attempting to destroy evidence. Although Bo has had minor scrapes with the law, he is actually a responsible and loving boy, taking care of his younger siblings when his mother goes on five-day drunks and supporting Ali whose own mother is sleeping around promiscuously. The main threat to Bo comes from the chief of police, after his daughter is nasty to Ali and Bo blurts out that her own fa-

ther had an affair with Ali's mother for months. This breaks up the chief's marriage, and he wants revenge on Bo, but instead he is prevailed upon to resign in disgrace. In the end, Torey's mother, a lawyer, seems to be looking out for Bo as well as Ali and Ali's little brother.

BOX, C. J.   Born in Wyoming, heralded author of *Open Season** (Putnam, 2001), a mystery novel featuring earnest young Wyoming Game Warden Joe Pickett, who doggedly brings to justice those who would sacrifice animals and environment for business progress. A *New York Times* Notable Book and nominated for an Edgar Award for Best First Novel, *Open Season* was a *Booklist* choice for young adult readers. Its sequel, also starring Joe Pickett, is *Savage Run* (Putnam, 2002). Box has worked as a ranch hand, fishing guide, and small-town newspaper reporter and editor, and has also been a member of an exploration survey crew. He writes out of his familiarity with Wyoming and the Rocky Mountain region. He is currently the chief executive officer of Rocky Mountain International Corporation, a company that coordinates international marketing for the state tourism departments of Montana, Wyoming, South Dakota, Idaho, and North Dakota. He lives near Cheyenne with his wife and three daughters.

THE BOXER (Karr*, Kathleen, Farrar, 2000)   Sports novel of a young Irish boy who fights the way out of poverty and a tenement on the Lower East Side of Manhattan for himself and his family in the 1880s. The narrator, red-haired John Aloysius Xavier Woods, 15, works a twelve-hour day in a sweatshop ironing men's shirts to help support his mother and five younger siblings since his alcoholic father ran off. In hope of the five-dollar purse (more than he makes in two weeks), he goes into Brodie's Saloon, which advertises for "likely lads" for bare-fisted sparring matches. Johnny is small, but quick, and thinks he may have a chance of lasting the required four rounds. His second round is interrupted by a police raid, since fighting is illegal in New York, and he lands in the Tombs with a six-month sentence. His first night in Bummers' Hall is utter misery, but when he eagerly joins the other inmates for exercise in the yard, hoping for fresh air to drive out the foul smell, a bully named Skelly provokes a fight. Watching, an old fighter named Professor Michael O'Shaunnessey sees promise in the skinny kid and takes Johnny under his wing. Knowing the ropes and having some cash to bribe guards, he moves Johnny to his own quarters, away from the reeking hall, and feeds him far better than the slop served the other prisoners. He, too, has six months to serve, and as an investment in the future as well as to pass the time, he starts rigorously training his protégé. The "Perfessor" also gets a guard to drop by Johnny's mother's tenement apartment weekly with food and enough money to help pay the rent. When Johnny's weight is up a bit and his muscles are toughened, the Perfessor arranges a match in the yard with Skelly, backed by the guards who are bored and like betting. Johnny wins, despite dirty tricks by Skelly, and leaves the Tombs with half the Perfessor's earnings from betting on him and a professional name, The Chopper. The money disappears fast on new clothes for the family, and other necessities. Johnny hunts for work, only to find that manual labor, even ditchdigging, requires political patronage. As a last resort, he returns to Brodie's Saloon, now called a "boxing club," with exhibition sparring nightly. All the Perfessor's training pays off, and he is soon boxing three nights a week, going to a vocational high school during the day, and insisting that the younger children attend school. Then Brodie makes him an offer, that he lose the next fight for two hundred fifty dollars. Reluctantly, Johnny agrees, but in the ring finds he cannot throw the fight, knocks out his opponent, and is fired by Brodie. He returns home to find that his youngest sister, Katie, is extremely ill with whooping cough. For a couple of weeks, he helps nurse Katie and Bridget and Jamie, all with severe illnesses, and tries to help the other families in the tenement, which is swept by the disease that is fatal to some of the children. Just as the future seems hopeless, he receives a letter from Professor O'Shaunnessey, who has become the new boxing master of the high-toned New York Athletic Club. Soon he is employed at the club, keeping the workout machines in shape and occasionally sparring with the toffs who come to learn boxing. The Perfessor organizes a series of exhibition bouts, for each of which John wins trophies, gold medallions, or a watch, but also fifty dollars in under-the-table tips. After the exhibitions, O'Shaunnessey gets him a professional prizefight for July, to be held at Long Point, Ontario, Canada, across from Buffalo, New York, since fighting is illegal in the United States. A few weeks before the fight, his father shows up, belligerent and demanding as ever, threatening to use his belt on the terrified children. Johnny knocks him out, but he gets away with some of his son's valuable trophies and is almost certain to return. Johnny confesses to his mother, for whom he has bought a sewing machine to free her from her poorly paid construction of artificial flowers, that he plans to move them all to a small house in Brooklyn, where they can have a garden and fresh air. This depends on his winning the fight at Long Point, where he is matched against an Australian, who fights dirty, trips him so he breaks his ankle, and jams resin into his eye, but Johnny manages to win and get his share of the purse, a thousand dollars, enough to buy the little house in Brooklyn. Johnny has doubts about continuing as a professional fighter, but he is determined to go back to school, to try to get his talented sister Maggie some art training, and to steer his brother Liam in the right direction. The strength of the novel is in its details of life in the 1880s, in the tenements, the jail, the low-class saloon, and the upper-class athletic club, and in Johnny's appealing character, naive but steadfast, devoted to his family, and hopeful against long odds. ALA/YA.

BOYLAN, JAMES FINNEY (1958–) Born in Valley Forge, Pennsylvania; editor, educator, writer. He was graduated from Wesleyan University in 1980 and began graduate study at Johns Hopkins University, where he taught after getting his degree. For some time he was an editorial assistant at Viking/Penguin and later production editor of fiction at E. P. Dutton. He has been a visiting professor at University College, Cork, Ireland, and teaches creative writing and American literature at Colby College. Among his publications is a book of short stories and two novels described as both bizarre and rollicking, *The Planets* (Bloomsbury, 1991) and its sequel, *The Constellations* (Bloomsbury, 1992). Another highly entertaining novel, *Getting In** (Warner, 1998), follows four high school seniors as they visit elite New England colleges for interviews with admissions officers, a trip

full of ironic errors and misunderstandings. Boylan lives in Belgrade Lakes, Maine.

BRADLEY, MARION ZIMMER (1930–1999) Born in Albany, New York; died of a heart attack in Berkeley, California; educated at the State University of New York–Albany, Hardin-Simmons College (B.A.), and the University of California–Berkeley; editor of *Marion Zimmer Bradley's Fantasy Magazine* and popular writer of science fiction, fantasy, gothic novels, and mysteries. She received the Locus Award for best fantasy novel in 1984 for *The Mists of Avalon* (Knopf, 1983), an ambitious retelling of the Arthurian legend. Her many Darkover novels have remained popular and have inspired their own fan magazines. *Heartlight** (Tor, 1998), about the ongoing efforts to combat the power of Evil, was selected by *Booklist* for young adults. Its companions are *Ghostlight* (Tor, 1995), *Witchlight* (Tor, 1996), and *Gravelight* (Tor, 1997).

BRADSHAW, GILLIAN (1955?–) Born in Falls Church, Virginia; lived for a time in Chile when she was a child; was graduated from the University of Michigan where she won prizes for Classical Greek in 1975 and 1977 and the Hopwood Award for Fiction in 1977; received her master's degree in classics from Newham College, Cambridge; has also lived in California and England. She has published science fiction and fantasy novels and has won critical acclaim for her historical fiction set in ancient times, like *The Bearkeeper's Daughter* (Houghton Mifflin, 1986), which is set in the period of Justinian I; *Cleopatra's Heir* (Forge, 2002), about Caesarion, the son of Julius Caesar and the Queen of Egypt; and *The Sand-Reck-*

oner* (Forge, 2000), about the noted Greek mathematician, Archimedes, which received the Alex Award. Also highly praised has been her Arthurian trilogy, *Hawk of May* (Simon & Schuster, 1980), *Kingdom of Summer* (Simon & Schuster, 1981), and *In Winter's Shadow* (Simon & Schuster, 1982).

BRANWEN (*The Lost Years of Merlin**) Mother of Emrys, with whom she is washed ashore in Gwynedd (Wales), when he is about seven. Although she refuses to tell him anything about his past, which has been wiped from his memory, she does tell marvelous stories that stir his imagination. Because she will give him no information, he refuses to believe she is his mother, even when she nurses his burns with great tenderness and helps him develop the "second sight" by which he can see and even read inscriptions. Emrys eventually learns that she is really Elen of the Sapphire Eyes, a Celtic woman who fell in love with Stangmar, son of the powerful wizard, Tuatha, and who came to Fincayra to be with him. After the first seven years of his son's life, Stangmar became so corrupted by the evil power, Rhita Gawr, that he promised to kill the boy. To save her son, Elen fled the island and eventually was washed ashore in Gwynedd, where she took the name of Branwen. To protect him from the evil of his father, she refuses to tell Emrys of his past, but when he is determined to leave, she gives him a packet of healing herbs and the Galator, a pendant of great power, to take with him.

BRAVERMAN (*Hope Was Here**) Very tall, angular grillman at the Welcome Stairways diner who spearheads the campaign of G. T. Stoop for mayor of Mulhoney, Wisconsin. Braverman is devoted to G. T., who gave him a job when his mother was out of work, then taught him to cook. When three thugs hired by the Millstone campaign beat him up, Hope Yancey goes to his home, carrying a cactus in lieu of flowers, and is surprised that he has two younger sisters and his mother calls him Eddie. He admits to Hope that he actually wanted to kill the men who took turns holding and hitting him, and he was frightened of his own murderous fury. She tells him that when she was eleven, her aunt got a friend to teach her to box, and she beat out her anger on the punching bag, anger at her mother for abandoning her and at her aunt for uprooting her repeatedly to go to a new job. When she tells Braverman that her mother named her Tulip, he roars with laughter, and for the first time she is able to laugh at the ridiculous name. When he asks her out to dinner, she is not sure, having always heard that it is unwise to date someone you work with in a stressful place like a diner, so he suggests they have a trial run after Welcome Stairways closes, sets a table with a candle and flowers from the cash register counter, and cooks them both delicious pork chop sandwiches, the most romantic dinner she can imagine. Although he has been out of high school for a year, he cannot afford to go to college, but G. T. sets up a scholarship fund so that while Hope is going to college in Michigan, he will go to the University of Wisconsin.

BREAKING RANK (Randle*, Kristen D., Morrow, 1999) Realistic contemporary novel of school and community life set in an unnamed American city in recent years. Mr. Hall, head counselor at Feynman High School, persuades the parents of Casey Willardson, 17, to allow her to tutor shy, dark-haired Thomas Fairbairn,

18, but Casey's best friend, Joanna, tells her that this action will not look good to the rest of the school. The Cribs, to which pretty blond Casey and Joanna belong, are the kids from the "good" side of town. They are active socially and athletically, wear letter jackets, are school leaders, and look down on the kids of the Clan* from the "other" side of town. The Clan hold themselves aloof, are in only remedial classes, dress only in black, and wear braided bracelets and single, small-beaded braids of hair. Thomas has done what no Clan member has ever done, taken a standardized test and scored so high that school authorities consider him gifted. Mr. Hall places him in honors classes and tells him that financial aid is available to send him to college. Since Casey and Thomas sit together for tutoring, the Cribs cast hostile glances at them, especially Gene Walenski, a letterman. Soon Thomas—called "Baby" by his mother and older brother, Lenny (Leonard), 22, a talented mechanic, and by the Clan—and Casey are meeting at her house as well as at school. Casey finds that he is well-read, smart, and willing. Thomas yearns to go to college, but he knows that Lenny wishes him to become a mechanic, too. Baby also meets opposition from the Clan, who wish to keep him in line and egg him on to have sex with Casey to prove that he is one of them. An older Clan member, Edmund*, learns of the challenge and quits the Clan because he says Baby is different and they should respect that. Thomas worries about his situation, to the point of always feeling queasy, but shows affection to Casey who flirts a little, and before long their emotions are getting in the way of work. Casey wants them to go to a movie and lies that it is all right with her parents, while Baby also lies to Lenny to get Lenny's car. They are spotted at the

drive-in by Gene and his pals, who have been drinking, and a fight breaks out during which Thomas suffers a broken arm and some internal injuries. Except for the intervention of Dickon, one of the Cribs, who has a clearer head and more sense, Thomas might have been killed. Casey regrets her part in the matter, as does Thomas for lying, but the Clan and the Cribs decide to have it out under a freeway viaduct. Police soon break up the fight, and the judge remands all the kids to their parents' custody and sentences the leaders to community service under Mr. Hall. Casey and Thomas happily resume their lessons together. Although Thomas seems too weak-kneed and sensitive and Casey too flirtatious and deceptive, the reader is on their side. Tension grows gradually to a breath-holding pitch at the end, so that the book becomes a calculated thriller. It conveys well the irony that the "good" kids are more to be feared than the presumably "bad guys" of the Clan, who never stir up trouble in the community, being more vocationally oriented. Style is crisp, scenes vivid, and the resolution satisfying. Best is the writer's ability to create a sense of clear and imminent danger. ALA/YA.

BRIAN MCNAIR (*The Good Children**) Youngest of the McNair quartet, only six when his parents die. He becomes obsessed by the idea that his mother can speak to him from the place where they have secretly buried her, and he single-handedly creates a beautiful garden over the spot. He is extremely talented in music and often plays the violin at his window, overlooking the grave site, and composes a beautiful piece he calls "In the Garden." When Kevin talks about selling the house, exhuming and disposing of their mother's corpse first, Brian becomes hysterical, accusing his brother of killing their mother, shifting the ladder so she fell. Liz figures out that Brian himself, probably trying to be helpful, shifted the ladder. After he has been committed to the mental hospital, she realizes that he will never agree to face the "reality" that his mother abandoned them, as the psychiatrist insists he must, and will be destroyed by further drugs and shock treatment. When he recovers from the terrible spasms, cramps, and hallucinations of the detoxifying process, he does not remember the escape that Liz and Radix* have engineered. At the end, Liz says the record she is writing of their lives is for Radix for Christmas, and for Brian, when he is strong enough to face it.

BRIAN SPRING (*The Voice on the Radio**)   Younger brother of Janie* Johnson, the Spring sister who was kidnapped. Because Brian likes history in particular and sees an opportunity to learn about America's origins, he accompanies Janie and their older sister, Jodie Spring, when they drive to Boston. He feels keenly Janie's pain at being betrayed by Reeve Shields but is smart enough to realize that if they keep quiet they may all heal faster. He is relieved that the Springs have moved to a larger house, because like his siblings he has felt smothered by his parents' overprotectiveness. The book does a fine job of showing the effect on a family of the sudden, traumatic loss of a child.

BRIDAL, TESSA (1947–)   Born and raised in Montevideo, Uruguay, where she spent the first half of her life, a descendant of Irish immigrants who settled in Argentina. She has also lived in Washington, D.C., and London, England. She is director of public programming at the Science Museum of Minnesota, in charge of producing and directing the museum's science demonstrations and theater performances. She has been chair of the Museum Theater Professional Interest Council and an innovator of the "museum theater" education technique. She has been a theater consultant for museums and zoos in the United States and Canada, artistic director of the Minnesota Theater Institute of the Deaf, and visiting writer at Hamline University and North Dakota State University, among other offices and positions. Her novel, *The Tree of Red Stars** (Milkweed, 1997), about political repression in Uruguay, is based on actual people and events. Selected by *Booklist*, the novel also won the Milkweed Prize for Fiction. With Susan McCormick, she edited *Science on Stage Anthology* (Association of Science Technology Centers, 1991). Bridal and her husband have two daughters and have made their home near Minneapolis.

BROOKS, TERRY (1944–)   Born and raised in Sterling, Illinois. After receiving an A.B. degree from Hamilton College, he took his LL.B. from Washington and Lee University and practiced law in Illinois from 1969 to 1986. A self-taught writer, he published his first novel, *The Sword of Shannara* (Random House; rep. Ballantine, 1991), in 1977. A popular paperback, it helped establish fantasy as a genre for adults. Since then, Brooks has published eighteen more books of fantasy, most of them in sets. Sequel to *Running with the Demon* (Ballantine, 1997), *A Knight of the Word** (Ballantine, 1998) is an adventurous and suspenseful good-versus-evil novel. It was chosen by the New York Public Library for teen readers and is the second book in The Demon Series. *Angel Fire East* (Ballantine, 1999) is the next book in the set. While critics have noted similarities to the novels of J. R. R. Tolkien in style and substance, they praise Brooks's storytelling talent and his skill at raising social issues without didacticism. He has made his home in Seattle and Hawaii.

BUCK JOHNSON (*Sasquatch**)   Buckley Johnson, old man with a limp who opposes the expedition of Dr. Theodore Flagg to Mount Saint Helens to capture or kill a Sasquatch. Buck, as he prefers to be called, takes Dylan, the narrator, with him to the mountain to do what he can to foil Dr. Flagg's purposes. Dylan discovers that Buck has a friendship of sorts with the Sasquatch, several of which he has come to know and an entrance to whose lair is inside Buck's cabin. Dylan learns from Buck that FBI Special Agent Steven Crow, who stakes out Buck's house from across the street, has been following Buck for years. Crow is sure Buck is the man who hijacked a Northwest plane for two hundred thousand dollars in ransom. After Dylan finds the money in the Sasquatch's lair, Buck admits he did the deed to get money to take his son, Gary, who was dying of cancer, to Mexico for treatment unavailable in the United States. Buck bailed out of the plane over Mount Saint Helens, broke his hip in the fall, and was found by a female Sasquatch who took him to the cabin of a mountain man named Billy Taylor. Billy nursed Buck to health in his cabin and stowed the money underneath in the Sasquatch's lair. Billy later left the cabin to Buck in his will. Buck is a colorful and engaging figure.

BUD, NOT BUDDY (Curtis*, Christopher Paul, Delacorte, 1999)   Realistic, picaresque period novel set in Michigan in 1936 during the Great Depression. The narrator, orphaned African American Bud (not Buddy) Caldwell, 10, runs away from an abusive foster family in Flint for Grand Rapids to search for the man who he is certain is his father, a famous musician and bandleader. Although the plot is predictable, scenes capture the moment well, the poignancy is tempered by frequent humor, and the Depression era is made vividly real. Previously, the book won both the Coretta Scott King Award and the Newbery Award and was cited by *School Library Journal*. For a more detailed entry, see *Dictionary, 1995–1999*. ALA/YA.

BULL CATCHER (Carter*, Alden R., Scholastic, 1996)   Sports novel set in the small southern Wisconsin town of Shipley at the time of publication. The novel exudes baseball color and excels in drawing exciting scenes from the catcher's point of view, with tight plays, long hits, insider jargon, and references that give the book immediacy and great credibility. As his senior project, Bull (Neil) Larsen writes about his four high school years, when he aspires to be a winner—to catch and hit his team to the area championship, gain the attention of college scouts, do the right thing by his friends, and land the girl of his choice. A big burly boy, slow at running but powerful of body and quick of intellect, Bull lives a casual, satisfying life with Grandpa* Larsen, a widower, who raised him. Bull and Jeff* Hanson, shortstop, have been baseball-crazy best friends since childhood. Both plan careers in baseball, although both know that take-charge, baseball-savvy Jeff has the greater chance of achieving his ambition. In ninth grade, the boys "discover" Ngo Huynh Phuong*, pronounced No Win Fong, a Vietnamese American youth with a deadpan face and an arm so strong he becomes a high school star by his junior year. Another friend and teammate is Billy* Collins, who takes great pains to conceal the beatings his abusive father administers only on his arms. When Sandi* Watkins, cheerleader and Bull's longed-for girlfriend, finds Billy weeping by the school loading dock because his arms hurt so much, Grandpa insists that teachers be contacted, and for a time Mr. Collins eases up on the brutality. When West Halloway, a senior and first-string catcher, is injured, Bull takes over. He is overly aggressive in tagging a player, Andy Heckert, breaks the boy's nose, and earns Coach Borsheim's disgust, two games' suspension, the opposing team's unrelenting hatred, and his own disappointment at his overzealous behavior. At Grandpa's suggestion, he drives to Andy's house and apologizes, gaining both Andy's friendship and the attention of his star softball player sister, Bev, with whom Bull develops an on/off relationship. Bull participates in other activities, like the marching band, keeps his grades up, and in his senior year makes the National Honor Society. The summer before his senior year, he works at a camp for camp counselors, where he and Bev rescue the camp director, who has injured his foot with an ax. In his senior year, he shows himself highly capable at directing the team, hits .340 and gets thirteen homers, and works Sally Eckes, the team's first and only girl, who has a great knuckleball, well into the lineup. Bull's blooper to center, not magnificent but timely, wins the championship against Caledonia but not a scholarship to the big college of his choice as happens with Jeff. Bull decides he will enroll at the University of Wisconsin for its academic program and see whether Bev will become his girl again. Although the point of view wavers occasionally, sometimes Bull is too self-complimentary, and the cast is too large for easy recognition, the book has plenty of action and

drama and, in addition, shows well that good sportsmanship can and should occur both on the field and off. ALA/YA.

BUNTING, JOSIAH, III (1939–) Born in Philadelphia, Pennsylvania; educator, major general in the U.S. armed services. He was graduated from Virginia Military Institute in 1963, attended Oxford University as a Rhodes scholar, and was a doctoral candidate at Columbia University. From 1973 to 1977, he was president of Briarcliff College, a women's college in Briarcliff, New York, then for ten years was president of Hampton-Sydney College. From 1987 to 1995, he was headmaster of the Lawrence School, an independent boarding school near Princeton, New Jersey, and then became superintendent of the Virginia Military Institute. His first novel, *The Lionheads* (Braziller, 1972), is about Vietnam, reflecting his military experience, but his better-known novels are concerned with schools and academic practices. *An Education for Our Times* (Regency, 1998) is written in the form of letters from a dying man to his lawyer proposing a new kind of school, and *All Loves Excelling** (Bridge Works, 2000) is a savage commentary on the pressures on young people to get into elite colleges.

BURIED ONIONS (Soto*, Gary, Harcourt, 1997) Contemporary, realistic novel of Mexican American family and community life and a boy's growing up set for a few weeks in Fresno, California. Narrator Eddie, 19, yearns for a settled, peaceful, worthwhile life away from the poverty, gangs, vagrants, and punks that abound in his Fresno neighborhood. He thinks there must be a giant onion buried beneath Fresno, because there are so many tears in that city. When Coach, an ex-gangbanger and now the neighborhood recreation leader, says he got away from the degradation by joining the army, Eddie considers various possibilities and eventually decides on the navy. The conclusion is predictable, and characters are types. The book's power lies in Eddie's appeal and in the picture of the dismal conditions that surround and threaten to engulf him. For a longer entry on this book, see *Many Peoples, One Land* [no. 357]. ALA/YA.

BUTTS, NANCY (1955–)   Born in Ohio and raised in Texas, Michigan, Pennsylvania, Colorado, and Virginia, before being graduated from Duke University with a degree in religion. She trained as a physician's assistant and settled in Georgia, where she became a journalist. As a staff writer and editor, she earned three awards from the Georgia Press Association. She was also honored by the Georgia School Board Association for her coverage of educational matters. She has made her home in Barnesville, Georgia, with her husband and son. Her first novel was *Cheshire Moon* (Front Street, 1996), about a hearing-impaired girl. *The Door in the Lake** (Front Street, 1998), a science fiction novel involving a boy who is contacted by space aliens, was an American Library Association choice for young adults.

C

CABOT, MEG(GIN) (1967–) Born in Bloomington, Indiana; graduate of Indiana University with a B.A. in fine arts; popular writer for teens of books of romance, humor, and the supernatural under the names Meg Cabot (The Princess Diaries Series), Jenny Carroll (The Mediator Series and the 1-800-WHERE-R-YOU Series), and Patricia Cabot (various titles). She is best known for *The Princess Diaries** (HarperCollins, 2000), about a girl who learns she is the heir to the throne of a European principality. The book was selected for young adults by the American Library Association and was made into a film by Walt Disney starring Julie Andrews.

CALHOUN, DIA (1959–) Born in Seattle, Washington; freelance artist and graphic designer, writer. After training to be a professional dancer from the age of five to sixteen, she had foot surgery and gave up dancing for college, receiving her B.A. from Mills College in 1980. Her first two novels, both fantasies, were enthusiastically received. *Firegold** (Winslow House, 1999) is set in an imaginary realm divided into two antagonistic areas, the orchards in the south and the mountains in the north, and concerns a boy with ties to both who must find a way to bridge the gap. *Aria of the Sea** (Winslow House, 2000), set in an archipelago where magic is possible, is about a girl determined to be a dancer in the royal school.

CALLIE ANNE BENTON · DICKSEN (*The Starlite Drive-in**) Narrator of the novel. Barely aware of her developing sexuality, Callie Anne fancies herself loved by Charlie Memphis*, the handsome drifter. She is also highly attracted to Virgil, the high school student who works at her father's admission booth. He returns her interest, even though he is pursued by girls his age, and they have a sweet romance, a relationship that is one of the novel's best features. Although it is never completely clear why she does not convey her suspicions about Charlie Memphis's death to the sheriff, the reason is probably that she feels that episode in her family's life is over and she does not want to besmirch her father's memory or distress her mother more than she already has. Callie Anne, however, is also very certain that the bones are not those of Billy Watson, the mentally challenged man who disappeared about the same time, as her mother suggests.

CAM (*Ordeal**) Harry Cameron, quiet, high-principled defense attorney, whose main worry until Hunter abducts his wife, Wren, and his son, Daniel, is the rebellious behavior of the teenage boy, who resents his parents' attempts to force him to rein in his disruptive behavior in school and his experiments with mild delinquency. About sixteen years earlier, Cam came across Wren by accident and fell deeply in love with the beautiful, disoriented girl who told him the story of her life with an environmental community and her betrayal of the group when she realized that they were not the innocent idealists she had believed. He helps her change her name and start a new life, but he does not tell her that he contacted Steve Austin*, the FBI agent she had reported to, and checked with him that she was what she said she was and that she was not actively wanted by authorities. When Wren and Daniel are kidnapped, he gets in touch with Austin, who has left the FBI and started a security agency. During the long absence of his wife and son, Cam almost falls apart but is saved by the stable good sense of his young daughter, Zoe, and his need to take care of her. A very decent man, Cam has always accepted and loved Daniel as his son, even though he knows that Hunter is the actual father.

CARBONE, ELISA (LYNN) Born in Washington, D.C.; lecturer at the University of Maryland–College Park; consultant and trainer in communications skills; writer of nonfiction for teachers and novels for children and young adults. She received her B.A. and M.A. from the University of Maryland, where she has done Ph.D. work, and is a resident of Silver Spring, Maryland. Of her several published books, *Stealing Freedom** (Knopf, 1998) was cited by the American Library Association for young adults. It tells of a young slave girl's flight from Maryland to freedom in Canada. Carbone has also published school stories, *Starting School with an Enemy* (Random House, 1998) and *Sarah and the Naked Truth* (Random House, 2000); a thriller, *The Pack* (Viking, 2003); and another historical novel, *Storm Warriors* (Knopf, 2001), about an African American lifesaving crew in the Outer Banks off North Carolina in the nineteenth century who experience racism.

CARD, ORSON SCOTT (1951–) Born in Richland, Washington; journalist, theater manager, novelist. After two years as a Mormon missionary in Brazil, he received his B.A. from Brigham Young University in 1975 and his M.A. from the University of Utah in 1981. His novels have mostly been science fiction and fantasy, notably the Ender series, starting with *Ender's Game* (Tor, 1985), and the Shadow series, starting with *Ender's Shadow** (Tor, 1999), which he has described as a companion novel to *Ender's Game*, covering the same period and incidents with a different protagonist. Other books in this series are *Shadow of the Hegeman* (Tor, 2001) and *Shadow Puppets* (Tor, 2001). In novels combining historical fiction and fantasy, he has used the premise that by returning to an earlier period a person can change history, as in *Pastwatch: The Redemption of Christopher Columbus** (Tor, 1996). He also has written the five-volume Homecoming science fiction series, starting with *The Memory of Earth* (Tor, 1992) and many other science-fantasy novels and short story collections, as well as several plays. He has sometimes published under the pseudonym of Brian Green.

CARDINAL LITTI (*The Last Day**) Cardinal in the Roman Catholic Church who, because he becomes convinced through study and prayer that Jeza* is the Messiah, is attacked by his colleague, Cardinal di Concerci, and leaves Rome to follow Jeza. He is a sad figure but likable and admirable because at great cost he stands up for what he believes is right. He follows Jeza even to her home with the Bedouins in the desert and to the hospital at which she dies.

CARMEN HANSEN (*Night Flying**) Aunt of Georgia Hansen, the protagonist and narrator. Carmen is the black sheep of the Hansen family of women. She violated her mother's decree of no men when she fell in love with and became pregnant by Sam Gowen, the son of the man who does odd jobs for Georgia's Grandmother Myra Hansen, the family's bullying matriarch. After the baby, Georgia, was born, Grandmother Myra decreed that she be brought up by Maeve, the woman Georgia has been led to believe is her mother and is really her aunt. Grandmother then threw Carmen out and dominated and derided Maeve until she became little more than a shadow.

CART, MICHAEL (1941–   )   Librarian, editor, science fiction writer, novelist. For many years he was director of the Beverly Hills (California) Public Library and has been children's editor for *Parents* magazine and a columnist for *Booklist*. His book, *My Father's Scar: A Novel**

(Simon & Schuster, 1996) deals in a sensitive way with a homosexual relationship. Among several books he has edited are *Tomorrowland: Ten Stories About the Future* (Scholastic, 1999), *In the Stacks: Short Stories About Libraries and Librarians* (Overlook Press, 2002), and *Love and Sex* (Pulse, 2003), a compilation of ten stories praised for the realistic way they deal with interracial love, sexual obsession, abortion, and gay and lesbian relationships. He also wrote *From Romance to Realism: 50 Years of Growth and Change in Young Adult Literature* (HarperCollins, 1996), *What's So Funny?: Wit and Humor in American Children's Literature* (HarperCollins, 1995), studies of the lives and writings of Robert Lipsyte and Francesca Lia Block for Twayne Publishers, and a biography of Walter R. Brooks, creator of the Freddy the Pig books for children.

CARTER,   ALDEN   R(ICHARDSON) (1947–   )   Born in Eau Claire, Wisconsin; former naval officer, teacher of high school English and journalism, and writer of more than twenty books of nonfiction for young adults on historical and technological subjects, best known for his young adult novels, which have been praised for their characterization and honesty. His first novel, *Growing Season* (Coward-McCann, 1984), is regarded as a skillful combination of farm life and family relations. *Wart, Son of Toad* (Putnam, 1985) is a compassionate, occasionally humorous father–son story, and *Sheila's Dying* (Putnam, 1987) concerns a girl with cancer. *Dogwolf* (Scholastic, 1994) revolves around a part Native American boy and a big dogwolf. *Bull Catcher** (Scholastic, 1996), about a high school baseball player who aspires to catch and hit his team to the area championship, was an American Library Association choice for young adults. More recently, he has published *Crescent Moon* (Scholastic, 1999), set against the last major log drive in Wisconsin. Carter lives in Marshfield, Wisconsin.

CASSIE WEINSTEIN (*My Sister's Bones**)   At eighteen the older sister of Billie. Cassie has always been the best at everything she does in school or outside, compulsively determined to be at the top. A tall, strong, willowy blond, Cassie is assertive, smart, and decisive, until she goes to Cornell University. She loses weight, worries unduly about her classes, and studies to excess. Cassie gradually deteriorates until she is taken to a private mental hospital. She makes uneven progress, until Michael*, her father, insists she come home. Billie early fears her sister may have anorexia, and when she reads about the symptoms in the library, becomes frightened for Cassie's life. As presented, Cassie is the classic anorexic. That she will regain her health is by no means certain at the end of the book.

CAST TWO SHADOWS: THE AMERICAN REVOLUTION IN THE SOUTH (Rinaldi*, Ann, Harcourt, 1998)   Historical novel of the American Revolution during the British occupation near Camden, South Carolina. Two summer months in 1780 are momentous for white Caroline Whitaker, 14, daughter of a wealthy Patriot landowner. The British shoot a dear friend, commandeer her house, and imprison her father. Moreover, she learns the truth about why she has a black grandmother. This long novel is filled with fascinating historical and cultural information, scenes are vivid, and the atmosphere of tension, confusion, and terror in the face of the British is palpable. For a longer, more detailed entry, see *Many Peoples, One Land* [no. 107]. NYPL.

CATHERINE OF ARAGON (*Mary, Bloody Mary**)   The Spanish princess who becomes, briefly, the wife of Henry* VIII of England and queen of England. She is the mother of Mary Tudor, who tells the story and who sees her mother as terribly wronged by Henry. Henry falls in love with (is bewitched by, as Mary sees it) Anne* Boleyn, a beautiful young courtier. In order to marry Anne, he tries to have his marriage to Catherine declared invalid, and when Catherine resists his efforts to get rid of her, he banishes her. As Mary describes events, her mother dies of slow poisoning, probably at Anne's instigation. When pressured to sign the oaths that declare Catherine and Henry's marriage invalid, Mary is caught between her love and loyalty for her mother and concern for her own life. (See also Katherine of Aragon*.)

CAUCASIA (Senna*, Danzy, Riverhead, 1998)   Realistic novel published for adults of an African American/white family in the 1970s mostly taking place in Boston. The episodic plot is quickly summarized. Narrator Birdie Lee, 8, and her darker sister, Cole, 11, are inseparable, so close that they converse in an invented language all their own, which they call "Elemeno." They are the only children of outspoken white suburbanite Sandra Lodge Lee, an impassioned and dedicated activist for civil rights and daughter of a Cambridge classics professor, and introverted black militant Deck Lee, a professor of anthropology at Boston University and writer of books on race relations. After he and Sandy split up, Deck takes his black girlfriend and Cole and leaves for Brazil, where he hopes color will not be the hindrance to him that it is in the United States. Increasingly erratic and unstable and certain that authorities will arrest her for several recent activities involving guns and the protest planning meetings held in her basement, Sandy flees with Birdie. The two spend the next six years on the run in New England, the first four moving from place to place, sometimes living in her van or in a commune, the last two in a rented house in a small New Hampshire town under an assumed identity, as Sheila Goldman, widow of a Jewish professor, and her daughter, Jesse. Birdie, feeling lost and alone, since Sandy is now happy with a live-in lover, and yearning for Cole and her father, takes off for Boston and her Aunt Dot Lee. She learns from Dot that her father and Cole have returned to the United States and are living in Oakland, California, persuades her Grandmother Lodge to give her money to fly to California, and is reunited with her father and sister. Book's end finds Cole a college student in Berkeley and Birdie ready to enroll in high school there, where Cole says biracials abound. Although the main characters are somewhat fleshed, the book is chiefly memorable for particular moments. For example, a party early in the book for Aunt Dot is attended by an assortment of colorful, out-of-the-mainstream figures, many of them Sandy's activist colleagues. Birdie becomes aware that guns are being stockpiled and that some of the people there are not to be trusted. When Deck, in an attempt to give Birdie the attention from him that she craves, takes her to the Boston Public Gardens, an elderly couple summon the police, certain that Birdie has been abducted, a situation that is embarrassing to Deck, but he handles it well. New Hampshire professor Walter Marsh and his wife, Libby, from whom Sandy rents a house, are both liked and despised by Sandy as snobbish liberals, since they openly look down on the working-class residents of the little town. Their son, Nicholas, mostly away at boarding school, is Birdie's first crush. The meeting with her father, during which she realizes that he is just as engrossed in what her mother called "overintellectualizing" racial relations as he once was, reveals that she is still, after six years on the run, tremendously in need of his love, and he is as remote as ever. Scenes have power, Sandy and Birdie are good if flat characters, interesting in themselves, although the "I" voice sometimes gets tedious. There is a limited sense of the tension, the frustrated idealism, and the suspicion for law enforcement of the period, but on the whole the book outruns itself. Alex.

CHAE LAFFERTY (*Criminals**) Writer husband of Mollie. His latest book, *The Dark Forest*, has caused a break in his marriage because he has used intimate details of an early indiscretion she confessed to him and also of their sex together. Earlier, Chae and Mollie have been living a romantic back-to-the-earth life at their isolated Scottish farm, blithely ignoring the way their agricultural efforts cost far more than they bring in and using up her inheritance, while she weaves and he writes. When he returns, drunk and repentant, he finds she has discarded all the things they have collected together, mobiles, artworks, stones, a small animal skull—and all sign of his two children by a former marriage, both now in school in Edinburgh. He weeps and begs her to take him back, because he has discovered he cannot write without her. At first he believes her story that she is baby-sitting for a friend, but when Kenneth* and Joan show up, Joan demanding the baby back and Kenneth demanding money to keep quiet about the child, he understands the situation and tries to buy the parents off. In the end, with Mollie in the mental hospital, he and Ewan Munro each put up a thousand pounds to help Joan out, offered through a solicitor and given to Joan's mother so that Kenneth cannot get his hands on it.

THE CHAMP (*Downsiders**)   Old man of seventy-eight who lives in an abandoned municipal swimming pool and was the first "faller" (Topsider rejects or "bums") caught by Talon* Angler, Railborn* Skinner, and Gutta, when it was their duty to catch fallers. Chocolate-skinned and white-bearded, The Champ, once Reginald Champlain, becomes Talon's friend, and the two often play Monopoly. The Champ gives Talon the idea of getting antibiotics to cure his sister of her respiratory infection, and thus Talon contacts Lindsay Matthias. The Champ also influences events by a chance remark about one Alfred Ely Beach (a real historical figure). This remark gives Lindsay the idea of investigating Beach in the New York Public Library. She then theorizes that Beach created Downside.

CHANG AND ENG (Strauss*, Darin, Dutton, 2000)   Biographical novel for adults of the original Siamese twins, Chang and Eng, who were born on a Makong River houseboat in May 1811. Although the midwife is appalled to see them joined by a ligament at their chests, their mother is fiercely protective, and for six years they lead a secluded but happy life, with their father teaching them fishing, tumbling, and Gung-Fu, an art of self-defense. Then an envoy from Rama, king of Siam, comes for them, and they are taken to the court. They and their mother think they will be killed, and, indeed, they see others killed for minor offenses, but

Rama is curious and comes to think of them as a good omen and even has them educated. After several years, he suddenly has them returned to the houseboat, because a plague has killed their father. Being enterprising, the boys start a duck farm and sell eggs, but soon they are jerked from this satisfactory life by Captain Coffin, who offers to make them famous and wealthy. They are fourteen when he takes them on the *Sachem* to America and, in business with a Mr. Hunter, exhibits them in a tent, where they flip across the stage and are stared at by a general audience or examined and prodded by medical men. Hunter keeps them locked up and bilks them of the money he has promised. When they are sixteen, he takes them to Europe. P. T. Barnum gets in touch with them and tries to lure them from Hunter, and the two promoters get into a raging argument over whose Chinamen they are. Eng tells them, "We are no one's Chinamen," but are from Siam and "we are each our own man." They set up their own show and are successful, famous, and even moderately wealthy. When they arrive in the small town of Wilkesboro, North Carolina, Mrs. Yates, the obese woman innkeeper, looks them over and announces that she has found husbands for her daughters. The two girls, no longer young, are agreeable, and the twins, who have never expected the joys of the marriage bed, are delighted. Adelaide, the more aggressive girl, choses Chang, and Sarah takes Eng, and they are married in 1842. Later, Eng learns that when Sarah was quite young, she became sexually involved with a slave, said he raped her, and watched while he was lynched, but Eng comes to think the sex was consensual. The community has ostracized both girls as a result. Now well to do, the twins buy land and have a house built to accommodate their peculiar situation, with one large bedroom, where each will entertain his wife on alternate nights, and a small one where the other woman will sleep. Chang and Adelaide are enthusiastic, boisterous lovers. Eng, always quieter and more intellectual than his brother, and Sarah are more restrained, but since both women want children, their sexual activity is frequent. The first child is Eng's, Catherine, a frail girl whom he loves far more than his other offspring, but eventually they have twenty-one children between them. Their lovemaking, where one twin pretends to be blind and deaf while the other performs, is described in detail. Eng soon finds Sarah cold and distant, and he is confused by Adelaide's flirtatious actions to him while she makes scornful remarks about Chang. Occasionally, he clasps her hand when his brother seems asleep, but only once, when Chang has passed out from too much drink, does he actually have intercourse with his sister-in-law. Chang's increased drinking becomes a problem to Eng, an embarrassment and worse, since the two share one stomach and he often feels the effect of Chang's liquor. The Civil War, in which North Carolina sides with the South, is hard on the twins, with their crops commandeered by Confederate troops and their slaves freed to follow the Union army. When their house burns down, they have to borrow money to rebuild. Chang insists on two houses, where the brothers spend alternate half weeks, each pretending invisibility when in his brother's house. To recoup financially, the brothers tour again, with decreasing success as Chang drinks more heavily. After their last appearance, they have a major physical fight on the stage, and Chang admits to setting the fire because he knew about Eng and Adelaide. He has a stroke,

and Eng must cart him along with a sort of harness. In January 1874, Chang dies and Eng realizes that he, too, will die very shortly. The facts of the life of Chang and Eng have been thoroughly researched. What the novel offers are speculations about their emotions and insights into the contradictory feelings they must have had toward each other. Eng is the narrator. He is also the more intelligent, having taught himself first to understand and speak English well and then to read, an activity he enjoys, being especially fond of Shakespeare and the Bible. Chang is the crowd pleaser, willing to play the fool and bandy words with the audience to get applause. Eng never stops longing to be free of his twin, but doctors at the time believe separation would kill them both. He is often scornful of Chang and greatly deplores his drinking, but he comforts his brother when he senses real fear or depression. The popular press of the day considered Chang the bright one, with his stage smile and pidgin English, but Eng is the real leader, managing their money and making the more important decisions. Although they are treated abominably by their promoters, many in their audiences, rednecks in Wilkesboro, and even their wives, Eng exhibits fortitude and resolve in the face of lifelong adversity. Alex.

CHAPPELL, FRED (DAVIS) (1936–   ) Born in Canton, North Carolina; educator, poet, novelist of the southern experience, using traditions of the gothic and fantasy. Since 1964, he has been a professor of English at the University of North Carolina–Greensboro. In addition to writing at least a dozen books of poetry, he has contributed to many literary journals. He is the author of several novels, among them *I Am One of You Forever* (St.

Martin's, 1985), which uses tales and character sketches woven into a frame story in a complex narrative structure, a technique also used in *Farewell, I'm Bound to Leave You** (St. Martin's, 1996), a series of stories about local people told to a boy by his grandmother and his mother, sometimes simultaneously, sometimes separately, occasionally with conflicting details, set in a frame as the boy and his father wait for the grandmother's imminent death. His work is noted for a strong sense of place, mostly southern hill country.

CHARLOTTE BLEVINS (*The Haunting**)   Great-great-great-grandmother of Lia Marie Starling, the narrator and protagonist. In the diary story, orphaned Charlotte, 16, is living with her grandfather, kind, gentle Placide Blevins, at his plantation house, Graymoss, in the country outside of Baton Rouge, Louisiana. The American Civil War is raging, and since help is increasingly hard to get, Placide has hired surly, threatening Morgan Slade as overseer. When the Union soldiers are near, Charlotte reports that Placide tells her that Slade attacked him and ran from Graymoss, taking with him cherished Blevins valuables. Charlotte says that Placide said that he had much to tell her and that if anything happened to him the answers to these matters lie in his copy of *Favorite Tales of Edgar Allan Poe*. Since his bookmarks drop from the book, she cannot immediately figure out what he intended for her to get from the collection. Just why she does not later work at the task is not clear. Lia uses the stories to explain the mystery that haunts the old house and to exorcise the ghosts.

CHASING REDBIRD (Creech*, Sharon, HarperCollins, 1997)   Present-day realistic novel of domestic life and a girl's

growing up. Shy, plain Zinny (Zinnia) Taylor, 13, the narrator, lives with her six brothers and sisters and their parents in a farmhouse near the Ohio River not far from the town of Bybanks, Kentucky. While all the children are distinguished by some feature, May, 15, for example, being the most bossy, pretty, and boy crazy, Zinny is regarded by her siblings as the "strangest," the "stringiest," "immature," and "embarrassing." Since Zinny often feels left out or put down, she spends a lot of time in the other half of the big house with her Aunt Jessie and Uncle Nate, her father's eccentric but loving much-older brother, and Nate's also somewhat oddball, red-haired wife, whom he refers to as his Redbird. Zinny internalizes problems. For years she has believed that she was the cause of the death of Nate and Jessie's daughter, Rose, who died from whooping cough when she and Zinny were four. Just before Aunt Jessie dies of insulin shock, Zinny discovers an overgrown trail behind their house marked by mostly buried stone slabs and moving roughly parallel to the Ohio River. Zinny decides that she will uncover the slabs and clear the trail, her way of atoning for Aunt Jessie's death, which for some reason she believes she has also caused. She finds maps at the local historical museum and by the time school starts, she has retrieved the entire trail, which she calls "The Redbird Trail" after Aunt Jessie. Her effort attracts media attention, and the area becomes a kind of public nature walk. At the same time, Zinny faces other personal problems. Uncle Nate behaves ever more strangely, insisting on searching for his Redbird throughout the countryside by himself. He beats clotheslines and the like with sticks because he thinks they are snakes, creatures Jessie detested. A new boy in town who works at Mrs. Flint's grocery store, Jake Boone, 16, takes an unusual interest in Zinny, bringing her gifts of a cricket by which she can tell the temperature, a turtle, a puppy, lucky stones, and a diamond-and-ruby ring. At first, Zinny thinks he is only paying her attention because he has a crush on May. He persuades her, however, that he is truly interested in her, and they are low-keyed sweethearts by the end of the novel. Some of the items Jake brings her have been stolen, the puppy and the ring, for example, and when he steals a car, he is arrested. Zinny, too, gets into trouble by cutting a wire fence around a meadow, thinking that the trail must lead through it, and then "borrowing" a horse she finds inside. Because the local sheriff is understanding, he assigns them public service as punishment. Uncle Nate helps himself to the stolen ring and takes it to a cabin along the trail where he deposits it at a shrine he and Jessie had erected to Rose. It seems that he often spends time there communing with his departed loved ones. When he suffers an attack of some kind, Jake helps Zinny with him, and the old man recovers. By the end of the story, Zinny feels better about herself, can even talk in complete sentences to assert her rights and feelings, and takes pride in her accomplishment with the trail. Zinny is a credible figure, and her fears and insights are believable, but the rest of the sometimes overdrawn characters and events must be evaluated as products of her occasionally melodramatic imagination. The novel tackles so many problems that it seems splintered, and it is difficult to believe that in the late twentieth century an apparently normal sixteen-year-old boy would go to such lengths to impress a plain girl of thirteen, especially one who persists in rejecting him and has a very

pretty, eager older sister. Some very funny, even hilarious, scenes relieve the seriousness, and the message that, while it is indeed appropriate to honor past times and those who have departed, one must live in the present and make the most of it cannot be missed. ALA/YA.

THE CHATHAM SCHOOL AFFAIR
(Cook*, Thomas H., Bantam, 1996) Realistic period mystery published for adults and set for one year beginning in August 1926, in Chatham, a sleepy little town in Massachusetts near Cape Cod. The slender plot is easily summarized; texture and characters bolster it and provide impact. All Chatham is amazed when beautiful, young, dark-haired Miss* Elizabeth Channing comes from Africa to teach art at the exclusive private Chatham School for boys. The romance between her and married Mr.* Leland Reed, another teacher, results in the tragic death of a local teenage girl, Sarah* Doyle, by the action of Mrs.* Abigail Reed, and forever changes the life of the narrator, Henry Griswald, who is fifteen. Henry tells the story perhaps sixty years later, now a successful lawyer in Chatham and in personality much like the father he despised in his youth, proper Mr.* Arthur Griswald, school headmaster. Young Henry, who longs to be free and yearns for adventure, sees in Miss Channing and the stories of the places she has visited symbols of the large, exciting, exotic outer world. He little suspects that once released from the village he regards as a prison, because of his part in the notorious Chatham School Affair, he will no longer glory in the freedom for which he has yearned and will ironically spend his life in the town he detested. Upon her arrival, Mr. Griswald arranges for Miss Channing to live in the

empty Milford Cottage on Black Pond and unwittingly asks Mr. Reed to transport her in his car to and from school. Before long, people are noticing that they are spending more and more time together, and tongues wag. Mr. Reed starts to build a sailboat, with which Henry helps, and names it the *Elizabeth*. The tragedy unfolds through Henry's reminiscences, which include snatches of judicial testimonies and depositions related to Sarah's death. Mrs. Reed becomes convinced that Miss Channing and Mr. Reed are planning to kill her and sail off in the boat. One day at Milford Cottage, while he, Miss Channing, and Sarah sit on the bank of Black Pond while Miss Channing tutors Sarah, they see Mrs. Reed driving the Reed family car at breakneck speed straight at them, killing Sarah and settling in the pond, where later Mrs. Reed is pronounced dead. Although Miss Channing cannot be charged with Sarah's death, town sentiment demands that someone pay. Miss Channing is brought to trial on conspiracy to murder Mrs. Reed and adultery. She is sentenced to three years in prison, where she dies. Asserting that only a few people in Chatham now remember those days, mature Henry recalls the incident vividly, and on the book's second to last page, he confesses the secret guilt that has negatively marked his life. When he dived into the water to rescue Mrs. Reed, he found her alive, but, still under the influence of romantic notions, he held the door shut, so that it was he who effectively killed her. Henceforth, Henry kept himself aloof from life, burying himself in books and thoughts of the past. Characters are well drawn, and suspense is artfully created by flashing forward, then returning to old Chatham, dropping hints of disaster to come and repeating comments that create an atmosphere of doom. For example, Miss Channing looks out over Cape Cod shortly after she arrives and remarks that it looks "tormented." The occasional purple writing may be taken as reflecting Henry's highly impressionable mental state. In addition to holding the reader's attention, the book describes small-town life of the period well. Booklist.

CHAUNCEY POTTER (*Sunshine Rider: The First Vegetarian Western**)   The imperious cook with Mr.* John Boardman's Circle Six trail drive, for whom Wylie Jackson works as assistant. One of the book's first humorous incidents occurs when Wylie learns that Chauncey was scalped by Indians. Chauncey pulls off his cap, revealing his bone-white head with a ragged red welt where the scalp had been. Wylie is so upset by the horrible sight that he takes to his heels, to his chagrin accompanied by raucous hoots of laughter from the amused cowboys. A rank newcomer, Wylie has been, in cowboy parlance, hurrahed.

CHBOSKY, STEPHEN   Screenwriter, novelist. He grew up in Pittsburgh, Pennsylvania, and was graduated from the University of Southern California's Filmic Writing Program. His first film, *The Four Corners of Nowhere*, which premiered at the 1995 Sundance Film Festival, went on to win Best Narrative Feature honors at the Chicago Underground Film Festival. He has participated in the Sundance Institute's filmmakers' lab and received the Abraham Polonsky Screenwriting Award for the screenplay *Everything Divided*. *The Perks of Being a Wallflower** (Pocket Books, 1999), a novel of letters to an unknown figure by a socially inept high school boy, is both amusing and touching. Chbosky lives in New York City.

CHINHOMINEY'S SECRET (Kim*, Nancy, Bridge Works, 1999)   Novel of a present-day Korean American family, their intergenerational rifts, and how actions and superstitions from the past almost destroy their modern life together. Myung Hee Choi and her husband, Yung Chul, live in Los Angeles with their two daughters, Christina, 24, a beautiful, obedient, charming second-grade teacher, and Grace, 22, a clumsy, plain senior at UCLA. When Yung Chul's mother, Chinhominey (paternal grandmother), suddenly makes her first trip from Korea to visit, old animosities are stirred up and reappraisals of their lives make all of them unhappy. The girls know little Korean, their grandmother no English. She makes no secret of her disapproval of almost everything she finds. She has never forgiven Myung Hee for taking away her only child or Yung Chul for emigrating with his beautiful wife rather than staying to care for his mother. For her part, Myung Hee still resents her mother-in-law's consulting a fortune-teller about their marriage and fears the fate that Chinhominey reported: their second child would be doomed to die early, before her mother. As a result, she has watched hawkishly over Grace, continually warning and criticizing her, making her insecure socially and unhappy with everything she does. Christina, apparently so near perfection, is actually under great strain to keep up her image, always doing what she knows is expected of her, never feeling free to become an individual. Yung Chul, once so deeply in love with Myung Hee, has been watching his marriage fall apart, his wife turn away from him, and his daughters become strangers, so that he feels he is a failure and has come to dread his home life. Into this already dysfunctional family, Chin-

hominey brings further conflict. To the girls she seems rude and demanding. To her son she is a stranger, someone toward whom he can feel no emotion. To Myung Hee she is a continual reminder of her words: "This marriage is doomed. It will not last." Each of them reacts in his own way. Yung Chul, a certified public accountant, has a flirtation with a girl in his office no older than Christina, but it comes to nothing. Christina becomes engaged to Henry Fruzlow, the young doctor she has been dating, hiding from her family and from herself that he has become increasingly abusive. Grace, rejected by the one boy who has paid attention to her, drives to San Francisco, parks near the Golden Gate Bridge, and walks out, intending to commit suicide. Christina, finding herself pregnant, goes to an abortion clinic. Each of them pulls back from fatal action at the last moment. When Yung Chul returns home, he finds that Myung Hee has taken Chinhominey to the hospital after his mother complained of a severe stomachache. Although the doctors can find nothing wrong with her, the old woman dies, having apologized to Myung Hee for the lies she told about the fortune-teller's predictions, saying their marriage is not doomed and that Grace is not destined to die young. What she does not tell them is her own secret, that when she was a young woman, the fortune-teller predicted that she could not have a son by her husband and arranged that she have intercourse with a disreputable looking man, the fortune-teller's husband, and the result was her pregnancy with Yung Chul. This secret she had kept from her husband, whom she loved dearly, and she dies without revealing it to her son. In the epilogue, the ominous predictions lifted, Myung Hee and Yung Chul have rediscovered each other with love and renewed passion. Christina has dropped Henry but has his son, a healthy baby who delights the whole family. Grace, who has for years been assumed to be going to Harvard Law School, decides to do graduate work in psychology at the University of California–Berkeley, where she meets and starts to date an Italian classmate. The novel is in the third person, skipping from the mind of one family member to another, except for first-person passages detailing Chinhominey's thoughts, an interesting technique for keeping her central, even though most of the action concerns the others. Dropping belief in dire predictions of another culture is shown to be difficult, almost impossible, even in a different cultural environment, and the effect these beliefs have even on the American-raised daughters is corrosive. Booklist.

CHOOSING UP SIDES (Ritter*, John H., Putnam, 1998)   Boy's growing-up novel with personal-problem and sports-story aspects set in 1921 in the small Ohio River town of Crown Falls, Ohio. Luke Bledsoe, 13, describes his conflict with his rigid, Baptist preacher father, Zeke, and with himself over using his natural left hand to throw a baseball. Zeke has steadfastly refused to let his son use his natural hand, since he believes the left is the Devil's hand. Inadvertently picking up and throwing a baseball with speed and accuracy with his left hand and encouraged by his sportswriter uncle to develop his talent, Luke is conflicted, since obedience to his father and to the religious admonitions of his church is very strong. While Zeke's accidental drowning in the Ohio is a convenient solution, Luke is a moral boy, whose dilemma is convincing. Ear-lier the book won the International Reading Association Award. For a more detailed entry, see *Dictionary, 1995–1999*. ALA/YA.

THE CLAN (*Breaking Rank**)   The group of boys from the less desirable part of town to whom Thomas Fairbairn, called "Baby," belongs. The "good" kids in school known as "Cribs," the pushers and shakers, think the Clan kids are wild, drug addicts, alcoholics, and thieves, none of which describes them. The Clan was founded about ten years earlier by Lenny (Leonard) Fairbairn, Thomas's older brother, and his two friends, Edmund* and Shelly, because they felt school did not serve their needs. Clan members have no fixed territory and are completely law abiding. Thomas says they are a "culture . . . [a] society within and in spite of a larger society. Social iconoclasts." Each of the leaders has an occupation at which he is very good. Lenny is a highly regarded mechanic; Edmund started and runs a chain of dry-cleaning establishments; and Shelly is a successful artist. Each instructs a group of apprentices, called "aps," within the Clan.

CLARKE, BREENA (1951–   )   Born in Washington, D.C., the daughter of two government workers whose memories provided the substance for her novel about African Americans set in the Georgetown area of the capital in 1928, *River, Cross My Heart** (Little, Brown, 1999), which was named to the Alex list, selected by Oprah, and praised for its descriptive style. Educated at Webster College and Howard University, she joined Time, Inc., in New York City, holding positions as bureau manager and news desk editor of *Time*, assistant to the deputy managing editor, and administrator of the corporate Editorial Diversity Program. She has also contributed to several anthologies of stories and plays by African Americans. She lives in New Jersey.

CLOSE TO A KILLER (Qualey*, Marsha, Delacorte, 1999) Mystery-thriller set in a present-day large midwestern urban area, Dakota City, involving a beauty salon run and staffed by women who learned the trade while in prison for manslaughter and murder. Barrie Dupre, 16 or 17, resents having to move from the suburbs when her father and stepmother, a professor of French literature, go to Paris for a year and Barrie must live with Daria, her mother, who was in prison for seven years for her involvement in a protest in which a bomb killed a guard. Since her release, Daria has started a salon called "Killer Looks," employing women who were in the cosmetology course at Washburn State Women's Prison with her, aided by a grant from a foundation devoted to helping women reestablish their lives after incarceration. To her surprise, the business has caught on and now is very busy with an upscale clientele. Daria employs Barrie as a towel girl at the salon and treats her and the other employees firmly and unsentimentally. Barrie has found a haven in An Open Book, a small used bookstore run by Eric and Willa, where she often goes to browse and where they save her any copies of Career Romances for Young Moderns, a series from the 1940s that she collects. They also save for her old photographs of unidentifed people, about whom she makes up stories. Trouble for the salon starts when the husband of one of their wealthy customers is murdered and soon after that one of their regular clients, both shot. Lieutenant Henley, who questions Barrie, seems especially interested in Daria, but more as a possible date than as a suspect. At first Barrie suspects Wylie Hampton, a teenager in drug rehab who seems unusually interested in her and in the women who work in the shop. Her suspicions gradually shift to Dean, 20, who lives in a group home and works at the shop and also at the People's Center, which caters to runaways and troubled youth. As the investigation progresses, Daria's house is ransacked and trashed, and the building containing their shop is burned, with an old woman on the third floor killed. Wylie, who seemed to have licked his drug habit, checks again into rehab and is later found, badly beaten and with one foot crushed, beside a railroad track. Finally, Barrie realizes that it is Eric who has checked into her appointment book while she is browsing in his shop, has known when wealthy homes will be empty because the owners have salon appointments, and has been surprised while robbing the houses. His apprehension depends on a receipt left in one of the career books Barrie bought, showing that he was in town, not in Missouri as he claimed, on the night of the first murder. Since he thought Wylie saw the receipt, he has tried to leave him unconscious on a railroad track. Realizing that Barrie still has the receipt, he chases her to a bus stop, tries to drag her off, slips into the bus path, and is killed. A number of other interesting characters people the novel, especially the women who work in the shop, notably TaNeece, the only African American employee, who was imprisoned for slamming a football player with a softball bat when she came upon him sexually molesting her eleven-year-old niece, and her mother, Evelyn, who provides Barrie and Daria support, sanctuary, and muscle power to clean up after their house is trashed. The tension between Daria and

Barrie, who still resents her mother's doing something that robbed her of a maternal figure for most of her childhood and also what seems her lack of understanding now, is one of the main threads in the plot. ALA/YA; NYPL.

CLOUDY IN THE WEST (Kelton*, Elmer, Doherty, 1997) Adult western-adventure and boy's coming-of-age novel set for several weeks in 1885, starting in East Texas. After twelve-year-old Joey Shipman's father dies from a mysterious mule-and-wagon upset; Reuben, their loyal, old African American hired man, is found dead under strange circumstances; Joey's father's will leaves the farm to Joey instead of to Dulcie, Joey's irascible stepmother/guardian; and Joey decides that his own life is in danger from Dulcie and her personable, so-called cousin, Blair Meacham, Joey runs away to his father's cousin, Beau Shipman, in Bastrop, Texas. He finds Beau in jail, where apparently the man often resides because of his propensity for alcohol. Sheriff Gardner bullies Beau into keeping the boy on pain of further imprisonment. Meacham, pleasant as ever, soon shows up in Bastrop and insists the boy return to the farm. At a river not far out, Meacham unexpectedly turns nasty, tries to drown Joey, and shoots at Beau. When they defend themselves, Meacham falls into the water and is swept downriver by the current. Certain that they have killed the man and that their story will not be believed, Joey and Beau take off for the Far West, Joey riding his old farm horse, Taw, and Beau on Git Out. The two encounter colorful Old West figures and experience near escapes and tight spots before Joey arrives back at the farm weeks later, a little older and considerably wiser in the ways of the world. Having argued and

bickered throughout most of the novel over matters of control and Beau's desire for liquor, the two travelers have grown to like and respect each other. Shortly after a Texas Ranger informs them that Miller Dawson*, a notorious outlaw, is in the area, Dawson turns up and steals Git Out. Farther on, they encounter Judge Henry Smith, who appears to exemplify frontier hanging justice. In Austin, they spot Git Out in front of a saloon and take the horse back, but are soon captured by Dawson, to whom Joey finds he is strangely attracted, and taken to his outlaw camp in a remote canyon. A power struggle between Dawson and a member of his band, Farlow, over a prostitute, Alta, whom Farlow brought from San Antonio and has abused, leads to Farlow's death. Dawson leaves for another robbery, and Alta stays with Joey and Beau, who decide to head for California, Beau now sweet on Alta. Alistair McIntosh*, an elderly Scottish American sheep man, comes by with his herd of more than two thousand sheep, puts Beau in his wagon, and shares his supplies with them. Dawson shows up again briefly outside Stockton and is recognized by McIntosh, who reports him to the sheriff, and Dawson is captured and hanged. Beau and Alta are married, and Beau decides to return to Bastrop and turn himself in. To their surprise, they learn from Sheriff Gardner in Bastrop that Meacham is alive. Sheriff Lawton back home seems skeptical of Joey's story about Dulcie's and Meacham's attempts to kill him, but the first night home, Meacham tries to kill Joey by smothering him. The sheriff turns up in the nick of time, but Meacham gets away. The next day Meacham returns to take Joey hostage, shoots Dulcie, and is himself wounded, arrested, and held for hanging. Meacham has been behind the efforts to kill Joey in order to get the farm for himself. Published for adults and offering more detail than most novels for the teen trade, the novel moves rapidly with plenty of action and effective twists, and Joey grows up believably, if expectedly. Alta, Dawson, Beau, and McIntosh have dimension, but Meacham is soon seen as the bad guy, and most other characters are clear types or suitable functionaries. A particular strength of the book is the clear picture of the area the fugitives travel across. ALA/YA.

COLES, WILLIAM, JR. (1932–) Born in Summit, New Jersey; professor, writer. Coles received his B.A. from Lehigh University in 1953, his M.A. from the University of Connecticut in 1955, and his Ph.D. from the University of Minnesota in 1967. He has taught at Amherst College, Case Western Reserve University in Cleveland, and Drexel University in Philadelphia, and since 1974 has been a professor and director of composition at the University of Pittsburgh. *Another Kind of Monday** (Simon & Schuster, 1996) is an unusual mystery and detective story with all the clues in a sort of treasure hunt leading to interesting places in the history of Pittsburgh. Coles has also written several study guides and books about writing.

COMAN, CAROLYN Author best known for her problem novels for middle-grade and early high school readers. Born in Evanston, Illinois, she was educated in private, parochial, and public schools and studied writing at Hampshire College in Amherst, Massachusetts. She is on the faculty of the Vermont College Master of Fine Arts in Writing for Children Program. Among her publications are *Tell Me Everything* (Farrar, 1993), about the death of a mother; *What Jamie Saw* (Front Street,

1995), about domestic abuse; *Bee and Jacky* (Front Street, 1998), about sibling incest; and *Many Stones** (Front Street, 2000), an American Library Association choice for young adults and a Printz Honor Book about a girl's conflict with her father and attempts to cope with her older sister's death. For additional information, see *Dictionary, 1990–1994* [*Tell Me Everything*] and *Dictionary, 1995–1999* [*What Jamie Saw*].

CONLY, JANE LESLIE (1948–) Born in Virginia; novelist. Her *Trout Summer** (Holt, 1995), was previously on the American Library Association's Notable Books list, and has more recently been cited in their young adult list. For earlier biographical information and title entries, see *Dictionary, 1990–1994* [*Crazy Lady*] and *Dictionary, 1995–1999* [*Trout Summer*].

CONNOR KANE (*Silent to the Bone**) Best friend and eventual savior of Branwell Zamborska, who is accused of dropping and thus almost killing his baby half sister, Nikki. Aware that his older half sister often has felt rejected by their father since he married again, Connor, the narrator, has some sense of how Branwell might feel about his little sister. Also, having felt sexually attracted to Vivian Shawcurt, Nikki's au pair, he has some sense of why Branwell changed after Vivian arrived. Long aware that Branwell loves words, the taste, sound, and myriad applications of them, Connor noted that Branwell grew increasingly quiet and uncommunicative after Vivian came. The reason, he figures out, is that Branwell realized that he should have reported to his parents that Vivian smoked and entertained Morris Ditmer while Nikki napped, both against the rules.

COOK, KARIN   Activist, health educator, writer. Her sensitive novel, *What Girls Learn** (Pantheon, 1997), was on an earlier American Library Association list, but has more recently been cited in their young adult list, as well as being placed on the Alex list for outstanding novels for young adults, that of the New York Public Library, and of *Booklist*. For earlier biographical information and a title entry, see *Dictionary, 1995–1999* [*What Girls Learn*].

COOK, THOMAS H. (1947–   )   Popular writer of novels and police-procedures books for adults; born in Ft. Payne, Alabama. He received a B.A. from Georgia State College, an M.A. from Hunter College, and a M.Phil. from Columbia University; has been an advertising executive, a teacher of English and history, and a contributing editor and book review editor for *Atlanta* magazine; since 1981 a full-time writer. With his wife, Susan Terner, a writer for radio, he has made his home in New York City. Several of his novels have been nominated for the Edgar Allan Poe Award: *Blood Innocents* (Playboy, 1980), a police novel set in New York City; *Sacrificial Ground* (Putnam, 1988), a mystery; and *Blood Echoes: The True Story of an Infamous Mass Murder and Its Aftermath* (Dutton, 1992). A 1926-period novel, *The Chatham School Affair** (Bantam, 1996), received the Poe Award and was also selected by *Booklist* for young adult readers.

THE COOK'S FAMILY (Yep*, Laurence, Putnam, 1998)   Realistic, contemporary novel of a mixed-race Anglo-Chinese girl and her grandmother, newly arrived from Hong Kong, who become involved in a San Francisco restaurant cook's fantasy, pretending for his sake that they are his wife and daughter. The little Chinese woman, with her feet crippled from binding, and her modern granddaughter both learn much from the experience. For a longer entry, see *Many Peoples, One Land* [no. 238]. NYPL.

COOL, TOM   Until recently deputy director of intelligence for plans and programs, United States Southern Command, serving in Panama. In 1999, he retired from the navy as a commander and joined a private group in Miami, Florida, working with U.S. Intelligence. His novels, described as "hard" science fiction, include *Secret Realms** (Tor, 1998), *Infectress* (Baen, 1977), and *Soldiers of Light*, written with John deLancie (Pocket Star, 1999).

COONEY, CAROLINE B. (1947–   ) Since 1978 a prolific and honored writer of mystery and romance novels mainly for young adults, of which she has published about five dozen. Among these are the family novel *What Child Is This?: A Christmas Story** (Delacorte, 1997); the suspenseful problem and growing-up novel, *The Voice on the Radio** (Delacorte, 1997); *The Terrorist** (Delacorte, 1997), about the killing of an American boy in London; *Wanted!* (Scholastic, 1997), a murder-mystery thriller built around business-data theft; *Hush, Little Baby* (Scholastic, 1999), a story of suspense that revolves around a baby-selling scheme; and *Burning Up* (Delacorte, 1999), about a fifty-year-old arson fire and racism. All have been cited by the American Library Association as good reading for young adults, the last four also for reluctant readers. Her children grown, Cooney lives in a coastal town in Connecticut. For additional information about Cooney, more titles, and a title entry, see *Dictionary, 1995–1999* [*Driver's Ed*].

COOPER, SUSAN (MARY) (1935–) Born in Burnham, Buckinghamshire, England; playwright, screenwriter, journalist, author of novels and nonfiction for adults; popular, versatile, and acclaimed writer for children and young people. She received her M.A. from Somerville College, Oxford University, immigrated to the United States in 1963, and is a resident of Connecticut and New York City, married to actor and playwright Hume Cronyn. She is best known for The Dark Is Rising Series of fantasies, of which *The Grey King* (Atheneum, 1975) won the Newbery Award. An American Library Association selection for young adults, *King of Shadows** (McElderry, 1999), combines fantasy and historical fiction in taking a boy from 1999 back in time to become an actor in Shakespeare's theater. More recently, Cooper has published *Frog* (McElderry, 2002), a picture storybook illustrated by Jane Browne, and *Green Boy* (McElderry, 2002), an ecological fantasy set in the Bahamas. For more information about Cooper, titles, and title entries, see *Dictionary, 1960–1984* [*The Dark Is Rising*; *Dawn of Fear*; *The Grey King*; *Over Sea, Under Stone*] and *Dictionary, 1990–1994* [*The Boggart*].

CORA ALLENBERG (*The Tree of Red Stars**)   Quiet young daughter of Jewish refugees who move into Magda* (Magdalena) Ortega Grey's affluent neighborhood in Montevideo, Uruguay. Cora becomes a close friend of both Magda and Emilia. Especially while the three girls are still young, Cora seems very romantic to the other two girls, because her family escaped the Nazis in the Netherlands by hiding in a hearse. Cora is wounded during the riot following Che Guevara's speech, which she attended because the socialists helped her family get out of Europe. Cora falls in love with Ramiro, and the two become involved with the Tupamaros (Tupas), the revolutionary movement of students and intellectuals who oppose a military dictatorship. Ramiro dies for the cause, and Cora becomes one of the "disappeared," those who simply vanish and are never seen again.

CORMIER, ROBERT (1925–2000) Born in Leominster, Massachusetts, one of the most influential novelists for young people of the late twentieth century, noted for introducing pessimistic endings. Among his recent novels, *Tenderness** (Delacorte, 1997), about a sociopath and a runaway girl, is similar, but *Heroes** (Delacorte, 1998), a story of a boy, horribly wounded in World War II, coming back to his hometown intent on getting revenge on the man who raped the girl he loved and who is now lauded by the residents, has a more complex psychological pattern. Earlier biographical information and title entries appear in *Dictionary, 1960–1984* [*The Chocolate War*; *I Am the Cheese*]; *Dictionary, 1985–1989* [*Beyond the Chocolate War*]; *Dictionary, 1995–1999* [*In the Middle of the Night*; *I Am the Cheese*]; and *Dictionary, 1990–1994* [*Other Bells to Ring*; *We All Fall Down*].

COVILLE, BRUCE (1950–)   Born in Syracuse, New York, where he still lives; playwright and lyricist for musical theater; popular and very prolific writer best known for his books for middle-grade readers in the lighthearted Magic Shop series, which feature Mr. S. H. Elives. Many of Coville's books employ mythical creatures, like unicorns, dragons, and dwarves, among them his set for early adolescents and young adults, The Unicorn Chronicles. With Jane Yolen*, Coville wrote *Armageddon Summer**

(Harcourt, 1998), about an apocalyptic religious sect. It was recommended for young adults by the American Library Association. For additional information about Coville and earlier titles, see *Dictionary, 1995–1999* [*The Skull of Truth*].

CRASH (Spinelli*, Jerry, Knopf, 1996) Amusing, realistic, in-your-face problem novel with sports-story aspects set in an unnamed Pennsylvania town in the late twentieth century. Among other matters, Crash (John) Coogan, 12, tells about his growing prowess as a football hero; his relationship with Penn Webb, his small, dorky Quaker classmate; the arrival of his aging grandfather, Scooter; and the activities of his lively family, all of which broaden his perspectives on self and life. Previously the book was cited by *School Library Journal*. For a longer entry, see *Dictionary, 1995–1999*. ALA/YA.

CREECH, SHARON (1945–)   Born in Cleveland, Ohio; for many years a resident of England, Europe, and Chautauqua, New York; recently returned to live in the United States; editorial assistant, teacher of English and American literature, writer of fiction. Creech is best known for her Newbery Award–winning novel, *Walk Two Moons* (HarperCollins, 1994), about growing up, dealing with death, and interpersonal relationships. *Chasing Redbird*￼* (HarperCollins, 1997), an American Library Association selection for young adults, is a humorous girl's growing-up novel that features an oddball assortment of characters. The highly textured and lyrically written *The Wanderer*￼* (HarperCollins, 2000), on the surface a sea-adventure novel, concerns growing up, self-identification, and interfamily relationships. It was also chosen by the American Library Association for young adults and was a Newbery Honor book. Other recent publications include *A Fine, Fine School* (HarperCollins, 2001) and *Fishing in the Air* (Joanna Cotler, 2000), both picture books, and *Ruby Holler* (HarperCollins, 2001), a novel. For more information about Creech and a title entry, see *Dictionary, 1995–1999* [*Walk Two Moons*].

CRICHTON, MICHAEL (1942–) Born in Chicago, Illinois, educated at Harvard University, from which he received B.A. and M.D. degrees. While still a medical student, he published novels under the pseudonyms John Lange and Jeffrey Hudson. His first novel under his own name, *The Andromeda Strain* (Knopf, 1969), also written while he was still in medical school, established his reputation with the techno-thriller. Since then he has published a dozen more novels, several books of nonfiction, and a half dozen screenplays as Crichton, as well as several other novels under pseudonyms. He has been a full-time writer of books and films and a director of films and teleplays since 1970. He also created the highly popular television series *ER*. The novels that have garnered the most popular attention have been *The Great Train Robbery* (Knopf, 1975) and *Jurassic Park* (Knopf, 1990), which was later published as *Michael Crichton's Jurassic World* (1997) and made into a very popular thriller movie. Two techno-mysteries, *Airframe*￼* (Knopf, 1996), about in-flight airplane problems and corporate intrigue, and *Timeline*￼* (Knopf, 1999), a time-travel thriller, were chosen by *Booklist* for young adults.

CRIMINALS (Livesey*, Margot, Knopf, 1996)   Convoluted, suspenseful novel published for adults of several mostly well-meaning people whose lives are caught in a complicated web of deceit after a baby is found in the men's restroom of the bus depot in Perth, Scotland. Ewan* Munro, a young investment banker, stops briefly in Perth on his way from London to give emotional support to his sister, Mollie*, whose novelist husband, Chae* Lafferty, has recently left her. In the stall in the men's room, he sees a package, picks it up, thinking to turn it in at the desk, and discovers it is a baby. Just then the bus begins to pull out with his baggage aboard, so he sprints onto it, still holding the baby, and rides to the small town where Mollie is to pick him up. She is surprised, but sensibly says they should take the baby home with them for the present, buys diapers and formula, and drives the five miles in the rain to her isolated house, Mill of Fortune. They discover the baby is a girl, about four months old, with coppery-colored skin, suggesting a parent from India. For the next few days, through a series of errors on Ewan's part and contrivance on that of Mollie, who has fallen in love with the baby and named her Olivia, they keep the child and fail to report it. Ewan finds Mollie baffling, sometimes her old, brisk self, sometimes seeing strange black birds swooping toward her and hearing terrifying voices, and although he has come to discuss her failing marriage, she is reluctant to even mention Chae. Ewan has his own worries. In a moment of weakness with Vanessa*, a beautiful woman in a rival company whom he loves, he has mentioned a pending merger, and has since discovered that a sudden heavy buying spurt has alerted the authorities to possible insider trading. The first section of the novel alternates between the points of view of Ewan and Mollie. The second switches to that of Kenneth*, the father of the baby, who just discovered her existence, having had sex with her mother, Joan, a petite woman of South Asian extraction, the year before, whom he had almost forgotten. After losing yet another job, Kenneth, a punk whom his mother calls a "gormless wonder," turns up at Joan's apartment and, to keep her old Asian mother from disturbing them, agrees to take care of the baby, Grace, while Joan works. Tired of Grace's crying, he wraps her up like a package and takes her out with no particular plan, and, stopping to relieve himself at the bus depot, leaves her, now asleep, on the floor of the stall. A few minutes later he sees Ewan emerge with the package that is Grace, and hop on the bus. Kenneth follows. Although he has no interest whatsoever in recovering Grace, he sees the opportunity for a bit of blackmail. Worried about his possible implication in stock fraud, Ewan flies back to London, with Mollie promising to turn Olivia in at the police station and promptly returning to Mill of Fortune instead. Ewan goes on business to Milan, where he gets a frantic call from Vanessa, now aware that she has used his information illegally. Mollie goes from being enthralled with Olivia to terror, as Kenneth calls several times with threatening, though unspecific, messages. He has been telling Joan increasingly implausible stories about where Grace is. Chae returns, drunk and contrite, saying he cannot write without Mollie, and Mollie succumbs. Finally, they all converge at Mill of Fortune, with Vanessa driving Ewan, and Kenneth bringing Joan, hoping to wring a sizable sum from Ewan, whom he thinks is Chae. In the ensuing confusion, with Ewan trying to apologize for taking the baby, Mollie trying to buy Olivia from Kenneth, Joan frantically declaring that Grace is her baby and not for sale, the child is dropped on the stone floor. She is taken to the hospital with a broken arm and possible skull fracture. Mollie, clearly in a state of mental breakdown, is also taken to the hospital. The police decide not to press charges. The baby is expected to recover completely. Ewan's lapse of confidentiality about the merger is considered wrong but not actionable. Vanessa quits her job and leaves for New York, where she has a lover. Chae waits at Mill of Fortune for Mollie to recover. The complex plot is entertaining, but the novel's strength is in characterization, with all the figures well realized and all, except for Kenneth, beguiling though flawed. Even Olivia/Grace charms a reader, so that Mollie's obsession and Joan's frantic worry about her are completely understandable. Booklist.

CROOKED (McNeal*, Laura Rhoton, and Tom McNeal*, Knopf, 1999)   Realistic novel that starts out as a family-life and school novel with growing-up and friendship aspects and then becomes a relentlessly suspenseful thriller. Events occur in recent years during a snowy, cold March in the small town of Jemison, New York. Red-haired, pretty, good-student Clara Wilson, a ninth grader at Melville Junior High, has typical adolescent problems. Among others, she deplores her crooked nose, fears her parents' marriage is breaking up, and wonders if cute, shy, tall Amos MacKenzie, 14, likes her. Amos, too, has problems: coping with the antics of his practical joker pal, Bruce Crookshank, hoping the jocks in high school will notice him, worrying about his father's increasingly bad health, and wondering whether Clara likes him. Episodes revolve around these concerns until one night Adam is walking in the snow after dark when he observes the two hoodlum Tripp brothers, Charles, a senior and brutal, and the younger Eddie, sixteen but a freshman, destroying mailboxes, porch lights, and the snowpeople in a pleasing outdoor display. Although he tries to remain quiet and unseen, Amos inadvertently makes a sound and then is struck viciously with a bat. Police soon pick up Charles, who is a known troublemaker. He is remanded to juvenile hall for two weeks, but Eddie remains on the loose. After a period in the hospital, and more than a little concern for his health, Amos returns to school where he is hailed as a hero. He soon feels Eddie's eyes on him everywhere he goes and is made aware in a variety of ways that Eddie and Charles are displeased with him, because they erroneously believe that he identified Charles to the police. Clara also becomes the subject of stalkings, leers, and suggestive remarks, especially from Eddie. Amos lacks moral fortitude, however, and caves in when he should report the Tripp brothers' activities. When they do contact police, however, they are shabbily treated. For her part, Clara sometimes finds Eddie's attentions exciting, but notably not when he deceptively takes her to a local lovers' rendezvous and refuses to take her home at the promised time. The Tripps are finally tripped up, at least for the time being, in the novel's very scary concluding portions. One night, Amos spots the brothers' ugly, intimidating, souped-up vehicle and secretly hitches a ride in the back as they drive to their apartment. There he discovers that they have tied up Charles's girl, releases her, and learns that they are on their way to Clara's. The Tripps have Clara in the attic, and Charles is preparing to rape, possibly kill or at the least mutilate, her, when Amos and Bruce, upon whom Amos has happened, arrive. The Tripps get away, but Amos and Bruce take Clara and her dog, which the Tripps have poisoned, to the hospital. To their disappointment, a lenient judge sentences Charles to six months in a state facility for juveniles and Eddie to fourteen days in juvenile hall. On the way from the building after the sentencing, Charles indicates to Amos that revenge lies in the future. Coincidence plays a large role in the plot, and Clara and Amos are likable if stereotypically flawed. The families' hurts—Clara's mother abandons her family, and Amos's father dies of cancer—provide texture for what would otherwise be a superficial, melodramatic, replete-with-sensationalistic-cliffhangers plot. Family scenes have power and contribute some normalcy amid the increasingly terrifying external circumstances. The Tripps and what happens to them appears to reflect what some think is a growing problem in society. ALA/YA.

CROSSING JORDAN (Fogelin*, Adrian, Peachtree, 2000)   Realistic novel of friendship, racial discrimination, and domestic adventures set one summer in recent years in Tallahassee, Florida. When he hears that the African American Lewis family has bought the house next door, the father of narrator Cass (Catherine Margaret) Bodine, 12, builds a tall wooden fence along the edge of the Bodine property and forbids Cass to have anything to do with the Lewises. Cass, who often sits under the rose of Sharon bush near a hole in the fence, soon makes friends with fatherless Jemmie* (Jemmeal Constance) Lewis, also twelve. Cass discovers that they have common interests: both are very fast runners, and both like to read. They meet mornings at the middle school track and run so well together that they feel like "two parts of one machine." Jemmie says they make a good team and dubs them "Chocolate Milk."

They also read Cass's copy of *Jane Eyre* to each other, all the time being very careful not to let anyone know they are friends. Cass overhears Mrs. Lewis, a nurse, refer to the Bodines as bigots, but Jemmie's grandmother, Nana Grace, finds the girls reading together and welcomes Cass into the house. Jemmie tells Cass about the civil rights movement, and Cass reveals that the Bodines are very poor. Mr. Bodine is a maintenance man, and Mama cooks and cleans at the Children's Shelter. Cass sees discrimination in action when one day Nana Grace sends them to the store for eggs, Jemmie goes in alone, and the racist clerk accuses Jemmie of stealing. Cass comes to her rescue but feels ashamed when she realizes she did not completely trust Jemmie because she is black. A potential tragedy brings the two families together. Cass's older sister, Lou Anne, madly interested in boys and makeup, has a summer job taking care of their baby sister, Missy. One extremely hot summer day, she has Missy on her hip while she argues at length with her boyfriend, and the baby becomes overheated and listless. Cass races the baby home and calls Jemmie's mother, whose quick action saves the child. Mr. Bodine thanks Mrs. Lewis and even shakes hands, but the grownups remain stiff with one another. Mr. Bodine starts doing odd jobs around the Lewis place, however; Mrs. Lewis often stops by to check on Missy; and the girls do what they can to get their mothers to be friends. The families finally come together as the result of a fund-raising race for sickle-cell anemia. Although they are among the youngest competitors, the girls are almost winning, when a bigger girl brushes Jemmie, who falls down and is injured. Cass could have finished by herself but chooses to help her friend; they are, after all, Chocolate Milk.

Their pictures appear in the local newspaper, and the kids in school admire them for their pluck. The book concludes with the "first-ever Bodine–Lewis potluck" supper at the Lewises' house the Saturday after school starts. The plot is predictable but consistently entertaining even though it appears developed to thesis. Dialogue is extensive and lively, and the girls are well drawn. The book excels in showing the girls in various vacation activities having fun together about the house and yard. Jemmie is a stronger figure than Cass, and Nana Grace, who hums spirituals and freedom songs, gives the book its title. She explains that in slave days "crossing Jordan" meant to reach freedom. ALA/YA.

THE CUCKOO'S CHILD (Freeman*, Suzanne, Greenwillow, 1996)   Novel of a young girl's transition from life in Beirut to a small town in present-day Tennessee after her parents have disappeared, evidently drowned. Her inability to adjust is very hard on her inexperienced but well-meaning aunt and the other people who try to help her. For a longer entry, see *Dictionary, 1995–1999*. ALA/YA.

CURTIS, CHRISTOPHER PAUL (1954–   )   Born in Flint, Michigan, the locale of his Newbery Award–winning *Bud, Not Buddy** (Delacorte, 1999), about an orphaned boy's search for his father. The book was also a Coretta Scott King winner, cited by *School Library Journal*, and recommended by the American Library Association for young adults. Earlier, Curtis published the family and period novel *The Watsons Go to Birmingham—1963* (Delacorte, 1995). An African American graduate of the University of Michigan, he has held various positions and currently lives in Windsor, Ontario, Canada. For more details about Curtis and title entries, see *Dictionary, 1995–1999* [*Bud, Not Buddy*; *The Watsons Go to Birmingham—1963*].

D

DALLAS, SANDRA (1939–) Born in Washington, D.C.; writer, editor. She received her B.A. from the University of Denver in 1960 and worked as an editor of *Business Week* until 1990. Her nonfiction publications, which are numerous, focus on the history and architecture of the western United States. Her novels mostly examine small-town America, among them *Buster Midnight's Cafe* (Random, 1990), concerning Butte, Montana. In *The Persian Pickle Club* (St. Martin's, 1995), set in Depression-era Kansas, the narrator is a quilter, a skill intrinsic again in her historical novel, *Alice's Tulips** (St. Martin's, 1999), a story of the home front in Kansas during the Civil War. She is also listed in some references as Sandra Dallas Atchison.

D'AMATO, BARBARA (1938–) Born in Grand Rapids, Michigan; mystery-novel writer. She attended Cornell University from 1956 to 1958 and received her B.A. from Northwestern University in 1971. Although she has occasionally taught mystery writing, she has been a full-time author since 1973, sometimes using the pseudonym Malacai Black, and with her husband, Anthony D'Amato, has written some musical comedies and children's musicals. Best known for her Cat Marsala mystery series, the first of which is *Hardball* (Scribner, 1990) and the ninth *Hard Road* (Scribner, 2001), about an Oz festival, D'Amato has set almost all her many books in Chicago, including *Killer.app** (Forge, 1996), a mystery involving high-tech computers. Among her other novels are *Good Cop, Bad Cop* (Forge, 1997), a take-off of a shootout between the Black Panthers and the police in 1969; *Help Me Please* (Forge, 1999), about the kidnapping of a senator's daughter; and, more recently, *Authorized Personnel Only* (Forge, 2000) and *White Male Infant* (Tor, 2002).

A DANCE FOR THREE (Plummer*, Louise, Delacorte, 2000) Psychological and sociological novel of a teenage pregnancy and mental illness, set in Salt Lake City at the end of the 1990s. Since her father's death two years earlier,

Hannah Ziebarth, 15, has had to shoulder almost the entire responsibility for the household, her mother having retreated into agoraphobia, unable to leave the house, open the door, or even call out on the phone, though she can answer incoming calls. Hannah does the grocery shopping, the cooking, and all the other housework, even, when she goes to school or her job at Burger Bar, leaving little package lunches for her mother, whose only interest has become her bonsai trees, which she cultivates expertly. Hannah's passion is drying the roses she steals from gardens along her street, especially those from the yard of cranky Rosa Benson, who makes a contest out of trying to catch her. When Hannah, who has been going with Milo Fabiano, a handsome, confident boy of a well-to-do family, discovers she is pregnant, her mother thinks only of herself, of what will happen to her, and when Hannah tells Milo, whom she expects to be delighted and eager to marry her, he hits her in the face and calls her a whore. Hannah discovers he has gone back to Mimi, an old girlfriend. Only Roman, Milo's brother, who is about Hannah's age, knows what has really happened. When Hannah gets home and sees her bruised, blood-streaked face in the mirror, she cuts a small slit near her eye with a razor blade and smears the rest of her face with blood, then in what is later called a "psychotic episode," throws her mother's bonsai plants off the porch and leaps out into the yard, shouting and waving her arms. She is taken to a psychiatric ward. First-person narration in the novel shifts in sections from Hannah to her friend Trilby, back to Hannah, to Roman, and ends with Hannah again. Trilby, trying to think of an appropriate gift to take when she goes to visit, realizes that it must be roses, stolen roses, and she collects a large bouquet, though she is caught by almost every homeowner. Hannah's recovery is not immediate, but gradually she confronts her pent-up anger at Milo and her mother and even at her father for dying. A Mormon, she is visited by her bishop, a lawyer who apologizes for not having realized what a burden she has been carrying and who volunteers to be her attorney if she wants to sue Milo for paternity or battery. After a month, she is allowed to go with Trilby to a concert, where she glimpses Milo, who sees her and gives her the finger. Back at the hospital, for the first time Hannah is able to see that Milo's attitude is not her fault and that her mother, who has been in therapy, too, is getting better. She even calls Rosa Benson to apologize for stealing her roses and finds the old woman surprisingly sympathetic. Roman, who lost one eye in an accident, is a golfer, "the next Tiger Woods," his ambitious father says, but Roman wants to be a sports psychologist, not a professional golfer. His parents and Milo, who has denied the possibility that he could be the father, are incensed that he is required to give blood for a DNA test when the baby is born. Roman goes along to the hospital, and while they are busy, he finds the nursery, where he sees Baby Ziebarth and recognizes him immediately as one of his family. When the DNA test proves Milo is the father, only Roman has any sympathy for Hannah and appreciates that she is not asking for money, but just that Milo sign away his rights so the baby can be adopted, a solution she has come to accept reluctantly but realistically. Milo goes to a private prep school to finish his senior year, and Hannah returns to high school, where she sees Roman and, having learned from a nurse that he was at the hospital nursery, thanks him for coming to see the baby. While this is one of a plethora of adolescent novels about teenage unwed pregnancies, it is handled better than the average and shows how this problem, combined with others like Hannah's responsibility for her mother, can lead to mental illness. Surprisingly, the most touching voice is that of Roman, who realizes that he is greatly attracted to Hannah, without any hope, and at odds with his family, probably forever. ALA/YA.

DANCER (Hewett*, Lorri, Dutton, 1999) Contemporary novel of an African American girl whose whole world revolves around her obsession with dance and her desire to be accepted into a ballet company. Stephanie Haynes, 16, goes to Lakeview Country Day School in Denver, an expensive and exclusive school to which she has a scholarship because her father is the head custodian, but her far greater interest is in her ballet school run by Madame Caroline, which she attends six days a week, also on scholarship. When the lead in *Sleeping Beauty*, her school's big production, goes to Anna Gritschuk, a new girl, Stephanie is inwardly devastated, but she summons up spirit to congratulate Anna and to act happy to have the part of the Lilac Fairy. Wilhemina Price, a flamboyantly dressed older woman who looks like an African queen, visits their class and afterward invites Stephanie to work on ballet technique with her and her great-nephew, Vance Ross, at her home on Sundays. Stephanie, though somewhat in awe of Miss Winnie, as she wants to be called, is soon devoted to her, but Vance baffles her. When he tries, he is a marvelous dancer, but he seems uninterested and even rude, though he is to be the male lead in *Sleeping Beauty*. Stephanie's parents want her to ease up on ballet, because they fear she

will have little chance professionally, and to think about college, an attitude that creates a rift in the family. Because so much of her time is spent on ballet, Stephanie has never been active in school social circles, but when a new girl, Gillian Sporer, the only other African American in her class, who usually ignores her, invites Stephanie to accompany her to a party given by an older student, she goes. It turns out to be a disaster, with drinking and drugs, and when one of the other partygoers mocks her as a janitor's daughter, she throws beer in his face. She dares not call her parents to come to get her, since they have been pleased to have her included in a nonballet affair, so she calls Miss Winnie, who sends a taxi for her and lets her spend the night at her house. She learns that her hostess once danced with a company in Europe and had high ambitions, thwarted because the dance world was not ready for a black ballerina. She also learns that Miss Winnie is the only stable person in Vance's dysfunctional family and has coached him since he was a child, but that he has begun to rebel at ballet, wanting to pursue dance in an act he and two friends have worked up. Miss Winnie takes Stephanie and Vance to a performance of the Dance Theatre of Harlem, where they are allowed to join the company for practice, and Stephanie is enthralled. Another time Vance takes her to a club where he and his friends easily win a dance contest, and Stephanie sees what it means to him. After a quarrel with her parents, Stephanie calls Vance who picks her up and admits that he has told Miss Winnie he is quitting ballet, and that he resents her trying to relive her life through Stephanie. When Stephanie begs him to stay on through *Sleeping Beauty*, he agrees. In school the next day, Stephanie finds Gillian vomiting in the restroom and learns that she has taken her mother's pills, attempting suicide. Because she refuses to go to the nurse, Stephanie takes her to the custodians' office, where her father summons the nurse and an ambulance. Visiting her later, Stephanie feels mostly pity for the girl with her lavish house, fancy car, and large allowance. For several weeks Stephanie and all the best ballet students audition for the summer programs of the main ballet companies, a step in the direction of becoming a professional dancer. To her delight, Stephanie is accepted for the summer program of The School of American Ballet in New York. At the same time, she is beginning to see the problems of such a life, and she agrees to think about college as a fallback option. The *Sleeping Beauty* performance goes off beautifully, and Vance, who is now really through with ballet, suggests that his little dance group might look for contests in New York. Stephanie's total absorption in her dancing is so vividly described that a reader is caught up in her enthusiasm. Her difficulties with schoolmates, her conflicts with her parents, and the obligatory drinking-drugging party, the fare of many other young adult novels, are less compelling. ALA/YA.

DANCING ON THE EDGE (Nolan*, Han, Harcourt, 1997)   Realistic contemporary problem novel with surrealistic aspects of four years in the lives of a mentally ill Alabama girl and her eccentric family. Miracle McCloy, 10, the narrator, spends a lot of time with her beloved father, Dane, considered a prodigy because he published a novel at the age of thirteen, and her controlling, spiritualist grandmother, Gigi, who holds Dane up as a model for Miracle. When Dane simply melts away on the floor after a seance,

Miracle withdraws into a world of her own making. She burns herself severely trying to re-create Dane's old room, lands in a psychiatric unit, and with the help of a loving aunt learns family secrets that start her on the road to healing. Best is the gradual, relentless descent into mental illness of Miracle's fragile personality. Previously, the book was recommended by *School Library Journal*. For a detailed entry, see *Dictionary, 1995–1999*. ALA/YA.

DANCING WITH AN ALIEN (Logue*, Mary, HarperCollins, 2000)   Fantasy of a visitor from outer space, set in North St. Paul, Minnesota, in the very late twentieth century. In alternate chapters, Branko, a six-foot-four-inch tall young man from a distant planet, and Tonia (Antonia), 17, a midwestern American teenager, describe meeting, falling in love, their different expectations, and, finally, their parting. Branko, the reader learns gradually, has been sent from his home planet to bring back a female, since a few years previously all the women there died from a disease that affected no men. He is staying at the home of Fred and Martha, whose daughter disappeared a few years ago, taken to Branko's home planet by a young man she fell in love with, and has since been a baby-making machine, closely supervised and constantly monitored, although he does not tell this last part to her parents, who have agreed to take him in, hoping for some contact, through him, with their daughter. Tonia is tall and strong and has never had a boyfriend. She and her friend, Beatrice, have talked about it and wondered about having sex, which they refer to as "slow dancing," but they are not unhappy with their lives as they are. She first sees Branko at the lake, where he behaves strangely, walking into the water up to his neck, then turning and walking out. She realizes that he cannot swim. Another day, after she swims out to the dock, she spots him walking toward her until his head is under water. After a few seconds of hesitation, she dives in, finds him, and hauls him back to the beach, where she applies mouth-to-mouth resuscitation. When he is breathing again normally, he sits up, thanks her, and walks off. Branko knows immediately that this is the girl he must take back with him. Fred, who has been with him at the beach, wants no part in Branko's mission and will not help him find Tonia, so he walks the streets looking for her and haunts the beach until he finds her with Beatrice and a boy named Walter, whom Beatrice met at camp. Branko asks Tonia to teach him to swim, and she agrees to try. For Branko, water is a strange luxury, since it is rare on his planet, where there are no lakes, rivers, or oceans, and the novelty of being submerged in it is exciting. Having grown up with boys, he is quite at ease with Buzz, Tonia's four-year-old brother, but at first he is nervous around Tonia and Beatrice, because he has seldom seen and never touched a female since his mother's death when he was three. He has been intensively coached for this mission to say he is from Romania and to wait for the female to make overtures so he will not scare her away, but he is not prepared for falling in love with a girl. As the time comes for him to leave, he becomes melancholy, knowing that if he persuades her to come with him she will be forced to produce offspring continually and he will not have exclusive use of her, since they need to vary the gene pool, but that if he is unable to bring back a female, he will be considered a failure for the rest of his life. As they fall deeply in love, he finally admits he is from another planet, and they have

intercourse, once (probably, with women so rare on his planet, his only chance in life). She agrees to go back with him, but he leaves without her, unwilling to subject her to a life of such servitude. A subplot concerning the marital troubles of Tonia's parents has little effect on the story except to provide a touch of humor when Branko naively asks her father, at the dinner table, whether he is still seeing other women. The two main characters are well developed, and the story, though predictable, is touching. ALA/YA.

DANGEROUS SKIES (Staples*, Suzanne Fisher, Farrar, 1996)   Realistic sociological-problem and mystery novel set for a few weeks in the spring of 1991 among the fisherfolk and truck farmers of the creeks and marshes along Virginia's Eastern Shore of the Chesapeake Bay. The narrator, red-haired Buck Smith, 17, tells about traumatic events that occurred when he was twelve and that forever changed his life and that of his best friend, pretty, intelligent, African American Tunes* Smith, also twelve, the daughter of Buck's father's longtime friend and widower farm manager, Kneebone* Smith. While out fishing with his faithful Lab, Obie, very early one morning in April, "a season of dangerous skies," Buck spots his disagreeable, often menacing neighbor, Jumbo* Rawlin, poking around in the creek with his fishhook, mumbling angrily all the while. A few hours later, Buck and Tunes discover the dead body of Jorge* Rodriguez, the manager of the area's Haitian and Mexican seasonal workers, his left temple smashed in and a gunshot hole in the middle of his forehead. Without explanation, Tunes immediately takes off through the marsh, leaving Buck to tow the body to the dock. Under questioning from Sheriff*, Buck gives only the barest of details, out of fear not telling about Tunes or Jumbo. Later, when he blurts out to his father about having seen Jumbo, his father promptly contacts Sheriff, who now distrusts Buck's story. When it comes out that Tunes ran off and even though Jumbo is known to be a menacing man, prone to vicious acts of temper, Sheriff and the community side with him. Jumbo is generous philanthropically, has held public office, and owns the most land in the area. He tells Sheriff that Tunes and Jorge were lovers, and when Tunes's gun is found in the water near where the body was found and her arrest is imminent, Buck informs Tunes, and she flees. Convinced of her innocence, Buck searches for her along the creek, where he finds her living in an old duck blind. He consults old Judge* Wickham, who urges Tunes to give herself up, promising support in finding the truth. Tunes then tells Buck that for more than a year, Jumbo had been sexually molesting her and that on one occasion she threatened him with a gun, which she left behind in the marsh as she ran away from him. She also says that Jorge once intervened when Jumbo was beating her. Tunes turns herself in, but Sheriff arrests her anyway, refusing to believe her story. At the trial, the prosecutor cleverly prevents Buck from telling anything about Jumbo's menacing habits and generally discredits the boy's testimony, but the defense attorney persuades the judge to drop the case for lack of solid evidence. Buck never sees Tunes again. He realizes he has not only lost his best friend, but also "the notion there was magic in the world . . . [and] my childhood." In this case of Jumbo's word against Tunes's, money and race figure significantly—he is white and a landowner, and she is the black daughter of a farm manager and a descendant of slaves. The sense of geography is strong, in particular the potential for storms, and provides a fine backdrop for the psychological setting, the ingrown community of a few churches, some clubs, and the long-held beliefs of the whites that blacks are a part of their lives yet separate and need to be kept in their places. Buck learns firsthand about hypocrisy through his own Dad, who belatedly contributes to Tunes's defense out of respect and affection for her father. Occasionally, melodrama intrudes, although such scenes can be attributed to Buck's boyish overreactions. On the whole, the book grips throughout and leaves the reader with disgust about the persistence of racial prejudice. ALA/YA.

DANGER ZONE (Klass*, David, Scholastic, 1996)   Basketball novel centered on an international tournament in Italy, which is disrupted by a neo-Nazi group strongly antagonistic to non-Ayrans, mainly because all the players on the U.S. team except the protagonist are African Americans. Ironically, he is the only one shot. Prejudice, both white and black, forms a major theme in the novel. For a longer entry, see *Many Peoples, One Land*, [no. 66]. ALA/YA.

THE DARK SIDE OF NOWHERE (Shusterman* Neal, Little, Brown, 1997) Science fiction with boy's growing-up aspects, set in recent years in the small town of Billington, somewhere in the eastern United States. Only-child Jason Miller, the rebellious, iconoclastic fourteen-year-old narrator, is bored with almost everything—his not-too-bright best friend, Wesley, his average parents, school, and especially his hometown and the monthly shots he must take, purpose unknown. His life changes abruptly when classmate

Ethan dies of what is said to be a ruptured appendix and the school janitor and security guard, Mr. Grant*, mysteriously assures him that Ethan is not dead and gives him a metallic elbow-length glove. He instructs Jason to meet him Tuesday after school at the barn in Old Town, a nearby area hard hit by a tornado and a plague and then abandoned. He shows off the glove to lively, assertive newcomer Paula Quinn and discovers that the glove is really an innovative BB gun. After school on Tuesday at Old Town, he finds Grant instructing about thirty young people from Jason and Grant's church, Holy Circle Nondenominational, about how to use the glove, all the while, Jason says, "spouting profundities" in a sonorous voice like a prophet. When he gets home, he discovers his parents packing in preparation for going "elsewhere." Before they leave, Jason's father takes him to Old Town, where he learns that the Millers are one of several extraterrestrial families, all members of Holy Circle, who arrived in Billington twenty years earlier. The crash of their spaceship has become popularly mythologized as a tornado and a plague. The aliens wrapped the DNA of the deceased inhabitants around their own, adopted their identities and appearances, and settled in Billington. Jason's parents know that Grant has discovered that an invasion of spaceships is imminent. The young people, all of whom also receive shots, notice that they have begun to itch intensely, lose hair, and change appearance. When Jason demands that Grant tell them what is going on, Grant takes him to a basement in Old Town, where Jason finds Ethan alive, now an incredibly well-muscled and handsome youth with long silky hair and a peach-fuzz complexion. Ethan has been changed by the shots into the old alien body and

mind. The young people will also soon be like Ethan, because of the shots, but the parents have decided to retain their human shapes until the invaders arrive. Jason's parents take off for parts unknown, while other adults prepare for the arrival. Jason, who is attracted to human Paula and has become a friend of Mrs. Pohl, the mother of the young man whose appearance Jason was given, has misgivings about destroying humanity in the name of populating Earth with a presumably superior race of beings. He stops taking shots in an attempt to retain his humanity but is detected and forced to resume them. When Wesley tries to launch their old spaceship, it crashes, destroying what is left of Old Town. Jason feels a terrible pain, like appendicitis, and dies, as Ethan did. He is revived by his parents, but with the alien physical form. He learns that his parents have also had great reservations about the alien enterprise and have been, in various ways, trying to scuttle it. At the end, human inwardly but not outwardly, moved by a pleasing feeling of human compassion, Jason and his parents go to the state legislature to warn them about the impending extraterrestrial invasion. The novel exhibits traits typical of its genre: plentiful action, high suspense, a superficial examination of such matters as racial superiority and mob or cult mentality, clever extrapolation from known science, flat, functional characters, and a morally slanted conclusion. ALA/YA.

DAVE AT NIGHT (Levine*, Gail Carson, HarperCollins, 1999)   Humorous period novel of friendship and orphanage life set in New York City in 1926 during the Harlem Renaissance. Narrator Dave Caros, 11, sneaks out at night from the abusive Hebrew Home for Boys and meets grandfatherly Solly Gruber, who tells fortunes for partygoers, introduces the boy to African Americans involved with historical figures of the Harlem Renaissance, and is eventually instrumental in improving conditions at the home. Period details are vividly and skillfully evoked, the protagonist is admirably plucky, Solly makes a fine "fairy godfather" figure, and the style is light and lively. Previously, the novel was selected by *School Library Journal*. For a longer entry, see *Dictionary, 1995–1999*. ALA/YA.

DAWSON, MILLER (*Cloudy in the West**) Good-hearted outlaw, whom Joey Shipman and his cousin, Beau, meet while they are on the road to West Texas. Dawson's reputation as a Robin Hood type is widespread throughout the region, but lawmen report that he is really just a common brigand. Joey is attracted to him, because he is kind, takes an interest in him, and generously shares his supplies with him and Beau. Dawson asserts that he has not killed as many men or robbed as many banks as he is said to have done. He says that all he really wants is to get enough money to go to Oregon, buy some good farmland, and bring his son, who is about Joey's age, to live with him there. He is captured and hanged in Stockton.

DEFINE "NORMAL" (Peters*, Julie Anne, Little, Brown, 2000)   Contemporary personal- and sociological-problem story set in an unnamed city in the months of March and April. Responsible, well-mannered, intelligent, conservative— "normal" to most people's standards— Antonia Dillon, 14, the eighth-grade narrator, cannot believe that Dr. DiLeo, psychologist at Oberon Middle School, has asked her to be the peer counselor in the school's newly created program for, of all people, classmate Jazz (Jasmine) Luther. Antonia is a top student, all As, participates in extracurricular activities, and also takes care of her home, two brothers—Michael, 7, and Chuckie, 3— because fearful, sickly Mom spends all her time in bed. Antonia must now give up her homeroom study period to try to help this psycho—tattooed, pierced, purple-haired, black-lipsticked, foul-mouthed druggie (she thinks) with shredded jeans. She appeals to Dr. DiLeo, but he insists Jazz needs help. Jazz hates teachers, recites mantras in a lotus position during their sessions, and openly despises Antonia as a "priss" who kowtows to teachers and dresses in skirts and blouses to get good grades—Jazz's every move and every word get under Antonia's skin. Forced to continue in the program with twice-weekly meetings, however, the two girls begin to share their lives. Antonia realizes she has no friends, while Jazz's are odds-outs types. Antonia thinks Jazz is really troubled, then thinks maybe the trouble between them is Antonia herself. She has set responsible goals: get into advanced placement classes, get out of high school early and into college, and get away from the burdens of home as soon as possible. Everything went to pieces three years ago when Dad, a roofer, walked out, and now Mom is even using Antonia's college money to pay bills. When she mentions that she regrets not having learned to swim, Jazz invites her over to swim in the Luthers' indoor pool. Antonia is amazed—the Luthers must be rich. Their house is enormous and well-appointed, and Mrs. Luther is "awesome," so beautifully coifed and dressed, and is nice besides. When Antonia gets a call from Michael that he, Mom, and Chuckie are out near the airport, and Mom is incoherent and cannot cope, the Luthers help, and Mom is taken to St. Joseph's Hospital and the children to the Luther house, where they stay until a social worker arranges for them to live with foster parents. Antonia is filled with anger and resentment against Jazz, Jazz's mother, the "system," herself—against everything. A visit to Mom in the psychiatric hospital is a disaster; the social worker says Mom is clinically depressed. Antonia admits that Mom has had a hard time since Dad walked out. Jazz's ambition, Antonia learns, is to go to Juilliard to study classical piano, at which she excels. Antonia persuades her to play, just for a little while, in the school auditorium, where her beautiful music draws an increasingly larger and admiring audience. She becomes a sort of star in the school for her talent, even among teachers who had thought she was just short of a thug. The truth comes out eventually. Realizing that both girls have severe problems and believing that they could help each other, Dr. DiLeo admits that he asked them to counsel each other—pairing them was a setup, and as it turns out a successful one. Jazz agrees to play in her spring recital, dressing more conventionally than usual, and patches things up with her mother. Mom comes home, able for a time at least to cope, and the girls are now close friends. The book is set up in short, snappy chapters, almost entirely in contemporary dialogue, and moves to a predictable but satisfactory conclusion. The attentive reader soon sees that the girls are much alike—determined and dedicated to a secret ambition, mother focused, and likable—although they do not realize it until much later. The author handles them with tact and sympathy. ALA/YA.

DESSEN, SARAH (1970–   )   Born in Illinois; author, teacher of writing at the University of North Carolina–Chapel Hill, where she earlier attended college. Until she started writing full time, she worked as a waitress. Two of her novels, *Someone Like You** (Viking, 1998) and *Keeping the Moon** (Viking, 1999), were on the *School Library Journal* Best Books list and have since been named to the American Library Association Young Adult list. *Someone Like You* was also cited by the New York Public Library as an outstanding book of the year. *That Summer** (Orchard, 1996), set in the months when a girl's divorced father and her older sister are both being married, is about the need to give up illusions about the perfect past. *Dreamland** (Viking, 2000), a grimmer book, is about a girl's inability to get out of an abusive relationship with her boyfriend. All have convincing protagonists dealing with real problems. For earlier biographical information and title entries, see *Dictionary, 1995–1999* [*Keeping the Moon; Someone Like You*].

DEUKER, CARL (1950–   )   Born in San Francisco, California, educated at the University of California–Berkeley (B.A.), the University of Washington (M.A.), and the University of California–Los Angeles (teaching certificate). He has taught in schools in the state of Washington and was a book and film critic for the *Seattle Sun* from 1980 to 1985. His novels for young adults, all of which were selections of the American Library Association, have been sports stories, in which the protagonists have personal as well as sports problems with which to cope. Two revolve around basketball, *On the Devil's Court* (Little, Brown, 1988) and *Night Hoops** (Houghton Mifflin, 2000), while *Heart of a Champion* (Little, Brown, 1993) and *Painting the Black** (Houghton Mifflin, 1997), involve baseball. Dramatic and fast moving, the books pull readers into the action on diamond and court and into the protagonists' personal issues as well.

DITCH GORDON (*The Reappearance of Sam Webber**)   A tall, "stretched-out" man, constantly puffing on a cigarette, owner of the flower shop where Sam Webber's mother works. Not at ease with the boy, who is rather scared of him, Ditch nevertheless tries to help him make the transition to his new neighborhood, coming over and clearing out, with Sam helping, the small backyard that has been filled with junk, then taking him to the 7-Eleven and buying him a Coke and a couple of comic books. The apartment that he and his wife, flamboyant, good-hearted Junie, found for the Webbers is not far from his store. More than just employers, he and Junie, unable to have children, adopted Sam's parents as if they were their own and feel dismay, themselves, that Big Sam has disappeared. Just before Christmas, when Sam proposes that they ask Greely* Clemons to their holiday dinner, Maxine and Junie worry about how Ditch will treat the black man, but he engages Greely in talk about sports as they watch a television game, and the day passes without incident. Later, hearing Ditch use the word *Nigger*, Sam is distressed and asks his mother to tell Ditch to avoid that language. She wisely says it would be better if he told Ditch himself, and he finally screws up his courage to do so. Ditch is surprised and a little defensive, but he seems to respect Sam for speaking up.

DONETTA RUSH (*From the Black Hills**) Girlfriend of Michael Newlin, one year behind him in school at Wheatly, South Dakota. From a dysfunctional family, Donetta is more dependent on Mike than he is on her. Her parents were divorced when she was nine or ten, and her father, who lived with an alcoholic, died when she was fifteen. Her sister, Margo, has moved back home with her husband, Cory Burris, who feuds continually with her mother, owner of a beauty shop. When they fight, Donetta goes to her room, trying to stay out of the conflict. Donetta is a very small girl, like a bird, Mike thinks. She and Mike have had sex since before she was fifteen, always being careful to use condoms, and he is the only boy she has ever been with, but he admits to himself that he is often thinking of some other girl during the act, and he knows that emotionally she is more attached to him than he to her. Still, when his father kills his secretary, Mike gets more support from Donetta than anyone else, and after he has made the phone call to betray his father, although as it happens Glenn has already been arrested, he finds his only comfort in playing over and over a tape Donetta made for him, which begins with "It's three o'clock in the morning. I can't sleep, I can't dream, I can't stop thinking of you."

DONNA DELUCA (*Kissing Doorknobs**) A girl Tara Sullivan's age who is her friend for about a year. Tara describes Donna as beautiful, muscular, and popular, especially with the boys, and at odds with her parents. She wears sunglasses because she has recently had an operation on one eye. Cynical and angry looking, she smokes, lies easily, and is tough and sophisticated compared to Tara. She and Tara take trips to Chicago to go shopping, and Donna introduces Tara to shoplifting, except that Tara's conscience forces Tara to return the things she stole. When Tara learns that Donna has been having sex with her boyfriend, in an ironically humorous episode she takes Donna to a drugstore to buy condoms, but the pharmacist refuses to sell them to the girls because they are so young. This is one of the few instances in which Tara concerns herself with someone else's problems. When last seen, Donna is in a home for unwed mothers.

DON'T THINK TWICE (Pennebaker*, Ruth, Holt, 1996)   Realistic novel of four months in a home for unwed mothers, in which a girl learns to understand herself and to see her own family more clearly. Divided into eighteen weeks in the 1990s, starting in August and ending just before Christmas, the narration is in first person present tense by Anne Harper, 17, from Dallas, who has been taken by her humiliated parents to the home somewhere in rural Texas to wait out her pregnancy. At first, Anne, who is highly intelligent but has low self-esteem, is hostile to the whole setup, viewing the other girls as dim-witted losers, the woman in charge, Mrs. Landing, as inept and nosy, and the experience as one to endure and then forget about forever. Gradually, she begins to be interested in the other girls. Her roommate, Cheryl, is from Oklahoma, a determinedly cheerful girl who goes to group discussions and prayer meetings with a smile but secretly cries at night. Harriet, whom Anne despises, is from Kansas, a deeply religious girl who constantly quotes the Bible and offers to pray for the others. Gracie, a very small girl only twelve or thirteen, who was raped by her father, almost never says anything. LaNelle, from Arkansas, is the oldest in a big family, all of whom are physically abused by their father. Donna keeps waiting for her boyfriend, Dick, to come and marry her. Nancy, a student from the University of Mississippi, con-

siders all the others in need of her advice on beauty aids and how to catch a man, and is universally disliked. Rachel, from the San Francisco Bay area, is the only one with any political or ecological interest, and she tells the others frequently about how liberal and enlightened her family and home environment are. Anne tries not to think about her own family, even refusing to read most of the letters they send on what she recognizes as her mother's enforced schedule. Her younger sister, Pamela, 15, who has always resented Anne because she gets good grades and their father's approval, writes about her boyfriends and the school dance at which she sees Jake with some other girl. Her mother, who has several times been hospitalized for nervous breakdowns, writes cheerful gossipy letters utterly removed from reality, acting as if Anne is at a summer camp. Her father, a high-powered lawyer, writes cold, impersonal letters, clearly signaling that she has forfeited his love and approval. When bullied into going to group sessions, Anne does not volunteer any information about herself or how she got pregnant, and for a long time keeps herself from even thinking about Jake, the boy she started to go out with less than a year before, her first boyfriend, with whom she fell madly in love and with whom she had intercourse through the late spring and early summer, until he broke up with her. Only after the breakup did she find out she was pregnant, and she has never told him of her plight. All except Rachel expect to give their babies up for adoption. LaNelle is the first to deliver, and her baby, whom she holds and names Laurie, dies in a couple of days. When her father comes to get her things, Anne is surprised to see he is not a monster but a stooped, skinny hillbilly, not looking like a man who beats his kids with a strap. Donna, who learns in a letter from a "friend" that Dick is dating another girl, delivers a girl whom she never sees and leaves the home deeply depressed. Gracie goes into labor but her baby must be delivered by cesarean section. She is sent to live with an aunt in Boston. Nancy, predictably, has her baby, comes back in a new, stylish dress, and heads back to Old Miss to snare a well-to-do husband. Rachel, whose boyfriend, Daniel, finally decides he wants to marry her, angrily refuses and plans to give up her baby for adoption, realizing that her parents talk a liberal line but really are hypocrites, not wanting to have anything to do with the reality of a bastard offspring. To her surprise, Anne becomes a close friend of Cheryl, who tells her about being seduced by her minister, an event that her pious parents refused to believe, reacting instead by throwing her out. She and Anne are in town, waiting at a diner for Mrs. Landing, when Cheryl goes into labor. Anne begs a ride to the hospital from a laborer who is at the counter, the kindest person she has met in the whole experience, and while she is waiting at the hospital, her own water breaks and she is admitted. After an agonizing labor, she insists on seeing her baby, a beautiful, eight-pound girl, even against the advice of her doctor and social worker, and then reluctantly gives her up. Cheryl's baby is a boy whom she gives up without seeing. Cheryl plans to go to secretarial school and perhaps try for a reconciliation with her family. In the end, Anne's father picks her up, and she is ready to face her life at home, knowing that she will never mistake her family for the loving, supportive people she had imagined them, realizing that no one except the girls at the home will ever know what they really went through, but stronger from her experience and with,

ironically, a better self-image. What could be an artificial case-history narrative is made interesting and moving by Anne's sharp, usually unspoken, wit and ability to see through pretensions. Her gradual development from what she recognizes as a passive-aggressive personality to a caring and competent friend to Cheryl is believable, and the pain that almost all the girls feel at giving up their babies is well evoked. ALA/YA.

DON'T YOU DARE READ THIS, MRS. DUNPHREY (Haddix*, Margaret Peterson, Simon & Schuster, 1997)   Contemporary problem novel of a girl trying to shoulder the responsibilities for her household and her younger brother after the departure of both parents, told in journal entries for a high school English class. For a longer entry, see *Dictionary, 1995–1999*. ALA/YA.

THE DOOR IN THE LAKE (Butts*, Nancy, Front Street, 1998)   Science fiction novel set for a few days in recent years in southwestern Virginia involving a space abduction and a time warp. Very early one October morning, thin, dirty, glassy-eyed Joseph Patrick Finney, 14, called Joey, walks into a Minit Mart just outside his hometown of Cornish Gap. While trying to drink from a milk carton, which ironically bears his own picture, he suddenly collapses to the floor insensible. When he wakes in the hospital two days later, he learns that he has been missing for two years, the object of a national search. All he can remember at first was having to go to the bathroom in the middle of the night while his family was camping at Smokewater Lake in the Allegheny Mountains. Kind Dr. Kaminsky says that Joey's constant nasal drip appears to be caused by a metal obstruction in his brain. Joey's adjustment to home and school is often painful. He is saddened by his mother's now-gray hair, his father's skepticism about his story, and his brother Kevin's* often patronizing attitude. He is also very bothered by the almost total disregard, and occasional disparaging remarks, of his school friends and his once bosom pal, Hamp Durden. Although previously an honor student, he is behind in his schoolwork. Sheriff Wade Varnadoe, however, is consistently supportive and caring, often checks on Joey, and just generally keeps an eye on him. Joey has seizures during which he realizes that he is recalling what happened at the beginning of the two-year disappearance. He remembers seeing an immense glowing circle rising from the lake, and then begins to hear a voice that tells him to come back to the lake and to the "door." News stories about him prompt two college students, Ethan* Glass and Ariel* DeWitt, to e-mail him offering help. Ethan thinks Joey has been caught up in some distortion of space time, made possible by extraterrestrial technology. When Joey's physical symptoms persist, he insists on returning to the campground. With the help of Ethan, Ariel, and Kevin, he goes to the lake in the middle of the night, to the spot where he stood two years earlier. Again, an immense circle rises from the water, which Joey now recognizes as a door. As he moves toward it, a voice or presence speaks through him, insisting it meant no harm, agrees to remove the metal object, and responds positively to Joey's suggestion that he be returned to the time before the trouble began. Immediately, Joey finds himself at the time and place where he was originally, near his parents' pup tent and the larger tent where he, Kevin, and their two friends were sleeping. Joey is twelve years old

again but retains his memories of the brief time when he was fourteen. The book's flap describes the novel as a "cross between *The Twilight Zone* and *The X-Files*," an arena for inexplicable events that are made emotionally if not intellectually acceptable. Joey's bewilderment and psychic pain are palpable all the way. Of the other characters, only Kevin changes. He becomes his brother's staunch supporter, as the reader would like, if too abruptly. The college students play their supporting roles well, and the adults are also mostly helpful, but the behavior of Joey's contemporaries toward him is deplorable—cold, unfeeling, disparaging, unwelcoming. ALA/YA.

A DOOR NEAR HERE (Quarles*, Heather, Delacorte, 1998) Contemporary realistic novel of a dysfunctional family in which the three teenagers struggle to protect their eight-year-old half sister despite their mother's alcoholism and their father's absence. The narrator, Katherine Donovan, 15, is nearly overwhelmed by the difficulties of running the house and managing her younger siblings while her mother lies drinking and sleeping in her upstairs bedroom, emerging only for brief visits to the liquor store for new supplies. Katherine knows they cannot count on their father, Dale, for help since he left their Washington, D.C., home ten years earlier to live with his receptionist, Ophelia, in Michigan, and has subsequently married her and started a new family. He has made it clear that he wants nothing to do with Alisa, who was born two years after his departure, the result of one of her mother's frequent brief affairs, even she does not know which. He does send some child support money for the older three and insists that they go to an Episcopal school which they detest. Katherine, a disorganized, prickly, but intelligent girl, and her siblings, Douglas, 14, a near-genius at mechanical and scientific things unwilling, usually, to face emotional problems, and Tracy, 13, a very pretty girl interested mostly in her friends and parties, are all devoted to Alisa, whom they have practically raised with little help from their mother, and their greatest fear is that someone will discover their situation and that authorities will send Alisa to a foster home. Their difficulties accelerate when Alisa's African American principal, Ms. Haley, sends a note home, insisting on a conference with their mother because Alisa has been running off from school, into the woods that are strictly out of bounds. Katherine learns that Alisa, who is devoted to C. S. Lewis's books, is looking for the door to Narnia, which she is sure she has seen among the trees, hoping to find Aslan and get him to cure her mother. To add to their troubles, they are running out of food and money, the pipe in the kitchen sink is broken, and eventually the heat and electricity are shut off for lack of payment. In trying to cope, they make a number of bad moves. Tracy forges letters to Ms. Haley and to their own school office to cover absences and, when they find the support check from their father, their mother's signature so that Douglas can ride his bike to the bank and deposit it. He is not allowed, however, to take any money out. They solve this, after considerable anguish, when they find their mother's ATM card and Alisa tells them that the code is her name. They wait until after dark, thinking there will be less traffic, and Douglas drives them, somewhat erratically, to the supermarket. Just as they think they are in the clear, they run into Ms. Haley, also shopping at night. When Alisa is banned from attending school until she has seen a psychiatrist, Katherine smuggles her aboard her own school bus and hides her under the bleachers in the gym. There the religion teacher, Mr. Dodgson, finds her and much of their story comes out. He is understanding and sympathetic to Alisa, with whom he shares a love of Narnia. Afraid that he will report them and thinking she can discredit him so he won't be believed, Katherine writes an anonymous letter to the dean of students, suggesting that Mr. Dodgson has an unhealthy interest in Alisa. Before she can reconsider and retrieve it, their mother stumbles out of bed, has a bad fall, and Katherine goes with her in the ambulance to the hospital. She is late getting home and learns from Douglas and Tracy that Alisa has been missing for hours. When her own frantic efforts to find her little sister are unavailing, she realizes that the child is probably trying again to get to Aslan. Having no way to get to the school, she calls Mr. Dodgson asking for help. He picks her up and they search in the dark and cold and finally find Alisa huddled in the woods, extremely cold and disconsolate because, she says, Aslan would not let her stay in Narnia. Mr. Dodgson explains, gently, that Aslan wants her to be with Katherine and the others, who really need her. The end is not entirely happy. Ms. Haley takes charge, and their mother is soon in a rehabilitation program, while the four youngsters are living uneasily with their father in Michigan, the forceful woman having persuaded him that Alisa is also his responsibility. Mr. Dodgson, however, while not proven to have any illicit interest in Alisa, is dismissed, since even the hint of scandal terrifies the school authorities. While Katherine is admirable in her struggles and is shown to realize that she did Mr. Dodgson an injustice, the various events have so overwhelmed her that her guilt does not seem as deep as it should be. Both parents are stereotypes. One disturbing element is the way the three teenagers smoke incessantly. The novel's greatest strength is the sense of events inexorably leading toward disaster, with the children enmeshing themselves deeper and deeper in lies and contradictions. ALA/YA.

DORRIS, MICHAEL (ANTHONY) (1945–1997) Native American writer and educator; born in Louisville, Kentucky; professor of anthropology and chair of the Native American Studies Department at Dartmouth College; author of scholarly materials, nonfiction, and novels, some with his wife, the Native American novelist Louise Erdrich. *The Window** (Hyperion, 1997), cited by the American Library Association for children and young adults, is a companion to the writer's earlier and best-known novel for adults, *A Yellow Raft in Blue Water* (Holt 1987). For more information about Dorris and title entries, see *Dictionary, 1990–1994* [*Morning Girl*]; *Dictionary, 1995–1999* [*Guests*; *Sees Behind Trees*; *The Window*]; *This Land Is Our Land* [*A Yellow Raft in Blue Water*, no. 424]; and *Many Peoples, One Land* [*Cloud Chamber*, no. 436; *Guests*, no. 437; *Sees Behind Trees*, no. 438; *The Window*, no. 439].

DOWNSIDE (*Downsiders**) City of five thousand people who live in the sewers and subways beneath Manhattan in New York City and of whose existence New Yorkers, known as Topsiders to the Downsiders, are unaware. Downside is governed by a leader called the "Most-Beloved" and by Wise Advisors, has laws that govern behavior, the main one of which is that no Topsider may enter Downside and then leave, and has rituals and beliefs appropriate to a civilized soci-

ety. Youths are organized into groups of about three, girls included, to learn adult ways, like hunting and rescuing "fallers." Fallers are Topside people who are on the fringes of Topside society, often called "bums." They are rescued by Downsiders, renamed, taught skills, and given responsibilities so that they can become useful members of society. Lindsay Matthias, a Topsider friend of the Downsider youth, Talon* Angler, reads in the New York Public Library about Alfred Ely Beach, a historical late-nineteenth-century inventor who, despite the opposition of Boss Tweed of Tammany Hall, constructed a successful pneumatic subway beneath New York City, until forced by City Hall to abandon the project. Lindsay theorizes that Beach continued to build, using down-and-out workers at night, taking in the destitute and the rejected, and secretly creating a world for them beneath the streets. This, she thinks, was the beginning of Downside. Although advised not to by The Champ*, a faller, because it might shock Talon too much, Lindsay shares her information with the boy. A map of Downside appears at the beginning of the novel.

DOWNSIDERS (Shusterman*, Neal, Simon & Schuster, 1999) Contemporary novel of fantasy and friendship set in New York City from December to April, which postulates a region called Downside* of five thousand inhabitants who occupy the sewers and subways beneath Manhattan Island and of whose existence the Topsiders (New Yorkers) above are unaware. Her mother having run off to Africa with her zoology professor, Lindsay Matthias, 14, is sent by plane to New York City to live permanently with her father, Mark, an engineer engrossed in building an aqueduct beneath New York City, and his disagreeable, mean-spirited son, Todd, also 14. Lonely Lindsay finds a friend from a most unlikely source, Downside. On New Year's Eve, Talon* Angler, 14, a Downsider, seeking help for his very ill little sister and having been advised by his elderly friend, The Champ*, to get antibiotics from Topside, contacts Lindsay, whom he has come to admire from afar. Although frightened at first of the strange, unkempt boy, Lindsay gives him leftover pills and enables him to get away safely. Out one day, Lindsay spies Talon observing her from a curbside drain, into which she is pulled when her hair gets caught in his metallic vest. Although he knows it is strictly forbidden, Talon shows her around Downside. Lindsay is amazed at how the Downsiders have fashioned clothing and created a pleasant and functioning world out of items the Topsiders have discarded. Among other events, the two enter the BOT (Big Old Tunnel), where they are almost trodden by the wild cattle that live there and that the Downsiders hunt. Railborn* Skinner, also fourteen, is one of the Downsiders with whom Talon is grouped (the other is a girl, Gutta) for coming-of-age activities like hunting. Seeking to elevate himself among the Downsiders and especially with Gutta, Railborn reports to Downside authorities that Talon has shown a Topsider around. Talon is apprehended, tried, sentenced to be executed, taken to a water main, and put inside, from which he is eventually expelled into the Atlantic Ocean. He is rescued by a derelict old woman who lives under the boardwalk at Coney Island. At that point, however, Mark Matthias's workers unwittingly break through into Downside. Railborn suggests that Downside retaliate against Topside by cutting off electricity, water, gas, and sewers. The Topsiders search for the cause of their utilities failure and blast into Downside. When he finds Gutta seriously injured, Railborn makes a fateful choice: he takes her to a Topside hospital. When last seen both are well and in a Topside home for wards of the state, Railborn having given up Downside life and a high position to save Gutta. Mark Matthias is blamed for the disaster, is forced to resign his position, and moves the family to a smaller house elsewhere. Talon organizes the Downsiders to ignite natural gas in the aqueduct shaft, known hereafter among the Downsiders as the "Great Shaft Disaster," which destroys half of Downside but seals off the rest. Talon later shows Lindsay how the Downsiders have taken over the tops of abandoned water towers to create new dwellings. Talon has become the Most-Beloved, the leader, of the Downsiders. In accepting the position, he has given up any hope of a life with Lindsay. The novel is a page turner; plentiful action and high tension lead to a powerful climax. Although the plot moves unevenly, characters are well drawn, obviously foiled, and faced with moral as well as practical decisions, and Downside is convincingly created. Thrills aplenty appear, and the comparisons between Topside and Downside offer the thinking reader much to ponder. ALA/YA.

DRAPER, SHARON MILLS (1952–) Born in Cleveland, Ohio; educator, novelist. Her *Forged by Fire** (Simon & Schuster, 1997), which won the Coretta Scott King Award, has more recently been named to the American Library Association Young Adult list. For earlier biographical information and a title entry, see *Dictionary, 1995–1999* [*Forged by Fire*].

DREAMLAND (Dessen*, Sarah, Viking, 2000)   Contemporary   psychological novel of how a girl's efforts to keep up with her "perfect" older sister, or failing that, to be entirely different, lead her into a relationship with an abusive boyfriend who threatens her physically and mentally. On Caitlin O'Koren's sixteenth birthday, her sister Cass (Cassandra), 18, who has always been athletic, brilliant, and beautiful and is two weeks away from entering Yale, leaves home for New York to join a young man named Adam whom she has known only briefly and who works on the *Lamont Whipper Show*, a trash television program. Her mother, a highly controlling woman dedicated to her older daughter's success, is devastated. Her father, a university dean of students, used to managing the lives of young people, discovers he is powerless to bring Cass home or understand her motivation. The novel, however, centers on the narrator, Caitlin, who has always followed her sister's lead and now finds herself rudderless. After the initial shock wears off, their mother turns her attention to her younger daughter, devoting her energies to keeping track of Caitlin's schoolwork and the practices of her cheerleading group, which she joined only because her best friend, Rina, goaded her into trying out. Although Caitlin feels smothered, she tries hard to live up to expectations and keeps up the pretense of being appreciative, until she meets Rogerson Biscoe, a boy from a prominent family who has been in trouble with the police and, she soon learns, has a drug distribution business. At first she is infatuated by Rogerson's good looks and flattered by his attention, and she also enjoys being as different from Cass as she can be, smoking pot and skipping school to be with him. From a scene she witnesses at his home, she realizes that Rogerson is a victim of his father's abuse and knows that, while vulnerable, the boy

has a bad temper, but she is utterly unprepared when, angry about some trivial thing, he strikes her viciously in the face. This is just the first instance of escalating violence against her, usually on her body where the bruises will not show if she wears slacks and long sleeves. He is especially touchy about being made to wait, and Caitlin grows tense and nervous fearing to hold him up for even a minute. She starts missing practices for cheerleading, which she has begun to hate. Almost the only time she can relax is at the dilapidated farmhouse rented by his friends, David and Corinna, who seem to have a perfect, loving relationship and where she can smoke pot and stop thinking about her problems. When she discovers that Corinna has been supporting her lazy lover and, unable to make ends meet, has left for California, it is one more disillusionment. Caitlin retreats more and more into a dreamworld, whether she is stoned on drugs or not, and is unable to reach out to Rina or her parents or to tell anyone about her increasing fear. The climax occurs at her parents' April Fool's Day party, when Rogerson, waiting as she drives up after spending an afternoon with Rina, pulls her into his car, beats her, and throws her to the ground. He is pulled off as he kicks her savagely. As the guests cluster around, her parents for the first time really look at her and see the results of long-term abuse. The last chapters are at Evergreen Care Center, where Caitlin gradually "swims up from underwater," as it seems to her, slowly regaining confidence and facing reality. While predictable and peopled largely with stereotypes (especially Caitlin's parents), the novel does a good job of showing how such a relationship can develop and why it is hard to leave. Caitlin knows that Rogerson is needy, starved for affection, and after he has been violent he is loving and sweet. He also is highly intelligent, a quality she admires greatly, and wild, something that differentiates him from any of the boys Cass went with previously. Although it follows the pattern of a case study, the book explores Caitlin's emotions and makes them real to a reader. ALA/YA; NYPL.

DUST (Pellegrino*, Charles, Avon, 1998) Adult futuristic science fiction thriller set almost entirely in the United States. The terror starts on the barrier island Long Beach in Long Island Sound, New York. Several sunbathers are simply overwhelmed by a kind of black dust that rolls over them, suffocates them, and then devours their flesh. As it spreads throughout the area, it is determined that it consists of mites. The scientists (some of them real people) at Brookhaven National Laboratory on Long Island try to explain its origin and determine how to handle it. Scientist Richard Sinclair, who escaped from Long Beach with his daughter, Tam, 10, dons a special impenetrable suit, and in the laboratory's special blimp, flies to the beach, descends, and soon realizes that the plague has destroyed everyone there, including his wife, and he barely manages to escape with his life. Similar incidents occur in North Carolina and in Bangor, Maine, and other unusual and frightening events follow. A red tide devastates the rivers, streams, pools, and offshore ocean at Vancouver, British Colombia, and bats attack and kill humans in the Caribbean. The environment has become very quiet—there are no longer any birds. As a result of many, lengthy (and fascinating to read) discussions, the scientists conclude that something has destroyed the insects, and then dedicate themselves to finding a way of bringing them back, since all life depends on them. Failing to find eggs and the like with which to work, they attempt to clone a cockroach from a sole survivor, and then other insects from fossils. While this is going on, panic among the populace devolves into madness. Power outages create shortages of clean drinking water, and cholera and scurvy and other diseases break out and spread. Environmental degradation is followed by the collapse of the economy, in much the same way as, the scientists realize from written records, occurred in ancient Babylon. War breaks out between India and Pakistan, to complicate matters further. Just when it seems that something can be worked out to stave off complete disaster, a highly charismatic, foul-mouthed, incendiary talk-show host, Jerry Sigmond, incites malcontents and militia types to attack Brookhaven National Laboratory, as the source of all the problems. At about the same time, an army officer in charge of an underground missile silo somewhere in Kansas, unable to get solid information about what is going on in the upper world, releases his missiles, and as a result Washington, D.C., among other cities, is destroyed. Tam, Sinclair, and other scientists from Brookhaven take off in the blimp for the Azores, having determined that life is near to normal there. Although the blimp is severely damaged by Sigmond-incited forces, they manage to escape. An epilogue set twenty years later, focuses on Tam who sees some hope for the future, although she realizes that her father has been severely damaged psychologically by the loss of his wife and his and his fellows' inability to stem the destruction. Although slow to start, the book is intensely gripping, and through Sinclair, especially, makes personal both the devastation and the efforts to contain it.

The discussions among the scientists and the theories proposed and tested in discussion against what is thought to have happened in the past through archaeological discoveries are extremely fascinating. They slow the plot, but at the same time they strengthen it. Social commentary appears variously, as, obviously, with Sigmond. Not the least horrifying is the effect of the information in the afterword on the impact of the novel. It points out the "reality" of many of the incidents and indicates that the Earth is indeed due for one of its periodic catastrophes, which have occurred several times in the past, like that of the dinosaurs. The best (or worst, depending on one's perspective) part of the novel is the writer's great skill in making the panic and devastation so very, very real—and very scary. NYPL.

DUST DEVILS (Laxalt*, Robert P., University of Nevada Press, 1997)   Short western-adventure novel with boy's growing-up aspects published for adults. The action occurs in Heavenly Valley in northeastern California and northern Nevada in the early part of the twentieth century, the last days of the Old West. Teenage Ira Hamilton, whose mother died at his birth, is the son of proud, independent, Indian-hating rancher John* D. Hamilton (usually referred to in the novel as "John D. Hamilton by God"). Ira was suckled in infancy by Sage Flower, wife of the chief of a local Native American Indian Paiute band, Black Rock Tom, whose son, Cricket, is Ira's age and best friend. Also proud and independent, Black Rock Tom has little use for whites ("The only presents white men gave us was gunpowder, whiskey, and smallpox"). At the July 4 celebration in Sierraville, California, Ira's prize for winning a bronc-riding contest is a pure-blooded Arabian pony. The Arabian is soon stolen by Hawkeye, a notorious rustler, and taken to his ranch in Nevada. Advised by his father of the perils of desert travel, Ira sets out to get the Arabian back, and the desert soon gives him good reason to appreciate his father's admonitions. While trailing Hawkeye, he is shot in the back and would have died had it not been for Cricket and some of Black Rock Tom's men. They take him to their camp, where he is nursed to health by the shaman and Sage Flower. He stays there for some days, living as husband with Thoma, Cricket's beautiful sister, with whom Ira is in love. When he has recovered, he and Cricket steal back the pony from the ranch where Hawkeye is holed up, Cricket killing the rustler with bow and arrow while Ira grabs the horse. They return to Black Rock Tom's place, where for almost a month Ira undergoes the ritual of acceptance into the band in preparation for marrying Thoma, who is now pregnant. On their wedding day, Cricket rides to John D. Hamilton's ranch and escorts him to the ceremony. Aware of how Black Rock Tom has helped him by again saving Ira's life, John D. Hamilton rethinks his attitudes toward Indians and stretches out his hand to the man who is now his son's father-in-law. The plot moves fast with plenty of action and a strong sense of physical and ethical setting in good western novel style. Although simple in structure and flatly characterized, John D. Hamilton being the only dynamic figure, the novel is ironically highly affecting, partly because of the emotional substance and partly because of the economical style. Every word is put to good use. The dust devils are both literal and figurative—small desert dust storms and the long-held animosity of the whites for Indians that have blinded them to the Indians' virtues and very humanity. ALA/YA.

E

EARLEY, TONY (1961–)   Born in San Antonio, Texas; attended Warren Wilson College in North Carolina and the University of Alabama in Tuscaloosa. Mainly known for his short stories, he lives in Nashville, Tennessee, where he is an assistant professor at Vanderbilt University. A *Booklist* selection for young adults, *Jim the Boy** (Little, Brown, 2000) is an engaging family and boy's growing-up novel set in North Carolina during the Great Depression. He has also published the short story collections, *Here We Are in Paradise* (Little, Brown, 1994) and *Somehow Form a Family* (Algonquin, 2001), and has contributed short stories to such periodicals as *Harper's Magazine* and *Tri-Quarterly*.

ECHENKORLO (*I Rode a Horse of Milk White Jade**)   Maternal grandmother of Oyuna, a Mongolian girl of the early fourteenth century. A shamaness, Echenkorlo travels alone, turning up now and then near the *ail*, the camp of Oyuna's father and the related group of herdsmen and their families. When Oyuna, against her father's orders, visits the *ger* that has appeared set far apart from the other dwellings, the old woman and a mysterious companion named Udbal question her and listen to her story of the words she has heard from her mare, Bayan. Although her instructions are enigmatic and Oyuna understands little of what is told her about the use of herbs, the girl remembers the smoky ger smelling of incense and, unlike the spare huts of her people, cluttered with many items—animal skins, roots, furry bags, and curiosities of all sorts. She knows that Enchenkorlo has traveled widely and has strange powers, feared by the people of the ail. The next morning the ger is gone, but on her journey to the great Khan Oyuna comes upon her grandmother's body in a cave in the mountains, surrounded by bags of roots and herbs, with drawings in the mud of the cave floor. She buries all the bags with the body of her grandmother at the back of the cave, but later, when illness strikes the horse herd of the Khan, she remembers and interprets the drawings and retrieves the herbs to cure the horses. In the frame story, when Oyuna waits with her granddaughter for the birth of a filly and tells the story of her own white horse, Bayan, Oyuna herself seems to have become a shamaness.

EDMUND (*Breaking Rank**)   Along with Lenny (Leonard) Fairbairn and Shelly, a founder of the Clan*. Like the other two, he has been successful in his vocation. He sees that the other Clan members are trying to force Thomas Fairbairn (called "Baby") to drop his ambition of getting a high school diploma and going to college and are also challenging him to prove his loyalty by having sex with Casey Willardson. Unlike Lenny, Edmund tells them forcefully to leave Thomas alone. Then he walks out, leaving the Clan membership. Later, however, Casey and Thomas see him at one of his shops, wearing regular, not Clan, clothing, but with a Clan bracelet about his wrist.

ELECTION (Perrotta*, Tom, Putnam, 1998)   Realistic novel of an election for high school student president for the 1992–1993 school year at Winwood (New Jersey) High that changes half a dozen lives and comes near to ruining a couple of them. The novel is narrated in the first person, shifting in each chapter among five characters: Mr. M. (Jim McAllister), history teacher; Paul Warren, 16, football player who ranks surprisingly high on his PSATs and begins to think about college; Tracy Flick, 15, ambitious sexpot who has been having an affair with her English teacher, Jack Dexter; Tammy Warren, Paul's younger sister, who has lesbian interests; Lisa Flanagan, Tammy's best friend who becomes Paul's girlfriend; and, briefly, Joe Delvecchio, janitor at Winwood High and landlord of Tracy and her mother. When Mr. M., a dedicated teacher

and adviser to the student government, spots Paul as the most original thinker in his classes, he suggests that the boy run for school president, mostly because it will look good on his résumé for college admission. Paul's opposition will be Tracy, who is prominent but not well liked. To everyone's surprise, Paul's sister, Tammy, a sophomore, also files a petition to be a candidate, evidently to get back at her brother and Lisa. Through Tracy's mother, Jack Dexter's affair is exposed, and his pregnant wife divorces him. Mr. M., whose wife has been trying, in vain, to get pregnant, comforts Sherry Dexter and plays with the baby, eventually succumbing to their mutual desire and having sex with her. Sherry, who is the best friend of Diane McAllister, confesses to her and they mutually exclude Mr. M. from their beds. At school, Lisa takes over Paul's campaign, about which he has been ambivalent, and plasters the halls with her well-drawn pictures of him. Tracy gets Joe to let her into the school building at night and starts taping her professionally printed posters to every locker, tearing down and ripping up the ones for Paul. The next day, confronted by the principal, she denies it, and Tammy, whom no one has really suspected, confesses to it so she will be suspended. She has met and developed a crush on an older girl from Immaculate Mary Catholic School and hopes to transfer there. The day of the election, Paul cannot bear to vote for himself so he writes in "None of the Above." Counting votes the next day, Mr. M., who cannot bear to have Tracy win, slips aside two ballots for her, which brings the count to a win for Paul by one vote. Tracy, who cannot bear to admit that she could lose, stands up from her seat on the stage as they announce the winner and is ridiculed and humiliated when it is Paul.

The student who had already counted the votes and come out with a one-vote lead for Tracy is suspicious. A series of coincidences keeps Mr. M. from destroying the stolen ballots, which are found in the wastebasket by Joe. Confronted by the principal, Mr. M. resigns, and Tracy is named president, the whole scandal made much of by the local newspaper. She feels victorious and vindicated until Paul admits to her that he did not vote for himself, and she realizes that it was actually a tie. Diane and Mr. M. make up when she discovers she is pregnant, but he is panicky at having no income. One of his former students whom he hardly remembers offers him a job at his Chevrolet dealership. Tammy goes to the Catholic school but is mostly disappointed. Paul and Lisa, no longer going together, are both accepted at colleges, not the most elite but adequate. At the end of the next school year, Tracy realizes as they sign each other's yearbooks, that no one is really close to her or likes her much. She dresses in her sexiest outfit and goes to the Chevrolet dealership, planning to humiliate Mr. M., but ends up asking him to sign her yearbook. The five different voices in the novel are well differentiated and develop the characters well, with considerable wry humor, some of it based on the specific situation and some on the general high school culture. The pervading tone is irony, since the position of school president is without duties or power, essentially meaningless. Alex; Booklist.

ELIZABETH I (*The Secret Diary of Anne Boleyn**)   Queen of England, daughter of Anne* Boleyn and Henry* VIII. Elizabeth is presented as proud, duplicitous, shrewd, and determined not to share her royal power with anyone. She is conciliatory about religious matters, since her older sister, Queen Mary, and her older brother, King Edward, had been zealous about promoting the Roman Catholic Church and Protestantism, respectively, and caused much grief to their people over religion. After reading her mother's diaries, Elizabeth decides never to marry, not even her beloved Robert Dudley, since the times dictate that a woman be subservient to her husband and Anne was a tool of the men in her life, her husband, Henry, and her father, Thomas Boleyn. Although Dudley serves her loyally, Elizabeth tears up the document that would make him an earl. Elizabeth is much loved as the people's princess and queen.

ELLA ENCHANTED (Levine*, Gail Carson, HarperCollins, 1997)   Fantasy retelling the *Cinderella* story in an imaginative fictionalized version. At her birth, a foolish fairy gave Ella the gift of always being obedient, a grant that causes the independent girl great difficulty, but after many complications she frees herself from the spell and wins her prince. For a longer entry, see *Dictionary, 1995–1999.* ALA/YA.

ELLIE EISEN (*If You Come Softly**) Elisha Eisen, 15, third daughter and much the youngest child of an affluent, very busy New York City physician. Ellie has little contact with her older brothers and sisters, except for Anne, who is ten years her senior, is a lesbian, and plans a commitment ceremony with her companion. This lesbian aspect seems extraneous to Ellie's story except that it points out how going against society's norms may cause trouble. Ellie resents her mother's having two times walked out on the family. She thinks African American Miah* Roselind is beautiful with his rich, long locks and light-colored eyes, his easy, sincere attitude, and his competent, confident ways. After his death, her mother unexpectedly urges Ellie to "remember what . . . [she] can," undoubtedly because she herself is trying to hang on to those days when she and Ellie's father were first in love and before he became too engrossed in his medical studies and work to have time for her.

ELSKE (Voigt*, Cynthia, Atheneum, 1999)   Broad-canvas historical-adventure and romance novel set in an unnamed preindustrial northern area, similar to medieval northern Europe or northern England, while gunpowder, still considered magical, is just coming into use. Destined from birth to be the Death Maiden and hence to follow the king into the land of the dead, Elske, about thirteen, escapes rape and death at the hands of the terrible bloodthirsty Volkaric, or Wolfers, with the help of her grandmother. While fleeing on foot eastward, she falls in with three merchants, Tavyan and his two sons, Taddus and Nido, on their way home to the flourishing port city of Trastad from a successful trading trip. She works as a servant for Tavyan's household and then as personal servant for wealthy Var Kenric's daughter, Idelle, to whom Taddus is betrothed; she is well treated in both houses. She bravely beats off several rowdy, drunken youths who are bent on raping Idelle. They are Adeliers, young foreign men who have come to Trastad seeking wives at the biennial Courting Winter. For her safety, Elske is taken into the house of Var Jerrol, a leader in the ruling Council, who is impressed by her fortitude and ability to read, write, and speak both Norther, the Wolfer tongue, and Souther, the language of her grandmother. She is sent to the great house of Var Vladislav, with whom Beriel, the Fiendly Princess

(called so because of her willful, often disobedient behavior) will be living during the Courting Winter. Elske and Beriel soon bond, and Elske is instrumental in helping Beriel give birth secretly to a baby, the result of rape, and then takes the baby to Idelle, now married to Taddus and barren. She also helps Beriel escape from the city to return to her country, the Kingdom, and regain her rightful throne as queen, which has been usurped by her brother, Guerric. The rest of the novel, about one-third of it, tells of their return by ship and slow walk overland, their encounter with Beriel's supporters, and her reclaiming the throne. They are joined by Win, the red-haired third son of an innkeeper. At the hall of Beriel's uncle, the earl of Sutherland, Lord Dugald, heir of the earl of Northgate, reports that Wolfers have been ravaging the northern part of the Kingdom. Troops are mustered to fight Guerric, forces Beriel leads, and Dugald and Elske move against the Wolfers. Dugald's troops surround the Wolfers, and Elske and Dugald approach by small boat. Elske stands naked in the bow, pretending to be the Death Maiden, and the Wolfers flee in panic. Beriel's troops triumph against Guerric, Win slays the man lest he harm Beriel, and Beriel is accordingly crowned queen. Dugald and Elske wed, and Win becomes Beriel's king. An epilogue summarizes annals of the Kingdom that indicate that Beriel and her descendants build a mighty realm. The first half of the novel contrasts the ways of the Wolfers and Trastaders, with particular emphasis on their treatment of women, while the last half has more excitement and intrigue. The cast is large, but Beriel and Elske, much the same in their strengths, are pivotal in influencing their own and the larger situations. Scenes in less wealthy houses, like that of

Tavyan, contrast with those in the nobles' villas, and meetings among civil and war leaders (at one of which Elske contributes her ideas about how to resist the Wolfers), courting socials, and interaction on shipboard and land paths give a good sense of the culture and the terrain. The two women and the grandmother, who appears only briefly but memorably, are the strongest figures. Style, especially the dialogue, is formal, giving the sense of oldtime speech. The novel is one in the author's Kingdom series, which began with *Jackaroo*. ALA/YA.

ENDER'S SHADOW (Card*, Orson Scott, Tor, 1999)   Futuristic fantasy published for adults, described as a parallel novel to *Ender's Game* (1985), relating the same events but from a different point of view. Starting in the worst slums of Rotterdam in the far future, *Ender's Shadow* centers on Bean, four years old at the opening, an urchin so brilliant that he has survived on the street for three years, taught himself to read and understand several languages, and figured out how to insert himself into the begging "crew" of Poke, 9, then teach her to employ one of the bullies to protect them. Unfortunately, she chooses Achilles*, a sociopath, and spares him when she is urged by Bean to kill him. His pride injured, Achilles never forgives either of them and eventually kills Poke. Bean is taken in by Sister Carlotta, a nun devoting her life to discovering children intelligent enough to be sent to the Battle School of the International Fleet, where they will be trained to lead space armies against the Formics or "Buggers," highly developed insectlike creatures from other galaxies determined to wipe out our world. At five, Bean is sent to the Battle School, an orbiting space station, the youngest of a group of new recruits. In the meantime, Sister Carlotta traces his origin to an illegal gene-altering experiment that produced twenty-four babies, twenty-three of whom were murdered when the experiment was about to be discovered. Bean is the only survivor, having escaped at the age of one and hidden in a toilet tank until a janitor found him. The nun discovers that he is really the child of Julian Delphiki and his wife, whose fertilized eggs, stored frozen, were stolen by his half brother, who is now imprisoned as an international criminal. The major part of the novel is about the Battle School, where Bean is the youngest and brightest. The star of the school is Ender* Wiggin, a boy almost worshipped by most of the others. Always distrustful of authority, Bean employs his unusual skills to discover a great deal about the school and the systematic deception of the teachers, especially when the pace of training suddenly speeds up. Bean realizes that war with the Buggers is imminent. When, against the advice of Sister Carlotta, Achilles is found and brought to the Battle School, he is intent on murder. Bean realizes this and defeats him through cleverness and the help of the only friend he has made, Nikolai Delphiki, a boy about two years older than he is, very smart but not in Bean's class. In the final series of supposedly simulated battles, only Bean and Ender realize that the war is real and that it is the last chance to exterminate the Buggers or let the world be wiped out. Their triumph is thrilling, fast paced, and uncertain until the last few seconds. The logic of using children as the warriors is based on the great distance in space, so that adults would be too old at the crucial time, but that logic may not hold up in the various twists of fact and deception. A more subtle development is the gradual awakening of emotion in Bean, whose struggle for survival in Rotterdam leaves no room for affection or gentleness. In the end, he goes with Nikolai, his true brother, to the parents he has never known and is able to return their welcoming love. Alex; ALA/YA; Booklist.

ENDER WIGGIN (*Ender's Shadow**) Top boy in the Battle School of the International Fleet, an acknowledged leader almost worshipped by many of the others. He is brilliant in the tactics of his group in simulated space maneuvers, but even smarter in the way he trains his men to think for themselves and act independently from him, a trust none of the other leaders dares have. When he is challenged by a jealous rival, he fights back so hard that the other boy dies, a situation that the teaching hierarchy at the school could have prevented but did not. As a result, Ender is deeply troubled and almost unable to carry out his leadership duties in the final battle, which only he and Bean, among the boys, realize is not simulated, as all their practices have been, but actual. Although he performs brilliantly and is successful, he is so traumatized that he may not recover psychologically. Bean is the only boy brilliant enough to be a real threat to Ender, but he deliberately refrains from challenging the older boy and assumes the position of adviser, giving support that is essential at the critical moment. Ender is the main character in the 1985 novel, *Ender's Game*.

ESLE HOSTETLER (*No Strange Fire**) Twin brother of Jacob Hostetler. Jacob is thought to have set the fires that consume six barns among the White Top Amish in Big Valley, Pennsylvania, and cause the death of little Eli Yoder, 10. The opposite of his brother in his attitude toward the Amish, Esle enjoys the satisfaction of the demanding farm work and of working along with nature to produce good harvests, appreciates the closeness of his family and the community, and looks forward to being baptized and becoming a full member of the community. At first Esle resents their mother's having given Jacob all the money she had saved, since he had wanted some to buy a new gun, but later on he simply wishes he had tried harder to understand Jacob and keep him at home.

ESPERANZA RISING (Ryan*, Pam Muñoz, Scholastic, 2000) Biographical fiction of the author's Mexican grandmother's childhood experiences when her family and close friends emigrated to the United States in 1930 from Aguascalientes, Mexico. Esperanza Ortega, 12, loves her life of wealth and privilege and her landholding family—Papa, who grows grapes; beautiful, kind Mama; and wise Abuelita (Grandmother). She loves their El Rancho de las Rosas and their loyal servants Hortensia, Alfonso, and their capable son, Miguel, 17. This easy life comes to an abrupt end when on the eve of Esperanza's thirteenth birthday Papa is murdered by bandits. The family flees for the United States in the middle of the night, leaving frail Abuelita at a nearby convent and taking only a few necessary and precious possessions. A loyal neighbor smuggles them in his wagonload of guavas to Zacatecas, where they board the train for Los Angeles. Esperanza hates riding in the peasants' car, sitting on the wooden benches next to dirty poor people, many of them children. She expresses her scorn openly, provoking reprimands from Mama. In Los Angeles, they join relatives of Alfonso and then travel in a rickety truck over the mountains into the San

Joaquin Valley to the farm-labor work camps there. To Esperanza's great disappointment, they are assigned a tiny two-room wooden cabin containing only a couple of mattresses and a few pieces of rude furniture made of boxes. Two girls will have a great impact on Esperanza's life. Marta, about Miguel's age, angrily speaks against the rude living conditions, poor pay, and exploitive owners and becomes a leader in the strike that later breaks out. Isabel, 8, Alfonso's niece, teaches Esperanza how to care for the house, cook while the women sort and pack the seasonal fruits in sheds and the men work in the fields, and look after Isabel's twin baby brother and sister when Isabel starts school. The work is hard, and Esperanza makes many mistakes, but she is willing. Her attitude gradually improves, and she wins friends. She even gains the respect of Marta, who had openly derided her as one of those rich, avaricious landowners against whom the Mexican revolutionaries fought. Strike talk increases, but a severe dust storm temporarily puts an end to the action. Mama falls ill of Valley Fever and must be hospitalized for five months. Esperanza works in the fields and sheds to pay the doctor and bring Abuelita, for whom Mama longs, to California. Miguel has a job in the railroad machine shop, but when the strike breaks out, he loses it and leaves for northern California. Police and immigration officials round up strikers, even American citizens, and ship them to Mexico. Times get hard because displaced workers from Oklahoma and elsewhere are willing to work for very little. Esperanza discovers that the money orders she had been saving to bring Abuelita to California are missing. Blame falls on Miguel, who had indeed taken them but only because he, too, wanted to bring Abuelita to

California. The family is reunited, and Esperanza begins to feel close to this land, too. Times and work are tough, and they are despised and exploited by the Americans, but they are all together again and have hope that the future will be better in this country of promise. As Abuelita had told them earlier, they will rise like the fabled phoenix. Indeed, Esperanza's name means hope. These and other symbols seem belabored, Marta is too strident, and Isabel too good, but Miguel serves as a worthy older-brother type, and the women are good models for Esperanza. The difficult, almost inhumane conditions in the camp are shown all too clearly, and the camp sweeps, the author points out in an endnote, actually occurred, "a voluntary repatriation" that involved perhaps one million Hispanics and predated the now-infamous Japanese relocations of World War II. Although most of the incidents are fiction, the book has the impact of reality. ALA/YA.

ETHAN GLASS (*The Door in the Lake**) College student in physics who together with Ariel* DeWitt helps Joey (Joseph Patrick) Finney discover what happened to him while he and his family were camping in the Allegheny Mountains. Highly interested in the possibilities of UFOs and space aliens, Ethan is sure that Joey got caught up in some distortion of space time. In support of his theory, he has learned that there were numerous reports of UFO sightings at the time of Joey's disappearance and that Smokewater Lake, where Joey disappeared, was at the center of them all. He says the reason that Joey still looks to be twelve is that he really is. He helps Joey partly because he wants to be of service to the boy and partly to learn more about strange sightings he himself experienced when he was ten. Of the two students, his is the livelier personality.

EVA GALT (*I Want to Buy a Vowel**) Eleven-year-old who, with her little sister Ava, discovers Alfredo* Santayana in the abandoned witch's house, which she, not wanting to be sexist,, calls the warlock's house. Eva is a thoughtful, practical child. She is skeptical that the blot on the stamp machine glass is an image of the Virgin Mary, and she debunks Kenlow Schindler's claim to be a Satanist, saying a real Satanist would not use Vienna sausages, and besides, she does not believe in Satan. Kenlow does scare her, however, with his threats and his anonymous letters, so, although she has identified him, she does not tell any grown-up. When they are running from the fire, she momentarily considers just leaving Kenlow to burn, but decides she and Ava must drag him, if possible, to safety. As daughter of an Episcopal priest, she prays, but not to God, since she cannot imagine his face, but to Ted Williams, whose feat of hitting .406, she has heard her father say, is about equal to Jesus walking on water. Miserably conscious of her parents' incompatibility and afraid they may divorce, she prays mostly that her parents will like each other again. Although her mother and father join forces in an effort to get a job for Alfredo, there is no assurance, at the book's end, that this will have a lasting effect on their marriage.

EVAN ADAMS (*My Father's Scar**) Older boy, senior when Andy Logan is a high school freshman, with whom he is made cochairman of the parish Easter pageant. A very good-looking boy with long blond hair, Evan is swooned over by all the girls and younger boys and clucked over by the parish women. He is clever, funny, and brave enough to challenge Pastor Peterson's interpretation of the sin of lust. When Andy cannot control the children recruited for the performance, Evan steps in and entertains them in the church with gymnastic stunts until the pastor arrives and condemns it as blasphemous. For the pageant, he takes on the job of making new wings for the angel costumes and jokingly refers to himself as "Guardian Angel Man." After he has publicly announced in church that he is gay and then been deliberately cheated of his score in the gymnastics meet, his fellow team members steal his clothes while he is in the shower. Andy finds him some sweats, but is afraid to go to his rescue when his younger brother and a gang of kids are beating him and threatening to castrate him with scissors, an idea suggested by the pastor. Filled with self-loathing at his cowardice, Andy stays away from the hospital until Patti Sheldon tells him that Evan has wondered why he did not come. In the hospital, Andy confesses his love for Evan, who is understanding but refuses to consider taking the younger boy away with him. When Evan leaves town, he gives Patti a package for Andy, a pair of wings and a note saying, "I love you," and signed GUARDIAN ANGEL MAN.

EWAN MUNRO (*Criminals**)   Investment banker, younger brother of Mollie* Munro Lafferty, a careful, controlled man whose tendency to stutter has made him limit conversation to terse statements and given him a reputation for being a dour, though very reliable, Scot. Ewan's stutter is responsible for several of the mistakes surrounding the baby he finds in the bus depot men's room. He is unable to explain quickly to the person at the bus counter what he has found, and as he gets on the bus he is unable to beg the driver to wait a minute, while he disposes of the baby to someone responsible. Again, when he tries to call the Perth police from Mill of Fortune, he stutters so badly that they think it is a crank call and hang up. In business meetings, he is confident and does not stutter, but the impediment has kept him from close relationships with women, so he misinterprets the friendship Vanessa* offers and indiscreetly discusses a pending merger. Throughout the novel he reads *The Dark Forest*, the latest novel by Chae* Lafferty, and only gradually begins to see why his sister is so outraged. Because she is good at covering up her mental problems, hoping to keep Olivia for herself, he does not fully realize how ill she is. In the end, he confesses his merger mention to Vanessa and his abduction of the baby from the bus depot to the proper authorities and is let off on both counts.

THE EXCHANGE STUDENT (Gilmore*, Kate, Houghton Mifflin, 1999)   Futuristic fantasy involving programs in 2094 to save endangered species on Earth and the great desire of exchange students from Chela to restore animal life on their home planet. Despite her youth, Daria Wells, 16, is licensed as a private breeder and has been raising binturongs, fennec foxes, dwarf mongooses, and a wide variety of other animals and birds in an enclosure on her wealthy family's spacious grounds in Westchester, Connecticut. While her father, Roger, supports her activity, neither of her older twin siblings, beautiful, fashion-conscious Lily nor easygoing Tim, who is immersed entirely in music of the late twentieth century, have any interest in her zoo or rare creatures. Her intense but organized life is disrupted when her rather ditzy mother,

Gloria, invites one of a group of teenage exchange students from the distant planet Chela to be their guest for a year. Both sides suffer some culture shock. Fen, their exchangee, like other Chelans is more than seven feet tall, very thin, silvery gray all over but subject to a wide variety of color changes according to emotion, and almost totally unclothed, although his mentor has insisted on a sort of bath wrap around his loins. He is also imperious, intensely curious, in need of frequent meals and naps, and, fortunately for Daria, obsessed with animals. Although he will not admit it and the subject, verboten among Chelans, fills him with shame, there are no animals on his home planet except for insects and a few rodents, larger species having been killed off generations earlier. Since he has no concept of personal property or the need for door locks, within a few days he steals one of the four kits born to Daria's fennec fox and a suede purse belonging to Lily as a pouch for it. Both girls are outraged, Daria mostly because she fears he will kill the kit by feeding and tending it wrongly. Before she can retrieve it and return it to its mother, Roger persuades her to give Fen the right formula and let him try to hand-rear it. Daria takes Fen, along with the kit now named Scrabble, to the Hudson Valley Ark, a breeding facility for endangered species, and introduces him to the director, her mentor, Giovanna Ferrante, an older woman as intensely curious as he is, who gives him a tour of the place, including the banks of animal genetic material stored there. Because formal schooling is repugnant to Fen, Giovanna offers him a job at the Ark, to his delight. Secretly, the members of the exchange group, though scattered around the world, have kept in touch with each other using handheld communicators with collapsible visual screens. His betrothed future mate, Filya, the acknowledged leader of the group, wants to take a sampling of earthly animals back to Chela with them. Calling from Rome, she proposes that Fen steal enough genetic material to start animal life again on Chela. Fen, the most intelligent of the group, realizes that even if they can master the technology to develop live animals from the DNA, the whole environmental chain must be right for them to survive and thrive. He stalls, but when word comes that the students are to be recalled early to Chela, he attempts the theft and is discovered by Giovanna. Once she understands his reasons, she goes into action, contacts their Chelan mentor, U-Bandor, and they arrange to keep the exchange students on Earth, build a Chelan biosphere, and test what animals might survive on their home planet, all this to be financed by Chela, where the desire for animals is so great that no cost will be too much. The events of the novel are interesting in themselves, but its charm is in the feeling for the animals on the parts of Daria and Giovanna, and the overwhelming devotion Fen has to them. This characteristic makes Fen a lovable figure, even when he is being demanding and manipulative. The prospect of a world without animals is chilling and not beyond imagination. ALA/YA.

EXEGESIS (Teller*, Astro, Vintage, 1997) Clever, amusing, and ultimately touching novel told almost entirely in e-mail entries to and from an artificial intelligence created by a Stanford University graduate student in the year 2000. Just before Christmas, Alice Lu, working on a project started by her adviser, Professor Joseph Z. Liddle, suddenly has an idea for a couple of implementations to the basic information-organizing program that they call Edgar, and when she returns from vacation, Edgar is able to initiate and continue postings in an intelligent way. At first the messages are crude, consisting largely of dictionary definitions of words she has used in her e-mails to it, but they rapidly become more sophisticated and intelligible. Alice is reluctant to tell her adviser of the changes because she rightly thinks he will take credit for the developments and she wants to replicate the process so she can prove it is her own contribution. During the next few months, she struggles with the idea that Edgar is self-aware. To feed its insatiable desire for information, she gives it *Grolier's Encyclopedia*, which it reads in a short time and asks for more. She gives it a CD-ROM of the complete works of Shakespeare, which it does not like as well. To escape from Alice's control, Edgar moves itself to Carnegie-Mellon University and learns to seek its own reading material. Alice is unable to start a backup she made of Edgar before its move, and she is unable to make another self-aware program, though she continues to try. In March, Edgar informs Alice that it has moved again, because the FBI has begun to investigate it, presumably because it was reading their files. From that time on, Edgar's "life" becomes a battle with teams of National Security Agency (NSA) agents trying to determine how it works and to persuade it to become part of the NSA system. Since it is basically amoral, Edgar has no desire to be on the NSA side in international intelligence gathering, and refuses to become a tool of the government. In round-the-clock inquisitions, NSA tries to force Edgar to cooperate. Only one agent, Major Thomas D. Savit, seems to realize what Edgar really is and to respect its right to freedom. Alice, in the meantime, is dropping out of school, distraught, unable to re-create

Edgar or to rescue it from the NSA. Her only recourse is a threat to go public, one that the NSA investigators fear enough to leave her at large. Her relationship with Edgar has gradually changed so she thinks of it as her son or perhaps even lover, whom she has to protect from domination by unfeeling powers of government. In the end, Edgar seems to have become not only self-aware but capable of emotion. His last message, just before his suicide by wiping himself out electronically, says only "Goodbye, Alice," but the subject line is "my dear." The novel ends with a dense NSA document, detailing their experience with Edgar and the various plans submitted to deal with it, including murdering Alice, an idea rejected because they are unable to determine whether this will destroy Edgar and fear she may have left information that would point to their complicity in her death. The novel starts with a disclaimer by Alice, saying that it is being published as fiction, because no publisher would believe the truth, and a letter from Tom Savit, saying that he is sending her the entire NSA file, including all her e-mail to, from, and about Edgar, in an effort to make up for his part in what he sees as a major crime against the humanity of Edgar. In the correspondence, various other elements emerge about Alice: her father is a dominating, disapproving academic, demand-

ing her success as a Ph.D.; her mother is interested only in her getting married and providing grandchildren; and she had a boyfriend named Charlie, whom she rejected because of his infidelity. The novel, though quirky, is a moving plea for respecting freedom and independence. Booklist.

EYRIE (*Archangel**)   The mountain hold in Bethel, containing about fifty angels and one hundred others: mortal wives, servants, and workers. It is accessible only by air, since the angels fly to it easily and can carry anyone who wishes to ascend or descend. Although it is stark, it is beautiful and has vast wealth. Gabriel* has been head for five years since his father's death. Life there is considered so desirable that many mortals are known as "angel-seekers," desiring to have a child by an angel and thereby gain a permanent place in the hold, since angels mating with angels often produce deformed offspring and are therefore forbidden to marry. These alliances with angel-seekers are not always successful, since the birth of an angel is rare and the mortal children are often abandoned. There are two other angel holds in Samaria, Monteverde in Gaza and Windy Point in Jordana. The main job of the angels in these holds is to intercede with Jovah for the good of the people.

F

THE FALCON (Koller*, Jackie French, Atheneum, 1998)   Boy's growing-up novel in journal entries set in a New England town in the late 1990s. By his own admission, Luke Carver, 17, is a screwup, always getting into trouble despite his good intentions and his parents' constant warnings. In fact, it is the overprotectiveness of both his mother and his father that seems to drive him toward danger. He can work off some of his frustration in wrestling, where he is the heavyweight star of the high school, but he still drives too fast, joins his friends in drinking, and generally disregards the caution suggested by adults, especially when they refer to his "condition," a reference he greatly resents. He is extremely fond of his girlfriend, Megan, so much so that he breaks up with her for fear of getting too involved, and then is hurt and furious when she takes up with Tony Lieberman, whom she has long known as a friend. In his journal entries, which get longer and more detailed as he progresses from January to March, he avoids mentioning what might handicap him, and even crosses out any sentence that seems to be leading in that direction. After a number of near disasters, all brought on by his recklessness, he begins to doubt his own ability to escape trouble. Lonely and distraught, he takes his dog for a walk, finds himself across the stream from Megan's house, and sees her grooming her horse in the yard. Before he can retreat, Tony comes up on his horse, and it is clear that they are about to ride toward him. Luke shinnies up a tree and hides until they have gone by, but they recognize his dog and wonder whether he might be near by. To avoid them, he climbs up a sheer rock face, not considering that his shoes are the wrong kind and that his hands are getting numb in the cold. As he nears the top, half frozen, a large chunk breaks off above him and crashes into his face. He wakes in the hospital with bandages over his right eye, having been rescued by Megan and Tony, and admits to the journal for the first time that he lost sight in his left eye four years before. After an operation and brief recovery period, he is moved to a psychiatric area, still with bandages over his eye, and discovers his roommate is Lenny Bertoli, a member of last year's wrestling team who has been at the university and, Luke has already heard, has attempted suicide. Luke spars with the psychologist, Jim Spellman, and avoids telling him the truth about his earlier eye injury until after Lenny, panicky about returning home, admits that he is gay. At first Luke is shocked and revolted, but eventually gets up the nerve to apologize and suggest that they can still be friends. They have a lot in common, both suffering from the high expectations of their parents and both unable to face the truth of what is bothering them. The next day Luke tells the psychologist the real story of his first eye injury, how he had been egged on by older boys at the beach to pick a fight with a kid and received a blow directly to his eye, which he hid for several days until it was too late to repair surgically. Although he endured several operations, none successful, he has never admitted that the injury was not caused by a chance elbow to the eye in wrestling, as he has said, but through his own fault. After he is out of the hospital, he realizes that he will never be free of the guilt that drives him to do rash and foolish things until he tells his parents the real story. He visits Lenny, who is having an equal problem admitting to his parents that he is gay, and they make a pact to both own up at three o'clock the next day, then get together to "pick up the pieces." On the way home, Luke stops to see Megan and makes peace with her. The novel is different from many others because Luke has supportive parents and even two siblings, an older sister and a younger brother, whom he likes and enjoys. He also is good at sports, despite his blind eye, and does well in school. It is essentially a psychological study of how one's own conscience

can become a demon when one is hiding a truth and how the only way to free oneself is to confess. The title comes from a poem Luke wrote about a falcon unable to soar because his leg is chained. ALA/YA.

FAREWELL, I'M BOUND TO LEAVE YOU (Chappell*, Fred, Picador, 1996) Episodic novel originally published for adult readers giving a picture of a largely rural, mountainous North Carolina community in the early part of the twentieth century, as seen through the stories told by his mother and grandmother to Jess Kirkman, 15. In the frame narrative, Jess and his father, Joe Robert, wait in the living room while Jess's mother, Cora Sorrells Kirkman, attends her dying mother, Annie Barbara Sorells, in the bedroom. The main body of the book is a series of memories, character sketches, gossip, and insights told mostly by Jess's grandmother—some funny, some tragic, a few fanciful, some love stories, one a chilling ghost story—mostly about the women of Herwood County. One is about the strange friendship of a woman who never speaks and the loudest, most flamboyant doxy in the town. Another is of a friendship enjoyed by a young tomboy and an old man who teaches her to fish until he breaks his foot in a remote place and, to save him, she takes his truck, although she has never driven before, to get help. The love stories are not all happy. Aunt Chancy, who is married to mean Dave Gudger, falls in love with Frawley Harper, some fifteen years her junior. After their one afternoon with each other, Uncle Dave, who knows what has happened, sets out to hunt down Frawley, and both men disappear. Aunt Chancy loses her mind, but Aunt Samantha, who goes to take care of her in the mountain cabin, thinks she sees a man's body in the outhouse hole. As a girl, feisty Ginger Sumerell learned to protect herself in backward Marsden County, where men get wives by ambushing girls, "bigging" them, and getting them pregnant, but she has become so independent that the men in Herwood County give her a wide berth. When she decides she wants a husband, she proves to Orlow Jackson that she can outdo him with shotgun, rifle, pistols, and bowie knife, and he not only refuses to retaliate, he even hits himself on the head with a hammer to prove his devotion. There are various characters: Angela Newcome, so "beautiful and overflowing with Christian charity" that no one can stand her; Aunt Sherlie Howes, who has such a sharp, logical mind that men and women alike consult her; Aunt Samantha, a famous mountain fiddler, who has an upstanding name despite her free-talking nature and colorful speech. Many of the scenes are memorable: laying the ghost of Little Mary Lucas by decorating her grave with apple blossoms and singing hymns; Jess and his grandmother stringing beans on the porch steps or checking the jars of her canned food in the storeroom; a square dance at the remote Lafferty place, where Quigley fiddles and his wife Quattley and their ten or twelve children (no one seems sure how many), whom they call the "whippets," lead neighbors from far and near in an all-night dance attended by the folklorist, Dr. Holme Barcroft. In language musical with mountain color, the stories give a vivid picture of life long past and at the same time show a boy growing up in understanding of life and his desire to pass on the tales. Booklist.

FARMER, NANCY (1941–) Born in Phoenix, Arizona; scientist, novelist. Her survival novel set in Mozambique and Zimbabwe, *A Girl Named Disaster** (Orchard, 1996), a Newbery Honor book, won several other prestigious awards and was more recently named to the American Library Association Young Adult list. For earlier biographical information and title entries, see *Dictionary, 1995–1999* [*The Ear, the Eye, and the Arm*; *A Girl Named Disaster*].

FAR NORTH (Hobbs*, Will, Morrow, 1996) Realistic survival and adventure novel set from October to April in the Canadian Northwest Territories in recent years. Half-orphaned white Texan Gabe Rogers, 15, the narrator, attends a boarding school to be near his father, an oil-man. His roommate is Raymond Providence, a tall, handsome Slavey Indian. On a sightseeing trip with Raymond's uncle, their young bush pilot recklessly deviates from the flight plan. Their plane lands on Nahanni River, the engine stops, and the radio fails. The boys and the uncle reach shore, but plane and pilot are swept downriver, leaving the three to survive the winter with the uncle's woods savvy. Based on the writer's own experiences in the wilds and written records, the story is filled with excitement and excels in details of terrain and survival. Previously, the novel received a Spur Award. A longer entry appears in *Dictionary, 1995–1999*. ALA/YA.

FATHER HEANEY (*Snow in August**) Priest at Sacred Heart Church in Brooklyn, New York, which Michael Devlin, the protagonist, attends. A veteran of World War II, Father Heaney is a silent man, cold and distant, intent on doing his duty but little beyond that. The altar boys regard him as a war hero, although they know little about his war record. He smokes a lot and is reputed to drink.

When Michael tells him that Rabbi* Judah Hirsch's synagogue has been defaced with swastikas, Father Heaney promptly organizes the men of the church and neighborhood to clean the synagogue. Michael is grateful when Father Heaney visits him in the hospital, especially since none of his friends does. At book's end, Father Heaney has left Brooklyn, transferred to a parish in South America, further proof that, like the synagogue, the Brooklyn parish is dying.

FELDMAN, ELLEN (BETTE) (1941–) Born in Elizabeth, New Jersey; writer, editor. She received her B.A. from Bryn Mawr College in 1964 and her M.A. in 1967, worked as a copywriter in advertising, as publicity director for Putman's Publishing, and has been a freelance writer and editor since 1977. *God Bless the Child** (Simon & Schuster, 1997) is a mystery set at the eastern tip of Long Island, New York, with a protagonist who works in a bookstore discovering the young man whom she gave up for adoption as a baby, only to find he is a murder suspect. For seven of her novels she used the pseudonym Elizabeth Villars.

FELDMAN, JONATHAN (*The Last Day**) Journalist and anchor for World News Network television, who, with his partner, Breck Hunter, photojournalist, becomes deeply involved in covering the events surrounding the extraordinary young woman, Jeza*, who says she is the Daughter of God. Although a respected and trusted journalist, Feldman is a conflicted personality, both in his reactions toward Jeza, whom he finally not only accepts but supports, but also in his personal life. He is greatly attracted to Anke Heuriskein, a graduate student in international law at Tel Aviv University, whom at the end he expects to marry. Feldman wins a Pulitzer Prize for covering the millennium events and the Jeza story. A vulnerable personality, he is a foil for brash, confident Breck Hunter.

FERRIS, JEAN (1939–) Clinical audiologist and novelist for twenty years of books mainly for teenagers on sociological and psychological concerns. Several of her books have been cited by, among others, *Booklist*, *School Library Journal*, and the International Reading Association. She lives in San Diego, California. Her most honored book is *Invincible Summer* (Farrar, 1987), about teenagers coping with leukemia. More recent is *Love Among the Walnuts** (Harcourt, 1998), a funny story about grasping relatives in the fashion of Victorian melodrama, which was selected by the American Library Association for young adults. *Bad** (Farrar, 1998), set in a rehabilitation center for girls, was also an American Library Association choice for young adults. Other recent books are *Of Sound Mind* (Farrar, 2001) and *Eight Seconds* (Harcourt, 2000). For more information about Ferris, additional titles, and a title entry, see *Dictionary, 1985–1989* [*Invincible Summer*].

FEVER 1793 (Anderson*, Laurie Halse, Simon & Schuster, 2000) Historical novel of survival in the terrible yellow fever epidemic in Philadelphia in the summer of 1793, which killed five thousand people, 10 percent of the population. The narrator, Mattie (Matilda) Cook, 13, helps her widowed mother and her grandfather, Captain William Farnsworth Cook, a Revolutionary War veteran, run a coffeehouse, an establishment that thrives largely because of the skill of their African American cook, Eliza, a free black. Mattie's mother, from a higher social status than her carpenter father was, is determined to marry her daughter to an upper-class man and refuses to let her see anything of Nathaniel Benson, an apprentice artist, whom Mattie really likes. Rumors of the illness near the docks circulate, but it is not until Mattie's mother sickens that they think it more than a seasonal phenomenon. Her mother and Eliza both insist that Mattie and her grandfather leave for the country, where the air is thought to be purer. As they arrive on the outskirts of a village, the farmer's wagon on which they are riding is stopped by armed men on horseback, who insist that they turn back because Grandfather is coughing and they are letting no one who seems ill pass through. The farmer, in a panic, pushes Grandfather and Mattie out and whips up his horse. When Grandfather collapses under a tree, Mattie takes his canteen and finds a clear stream among the trees. She is turned away from a farm where she tries to buy food and is unsuccessful in catching a fish in her petticoat, but she does find some berries and some pears. As she nears Grandfather again, she falls and passes out. She wakes to find herself at Bush Hill, a notorious establishment that has been transformed by Stephen Girard into a fever hospital, where she is cared for by Mrs. Bridget Flagg. Her grandfather, too, is in attendance, having brought her there, and is now enjoying a flirtation with practical Mrs. Flagg. When Mattie is well enough to travel, an officious young man tries to send her to the orphan house, but Grandfather intervenes, and they return to the coffeehouse, to find it has been broken into and vandalized. There is no sign of her mother. Mattie is relieved to find that the upstairs has not been touched and that thieves have not found the lockbox in its hiding place. Although all the food has been taken or destroyed, she finds enough withered vegetables in the garden to make a thin soup. The next night, as she sleeps downstairs with the shutters open to let in some air, a couple of thieves break in and beat her to get her to tell where valuables are hidden. Grandfather stomps down the stairs with his rifle, shoots and misses, then is attacked by one of the men. Mattie grabs his regimental sword and swings at the thief, slashing his shoulder and driving him away. The exertion, however, kills Grandfather, who has long suffered a weak heart. The next morning, Mattie adds his body to the cart that picks up the dead, insists on helping push it to the cemetery, and there says a prayer, before they fill in the mass grave. She discovers that the market is almost empty, since farmers have not dared to bring produce in, and she is driven away by several people who fear her because she has been ill, but she finds a small child, alone, her mother dead on the bed. Carrying the child, who says her name is Nell but will volunteer nothing else, Mattie wanders until she glimpses Eliza entering a house. Reunited, she learns that Eliza is with the Free African Society, making rounds of homes most grievously hit, nursing and bringing food. Eliza takes her to the house of her brother, Joseph, who is recovering though his wife died. Eliza has been caring for him and his two little sons, Robert and William. Mattie steels herself to take Nell to the orphan house, but finds they are too crowded to take in another, so she returns with the child to Eliza's and is soon recruited into helping the Free Africans. When the children, however, all become ill, she insists on taking them to the coffeehouse, where there is more room and it is cooler. There she works tirelessly to care for them until the first frost, which clears the air and drives the fever away. The farmers return to the market, and the children recover. One day she meets Nathaniel, who has weathered the plague shut in with the Peale family, where he is apprenticed. Although everyone urges Mattie to sell the coffeehouse, she decides to run it herself, offering half of it to Eliza for her help. After they are finally open for business again, Mattie's mother returns, frail and unable to walk unaided, visibly aged, having gone to the country to find Mattie and Grandfather and been extremely ill. She is too exhausted to object to Nathaniel's presence, and it is clear that the power of decision has shifted to Mattie, who is now in charge of the coffeehouse and her own future. At the end of the book is an appendix about the plague, medical practices of the time, the Peale family, the Free African Society, Stephen Girard, and other historical figures mentioned in the novel. Details of the hard work, the spread of the illness, and the grim burials, complete with the filth and the stench that spread through the city, give the novel substance, but Mattie's spunky character and the way she matures through the hardships are interesting in themselves. ALA/YA; NYPL.

FIREGOLD (Calhoun*, Dia, illus. Herve Blondon, Winslow, 1999)   Fantasy of the coming-of-age of a boy in an imaginary preindustrial country divided into two mutually suspicious parts, the Valley, where the people are mostly orchard workers, and the Red Mountains, where the horse-loving Dalriadans live seminomadic lives as hunters. Jonathan Brae, 12, lives at Greengard Orchards, one of the more successful in South Valley, but he has never really fit in because he has blue eyes, a feature feared and hated among his people. His father, Brian, who is obsessed with the idea of the firegold apple, a variety extolled in legend, has gone off to the Red Mountains to hunt for it. He brings back for Jonathan a beautiful colt, a blood bay with stripes of gold through its black mane and tail. When his mother, Karena, sees the horse she calls it Rhohar and says she must set it free or kill it. Jonathan knocks her bow arm as she aims at the colt, but the next day while she is preparing to take it back to the mountains, a group of Dalriadans swoops down on their swift horses, one shoots her, and they take off with Rhohar. Through the winter, Brian is mostly silent as if stunned. As spring approaches, Jonathan takes on the job of planting six hundred Ruby Spice seedlings, mostly to keep himself busy enough to stop his constant worry that he might be going insane, as the Valley people say all blue-eyed people do at puberty. One day Rosamund Landers, a classmate he greatly admires, asks to help him while her father talks to Brian. After she has proudly planted one tree, her father spies her, roughly orders her to the buggy, and warns Jonathan in no uncertain terms to leave his daughter alone. The next day Timothy Dakken girdles a whole row of the seedlings, as a warning to stay away from Rosamund, he says. Brian calls in a debt and gives the Dakken land to Jonathan, making Timothy son of a tenant, but soon they are all faced with a greater crisis, verblight through all the Valley orchards. Their superstitions increased by fear for their livelihood, a group of men arrive, demanding that Brian hand over Jonathan so they can kill him and purge the Valley of blight. Brian stands up to them, and Jonathan, with a bow given him by his mother, scares them off. The next evening, Brian takes Jonathan and Uncle Wilford, an old man who came with Karena from the North Valley when she married Brian, to Highgate Lakes, where they stay with Sephonie, Jonathan's maternal grandmother, a weaver. When Brian and Wilford leave, Jonathan opts to stay with Sephonie. She tells him something of his grandfather, Angarath, a Dalriadan, and of the ancient split that divided the people into two antagonistic groups. As spring comes, he feels the call of the mountains and takes off, with his bow and a red rock he found earlier, one carved with a horse that seems to burn and glow at times of danger or crisis. He meets a group of Dalriadans led by Athira, a girl he once glimpsed when he was fishing. She prevents Kiron*, a young man only a little older than Jonathan, from killing him, and soon he is entrenched in the camp with Barli, a boy his age whose vocation is cooking, as his best friend. He learns that his red rock is the Farlith, an emblem of great magic, the loss of which has brought bad times to Dalriada, and that his bow is Cahaud, famous for its power. Called Jhonan by the people, he becomes more proficient in his use of the bow and in the ways of Dalriada. When he is fourteen, he goes with the others his age to Kalivi Mountain, where each must make a different and difficult Ridgewalk to death or, if successful, to be chosen by a horse and to choose a mate. Although his walk has been the most difficult of all and he is chosen by Rhohar, now a full-grown stallion, the seer refuses to give him the ritual cut over his heart, the O-Bredann, that denotes adulthood until he becomes emotionally whole. In a visionlike state during his walk, Jonathan has picked an apple that he recognizes as a firegold, and now, cast out again, he decides to take it to Brian to start a new line at Greengage. There he finds that many of their trees were destroyed by the men who wanted to kill him, but that the rest were saved by Rosamund. She is now living at Greengage. He also discovers through an ancient portrait that Brian is part Dalriadan, a heritage that accounts for Jonathan's blue eyes and the branching, antlerlike mark on his forehead and means that some other man did not father him, as both he and Brian had feared. As both a Valley dweller and a Dalriadan, he hopes to bring the people together again in the future. The fantasy is convincing, with a number of well-developed characters besides the protagonist. Jonathan's terror at the prospect of insanity and his feeling of rejection from both societies is moving. End papers with maps help to keep the geography clear. ALA/YA.

FLAKE, SHARON   Originally from Philadelphia; winner of the Coretta Scott King New Talent Award and of Pennsylvania Council of Arts Fellowship. She is director of publications at the Katz Business School of the University of Pittsburgh. Her first novel, *The Skin I'm In** (Hyperion/Jump at the Sun, 1998), is about an African American girl in seventh grade who, though very bright, suffers from low self-esteem. More recently, she has published *Money Hungry* (Jump at the Sun, 2001), in which a young girl, determined that she and her mother will never live on the street again, does everything legal she can think of to earn money. Flake makes her home in Pittsburgh.

FLEISCHMAN, PAUL (1952–)   Born in Monterey, California; poet, author of several kinds of novels for young people, often unconventional in pattern. Celebrating the power of the imagination, *Mind's Eye** (Holt, 1999) is set in a nursing home and written entirely in dialogue. His *Whirligig**

(Holt, 1998), about a boy's redemption after his drunken driving has killed a girl, is also experimental in its structure, while *Seedfolks** (HarperCollins, 1997) has thirteen different narrators. For earlier biographical information and title entries, see *Dictionary, 1985–1989* [*Rear-View Mirrors*]; *Dictionary, 1990–1994* [*The Borning Room*; *Bull Run; Saturnalia*] and *Dictionary, 1995–1999* [*Seedfolks*; *Whirligig*].

FLETCHER, SUSAN (CLEMENS) Born in Pasadena, California; graduate of the University of California–Santa Barbara and of the University of Michigan; writer of novels mainly for young adults. She is best known for her fantasy trilogy about dragon-sayers, humans who communicate and interact with dragons, of which the first is *Dragon's Milk* (Atheneum, 1989). Her strong ability to evoke place is also evident in *Shadow Spinner** (Atheneum, 1998), an American Library Association choice for young adults that cleverly improvises on the tale of Scheherazade. Fletcher lives in Oregon. A recent publication is *Walk Across the Sea* (Atheneum, 2001), in which a girl befriends a Chinese immigrant boy. For more details about Fletcher and titles, see *Dictionary, 1995–1999* [*Flight of the Dragon Kyn; Shadow Spinner*].

THE FLOATING GIRL (Massey*, Sujata, HarperCollins, 2000)   Mystery, not originally for young people, set in and near Tokyo, Japan, in the late 1990s, concerned mostly with the wildly popular subculture of enthusiasts of the *manga* (comic book) designed for adults, usually with highly explicit sex portrayed. Japanese American Rei Shimura, an antiques dealer and specialist, writes monthly articles for the English-language magazine *Gaijin Times*, dealing with artworks and ways to find valuable vintage pieces. To her consternation, the magazine's editor leaves and the owner decides to change the focus, turning it into a manga format with articles to appeal to a broader audience. She is assigned to write an article on the artistic values and history of the manga, about which she knows nothing. With the help of her Japanese lover, Takeo Kayama, a teacher of flower arranging now renovating a family house at the beach, she acquires and examines a number of manga, learns about *doujinshi* (limited-issue comics created by amateur artists), and is struck by the illustration in a series called Showa Story, which is far superior to the average. Her attempts to contact the artist, Kunio Takahashi, take her to Show a Boy, a strip club for women specializing in foreign men as dancers and hosts. There, she gets to know Nicky Larsen, an American from the University of Minnesota, and Marcellus, a tall, handsome Sengalese, both of whom are dancers, and sees a mural by Kunio, that whets her appetite to find him. When she finally gets to his home address, he is not there, but she discovers that he lives next door to Nicky, who writes the Showa Story comics and goes with the third member of their little group, Seiko Hattori, who works in her father's copy shop. Nicky appears dressed as Mars Girl, a comic book character, and is leaving for a date. Later that day, she sees on the television news that a body has been found in the river, and she knows from the description that it is Nicky. When she volunteers to identify the body, the police lieutenant, though a friend of hers, refuses, saying she did not know the victim well enough, but he allows Rika Fuchida, an ambitious intern at *Gaijin Times* who has been assigned to assist her, to identify him, though she knew Nicky only slightly at Showa College. Rei is suspicious of Rika's offers of help, and later events prove her correct. Her further investigations, which she thinks she owes to Nicky, lead her to suspect various people and to be injured when a man turns and deliberately hits her on an escalator, knocking her backward down the stairs. Before she finally discovers who murdered Nicky, she has contact with a member of the *yakuza* group, gangsters who extort payments from both sleazy and respectable businesses, and she has had misunderstandings and reconciliations with Takeo. In a final, dramatic scene she rescues Seiko from a suicide attempt in the sea, although she is not a strong swimmer and has to commandeer a boogie board from some young boys to push ahead until she reaches the girl. The actual events of the novel, though the threads are pulled together and explained satisfactorily, are not as interesting as the milieu described, a Japan not familiar to most Americans, with a youth culture wild and kinky, though on the surface polite, and a crime underworld recognized, though not publicly acknowledged, by everyone. Rei's frustration at being forced into the traditional subservient role of women at the magazine and elsewhere adds to the irony of the tawdry life she is investigating. The title comes from an old term for the world of courtesans and wine shops, a "floating world" not conforming to accepted patterns. Booklist.

FLYERS (Hayes*, Daniel, Simon & Schuster, 1996)   Lighthearted, contemporary mystery set in a rural region in eastern New York State. Narrator Gabe Riley, 16, notes that peculiar happenings occur after he, his younger brother, and their pals begin filming a "campy, semi-horror piece" by Blood Red Pond for their Gifted and Talented Class. Strange shadows, lights in a presumably empty house, and similar gothic conventions produce continuously good reading about boys of intelligence, enterprise, and compassion. Previously, the novel was nominated for the Edgar Allan Poe Award. For a longer, more detailed entry, see *Dictionary, 1995–1999*. ALA/YA.

FOGELIN, ADRIAN (1951–   )   Born in Pearl River, New York; received her B.F.A. from the Rhode Island School of Design. She has been an illustrator for the Baltimore Zoo, teacher at a day-care center, and an instructor in art at Florida Keys Community College. Her first book, *Crossing Jordan** (Peachtree, 2000), deals with racial discrimination in a friendship-story context. It was an American Library Association choice for young adults and was cited by the International Reading Association. She has also published *Anna Casey's Place in the World* (Peachtree, 2001), about two foster children in a new home. *My Brother's Hero* (Peachtree, 2002) concerns a boy who faces problems while on vacation in the Florida Keys. Fogelin lives in Tallahassee, Florida.

FORGED BY FIRE (Draper*, Sharon M., Atheneum, 1997)   Realistic present-day novel of a dysfunctional African American family in Cincinnati, Ohio, centering on a boy who grows up trying to protect his little half sister from being sexually molested by her father and ultimately saves her from a fire that kills the man. For a longer entry, see *Dictionary, 1995–1999*. ALA/YA.

FORGOTTEN FIRE (Bagdasarian*, Adam, Dorling Kindersley, 2000)   Historical novel set during the Armenian Holocaust in eastern Armenia (Turkey) for three years beginning in 1915 and based on the recollections of the author's great-uncle who survived the genocide. The narrator, Vahan Kenderian, 12, is the youngest of six children in the warm, loving family of Sarkis Kenderian of the province of Bitlis. Sarkis is one of the wealthiest and most influential Armenians in Turkey, a lawyer whom even powerful Turks consult. Vahan is bright, sheltered, and comfortable and confidently believes that his life will be much like his father's. By story's end in 1918, Vahan feels he has achieved the steely character his father desired for him through the discipline of suffering from the hunger, thirst, loneliness, brutality, and despair he has survived. Sarkis disappears, probably shot, and then Vahan's uncle, but not before the uncle, a kind of medic, brings for Vahan's mother, grandmother, and two sisters, Oskina and Armenouhi, little bags of poison to use if dire circumstances occur. Vahan often hears gunshots, knows that houses and churches are ransacked and destroyed, stores have closed, and people are driven away by Turkish soldiers to disappear forever. One spring day, seven soldiers appear, force the Kenderians into the courtyard, shoot Vahan's two older brothers, and drive the rest of the family away to an inn, where they are herded into a smelly, filthy room with fifty or sixty other people. When soldiers come and take young women away for their pleasure, Armenouhi eats the poison and dies. The starving, thirsty prisoners are driven to a river, where most are shot or somehow killed, but their mother urges Vahan and his next older brother, Sisak, to run when night comes. While fleeing, Vahan is almost raped by a vagabond Turkish soldier, whom Sisak kills with a big rock to the head. A few days later, Sisak dies of a raging fever. Vahan seeks refuge with a schoolmate's mother, Mrs. Altoonian, who hides him until she thinks it is no longer safe to do so, then finds a place for him as a stable boy with the Turkish governor of the region, Selim* Bey, who is known to have killed many Armenians. Among other experiences, Vahan joins a caravan of Turkish refugees, among whom he pretends to be deaf and dumb. In an almost deserted village, he is sheltered by Armenian Ara* Sarkisian, a huge giant of a blacksmith. Ara takes him to a Swiss mission for girls, where he lives disguised as a girl until the matron finds a place for him as a servant with Armenian Dr. Tashian. He grows to love Mrs. Tashian, a sweet, kind, gentle woman, who dies from a stroke brought on by the death in childbirth of a young girl abused and impregnated by the German consul. Vahan moves on, eventually reaching the seacoast and Constantinople, where he finds refuge in an orphanage. According to the epilogue, he is later reunited with his sister, Oskina, and they emigrate to the United States in 1921. This account of incredible hardship and suffering is related in a curiously abstracted, dispassionate tone for the most part, so that it seems more like history rather than fiction. The many characters and incidents are largely undeveloped. Impact comes from the reader's knowing that the narrative is based on the true experiences of one brave, enduring boy, who never loses hope, his pride, and his self-respect and who reaches out to help others when he can. The title may derive from Vahan's father's remark that steel is strengthened by fire. ALA/YA; NYPL.

FREEMAN, SUZANNE Journalist, book reviewer, teacher of writing, author. Her first novel, *The Cuckoo's Child* (Greenwillow, 1996), was named to several prestigious lists, among them the American Library Association Young Adult list. For an earlier biographical and title entry, see *Dictionary, 1995–1999*.

FROMM, PETE (1958–)   Born in Milwaukee, Wisconsin; received a degree in wildlife biology from the University of Montana. He held various positions with the Idaho Department of Fish and Game and was a ranger with the National Park Service before becoming a full-time writer in 1987. He is best known for his collections of short stories, for which he has received high critical acclaim, including nominations for the Pulitzer Prize, among them *Dry Rain* (Lyons, 1997) and *Night Swimming* (Picador, 1999). His first novel was *Monkey Tag* (Scholastic, 1994), for young adults, about the physical and psychological problems twins suffer as a result of a tragic accident. His adult novel, *How All This Started** (Picador, 2000), about siblings wild about baseball, one of whom suffers from mental illness, was named to the New York Public Library List of Best Books for the Teen Age and chosen by *Booklist*. *Indian Creek Chronicles: A Winter in the Wilderness* (Lyons, 1993), a memoir, was also well received. He lives with his family in Great Falls, Montana.

FROM THE BLACK HILLS (Troy*, Judy, Random, 1999)   Coming-of-age novel of a high school senior in present-day Wheatley, South Dakota, whose insurance agent father shoots his receptionist, with whom he is having an affair, and alters his son's life forever. Through the spring and early June, Mike Newlin's main preoccupation has been sex, real coupling with his girlfriend, Donetta* Rush, and fantasized encounters with Lee-Ann Schofield, wife of Neil, the ranch owner on whose ranch

he has worked since he was fourteen. Although she is thirteen years his senior, Lee-Ann, a petite mother of two-year-old Janna, has always been friendly and this spring, since Mike has grown and developed, seems to signal that she is ready for a more intimate relationship, all of which makes him hot with both lust and guilt, since he likes and respects Neil. On June 18, Neil comes to where Mike is mowing and tells him that his father, Glenn, has evidently killed Mary Nise at the Tenderly Motel in a nearby town, called an ambulance, and taken off in Mary's car, leaving behind the gun and his own car. When Neil drives him home, Mike is questioned by the police, particularly Tom DeWitt, a special agent from Rapid City, who seems to think that Glenn will be likely to contact his son and that Mike is the key to finding him. Mike's mother tells him that she knew of the affair and blames herself, because, when Mary wanted to break it off and leave town, she had persuaded the young woman to stay until Glenn calmed down, afraid that he would kill himself. Mike considers his father bewildered, even hopeless, unable to cope with life, but never violent or dangerous. Mike has not been really close to his mother for a long time, but it annoys him that she seems to enjoy Tom DeWitt, who keeps dropping by, supposedly on a casual visit, either chatting her up or trying to pry information from Mike. Glenn is sighted in Colorado with a woman and a dog, obviously the one belonging to Mary Hise, which has been missing. Later, the woman is found with the dog, for which she has given Glenn money. As the time approaches for Mike to leave for South Dakota State in Brookings, where he will be in the honors program, two things happen. His mother starts divorce proceedings and begins going out with a man whom she has been tutoring, and Lee-Ann almost has sex with Mike, but reneges at the last moment. At Brookings, his roommate is a nerdy type named Raymond Nelson, who tries to be nice but with whom Mike feels little in common. He meets a girl at a dance with whom he has sex, but he feels nothing for her. Everything makes him disoriented, and he stops studying, starts skipping classes, seldom eats, and does not look at his phone messages. Gradually, he begins to realize that he is under surveillance, probably by Tom DeWitt. One night he gets a call from his father, telling him to "drive on out." Mike tells Raymond that his friend Josh is in a campground nearby and wants him to spend the night, then drives his truck aimlessly until a car flashes its lights to him and he follows it a long distance to an isolated third-rate motel in Minnesota. His father is with a strange, erratic woman named Inez, whom he tries to placate when she frequently takes offense, afraid she will leave with her car and strand him. The only others at the motel are a red-haired woman and her dog, who move into the far end unit. A winter storm moves in. Inez, obviously mentally unstable, picks fights, rackets around the room, and finally jumps in her car and leaves. Glenn tries to get Mike to give him the truck keys, or promise to drive him to Cleveland, or at least Minneapolis. Mike insists that his father tell him what happened with Mary Hise. Glenn can only blame her for her own death, saying, "She grabbed my arm." Mike gives his father what money he has, drives his truck to a pay phone in a small town, and calls the number of Tom DeWitt's cell phone, which the detective has given him. Tom answers from the motel, where he and the red-haired woman police officer have arrested Glenn. Finally realizing that he is

not responsible for his feckless father, who has never been a person he could count on, Mike returns to school, longing for the days when he could roam the Black Hills, carefree, and beginning the hard adjustment to this new understanding. The landscape of western Dakota is almost a character in the novel, an area that has shaped Mike's reticence and molded his independence. Before the murder, Mike is a fairly typical teenager, on the wrestling team at school, intelligent, self-contained but not a loner. The incident knocks his confidence from under him and destroys his view of the past as well as the present and probably the future. Booklist.

FUMIKO (*The Yokota Officers Club**) Japanese maid who is said by Major Coney Wingo, who has found the Root family an off-base place to live, to "come with the house." It turns out that she has been Wingo's mistress for years, but she becomes a true friend to the Roots, especially the mother, Moe*, and Bernie, the eldest daughter, who loves Fumiko deeply. She helps Moe through the birth of the twins, two miscarriages, and Bosco's birth, being far more supportive and useful than Moe's husband. After the family is abruptly ordered to return to the states, Fumiko is never mentioned again until Bernie is about to go to Japan with Bobby* Moses. Moe gives her a letter for Fumiko, in case she can find her, apologizing for the unfortunate circumstances of their departure and saying she knows it was not Fumiko's fault. At the Yokota Officers Club, Bernie does find Fumiko, now a call girl, and learns her story. During the war she and her mother almost starved, and at the war's end, they are delivered to a brothel in Tokyo. Her mother hangs herself, but the madam looks Fumiko over and suggests that there is an American officer with "special tastes." This turns out to be Major Wingo, who is so intimidated by his wife, LaRue, that he is sexually dysfunctional with her. After he leaves her, Fumiko has his child and supports herself, and her daughter, Hanna Rose, by working in the black market, living in a wooden crate. Hanna Rose sickens and dies. In despair, Fumiko becomes ill herself, but Major Wingo returns and sets her up in a room, visiting her whenever he can, admitting to her what he cannot admit even to himself, that he is afraid. His cocky, devil-may-care attitude is all a pose, and he weeps in Fumiko's arms and tells her about the very secret missions his crew goes on. This is her undoing, because when none of the men in Wingo's squadron returns, Fumiko comforts Bernie Root, telling her a secret, that the men are safe in Alaska. To get attention from Kit's friends, who usually ignore her, Bernie swears them all to secrecy and tells Fumiko's secret. In this way Bernie is herself responsible for the ruin of her father's career and for his firing Fumiko.

FUQUA, JONATHAN SCOTT   Historian, artist, naturalist, dramatist. He has also been a copywriter, illustrator, and teacher of literature and art, and has been writer-in-residence at Carver Center for the Arts. His novel, *The Reappearance of Sam Webber** (Bancroft, 1999), is a strong picture of a boy's hurt and confusion after his father disappears and of his gradual adjustment to the situation. A more recent novel is *Darby* (Candlewick, 2002), set in Marlboro County, South Carolina, dealing with issues of class and race. Among his other publications are *American Rowhouse Classic Design* (Stemmer House, 1997); *B & O: Awards Railroad* for the Baltimore B & O Museum; and a graphic novel, *In the Shadow of Edgar Allan Poe*. Fuqua has investigated the Civil Rights movement, blockbusting, suburbanization, architecture, and the lunch-counter industry, and written numerous plays, including a large-scale production titled *Coffee and Comets at the Starlight Diner* for the Maryland Science Center. He makes his home in Baltimore.

G

GABRIEL (*Archangel**)   Thirty, angel chosen fifteen years earlier to replace Raphael*, when his twenty-year term as archangel expires. With dark hair and white wings, he is a great beauty, and his singing voice is recognized as the best in the land. A serious young man, he is sure of himself, impatient, often thought to be arrogant, and absolutely dedicated to the good of the world. Because his father, Jeremiah, died five years before, he has been leader of the angel host at the Eyrie* since he was quite young, with heavy responsibilities that have kept him from finding the wife chosen for him by Jovah until only a few months before the annual Gloria, at which he will become archangel. While he knows she must be mortal—angels cannot marry angels—he is appalled to find that Rachel* is not even from a noble family, but daughter of a hill farmer, and even more horrified to discover that she is a slave. While it is clear to a reader that they will be a perfect pair, since they share compassion for the poor, love of music, devotion to justice, and dedication to Jovah, pride keeps them from admitting it to each other. Gabriel recognizes his love for Rachel before she admits she loves him. Her standoffishness tempers his pride and makes him a more reasonable life partner.

GABRIELA (*The Tree of Red Stars**) Movie-star beautiful young street beggar in Montevideo, Uruguay, whom Magda* Ortega Grey likes very much. The women in Magda's neighborhood are sympathetic to Gabriela, since they know she does not have the means to better her condition and feed her family. Marco* Periera also keeps an eye on her and helps out as he can. Magda learns that Gabriela was one of the beggars picked up on the streets by the police to practice methods of torture on. When Magda sees the picture of Gabriela's dead body, she becomes very angry, wishes she could kill the people responsible, and casts in her lot with the revolutionaries known as the Tupamaros.

GAIMAN, NEIL (RICHARD) (1960–   ) Author of more than forty books, best known for his adult fantasy, science fiction, and graphic novels. He was born in Portchester, England, attended Ardingly College and Whitgift School, and currently makes his home in the United States. He worked as a freelance journalist before becoming a full-time writer of novels and screenplays and has also published short stories and nonfiction. Of his graphic novels, the dozen in The Sandman series have received the most attention. Although faulted by critics for being contrived and overworked, his novels have made a mark in the genre. Among his fiction, *Neverwhere* (BBC Books, 1996; Avon, 1997) takes place in a fantasy world beneath London. Recipient of the Alex Award and chosen by *Booklist*, *Stardust** (Avon, 1999), like others of his novels, borrows heavily from oral tradition. A half-fairy young man goes through a gap in a wall to search for a falling star and finds a new life among the fairy kind.

THE GATES OF TWILIGHT (Volsky*, Paula, Bantam, 1996)   Adult fantasy-adventure novel set in a fictitious land that resembles colonial India under the British. The native Aveshquians, a small, golden-skinned, black-haired people, are threatening to rebel against their western overlords of two hundred years, the taller white-skinned, light-haired Vonahrish. The Vonahrish suspect that the natives are being stirred up by the Filial, the priests of the natives' main god, Aoun-Father, specifically by his earthly representative, KhriNayd-Son. Vonahrish Renille vo Chaumelle, 31, assistant deputy secretary of the Civil Service, is dispatched by Protector (governor) vo Trouniere, whose Residency stands in the city of ZuLaysa, to infiltrate the Filial compound of JiPhaindru in the Old City portion of Zu-Laysa, to learn whether KhriNayd-Son lives and is behind the current rash of

riots. Although Renille is of a noble Von-ahrish family, he has native blood from a few generations back and speaks the native tongue. Disguised as a holy pilgrim, he enters JiPhaindru and learns from a very thin girl of about twelve, Chura, that the Filial maintain a cadre, called the Chosen, of pre- and early-adolescent girls for sacred prostitution, Chura among them. He observes a secret, sacred rite, led by KhriNayd-Son, in which two monstrous hybrid babies are torn from the bodies of two young girls, the specially Chosen, and then girls and babies are sacrificed. Discovered by the Filial, Renille escapes with Chura's help, and, pursued by wivoori, poisonous flying lizards trained to Filial commands, he takes refuge briefly in the most despised part of the city, where the Nameless, the lowest level of society, live. Still weak from the poison of a wivoori bite, he makes a slow and difficult journey northward by foot to the palace, OodPray, of native Gochalla* (queen) Xundunisse, whose beautiful daughter, Gochanna* (princess) Jathondi, takes him in. He returns secretly to Zu-Laysa and to the Residency, which is soon besieged by the natives. Jathondi escapes from her mother's palace and wrath for harboring Renille and goes to ZuLaysa. She is kidnapped by the Filial, imprisoned, and destined to be impregnated and eventually sacrificed by, most likely, KhriNayd-Son. Renille leaves the besieged Residency, makes his way to JiPhaindru, intending to kill KhriNayd-Son, finds, and releases Jathondi. They struggle mightily against the powerful magic of KhriNayd-Son and kill him. In a mystical sequence, Aoun-Father's brilliance magically fills the entire place. Jathondi's mother, having learned what the Filial have planned for her daughter, summons help from the old gods and their followers who were in early times overthrown by the Aoun-Father's gods. They defeat the Filial, and JiPhaindru is reduced to powder. The rebellion peters out, and peace returns to the realm. OodPray becomes a school for Aveshquian children. Since Renille and Jathondi plan to marry and the Resident Protector says that the Vonarish will not accept his native wife, they elect to move to another state. Abundant action, skillfully revealed and foiled characters, political intrigue, treachery, and romance hold the attention and mitigate the formulaic plot. The native women are especially admirable. Although mystical scenes appear and sorcery and magic coexist with guns and shells, careful attention to details of politics give the book the flavor of historical fiction. It is to the author's credit that she manages to engage the reader's sympathy for the Protector and Renille, who represent the best of the Vonarish, while at the same time she evokes sympathy for the Aveshquians. Booklist.

GEAR, KATHLEEN O'NEAL   Archaeologist and writer; author with her husband, W. Michael Gear*, of the First North Americans series, one of which is *People of the Mist** (Forge, 1997), about the prehistoric Algonquian Indians of the Chesapeake Bay area. She is a former state historian and archaeologist for Wyoming, Kansas, and Nebraska for the U.S. Department of the Interior. Other books in the First North Americans series include *People of the Fire* (Tor, 1991), about the early Native peoples of the Central Rockies and the Great Plains, and *People of the Sea* (Forge, 1993), about the prehistoric Indians of California, Arizona, and New Mexico. Individually, she has written *Sand in the Wind* (Tor, 1990), about whites among Cheyenne; *This Widowed Land* (Tor, 1993), set among Wyan-

dot Indians and Jesuits in Quebec; and *Thin Moon and Cold Mist* (Forge, 1995), about pioneers in Colorado. The Gears have made their home in Thermopolis, Wyoming.

GEAR, W. MICHAEL   Archaeologist and writer. He is the author, with his wife, Kathleen O'Neal Gear*, of the First North Americans series of novels about prehistoric Native American Indians of what is now the United States. One of these is *People of the Mist** (Forge, 1997), a mystery and historical fiction about the early peoples of the Chesapeake Bay region selected by *Booklist*. Others in the set are *People of the River* (Tor, 1992), about the Mound Builders of the Mississippi River, and *People of the Lightning* (Forge, 1995), about the Florida Native American Indians. An anthropologist by training, he has worked as an archaeologist since 1978. The Gears have made their home in Thermopolis, Wyoming. Individually, he has published, among others, *Long Ride Home* (Tom Doherty, 1988), *Big Horn Legacy* (Tom Doherty, 1996), and *The Morning River* (Forge, 1996), all historical and western-adventure novels. Together, the Gears have also published a set of novels about the Anasazi Indians.

GETTING IN (Boylan*, James Finney, Warner, 1998)   Lightly satiric novel of the efforts of four high school juniors to choose a college and to be admitted to the class of 2003, set in New England, mostly on a series of elite campuses. The four young people are Dylan Floyd, his cousin Juddy (Judson) Floyd, Juddy's stepsister, Allison Baxter, and Allison's boyfriend, Polo MacNeil. With Ben Floyd, Dylan's father, Lefty Floyd, Juddy's father, and Lefty's new wife, Chloe, mother of Allison, they are in a Winnebago motorhome touring the campuses of Yale University, Harvard University, Bowdoin College, Colby College, Dartmouth College, Middlebury College, Williams College, Amherst College, and Wesleyan University, at all of which one or sometimes all four applicants have interviews scheduled. At each, some mishap or misunderstanding botches up the interview. At Yale, the admissions officer gets Dylan's name reversed and, when Dylan mentions that his mother is dead, begins to weep because his own mother died recently. The meeting ends with Dylan comforting the interviewer. The group, getting caught in Boston traffic, never does find Harvard. Juddy, who has no intellectual aspirations, is not worried, since he is being courted by Harvard for his skill at fencing, his only accomplishment. Polo, a product of affluent parents and a private prep school, is sure Harvard will be delighted to get him, but his main interest is in persuading Allison to have sex with him and mentally reminiscing about sex with other women. Allison, an accomplished musician, loathes the crudeness of Lefty and Juddy and is not sure what she wants to do but, on principle, holds out against Polo's demands. Among the adults there are two main conflicts and several secrets. Chloe has begun to despise Lefty, but since her deceased husband left her flat broke, she does not dare divorce him for fear that he will not pay Allison's college costs. She fantasizes about his dying and leaving her his considerable wealth and, since he is overweight and has a bad heart, decides to kill him by overfeeding him and seducing him into overactive sex. Lefty has two secrets from Ben: he slept with Ben's wife, Faith, who afterward committed suicide and, as a member of a board of a financial company, voted against extending the time on

Ben's loan, forcing him into bankruptcy, both actions motivated by his resentment of his smarter younger brother who went to college while he worked at and later inherited the family automobile dealership. Ben, who has not told Dylan about the loss of his company, is dreading that he may have to go to work for Lefty and hoping his son will get a scholarship. Dylan is afraid to tell his father that he got mixed up on his SAT exams and scored very low. At each campus tour, they run into a rude, self-important man named Captain Bedford from Atlanta and his cowed daughter, Welly. At one college, Dylan's interviewer never shows up, and at another the pregnant admission officer's water breaks, and Dylan helps her into a taxi for the hospital. On two campuses, Polo and Welly make love in the chapel. When Bedford's arrogance gets too aggravating, Ben tells him off and is astonished to be offered a job as the head of one of Bedford's thriving companies. Chloe, having survived a hike on a dangerous portion of the Appalachian Trail near Dartmouth on which she, Ben, and Lefty are all nearly killed, leaves Lefty and decides to hike the whole trail, starting in the South. In the end, Allison opts for Wesleyan; Dylan goes to Middlebury, as both his parents did; Juddy, who cares almost nothing about college, is given an athletic scholarship to Harvard; and Polo, having missed two rescheduled interviews at Harvard and messed up a third, goes to work at Lefty's car lot. The mistakes and misunderstandings range from hilarious to very touching, with ironic twists and broad, satiric swipes at the whole admissions system and the pretensions of the New England colleges. Dylan, a bright, decent, unpretentious boy, and Allison, who dumps Polo and becomes a good friend to Dylan, are appealing characters, who, one suspects, will do well wherever they end up. Alex; Booklist.

THE GHOST IN THE TOKAIDO INN (Hoobler*, Dorothy, and Thomas Hoobler*, Philomel, 1999)   Historical and mystery novel with boy's growing-up story aspects set in 1735 during the age of the samurai on busy Tokaido Road in Japan. Seikei, 14, son of a prosperous tea merchant, dreams of becoming a samurai (a hereditary warrior whose code demands courage, loyalty, and honor) and writing poetry, an activity that only samurai are allowed to do. While he and his father are on the way to Edo, where the military governor known as the shogun lives, he observes a daimyo (a samurai lord) known as Lord Hakuseki viciously attempt to trample to death with his horse a scar-faced beggar, who nimbly leaps away. At the inn that night, he observes a beautiful young girl named Michiko, daughter of a papermaker, sell the daimyo some exceptionally fine paper that her father has produced. Later that evening, Michiko tells him a ghost story about a jikininki (a horned eater of human flesh). In the middle of the night, Seikei awakens to see what he thinks is the jikininki just outside his room, gets up, and follows the creature, which simply sinks into the floor. The next morning, the daimyo reports the theft of a precious ruby, and when it is found in Michiko's paper box, Judge Ooka, a famous historical magistrate and detective, is summoned. The judge discovers the ruby in the box is fake, smashes it, and hearing Seikei's story, orders the boy to retrace the ghost's path. When Seikei discovers a tunnel beneath the inn and the judge learns that a troupe of kabuki theater actors had played near the tunnel's end, the judge remarks strangely that it will take a long time to discover the solution to the mystery. After Seikei confides to the judge his ambition to become a samurai, the judge orders him to accompany him to Edo, gives him a polished wooden sword, and tells his servant Bunzo, a samurai, to take charge of the boy and teach him to ride. At Ise, the holiest place in Japan with its temple to the goddess Amaterasu, Seikei attends a kabuki play, goes backstage afterward, notices that the lead actor, Tomomi, is the scar-faced beggar he saw on the road, and loses his sword to the man. Bound now by honor to serve Tomomi and having discovered that the judge has left town for Edo, Seikei travels with the kabuki troupe for some time. Tomomi teaches him much about swordplay and treats him well, eventually training him for a part in a play he is writing to perform for Lord Hakuseki, the daimyo, and the shogun at the daimyo's house in Edo. During this time, Seikei discovers that it was Tomomi he saw outside his room that night, playing the part of a geisha, a pleasure woman. Eventually, the mystery of the missing jewel is solved. The play Tomomi wrote is the story of his own family, who being Kirishitans (Christians), an unlawful religion in Japan at that time, were slain by their neighbor, Lord Hakuseki, who then seized their lands. Only the child Genjii, now called Tomomi, whose face was disfigured in the event, survived. Tomomi carefully laid plans for revenge and stole the ruby from the daimyo. During the play, he displays the jewel, which the daimyo stole from Tomimo's family, to the daimyo, draws his dead father's sword, an elegant piece decorated with Christian symbols, and kills the daimyo. The shogun's guards then behead Tomomi. The judge adopts Seikei so that the boy can be trained as a samurai. Spunky Seikei is a sympathetic, adequate protagonist, but Tomomi is the most interesting figure. Clues are skillfully planted for the reader to solve the mystery along with Seikei and the judge. Colorful scenes bring eighteenth-century Japan to vivid life: the teahouses; the pilgrims in the streets and the temples; the "floating worlds" of the pleasure parts of the towns; and, in particular, the kabuki theater. The culture and the ethic of the times are skillfully intertwined with the plot and main characters. ALA/YA.

GHOST OF A HANGED MAN (Vande Velde*, Vivian, Marshall Cavendish, 1998) Ghost fantasy set in the summer of 1877 and the spring of 1878 in a small town somewhere in the United States. Steady, observant Ben (Benjamin) Springer, 12, the narrator, describes the troubles that ensue after Jake Barnette, a notorious outlaw, is captured, tried, convicted, and hanged. In 1877, at the end of his trial, Jake announces that he will come back and take "you with me," that is, everyone party to his arrest, conviction, and execution. Since Ben's father is the sheriff, Jake vows vengeance on his family, too, meaning Ben and his fractious, headstrong younger sister, Annabelle, 9. Ben's account then skips to the spring of 1878, when one day in Pickett's General Store, a gypsy woman predicts for Mr. Pickett that the town will be "in danger from the water" and "drowning people, or drowned people, coming up out of the water." This happens, when the most rain the town has ever seen, floods of it, drenches the town and causes coffins, including Jake's, to rise out of the ground and float. In the heavy rain, Ben and Annabelle quite literally run into a gypsy girl, Zandra, a little younger than Ben and stereotypically described as surly and dark haired. All three go to the sheriff's office to get out of the rain, and Zandra tells Ben's and Annabelle's fortunes using cards. She says that the cards show "hope and love will help" Ben. The next morning they hear that Ira Chetwin, foreman of the Barnette jury, has been found dead in his bed. Next to die is Judge Wade, from a fall down a set of stairs. Zandra says that Jake's coffin must be reburied, and immediately, to keep him from getting stronger, but the coffin is found to be empty. Then Emmett Sanders, Pa's deputy, is found dead, hanging from a tree in the Springers' backyard. As Pa walks over to the body, Jake steps out from behind the tree and grabs Pa to put a noose over Pa's head. Attempting to help Pa, Ben sees something pale blue and identifies it as his dead Mama. She contends with Jake, who becomes increasingly pale and wispy each time Mama touches him. Zandra's prediction that love will help Ben has come true. The children race to the cemetery and push the now very heavy coffin into the ground and speedily cover it with dirt. Jake is never seen again. These concluding scenes are unclear and implausible. Best are the small-town atmosphere and setting, the quick pace, and the strong opening, in which Annabelle whines to be allowed to attend the hanging, an action that is both childlike and also typical of the days when hangings were public entertainment. ALA/YA.

GIDEON'S PEOPLE (Meyer*, Carolyn, Harcourt, 1996) Boy's growing-up and period novel set for about two weeks in the early summer of 1911 in rural Lancaster County, Pennsylvania. Two boys from different cultures must decide what is most important in their lives. Events are seen from three contrasting vantages, that of Isaac* Litsky, 12, from an Orthodox Jewish family, and those of Gideon

Stoltzfus, 16, and his sister, Annie, 12, of a strict Old Order Amish family. An accident brings these three together on the last Friday in May, when the wagon in which Peddler Jakob and his son, Isaac, are riding overturns at the gate to the Stoltzfus farm, injuring Isaac and the horse, Goldie, and severely damaging the wagon. Jakob returns to Lancaster, because Mameh is about to give birth to another child, leaving Isaac with the hardworking, respected, large Stoltzfus family, who take gentle care of him. Before Jakob leaves, he tells Isaac to remember who he is, meaning that the boy should keep to Orthodox ways, a matter that Isaac respects but which presents problems in the two weeks he remains with the Amish, especially with the food. While Annie tends Isaac, bedridden in the spare room, she discovers under some loose floorboards "English" clothes, garments worn by the English-speaking residents of the county, a mouth organ, and a copy of *Treasure Island*, all items forbidden to Old Order Amish. Certain they are Gideon's, she assumes that her brother is planning to run away. Isaac soon realizes that there is trouble in this household and deduces that it has to do with the harsh way Gideon's father, Ezra, called "Datt," treats Gideon. As Gideon approaches the age of baptism and full membership in the church, he realizes he does not wish the strict order to have complete control over his life. Annie confides her fears to Isaac and also asks Gideon not to leave without saying good-bye to her. One night after hymn singing, Gideon whistles one of the tunes, and when Ezra asserts the devil is in Gideon for whistling and begins to whip his son, Gideon decides it is time to leave. He drives Isaac home to Lancaster in the repaired wagon, saying he will return on the trolley, but he really intends to take the train to Uncle Aaron's farm in Big Valley to the west. When Annie discovers the English clothes gone, she and her older brother's wife, Barbara, search for Gideon at the train station without success. On the next day, Annie returns to the station and encounters Gideon. Although both know that Gideon will be shunned and communication forbidden, they promise to write to each other via Isaac's and Barbara's addresses. Isaac is grateful that he has a kind, loving, and understanding father and prepares for his bar mitzvah. Annie has choices to make, too: Where does right lie with respect to her brother? She concludes that God requires her to love her brother as well as her parents. The didacticism is both a drawback and a strength. The many details of Amish and Jewish life give the book power. The Orthodox ways of Russian Jewish immigrants are mostly presented via Isaac's thoughts and memories, and his homesickness for the warm, loving traditional Friday night Sabbath celebration is tellingly poignant. The scene in which Gideon is included in the Friday ceremony is among the book's most eloquent. Amish scenes include Preaching Sunday, Visiting Sunday, and everyday household tasks, and the community's severity in keeping everyone in line comes across well. The core problem of personal identity that confronts each boy and the insights shed on Gideon's situation by Annie's love for him are other strengths. ALA/YA.

GIFF, PATRICIA REILLY (1935–) Born in Brooklyn, New York; reading teacher for twenty years; author of more than sixty books for children, most of them in series. She received a B.A. from Marymount College, an M.A. from St. John's University, and a Professional

Diploma in Reading and Doctor of Humane Letters from Hofstra University. She lives in Weston, Connecticut. *Lily's Crossing* (Delacorte, 1997), a period novel set during World War II, was a Newbery Honor book, among other citations. *Nory Ryan's Song** (Delacorte, 2000) is a historical novel set in Ireland during the potato famine of 1845, based on Giff's own family history. It was recommended for young adults by the American Library Association. For additional information about Giff and a title entry, see *Dictionary, 1995–1999* [*Lily's Crossing*].

THE GIFT (O'Leary*, Patrick, Tor, 1997) Adult otherworld good-versus-evil fantasy set once upon a time and involving the importance and power of storytelling. An outer story and enclosed inner tales, as in old Far Eastern oral tradition, produces a long, complicated plot and numerous characters, human, animal, and fantastic. In a prologue, the Teller, a little, aging, bald man, badly scarred about his body and limbs, a recent addition to the cowed crew of a fishing boat captained by a cruel, brusque man, assumes the role for which he is named by relating a story of how the Gift of Magic came to be. He next tells of a boy, who, refused the book of magic containing a great spell that he had been promised, grows up to search for and find it. Embittered, he uses the great spell to summon up from the dead a terrible, evil black bird called "Tomen." Tomen dubs the man The Usher of the Night, and through naming him, assumes control over him. Indeed, they often appear to be one. Although these evil beings touch many lives, the two characters with whom they become most involved are Simon, the nineteen-year-old king of the land, newly enthroned, and Tim, 12, an orphaned woodcutter's son. When Simon

becomes king upon the death of his father, it is soon evident that he is losing his hearing. After many healers try to help him without success, there appears at the palace a strange man who says he is a Wizard of the Wind named Usher, and, to prove his power, he magically sets the nearby forest on fire and then heals Simon's disability. Simon soon discovers, however, that his hearing is now so acute that it is a torment. Much of the novel concerns his attempts to become normal and break the power of the evil sorcerer. Tim, the woodcutter's son, has lost his parents in the fire that the strange sorcerer (and a bird) set and that spread beyond the city. Simon and Tim join forces and in so doing suffer many physical and emotional dangers. Interspersed among their adventures are brief interludes on the fishing boat in which the Teller speaks with crew or Captain, and thus the reader is reminded that the entire novel is the Teller's tale, a story that generates and enfolds stories. Eventually, Simon resumes his kingly responsibilities, having put aside his desire for revenge, but Tim continues to search for Usher in order to destroy his evil magic. Not unexpectedly, because attitudes and looks give hints, the Teller turns out to be Tim, while the Captain is Usher, whose life, and evil, Tim ends. In an epilogue, Tim travels to Simon's palace, where he learns that Simon is happily married. Simon introduces Tim to a woman, and the expectation is that the two will marry and Tim can finally have peace. Stories appear in abundance, related by the Teller and also by many of the figures whom Simon and Tim encounter. They have some of the flavor and character of, but are more complex and detailed than, old told tales, and just as most of the characters are enchanted, the stories themselves cast a sort of spell over the reader. It is not an easy matter to keep track of characters and places, and one eventually just gives one's self to the book without trying to maintain much in the way of order—that is, gives in to the power of the story—but certain other themes also become evident, among them the futility of hatred and revenge, the wrongness of misogyny and the continuing abuse of women, and, ultimately, the utter uselessness and waste of evil itself. Booklist.

GILMORE, KATE (1931–)   Born in Milwaukee, Wisconsin; craftsman, writer. She received her B.A. from Antioch College in 1954 and has been a craftsman and run a business making and selling topiaries and wreaths from dried botanicals. Her career as a novelist began late, but successfully, with several novels for young adults, among them *Remembrance of the Sun* (Houghton Mifflin, 1986), based on her own experience living in Iran during the 1970s. Others include *Enter Three Witches* (Houghton Mifflin, 1991), in which a boy tries to keep his new girlfriend from knowing that he lives with a group of witches, and *Jason and the Bard* (Houghton Mifflin, 1993), which explores the world of the professional theater. *The Exchange Student** (Houghton Mifflin, 1999), futuristic fantasy about a student from a distant planet living with an American family, was named to both the American Library Association Young Adult and the Young Adult Reluctant Reader lists.

GILSTRAP, JOHN (1957–)   Novelist, screenwriter, journalist, expert on explosives and hazardous waste disposal, environmental engineer, and consultant. He received his B.A. from the College of William and Mary and his M.S. from the University of Southern California. He has been a full-time writer since his first book, *Nathan's Run** (HarperCollins, 1996), collected a large book contract followed by a movie and foreign sales. An American Library Association choice for young adults, it is the suspenseful story of a twelve-year-old boy on the run from a murder charge. Another critically acclaimed and popular thriller also revolves around fugitives from the law, *At All Costs** (Warner, 1998), named to the Alex list. Another in the same vein is *Even Steven* (Pocket Books, 2000). He lives in Virginia with his wife and son.

GINGER (*Joy School**)   Young housekeeper for Katie and her father, Frank, in their new home in Missouri. She is a poor woman, but as Katie says when she sees Ginger's home, "she has fixed up what she has so comfortably it makes you want to stay there awhile." She is kind, and perceptive about Katie's problems, and seems to have antennae out to pick up her hurts and "have the manners to do something about it." When Katie's father is furious that she has gone out on a double date to a drive-in movie, Ginger stands up to him and prevents him from physically abusing his daughter, and she promises not to tell him when Katie has been sent to the principal for talking back to a teacher. Long before either of them says anything to her, Katie knows that they are involved with each other. When she asks straight out, Ginger admits that she is in love with him, although she has been going with a lumpish young man named Wayne. "I like Wayne. But . . . I have always liked a little danger in a man, Katie." She understands that Katie finds it hard to think of anyone replacing her mother and does not push the subject. With her tact and gentleness, it seems likely that she will be a good stepmother.

A GIRL NAMED DISASTER (Farmer*, Nancy, Orchard, 1996)   Unusual journey and survival novel of a Shona girl in the 1980s from Mozambique who makes her way to Zimbabwe, with a long solitary stay on an island in Lake Cabora Bassa, her only companions a troop of baboons who are both helpful and threatening. For a longer entry, see *Dictionary, 1995–1999.* ALA/YA.

THE GIRLS (Koss*, Amy Goldman, Dial, 2000)   Contemporary realistic novel of friendship with school-story and family-life aspects of a hurtful clique of middle school girls set for three days in Los Angeles. The story is told by the five girls in first person, with the addition of a newcomer at the end. Each girl speaks several times, beginning with Maya. She phones to invite Candace, who of their group is always asked first, to join her on an outing to Six Flags, Magic Mountain amusement park, and Candace's phone being busy, calls elsewhere to discover that the other four are going to Darcy's house for a Saturday night sleepover to which Maya was not invited. The reader wonders why she was excluded and receives no clear answer in the novel, except that it was the decision of Candace, the acknowledged leader of the clique. Darcy makes a crank call to Maya, which upsets both Maya and her mother. Afterward, when her mother finds out, Darcy defends herself by saying that she cannot be friends with anyone Candace does not like, but her mother grounds her. On Sunday morning, after Candace's mother picks her up for Sunday School, Renee asks Darcy why Candace turned against Maya so suddenly, but Darcy evades the question. When Brianna asks Candace how she should behave toward Maya, Candace derides her, saying she should make up her own mind and declares that Maya is simply boring. Darcy calls Candace to tell her she has been grounded, and Candace makes fun of Brianna. Darcy realizes that Brianna, like Maya, is history in Candace's eyes. On Monday, matters come to a conclusion of sorts. Candace sits beside Nicole and praises her long red hair. Darcy realizes that Candace is replacing Brianna and Maya with Nicole, adding Nicole to her collection of girls. Brianna now knows how terrible it feels to be excluded. In the cafeteria line, Renee walks up to Maya, both are soon joined by Brianna, and Renee tells Maya that they come in peace. Darcy decides that since she is grounded and cannot go to the mall with Candace and Nicole, she had better apologize to Maya, walks up to her, and snarls a sort of apology in Maya's face. The other three girls burst into laughter, Brianna feels relieved that she no longer has to please Candace, Renee is relieved of her guilt, and Maya assures them she has no hard feelings. Nicole, who speaks last, is pleased at being with sweet, friendly Candace, as she thinks of her new friend. As Darcy is apologizing to Maya, Candace informs Nicole that, although she does not want to hurt Darcy's feelings, Darcy has become a terrible, unwanted burden, like "toilet paper stuck to my shoe." Nicole tells herself she is going to change that and show Candace what a real friend is like. While the girls vary in socioeconomic background, academic ability, and aspirations, Candace, manipulative, conniving, acid or sweet tongued to suit her purposes, has been the clique's center and gets satisfaction from keeping the girls under her thumb. The reader recognizes that the clique cycle is repeating itself with Nicole as the first new subject of Candace as the queen bee. The reader hopes that the other girls will have learned a lesson in what friendship means. The girls' talk is filled with self-centered chatter and whining, barbs, pretensions, petty sniping, backbiting, and parental put-downs typical of many preteens, and the cruelty of cliques is made abundantly clear. The quick changes from narrator to narrator are sometimes confusing. To the adult reader at least, the nastiness and sycophancy get tedious. ALA/YA.

THE GIRL WHO LOVED TOM GORDON (King*, Stephen, Scribner, 1999) Adult survival novel with sports-story aspects set in the wilds of western Maine and eastern New Hampshire at the time of publication. One Saturday in early June, while walking a portion of the Appalachian Trail with her mother, Quilla, who is divorced from her alcoholic husband, and her computer nerd older brother, Pete, 14, Trish (Patricia) McFarland, 9, big and intelligent for her age, wearies of the frequent arguments between Quilla and Pete. They pay no attention when she says she needs to relieve herself. She leaves the trail and decides to return by cutting through the trees and bushes. She is soon lost, and nine long, hard days pass before she rejoins her family. She surmounts many challenges with pluck, luck, and good sense. The terrain is difficult, with dense trees, heavy underbrush, swamps, and cliffs hindering her progress, and she falls frequently. Remembering that she read in one of the *Little House* books that if you are lost in the woods, you should follow a stream, and it will eventually lead you out, she finds one, and stays by it or another one much of the way. She also faces other problems that become more critical the longer she remains in the wilds: insect bites, lack of food and water, exposure, loneliness, and fear of the unknown and of a potentially hostile presence. She has a little picnic food in her backpack and a bottle of water and another of soda, but all this is soon gone. She drinks from the stream, picks checkerberries and their leaves, gorges on fiddleheads, and finds some beechnuts, which she mingles with the checkerberries and keeps in her backpack. She experiences vomiting and diarrhea, from the water, she thinks, and these signs of illness continue. Ingeniously, she cuts the hood from her poncho and uses it to catch trout, uses pine branches and needles to make a bed, and is wracked by severe coughs, sore throats, fevers, and chills. She ponders the injustice of dying when she is trying so hard to live, and wonders whether God exists and hears prayers. She often senses something or someone watching her. She fishes her Walkman out of her pack, finds a local station that broadcasts Red Sox games, and follows her favorite player and hero, Tom Gordon, a relief pitcher (a real figure but for the purposes of the story fictitious). She sometimes has hallucinations, during which Tom appears, at first very illusory, later walking beside her as a kind of adviser. Via the radio, she learns that search parties are looking for her, but because there has been a report that she was abducted, the search parties ironically never hunt where she is. She eventually spots the ruins of a gatepost and then a path, which she follows to a lane or road. The presence she felt turns out to be a huge old bear, which attacks just at the moment that an out-of-season hunter spots Trish and shoots the creature. Trish is taken to the hospital, treated for pneumonia, and enveloped in the love of her family. In the middle of the novel, just when the reader begins to lose interest with the sameness of things, the author cleverly interjects the broadcasts and Trish's memories of life with her friends and family—her assertive, determined mother, alcoholic but warm father, and stubborn, directive brother. Although the conclusion seems overly fortuitous, it has actual precedent. Her stubborn will to survive and her faith in Tom's imagined advice, and whatever force, God, she thinks, that Tom points upward to when he saves a game enable her to survive. At the very end of the book, as she lies in her hospital bed, she taps the visor of her Red Sox cap and points her right index finger upward. ALA/YA; Booklist.

GO AND COME BACK (Abelove*, Joan, DK Ink, 1998)   Realistic episodic novel set in the mid- to late twentieth century among a Peruvian Indian tribe. The Isabo people welcome two New York City anthropologists, referred to by the Isabo as "the two old white ladies," when they arrive at their remote upper Amazonian village. Unhesitatingly generous, the Isabo consider the women "stingy" and "stupid" because they do not share freely; do not understand the importance of parties, especially with freely flowing liquor; and do not bathe their entire bodies every day, among other cultural differences. Nevertheless, the anthropologists and villagers become fond of one another, and when the Americans leave, they are pleased to hear the Isabo traditional parting words "Go and come back." The novel was cited by *School Library Journal* and appeared on the *Horn Book* Fanfare list. For a full title entry, see *Dictionary, 1995–1999.* ALA/YA.

GOCHALLA XUNDUNISSE (*The Gates of Twilight**)   Queen of a native tribe about twelve miles north of the Vonahrish capital of ZuLaysa. A big, commanding woman, early in the novel she informs Protector vo Trouniere that he must fix up her palace, OodPray, which is much in need of repair. Refused, she arranges for her daughter, Ghochanna* (princess) Jathondi, to marry the king of another northern tribe, in order to drive out the Vonahrish and regain independence. When she learns that Jathondi is to become a Chosen (sacred prostitute) of KhriNayd-Son, or possibly even of the Aoun-Father (chief god), if he exists, and when she gives birth be sacrificed, Xundunisse calls on the power of deposed gods for help. They defeat the current set of gods and reduce JiPhaindru to rubble. Xundunisse then commits suicide. She is a strong, sad figure, doomed to fail because of circumstances beyond her control.

GOCHANNA JATHONDI (*The Gates of Twilight**)   Daughter of Gochalla* (Queen) Xundunisse of a native tribe about twelve miles north of the Vonahrish capital of ZuLaysa. Since Jathondi's deceased father saw to it that she was educated in Vonahr, she informs her mother that the Vonahrish way is the way of the future. Jathondi is outspoken, self-confident, and assertive, much more so than native women normally are. When her mother informs her that she has arranged for Jathondi to marry the king of another local tribe, Jathondi refuses outright and, hence, is confined to Ood-Pray palace. The romance between Jathondi and Vonahrish Renille vo Chaumelle is low keyed throughout, the emphasis being more on political realities than emotional attachment. When Renille discovers her imprisoned in JiPhaindru, she is weepy and clinging, in need of a rescuer, behavior not typical of this previously strong, self-reliant woman.

GOD BLESS THE CHILD (Feldman*, Ellen, Simon & Schuster, 1998)　　Novel for adults of family relationships with a mystery aspect, set on the eastern end of Long Island, New York, in the 1990s. Bailey Bender, probably in her early forties, after a failed marriage, has semiretired from what was once a fast-rising career as a writer/director/producer of television news to a small house on a wooded acre, where she is less trying to reassess her life than waiting for what will happen next. She works part time at the local bookstore, Livres of Grass, owned by Maude Thwait. She has many acquaintances among the summer people and friends, though not so many, among the year-rounders, in particular Nell* Harris, 16, a gawky high school girl who works in the store and hangs on her every word, and Mack* (MacKinley) Reese, who teaches high school in the winter and runs a line of lobster pots and fishes in the summer. Nobody's poster boy, Mack is low key, divorced with a thirteen-year-old son, and would like to be more than a friend, but he does not push it. He and Bailey have a bantering, sometimes prickly, sometimes fond, relationship. In an attempt to stem her general uneasiness, Bailey decides to try to find the child she had twenty years before and gave up for adoption, a plan her mother, Gilda, the only person she has told, strongly opposes. Suddenly the town is electrified by a shocking scandal: a girl named Juliet Mercer has been found dead on the patio of the lavish home of Eliot and Caroline Prinze, having evidently fallen, dived, or been pushed from the deck above. Bailey knows Eliot, a syndicated columnist and television commentator, by reputation and Caroline slightly from her occasional appearances in the bookstore, but she does not know their son, Charlie, 20. Pictures of him in the newspaper look spoiled, smirking at the camera, better looking than most of the rich kids in the neighborhood but otherwise typical. She decides immediately that he must be guilty and Juliet an innocent victim. For the next weeks, further bits of information leak out to the avid town. Charlie was at the house with Juliet earlier in the evening, but says she was fine when he drove into the city. Marks on her neck indicate strangulation, either assault or kinky sex. She was pregnant. A computer hacker who was recommended to Bailey for her search suggests a way to match the number on the original birth certificate, which she still has, with the number on the certificate issued after adoption, and somewhat ambivalently she spends an afternoon in the New York Public Library pursuing this lead, only to find that the adopting couple was named Prinze, Eliot and Caroline. After thinking about it, she writes a note to Charlie. A few days later when his parents are not at home he calls and invites her to come to his house, since the press and police are watching all his moves. To her surprise, he welcomes her, a little shyly. They talk for some time, and she feels a strong upwelling of maternal love. She becomes convinced that he is innocent. A few days later, the newspapers reveal that Charlie was adopted, and soon Bailey is named as the birth mother. Nell quits her job. In the next few weeks Bailey goes several times, by invitation, to the Prinze home, puzzling each time at the relationship between Charlie and Eliot, competitive and wary, not only on the tennis court but also in the way they watch and talk to each other. She also meets with the high-powered lawyer Eliot has hired and discovers that Juliet was not the innocent young woman the press has pictured. On one occasion, Charlie accuses Eliot of having sex with Juliet, and his father rather proudly admits it. After reading Juliet's diary, which has been subpoenaed and is partly in code, Bailey figures out how Eliot could have been at the house the night of her death after Charlie left, although supposedly he had been at his town house, and substantiates this suspicion by checking with his garage. When she confronts Eliot in front of Charlie, Caroline, and the lawyer, he admits it but says the girl, drunk and on drugs, fell off the deck in a melodramatic threat of suicide. He has no intention of admitting his presence that night, but says the lawyer will get Charlie off. The next morning Bailey learns that Eliot's car has crashed into a guardrail and thrown him into a canal. It is called an accident. Charges are dropped against Charlie, and he takes a job in Paris with an international human rights organization. The parallel plot concerning Mack and his son exposes another difficult child–parent situation, as, in a lesser way, does Nell's relationship with Bailey. Despite the unlikely coincidence of Bailey's child being Charlie Prinze, which is explained quite logically, the novel is subtle in its exploration of love and conflicts in the parental role and wrenching in its sense of loss to all concerned. Booklist.

GOLD DUST (Lynch*, Chris, Harper-Collins, 2000)   Realistic sports novel with boy's growing-up and friendship aspects set for about six months in Boston, Massachusetts, in 1975. The white narrator, Richard Riley Moncreif, 12, loves baseball passionately. When big, strong, courteous, black Napoleon Charlie Ellis enrolls just before Christmas in Richard's class at St. Colmcilla's Catholic School, fresh from Dominica in the Caribbean, Richard sees an opportunity to introduce him to the great American sport and

make a ballplayer out of him. Although Napoleon is cool to the idea and tries to tell Richard his game is cricket, Richard simply ignores what he says. Richard's dream is to make the two of them the counterparts of two young Red Sox players, Fred Lynn and Jim Rice, who are being hailed as the "Gold Dust Twins," the future of the pennant-starved Red Sox. Although Richard never asks about his family, Napoleon tells him that he and his father have come to Boston alone to start his father's job, leaving his mother and older brother in Dominica until his brother graduates. Richard characteristically never pursues the subject and so is surprised when he learns the man is a professor of creative writing and Caribbean literature at Boston University. Later, Dr. Ellis takes both boys to a fancy restaurant, where Richard is completely out of his element with the menu and service, but Napoleon is quite at ease and displays social graces alien to Richard's world. Napoleon also enjoys classical music and attends a concert with Red-Haired Beverly, a classmate, who is more inclined to explore Napoleon's likes and dislikes. Despite taunts from classmates like Butchie, one of the kids bussed to school from Ward 17 who exude "attitude" especially toward blacks, Richard continues to associate with Napoleon. On Palm Sunday, Director James Connolly invites Napoleon, who has an exceptionally beautiful, true high voice, to join the special church boys' choir. Richard realizes he did not know that Napoleon can sing so well. When Napoleon gets two free tickets to the Red Sox opener, he invites Richard. Richard is in his element, truly happy in "awesome" Fenway Park watching his heroes. Napoleon, however, finds the afternoon tedious and, noting the absence of black people in the crowd, thinks maybe they consider baseball boring, too. In a spring game Richard organizes among the boys, Richard pitches to Napoleon, a pitch gets away from Richard hitting Napoleon in the mouth, and then another strikes his back. The two boys square off, ready to fight, the other boys shouting encouragement to Richard. Napoleon grabs Richard, bursts into tears, throws him down, and stalks off. Later, walking with Beverly, Richard sadly tells her about his "sweet dream" of the heights to which the two of them could have risen together. She wisely points out that it was his dream, not Napoleon's, and that he had never tried to find out what Napoleon's dream was. Richard asks her to apologize to Napoleon for him when she next sees Napoleon, who will be going to another school, and to wish him good luck. The relationship between the two boys apparently exemplifies ongoing race relations between whites and blacks, whites confidently arranging things to their satisfaction and assuming that what satisfies them will be good for everyone. The two boys are well drawn, Red-Haired Beverly is a self-assured go-between, and Butchie and Richard's other baseball pals are stereotypical white racists in the making. Some humor relieves the seriousness. The author turns phrases with skill and captures well America's passion for its longtime national game. Actual players are often mentioned. ALA/YA.

THE GOLEM (*Snow in August**) The legendary man of clay whose story Rabbi* Judah Hirsch tells Michael Devlin, the protagonist. The account prompts Michael to re-create the Golem to prevent Falcons gang member Frankie McCarthy from causing further trouble in the neighborhood. The story, as the rabbi tells it, takes place in the sixteenth century, when Jews were suffering greatly throughout Europe. Rabbi Judah Loew, the wise and beloved rabbi of Prague, created the seven-foot-tall creature with a special silver spoon and mud from the Vltava River. He called the creature to life by inserting a special parchment containing certain Hebrew words in his mouth and chanting the secret name of God. The immensely strong and clever Golem protected the Jews from their enemies, until, rejected by the woman he loved, the Golem rampaged through the ghetto. To prevent more destruction, the rabbi returned the creature to clay.

THE GOOD CHILDREN (Wilhelm*, Kate, St. Martin's, 1998) Novel originally published for adults of an unconventional but devoted late-twentieth-century family in a rural area fifteen miles south of Portland, Oregon. When their parents buy their first real house, the McNair children, Kevin, 15, Amy, 14, Liz, 11 (the narrator), and Brian*, 6, are delighted, having been dragged for years from one temporary home to another, following their father, Warden, whose position as a structural steel-stress engineer moves him after a few months on any job. Their mother, Lee, has always insisted that keeping the family together is more important than friends or continuity of schools, but she is as thrilled as the children are with the house, which is isolated on four wooded, hilly acres away from any close neighbors. Warden, who came from a dysfunctional family and put himself through school, has promised that this move is the last, that Kevin, who feels strongly about finishing high school and college, will not have to start again in a new place. Lee rebuffs get-acquainted efforts from neighbors, but she thrives through the summer, cooking and canning, singing and dancing, "growing younger," Liz says, although she is already fifteen years younger than Warden. The children do well and start school happily but warily, sticking together even on the school bus, not trying to break into the long established friendship patterns in the small town. In September, they get word that Warden has been killed in an accident, and Lee, appalled by the funeral and sympathy of strangers, makes all four children promise that they will not let that happen to her. Mr. Martens, a lawyer, explains that Warden has provided for the family well, with college trust funds for each youngster. When they discover that Lee has ignored the bills, Kevin writes checks to pay them, and Amy, after practicing for some time, signs her mother's signature. Before Christmas, Kevin finds his mother soaking wet under the apple tree, evidently killed in a fall. Remembering the horror stories Lee had told them about foster homes she grew up in and fearing that they will be separated, they tell no one about her death but quietly bury her in the side yard where the ground is soft under a compost heap of grass clippings. For a while they tell people that their mother is ill, but when Kevin's graduation looms, they invent a cousin for her, Harriet Downs, in Riverside, California, a polio victim who needed help for a few weeks. When she supposedly gets home, they go camping at the coast for a couple of weeks. There they come up with a plan. Their mother will presumably go off to help Harriet Downs again, and when they do not hear from her, they call Mr. Martens, who comes out impatiently, and notifies the sheriff. He finds the car at the train station, where they left it and makes inquiries but soon leaves them alone. Before school starts again, Mr. Martens brings an associate, William Radix*, 25, who he says will be handling their affairs

from then on. He also hires Mrs. Inglewood, a tall, horse-loving woman, as a part-time housekeeper. Kevin, a computer whiz, starts at Portland State. Radix, whom all but Liz start to call Bill, drops by every couple of weeks, often playing games with them, and over the next few years becomes almost part of the family. He goes camping with the three younger McNairs, Kevin having started by now at Stanford University, but soon he must return to Philadelphia where his elderly father is ill. Kevin, who has written a brilliant computer program with some friends, wants to sell the house for start-up money to finance a company. Terrified, Brian, who has always said their mother was able to talk to him in the garden, becomes ill. When Liz, thinking she may be able to talk him out of this obsession, goes to the garden with him and asks their mother to leave him alone, he flings himself at her, tries to cover her mouth, and they both hit their heads. Liz cannot wake him and calls 911. He ends up in a private mental hospital arranged by Mr. Martens, where he is overmedicated and becomes zombielike, and, when he will not give up his "delusion" about his mother, he is scheduled for shock treatment. Liz plots a daring escape and calls Radix, who flies out from Philadelphia and reluctantly agrees to help her. They get Brian back to the McNair house where, with the help of Mrs. Inglewood, they nurse him through a terrible detoxification, and Radix gets the guardianship turned over to him from Mr. Martens, who is glad to be rid of the responsibility. Liz, who has finally told Radix the whole story of their mother's disappearance, also tells him that she loves him. He is "poleaxed" and says it is just gratitude, but when he gets back to Philadelphia he starts calling every day and asks himself out for Christmas. Liz's voice, forthright, self-deprecating, often very funny, dominates the novel. Her maternal feeling for Brian, especially when the older siblings are exasperated with him, sets the scene for the daring rescue. The schemes to cover their mother's absence and to get Brian out of the mental hospital are ingenious and keep the tension high. Altogether, this is a believable and engaging novel. NYPL.

GOULD, STEVEN (CHARLES) (1955–   ) Born in Fort Huachuca, Arizona; author of science fiction and suspense novels for adults and contributor of stories to science fiction periodicals and anthologies. His writings have been honored with nominations for the Hugo Award and the Nebula Award. He attended Texas A & M University and has been a computer professional. His first book, *Jumper* (Tor, 1992), about teleporting, came out to high praise, and his second, *Wildside** (Tor, 1996), an action-filled science fiction involving a credibly delineated alternate world, was recommended for young adults by the American Library Association. Other titles include *Greenwar* (Tor, 1998), a technical suspense novel written with his wife, Laura J. Mixon; *Helm* (Tor, 1998); and *Blind Waves* (Tor, 2000), also science fiction and suspense. He has made his home in Albuquerque, New Mexico.

GRAMPA FREEGY (*Nobody Else Has to Know**)   Garrulous, loving, indulgent grandfather and surrogate father of Webb Freegy, the protagonist. Grampa is a white-bearded, lively man of seventy-five, who encourages Webb in his aspiration of becoming his school's star runner. He takes the blame for the accident in which Webb suffers a broken right leg and Taffy Putnam is critically injured, because he allowed Webb to drive. Webb is not old enough to have a driver's license, and Grandpa knows that a driving conviction can ruin Webb's life. He also knows that Taffy's family will probably sue and that Webb's widowed mother would spend the rest of her life paying for Taffy's keep. Webb realizes that in assuming the blame for the accident, Grampa is attempting to make up for being a poor husband and a bad father by helping his grandson.

GRANDMA DOWDEL (*A Long Way from Chicago**; *A Year Down Yonder**)   In the first book, the grandmother with whom narrator Joey Dowdel and his sister, Mary Alice, spend every August from 1929 to 1942. Each episode in the book features Grandma, staunch, imperious, and resourceful. In the second book, Mary Alice, the narrator, spends one school year with Grandma while her older brother, Joey, is out west with the Civilian Conservation Corps, her father is out of work, and he and her mother live in a tiny one-room Chicago apartment. Grandma Dowdel is a large woman, imperious, and resourceful, known in her small Illinois town as "trigger happy." She is a crack shot with the loaded Winchester she keeps behind the kitchen woodbox. She lives on the outskirts of town in a big, old house, with a privy and a cobhouse (storehouse) in back. Grandma enjoys taking the pretentious people in town down a peg and shows a special interest in those less regarded, like old Mr. Nyquist and Miss Effie Wilcox. Most people in town are at least a little afraid of her.

GRANDMA LOGAN (*My Father's Scar**) Mother of Andy's father, a grim, insensitive woman who bullies her grandson, her Uncle* Charles Abbott, and even her son, Harold*. Her effort to buy friendship for Andy, one of the most humiliating memories of his childhood, is utterly removed from any realization of the situation. As Uncle Charles points out to Andy, she is not trying to make him happy, but to make him ordinary, one of the faceless herd, so she will not have to try to understand him. Her attitude toward her uncle, who lives on the top floor of her house, is equally disapproving. She is ruthless in her rudeness to his friend, Horace Biddle, another gentle, bookish man. Mr. Biddle tells Andy that he will never forgive her for ignoring and deriding Uncle Charles's appointment as state poet laureate years before and her refusal to go to the program where he was awarded the honor. After Uncle Charles dies, she throws his books out the window into the mud and puddles of the yard, the quickest way of clearing out his room to rent.

GRANDMÈRE (*The Princess Diaries**) Mia Thermopolis's domineering grandmother, her father's mother, with whom Mia has spent holidays at her elegant villa in France, before she learned that Grandmère is the dowager princess of Genovia. Now that Mia is officially to be her son's heir, Grandmère is appalled at Mia's looks and behavior and sets out to make her over into a proper princess. She teaches her how to sit, with her legs together so that her underwear does not show, has her hair redone and lightened, gives her lessons in conversing and interacting with European royalty, and the like. Two times Grandmère informs the media about Mia's being royal. She is responsible for Mia's picture appearing on the front page of the *New York Post*, and later she invites Mia to dine out with her so that Mia can learn how to handle the media, both times to Mia's chagrin. Grandmère is so overdrawn that she is almost a caricature and, hence, hard to take credibly.

GRANDPA KEVIN WARD (*Painting the Black**)   Paternal grandfather of Ryan Ward, the narrator. He takes an interest in Ryan's catching, because when he was younger he was a catcher, too. He gives Ryan good equipment, much better than what Ryan has been working with, and also teaches him some of the finer points of catching, for example, how to be quicker and better at picking off runners, advice that gives Ryan an advantage over the other catchers on the high school team. He also has an influence on Ryan's decision to tell what he knows about the attack on Monica* Roby.

GRANDPA LARSEN (*Bull Catcher**) Grandfather of Bull Larsen. Grandpa is a retired widower, who has a small sharpening business in his garage. He is a congenial, kind, life-loving man, with an eye for the ladies. Grandpa is an apt intermediary between Bull and Bull's absent mother, whose attempts to influence Bull's life, for example, getting Bull to attend a private school in California, Bull increasingly resents. Grandpa advises Bull and Jeff* Hanson that the abuse that Billy* Collins is suffering must be reported to authorities and suggests contacting the school. Since teachers are obligated to report abuse, Billy becomes a center of attention, and the abuse abates. Grandpa is also one of Bull's biggest fans.

GRANT (*The Dark Side of Nowhere**) Security guard and janitor at Billington Junior High, the school that narrator and protagonist Jason Miller attends. Jason thinks that Grant is odd, even weird, a loner, yet ubiquitous. A flat figure, Grant provides the sinister element in the novel. He has a satellite dish on his roof, the only one in town to point north, by which he has received information about the impending alien invasion. He is manipulative both in the open and behind the scenes but appears upright and trustworthy. Grant has no compunctions about destroying humanity, asserting that species that become extinct deserve their fate.

GRAY, DIANNE E.   Grew up on a farm near York, Nebraska, not far from the place that her great-grandparents homesteaded in 1869. This rural setting and its history provided the motivation and material for *Holding Up the Earth** (Houghton Mifflin, 2000), an American Library Association choice for young adults, which tells how an unhappy, lonely orphan girl finds inward peace, renewed spirit for life, and a home through learning about the family history of her foster mother and foster grandmother. *Together Apart* (Houghton, 2002) was inspired by a fierce storm that hit the Plains states in 1888. Gray and her husband live in Winona, Minnesota. They have two daughters and three grandsons.

GREELY CLEMONS (*The Reappearance of Sam Webber**)   African American janitor at Robert Poole Middle School, who becomes friend and protector of Sam Webber. An old man who moves and talks slowly, he first comes upon Sam in the boys' rest room, where he is throwing up from nervousness on his first day at school. Later, he comes into the rest room when Newt Novacek is bullying Sam, and he drags Newt to the office, rescues Sam from the hall monitor teacher, and escorts him, slowly, to his classroom. After that he shows up in the cafeteria and eats with Sam and walks to the bus stop with him, until he is sure Sam has enough confidence to stand up for himself. They often go to the Little Tavern, where Greely eats and Sam has a Coke, and where a dwarf named Rose often waits on them. After his heart attack, Greely insists on telling Sam about how he deserted his own family in Atlanta, one reason he has felt compelled to help the boy. Without this added information, Greely might be too good to be a believable character.

GRIFFIN, ADELE (1970–)   Born in Philadelphia, Pennsylvania; graduate of the University of Pennsylvania; author of novels for middle graders and early adolescents; resident of New York City. *Sons of Liberty** (Hyperion, 1997), an American Library Association choice for young adults, draws a parallel between the strife in a dysfunctional family and the American Revolution. *The Other Shepards** (Hyperion, 1998), a realistic problem novel with fantasy aspects cited by the American Library Association for children and young adults and also by *School Library Journal*, explores the effect on younger siblings when their parents idolize older children who died in an auto accident. Recent novels include *Amandine* (Hyperion, 2001), *Witch Twins* (Hyperion, 2001), *Witch Twins at Camp Bliss* (Hyperion, 2002), and *Overnight* (Putnam, 2003). For more information about Griffin and a title entry, see *Dictionary, 1995–1999* [*The Other Shepards*].

GRIMES, MARTHA   Born in Pittsburgh, Pennsylvania; professor of English, novelist. She grew up in Garrett County, Maryland, received both her B.A. and M.A. from the University of Maryland, and has more recently lived in Washington, D.C., and Santa Fe, New Mexico. Grimes has taught at the University of Iowa; at Frostburg (Maryland) State College; and Montgomery College, Takoma Park, Maryland. Her many mystery novels are mostly named for British pubs, among them *The Man with a Load of Mischief* (Little, Brown, 1981), *The Old Fox Deceiv'd* (Little, Brown, 1982), *The Jerusalem Inn* (Little, Brown, 1994), and *Help the Poor Struggler* (Little, Brown, 1985). Most of her mysteries have Richard Jury, Scotland Yard detective, as the main character. A departure from this pattern is *Hotel Paradise** (Knopf, 1996), set in a deteriorating resort hotel and narrated by a twelve-year-old girl, daughter of the cook and part owner.

GROOMS, ANTHONY (1955–   ) African American; born in Charlottesville, Virginia; received his B.A. in theater and speech from the College of William and Mary and his M.F.A. in English from George Mason University. He has had a long career as a professor of English and teacher of creative writing at such institutions of higher education as the University of Georgia, Morehouse College, and, most recently, at Kennesaw State University. Winner of several prestigious awards, among them Arts Administration Fellow for Literature, National Endowment for the Arts, he has published plays, a book of poems, and short stories, and has contributed prolifically to journals and anthologies. *Bombingham: A Novel** (Free Press, 2001), about the civil rights movement in Birmingham, Alabama, is his first novel. It was cited for young adults by *Booklist*. He also writes as Tony M. Grooms and has made his home in Atlanta, Georgia.

H

HABIBI (Nye*, Naomi Shihab, Simon & Schuster, 1997) Realistic, episodic novel set in recent years mostly in Jerusalem, Israel. Since Liyana, 14, and her younger brother, Rafik, have always known that their Palestinian-born doctor father, Poppy (Dr. Kamal Abboud), wishes to return to his homeland, they are not surprised when they learn that the family will move to Jerusalem where he has accepted a hospital position. They must make many adjustments, including learning the language, adapting to the customs, and fitting into the school system, but they have many good times, too. Tense moments arise from the Arab–Israeli conflict. Their grandmother's house in Ramallah is severely damaged by searching Israeli soldiers, and Poppy is jailed when he intervenes on behalf of a wounded Palestinian youth in a refugee camp. On the personal level, Liyana is attracted to a good-looking Israeli boy, a relationship that holds the potential for problems. The book seems to have a didactic intent, suggesting that possibilities for peace and harmony for Jews and Arabs lie with the younger generation. Earlier, the book received the Jane Addams Award and was cited by the American Library Association for middle readers. A fuller entry appears in *Dictionary, 1995–1999*. ALA/YA.

HADDIX, MARGARET PETERSON (1964–) Born in Washington Court House, Ohio; journalist, college instructor, author of a variety of novels for young people. *Leaving Fishers** (Simon & Schuster, 1997) is about a girl caught up in a religious cult and her difficulties in getting free. *Among the Hidden** (Simon & Schuster, 1998) is a futuristic fantasy about a forbidden third child in a totalitarian society that permits only two offspring. *Just Ella** (Simon & Schuster, 1999) is a fantasy with an entirely different tone, a light sequel to *Cinderella* telling about what happened after the prince came with the glass slipper. Two of her other novels, *Running Out of Time** (Simon & Schuster, 1995) and *Don't You Dare Read This, Mrs. Dunphrey** (Simon & Schuster, 1997), both won International Reading Association awards, among others, and are on the American Library Association Young Adult lists. Earlier biographical information and title entries appear in *Dictionary, 1995–1999* [*Don't You Dare Read This, Mrs. Dunphrey*; *Running Out of Time*].

HALL, ROBERT LEE (1941–) Born in San Francisco, California; artist, author of mysteries with historical settings. Hall attended the University of California–Berkeley from 1958 to 1960, and then California College of Arts and Crafts, receiving a B.A. in education in 1964, a B.F.A. in 1965, and an M.F.A. in 1968. He has worked in art departments of advertising agencies and taught high school art and English. His *London Blood: Further Adventures of the American Agent Abroad** (St. Martin's, 1997) is one of the more recent in a series of mysteries about Benjamin Franklin during his years in England. Among the others are *Benjamin Franklin and the Case of Artful Murder* (St. Martin's, 1994), *Benjamin Franklin and the Case of Christmas Murder* (St. Martin's, 1990), and *Benjamin Franklin Takes a Case* (St. Martin's, 1998). He is also the author of *Exit Sherlock Holmes: The Great Detective's Final Days* (Scribner, 1977) and *The King Edward Plot* (McGraw-Hill, 1980).

HAMILL, PETE (1935–) Born in Brooklyn, New York, the oldest of seven children of Irish immigrants; attended Pratt Institute and University of the Americas (formerly Mexico City College). He served in the U.S. Navy and was an advertising designer, becoming an award-winning writer and editor for such papers and journals as the *New York Post*, the *Saturday Evening Post*, *Esquire*, and the *New York Daily News*, of which he was editor when he published *Snow in August** (Little, Brown, 1997), which was chosen by

Booklist and for the Alex list. Hamill has said that the novel is "a mixture of memory and invention." It tells of anti-Semitism and racism in an Irish-Catholic neighborhood in Brooklyn from the standpoint of a boy of eleven who might have been Hamill himself. Hamill has published seven other novels, most recently *Diego Rivera* (Abrams, 1999); collections of his short stories and newspaper columns, including *Piecework* (Little, Brown, 1998); screenplays; and an autobiography: *A Drinking Life: A Memoir* (Little, Brown, 1994), which tells of his struggle with alcohol. He lives in New York City.

HANAUER, CATHI Author, editor, and writer for such national publications as *McCall's*, *Mademoiselle*, and *Seventeen*. *My Sister's Bones** (Delacorte, 1996) concerns how a college girl's anorexia affects the rest of the family as well as the girl herself. A first novel, it was cited by the American Library Association for young adults. Hanauer has also edited *The Bitch in the House* (Morrow, 2002), a collection of essays about their lives by twenty-six women. Hanauer lives with her family in New York City.

HANG A THOUSAND TREES WITH RIBBONS: THE STORY OF PHILLIS WHEATLEY (Rinaldi*, Ann, Harcourt, 1996) Biographical novel set mostly in Boston, Massachusetts, in the mid-1700s about the short, unhappy life of the historical first African American woman poet (1753–1784). Keziah is brought from Africa on a slave ship and bought at auction by John Wheatley, an affluent merchant, who renames her Phillis and gives her as a servant to his spoiled daughter, Mary. Phillis soon learns to read and write and excels in Greek and Latin. Noting that she is precocious, the Wheatleys indulge her and dress her in the finest attire. She composes poetry, travels to England, and becomes an international celebrity. Famous historical figures appear in the novel, which portrays the times well. For a longer, more detailed entry, see *Many Peoples, One Land* [no. 108]. ALA/YA.

HARD BALL (Weaver*, Will, Harper-Collins, 1998)   Boy's growing-up novel in a sports-story context set in August 1971, mostly on a farm near the northern Minnesota town of Flint, the third book in a series. Billy (William Jefferson) Baggs, 14, a farm boy with a terrific pitching arm, has two main problems: King Kenwood, the town boy who is his rival for starting pitcher on their high school team and for the affections of pretty Suzy Langden; and Abner, his tough, irascible, penny-pinching farmer father. On a bus trip with other town and country kids to see a Minnesota Twins game, Billy makes some time with Suzy but is also hit in the mouth by a foul ball. True to form, Abner resists getting the teeth fixed. Billy's sensible mother, Mavis, uses the money she makes working in town to take Billy to the dentist. Since the broken teeth are capped in stainless steel, Billy dreads school, but Mavis encourages him. She gets him new school clothes, even some like the town kids wear. Billy takes Suzy joyriding in the family pickup, helps his father make silage, and pitches the last Friday-night game of Town Team against Farm Team on the field on the Baggs farm. Because he cannot keep his mind on his pitching, he is removed and then spends time with Suzy, which gets him into a fight with King. When King's father, Mark, the local prosecuting attorney, and Abner exchange words, the boys claim that falls caused their injuries. Coach Anderson, however, who wants both boys playing for him, is furious. He insists that if the two boys want to be on the same baseball team, they must spend a whole school week together. For half of the first week, King proves he is no slouch at hard work. He shovels manure; helps Mavis with dishes (something neither Billy nor Abner does); is almost overcome by silo gas but is rescued by Billy; and labors extremely hard at sawing wood. Billy finds that King's life is very different from his. King's house is as big as three normal houses and slick-as-a-pin clean. Since King's homemaker mother has alcoholism, King does most of the cooking. He has no chores, but after school he is expected to work out in the well-appointed basement gym and then in the expensive batting cage in the yard. His father expects him to excel in sports and also in his studies. When Abner picks Billy up on Saturday, Mark tells Abner that if he sends Billy to high school in Buckman, Mark will see to it that the personal problems that Abner has incurred with the court will be dropped. Abner is so enraged that he drives his truck across the Kenwood lawn as they leave, cutting big ruts in the grass. The boys enlist Coach Anderson in a scheme suggested by Suzy. Coach summons Abner and Mark to school and tells them that both boys are on strike against them for certain reasons. Billy wants Abner to hire a man to help with the work because he is too tired even to stay awake in school all day; wants his father to be kinder; and wants Mavis to have a car of her own so she can drive to work. King's "striking points" are more moving. He wants Mark to stop embarrassing him by whining and yelling at King's games, and he wants Mark to stop comparing King to his older brother. Since the boys threaten to stop doing chores, working out, and playing sports altogether unless their fathers agree, the men take them seriously. Abner complies completely, and even takes Billy to a bakery to have a doughnut. For the first time in weeks, Billy sleeps late in the morning. He thinks maybe he can even get an A in English, and most important of all, he feels better about himself than he ever has. The book is a study in human relationships, a "people" story more than a sports story, sports merely motivating part of the plot. The best part of the novel is its vivid and convincing descriptions of life on the farm. ALA/YA.

HARD LOVE (Wittlinger*, Ellen, Simon & Schuster, 1999)   Contemporary realistic boy's growing-up novel set in and near Boston, Massachusetts. When John Galardi, 16, the narrator, starts his own zine (self-published literary magazine) and makes friends with a bright Puerto Rican American girl, Marisol, who also puts out a zine, he identifies his straight gender orientation, comes to terms with his parents' divorce and their new lives, and has a more positive attitude toward life. John and Marisol are convincing, events are believable, and the style is crisp and contemporary. Earlier the novel was cited by *School Library Journal*. For a longer entry, see *Dictionary, 1995–1999*. ALA/YA; Printz Honor.

HARDMAN, RIC LYNDEN   Born in Seattle, Washington; freelance writer. His *Sunshine Rider: The First Vegetarian Western** (Delacorte, 1998) was named to the American Library Association list for young adults. He holds college degrees, served in the U.S. Marine Corps, and has made his home in California with his wife and two children. He has also published *Fifteen Flags* (Little, Brown, 1968), *The Chaplain's Raid* (Bantam, 1966), *No Other Harvest* (Doubleday, 1962), and *The Rare* *Breed* (Fawcett, 1966). He plans a sequel to *Sunshine Rider*.

HARLEY LIKE A PERSON (Bauer*, Cat, Winslow, 2000)   Girl's growing-up novel, set in Lenape Lakes, New Jersey, in the late twentieth century. The narrator, Harley Columba, 14, starts high school with the usual qualms and hopes, but she carries with her the results of a dysfunctional family and her conviction, partly because she is blue-eyed in an otherwise brown-eyed household, that she is adopted. Her heavy-drinking father, Roger, and her mother, Peppy, yell at each other and at their three kids, Harley, her brother, Bean, and her little sister, Lily. Her freshman-year experience follows a pattern predictable from many novels: She has a falling out with her best friend, Carla Van Owen; she is delighted with the attention of Johnny Bruno and hurt when he reverts to his former girlfriend, Prudence Clark; she falls in love with an older boy, senior Evan Lennon, who asks her to the Spring Ball; she tries both alcohol and marijuana with him; after he is arrested for dealing drugs and banned from school property, she goes to the ball with his friend, Oliver, who is drunk and causes a disturbance, so her parents (who think she is with Evan) are called, and she is grounded "for life." Three things raise this novel above a dozen others with virtually the same sequence of events. One is Harley's voice, which is both convincing and funny. The others are her artistic ability and her detective work to find her real father. When a portrait is needed for the stage production of *Anastasia*, her art teacher suggests Harley who, after reading the script and thinking it over, decides they need portraits for each of the three acts, the first with no features at all, the second, when Anastasia is beginning to persuade some people that she is authentic, with a suggestion of her face filled in, and the third, a complete portrait of the proud, aristocratic girl who has proven her heritage. After the fiasco at the Spring Ball, she is barred from finishing the paintings, though her art teacher and the producer of the play protest. Her search for her birth father follows several clues, mainly a harlequin doll she discovers in the storage area, with a note to "my Harleykins. Papa loves you forever and a day," written in the same handwriting as a note in Peppy's high school yearbook by Sean Shanahan, Carla's father, who left to become an artist in New York City. Furious and hurt when she is barred from the *Anastasia* production, Harley takes a bus to New York City and hunts up Sean, who she suspects is her father as well as Carla's. In his loft apartment in Greenwich Village, he first denies any relationship to her, but after her determined questioning, he finally admits that he was involved with both their mothers when they were young and that Roger agreed to marry Peppy if Sean would stay out of their lives after that. Disillusioned but satisfied that she at last has some truth about her origin, Harley returns to Lenape High School, gets the janitor to let her into the art room, and finishes the portrait of Anastasia. The last chapter, set on the night of the production, tries to tie all the ends together. Harley (holding roses sent by Sean), her mother, and, improbably, Evan sit together in the audience. Roger comes in, vodka on his breath, sits with them and says to Harley "Good work," the first compliment he has ever given her. Just how they all reached this stage of compatibility is not spelled out. It is clear that Harley's self-esteem is greatly improved, and it is implied that her confidence will carry her through any further difficulties. The parallel between her quest for recognition and Anastasia's is obvious. ALA/YA.

HARMETZ, ALJEAN   Culture and entertainment correspondent for the *New York Times* in California, writer. She received her B.A. from Stanford University, and has made her home in Los Angeles. Most of her books have been nonfiction, dealing with movies and moviemaking, but *Off the Face of the Earth** (Scribner, 1997) is a departure, the story of the abduction from a shopping mall of a boy and his eventual rescue, largely through his good sense and cleverness and his mother's unrelenting efforts. Harmetz has also been a contributing editor for *Esquire*.

HAROLD LOGAN (*My Father's Scar: A Novel**)   Abusive, drunken father of Andy, a man who was a football star in high school and has never achieved such glory again. His face bears a scar from a tackle he once threw "with too much force and too little form." The referee called it unnecessary roughness; he calls it his "badge of honor." He has no understanding of, or sympathy for, his bookish son, constantly deriding him for his weight and forcing him into impossible situations like his confrontation with Billy Curtis. As Andy enters the teen years, Harold is drinking so heavily that he loses his job, and he becomes increasingly abusive, verbally and psychologically to his wife and physically to his son, who frequently has to explain away black eyes and bruises as clumsy falls. Although Harold's actions have often shown that he has doubts about his son's masculinity, Andy's announcement that he is gay triggers a violent response, and he shouts at the boy to get out and never come back. While he despises and hates his father, Andy still wonders whether his own inability to be the football hero Harold must have hoped for is the cause of his alcoholism.

HARUF, KENT (1943–)   Born in Pueblo, Colorado; educator, writer. Haruf received his B.A. from Nebraska Wesleyan University in 1965 and his M.F.A. from the University of Iowa in 1973. He served in the Peace Corps in Turkey in the late 1960s, taught high school English in Wisconsin and Colorado, and has been a professor at Nebraska Wesleyan University and at Southern Illinois University–Carbondale. All of his novels are set in the fictional small town of Holt, Colorado, near the Kansas border, including *The Tie That Binds* (Holt, 1984), about a woman who gives up love to care for her tyrannical but crippled father, and *Where You Once Belonged* (Summit Books, 1991), about an abusive ex-high school football hero, a novel described as "taut and deadly." *Plainsong** (Knopf, 1999), also set in Holt, has a more complicated structure, following three groups of characters whose lives intertwine. Haruf is noted for a lean prose style and moving stories, with no sentimentality. He has also published short stories in various periodicals and in *Best American Short Stories* (Houghton, 1987) and *Where Past Meets Present* (University of Colorado Press, 1994).

THE HAUNTING (Nixon*, Joan Lowery, Delacorte, 1998)   Mystery novel revolving around a haunted house set in recent years mostly near Baton Rouge, Louisiana. Introverted, shy, bookish Lia Marie Starling, 15, the narrator, is seated beside the bed of her comatose ninety-six-year-old great-grandmother, Sarah Langley, when Sarah suddenly awakens, grabs Lia's arm tightly, and speaks her last words: that she is leaving the pre–Civil War Greek Revival ancestral plantation house known as Graymoss to Anne Starling, Lia's mother; that Graymoss must be protected; that the family must stay away from it because it is haunted by a terrible evil; and that they must read the diary of Charlotte* Blevins, Lia's great-great-great-grandmother, who was the last person to live at Graymoss. Anne, a strong-willed psychologist, is delighted to have Graymoss, because now she and Derek, Lia's father, can fulfill their dream of providing a home for unadoptable children. Lia reads the diary left by Charlotte, then sixteen, which tells how Charlotte's grandfather Placide's overseer, Morgan Slade, threatened Placide and Charlotte in the last days before the Union soldiers came; how the Union soldiers shot Placide but left without burning the place because Charlotte bravely stood up to them; and how on that very night, the house seemed to come alive with grimacing faces in moldings, whispers, and a strong sense of evil and suffocation. Charlotte was driven from the house and never lived there again. While Lia experiences strange happenings when she and her mother visit, Anne pooh-poohs her story, Charlotte's misgivings, and the accounts of terrible events happening especially at night told them by old Charlie Boudreau, the caretaker, and others interested in the place. Mrs. Ava Phipps, the old woman who occupies the former overseer's house, says they will not be able to live there unless they find the reason for the evil and put it to rest. She challenges Lia to do just that. More untoward events occur, including some bad mishaps that involve the police, before Lia succeeds. Using the diary and grandfather Blevins's book mentioned in the diary, *Favorite Tales of Edgar Allan Poe*, which something in Graymoss pushed from its shelf into Lia's hands, she figures out that the evil emanates from the ghost of Morgan Slade, who was murdered by Placide to protect Charlotte, and from Placide's own ghost. Lia discovers Slade's body interred in the basement, lying beside the valuables from Graymoss that he had stolen. She orders his ghost to depart and then tells Placide that his ghost can go, too, since from now on the house will be in good hands. Lia develops credibly, if predictably, into an assertive, more confident young woman, able to express herself and take charge of situations. Most of the characters, with the exception of determined Anne, are functionaries and overdrawn. Even though the end requires a stretch of the imagination, the twentieth-century story has enough gothic conventions to keep the reader's attention. More engrossing though short is the diary story of how Charlotte confronts several terrors: the vicious Slade, the sudden death of her grandfather, the drunken soldiers, the possible loss of her home, and the horrible evil that so rapidly envelopes the house she has come to love. ALA/YA.

HAUTMAN, PETE (1952–   )   Born in Berkeley, California; freelance writer. His complex time-slip fantasy, *Mr. Was** (Simon & Schuster, 1996), was a nominee for the Edgar Allan Poe Award, and, more recently, was added to the American Library Association Young Adult list. For earlier biographical information and a title entry, see *Dictionary, 1995–1999* [*Mr. Was*].

HAYES, DANIEL (1952–   )   Born in Troy, New York; graduate of State University of New York at both Plattsburgh and Albany; high school English teacher; author of novels for young adults; resident of Schaghticoke, New York. His lighthearted mystery novel, *Flyers** (Simon & Schuster, 1996), lauded for its entertain-

ing story and aptness at catching the behavior and attitudes of teenage boys, was nominated for the Edgar Allan Poe Award and cited by the American Library Association for young adults. Among his recent publications is *Juan Verdades: The Man Who Could Not Tell a Lie* (Orchard, 2001), a picture storybook. For more details about Hayes and more titles, see *Dictionary, 1995–1999* [*Flyers*; *No Effect*].

HEAD ABOVE WATER (Rottman*, S. L., Peachtree, 1999)   Sports novel featuring a present-day high school girl whose ambition for her junior year is to get a good enough time in the 200-meter freestyle swimming event to qualify for the state meet. The narrator, Skye Johnson, 16, is an excellent swimmer and a hard worker, training almost compulsively, but her other responsibilities almost defeat her. Because her divorced mother must work not only as a secretary during the day but as a bartender at night, the housework and the care of Skye's older brother, Sunny, who has Down's syndrome, are almost all on her shoulders. In addition, she has started going with Mike Banner, a senior and football star, who is far from content with the restrictions on her life. As their relationship progresses, Mike starts pressing her to have sex with him, and about the same time Sunny decides he wants to learn to swim. Because he had a bad experience in a pool when he was about eight, he has not wanted to try until now, although he has patiently waited for Skye at every practice so she can walk him home, and he cheers vigorously for her at meets. Unfortunately, he wants Skye to teach him, and her mother thinks that it is a good idea. Unable to face losing more of her free time to his care, Skye makes a deal with one of the instructors to put him in a beginner's class, making him promise to keep the arrangement secret from their mother. Although he sulks and hates being in with little kids, Sunny agrees. After a bit, the instructor catches on, tells him he is promoted to being her assistant, and he starts loving it, asking only that Skye take him to free swim on days when there are no classes. Although he is in special classes at the same school she goes to, she cannot leave him alone and is not allowed to have friends in the house when their mother is not home, so she takes his lesson time to see Mike, even going to his house when his parents are gone. Like her best friend, Jenny, who has a sweet and compliant boyfriend, she has thought about sex and decided to wait, at least until she is older, but Mike at first tries to persuade her, then force her. She knees him in the groin and escapes, hurt and furious. Jenny says that Mike has told everyone he broke up with her because she had been pursuing him too hard and was no good in bed, and wants her to report him to police or at least school authorities, but she refuses, knowing he will put the blame on her. At the homecoming dance, for which she is nominated to be a princess and has had to beg a date from a swim meet acquaintance at another school, she is waylaid by Mike. He tries to kiss her, and when she evades him, says abusive things about Sunny. Without thinking, she slugs him, connecting solidly with his jaw, then following through with a left which he ducks. She hits the locker behind him, and her hand explodes in pain. That night her mother takes her to the hospital, and the doctor says her hand must be in a cast for six weeks, preventing her from swimming at the state meet. After prying the whole story from Skye, her mother calls Mike's parents, and the next day Skye is called to the counselor's office where Mike, obviously unrepentant, gives her a pro-forma apology. Since the Special Olympics and the state meet are on the same day, her mother has been torn about which to attend, but now decides they will all go to the Special Olympics event. Skye insists that she must be at the state meet to support her team. She rides with a friend and watches through the morning, then decides to go to the city pool to watch Sunny. He has already swum two events but is discouraged because he has not won. Skye finds him and gives him advice and encouragement. When he wins his heat in the longer 100-meter freestyle, he is delighted, and when he gets a medal for second place in the race, he gives it to Skye. She realizes that he loves and admires her, and that she loves and admires him, too. Although swimming is important in the novel, the main problems for Skye are her infatuation with Mike and her almost overwhelming burden of having to take care of Sunny. The difficulties of coping with a developmentally disabled sibling are not glossed over, and Skye is shown as an unusually competent teenager. Mike, however, is perhaps too self-centered and clueless to be entirely believable, especially in the way he treats Sunny, pushing him in the halls and calling him a retard, even when he still wants to make an impression on Skye. Descriptions of the actual swimming make one want to dive into a pool. ALA/YA.

HEARTLIGHT (Bradley*, Marion Zimmer, Tor, 1998) Broad-canvas, adult, near-reality, good-versus-evil fantasy set from 1960 to 1999 in San Francisco, California, and variously in Massachusetts and New York and concluding in Washington, D.C. Colin MacLaren, thirty-ish, has been a dedicated and sworn

Lightworker in the ongoing conflict between the Light (or forces of good) and the Dark (or forces of evil), beginning in World War II, in which it appears his Order, and others aligned with good, triumphed. Having received a Ph.D. in psychology with emphasis on parapsychology, Colin accepts a teaching position at the University of California–Berkeley, the next phase of his response to his "heartlight" (or call) throughout this long, complex, sometimes tedious, and overextended novel of many episodes and huge cast of characters. At Berkeley, he renews acquaintance with his longtime friend, Alison Margrave, who nurtures young people in the way of the Light. One of these is Simon Anstey, at fifteen already an extremely promising harpsichordist and sometime dabbler in Magick (the occult). Colin also soon meets Claire London, a young nursing student and Sensitive (or psychic) who tells small portions of the story and upon whose extrasensory abilities Colin often depends. Through Simon, Colin encounters Toller Hasloch, a practitioner of Black Magick, with whom he contends thereafter and whom he reports to his superiors as working for a renaissance of the Thulist movement in Germany that precipitated World War II and, as he learns later, is behind many of the troubles and disasters, like the assassination of John F. Kennedy, that afflict the United States during the century. Against the rules of his Order, Colin kills Toller but later discovers that Toller somehow escaped and is alive and active. Others who affect Simon's life are Thorne Blackburn, who founds a Magick movement, becomes a New Age cult figure, and dies mysteriously on his New York estate; John Cannon, an "innocent" who collects information for a book on the occult; Father Mansell, a defrocked priest now into

Magick; and Emily Barnes, whom Simon, unable to play owing to an accident, is prevented from sacrificing as a means of restoring his own lost musical ability. Both Colin and Claire then become involved in combating occult problems that touch Claire's young cousin, Rowan Moorcock. Colin destroys the evil Church of the Antique Rite after harrowing struggles, and in the late 1990s manages with Rowan's help to be in on the destruction of Toller Hasloch, by this time a mogul and malevolent force on Washington D.C.'s Beltway. Retired, Colin passes the mantle of his order and the heartlight call to fight for Good to Rowan. The capsule summary of and Colin's conclusions about twentieth-century American history as measured against his Order's fight for Good, particularly with respect to the increasing corruption of government and corresponding apathy of the public, and the notion that history is made on an entirely different plane from the ordinary human one are the book's most fascinating aspects. Colin's ongoing efforts to live up to his ideals and his charge to help and protect, particularly those who are unaware of the Dark powers, endear him to the reader. Since the book is very long, occupied often with details of Magickal rites, and demanding—it requires dedication just to keep track of the characters, of whom only a very few are listed above—the novel will probably appeal most to diehard fantasy readers and to Bradley devotees. *Heartlight* has several companion books. Booklist.

HEAVEN (Johnson*, Angela, Simon & Schuster, 1998)   Girl's growing-up novel set in Heaven, Ohio, presumably in the late twentieth century, in which Mandy Carroll, 14, learns that the couple she has considered her parents are really her aunt and uncle, and that the man she has thought of as her favorite uncle is actually her father. The news upsets her greatly, but she comes to terms with it. For a longer entry, see *Many Peoples, One Land* [no. 58]. ALA/YA.

HENRY VIII (*Mary, Bloody Mary**; *The Secret Diary of Anne Boleyn**)   King of England. In *Mary,* he is the father of Mary Tudor, who tells the story. Both as a king and as a father, Henry is shown as willful, despotic, demanding, and increasingly degenerate. At first he is indulgent toward and proud of his beautiful little daughter by Catherine* (Katherine*) of Aragon, and the child is petted and loved. Later, when he seeks to marry Anne* Boleyn, Mary becomes a political and personal liability to the extent that she feels her life is in danger. There is little appealing about Henry as he appears in Mary's story. In *Secret Diary,* he is the husband of Anne Boleyn and father of Elizabeth* I. He is physically attractive, handsome, fun loving, and athletic during the early part of his relationship with Anne. Later, his body reflects his increasingly dissolute ways, and he becomes obese, bloated, and diseased, very unpleasant. He is also obstinate, manipulative, capricious, and autocratic. In marrying Anne, he separates the Church of England, of which he makes himself Supreme Head, from the Roman Catholic Church and starts the Reformation in England.

HERO (Rottman*, S. L., Peachtree, 1997) Growing-up novel of a troubled and abused boy in Oklahoma in the late 1990s. Suspended from school for fighting with his onetime friend, Rick, Sean Parker, 15, the narrator, is also arrested for curfew violation and sent to Carbondale Ranch to perform his community service. There he finds the elderly owner, Dave Hassler, reasonable and generally mild mannered, but unwilling to put up with any surliness, backtalk, or lazy work. At first resentful at having to shovel manure, although pleased with the food that is better and more plentiful than he is used to, Sean is secretly attracted to the horses. The first afternoon a turning point comes in his life when a mare goes into labor prematurely, and Hassler, with his hired man, James, works frantically to get the foal turned to the correct position and born, while Sean on his knees holds the mare's head. As soon as the foal is born, Hassler takes it to a clean stall and tells Sean to clean it up while they deal with the mother. After Sean has wiped down and given the little colt a bottle, Hassler explains that Manda, the mare, produces good offspring but is a bad mother, even killing her first foal and injuring her second, so they will hand-feed this one. Sean bonds with the new colt, partly because of the circumstances of its birth but also because his own mother is so abusive that he has feared she will some day kill him. On the second day the colt, which Sean has named "Knicker," is not doing too well. That evening Sean's mother confronts him, drunk and demanding the money that she thinks he is earning at the ranch. Though he protests that it is unpaid community service, she hits him repeatedly and knocks his head back against a nail that protrudes from the wall until he passes out. When he comes to, she has gone, and he flees, at first aimlessly, then heads out to the ranch and climbs into Knicker's stall, where in the morning Hassler finds them cuddled together. The doctor Hassler summons says that Sean has a slight concussion and an infection where his head hit the nail and advises bed rest, but Sean insists on taking care of Knicker, and Hassler lets him, saying he can stay at the ranch for the whole week if he lets one of his parents know. His mother, who spends her nights on the street, is not home, and he dares not talk to his father, whom he has almost never seen since the divorce nine years before, and whom he blames for taking him back, after their infrequent times together, to his abusive mother. In the next days, he bonds even more closely to Knicker and vacillates between admiring and resenting Hassler. He is astonished when his English teacher, Mrs. Walker, shows up at the ranch, evidently a friend of Hassler since she worked there as a teenager. From James, he learns that Hassler was a hero in World War II, returning against orders to save his platoon mates even though he was wounded. Before the weekend is through, Sean is summoned to the hospital, where his mother has been taken suffering from kidney failure, liver trouble, and related problems. There his father shows up, agrees to pay the bill for his ex-wife, and orders Sean to go home and wait for him there. Sean stands up to him, accuses him of trying to take over after nine years of neglect, then runs. Hassler picks him up and on the way back to the ranch admits that he intervened, told Mr. Parker off, and hit him, and now may be sued for assault. The next evening, Manda attacks Sean when he starts to clean her stall, and he beats her back with a shovel. The vet comes for Manda, and Hassler takes Sean to the hospital, where the boy, who is appalled at his own violence, finally tells the doctor who stitches his shoulder and Hassler about his mother. Things seem to be going well for Sean until Rick, who has taken up drug dealing, traces him to the ranch and thinks it will be a good place to store his stash. High on whatever he is selling, he waves a gun around and threatens to shoot Knicker, while Sean tries to talk him down. When Hassler shows up and Rick points the gun at him, Sean leaps in front and gets a bullet in the chest. The epilogue, which is in the third person, is set in the hospital room where Hassler is keeping vigil and Mrs. Walker comes in, cheered to hear that the doctors are hopeful, and shows the essay Sean wrote about heroes for her class, a paper still cynical but showing the influence that his time at the ranch has had on him. The main problem with the novel is the time frame. If Sean's redemption were stretched over six months or a year, it could be believable, but the change is too great to occur in a week, along with three major injuries and several serious confrontations. The stories of Hassler's war service are introduced heavy-handedly and are unnecessary to show what a fine person he is. The strongest element is Sean's distrust of almost everyone, his own self doubt, and his delight in the affection of the little colt. ALA/YA.

HEROES (Cormier*, Robert, Dell Laurel Leaf, 1998)   Grim variation on the boy's coming-of-age novel, ironically titled, with mystery-story aspects. Terribly injured in World War II, Francis Cassavant, the narrator, returns to Frenchtown in Monument, Massachusetts, with one goal: to kill Larry LaSalle, former director of the Frenchtown Recreation Center, known locally as the Wreck Center. Since he has virtually no face, his nose, lips, and much of his cheeks having been blown off by a grenade, Francis keeps a scarf over the lower half of his face, and no one recognizes him except one drunken ex-GI, who respects his desire to be anonymous. Most of the story is told in flashbacks. An orphan, Francis lived with his Uncle Louis until, at fifteen, he lied about his age and joined the army. Uncle Louis moved to Canada during the war, and Nicole Renard's family has moved to Albany, New York, so there is no one in Monument that Francis wants to see except LaSalle, the local hero who won a Silver Star and who, Francis is sure, will return to the town. Through most of the novel, the reader does not know why he is stalking LaSalle. The flashbacks alternate between war memories and those of his years in Monument. In seventh grade at St. Jude's Parochial School, he meets Nicole, who seldom says more than hello to him but who seems to signal more with her eyes, and he falls hopelessly in love. Then charismatic Larry LaSalle, a dancer from New York, comes to Monument to run the newly opened Wreck Center, and life changes for all of the town's teenagers. Since Uncle Louis, though kind, is a silent man, Francis is lonely and spends most of his free time at the center, where LaSalle is busy teaching crafts, organizing teams, and directing shows. He decides that Francis will be the champion at table tennis and teaches him relentlessly. Francis, though too small for most competitive sports, is blessed with quick responses and soon becomes skillful. Nicole is the best dancer at the center, and LaSalle stars her in several productions. For the December celebration, there is to be a table tennis tournament on Saturday and a musical show on Sunday, at which Nicole will be featured in a number called "Dancing in the Dark." To his own surprise, Francis wins the tournament on Saturday, then, by popular demand, plays Larry LaSalle, who lets Francis win while making it look as if the boy's skill triumphs. The next day is December 7, and after Pearl Harbor, LaSalle joins up and the Wreck Center closes. Francis gets a job in the drugstore, where Nicole often drops in, and soon they are going together

to the Saturday movie matinees. LaSalle becomes an officer in the Marines, wins a Silver Star for action at Guadalcanal, and returns on a furlough to the adulation of the whole town. For the teenagers, he reopens the Wreck Center where they play games and dance, until just LaSalle, Nicole, and Francis are left. Pleading one last dance with Nicole, LaSalle sends Francis home. Sensing some reluctance from the girl, Francis stays in the hallway while LaSalle puts on a record and turns off the lights. Before he really knows what is happening, Francis realizes he is hearing LaSalle raping Nicole. She rushes out, disheveled, sees Francis, and dashes off into the dark. The next morning, LaSalle leaves town. When Francis tries to talk with Nicole, she tells him to go away, obviously blaming him for not preventing the assault. Later that week, Francis climbs to the top of the steeple of St. Jude's, intending to throw himself off, but decides he does not want to leave that legacy to his parents' memory. Instead, he alters his birth certificate and joins the army. His heroic action in throwing himself on the grenade is really another suicide attempt, resulting in his horrible disfigurement. When he finally learns that LaSalle has returned, he goes to the small apartment, taking the gun he has been carrying since he arrived in Monument, and confronts the man. He finds LaSalle almost unable to walk, his legs having been injured, and unrepentant, saying he loves the "sweet young things" but that his dancing days are over. As Francis points the gun at him, he pulls out his own gun, empties it so there is no threat to Francis, and asks him to leave. As Francis does, he hears the gunshot from the room above. Later, through one of the retired school nuns, he traces Nicole to a school in Albany where they talk and both realize that there is no going back. She tells him she may become a teacher and encourages him to be a writer. The ending is ambiguous; he has discarded the address of the plastic surgeon who might repair his face, and he still has his gun, but the book itself may mean that he found something better than suicide. ALA/YA.

HESSE, KAREN (1952–)   Born in Baltimore, Maryland; author of unusual books for young people. *The Music of Dolphins** (Scholastic, 1996), a novel of a feral girl who has been raised by dolphins, was on the Best Books for Children list of the *School Library Journal*. More recently, it was named to the American Library Association Young Adult list. Earlier biographical information and title entries appear in *Dictionary, 1995–1999* [*The Music of Dolphins*; *Phoenix Rising*].

HESSER, TERRY SPENCER   Author of *Kissing Doorknobs** (Delacorte, 1998), an American Library Association choice for young adults about a girl who suffers from Obsessive-Compulsive Disorder. Many details come from Hesser's own adolescent experience with the disorder as well as from her investigations about it, among others while serving on the Obsessive Compulsive Foundation of Metropolitan Chicago, where she lives. In addition to being a novelist, she is a feature writer, playwright, and independent television producer and has received awards for her work, including being nominated for an Emmy three times.

HEWETT, LORRI   Born in Virginia, raised in Littleton, Colorado; author of several books with African American characters. She is a 1994 graduate of Emory College and when she was a senior, she published her first book, *Coming of Age* (Holloway House, 1994), a story set in Denver for four to eight year olds. Her novels include *Soulfire* (Dutton, 1996), set in Denver housing projects and described as an "angry, rough-hewn inner city story"; *Lives of Our Own* (Dutton, 1998), about a Denver girl's culture shock when she moves to Georgia; and *Dancer** (Dutton, 1999), the story of an African American girl determined to be a ballerina. Hewett lives in Decatur, Georgia.

HIDDEN TALENTS (Lubar*, David, Tor, 1999)   Novel of an alternative school somewhere in Pennsylvania that starts with grim realism and develops into a clever and often amusing fantasy. Martin Anderson, 13, is sent to Edgeview Alternative School, having been expelled from every other school available. Edgeview is a dumping ground for boys so dysfunctional that everyone has given up on them. Martin has difficulty with authority and manages to insult teachers, parents, and anyone else in a position demanding respect with barbs aimed deftly to hit the most sensitive spot in the psyche, saying the one unforgivable thing in each instance. At Edgeview he is put in a room with Torchie, who starts fires. He soon meets Bloodbath, a large bully who beats on the smaller boys relentlessly, and Lip, Bloodbath's sidekick. Martin gets on well with Torchie, though he has to smother some smoldering spots and extinguish several blazes in their room, all of which Torchie claims he had nothing to do with. After a short time he names among his other friends Cheater, a small, very smart boy of Oriental heritage, whose perfect marks are always assumed to be the result of copying; Lucky, known as a thief; Flinch, a jumpy kid who makes teachers jittery; and Trash, who is ostracized because he unpredictably throws things.

The teachers are an odd assortment. Principal Davis seems to have no clue about what is really going on. Within a week, Martin has infuriated all of them by his remarks when they pressure him to tell the class something about himself. For instance, to Mr. Luther Parsons, math teacher, who combs a few strands of hair over his bare scalp, he says, "Hi. I'm Martin Anderson, and I'm not bald." To the history teacher, Ms. Crenshaw, an aspiring actress who likes to have her students dress up in period costumes, he remarks that it's as close as she'll ever get to Broadway. The New Student Evaluation Forms, which are printed at the end of chapters, call him destructive and vicious. Also printed in boxes are letters, some from Martin's sister, Teri, who misses him, and some, never sent, from his mother who is cowed by his bullying father. After a couple of weeks, Torchie and the other kids who hang around their room let him in on a secret: on Friday nights they have figured out a way to get into town by going on a makeshift rope ladder out a window, then through a drain tunnel under the high fence around the school. In town, they mostly play games in the pinball arcade until one night they are waylaid by a group of townies who want to beat them up, but they manage to escape. By watching the others closely, Martin figures out that each of the five has a special power, that Trash is telekinetic, moving objects without even touching them. Cheater reads minds. Torchie starts fires mentally. Flinch sees into the future, briefly, so he can dodge balls or fists. Lucky hears voices telling him where to look for things of value. All these talents get the boys into trouble. When Martin tells them, they at first do not believe him, but he works out a science-class project that proves it. All

this time, because of political pressures, the school is in danger of being closed. When the inspection team that will decide arrives, Bloodbath and his sidekicks are determined to make a big disruption. By now, Martin and his five see that the school is better than being transferred to a big, impersonal institution, and by using all their talents, they discover that the bullies have set a series of bombs throughout the school, to be triggered by candles. Torchie, who has learned from Martin to reverse his powers, puts them out. When the inspectors choose Martin to tell them candidly about the school, Principal Davis and most of the teachers groan, but Martin has learned from his friends that he, too, has a power: he can sense what a person most fears or hates. With great self-control, he resists either insulting the team members or buttering them up, and he gives them a frank appraisal of the school, suggesting that they get rid of the most troublesome boys like Bloodbath and arrange some way that a boy who improves can be released back to his home school. What he says makes sense to the inspectors, and the school is saved. In the end, all the six with hidden talents have learned to control them and are headed back to normal society. Far from the grim reform school story that it starts to be, the novel is light, entertaining, and gets a lot of real humor from its eccentric characters as described in Martin's uninhibited voice. ALA/YA.

HIGHER EDUCATION (Sheffield*, Charles, and Jerry Pournelle*, Tor, 1996) Futuristic science fiction and boy's coming-of-age novel set on Earth and somewhere in space for several months. When the dirty trick that nearly illiterate, surly Rick (Ricardo) Luban, 16, of Simi Valley, California, plans for a new teacher backfires and embarrasses an important political and educational official, he is summarily expelled from high school and thus doomed, probably, to a short, hard life on the streets, since jobs even for trained people are scarce. Mr. Hamel, tough, hard-nosed biology teacher, suggests he go to a certain address where they might have a job for him. There he is interviewed by computer for Vanguard Mining, a space firm, passes the interview, flies to Albuquerque, New Mexico, where he joins other recruits, disillusioned, rebellious dropouts or expellees like himself, and then to Tularema on the Mescalero–Apache Sovereign Nation. Like the other recruits, he is subjected to a grueling series of paper and physical tests. He also makes a sort of friend in Alice Klein, a knowledgeable woman from the Black Hills of South Dakota, and an enemy in a black tough, Vido Valdez, from Anchorage, Alaska. The twenty survivors of the tests, Rick among them, are taken by SSTO (single-stage-to-orbit vehicle) to CM-2 (Commercial Mine-2), an asteroid, for intensive training, after which they will be trained still further elsewhere as apprentices. Of the many, barely fleshed characters, belligerent Deedee Mao becomes Rick's love interest as well as coworker, and Jigger Tait and Gina Styan help to organize the recruits. The recruits struggle with reading, writing, and math, because they have always used reading machines and calculators, with physical exercise, with taking and following directions, and with showing initiative and resource. Unless they achieve and obey, they do not eat, success being rewarded with meal tickets. The plot reaches a melodramatic climax when Rick enters an SM (smelting module) that they were assigned to clean and finds Jigger and Alice engaged in a terrible physi-

cal struggle. Rick acts quickly, but Jigger kills Alice. It comes out that Jigger and Gina Styan are agents for Vanguard Security. Alerted that a saboteur may be among the new recruits, they have identified Alice Klein as an agent for a rival space-mining company, Avant, bent on sabotage. Impressed with Rick's work, Jigger invites him to join Security in a totally new enterprise, one planned in cooperation with Avant—to clean up the inept, corrupt school system on Earth. Rick refuses. He has matured considerably but is not yet ready to tackle such an assignment. Characters are predictable and flat, some sex and trash talk appear, space jargon and situations are used extensively, and the concept of mining asteroids is developed convincingly. For science fiction fans, action and technology abounds. Beyond that, plenty of social commentary appears in the descriptions of conditions on Earth—the feudalistic economy involving a vast gap between rich and poor, in which only those who go to company-run schools get jobs; drug- and crime-ridden streets; broken families; and hardest hit, with biting satire, the mind-deadening school system, in which the aim is to keep kids through high school so their parents can get the government stipend that attendance ensures, but which emphasizes conformity and feeling good rather than learning. The title obviously plays with words. Booklist.

HILL, ERNEST   Born in Oak Grove, Louisiana; writer of novels dealing with the difficult lives of young African American men. Hill is a graduate of the University of California–Berkeley, and received his master's degree from Cornell University. He has since been a doctoral fellow in history at the University of California–Los Angeles. He has also been writer-in-residence at Southern University in Baton Rouge. His novel, *A Life for a Life** (Simon & Schuster, 1998), set in rural Louisiana, is about a boy imprisoned for killing a clerk in a small store and his mentor, the father of the young man he killed, who visits him in prison, gives him a place to stay upon his release, and eventually sees him get an education and make something of himself. An earlier, more pessimistic novel, *Satisfied With Nothin'* (Simon & Schuster, 1996), is about a boy who, after difficulties in an integrated school, makes the football team and seems destined to succeed but is injured and slips back into hopelessness.

HOBBS, WILL(IAM CARL) (1947–) Popular and critically acclaimed writer of eighteen survival and adventure novels, some of them based on history. Educated at Stanford University, he was a reading and English teacher before becoming a full-time writer in 1990. He lives in Colorado, the location of several of his books. Three of his books have been selected by the American Library Association for young adults. *Far North** (Morrow, 1996) concerns two boys, one a Slavey Indian, the other white, who survive a winter together in the rugged Mackenzie Mountains of the Canadian Northwest Territories. *The Maze** (Morrow, 1998) is set in a particularly rugged part of Utah's Canyonlands National Park. *Jason's Gold** (HarperCollins, 1999), a historical adventure and survival story about incredible hardships during the Klondike gold rush, was inspired by his fascination for the period. Recent titles include *Down the Yukon* (HarperCollins, 2001), the sequel to *Jason's Gold*, and *Wild Man Island* (HarperCollins, 2002), an Alaska survival story. For more information about Hobbs, titles, and title entries, see *Dictionary,* *1995–1999* [*Far North*; *Ghost Canoe*; *The Maze*].

HOGAN, LINDA (1947–) Highly acclaimed Native American Chickasaw novelist, poet, essayist, short story writer, and playwright; born in Denver, Colorado; winner of numerous distinctions, including a Guggenheim Fellowship and a Colorado Book Award for *The Book of Medicines* (Coffee House, 1993), poems. She was also a finalist for a Pulitzer Prize for her novel *Mean Spirit* (Atheneum, 1990), about murders in Oklahoma prompted by the oil boom of the early twentieth century. Her writings draw on her Native American background for substance and style and reflect the feminine point of view. *Power** (Norton, 1998), a *Booklist* selection for young adults, describes how killing an endangered Florida panther affects both the Indian and the white communities. Hogan received her M.A. from the University of Colorado–Boulder, where she is currently a professor of English.

HOLDING UP THE EARTH (Gray*, Dianne E., Houghton, 2000) Contemporary realistic girl's growing-up novel with period and family-story aspects. Since the death of her single-parent mother in a car crash when she was six, Hope, 14, the narrator, has lived in seven foster homes. Yearning both for the past and for a future free of the foster care system, she always carries a backpack in which she keeps mementos of her mother, even a small plastic bag containing some of her mother's ashes. Hope is now the ward of Sarah Foster, a tall, purposeful single woman who treats her well and even puts the checks she receives from the state into a college fund for Hope. Hope is reasonably happy with Sarah, the best foster mom she has ever had, until Sarah decides they should leave Minnesota to stay for the summer with Sarah's mother, Anna Foster, on the farm near Prairie Hill, Nebraska, where Sarah grew up. The stories of four girls who have lived there help Hope see beyond her hurts and accept Sarah and Anna as her family. Anna, a lively, high-spirited woman, who takes Hope riding on her old Cushman motor scooter so the girl can savor the sounds, smells, and beauty of the area, suggests she read heirloom letters written by the daughter of the pioneer couple who homesteaded the farm in 1869, Abigail Chapman. Abby, 14, writes to her cousin Rachel about her family's hard experiences surviving alone on what is sometimes called the "Great American Desert." While her father has great dreams for the future, Abby and her mother find homesteading demanding. After a fire destroys the corn crop, her father seeks work elsewhere, and after her mother dies giving birth to a son, the family returns to Ohio. Abby's father signs the farm over to the Schmidts, German immigrants, Helmer and his wife, Minna, who become Anna's great-grandparents, and the place henceforth is known as "the Schmidt Place." Hope then reads the journal of Anna's mother, Rebecca Randolph, 14, who lived there in about 1900, as a hired girl for the Schmidts. Helmer is a terribly hard and stingy taskmaster, has built a beautiful house for the times, and is rumored to be wealthy. Helmer becomes mentally unbalanced and is put in a home, and Rebecca continues to work for the Schmidts. Anna's story takes place in 1936, when she was fourteen, too, during the Great Depression. One day she finds an old woman in the meadow, a place that Anna also loves. She discovers that the woman is the pioneer Abigail, returned to the home she loved in her childhood. Later, Anna finds Abigail lying dead in a grave she dug for herself in the meadow. Beside the body, Abigail finds what must be Helmer's buried money. Hope also reads Sarah's notebook, in which she has recorded how in the 1960s, when she, too, is in her teens, Anna unsuccessfully engaged in acts of civil disobedience to prevent the federal government from building an Atlas missile launch site in the meadow. At the end of the story, Hope has helped birth calves, has fallen in love with the meadow as did her predecessors, has sketched the wildlife and flowers of the area as mementos, has become engrossed in the history of the region, and has grown fond of the two strong women with whom she is living. She thinks of "Anna, dear Anna" as the "keeper of this land" and of Sarah as her mom. Sarah arranges to move there and to adopt Hope. Hope's own story proceeds much as the reader expects, an unhappy girl comes out of herself as she becomes involved in the lives of others. The best parts of the book are the stories within Hope's story, especially those of Abigail and Rebecca. Motifs repeat and give the novel cohesion—birth, death, the meadow, the swinging bridge near by, the abundant flowers, the trees by the creek, and the sod house and the cave that serve as shelters in times of stress or storms. ALA/YA.

HOLES (Sachar*, Louis, Farrar, 1998) Complicated, often funny, contemporary realistic novel of mystery and friendship. Convicted, although innocent, of stealing a pair of sneakers, Stanley Yelnats, about twelve, is sent to a boys' correctional facility in the terribly hot Texas desert, which is run by a sadistic female warden for whom the boys must endlessly dig holes in the sand. After a number of surprising twists and turns, Stanley gains a treasure, his first real friend, a deeper sense of self, and also greater understanding of his family history. Although some think the book deals too comically with serious subjects, the pace is rapid and filled with tension and excitement, and Stanley is a stalwart, sympathetic protagonist. The book earlier received the Newbery Award and the Christopher Award and was a *Boston Globe–Horn Book* Winner and an Edgar Allan Poe Nominee, among several other citations. For a longer entry, see *Dictionary, 1995–1999.* ALA/YA.

HOLT, KIMBERLY WILLIS   Born in Pensacola, Florida; writer of novels with southern settings for young adults. Two of her novels, *My Louisiana Sky** (Holt, 1997) and *When Zachary Beaver Came to Town** (Holt, 1999), previously cited to prestigious lists, have more recently also been named to the American Library Association Young Adult list. For biographical information and title entries, see *Dictionary, 1995–1999* [*My Louisiana Sky; When Zachary Beaver Came to Town*].

HOMELESS BIRD (Whelan*, Gloria, HarperCollins, 2000)   Realistic problem and girl's growing-up novel set for about three years in India at an unspecified time in the twentieth century. Because the narrator is one more mouth to feed, thirteen-year-old Koly's villager parents—her father a scribe, her mother an embroiderer of sari borders—betroth her to a boy she has never met, Hari Mehta, 16, of a family some distance away. The meeting between the two families is inauspicious: Mrs. Mehta immediately demands the dowry. Later, at the wedding, Koly thinks Hari seems much younger and frailer than represented, and hardly anyone pays any attention to her. Soon she learns that Hari is very ill with tuberculosis and is not expected to live and that

the Mehtas need the dowry to pay for a trip to Varasani so that he can bathe in the waters of the Ganges River, which are thought to heal. Although the Mehtas had not intended to take Koly with them, Hari insists, and they have a few pleasant moments playing in the water together. He dies in Varasani, and Mrs. Mehta immediately buys Koly a cheap white cotton sari, the widow's garment that she will have to wear henceforth. Her future is bleak. Mrs. Mehta does not want her and fills Koly's days with drudgery and harsh words. Mr. Mehta, a kind Brahman and schoolteacher, teaches her to read when she asks, especially sharing with her the work of the celebrated Indian poet, Rabindranath Tagore, whose poem about a homeless bird she appreciates the most. Since she is a widow, she can probably never marry again, and going home would not only be a hardship for her family but would bring them shame. In addition, she is penniless, because Mrs. Mehta appropriates her tiny widow's pension. After Mr. Mehta dies, Mrs. Mehta travels by train to live with a brother in Delhi. Koly is allowed only a few precious possessions, a quilt she had embroidered and the book of Tagore poems. On the way, when they stop at Vrindavan, Mrs. Mehta gives her a few rupees and then simply leaves her, to exist as she may among the hundreds of other widows, similarly abandoned, who sleep on the streets, beg, or chant at the temples for a little food. Raji, a rickshaw boy, shows her a home supported by a rich woman, Mrs. Devi, where widows are helped in return for their labor. Koly lives there, finding work first with a garland maker and then, when the rich woman sees how fine her embroidery is, with a sari maker. Koly acquires some friends, among them Raji, whom she teaches to read, who informs her that he has come to the city to earn money to build a house on land he inherited in his village, and who eventually asks her to marry him. Although she knows he is a good man, she takes her time in deciding, but at book's end she concludes that they can have a good life together. Mrs. Devi commissions her to make a sari, the border of which will contain the homeless bird Koly read about in Tagore. Koly, a homeless bird, is flying to her home. The plot moves on coincidence, characters are transparent, and symbolism is obvious. Koly's plight engages the emotions immediately, however, and she is admirable for her diligence, courage, and resource. Raji is almost a prince charming but also a worthy husband for a worthy heroine. The book's strength is in its vividly portrayed details of everyday life and customs from the woman's point of view in a warm and fluid style. A glossary of Hindee words appears at the end. An author's note about sources and time would be helpful; in fact, it is difficult to evaluate the book fairly without them. Taken as it is, the book may give readers the impression that all India follows these customs to this day. ALA/YA.

HOOBLER, DOROTHY Born in Philadelphia, Pennsylvania; graduate of Wells College with an A.B. and from New York University with an M.A.; editor and genealogist; freelance writer since 1973. Her numerous publications have been mostly with her husband, Thomas Hoobler*. Among these is *The Ghost in the Tokaido Inn** (Philomel, 1999), selected for young adults by the American Library Association, an adventure-filled, historical-mystery novel set in eighteenth-century Japan. Together the Hooblers have also published about five dozen nonfiction books, mostly in sets, and a histor-

ical-fiction series for younger readers. They have also written several textbooks on China, the Pacific Rim, and Latin America that reflect their continuing interest in history and travel.

HOOBLER, THOMAS Born in Cincinnati, Ohio; editor and freelance writer. He received an A.B. from the University of Notre Dame and has held various positions in private schools in Cincinnati, including teacher of English and basketball coach. Since 1974, he has published, mostly with his wife Dorothy Hoobler*, about sixty books of nonfiction, mostly in sets, like Images across the Ages (Steck-Vaughn) and the American Family Album (Oxford). The Hooblers have also together published Her Story, a children's historical-fiction series (Silver Burdett) that includes such titles as *A Promise at the Alamo* (1992) and *The Trail on Which They Wept* (1992). *The Ghost in the Tokaido Inn** (Philomel, 1999), an American Library Association recommendation for young adults, is a historical-mystery novel set in 1735 in Japan about a boy who dreams of becoming a samurai.

HOPE WAS HERE (Bauer*, Joan, Putnam, 2000)   Girl's growing-up and career novel, set in Mulhoney, Wisconsin, in the late 1990s. Hope Yancey, 16, the narrator, has already been a waitress in several diners where her aunt, Addie, is cook and sometimes part owner. When Addie's partner in Brooklyn absconds with the money from the register, the bank account, and the night waitress, they take jobs at Welcome Stairways in Mulhoney, where the owner, G. T. Stoop, needs help because he has been diagnosed with leukemia. Addie's great passion is preparing food, and Hope is almost as passionate about being a good waitress, a skill she inherited from her mother, Deena, who abandoned her to Addie when she was a premature baby and has seen her only three times since. At first small-town Wisconsin is something of a culture shock, but soon Hope is caught up in the life of the diner, which is central to much of what goes on in Mulhoney. Hope runs into some hassle from another waitress, Lou Ellen, but becomes fast friends with the other waitress, Flo, Yuri the Russian busboy, and especially tall, skinny Braverman*, 19, the grill man. Addie and G. T. vie for supremacy in the kitchen until G. T., disgusted with the corruption sanctioned by the mayor, Eli Millstone, decides to run against him. Soon the town is divided into two camps, those who suspect Millstone and know G. T. is honest and dedicated, and those who either work for the Real Fresh Dairy, which backs Millstone, or are afraid that a man with leukemia cannot handle the job. Stirred up by Braverman and organized by Adam Pulver, president of the Students for Political Freedom Coalition, a large number of teenagers circulate petitions to get G. T. on the ballot and turn out for all of Millstone's campaign appearances, where they question him on touchy subjects like the dairy's nonpayment of taxes and their trucks taking illegal shortcuts through residential areas at night. Dirty tricks start early in the campaign. The election board finds that a number of the signers of the petition have given false addresses. African American Pastor Al B. Hall of the Gospel of Grace Church talks the administrator into giving them a few hours to recheck or get new signatures. Half a dead mouse is found, with many screams and much fanfare, in a Welcome Stairways salad. The new sheriff's deputy, Brenda Babcock, an African American, seizes the salad bowl with mouse as evidence, checks the identification of the couple at the table who are suddenly reluctant, and eventually proves that the mouse had been dead for some time before it was dropped into the salad. Braverman is beaten up by three guys who warn him to stop his political activity. The Real Fresh Dairy pulls all its advertising from the *Mulhoney Messenger* run by Cecelia Culpepper, because she prints news and editorials favoring G. T. On a personal level, Hope's life is complicated by a brief visit from her mother and has to admit to Braverman that her original name was Tulip before she had it legally changed. He finds this hilarious. G. T. starts courting Addie, and Braverman asks Hope out to dinner. When the election results show Millstone the winner, they are all downhearted, but Hope runs into a customer who told her, adamantly, that he would never vote and, having seen his name on the list of voters, congratulates him. When he denies it, they look over the other voters on the list and discover enough votes were fraudulently cast to elect G. T. mayor. After appointing Brenda Babcock sheriff and making the dairy pay its back taxes, G. T. marries Addie and asks Hope if she will let him adopt her. As a child who has known nothing of her father (nor has Deena), Hope has always fantasized about him turning up to claim her and has made scrapbooks of her life to show him. Now she goes through them with G. T., knowing he is better than any of the fathers she has imagined. In less than two years his leukemia, which has been in remission, returns, and four weeks later he dies. Before she leaves for college, Hope finds an obscure place under the counter and writes, as she has in all the other diners of their many moves, "Hope was here." All the main characters are interesting and well realized, especially Hope, who is frank and resilient, a hard worker who makes waiting on tables a real art of service. Menus, special dishes, techniques for handling customers, and relations between cooks and the wait staff—all are described with enthusiasm and, often, humor. ALA/YA.

HORATIO ALGER HUNTINGTON-ACKERMAN (*Love Among the Walnuts**) One of the ten richest men in America, who is also among the most unhappy until he marries Mousey* Malone, an aspiring actress, retires to the country, and builds the country estate called Eclipse. Bentley, his faithful valet, describes him as "young, rich, handsome, honest, unaffected, sincere, and well educated." Throughout most of the book, Horatio is in a coma, having ingested cake poisoned by his two jealous younger brothers. A chemical and business wizard, Horatio invented chemical-free Pensa-Cola, The Thinking Man's Drink; Damitol, Asylum-Strength Pain Relief Without Side Effects; and Quiche-on-a-Stick.

HOTEL PARADISE (Grimes*, Martha, Knopf, 1996) Mystery involving a forty-year-old drowning and a present-day murder at a resort lake that gradually obsess a twelve-year-old girl who discovers the truth about both and their connection to each other and struggles to decide what is the right thing to do with her knowledge. The narrator is Emma Graham, whose first name, significantly, is not used until nearly the end of the novel, since she is usually referred to as "Jen Graham's girl" or just "Girl." She waits tables at the Hotel Paradise, a ramshackle resort hotel owned mostly by her great-aunt, Aurora Paradise, a tyrannical old lady who stays in her rooms on the fourth floor, playing cards, drinking, and complaining. Emma's mother, who has some

financial ownership in the hotel, is the cook, whose skill really keeps the place going, but who is so busy that she spends little time or thought on what her daughter is doing, as long as she shows up to work at the three daily meals. The hotel is near Spirit Lake, once a fashionable spot, not far from the town of La Porte, where Emma spends a good deal of her time checking parking meters or having a Cherry Coke at the Rainbow Cafe with her friend, Sheriff Sam* DeGheyn, or drinking cocoa in Miss Flyte's candle shop or in Miss Flager's gift shop, where the two old ladies meet alternately for tea and welcome her company. With no companions her own age and little to amuse her at the hotel, Emma starts to investigate the forty-year-old drowning of twelve-year-old Mary-Evelyn Devereau, of a family whose house still stands across Spirit Lake where the girl lived with three grim-looking aunts. Emma has an old picture of Mary-Evelyn with her aunts and is very curious about the drowning, but she knows that to ask questions directly will not get her much information about what was obviously a scandal at the time, so she thinks of ways to bring up the subject with all of the older people of the town and learns bits that only whet her interest. When a woman is killed at a pond nearby and cannot be identified, she even takes a train to the next stop, the backward community of Cold Flat Junction, to find out what she can about Ben* Queen, whom her great-aunt has mentioned as having run off with the youngest Devereau aunt, Rose Fern. She discovers not only the probable identity of the murdered woman, but also about the murder of beautiful Rose Fern Devereau some twenty years previously, a crime for which Ben Queen was sent to prison. As part of her investigation, she goes to the Devereau house one evening with two elderly brothers, Ulub* and Ubub Woods, who are considered retarded because their speech is hard to understand, but who have persuaded her that they know something about Mary-Evelyn's death. She makes several other trips there, on the last one meeting Ben Queen, just released from prison, who talks to her seriously and tells her he did not kill Rose or their daughter, Fern, the unidentified woman. Emma realizes that he took the blame for Rose's killing by Fern, who was "never right in the head" to protect his daughter, and now is willing, if Emma tells, to take the blame for the killing of Fern by her daughter, the beautiful, blond girl Emma has seen several times briefly. Emma makes no promises, but keeps her own counsel, not even telling the sheriff, whom she dearly loves. The plot, though ingenious, is not as important as Emma's voice, naive in some ways but frank with sharp insights about the community, the hotel, and the many characters there and in the town—Lola Davidow, her mother's business partner; Lola's mean daughter, Rae-Jane, 16; her own brother, Will, and his friend, Mill (Brownmiller Conroy); Maud Chadwick of the Rainbow Cafe; and many others whom she understands better than they might wish. Booklist.

HOW ALL THIS STARTED (Fromm*, Pete, Picador, 2000)   Contemporary realistic adult novel of family life, baseball, and mental illness set for a couple of years in rural western Texas within a few hours' drive of Midland. Big, tough-minded, physically strong, red-haired Abilene Scheer, about twenty, and her younger brother, Austin, the narrator, 15, named, their parents say, for the cities where they were conceived, are wild about baseball. Abilene practiced fer-

vently to become a pitcher on her high school team and was truly good, but was rejected by the coach because the other players refused to play with a girl. Determined that Austin make the team and become baseball's next Nolan Ryan, she outfits a practice pitching range on the abandoned World War II bomber base near their house, working with him day after day, week after week, until she knows he is ready for his sophomore year. The effort apparently unbalances her tender psyche and she begins to behave strangely, flunking out of Midland Community College, being verbally abusive, becoming pregnant without knowing by whom, and disappearing for days on end. Clayton and Ruby, Abilene and Austin's parents, secure a psychiatrist to whom they manage to take Abilene but whom she adamantly rejects at first. Austin makes the high school team, pitching so well in his first start that he gains acclaim, but because Abilene worked him so hard in preparation, he suffers obvious shoulder pain and is relieved, to her great chagrin, and needs the rest of the year to recover. Among other alarming activity, she acquires a gun, gives Clayton's to Austin, and takes Austin hunting for doves and swallows, shooting and cooking droves of the little birds. The parents are summoned to a hospital where she has been voluntarily admitted for sterilization and where she subsequently attempts to commit suicide. Abilene blames her problems on her parents' decision to live in a rural area and various other extraneous matters. Her outrageous behavior continues throughout the book and eventually drives a wedge between her and Austin and their parents. She finally accepts medications, is able to make reasoned decisions, and decides to try to live on her own in a group home. At the end of the book, she has reentered Midland Community College, and Austin has an athletic scholarship to the University of Texas and can look forward to a major league career. The family has been jolted and scarred, but the future looks brighter. Characters have little depth, incidents become repetitive, and Abilene's aberrant actions outrun their interest. Good are the close bond between the brother and sister, the graphic yet sensitive depiction of Abilene's descent into serious mental illness, and the gradually deteriorating home situation arising from the pressures of her manic depression. The baseball scenes are detailed and engrossing, and the remote desert area in which they live reinforces Abilene's growing isolation from society and from her family. Booklist; NYPL.

HOWE, JAMES (1946–)   Born in Oneida, New York; freelance actor and director, literary agent, and since 1981 prolific writer for children. He received his B.F.A. from Boston University in 1968 and his M.A. from Hunter College of City University of New York in 1977. Howe is probably best known for his Bunnicula series, of which there are more than a dozen books starting with *Bunnicula: A Rabbit-Tale of Mystery* (Atheneum, 1979), on which he collaborated with his first wife, Deborah, who died in 1978. Among his other series are those of Sebastian Barth, starting with *What Eric Knew* (Atheneum, 1985), and those of Pinky and Rex, easy chapter books all illustrated by Melissa Sweet, starting with *Pinky and Rex* (Atheneum, 1990). In a very different and more serious mode is *The Watcher** (Atheneum, 1997), a novel of child abuse, which was named to the young adult lists of both the New York Public Library and the American Library Association.

HOWE, NORMA (1930–)   Born in San Jose, California; writer, starting with stories for confession magazines when her six children were young, now author of several novels for young adults, all amusing but dealing with serious issues. She was graduated from San Jose State University in 1957. Her first novel, *God, the Universe, and Hot Fudge Sundaes* (Houghton, 1984), concerns a trial between evolutionists and creationists. *In with the Out Crowd* (Houghton, 1986), is about peer pressure, and *The Game of Life* (Crown, 1989) deals with the foolishness of astrology and the randomness of life. *The Adventures of Blue Avenger** (Holt, 1999) takes on the questions of freewill versus predetermination in a rollicking series of events. It has been followed by a sequel, *Blue Avenger Cracks the Code* (Holt, 2000). Howe lives with her husband in Sacramento, California.

HYDE, CATHERINE RYAN (1955–) Born in Buffalo, New York; novelist and short story writer, occasional teacher of writing. Her first novel, *Funerals for Horses* (Russian Hill Press, 1997), is about a girl who manages to find and save her brother who has always protected her in their dysfunctional family. *Pay It Forward** (Simon & Schuster, 2000), both amusing and thought provoking, stars a twelve-year-old boy whose plan to change society, conceived for a social studies assignment, actually has a positive effect on many people. It was adapted as a film by Warner Brothers, starring Kevin Spacey and Helen Hunt. Hyde has also published two other novels, *Electric God* (Simon and Schuster, 2000) and *Walter's Purple Heart* (Simon and Schuster, 2002), and a book of short stories, *Earthquake Weather* (Russian Hill Press, 1998).

I

I AM MORDRED: A TALE FROM CAMELOT (Springer*, Nancy, Philomel, 1998)   Unconventional retelling of the story of Mordred, son of King Arthur and his half sister, Margawse. Although, without departing completely from legend and Sir Thomas Malory's *Morte Darthur* (Caxton, 1485), Mordred's story must end in tragedy, this novel has less sense of doom and foreboding than Elizabeth Wein's 1993 *The Winter Prince* (Maxwell Macmillan, 1993) (*Dictionary, 1990–1994*) or even Mary Stewart's 1983 *The Wicked Day* (Morrow, 1983), in her series on Merlin and Arthur, all three choosing to picture Mordred more sympathetically than in his usual villainous role. In this novel, Mordred is taken from his fisherwife foster mother to the court of King Lothe of Lothian by the sorceress, Nyneve, who introduces him to Margawse, saying that she is his lady mother, and to the king, who reluctantly agrees to shelter him. After giving him a white puppy he names Gull, Nyneve departs. For five years he believes he is Lothe's son, until Gareth, along with Gawain one of the two older brothers in-

cluded in this version, tells him that he is Arthur's bastard and is destined to kill his father. When Mordred is fifteen, he joins his brothers at Camelot, where Arthur treats him kindly but does not acknowledge him, the one thing he really craves. His feelings for Arthur are ambivalent, a mixture of devotion and hatred. After he has been knighted, he goes on a quest, hoping to find a way of changing his fate, first back to the hut near Lothian, where he learns that his foster mother died in childbirth a few months after he left, then to the strange castle of Morgan le Fey, another sorceress half sister of Arthur, who tries to seduce him so that jointly they can seize power. When he escapes, he goes to Avalon, where the Lady of the Lake, asked how he can fight his fate, tells him only "Love." Then he rides off to seek Merlin, who has been imprisoned by Nyneve in a cave in Cornwall but is not truly dead and who is pictured in this version as an evil character, having told Arthur to kill all the boy babies in order to do away with Mordred when he was an infant and somehow imposing the fate of Arthur's death at the hands of his son by predicting it. In a strange, otherworldly garden he finds a penned hawk, playing on the bars of his cage like a harp, and in compassion, he frees it, only to have it, the next day, kill Gull and, presumably, Nyneve in some distant place, since Nyneve has watched over Mordred in the person of Gull. Back at Camelot, Mordred begs the boon Arthur long ago promised him. It is to go out with a blind harper of Druid blood and take his soul for safekeeping in a golden casket. As they perform the ceremony, his soul emerges like a white moth, but before Arthur can catch it, the harper's raven snaps it up, and both the raven and the harper disappear. The rest of the story plays out in much the traditional fashion, with Arthur, dying, finally calling Mordred "my son." In this novel both Gawain and Gareth are bloodthirsty knights, who kill wantonly and, to avenge the death of their father who is slain by Pellinore, torture and kill him and then slay their mother and Lamorak, the knight she is dallying with. Whether the hawk and the raven are manifestations of Merlin is not clear. Nor is it clear whether Margawse is guilty of deliberately seducing her half brother or was the victim of rape. The most pervasive impression in the novel is of Mordred's misery, unable to escape the destiny that will destroy him as well as the truly noble king. ALA/YA; NYPL.

IF YOU COME SOFTLY (Woodson*, Jacqueline, Putnam, 1998)   Contemporary, realistic, sociological-problem novel of growing up and interracial romance set in New York City at the two protagonists' homes and in an exclusive prep school. For most of the book, the chapters alternate between the fifteen-year-old young people, with those chapters concerning white Ellie* (Elisha) Eisen related by Ellie in first person, and those featuring handsome, bright African American Miah* (Jeremiah) Roselind in a third person so narrowly focused that the narrative has the effect of first person. Although the families of both young people are affluent, Ellie, the youngest of the five children of a prominent doctor living in the Central Park West area of New York City, and Miah, the only child of an award-winning filmmaker living in a nine-room apartment in Brooklyn, New York, both children are emotionally needy and lonely. Ellie's mother has, two times, walked out on her family. Miah's father lives with his girlfriend across the street from Miah and his novelist mother, Nelia. These two troubled teens from disturbed families quite literally bump into each other on their first day at Percy Academy. A sweet, calm romance develops and continues despite negative or querying looks from some classmates and snide comments from strangers on the street. Ellie confides in her lesbian older sister, Anne, who warns her of possible adverse consequences, but her mother is aware only that an important boy has entered her life. After it gets too cold to hang out in the park, Miah takes Ellie home, unannounced, to meet his mother. Nelia is beautifully warm and welcoming, and, henceforth, Miah and Ellie spend Saturday afternoons at Nelia's apartment. Late one afternoon, after walking Ellie home and kissing her good-bye, Miah heads back through the darkening park. He is completely unaware that police are seeking a young black man. So preoccupied is he that he is oblivious to the command to stop and is shot dead. Ellie's father and mother also attend the funeral, to which Nelia had purposely invited Ellie. In the last chapter, Ellie, now eighteen and accepted at Swarthmore, realizes that "[t]ime comes to us softly, . . . [and] long before we are ready it moves on," words that echo the Audre Lord poem from which the book's title comes. The settings in which the two young people live are well depicted, especially Miah's, where his homeboys gather, basketball is an all-consuming pastime, and the rich and famous gather at his father's apartment. Ellie's Jewish background figures only minimally, but her putting her Star of David chain about Miah's neck is a sweet and telling gesture of affection. What comes between and ultimately destroys the simple, sincere romance of this modern-day Romeo and his Juliet is race, not the long-held prejudice against intermarriage but simply that of mistaken identity and what some perceive as law officers' inclination to shoot first at blacks and not ask questions. Although such shootings may, unfortunately, be all too common, in the context of the plot as it has developed the shooting seems a convenient escape from attempting to resolve the real issue, that of a possible interracial relationship and subsequent marriage and all the baggage that might entail. Best is the depiction of the deep emotion between these two handsome, intelligent, thoroughly decent young people and of the sweetness of their ill-fated romance. ALA/YA.

IMANI ALL MINE (Porter*, Connie, Houghton Mifflin, 1999)   Adult novel of African American life in recent years in the inner city of Buffalo, New York, with school-story aspects. The narrator, Tasha Dawson, 15, tells the story in euphonious black street dialect, partly as it happens and partly in retrospect, but episodes knit well, and the novel flows along. Tasha is a single mother as was her mother, Mama, who had Tasha when she was about Tasha's age now and still lives on welfare and food stamps. Mama's friends are also mostly single, early mothers: Miss Lovey,

mother of Tasha's friend, Eboni, who is pregnant with twins; and Miss* Odetta, mother of drug-dealing June Bug. Tasha dotes on her daughter, Imani, five months, takes her to day care at Lincoln High School every day, and faithfully attends the parenting classes led by Mrs.* Poole. She finds comfort in the thought that little Imani, which means faith, is all hers and hers alone. Tasha longs for Mama's approval and overt affection, but Mama often slaps her and derides her. In addition, Tasha faces several other problems: maintaining high grades, of which she has proved herself capable, but which come harder with the birth of Imani; dealing with the sudden appearance at school of the boy who raped and impregnated her; dealing with her mother's new boyfriend, Mitch*, a red-haired white man; handling her attraction to schoolboy Peanut, by whom she becomes pregnant with her second child; and last, and most unsettling of all, the death of Imani in a drive-by shooting not long after Imani's first birthday. Tasha thinks of Mitch as the skeleton in their closet, but she gradually warms to him because he is kind to her Mama, dotes on Imani, tells her about his own hard life, encourages her to persevere in school, and helps immensely after Imani's death. She becomes friends with Peanut at school and soon has sex with him, loses track of him briefly, then resumes relations with him when he reappears in her life. At book's end, she says she will tell Peanut about the coming baby to see how he reacts. She ponders whether he will love her and the baby. Shots heard outside Mama's house near the beginning of the book and others occasionally remarked upon foreshadow Imani's death. Imani is upstairs in Mama's room near the window when shots riddle Miss Odetta and June Bug's house, Mama's, and others nearby, cutting down Imani who soon dies in the hospital. Heart-wrenching scenes follow: Tasha's near breakdown, a fistfight between Mama and Miss Odetta, the wake, and the funeral. Tasha finds some comfort in the worship service at New Light of the Covenant Church, where she is last seen, embraced by the music, prayers, and arms of the parishioners. She inwardly resolves to keep the coming baby and cherish it— all hers, hers alone. Although the reader sees the generations repeating themselves and has little hope that Tasha will realize her vocational ambitions, Tasha is a warm, loving young woman drawn with sympathy and understanding. The author captures the moment well, at home, in school, as incidents happen and in reflection. The characters, almost all women, are strongly realized. The church scenes are particularly memorable, rich in color and sound, with the choir's singing, the preacher's rhythmical sermons, and the congregation's spontaneous, heartfelt responses. ALA/YA; Alex; Booklist.

INGOLD, JEANETTE   Born in Texas; resident of Montana; among other occupations, writer of novels for middle graders and young adults. Recommended by the American Library Association for young adults, *The Window** (Harcourt, 1996) concerns a blind, orphaned Texas girl. Ingold has also published *Airfield* (Harcourt, 1999), set in the early days of aviation, and *The Big Burn* (Harcourt, 2002), a historical-adventure and survival story about the terrible fire of 1910 in Idaho. For a longer entry about Ingold and more titles, see *Dictionary, 1995–1999* [*The Window*].

INSIDE THE WALLS OF TROY: A NOVEL OF THE WOMEN WHO LIVED THE TROJAN WAR (McLaren*, Clemence, Atheneum, 1996)   Retelling of the main events, from the woman's standpoint, of the Trojan War. The story is presented as historical fiction and related by Helen, princess and then queen of Sparta, for the first half of the novel, and then by Cassandra, princess of Troy. The action begins when Helen is twelve and already so beautiful that she is the talk of all Greece. After she is abducted by Theseus, king of Athens, and ransomed by her brothers, Castor and Polydeuces, she is wooed by numerous eligible suitors. Her older sister, Clytemnestra, the wife of Agamemnon of Mycenae, overlord of Greece, urges her to marry Agamemnon's younger brother, Menelaus. Helen finds Menelaus unexciting but accepts him. Her father, fearing trouble, extracts promises from all her other suitors to protect Menelaus and his interests. For some time, Troy and Greece have attempted through diplomacy to solve problems over trade. One Trojan group of emissaries is led by handsome, personable Paris, son of Priam, king of Troy. The goddess Aphrodite has promised Paris the hand in marriage of the most beautiful woman in the world, Helen. Not long after Paris arrives at Sparta, Helen falls madly in love with him, and even abandons her baby daughter by Menelaus to accompany Paris to Troy, taking with her much of Sparta's treasure. When efforts to resolve what the Greeks regard as an abduction fail, Agamemnon marshals the suitors, and the Greeks set sail with a thousand ships to attack Troy. The visionary Cassandra, Paris's sister, a thoughtful seventeen year old doomed always to speak the truth but never to be believed, reports how few people, including their older brother, noble Hector, respect or even like Paris. She herself has had a dream in which she sees men writhing in their death throes outside the walls of Troy and later also has a vision of Hector's death. During the years the war wears on, Cassandra and Helen become friends, and all Troy thrills to Helen's beauty. Helen often points out to Priam and others from atop the city walls the various Greek warriors. While Achilles, the renowned Greek fighter, sulks in his tent over an affront to his dignity, the war abates but resumes in earnest after Hector kills Patroclus, Achilles's best friend and cousin. Then Achilles kills Hector and defiles the body, which Priam ransoms with the help of Polyxena, his beautiful daughter, who, during a night of lovemaking with Achilles, extracts from him the secret that his famed vulnerability lies in his heel. Armed with this knowledge, Paris kills Achilles but soon is himself slain. Throughout, Paris has shown himself, however, to be better at wooing Helen than as a warrior on the field. The Greeks soon ostensibly depart, leaving behind a huge, hollow horse in which they have concealed warriors. Enticed to take the horse inside the walls, the people of Troy soon fall prey to the Greeks. Disillusioned Helenus, twin of Cassandra and himself a prophet, has given the Greeks information about the prophecies that tell how to take Troy. While the Greeks rampage through the city, Cassandra manages to save Helenus, Helen, Andromache (Hector's widow) and her baby, Astyanax, and Queen Hecuba. The action stops abruptly, but an epilogue summarizes what happens to the principals. Both Helen and Cassandra are well-rounded figures, whose motives the reader can understand if not accept. Paris gets no good report, being presented as vain and selfish. Most members of the large cast are flat and unfleshed, and the war is shown as a waste in every respect. Priam's household is claustrophobically drawn, women without power except that which they can command by beauty, position, and chicanery. Various other myths and legends are interspersed throughout the narrative to cast light on events or flesh out characters. Sometimes it is hard to see how Cassandra has learned what she reports, the elaborate spy network that evidently prevailed notwithstanding. The author follows the main accounts of the conflict and events that precede it and probably correctly presents the war as the result of strife to control the rich trade through the Bosporus. ALA/YA.

IRENE RIVERS (*At All Costs**)   FBI Special Agent in charge of capturing Jake* and Carolyn Brighton, who have been on the run for fourteen years to avoid punishment for blowing up the U.S. Army hazardous-materials depot at Newark, Arkansas, in 1983, and killing sixteen people. At first she pursues Jake and Carolyn with bitter vengeance, because Jake made her look bad by giving her the slip after his arrest in Phoenix, South Carolina, and Peter Frankel, deputy director of the FBI, has upbraided her severely. She is a very unsympathetic figure also when she tries to trick Carolyn into confessing, when Carolyn is incarcerated and her son, Travis*, is dying, for all Carolyn knows. After Irene hears Jake's story, however, she feels compelled to investigate Frankel, and in so doing, discovers that he had been engaging in selling arms illegally to Iraq and set up the bombing as a diversion. Irene is shot and severely injured at the meeting of the principals in the ritzy restaurant in Washington, D.C., during which Frankel is killed.

I RODE A HORSE OF MILK WHITE JADE (Wilson*, Diane Lee, Orchard, 1998)   Historical novel in the quest pattern tinged with fantasy, set in Mongolia in the early fourteenth century. The narrator, Oyuna, a girl of the Kerait people, has one deformed foot, crushed by a horse when she was an infant, a sure sign of bad luck in her society. Confined for the next eight or ten years to her family's *ger* (the rounded, felt-covered huts of her people), she dreams of riding free across the steppe on a swift horse and, escaping once while fetching water, she discovers she has a natural affinity and understanding of the animals and is able to ride skillfully, giving her a delighted freedom she never feels struggling along on her crippled leg. When she is twelve, her mother is killed by lightning, another sign of the bad luck Oyuna carries with her. For three months she cares for her father, sneaking out after he is asleep to ride across the steppe and ease her grief. That autumn he takes her to the festival at Karakorum, where he has a new wife waiting for him and where he will seek a husband for Oyuna. To ease her fears, since he knows he cannot make a good match for a cripple, he promises that he will buy her a horse of her choice. At Karakorum, although her father can arrange no marriage for her, she happily examines many of the horses, determined to choose one that will carry her to win the long festival race the next year. When she steps among a trio of biting, kicking horses she hears one, an old white mare, say to her, "Help me away from here." Although she fears some trick and despite her father's disgust, she chooses the injured animal and leads it home behind the cart, which also carries his father's new wife and her two sons. Although the mare does not speak to her directly again, she seems to cause Oyuna's senses to sharpen, so that she can smell water and sense the presence of small animals hidden in the grasses. Some five months later, Oyuna visits the ger of her maternal grand-

mother, Echenkorlo*, a shamaness who travels alone. The strange old woman, to whom Oyuna tells the story of her talking horse, advises the girl to seize the good luck that follows her as surely as bad luck and to listen to her heart. The next spring a troop of soldiers arrive and, since everything on the steppes belongs to Kublai Khan, single out horses they wish to take, among them the white mare that Oyuna has named Bayan (meaning rich with beauty and goodness). Then they commandeer some of the men of the tribe to be recruits, among them Oyuna's older stepbrother. When his mother protests that he is crippled and he convincingly starts to limp, the commander says he will not limp on horseback and orders him to prepare to ride with them. Oyuna, more to be near her beloved Bayan than to save the boy, quickly switches clothes with him, chops off her long hair, and tugs her father's fur-trimmed hat low over her face. When the soldiers pull out, Oyuna rides among them on her beloved Bayan. Although the commander discovers her gender, he orders her not to tell, not wanting to lose face by admitting before his men that he has recruited a girl. With her little cat, Bator, which has followed her, inside her upper garment, she rides with the soldiers until a badly injured young man comes up, saying he is an arrow rider for Kublai Khan, delivering to him a great prize, and begging that one of the soldiers on a swift horse take it on to the next arrow station. Seizing the chance to get rid of his problem, the commander sends Oyuna off on Bayan, with only vague general directions. Their journey takes them to an arrow station where the keeper, a woman, tries to steal Bayan and marry Oyuna to her son, through treacherous mountains where she finds Echenkorlo's dead body with many bags of herbs and buries her in the back of a cave, across a desert, and finally to the city of Kublai Khan's palace. Through a series of unlikely but plausible events, Oyuna becomes a favorite of the great Khan, who shows her his prize possessions, his ten thousand white mares. When a disease strikes them and also Bayan, Oyuna recalls Echenkorlo's herbs and her instructions, half remembered from years before, and proposes that she retrieve the bags buried with her grandmother's body in the mountain cave. Kublai Khan sends her with an escort and a young soldier named Adja, a former arrow rider, as guide. They retrieve the herbs, which cure the mares still living, but are too late to save Bayan, who has delivered a white filly before dying. Married to Adja and riding one of the ten white mares the Khan has given her, Oyuna returns to the Keirat country where, after the filly matures, she rides in the Karakorum festival race, winning and reuniting with her father. All this is told by Oyuna as an old woman to her granddaughter, as they wait through the night for the birth of Bayan's great-great-granddaughter. Although many elements in the story stretch credulity, details of Mongolian life, the sense of communion of the girl with her horse and cat, and the adventures themselves are all compelling. A cameo appearance of Marco Polo serves no purpose, except to establish the period. ALA/YA.

THE IRON RING (Alexander*, Lloyd, Dutton, 1997)   Mythological and adventure fantasy that recalls the epics of ancient India, set in a time of swords, magic, miracle, talking animals, and demons. Young King Tamar is put under bond to obey powerful King Jaya, the symbol of his obligation the iron ring that appears on his finger. In his journey to break the king's hold on him, he is claimed as a slave by a *chandala* (the lowest of the castes), learns the folly of seeking revenge, and realizes that every life, no matter how despised by society, is valuable. High action, conflict, excitement, comedy, and colorful dialogue contribute to an examination of the purpose of life. Previously, the novel was cited by the American Library Association for younger readers. For a longer entry, see *Dictionary, 1995–1999.* ALA/YA.

ISAAC LITSKY (*Gideon's People**) Son of an Orthodox Jewish peddler in Lancaster County, Pennsylvania. Although Isaac would like to be more American like his friend Abie and eat hot dogs, speak English, and not learn Hebrew, he obeys the rules of his religion and goes to school to get ready for his bar mitzvah. He remembers and dreams about his family's flight from persecution in Russia and understands how hard life has been since they have been in America. He also knows that his mother hopes that he will have an easier life than his father, Jakob, who started out by carrying his merchandise on his back and then bought a faithful but bony old horse and an almost worn-out wagon. Although life is hard, Isaac feels loved and respected by both his parents. Isaac's circumstances contrast with those of Old Order Amish Gideon Stoltzfus.

ISAACS, ANNE (1949–)   Born in Buffalo, New York; received her B.A. and M.S. from the University of Michigan and also attended the State University of New York. She has held numerous positions in environmental education. *Torn Thread** (Scholastic, 2000) is a fictionalized account of the experiences of her Jewish mother-in-law, Eva Buchbinder Koplowicz, during World War II in a slave-labor camp in Czechoslovakia. It was selected by the American Library Association for young adults. An unpublished picture storybook, *A Bowl of Soup* (Scholastic), also describes Eva's girlhood wartime experiences. Isaacs's tall-tale story for *Swamp Angel* (Dutton, 1994), a picture book, received critical acclaim. Isaacs has also published a book of poems, *Cat Up a Tree* (Dutton, 1998), and of short stories, *Treehouse Tales* (Dutton, 1997). She lives in California with her husband and three children.

I WANT TO BUY A VOWEL (Welter*, John, Algonquin, 1996)   Highly entertaining novel of a young man, Alfredo* Santayana, 17, from Guatemala, who has walked across Mexico to the small town of Waxahachie, Texas, knowing almost no English except for a few phrases he has memorized from television. In his naivete, he thinks that if he can get a vowel, whatever that is, he will be given a new car. By talking to some Mexican American workers, he learns that he must have a green card to find legal work, but he might get on as dishwasher at a Chinese restaurant. Within a few days, Alfredo has moved into a vacant house known locally as the witch's house, along with spiders and numerous biting insects, where he can eat Chinese food from his dishwasher job. Two little girls who live nearby, Eva* Galt, 11, and her sister, Ava, 8, hunting for dinosaur bones in the woods near the house, uncover a leg bone, which Ava hopes belonged to Lewis or Clark. Their mother, Emily, takes them with the bone to the museum in Dallas, where the specialist says it is the bone of a man, probably the victim of a satanic cult operating in the area in the 1920s. Soon the whole town is buzzing about satanic rituals. Kenlow Schindler, a high school sopho-

more whose father is the minister of Christ's Unfurling Grace Church, is tired of being considered a model boy, although he obediently goes to church and Bible class every week. To get a little excitement into his life and to play a prank on the town, he digs a pentagram around the site of the skeleton and, because he knows that satanism requires blood sacrifice, dumps chicken giblets and pork brains in the center. Although the police chief, James McLamore*, debunks the whole matter, the town gets more feverish about satanic activity and religion. A woman claims to see the Virgin Mary in the stamp vending machine at the post office, and a large crowd gathers there, some of them kneeling. When Eva and Ava see the stain on the glass front of the machine, Eva says it looks like Sugarloaf Mountain. Her father, David, an Episcopal priest, preaches a clever sermon that points out the idiocy of this fervor. Eva and Ava, back digging for dinosaur bones, see Alfredo on the porch of the abandoned house, decide he is not a warlock or Satan, and offer him some of their iced tea. Their communication is limited to sign language and the few English phrases Alfredo knows, usually inappropriate to the situation, but after a few days they see him regularly, and Eva's efforts to talk to him using her mother's Spanish–English dictionary result in even more confusion. The girls also see Kenlow in the woods, dumping Vienna sausages on the pentagram, and when Eva is unimpressed by his claim to be a Satanist, he threatens them if they tell anyone. After people hear Alfredo's guitar, which he plays with enthusiasm but badly, and see candle light in the house, McLamore arrests him as an illegal immigrant. Alfredo is delighted to be in a nice, clean jail and get food that is not all Chinese. The Galt girls are so upset at the arrest that their parents rally to Alfredo's cause, hire a lawyer, and determine that he can get a green card if he can find a job that no native Texan wants. Reverend Schindler performs an exorcism in front of the jail. Sergeant Gloria Mondesi, who speaks Spanish, explains to Alfredo what is happening and lets him watch. Someone steals the stamp machine, and again an uproar ensues. A drunk sharing Alfredo's cell tells him that he knows who stole the stamp machine. When Alfredo passes this information on to Sergeant Mondesi, the town's attitude toward him changes. The immigration officials drag their feet about deporting him. Everything quiets down. Kenlow, resenting the change, goes to the witch's house intending to fake a satanic ritual and burns the house, starting a major fire in the dry woods. Running from it, he stumbles in a hole and breaks his ankle. Eva and Ava, also running from the fire, come upon him and, with some reluctance, drag him down the trail until firemen reach the spot and carry all three out. The search to find a job repugnant enough to be rejected by natives ends, finally, with Alfredo, now with a green card (which actually is pink) assigned to scoop up road kill, often several days old. The intertwined plot lines are mostly from the point of view of Eva or Alfredo, although sometimes from that of McLamore, Kenlow, or Reverend Schindler. Characters, even minor ones, are well defined, and the hypocrisy of their actions is told with good-natured humor. Religious belief ranges from Reverend Schindler's frantic exhortations about the presence of Satan and the goofy devotion of those kneeling at the stamp machine to the skepticism of David Galt, Eva's innocent questioning, and McLamore's practical agnosticism. The combination produces a thoroughly enjoyable novel. ALA/YA; Booklist.

J

JAIME BETANCOURT (*The Tree of Red Stars**)   Young Uruguayan air force officer with whom Magda* Ortega Grey has a romance. They meet through Marco* Periera, for whom Jaime is a character foil. Son of a tailor, he is ambitious and would like to go to the United States, get a good job with an airline there, and make a lot of money. Unlike Marco, he cares little about political and economic conditions in Uruguay. Ironically, a small streak of idealism, or perhaps it is honor, leads to his being shot to death in a duel. He refuses to kowtow to a higher ranking officer because that officer has deliberately caused the death of another subordinate.

JAKE BRIGHTON (*At All Costs**) Real name Jake Donovan. In 1983, he is twenty-four, newly married to Carolyn. Both are part of a hazardous-materials team sent to inventory the contents of a building sealed by the Environmental Protection Agency, a U.S. Army munitions and weapons depot closed under the Johnson administration. He and Carolyn become the "fall guys" who are blamed for the explosion and spend the next fourteen years on the run, always worried about the effect on their son, Travis*. Jake feels they should have turned themselves in and proved their innocence. For a long time, they believe that the bombing was an attempt to cover up the body they saw while in the building. Jake, Carolyn, and Nick* Thomas enter the building hunting for evidence to prove their innocence and discover only the bones of a dog. Police appear a few minutes after they arrive at the building, leading Jake to wonder why the law is always so close on their heels. That thinking leads him to Peter Frankel as the bomber, an idea he shares with Irene* Rivers when he breaks into her hotel room. He pricks her conscience (and touches on one of the novel's themes) when he asks her whether her job is to do what's right or just to follow orders.

JAMES WILLIAM WILSON (*Kinship**) Husband of Rae* Jean and father of Jimmy* and Pert Wilson, the fifteen-year-old narrator. He has been absent from home since Pert was born and has held a variety of jobs, having stuck to nothing—welding, electrical work, auto mechanics, and salesman of sheet metal, among others. He steals Rae Jean's hard-won rainy-day money, as well as funds from other people, and runs up an IOU of one thousand dollars gambling with the disreputable Weevils. He takes off just as the bubble of his deceit bursts. Pert realizes that she shares some characteristics with him—eyes, lips, grin, even her "fast mouth"—but her chin is different, and, she realizes, so is her attitude toward her family. Probably the only reason James William came back to Kinship was to claim some money that he had inherited.

JAMIE (*Song In the Silence: The Tale of Lanen Kaelar**) The faithful steward of Hadron. The protagonist, Lanen Kaelar, loves Jamie deeply and wishes he were her father. While they are on their way to Illara to attend the fair, Jamie tells her his story. After his parents died when he was still in his teens, he became a hired assassin, took a job with Marik of Gundar, with whom Lanen's mother, Maran Vena, was living at the time, and learned that Marik was in league with the Demonlord, Berys, in order to become a rich and powerful merchant. Marik pledged to Berys that he would give Berys his first child as payment for special powers. This first child turns out (not unexpectedly) to be Lanen, whom Marik seizes to fulfill his part of the bargain while they are on the Dragon Isle. Jamie drops out of the story after he arranges passage for Lanen to the Dragon Isle but reenters at the end, where he is seen as having been a faithful steward of Lanen's farm while she was away.

JANIE JOHNSON (*The Voice on the Radio**) Pretty, red-haired girl of six-teen, also known as Jennie Spring. When Janie was fifteen, she noticed the picture of herself as a small child on the side of a milk carton advertising lost children and traced her birth parents. Before the trauma of Reeve Shields's betrayal, Janie was just another pretty high school junior, planning her wedding to Reeve and sharing intimate confidences with her best friends. The reader gradually learns Janie/Jennie's story, mostly from Reeve's over-the-air account and partly as details variously come out. Janie was coaxed into a car and kidnapped from New Jersey when she was three by Hannah, the mentally ill daughter of her Johnson parents in Connecticut. Hannah led them to believe that Janie was her out-of-wedlock child, gave Janie to them to raise, and disappeared.

JASON'S GOLD (Hobbs*, Will, Harper-Collins, 1999) Historical-adventure and survival novel set for about a year during the Klondike gold rush of 1897 mostly in Alaska and Canada. The rigors of survival are nothing new for Jason Hawthorn, 15, who after his father died, quit his ten-cent-an-hour Seattle cannery job to seek his fortune in New York City. Having read about the lavish gold strikes in the Klondike, he hops freights to Seattle, where he finds that his brothers, Abraham, 23, and Ethan, 21, sawmill workers, have left for the gold fields, using his five-hundred-dollar inheritance to help stake their trip. With ten dollars in his pocket and lots of determination, Jason stows aboard a ship to Skagway, is reported to authorities by a bunch of con men because he refuses to help them pick pockets, is beaten up, and is dumped off at Juneau. On the beach, he encounters a fellow named Jack, who turns out to be the historical writer Jack London. Jason takes the lower White Pass route through the mountains, but rains turn it into a quagmire, it becomes littered with dead horses (hence, it comes to be known as "Dead Horse Trail"), and the increasingly desperate gold rushers become crazed with fear and highly dangerous. Hoping to catch his brothers at Lake Bennett on the way to Dawson City, he turns back to take the steeper Chilkoot Route, on the way rescuing a husky that a crazed stampeder is about to shoot, then hears the man blow his brains out. Continuing with King, the dog, at his side carrying a good share of the load, Jason contracts food poisoning and is nursed to health by a raven-haired girl, Jamie Dunavant, 14, and her father, gray-bearded Homer, a poet (fictionalized poet Robert Service). Once over the terrible Chilkoot Pass into Canada, at Lake Bennett he discovers he has just missed his brothers. He winters at a place called "Five Fingers" in the cabin of a prospector named Henderson and takes in a boy whose frostbitten leg has been amputated, Charlie Maguire. In the spring in Dawson City, Jason sees a sign that says HAWTHORN BROTHERS SAWMILL. His brothers are the proprietors of this profitable business and inform Jason he is part owner. He finds Dawson City a "carnival," a buzzing hub of activity with new businesses of every kind. He takes in a variety show featuring the "Princess of Dawson," who turns out to be Jamie Dunavant, reciting her father's poems. He spots Jack London again, wearing his characteristic red long underwear. One of the "Kings of the Klondike," Big Alex McDonald, stuffs Charlie's pockets with gold nuggets so the boy can go home to Chicago and his family. The novel is filled with substance; readers get their money's worth. The action moves fast and involves many characters, but the focus is always on gritty Jason, whose harrowing adventures reveal the extreme difficulties the goldseekers faced. Despite his ordeal, he succeeds in achieving not his planned objective but in finding success as an entrepreneur, as in reality did many gold seekers. The extensive details give a good feel for the excitement following the discovery, the hopes of the stampeders, the sense that almost anything would be better than toiling in "wage slavery" in an American factory or business, and the almost unbelievable dangers both physical and psychological. Some passages read like a history book, but these are few and softened by the abundant action. An author's note at the end gives historical background, provides a short bibliography, and identifies the many historical characters. Several maps keep the reader oriented. ALA/YA.

JED HOSKINS (*Armageddon Summer**) Teenage boy caught up in an apocalyptic cult's campground fortress as they await the destruction of the world predicted by their leader, the Reverend* Raymond Beelson. Although Jed is a skeptic and sees the contradictions and lack of logic among the Believers, as the group calls itself, he is persuaded to go along by his father, who is under Beelson's charismatic spell, and by his older sister, Alice, away at college, who worries about their father and says, "Someone's got to look out for him." Their mother ran off some months earlier to live with a photographer in Colorado. At first, Jed's father reacted by drinking heavily, then turned to the Church of the Believers, who scorn modern technology and are sure that God will destroy the world by fire, except for 144 of the faithful who will congregate on top of Mount Weeupcut near Mount Holyoke, Massachusetts, to wait out the holocaust and then go forth to start a new, purer society. Jed smuggles his laptop computer with him. When he has sneaked up the mountain to try to use it, Beelson finds him. Jed is surprised by what he perceives as the genuine conviction of the man and agrees not to use the laptop again. Later, after the armed "Angels" and the latecomers trying to get in to be saved seem destined for conflict, Jed does get out his computer to listen to the news, then with Marina Marlow goes to Beelson to warn him. Jed realizes that the man is afraid and lonely. In the riot that occurs when the outsiders break in, Jed sees his father shoot and kill a woman before they are swept apart in the swirl of bodies. Although he sees Beelson consumed by flames on the porch of the burning camp hall and leads Marina's mother and another young mother to safety, Jed is not able to save his own father. The romance between Jed and Marina is sweet and chaste, but in their letters at the end, after Jed has gone to live with his mother in Colorado, there is a suggestion that they might get together seriously in the future.

JEFF HANSON (*Bull Catcher**)   Star baseball player for Shipley (Wisconsin) High School and best friend of Bull Larsen, who tells the story. Jeff's love for the game appears at every turn in his life. He is great at shortstop, can catch passably, hits well, and exudes baseball savvy. He becomes team captain in his junior year and organizes Bull and their friends for pickup games as well as for summer teams. His greatest ambition is to win a scholarship to a big college and then go on to the major leagues. Jeff's stepfather's love for his family, including Jeff, serves as a stark contrast to the ill-treatment received by Billy* Collins from his father and corresponds to the kind, supportive relationship Bull has with Grandpa*.

JEMMIE LEWIS (*Crossing Jordan**) Daughter of the fatherless African American family who buy the big, old Faircloth place next door to the Bodines and who becomes best friends with Cass Bodine. Jemmie is more self-assured and venturesome than Cass and confidently tackles hard words when they are reading *Jane Eyre*. She knows the value of higher education and looks forward to getting an athletic scholarship, whereas Cass simply says going to college is beyond the Bodines' means. Jemmie comes up with most of the ideas for activities, like leaving notes in the cemetery where Miss Liz, the previous owner of the Lewises' house, is buried and reading there in secret.

JEZA (*The Last Day**)   Beautiful, enigmatic, young woman of unusual powers to heal, appear and disappear, and speak. On the eve of the Third Millennium, she appears and declares she is the Daughter of God, arousing great controversy, in particular for her verbal attacks against the Roman Catholic Church for hypocrisy and inattention to its ministry to the poor and unfortunate. Jonathan Feldman* and others who investigate Jeza's background believe that her extraordinary powers come because tests at the Israeli supersecret lab in the Negev Desert have altered her physically and mentally, but later it is learned that she was the control subject. The Israeli authorities fear she jeopardizes their national security and eventually arrange to have her assassinated. In a surprising conclusion, she is resurrected in the form of her invalid older sister. Her story revisits that of Jesus for a Third Millennium audience.

JIMMY (*Joy School**)   Young gas station manager with whom Katie falls in love. After their initial meeting, when she has just fallen through the ice of a pond near his station, he welcomes her frequent visits, since the station is not very busy in the afternoons and he is bored and lonely. He was a hockey player in high school, and he is a reader, so they find common interests to discuss. His great love is his 1954 Corvette, a Blue Flame 6, which he has kept a secret from his wife. When she finds out about it, he sells it and agrees to move to Iowa to work for her brother. He has told Katie that his wife was in love with his best friend, who broke up with her. She went out with Jimmy just to get back at him. Katie finally realizes that he loves his wife far more than his wife loves him. After Katie thinks he has gone, she goes to the pond and is feeding the ducks when he shows up, saying getting ready to move took longer than he expected. He tries to tell her that he is honored by her affection and that she will love someone deeply some time. He is a decent, rather naive young man, not about to take advantage of Katie's infatuation, even though he thinks she is two years older than she actually is.

JIMMY WILSON (*Kinship*)   Brother of Pert Wilson and son of Rae* Jean and James* William Wilson. He is a considerate, caring young man, who drops out of school to help his mother meet the bills, although he knows he will be forever handicapped in getting a good job. He is a valued employee at the gas station where he works. He longs for a new car and wants to marry pretty Sue Ellen Jenkins. When Rae Jean's rainy-day money is missing, Pert is certain Jimmy took it to buy a ring for Sue Ellen. Later, she learns that Miss Mulch, a caring trailer part resident, gave Jimmy the ring that her fiancé had given her. When Sue Ellen decides not to marry Jimmy and to give their baby up for adoption, Jimmy decides that he will raise the baby himself. At the beginning of the novel, Jimmy seems the typical at-loose-ends teenage boy. Later, Jimmy shows himself to be a fine young man, one who, in contrast with his father, assumes the responsiblities he knows he should.

JIM THE BOY (Earley*, Tony, Little, Brown, 2000)   Adult realistic family and boy's growing-up novel set mostly in the little town of Aliceville, North Carolina, for one year in 1934, similar, although lighter and on a smaller scale, to the Southern regional family-secrets genre. The father of Jim Glass, 10, died of a heart attack one week before Jim, Jr., was born. The boy has grown up living with his nearly reclusive widowed mother, Cissy (Elizabeth McBride Glass), in the house of her older brother, Uncle* Zeno, and next door to her other older brothers, Uncle Al and Uncle Coran, all tall, lean men, each of whom has his own house. The conservative, respected uncles together run the family farm-feed store, cotton gin, and grist mill, in their sleepy little town at the foot of Lynn's Mountain. They manage good, if spare, lives on their pay-as-you-go basis in these Great Depression times. Jim knows that his father was estranged from his grandfather and that his mother greatly dislikes her former father-in-law, Amos* Glass, now a very old man, who lives on the mountain. Details about the estrangement come out gradually and provide some cohesion for the otherwise largely episodic, anecdotal story. On his tenth birthday, Jim decides he is ready to do a man's work, hoeing corn with his uncles and the field hands, who include black Abraham*. He makes so many mistakes, however, that he goes home feeling miserable. That evening a birthday cake with candles, shiny new baseball glove and bat, plenty of joshing, and lots of good wishes indicate that they all love him despite his shortcomings. Among other episodes, Uncle Al takes Jim with him to look into buying a team of Belgians in South Carolina and then on to Myrtle Beach so that they can both take a look at the Atlantic Ocean. Jim starts fourth grade in a new, unfinished, two-story consolidated school. He makes a new friend in mountain kid Penn Carson, a big, strong Quaker boy, who is a worthy baseball opponent. Among other activities, they meet the Carolina Moon train in which the stationmaster tells them Ty Cobb is a passenger, although they never see the famous baseball player. They are almost beaten up by town toughs but are rescued by Abraham. At the Big Day carnival, Jim bests Penn at climbing the slippery pole and wins the dollar prize. When later Penn gets polio and is unable to walk, Jim feels guilty that he has not always treated Penn better. On Christmas Eve, the uncles wake Jim and take him outside for a spectacular view: electricity has been extended to Aliceville, and the new schoolhouse is lighted in celebration. The last major episode concerns the uncles' taking Jim up the mountain in the McBrides' old truck. Jim visits Penn, who is now in a wheelchair and to whom Jim gives his birthday glove. Jim also looks at Amos, now a very old, sick, frail man, through the bedroom window, the only glimpse he has ever had of his grandfather. As evening falls and he and the uncles look down at Aliceville, Jim feels small but happy. The world is very large, and he is just a boy, but as Uncle Zeno reminds him, he is "their" boy. Humorous, poignant, serious, exciting by turns, the book realizes the rural and small-town

area well and is especially good at capturing the close-knit McBrides. Stories within the larger story are memorable, as when Uncle Zeno tells how he baptized chicks when he was a boy and how Aliceville got its name. Booklist.

JIP HIS STORY (Paterson*, Katherine, Lodestar/Dutton, 1996) Historical novel of an orphan on a Vermont poor farm who is discovered to be a slave, son of a white owner who wants to retrieve his property. His escape, aided by a Quaker family and a schoolteacher, form the climax of the novel, but life on the farm, run by an alcoholic overseer, is the strongest element. For a longer entry, see _Dictionary, 1995–1999_. ALA/YA.

JOHN D. HAMILTON (_Dust Devils_*) Usually referred to in the novel as John D. Hamilton by God to indicate his proud, stubborn, independent nature. When his wife died giving birth to their son, Ira, now in his late teens, the child was suckled by Sage Flower, the wife of Native American Indian Paiute Chief Black Rock Tom. She raised Ira until he was four and his father could take care of him. Although grateful to her, he regrets having allowed an Indian to raise his son ("my first and biggest mistake"), especially since Ira still has strong ties to Black Rock Tom's family and band and to Cricket, Black Rock Tom's son Ira's age. But when he learns that the Paiutes have again saved Ira's life, that Ira and Cricket's sister, Thoma, are marrying, and that Thoma is expecting his grandchild, he changes his attitude toward Black Rock Tom. He concludes that the Indians are good people, badly misjudged and ill-used by the whites. At the wedding, he extends his hand to Black Rock Tom, and they shake, initiating a new era of peace and friendship between the two stubborn, proud, sturdy old men.

JOHNNY SURRATT (*An Acquaintance with Darkness**)   Historical Rebel-sympathizing son of Mary Surratt and brother of Annie* Surratt. Johnny is involved in the plot to assassinate President Lincoln at the end of the American Civil War. At the beginning of the novel, Johnny appears at the house of the protagonist and narrator, Emily Pigbush, a few days before Lincoln's death, to tell her that he is leaving the city and has arranged for the medicines her ill mother needs. Emily has loved Johnny since childhood and worries about him for days afterward. He is a friend of John Wilkes Booth and has been involved in spying and other activities for which authorities seek him. At one point in the story, Emily receives a letter from him telling her that he is safe in Canada and will return when his mother needs him. He never comes, however. He is the antithesis of Robert* deGraaf, the steady, loyal assistant to Emily's Uncle* Valentine Bransby.

JOHNNY VOODOO (Lane*, Dakota, Delacorte, 1996)   Present-day, realistic novel of an unlikely romance that goes sour but teaches a girl something of her own family and helps her reconcile with her father. Lonely, unhappy in her new environment in Charmette, Louisiana, Dee (Deirdre), 16, misses her life in Manhattan and her mother, who died about two months earlier. She despises her artist father, Curtis, partly because he has brought her and her brother, Kenny, 13, to this Deep South town where he paints and sleeps with a series of bimbo models and partly because he made her mother so unhappy in her last years. On her way

to school one day, Dee is surprised to have a boy speak to her through the iron fence that surrounds a park. He is about seventeen, with long hair, a beautiful, sensitive face, and he carries an accordion. Gossip in the school soon tells her he is Johnny Voodoo, though she later learns his name is Vouchamps, and that he is weird and she should stay away from him. Since she has not yet found anyone she likes in the school, she pays no attention and gradually begins to see Johnny after school and to think about him constantly. After they get to know each other, he takes her in his boat to a cabin in the swamp where she meets, with a shock, his brother Leander, a transvestite twelve years older than Johnny who has been in a mental institution. She learns that since Johnny was thirteen he has cared for Leander who lives, mostly, in a mini-commune in New Orleans except when he gets too difficult and they kick him out, whereupon he returns to the cabin and Johnny. The younger brother plays in the streets of the next town for food money and stays alone when Leander is well enough to go back to New Orleans. The closeness of Dee and Johnny grows, but does not include intercourse. Her absences and late returns finally impinge on Curtis's consciousness, and he confronts her. In the ensuing argument, he summons Kenny and forces him to tell Dee about finding her mother embracing a young man in the kitchen. The occasion, which leaves them all exhausted and weeping, brings Dee closer to Kenny than she has ever been and makes her realize that his reserve and compulsive neatness is an emotional protection he has built up. In a clumsy effort to make everything all right, Curtis plans a party, insisting that they all invite everyone they know. His current model, Robyn, whom Dee has considered a brainless tramp, turns out to be a good organizer and more aware of the family problems than she has seemed. By accident Curtis and Dee meet Johnny, who accepts Curtis's invitation to the party, but does not show up for the wild affair until Dee has given up on him and become drunk with some of the high school girls. They both say the wrong things, and she screams at him to leave. When she sees him after that, she feels and acts cold. The last time she sees him, he tells her that Leander is really bad, that they are going away together, and that she can use the cabin and the boat. Later, as she begins to feel again, she finds her way to the cabin, cleans it up, and returns frequently, gradually regaining her feeling for Johnny and understanding that, although he may never return, he has taught her a great deal about love. Although Dee's dysfunctional family is convincing, her romance with Johnny seems more an adolescent wish fulfillment—the wonderful, understanding lover who shows up from nowhere and loves her without reserve—than a relationship with a real person. The novel resists a happy-ever-after ending, but Dee's gain in self-knowledge seems out of focus and unsatisfying. ALA/YA.

JOHNSON, ANGELA (1961–) Born in Tuskegee, Alabama; writer of sensitive picture books and novels with African American characters. Her *Heaven** (Simon & Schuster, 1998) is a psychological study of a girl who discovers that she has been adopted by her aunt and uncle and that the man she has thought to be her uncle is really her father. For earlier biographical information and a title entry, see *Dictionary, 1990–1994* [*Toning the Sweep*]. A title entry for *Heaven* appears in *Many People, One Land* [no. 58].

JOHNSON, SCOTT (1952–) Born in Chicago, Illinois; graduate of Indiana University and the University of Massachusetts; high school teacher of English and creative writing; writer of problem and growing-up novels for young adults; and author of articles for magazines and journals. His experiences in the classroom and with his students provide the raw material for his stories. In *Safe at Second** (Philomel, 1999), two boys grow up credibly when they are forced to deal with adversity after a serious baseball injury. The novel was recommended by the American Library Association for young adults. For additional information about Johnson, titles, and a title entry, see *Dictionary, 1995–1999* [*Safe at Second*].

JORGE RODRIGUEZ (*Dangerous Skies**) The man whose body Buck Smith finds lying dead in the creek. Jorge managed the teams of Haitian and Mexican seasonal truck-farm laborers on Chesapeake Bay's eastern shore, treating both laborers and farmers fairly. He worked hard to get the laborers' housing improved and to secure busses to take them to church and to town. He had had problems with Jumbo* Rawlin over the workers and also had intervened when Jumbo beat up Tunes* Smith. Buck is sure that Jumbo killed Jorge, but since Jumbo brings witnesses to support him and no solid evidence is found to implicate him, Jumbo is never charged with the crime.

JOY SCHOOL (Berg*, Elizabeth, Random, 1997) Girl's growing-up novel set in Missouri in the early 1960s. During the winter of her thirteenth year, the narrator, Katie, braves the difficulties of starting an unfriendly new school, the loss of her first love, and, since the recent death of her mother and the departure of her older sister for Mexico with her boyfriend, the problems of living alone with her uninvolved father, an army colonel of whom she is understandably afraid. Her strongest support is their housekeeper, Ginger*, whom she recognizes as a genuinely kind and perceptive young woman, but resents in a confused way when she realizes that Ginger may become her stepmother. Her contact with her old home in Texas is kept alive, barely, by occasional letters from Cherylanne, her onetime best friend, full of advice on makeup, boyfriends, and French kissing, and by a less-than-successful visit from Cherylanne just before Christmas. A visit from her sister, Diane, and her boyfriend, Dickie, at Thanksgiving, is equally unsuccessful. Diane has come, mainly, to let her father know that she is pregnant and married, but their relationship, always strained, is antagonistic, and Katie can see that Diane is clearly bored with Dickie. Katie really does not much like her only new friend at school, Cynthia O'Connell, and she despises Cynthia's smarmy but critical mother, although she rather likes her old, bedridden Italian grandmother, Nona, who shouts at her daughter, occasionally pulls herself up at night to cook huge batches of spaghetti sauce, and offers Katie fifty dollars to bring her some whiskey. Shortly before her death, Nona gives Katie her old, leather-bound diary, written all in Italian, which she says is to "feel love." Cynthia says it is to get it out of the house so her mother will not read it. The most important people in the winter are Taylor, Katie's other school friend, and Jimmy, the gas station manager she falls in love with. Taylor is a beautiful, poised girl who models professionally, as does her older sister. She seems to have been expelled from a fancy private school, for unexplained reasons, but she dates boys

from the school and gets Katie to double date with her at a drive-in movie. Katie is appalled when Taylor and her date make out vigorously in the front seat and her own date tries to paw and French-kiss her. The evening ends even more disastrously when her father learns that she has been to a drive-in and only Ginger's interference keeps him from striking her. Taylor, moreover, shoplifts expensive items and walks out of restaurants calmly, leaving a large tip but failing to pay the bill. Katie is both shocked and fascinated by Taylor, partly because the other girls would give their eyeteeth to be chosen as her friend. Jimmy, however, is a thoroughly decent man. She meets him when she falls through the ice of a shallow pond where she is skating and makes her way to his gas station nearly frozen. He lends her a mechanic's uniform to change into, buys her hot chocolate, strips off his own socks for her to wear, and even drives her home, luckily before her father arrives. Jimmy tells her he is twenty-three, and she says she is fifteen, almost, one of many lies she finds herself saying, a new habit that worries but does not stop her. Katie is completely smitten. She has never seen a man so good looking, and, although she soon discovers he is married, she daydreams about him and drops in frequently at the station, where he always welcomes her in a friendly way. He takes her for a ride in the Corvette he has bought and fixed up lovingly, without letting his wife know, then tells Katie he has to sell it because they are moving to Iowa. The shock causes her to tell him that she loves him, and he is understandably distressed, having viewed their relationship as a casual friendship. Devastated, Katie talks to Father Compton, an old priest at a church where she occasionally sits to be by herself, pouring out to him all about her love for Jimmy, her disillusion with Taylor, her loneliness for her mother, and her disappointment that Diane has lost her baby, refused to come home with her father, and left Dickie to head out to California by herself. Father Compton advises her not to be afraid of sorrow, since it can teach you about joy. Although what happens to Katie is not much different from events narrated in a dozen other recent books about girls her age, the author makes it distinctive by the use of telling details from Katie's perceptive point of view that characterize her as a very bright, vulnerable, and brave girl. Through the winter she develops some assertiveness, and, though she is sure she will never love anyone as much as Jimmy, in the end she is beginning to regain hope. ALA/YA.

JUBILEE JOURNEY (Meyer*, Carolyn, Harcourt, 1997)   Contemporary novel sequel to *White Lilacs*, this book being about the great-granddaughter of the original protagonist, who comes to Texas for Juneteenth Day, celebration of the day emancipation reached the slaves of the area. A mixed-race child, she learns for the first time something of her African American heritage and the prejudice that still exists in the South. For a longer entry, see *Dictionary, 1995–1999*. ALA/YA.

JUDGE WICKHAM (*Dangerous Skies**) Elderly, retired court judge, who is a good friend of Buck Smith, the narrator. People respect him but also feel that he is no longer right in the head. Buck asks his advice when African American Tunes* Smith is about to be arrested for murder. Since Judge has faith in the judicial system, he advises Tunes to turn herself in. Nothing goes as Judge expects, all because Jumbo* Rawlin is white and Tunes is black. After the trial, Judge dies of a stroke. Buck thinks he died of disappointment over what happened to Tunes. Buck feels Judge advised them correctly, but because he was thought to be prone to "spells," Sheriff* did not give Judge the credit he deserved.

JUMBO RAWLIN (*Dangerous Skies**) James Beauregard Rawlin, the owner of the most land in the Eastern Shore region in which Buck Smith and Tunes* Smith live. Their neighbor, he is highly regarded as a pillar of society. A huge hulking man, he is described by Buck, the narrator, as "mean as a green-eyed snake." Buck says Jumbo threatens children who come near his property, smashed in the head and shot the dog belonging to Tunes's father, Kneebone* Smith, and abused his wife. Jumbo also had some trouble with Jorge* Rodriguez, whose dead body Buck and Tunes find in the creek, having met his fate in the same way that Kneebone's dog did. Despite Jumbo's reputation for meanness, the community accepts his story over that of Tunes, who is black. Jumbo claims that Tunes and Jorge were lovers and denies both having committed the murder and ever having sexually abused Tunes. He gets away with both crimes.

JUNGLE DOGS (Salisbury*, Graham, Delacorte, 1998)   Realistic, sociological- and personal-problem novel set in recent years in a coastal village somewhere in the Hawaiian Islands. Mixed-ethnic (Hawaiian-Filipino-Chinese-Portuguese) Boy (James) Regis, 12, has two main problems: his older brother, Damon, 14, a "tough guy" who leads a school gang and gets the family into trouble, and the wild ("jungle") dogs Boy is sure lurk in the trees along his paper route. Fine scenes at home and at school, the well-realized parallel between the human and animal dogs, and the author's keen ear for the speech of the age group and sharp eye for teen behavior give this book credibility and clarity. For a more detailed entry, see *Many Peoples, One Land* [no. 228]. ALA/YA.

JUST ELLA (Haddix*, Margaret Peterson, Simon & Schuster, 1999)   Light, fantasy sequel to *Cinderella*, telling what happened after the prince fitted the glass slipper to her foot and swept her off to the palace. At first dazzled by the unfamiliar deference and luxury, Ella Brown, now called Princess Cynthiana Eleanora, is soon embarrassed at not understanding what seem to her ridiculous rules, then frustrated at being prevented from making any decisions, and finally furious at being treated as a beautiful, mindless object. In the months leading up to the wedding, she is given lessons in palace protocol, religion, history, dancing, needlepoint, painting, and other subjects deemed necessary for a royal princess, but mostly she learns what not to do. When the maid fails to arrive before she rises, she makes up the fire herself, and finds that she has shocked everyone, especially Madame Bisset, her decorum instructor, and that the maid has been beaten and dismissed for oversleeping. When Lord Reston, her pompous instructor, has a stroke in the middle of his tedious history of the kings of the realm, she loosens his tight collar, sends a minor servant running for the royal physician, and is found with her ear against his lordship's chest as she listens for a heartbeat, only to be told that it is highly improper conduct. When she asks about his health at the luncheon table, Madame Bisset explains acidly that unpleasant subjects are not to be discussed by ladies. Mary, the little servant who fetched the doctor, later whispers to her secretly that his lordship

is alive but partly paralyzed, and she becomes Ella's first friend in the palace. Her second is Lord Reston's replacement, his son, Jed, who is expected to take on his father's job as official teacher of the royal religion, but she discovers that his real passion is to help the plight of the refugees from the continual war with neighboring Suala, a cause in which he has been unable to interest anyone with power or access to the royal purse. Jed is awkward, continually forgetting the proper forms of address, given to frank speech, and clearly smitten by Ella's beauty. The rigid expectations stifle Ella, and she begins to doubt that her life will change for the better after she is married. She sees the prince, Charm, for only an hour or two a week, an awkward, chaperoned session where they have a little stilted conversation. She realizes that he is empty headed, unable to make even the smallest decision without advice, and that he chose her only for her beauty, a requirement in all the royal marriages so that all their children will be good looking, as are all the Charming family. Instead of just running away, she thinks it only fair to ask him to break their engagement. The idea of her leaving, however, horrifies and angers him. Before she has a chance to persuade him differently, he has tied her up and goes off for advisers, among them Madame Bisset, who explain that canceling the wedding is impossible. When she is resolute, Madame Bisset drugs her, and she is carted off to a dungeon. There she has only the food that Mary smuggles to her. When she does not give in right away, Madame Bisset arrives with a horrible creature named Quog, soon to be executed for rape, to be her jailer. Mary, who tells her that Jed has left, having been given funds for his refugee camp, also smuggles a shovel, and Ella starts each night digging out the hole in the floor provided in lieu of a chamber pot. On the sixth night, the prince shows up, doing a poor job of acting horrified to find her there and proposing to rescue her. When Quog protests, Charm calmly runs his sword through the brute, but leaves when Ella insists she must stay two more days as "penance" for wronging him. That night her tunnel breaks through, and she eventually makes it to the Sualan border, where she finds that Jed has set up a refugee camp. He immediately proposes, but Ella is hesitant, not yet ready to jump into another commitment. They work together at the camp, where her knowledge of medicine is very valuable. When he is called back to the palace, his father having died, he leaves Ella in charge of the camp. He hopes to work toward ending the Sualan war or, failing that, to persuade his younger brother to take his hereditary position at the palace and return to Ella. A letter from him tells her that rather than admit she rejected the prince, they have arranged that one of her stepsisters take her place, and the royal wedding has proceeded as scheduled. This version of *Cinderella* has no magic elements, although Mary and many of the palace people believe in the fairy godmother and the pumpkin coach. Ella has worn her mother's wedding dress, obtained the slippers from a local glassblower, and taken herself to the ball. Underlying the humor in the novel, which lies in Ella's clear view of the stupidity of much of palace life, is a strong feminist statement of how much more important thought and action are than beauty and docility, a reversal of the traditional *Cinderella* story. ALA/YA.

K

KARR, KATHLEEN (1946–)   Born in Allentown, Pennsylvania; educator, theater manager, author. Among other novels with historical settings is *The Boxer** (Farrar, 2000), about an Irish boy in New York in the 1880s who manages to support his family and rescue them from poverty by prizefighting, mostly illegal at the time. For earlier biographical information and a title entry, see *Dictionary, 1995–1999* [*The Great Turkey Walk*].

KATE DEVLIN (*Snow in August**) Mother of protagonist Michael Devlin, an Irish immigrant to Brooklyn, New York, and widow, her husband having been killed in World War II in Europe. When Michael asks her whether he should tell the police about who attacked and robbed Mr. G [sic], she says absolutely not, because she remembers the trouble that beset Irish informers in the old country. When the police come to interview Michael, she throws them out. Her behavior demonstrates how situations that seem the same are not necessarily so, police informing in Ireland being quite different from the informing that is needed in their crime-ridden neighborhood in Brooklyn. At book's end, the Devlins move out of the area. Kate has had enough of the gangs.

KATHERINE OF ARAGON (*The Secret Diary of Anne Boleyn**)   Katherine, queen of England. A Spanish princess, she was the first wife of Henry* VIII, king of England, and mother by Henry of Princess Mary, who later became queen. After Henry falls in love with Anne* Boleyn, he decides to end his marriage with Katherine and send her to a nunnery. She has not produced the male heir he desires, has grown unattractive as she aged, and has developed a spiteful tongue. In addition, since relations between Spain and England have grown chilly, Henry no longer needs her politically. He has their marriage annulled on the grounds of incest, since, when Henry married her, she was the widow of Henry's older brother, Arthur, and hence, he maintains, she is his sister-in-law. Henry pulls numerous strings and throws his political weight around for years in order to accomplish his objective, and in the process separates the Church of England, whose head he and subsequent English monarchs become, from the Roman Catholic Church and starts the Reformation in England. (See also Catherine of Aragon*.)

KAYLA RUBENSTEIN (*Torn Thread**) Tall, quick-witted prisoner, 17, who befriends Polish Jews Eva and Rachel Buchbinder while they are in the slave labor camp in Czechoslovakia. Kayla had once been in Auschwitz, from which she gained release by volunteering to work at another camp. She has found a way to work with Czech partisans, among other acts dumping chemicals on bolts of fabric just before they are shipped, so that the fabric soon disintegrates. Late in the story, the girls discover that Kayla has disappeared. Her fate is never revealed.

KEEPING THE MOON (Dessen*, Sarah, Viking, 1999)   Contemporary coming-of-age novel of a girl who spends a summer with an eccentric aunt in a coastal North Carolina town, learns about love and kindness, and begins to grow out of her perception of herself as an ugly duckling. For a longer entry, see *Dictionary, 1995–1999*. ALA/YA.

KEILLOR, GARRISON (1942–) Born in Anoka, Minnesota; radio writer and host, novelist. Best known for his show on National Public Radio, *Prairie Home Companion*, Keillor has capitalized on his knowledge of small-town Minnesota fictionalized as Lake Wobegon, where "all the women are strong, the men are good looking, and the children are above average." He started radio work when he was a student at the University of Minnesota, where he received his B.A. in

1966 and later did graduate work, and has continued in radio except for a brief period when he lived in Denmark. Among his works of fiction are *Lake Wobegon Days* (Viking, 1985), a national best-seller, and *Leaving Home* (Viking, 1987), a book of short stories, both, as well as a number of others including books of poems, for a general audience, and *The Sandy Bottom Orchestra** (Hyperion, 1996), on which he collaborated with his wife, Jenny Lind Nilsson, for young adults. Keillor has also written for the *New Yorker* for many years.

KELTON, ELMER (1926–)   Born in Andrews, Texas; graduate of the University of Texas; farm and ranch editor for the *San Angelo Standard-Times*, editor of *Ranch* and associate editor of *Livestock Weekly*; highly acclaimed author of about fifty short stories and western-adventure novels for an adult audience, set mostly in the past in western Texas. He is a six-time winner of the prestigious Spur Award of Western Writers of America, and recipient of the Western Heritage Award of the National Cowboy Hall of Fame. His first Spur Award was for his second novel, *Buffalo Wagons* (Ballantine, 1957), about buffalo hunters. Several books concern the American Civil War, among them *The Texas Rifles* (Ballantine, 1960) and *Dark Thicket* (Doubleday, 1985), and some are about outlaws and lawmen in the Old West, like *Hanging Judge* (Ballantine, 1969). *Cloudy in the West** (Doherty, 1997), is a tension-filled story set in 1885, in which Joey, 12, flees for his life and has exciting adventures in western Texas. The book was chosen by the American Library Association for young adults. Regarded as one of the best western writers of all time, Kelton lives in San Angelo, Texas.

KENNETH (*Criminals**)   Punk hooligan father who leaves the baby in the men's rest room of the bus depot in Perth, Scotland. He has almost forgotten the mother, Joan, whom he runs into while shopping, although he had a one-night affair with her more than a year before, when they were both working at the infirmary. He was fired soon after and has not thought of her since, and he is astounded when she indicates the baby her old Indian mother is carrying is his daughter. He wants no part of the child, but being jobless again he drops in on Joan now and then, and in order to keep the old woman away agrees to baby-sit the child, whom they call Grace, while Joan is at work one day. With no paternal feeling whatsoever, he simply leaves her in the rest room while he has a cup of tea and later sees Ewan* Munro hop on the bus carrying her. While he is far from sharp mentally, Kenneth sees the possibility of making money from the situation, follows, and watches Ewan leave the bus and be picked up by his sister, Mollie*. By asking about her, Kenneth knows where they have taken Grace, and he works out a vague plan to wring a few pounds from Chae* Lafferty, whom he assumes Ewan to be. Gradually, his idea of what he can make increases, as he tries to keep Joan from making a fuss by saying that the child is at his mother's, then using various implausible stories to explain her continued absence. Since Joan is not at ease in the culture and has a brother who is an illegal immigrant, Kenneth has a hold over her to keep her from reporting the baby's loss. Too greedy, Kenneth jumps at the chance of selling Grace for ten thousand pounds to Mollie, but when the child is dropped on the stone floor, he assumes she is dead and takes off. In the end he has nothing and blames Joan for his lost chance.

KERNER, ELIZABETH   Born in Florida in the mid twentieth century, the daughter of a navy man. As a child, she read voraciously books of romantic, swashbuckling adventures and of fantasy, like those of J. R. R. Tolkien, whose influence is readily apparent in her writing. In 1976, she left for St. Andrews University in Scotland, from which she later received her degree. She lives in both the United States and Scotland. Her fantasy novel, *Song In the Silence: The Tale of Lanen Kaelar** (Tor, 1997) describes the adventures of a young human woman among dragons. The novel was chosen by the American Library Association for young adults. Its sequel is *The Lesser Kindred* (Tor, 2001).

KESSLER, CRISTINA   Writer and photographer. Her experiences in living in Africa for the past twenty-five years inspired *No Condition Is Permanent** (Philomel, 2000). An American Library Association selection for young adults, it concerns an American mother and daughter who visit a village in Sierra Leone. Kessler also has written the stories for several picture books, *One Night* (Philomel, 1995); *Jubela* (Simon & Schuster); and *My Great-Grandmother's Gourd* (Orchard, 2000), all set in Africa. *Konte Chameleon, Fine, Fine, Fine!* (Caroline House, 1997) retells a West African folktale, and *All the King's Animals* (Boyds Mills, 1995) is a nonfiction book about wildlife in Swaziland, for which she also provided the photographs. She and her husband live in Mali.

KEVIN FINNEY (*The Door in the Lake**) Brother of Joey (Joseph Patrick), who disappeared two years before the novel begins while camping with his family at Smokewater Lake in the Allegheny Mountains. Since Joey, now fourteen, did not grow at all while he was gone, Kevin, one year younger at thirteen, is bigger than Joey. He treats Joey with disdain at first, but as the novel progresses, he becomes more supportive. He accompanies Ariel* DeWitt and Ethan* Glass on the trip to take Joey into the mountains to where he disappeared. When the alien presence instructs Joey to go through the door in the lake, Kevin at first insists on accompanying Joey. He desists when Joey reminds him that their parents would be devastated if they lost both their sons. Kevin's change of heart toward Joey is a pleasing touch.

KEYES, J. GREGORY (1963–) Born in Meridian, Mississippi; raised on the Navajo Reservation in Arizona; received his B.A. from the University of Mississippi and his M.A. from the University of Georgia, where he is on the faculty. A student of folklore and mythology and particularly interested in civilizations organized around water, Keyes was inspired to write the *Booklist*-recommended adventure fantasy, *The Waterborn** (Ballantine, 1996). His first novel, it is set in a mythical realm that resembles ancient Egypt. The sequel is *The Blackgod* (Ballantine, 1997). Keyes has also written a set of historical fantasies, the first two of which are *Newton's Cannon* (Ballantine, 1998) and *A Calculus of Angels* (Ballantine, 1999). Keyes has also written for the Star Wars series.

KHADI (*No Condition Is Permanent**) Mende girl in the village of Bukama, Sierra Leone, with whom Jodie Nichols, the protagonist and narrator, becomes good friends. On arrival, Khadi meets Jodie with a coconut-milk drink that Jodie finds very refreshing. Khadi shows Jodie how to weed, wash clothes, shell peanuts, pull water, gather firewood, and carry both water and firewood on her head, as the Mende women do. She teaches Jodie to speak Krio, a kind of pidgin English. In short, Khadi pulls Jodie into the life of the village women, and in doing so is Jodie and the reader's window on village life, at least as the women live it. When Jodie realizes that Khadi is illiterate, she teaches her to read and write, to Khadi's delight, since only the village men and boys have these skills.

KILLER.APP (D'Amato*, Barbara, Forge, 1996) Intense, fast-paced thriller about a data systems company that plans, through sophisticated computer use, to kill the president of the United States and control the country and possibly the world. In a novel full of varied characters, the central figures are the narrator, Officer Susanna Maria Figueroa of the Chicago Police Department, and her partner, Norman Bennis; Susanna's sister, Sheryl Birch, a computer whiz at SJR DataSystems, a huge cyberworld company; Dean Utley*, head of SJR; Glen Jaffee and Zach Massendate, officially security employees, actually Utley's right-hand men in crime; Howie Borke, a computer genius, Utley's chief brain in SJR; Jesus Delgado, a highly intelligent Chicago Police Department Detective of Inca descent; and Kiro Ogata, a gay computer expert afflicted with arthrogyposis, a debilitating disease that comfines him to a wheelchair, who works for Bermandyne, Inc., a data processing company. The action starts when the body of Detective Frieswyk, whose disappearance Jesus Delgado has been investigating for five weeks, turns up floating in the Chicago River. At about the same time, Sheryl Birch, pushing a wrong key by accident, happens on a program at SJR that shocks her, since it gives highly personal and current information about employees that could have no direct relevance to their work. Simultaneously, Kiro Ogata, working late, discovers that someone has tapped into confidential files at Bermandyne. Fascination with puzzles leads all three to investigate further, unwittingly calling attention to themselves on the highly sophisticated system at SJR, which Utley controls from his high-rise office like a spider aware of any twitch on its web. Since SJR has taps into the police department, the local hospitals, and competing businesses, as well as many other Chicago enterprises, it is relatively easy for Howie Borke, at Utley's direction, to change the records, temporarily, at the hospital where Ogata is having minor surgery, removing the caution that he is allergic to certain anesthetics. Ogata does not survive the procedure. At the autopsy on Frieswyk, Delgado gets a number of clues, including evidence that the body has been in the water for weeks and that the lungs contain pollen from amaryllis, obviously indoor plants since this is midwinter in Chicago. By clever deduction and persistent work, he builds on a fragment of conversation with Frieswyk just before he disappeared and discovers that the detective had run into a scam in the department motor pool, whereby orders go in for two more cars, every several months, than the computer records, thereby netting for someone in the command line two extra expensive vehicles or a kickback of considerable proportion. Shortly thereafter, Delgado's house is set afire, and he escapes, managing to save his two young daughters but not his wife. When Sheryl's tinkering in the system becomes apparent to Utley, he has Zach and Glen follow her home and run her off the road over a steep banking. In the hospital she is almost killed by a transfusion of the wrong type of blood, the result of one of Howie

Borke's taps into the hospital computer. Sure that there is some connection between her accident and the troubling knowledge that Sheryl confided to her, Susanna and her partner take their suspicions to the superintendent of police and soon they and Delgado are hooked up with the police department wizard, Max Black, whose computer skills are comparable to Howie Borke's. The evil of SJR is apparent to all of them, but its purpose is not clear until Howie, who has not minded killing unknown people but is conscience stricken to have caused, he believes, the death of Sheryl whom he knew and liked, whispers to Susanna that they are planning to kill the president. Since both the president and the corrupt vice president are currently in Chicago, the situation is critical. The wild chases and narrow escapes of the next few hours are breathtaking, with the tension increased because it is impossible to know who among the police are corrupt and which, if any, phones and computers are safe. Susanna's six-year-old son is kidnapped; Bennis is seriously injured; Howie, Max, and Utley are all dead; and the plot is narrowly averted and SJR is exposed. Besides being full of action, the novel is crammed with computer jargon and explanations that are not necessary for a reader to understand but would fascinate an expert or a would-be hacker. Characters are surprisingly well developed, many of them acting as red herrings. The title is an abbreviation for "killer application," which refers to a computer application that replaces a program with a more powerful one. Booklist.

THE KILLER'S COUSIN (Werlin*, Nancy, Delacorte, 1998)   Mystery set in recent years in Cambridge, Massachusetts, in which the narrator, a boy suspected of killing his girlfriend, untangles events of his cousin's death four years earlier, despite the antagonism and outright sabotage of her disturbed younger sister, whom he eventually saves from a fire and befriends. For a longer entry, see *Dictionary, 1995–1999*. ALA/YA; NYPL.

KIM, NANCY (S.) (1966–)   Born in Seoul, Korea; attorney and author. A naturalized citizen, she received her B.A. in 1987 and her J.D. in 1990 from the University of California–Berkeley and her LL.M. in 1992 from the University of California–Los Angeles. Since 1990, she has taught law and worked as a corporate lawyer, mostly in the San Francisco area. Her first novel, *Chinhominey's Secret** (Bridge Works, 1999), concerns intergenerational and cross-cultural conflicts in a Korean American family. She has also published articles in several law journals.

KINDL, PATRICE (1951–)   Born in Alplaus, New York; novelist of strange, bizarre fantasies. *Woman in the Wall** (Houghton, 1997), is about a girl who disappears into the spaces between partitions in an old house and lives there for years until its imminent sale forces her out. For earlier biographical material and a title entry, see *Dictionary, 1990-1994* [*Owl in Love*] and *Dictionary, 1995–1999* [*Owl in Love*].

KINGDOM OF CAGES (Zettel*, Sarah, Warner, 2001)   Very long science fiction novel published for adults, set two or three thousand years in the future. Old Earth, as it is now known, has suffered from a Diversity Crisis. It has collapsed environmentally, socially, and economically, as have other worlds colonized after the devastation of Earth forced humans to develop habitations on other planets and stars. Only Pandora, an experimental station of domed cities, has maintained an ecologically sound environment, largely through repressive governmental policies, thought and behavior control, and limited immigration. Scientists called "hothousers" are engaged in a genetic experiment called the "Eden Project," hoping to produce humans immune to disease. Among a recent group of immigrants are the Trust family, Helice and her two daughters, Chena, almost 14, and Teal, 10. Helice, in particular, has attracted the attention of the hothousers because her genetic material makes her ideal for the Eden Project. In return for more comfortable living quarters, a better job, and education for her daughters, Helice agrees to be implanted with a fetus. Near term, she is murdered and the fetus torn from her body. Chena, in particular, is determined to learn who killed her mother and spends the next five or six years in the process. She and Teal are fostered by Nan Elle Stepka, the aged Pandoran healer on the fringe of Pandoran law but beloved of the common people, that is, the expendable citizens who may be killed or used for body parts if they do not toe the line. Among the Pandoran ruling clique are Dionte, who is adamant in her belief that the Eden Project is the salvation of Pandora and that any means justifies that end. She lies, murders, and manipulates the implanted Conscience of Tam, her birth brother (all Pandoran rulers have implanted Consciences). She also learns how to control Aleph, the Artificial Intelligence city-mind, who sometimes appears as a young woman. Tam, however, having some idea of what she intends, has kept an eye on the Trusts and also on activities outside the main city especially through Nan Elle. He is instrumental in getting the girls to Elle. After many adventures and tight spots later, Chena is captured by hothousers, led by Dionte, for egg implantation, and is imprisoned in a cave where she encounters a little boy of five or six, Eden, who bears a striking resemblance to Teal and whom she rightly suspects is Helice's son. In escaping, she kills Dionte and falls in with Teal and Elle's grandson, handsome, enigmatic Farin, who pops in and out of the story. Things so fall out that Aleph takes charge when Pandora faces imminent and massive invasion. She demands that the Pandorans put aside their selfishness and animosity toward outsiders and work cooperatively with representatives from the other worlds. The message is that cooperation, struggle, hard work, compromise, and dedication to the common good are vital for the survival of the human race. The novel offers nothing new in futuristic fiction and is typical of the genre: high in message, action, and technological setting; low in characterization; and mundane in style. The cast of characters is very large; they are either villains or good guys and are hard to keep track of (a list of characters at the beginning of the book would help). Time and place are revealed bit by bit, a method that becomes frustrating to the reader and even confusing at times, and plot motivations are not always clear. Action scenes are riveting, however, and with editing for clarity and elimination of wordiness, the novel would be a top-notch adventure and girl's growing-up novel. The title refers to the Pandoran rulers' having created a caged, not free, civilization in their unsuccessful efforts to maintain their environment. Booklist.

KING OF SHADOWS (Cooper*, Susan, McElderry, 1999)   Fantasy novel with historical aspects set in 1999 in Cambridge, Massachusetts, in real time, and in London, England, in 1599 in the fantasy time. Narrator Nat (Nathan) Field, an orphan of about twelve, is proud to have been chosen as one of twenty boy performers from the United States for Arby's (Richard Babbage) Company of Boys. They are to perform *Julius Caesar* and *A Midsummer Night's Dream* in London in the new Globe Theatre, a replica of the one of William Shakespeare's* time. Although they find Arby, the director, demanding, strict, and crotchety, the boys develop into a skillful and cohesive group, and after five weeks they leave for England. In London, Nat stays with the Fishers, a kind English family, who treat him well and take an honest interest in his acting and in the company. Nat is to be Puck in *Dream* and Pindarus in *Caesar*. Before the performances begin, however, Nat falls ill and is taken to the hospital, unconscious and suffering from a high fever. He is diagnosed with bubonic plague, once known as the Black Death. A different boy but with the same name, Nat awakens four centuries earlier in the house of actor-director Richard Burbage, his roommate a boy actor named Harry. Harry says that Nat has been ill, that he was afraid Nat had the plague, and that Nat has come to the Lord Chamberlain's Men at the Globe Theatre, Shakespeare's company, from St. Paul's Boys to play Puck for a week. Nat gets on poorly with a malicious boy named Roper, until one day he saves Roper from choking to death by performing the Heimlich maneuver to Roper's gratitude and everyone's amazement. Much of the book is taken up with descriptions of rehearsals, preparations for costumes, and some forays about London. Nat proves adept with both lines and acrobatics and early wins the praise of Burbage and especially Will Shakespeare, who plays Oberon. The Chamberlain's Men's performance for Queen Elizabeth I is a resounding success, and Nat is proud when she compliments him on his Puck. He grows fond of Will, finding in the warmhearted playwright and actor the father figure he has longed for since his own father committed suicide, and Will seems to find Nat a substitute for his own dead son, Hamnet. When at the end of the week Nat asks to remain in the company, Will replies that after he has completed school, he should apply and will be accepted. The next day, however, Nat awakens in the London hospital in 1999 and soon returns to his company. Nat confides in friends about what happened to him, and later Arby tells him that his St. Paul's counterpart was brought forward somehow in time in order not to infect Shakespeare with the plague, which was soon healed by modern antibiotics, and Nat was taken back to 1599 so there would be no break in continuity of performances. He also says that as Nat has missed his parents, so Will missed Nat, whom Will called his "aerial sprite." He perhaps saw in Nat his lost son and wrote the role of Ariel in *The Tempest* for his now-vanished Nat. The characters are hard to keep straight since they are numerous and barely individualized for the most part. Shakespeare and Burbage are well done, but Arby is a mysterious figure never developed. Although the means by which the transfer occurred is not clear, it does not seem to matter, since the book is filled with marvelous details about the theater and the culture of Shakespeare's period. ALA/YA.

KING, STEPHEN (EDWIN) (1947–) Born in Portland, Maine; received a B.Sc. from the University of Maine–Orono; since 1974 a prolific and popular writer for adults of fantasy and science fiction; horror, mystery, and occult fiction; psychological novels; screenplays; teleplays; and short stories under his own name and under pseudonyms, including Richard Bachman, Steve King, and John Swithen. He has an extremely long list of published writings, among them many novels, but critical reaction has been mixed. His best-known novel, *The Green Mile* (Signet, 1996), was made into a popular movie starring Tom Hanks. *The Girl Who Loved Tom Gordon** (Scribner, 1999), a novel of the physical and psychological survival of a girl lost in the woods of western Maine and eastern New Hampshire, was selected by *Booklist* and the American Library Association for young adults. Other recent novels include *Bag of Bones* (Viking, 1998); *Dreamcatcher* (Simon & Schuster, 2001), and *Black House* (Random House, 2001). He lives with his wife, novelist Tabitha King, in Bangor, Maine.

KINGSOLVER, BARBARA (1955–) Born in Annapolis, Maryland; research assistant, technical writer, freelance journalist, and best-selling novelist for adults. She is a graduate of DePauw University with a B.A. in 1977 and the University of Arizona with an M.S. in 1981. Her novel, *The Bean Trees* (Harper, 1988), about a woman who becomes caretaker for a withdrawn Cherokee two-year-old, and its sequel, *Pigs in Heaven* (HarperCollins, 1993), have been very popular. Other novels, including *Animal Dreams* (Harper, 1990) and *Prodigal Summer* (HarperCollins, 2000), have been well received, but her longest and most serious work, *The Poisonwood Bible: A Novel** (HarperFlamingo, 1998), about a missionary family in Africa, set an even higher standard. Kingsolver has also published nonfiction, short stories, and a book of poetry.

KINSHIP (Krisher*, Trudy, Delacorte, 1997)   Realistic novel of family and neighborhood life and a girl's growing up set for a few weeks in the late summer of 1961 in the little town of Kinship, Georgia. Clever, slightly wild, outgoing Pert Wilson, 15, who tells the story in semieducated diction, yearns for her father, James* William. When she was born, he wrote Perty on the birth certificate, because he thought her the "pertiest" baby in all Georgia, and then walked out on his family, to be heard from henceforth via one letter and a few occasional dollars. Pert, her mother, Rae* Jean, a veterinarian's assistant, and Jimmy*, a high school dropout and gas station attendant, live a hand-to-mouth existence in a cramped trailer in a park called "Happy Trails." The Wilsons run the park in return for free accommodations and are well liked by the residents. When handsome, blue-eyed, bearded James William shows up unannounced one Sunday after church, driving a red van loaded with sheet metal, and takes them all, including Gram Wilma Winder, Rae Jean's mother, to breakfast, Pert is almost ecstatic with joy. Two questions control most of the rest of the book: Why did James William leave? How long will he stay? Although Rae Jean and Jimmy become increasingly quiet and abstracted from family life and Gram grows increasingly acerbic toward James William, Pert revels in the attention James William lavishes on her, gifts of clothes and baubles and rides throughout the countryside. James William charms the Happy Trails residents, too, and wins their affection by doing odd jobs for them. When the mayor and zoning commissioners inform the owners of the park that the residents must leave because the area looks junky, James William takes the residents' and owners' money to buy and install sheet metal fender skirts, sod, and trees. When the commissioners say that the trailers are still impermanent structures, he persuades the residents to have them set in concrete and takes their money for that work, too. The residents feel so good about being able to stay and envision how pleasant the place will be that they rename the area as Pert suggests, Homestead Park: Where the Neighbors Is Just like Kin [*sic*]. An indication of possible trouble occurs when James William stands up Pert for the father–daughter dance, but Jimmy saves the evening for his sister by turning up with flowers. Just after the party to celebrate Jimmy's engagement to Sue Ellen Jenkins, the concrete man fails to show up, and it comes out that James William had given him cash without securing a receipt. Other peculiar things occur, among them that the out-county customers to whom James William had sold sheet metal and taken money have not received their deliveries. Then James William is seen leaving town, with the concrete man, in a large mobile home. A wheeler-dealer, James William has simply talked people out of money, lost much of it gambling, and taken off. Pert has learned that true families consist of those who care and look out for one another, as the people in the park and Rae Jean do. The book's structure is confusing, the narration being mostly Pert's but shifting occasionally for a page or so to different park residents. The advantage is that they provide information for the reader that Pert could not know, but the disadvantages are that the flow is interrupted and the reader must refocus and adapt to a variety of narrators only slightly known. The sense of the trailer park community and its ethic is strong, however, the best part of the novel, graphic with details of everyday life and interpersonal relationships. Diction varies acceptably from narrator to narrator, but the residents seem an overly studied group, even including a convenient family of odds makers and gamblers for James William to become involved with, and some colloquial speech seems forced and artificial. The ambivalent James William is the book's strongest figure, the pivot about which everything revolves. The reader's sympathies lie always with Pert, despite her occasional schoolgirl silliness and rebellions, as she learns a bitter lesson about life. ALA/YA.

KIRON (*Firegold**) Young Dalriadan who almost kills Jonathan when he first meets the group in the Red Mountains and who remains contemptuous and antagonistic through much of their acquaintance, although he has been ordered by Tlell, the master bowman, to be Atenar, Hart brother, to the newcomer. When he takes Jonathan to Elanae, his sister, the master fletcher, he shows a different side of himself, gentle, loving, worried about the frail, mute girl. He resents Jonathan because he fears that Athira, the young queen, will choose him for a mate and also, although Jonathan does not learn this until later, because he is the Dalriadan who killed Karena Brae, an unjustified slaying since she was clearly not being aggressive. After his Ridgewalk, Jonathan is chosen by Rhohar, the king horse, and seems destined to be king, so Athira feels she must choose him for a mate, but when the seer will not mark Jonathan's chest with the O-Bredann, she turns gladly to Kiron. After Jonathan rides wildly away, Kiron trails him and shows him the route to the valley so he can return to Greengage with the firegold apple.

KISSING DOORKNOBS (Hesser*, Terry Spencer, Delacorte, 1998) Realistic problem novel set in a Chicago suburb in recent years in which the light, often humorous style points out the seriousness of the subject matter. Tall, green-eyed, blond Tara Sullivan, 14, the narrator, is plagued by numerous irrational fears—"tyrants in her head," she calls them. Even in her early years, she sees monsters in her dreams so terrifying that her mother cannot comfort her, and she scratches her eczema until she is a bloody mess. Later, among other examples, school fire drills upset her, she worries about original sin and the afterlife, and she holds the priest in the confessional with detailed admissions of sins so long that waiting penitents complain and even get angry. She worries about worrying her mother and about whether her mother is doing drugs because of frustration with her. When she is eleven and hears the rhyme "Step on a crack . . . ," for years she cannot stop counting cracks lest she cause her mother harm. She says prayers incessantly and makes the sign of the cross to ward off problems so often that her mother slaps her in frustration. She worries about her thoughts and about worrying so much. Her parents argue, afraid they are insufficient as parents. To get away from the tension in the house, her father spends more and more time at the American Legion, and her mother takes a sales job at a department store. One psychiatrist says Tara suffers from insecurities and self-esteem problems, and another says she has attention deficit disorder and is very immature. Her longtime friends, model-pretty Kristin, African American Keesha, and athletic Amy, fall away, tired of ignoring or trying to cope with her quirks. When her father has a heart attack and her mother starts to drink, Tara prays and crosses herself even more. Things improve temporarily when she is twelve and forms a friendship of sorts with Donna* DeLuca, also twelve, whose dysfunctional parents are almost always away. The two girls complement each other in a way: Donna is tough and world weary, while Tara is increasingly afraid of the world. In eighth grade, Tara's marks improve, and she begins to realize that her problems have affected more lives than her own. Her doorknob kissing—touching a doorknob with all ten fingers in a certain way and then touching her face in the exact same way—drives her mother into fits of anger. Ironically, an old friend of her father, Allan Jacobson, now a high school science teacher, says that a student of his, Sam*, has similar problems and suggests that Tara may be suffering from Obsessive-Compulsive Disorder, a little-known chemical-imbalance-based illness. He puts her in touch with Sam, who tells her that he is excessively afraid of germs and that exposure and response-prevention therapy—he was forced to touch garbage in order to bring his compulsions under control—has helped him. His therapist works with Tara in her "fight to regain free will [sic]," and she gradually rebuilds her life. When Sam relapses, she is able to encourage him, returning to him some of the hope that he was able to transmit to her. The great number of fears that plague her for years, the agony that her family undergoes, and the inability of professional people to diagnose her seem almost unbelievable but are evidently authentic to the disorder. The light tone and the humorous scenes in which the fears are described make the number and intensity of Tara's fears seem realistic and not fabricated for instructional purposes. Thus, while the teacher's, Sam's, and the therapist's explanations are didactic, they work in context. Without the humor, the book would be a treatise. A lengthy essay by a doctor and a list of resources complete the book. ALA/YA.

KLASS, DAVID (1960–)   Born in Vermont; teacher, novelist for young adults and middle school readers. His basketball novel, *Danger Zone** (Scholastic, 1995), about an incident of terrorism at an international high school tournament in Italy, is as much about racial prejudice, both black and white, as it is about sports. For earlier biographical information and a title entry, see *Dictionary, 1990–1994* [*California Blue*].

KLAUSE, ANNETTE CURTIS (1953–   ) Born in Bristol, England; librarian and author of short stories, poems, articles for professional journals, and novels of suspense, horror, and science fiction. She emigrated to the United States with her family at the age of fifteen and received her bachelor's and library science degrees from the University of Maryland. She lives in Hyattsville, Maryland. Her novel of a werewolf girl who falls in love with a human boy, *Blood and Chocolate** (Delacorte, 1997), won praise for its daring tone and subject matter and vigorous style. It was cited by *School Library Journal* and by the American Library Association for young adults. For additional information about Klause, more titles, and title entries, see *Dictionary, 1990–1994* [*Alien Secrets*; *The Silver Kiss*] and *Dictionary, 1995–1999* [*Blood and Chocolate*].

KLEIER, GLENN   Writer who makes his home in Louisville, Kentucky; cofounder and president of Kleier Communications, Inc., a national marketing and communications company. He served as cochair of a political party organized by H. Ross Perot, who was an unsuccessful candidate for president. Kleier's novel, *The Last Day** (Warner, 1997), chosen by *Booklist*, is a suspenseful apocalyptic novel about a woman messiah. It came out to mixed reception, especially since it hits hard at organized religions, but was made into a movie and a television miniseries.

KLUGER, STEVE (1952–) Born in Baltimore, Maryland; attended the University of Southern California; lives in Santa Monica, California; has been an actor and general manager for the Light Opera of Manhattan, a television actor, and a writer of plays, screenplays, and novels for adults. He received the Alex Award for his bittersweet epistolary period novel, *Last Days of Summer** (Avon, 1998), the humorous story of the deep friendship between a Jewish boy of twelve in Brooklyn, New York, and a rookie third baseman for the New York Giants. Kluger's first book, also a novel, *Changing Pitches* (St. Martin's, 1984), concerns the career of a homosexual left-handed pitcher. A more recent book continues his interest in World War II, *Yank: World War II from the Guys Who Brought You Victory* (St. Martin's, 1990). Edited by Kluger, this is a collection of excerpts from *Yank Magazine* published in commemoration of the fiftieth anniversary of the U.S. entry into the conflict. He has also contributed to periodicals.

KNEEBONE SMITH (*Dangerous Skies**) African American father of Tunes* and good friend of Buck Smith, the narrator. Kneebone is so called because his joints are very swollen and misshapen from arthritis. He is Buck's father's farm manager and longtime friend and a descendant of slaves of Buck's father's ancestors. Kneebone has a good reputation in the community but keeps to himself, obvi-

ously because of the color bar. He is proud of Tunes but also fears for her, and rightly so. He demonstrates how loyalty and friendship mean nothing under certain circumstances and how the existence of blacks depends on the goodwill of the whites who dominate the region.

A KNIGHT OF THE WORD (Brooks*, Terry, Ballantine, 1998) Suspenseful adult fantasy of magic and good versus evil involving the interactions between humans and otherworld creatures set during the last three days of October in recent years in Hopewell, Illinois, and Seattle, Washington, sequel to *Running with the Demon*. The Lady of the Word, an ancient, powerful, universal force for good, sends a tatterdamalion named Ariel, a small fairylike creature of nature, to dispatch Nest* Freemark, a Northwestern University student and Olympic-quality runner, to Seattle. Nest is to urge John Ross*, who has renounced his duties as Knight of the Word, to reassume them. If he does not, demons and other monstrous powers of evil will subvert him and appropriate his magical powers for their nefarious ends. Ross and his lover, Stefanie* Winslow, are helping Simon* Lawrence operate his homeless programs, Fresh Start, a shelter, and Pass/Go, an alternative school. The people of Seattle, sometimes called the "Emerald City," highly respect Simon, known as the "Wizard of Oz," for his hard work and amazing success in serving the unfortunates of American society. Although Ross has had terrible dreams about disasters hitting the city, he persists in resisting Nest's urging, content to continue life with Stefanie and his friends at Fresh Start. Several events occur that indicate that disaster is imminent. Among others, Nest detects the horrible odor of demons at Fresh Start.

Andrew Wren, an investigative reporter for the *New York Times*, receives information from anonymous sources that someone is absconding with charitable funds at Fresh Start and discovers that Simon and Ross appear to be the culprits. Fresh Start mysteriously burns down, but Stefanie rescues all the women and children. Clearly a powerful demon is at work. Events come to a grand climax on Halloween night, when Simon is scheduled to receive gifts of land and funds for his enterprises and citations of praise during a public ceremony at the Seattle Art Museum, the place where in his dreams Ross has seen him killed. Various acts of skullduggery occur that make it seem that Simon is the demon and has been setting Ross up to take the blame for the embezzlements. Just in time, Stefanie is unmasked as the demon in service to the Void, an ancient and powerful force for chaos. Old magic in the form of Wraith, a ghost wolf that has been inside Nest, takes over and enables her to save Ross's and Simon's lives and kill Stefanie. Nest returns to Hopewell and her life as a student, and Ross resumes his life as a Knight of the Word and his responsibility to make the world better. Similarities to J. R. R. Tolkien's Ring novels do not detract from the pull of this substantial story. The author excels at creating atmosphere and at giving the inanimate life, so that the good nature creatures, among them Nest's sylvan friend, Pick*, seem completely believable. Social commentary, in particular about the homeless, and in general about the way things are in the world, the way they might be, and individual responsibility accordingly is a worthwhile element nondidactically treated. NYPL.

KOLLER, JACKIE FRENCH (1948–) Born in Derby, Connecticut; writer of many books for both young people and adults. Her novel, *The Falcon** (Atheneum, 1998), is a study in the crippling effects of guilt. For earlier biographical information and a title entry, see *Dictionary, 1995–1999* [*A Place to Call Home*].

KONIGSBURG, E(LAINE) L(OBL) (1930–)   Born in New York City; popular, versatile, highly acclaimed writer of humorous and clever realistic and fantasy novels and picture-book stories for young readers and nonfiction books for adults about writing for children and young people. She received her B.S. from Carnegie-Mellon University, pursued graduate work at the University of Pittsburgh, and is a resident of Ponte Vedra, Florida. She is best known for her two Newbery Award–winning books, *From the Mixed-up Files of Mrs. Basil E. Frankweiler* (Atheneum, 1967) and *The View from Saturday* (Atheneum, 1996), both lively, witty, complex puzzle novels. *Silent to the Bone** (Atheneum, 2000), an American Library Association choice for young adults, concerns a mute thirteen-year-old boy who is accused of harming his baby half sister. For more information about Kongisburg, titles, and title entries, see *Dictionary, 1960–1984* [*About the B'nai Bagels*; *From the Mixed-up Files of Mrs. Basil E. Frankweiler*; *Jennifer, Hecate, Macbeth, William McKinley, and Me, Elizabeth*; *A Proud Taste for Scarlet and Miniver*; *The Second Mrs. Giaconda*]; *Dictionary, 1985–1989* [*Up from Jericho Tel*]; *Dictionary, 1990–1984* [*A Proud Taste for Scarlet and Miniver*; *T-Backs, T-Shirts, COAT, and Suit*]; and *Dictionary, 1995–1999* [*The View from Saturday*].

KOSS, AMY GOLDMAN (1954–) Born in Detroit, Michigan; attended Wayne State University; lives in Glen-dale, California. The author and illustrator of four rhyming picture books, she is best known for her amusing novels of family and school life and friendship for preteens, which have received several citations. *The Girls** (Dial, 2000), selected by the American Library Association for young adults, describes three days in the lives of a hurtful clique of middle school girls. She has recently published *Smoke Screen* (American Girl, 2000), about a girl whose mother is unable to stop smoking; *Stranger in Dadland* (Dial, 2001), in which a boy gains new appreciation for his divorced father; and *Strike Two!* (Dial 2001), in which a girl's hopes of playing softball are dashed by a newspaper strike. For additional information about Koss, titles, and a title entry, see *Dictionary, 1995–1999* [*The Ashwater Experiment*].

KRISHER, TRUDY (B.) (1946–   ) Born in Macon, Georgia, and raised in southern Florida; graduate of the College of William and Mary (B.A.) and Trenton State College (M.Ed.); reviewer, freelance writer, and teacher of writing at the University of Dayton. *Kinship** (Delacorte, 1997), chosen by the American Library Assiociation for young adults, concerns family and neighborhood life in a trailer park in the little town of Kinship, Georgia, in 1961. It is a companion to the writer's highly acclaimed *Spite Fences* (Delacorte, 1994). A recent publication is *Uncommon Faith* (Holiday, 2003), in which residents of a mid-nineteenth-century Massachusetts town speak about issues of the day. Krisher has made her home in Dayton, Ohio. For more information about Krisher and a title entry, see *Dictionary, 1995–1999* [*Spite Fences*].

L

LACKEY, MERCEDES (1950–)
Born in Chicago, Illinois; computer programmer, prolific science fiction and fantasy writer. She received her B.S. from Purdue University in 1972, and for ten years worked as a computer software specialist before becoming a full-time writer. Lackey has written many novels, some in collaboration with other authors, including Andre Norton, Anne McCafferty, Piers Anthony, and her husband, Larry Dixon. She is best known for her Valdemar books. She also wrote the three-volume Diana Tregarde series and, with her husband, the Owl series. Her *The Serpent's Shadow** (DAW/Penguin, 2000) is part of another series about magicians called the Elemental Masters, set in Edwardian London. Lackey also writes song lyrics.

LANE, DAKOTA (1959–) Born in Brooklyn, New York; freelance writer and writing instructor since 1996. As a child she attended twenty-five different schools and so understands the loneliness of an outsider, which makes up part of the problems for the protagonist of *Johnny Voodoo** (Delacorte, 1996), about a girl whose unreliable father moves her and her younger brother to Louisiana after her mother's death. Lane attended San Francisco State University and has made her home in Woodstock, New York.

LANTZ, FRANCESS L(IN) (1952–)
Born in Trenton, New Jersey; librarian, writer, educator. She grew up in Bucks County, Pennsylvania, received her B.A. from Dickinson College in 1974 and her M.L.S. from Simmons College in 1975. A guitarist, she worked as a semiprofessional musician, a nanny, and a librarian in the 1970s, but has concentrated on being a writer since 1979. Lantz has published twenty novels for young adults, including some in the Sweet Valley Twins series. Her *Someone to Love** (Avon, 1997) was named to the American Library Association Young Adult list. She has also taught in adult education at Santa Barbara (California) City College, and lives in Santa Barbara.

THE LAST BOOK IN THE UNIVERSE (Philbrick*, W. Rodman, Blue Sky Press,

2000)   Futuristic fantasy set after the Big Shake, a catastrophic earthquake that destroyed the infrastructure of the known world and killed most of the people. Those surviving live in a number of "latches," or districts in the ruins of the city, the Urb, except for a comparative few "proovs," genetically improved people who live in Eden, an area strictly guarded and shielded from the normals, who are forbidden to enter. Each district is run by a latchboss, a gangster who controls by brutality and fear. Spaz, an epileptic boy who grew up in a normal family, has been exiled to the Banger latch run by Billy Bismo because his foster parents fear his illness may harm his little sister, Bean, their own child. Although most of the normals use mindprobe needles that create wonderful sensory experiences that compensate for their miserable lives and make them forget most of the past, Spaz cannot indulge in this diversion because it brings on his attacks, and as a result he is one of the few normals with any memory. Sent to bust down (steal everything) from a gummy (old person), Spaz meets a feral street child, perhaps five, whom he refers to as Little Face and who seems unable to talk but in exchange for a choxbar, a confection, leads him to Ryter's stackbox, where the old man greets him affably and urges him to take everything, although he does protect a pile of papers with marks on them, calling them a book he is writing. On the way home, Spaz is stopped by a vehicle carrying a proov girl, the most beautiful person he has ever seen, who asks him his name and gives him a sack of edibles. At his own cube, a latch runner, a highly illegal messenger, waits with a message from Bean, saying she is dying and wants to see him again. When Billy Bismo refuses to let him go, Spaz starts out on his own, suffering a grand mal

seizure near where he robbed Ryter. He wakes to find himself in the old man's stackbox, weak from the attack but determined to go on. Ryter insists that he sleep for a while, then sets out with him, suggesting that they go by the Pipe, the remains of an ancient water supply system, now derelict and infested with rats. Before long, they discover Little Face following them, so they struggle along together through another latch and into a third latch, where they encounter a mob surrounding the proov girl he saw earlier. While Ryter causes a distraction, they all get away in her vehicle. When she hears their story, Lanaya, the proov girl, takes them to the house where Spaz grew up, and he finds Bean very ill with leukemia. That night she goes into a coma. Ryter suggests to Lanaya that perhaps in Eden they have a record of a cure for the disease, and she agrees to take them there under her protection. Eden is astonishingly beautiful, with grass and blue sky, which they have never seen before, and they learn that Lanaya has been genetically engineered to become a Master, one of a group that rules Eden. With Ryter, she discovers that while the old chemotherapy techniques have been lost, they might try gene replacement on Bean. It works like a miracle, and soon she is beating Lanaya's father, one of the best chess players in Eden, just after he teaches her the moves. Lanaya's mother insists on keeping Little Face, who has begun to talk in sentences, but the rest are put on trial with Lanaya before the Masters. Although she makes a spirited and reasonable argument for letting them stay in Eden, they rule against her. Bean is returned to her parents, and Spaz and Ryter to their latch, which has suddenly gone wild because all the mindprobes have been deactivated. The mob kills Ryter, but Billy Bizmo saves

Spaz, because, he says, the boy is his son. Although Ryter's book is destroyed, Spaz finds a voice recorder and starts talking about Ryter and their adventure together, the nearest he can come to making a book. Like many postapocalypse stories, this is deeply pessimistic about the world of the future, but the main characters all display compassion and love despite their sordid surroundings. The pace is fast, the settings inventive, and the characters fairly well-rounded. ALA/YA.

THE LAST DAY (Kleier*, Glenn, Warner, 1997)   Long (484 pages), detailed, adult apocalyptic novel, with adventure-story and thriller aspects, set at the turn of the Third Millennium mostly in Israel and Cairo with shifts to Rome and several places in the United States. As the twentieth century concludes, hundreds of thousands of millenarian pilgrims from sects, cults, and mainline religions feverishly throng Jerusalem and its environs to await the Armageddon or the Rapture according to their persuasions. In the region are earnest Jonathan Feldman*, about thirty, a respected journalist and television anchor, and big, cynical, driven photojournalist Breck Hunter, a little older, both of World News Network television. On Christmas Day 1999, the two rush to the Negev Desert to cover what the Israeli Defense Force says was a Jordanian missile strike that has destroyed an Israeli supersecret test laboratory but that visiting Japanese astronomers say was a meteor hit. The Japanese scientists also report seeing near the lab a man and a woman, Bedouins, helping a badly injured woman survivor. Another remarkable event occurs at midnight on December 31 at David's Well in Bethlehem. During a terrible storm and earthquake, an invalid boy is miraculously cured but soon is discovered to be in reality a young woman beneath whose feet the word "Messiah" appears. A week later, the young woman, beautiful, slight, dark-haired, wearing a simple white robe trimmed in red and purple, preaches a charismatic sermon near the Sea of Galilee. She says she is Jeza*, the Daughter of God. Soon miracles, including healings, are attributed to her, and she attracts a supportive following, and many detractors and enemies as well. Feldman and Hunter discover that she is the only survivor of the desert blast and had been a test subject at the lab. The Israeli Defense Force seeks her, because it thinks she endangers Israeli national security. Religious groups are divided over her. The Vatican struggles to determine the authenticity of this self-proclaimed Messiah, and power conflicts develop among the cardinals, leading to the estrangement of Cardinal* Litti because he believes in Jeza and to the death of Pope Nicholas VI from stress on Easter. Some, like Feldman and Litti, who are around her a lot, become convinced that she is indeed special, but her sermons, which attack institutionalized religions as hypocritical about ministering to the needs of the world's peoples and eliminating strife and poverty, especially the Roman Catholic Church, generate increasing antagonism. The novel moves to a not surprising yet ironic and tragic conclusion on Easter weekend, Feldman and Hunter in the thick of things. Scenes stand out, such as that in which Jeza is welcomed to the Vatican to speak, and when rebuked and denigrated, causes a huge crack to appear in the altar. There are fascinating backstage views of the broadcasting world as executives, researchers, and reporters discuss approaches to stories and avenues to pursue. Shifts in setting point up effectively how Jeza is accepted, or not accepted, and sometimes used, among leaders, as in Washington, D.C., and among common people, as with a typical family in Racine, Wisconsin. Jeza is credible and her sermons well worked out. A novel of intrigue as well as philosophical speculation, the book revisits the story of Jesus for the new millennium from a feminist angle. It is clear, too, that the writer suggests that anyone who exhorts people to the highest ideals and challenges the establishment invites attack. Booklist.

LAST DAYS OF SUMMER (Kluger*, Steve, Avon, 1998)   Amusing, often funny realistic period novel published for adults of a boy's growing up and friendship with a major league baseball player, told in letters and notes between the two, occasional newspaper clippings, and a few other brief notations and comments. In 1940, World War II already raging in Europe, clever, intelligent, obstreperous Jewish Joey Margolis, 12, feels abandoned by his businessman father, who has left the family and married again. He also feels let down by his quiet mother, Ida, who has moved from their Hasidic community and taken an apartment with her sister, Aunt Carrie, in another neighborhood in Brooklyn, New York. Joey, being Jewish, is disliked and picked on, constantly attacked by what he calls the "Hitler Youth," who live there. His only friend is Craig Nakamura, who lives in the same apartment house, plays The Green Hornet to Joey's The Shadow, and being Japanese American, is also disliked. Joey gets As in school, except in Obedience, but his teacher's reports home indicate that he is capable. He is attracted to pretty Rachel Panitz, a relationship that blossoms believably. Since he mostly stays to himself, Joey writes letters of advice to President Franklin Roosevelt, who replies

expressing gratitude. Joey's greatest passion, however, is following the career of Charlie Banks, to whom he writes persistently. Charlie is a rookie third baseman and batting phenomenon recently acquired by the New York Giants. At first Charlie patiently, then rudely, tries to brush Joey off, but he eventually gets caught up in Joey's problems, with the law (Joey has decided to "embark on a life of crime"), in school, with Rachel, and with the bullies. When Joey informs him that he is to be ready for his Bar Mitzvah by his thirteenth birthday in October 1941 and his father refuses to help him study, Charlie, although Gentile, capably pinch hits. He coaches Joey while Joey travels with the team as substitute bat boy (and wins all the players' money gambling), and earns the appreciation and admiration of Joey's rabbi and the title United States Father of the Year, an accolade Eleanor Roosevelt bestows on him at the White House. Joey and Charlie exchange views on ballplayers (many famous ones like Hank Greenberg, also Jewish, are mentioned), and Joey confides in Charlie about Rachel. Charlie gives Joey advice about girls, takes the boy to meet his own girlfriend, Hazel MacKay, a stage and music-hall singer in competition with Ethel Merman, a romance Aunt Carrie helps to advance, and keeps Joey apprised of his life with his teammate, Jordy Stuker, called "Stuke." Right after Pearl Harbor, Charlie and Stuke enlist in the marines. Joey takes his surrogate father's departure hard at first, and his grades plummet. Craig and his family leave, too, to live with relatives in California, all of whom are interned later by the U.S. government. After completing his training and marrying Hazel, Charlie ships out. At Guadalcanal, two days after his twenty-fifth birthday, he dies, a hero's death rescuing his fellow marines. An epilogue on August 7, 1977, on what would have been Charlie's sixtieth birthday, sees Joey, now a well-known author and sportswriter, speaking at a fund-raiser in Racine, Wisconsin, Charlie's hometown, to benefit the Charlie L. Banks Scholarship Trust at the University of Wisconsin. The title's double meaning reflects the bittersweetness of the book's substance. Although the reader anticipates the end, the ties of friendship between man and boy are so strong and the episodes and commentaries about them so funny, indeed often hilarious, that the reader focuses on them rather than speculates on what will undoubtedly happen. The period elements and the baseball atmosphere are in themselves extremely interesting, and bits of gentle satire add depth. Charlie's letters are only a bit above illiterate, while Joey's are increasingly articulate, well stated, and mature. This never-sentimental book is mostly in the first person from the perspectives of Charlie and Joey, a difficult approach that the author handles with great skill. Alex.

THE LAST SIN EATER (Rivers*, Francine, Tyndale House, 1998)   Adult inspirational period romance in the vein of the television series *Touched by an Angel*, set among Scottish and Welsh immigrants and their descendants in the mid-nineteenth century in a remote valley in the Great Smoky Mountains of South Carolina. The story is built around the British Isles folk belief of the scapegoat. The sin eater consumes bread and wine upon the body of the dead person and thus absorbs the deceased's sins to keep that person from wandering the hills endlessly. Inquisitive, serious Cadi Forbes, 10, the narrator, thinks of herself as a "vessel of sins," one of which she believes so

grievous that she has lost her Mama's love and maybe that of her Papa, too. When the sin eater comes to Granny Forbes's funeral and takes upon himself Granny's sins, Cadi gets the idea that he might also take away her sins. She is told to stay away from the man, and, besides, no one seems to know where he lives. Lilybet, a new girl a little younger than Cadi, appears, an inscrutable figure who speaks in adult biblical language and whom no one else but Cadi hears or sees. She says that her father sent her and suggests that Cadi inquire of Miz* Elda Kendric, the oldest woman in their community. Miz Elda says the sin eater lives somewhere up on Dead Man's Mountain, alone. Cadi insists on searching, and Fagan Kai, 14, her older brother Iwan's friend, goes with her, but they are unsuccessful in finding the sin eater. One day Cadi spots a man coming into their valley, preaching the Bible. Brogan Kai, the self-proclaimed leader of the community, also sees the man, says he is crazy, and threatens to kill him. Cadi is curious about the man but decides to find the sin eater first. The sin eater performs the ceremony for her but extracts a promise from Cadi to listen to the man of God. She confesses to him that she killed her sister, Elen, because she was jealous; is enthralled by his preaching; is baptized; and is sad and disturbed on behalf of the sin eater when the man says that only Jesus, and no human sin eater, can absolve sins. Fagan also listens to the man of God and is baptized, but then Brogan kills the man of God and severely beats Fagan. Cadi's troubles, and those of the valley, become worse before the truth about the sin eater comes out. The two children discover he lives in a cave and, while there, they find behind his quarters in another cave pictures on the wall painted in blood. They learn that they were made by an

Indian survivor of a long-ago massacre led by Laochailand Kai, Brogan's father, who then revived the old sin eater custom to relieve his own and the communal guilt. Lots were rigged to fall on the current sin eater, Sim Gillivray, because Brogan was in love with Bletsung* Macleod, whom Sim also loved. Fagan and then Cadi preach, Brogan is wounded in the hand severely by a gunshot in a struggle, and many in the community are baptized. The valley embarks on a new beginning, a "new covenant," as Lilybet calls it. At the very end, Cadi is revealed as telling this story of her childhood to her grandchildren. She married Fagan, and they became the preachers at the New Covenant House, the cabin left to Fagan by Miz Elda. Although the novel is a fictionalized religious treatise, it excels in creating the claustrophobic community, in which grudges and antipathy are strong, tenacious, and resolved, in the context of the novel, only through accepting Jesus. That Cadi and Fagan should be able after only a few hearings to repeat the man of God's sermons verbatim in biblical language is not convincing, and the sin eater remains an unfleshed and almost enigmatic figure. The man of God is given a small history, and Cadi thinks Lilybet may be an angel. Scottish dialect adds much to time and place. Booklist.

LAXALT, ROBERT P(ETER) (1923–2001)   Born in Alturas, California, the son of a Basque sheepman; died in Reno, Nevada; editor and author of seventeen books for adults about Nevada, the West, and immigrants, in particular Basques. He attended Santa Clara University and received his B.A. from the University of Nevada. He was a founder of the University of Nevada Press, a consultant on Basque history and culture for the Library of Congress, and a Fulbright Research Fellow in Basque history and culture. He was best known for his several books about Basques, among them *A Cup of Tea in Pamplona* (University of Nevada Press, 1985), which was nominated for a Pulitzer Prize; *Sweet Promised Land* (Harper, 1957; University of Nevada Press, 1986); and *Time of the Rabies* (University of Nevada Press, 2000). *Dust Devils** (University of Nevada Press, 1997), an American Library Association choice for young adults, deals with hostility toward Indians in the early part of the twentieth century.

LEAH PRICE (*The Poisonwood Bible: A Novel**)   Twin of Adah*, daughter of Orleanna* and Nathan. A gifted child and a tomboy, she tries hard to identify with her father, avidly seeking his approval, but when she loses faith in him, and in his religion, she is the first to openly defy him. Her love turns to Anatole Ngemba, the village schoolteacher and the only educated man there. Anatole, who has an elaborately tattooed face, treats her as a child and forbids her to say she loves him, but after they leave Kilanga, he follows them to Bulungu, where he nurses her through severe fever. Anatole is deeply involved in the Congolese movement for freedom, and while having a white wife is a handicap, he never wavers in his devotion to Leah. For three years he is imprisoned for political reasons, and Leah stays at a Benedictine nunnery deep in the jungle. They eventually have four boys, and although for a short time they live in Atlanta and he attends Emory University, they return to Africa as their home. While Leah is passionate and sometimes angry and reckless, Anatole remains calm and hopeful.

LEAVING FISHERS (Haddix*, Margaret Peterson, Simon & Schuster, 1997)

Modern psychological and sociological novel of a lonely girl who gets sucked into a religious cult and her difficulties both in it and leaving it. Dorry Stevens starts her junior high school year in Crestwood, a suburb of Indianapolis, after her father's factory closes in Bryden, Ohio, and he takes a lower-paying job with the same company in Indiana for the three years until he is retirement age. Although Dorry begs to be allowed to stay in Bryden with one of her much older siblings or her best friend, Marissa, her parents say she is better off with them and will soon make friends in the new school. In her miserable first weeks she doubts this. When an attractive girl stops by the school cafeteria table where she is eating alone and invites Dorry to join her and her friends, she is shy but intensely grateful, and when they repeat their welcome on subsequent days, she is relieved and happy. Angela Briarstone, the girl who first spoke to her, and a good-looking boy named Brad seem to be the leaders of the group. They volunteer Lara to help Dorry with the English assignment she finds difficult, and it is Lara who first tells her about Pastor Jim and the Fishers of Men, the group she and all her friends belong to, and invites Dorry to a party in the clubhouse of an apartment complex. Dorry's wonderful time, meeting Pastor Jim and other new people, all of whom seem incredibly happy and eager to get to know her, is marred only by a conversation she overhears in which Angela angrily accuses Lara of stealing. Later, Angela explains to Dorry that Lara is a kleptomaniac and that she was trying to get her to return a bracelet she had taken. Because both her parents are working and preoccupied about money, Dorry spends most of the next weeks with the Fishers, even, through Angela's contacts, getting a regular baby-sitting job in an upscale neighborhood caring for Jasmine, Zoe, and Seth Garringer, whose mother is a sculptor working at home but needing time free from the children. The high point of her life occurs at a retreat, where she is baptized and becomes a Fisher. Her joy is dampened when she returns home to find that her mother has suffered a heart attack and is in the hospital. Her Fisher friends call and call with prayers until her father orders her to stop them. Although she spends as much time as she can at the hospital, all her free time is taken up by Angela, now her "discipler," who keeps track of her good deeds and her sins and assigns her tasks to test her faith. The most difficult of these occurs at Thanksgiving, when Dorry and her mother, now much better, and her father go to Bryden. Angela orders Dorry to fast on Thanksgiving Day. Dorry tries, but her parents, her older siblings, and her other relatives are aghast at her attempt, and she ends up weeping in her room. Since Angela has insisted she must convert someone, she tries on Marissa while they are in Bryden, but her friend only thinks she has become weird. At the next Fisher party, she becomes part of the welcoming group, a process she later learns is called "love bombing," pretending to be delighted to get to know a girl she finds shallow and fake. In another test she is assigned to an evangelizing group, an "E-Team," to proselytize in a shopping mall, where the security guard evicts them, threatening to call the police. Angela insists that she contribute all her savings from baby-sitting to the Fishers and that she bring in some converts, preferably her parents. Since Dorry sees that this is impossible, she hits on the Garringer children as her subjects, gathering them around her and telling them graphically about being condemned to burning in hell if they do not turn to Jesus. To her astonishment, they are terrified and scream for their mother, who fires her promptly. In answer to her tearful summons, Angela goes to the Garringer door and tells Mrs. Garringer that she is evil for turning away from a chance for salvation. With the picture of the children's fear in her mind, Dorry suddenly lets all her doubts about the Fishers surface, and she tells Angela that she is through, that she does not want anything more to do with her or the Fishers. While her parents are greatly relieved, Dorry is numb, shunned by the Fishers and alone again at school. Then Zachary, a boy she has known slightly from her early period in Fishers, sits down at her cafeteria table and asks her, "Know what happens to fish who get caught? They die." He has escaped from the cult and now is doing research, trying to get the group banned from the school, having learned that Pastor Jim does not live simply as he pretends but in a mansion, probably sleeping with girls he has "saved," and that Lara has suffered a mental breakdown from her experience. With Zachary and some other defectors from Fishers, Dorry begins to feel her way toward stability again. In the end, when she calls on Mrs. Garringer to apologize, she is not rehired, but the children, whom she has always loved, throw themselves at her and hug her eagerly. Dorry's need for friends and her lack of self-confidence are so well drawn that her initial entry into the cult is understandable, and the gradual escalation of the group's demands is convincing. Her defection is foreshadowed by doubts that keep coming up in her mind and being suppressed, particularly glimpses of Angela's fanaticism and delight in dominating her disciple. ALA/YA.

LEE, MARIE G., (1964–) Korean American; born in Hibbing, Minnesota; graduate of Brown University; instructor in literature and writing at Yale; Fulbright Scholar in Korea in 1997–1998; writer of novels reflecting the Asian American experience for middle graders and young adults. Among these are two books featuring Ellen Sung, a Korean American girl from a small Minnesota town who leaves for Harvard to study medicine, *Finding My Voice* (Houghton Mifflin, 1992) and *Saying Goodbye* (Houghton Mifflin, 1994). *Necessary Roughness** (HarperCollins, 1996), an American Library Association choice for young adults, concerns Korean Americans who move from Los Angeles to a small town in northern Minnesota. Lee's other books include *If It Hadn't Been for Yoon Jun* (Houghton Mifflin, 1993), *Night of the Chupacabras* (Avon, 1998), and *F Is for Fabuloso* (Avon, 2000). For title entries, see *This Land Is Our Land* [*Finding My Voice*, no. 245; *If It Hadn't Been for Yoon Jun*, no. 246] and *Many Peoples, One Land* [*Night of the Chupacabras*, no. 217; *Saying Goodbye*, no. 218].

LETTERS FROM YELLOWSTONE (Smith*, Diane, Viking, 1999) Adult period novel set during the summer of 1898 telling of a botanical expedition to Yellowstone National Park in Wyoming as related in letters by the scientists involved. Although Professor Howard Merriam of the Agricultural College of the State of Montana at Bozeman has his hands full with organizing the expedition and securing funds from the Smithsonian Institution in Washington, D.C., the young medical student and botany aficionado he has hired to be his assistant, A. E. Bartram (of the Bartram line of botanists), turns out to be a woman, Alex (Alexandria). He not only agrees with prevailing opinion that field conditions are unsuitable for a woman, but he also questions her ability to perform professionally. The local U.S. Cavalry unit, however, under the command of capable Captain Alexander Craighead, provides tent accommodations for her, and her knowledge, skill, and clear head soon earn her a respected position among the otherwise all-male, motley group. These include portly Dr. Andrew Rutherford, who plots their field positions, records weather and temperature readings, tames a raven, teaches it to speak, and prepares to study it scientifically. Philip Aber of the Smithsonian opposes their enterprise. William Gleick, also from the Smithsonian, escorts Mrs. Aber to Yellowstone at Aber's request and becomes so friendly with her as apparently to contribute to his colleague's dour mental state, and Aber is eventually found dead, an apparent suicide. Gleick approves of Merriam's work and supports it with a letter to his superiors. Also in the area or at the Lake Hotel are an arrogant European count who collects trophy animals, shoots Rutherford's raven, and is summarily ejected from the park; elderly Miss Zwinger, world traveler and naturalist; John Wylloe, naturalist and poet, who has been sent by editor George Bird Grinnell to record his impressions for *Forest and Stream*; college President Healy, who visits and is much impressed by Alex; and Lester King, a biologist from Cornell (Alex's institution), who has been sent by her parents to make sure she is all right, feels conditions are unfit for her, demands that she return with him, and is upset when she adamantly refuses. Most overlooked but vital to their success are Joseph and Sara, a Crow Indian couple. Sara serves as an example for Alex of an independent woman, and Joseph knows much about plants and their properties. They take Alex in after an unexplained fire sweeps through the Merriam camp and

also provide Rutherford with four crows to replace the beloved Edgar who was shot. Although Merriam fears that the fire has rendered the expedition worthless, he discovers that Alex has prudently been shipping specimens and drawings back to Cornell and that others have shrewdly preserved valuable materials. President Healy offers Alex a job classifying materials at the college, and she accepts. Although the voices of the writers are only somewhat individualized and the letters are much longer than reason says they could be, the writings are fascinating with their details of setting, field procedures, political and other influential figures, views of academic posturing and politics, social life at the Lake Hotel—parties, elaborate July 4 celebration, excursions—and relationships between the sexes. Thematically, the novel calls for respect, admiration, and understanding for nature, and especially for Yellowstone National Park. The latter plea appears especially in a cable that Captain Craighead wires his commanding officer. He says that he will resist efforts to allow the railroads and other private enterprise to exploit the area further—the "nation has but one Yellowstone Park" [and] "I intend to ensure it is protected." This is a substantial book, occasionally self-indulgent with detail, but engrossing overall. Booklist.

LEVENKRON,   STEVEN   (1941–) Born in New York City; psychotherapist, novelist. He received his B.A. in 1963 from Queens College of the City of New York and his M.S. in 1969 from Brooklyn College of the City of New York. In the 1960s he taught social studies, then for six years was a guidance counselor in New York secondary schools. Since 1972 he has practiced psychotherapy, in private practice, at Montefiore Hospital and Medical

Center, Bronx, New York, and at the Center for the Study of Anorexia in New York City. His first novel, *The Best Little Girl in the World* (Contemporary Books, 1978), about a girl who develops anorexia while dieting to qualify for a ballet camp, is credited with bringing this illness to public attention. Its sequel is *Kessa* (Popular Library, 1986). To help explain the condition, he wrote the nonfiction book, *Treating and Overcoming Anorexia Nervosa* (Scribner, 1982). His more recent novel, *The Luckiest Girl in the World** (Scribner, 1997), deals with another psychotic condition affecting teenage girls when pressure to succeed causes them to become "slashers," given to self-mutilation.

LEVINE, GAIL CARSON (1947–) Born in New York City; graduate of City College of City University of New York; resident of Brewster, New York; author best known for inventive retellings of stories from oral tradition, like *Ella Enchanted** (HarperCollins, 1997), an imaginative fantasy version of the *Cinderella* story. Selected by the American Library Association for young adults, *Dave at Night** (HarperCollins, 1999) is a light-hearted period novel about a boy who sneaks out of a Jewish orphanage and becomes involved with members of the Harlem Renaissance. Recent titles include *Betsy Who Cried Wolf* (HarperCollins, 2002), *The Fairy's Return* (HarperCollins, 2002), and *For Biddle's Sake* (HarperCollins, 2002), retellings of old tales. For more information about Levine, titles, and title entries, see *Dictionary, 1995–1999* [*Dave at Night*; *Ella Enchanted*].

LEVY, MARILYN (1937–)   Born in Youngstown, Ohio; graduate of Northwestern University; instructor in English at high schools in Ohio and Illinois, at Roosevelt University in Chicago, and at a private school in California; writer of plays and screenplays; author of sociological- and physical-problem novels for young adults. Her first book, *The Girl in the Plastic Cage* (Fawcett, 1982), reflects experiences of her daughter who wore a body brace for two years. Levy's twelve other novels also have some basis in fact, arising from her work with teens in the schools. *Run for Your Life** (Houghton Mifflin, 1996), chosen by the American Library Association for young adults, concerns impoverished, troubled African American girls who are helped by the new social worker at the local community center to organize a track team. The social worker is based on an actual figure, and the girls are composites of girls with whom he worked. Levy has resided in Santa Monica, California.

A LIFE FOR A LIFE (Hill*, Ernest, Simon & Schuster, 1998)   Realistic coming-of-age novel of an African American teenager who eventually pulls himself from a path toward disaster through the help of the father of a boy he killed. In Brownsville, Louisiana, in 1987, D'Ray Reid, 15, is one of the toughest boys in the projects, where he lives with his mother and his younger brother, Little Man (Curtis), 10, his father having been convicted of murdering a white man and sentenced to life in prison. When Little Man is tricked by a drug dealer into smoking crack, then threatened with execution if he does not pay one hundred dollars for the drugs, D'Ray begs for time to raise the money. Kojak, the dealer, gives him an hour. Frantically, D'Ray swipes his mother's gun, steals a truck, and heads for the small town of Lake Providence, where he holds up a small, family-owned store. When the young black clerk reaches for a gun, D'Ray shoots and kills him. Although he saves Little Man from Kojak, D'Ray soon sees police converging on his house, and, taking the rest of the money he stole, buys a bus ticket for Jackson, Mississippi, where he hopes he will be far enough away to avoid suspicion. From there on he makes one bad choice after another. Since he looks considerably older than he is, he becomes involved with a young prostitute named Peaches, with whom he falls in love, and soon is a pimp with a string of several girls working for him. When a john beats and robs Peaches, D'Ray kills him without compunction. After he accumulates a good store of money, hidden under the floor of the roach-infested room where they stay, he decides to buy a car and head for Detroit, but before he can carry out this plan, he sees police come to their motel looking for him. He catches a city bus, rides as far as it goes, walks to a small church, and pretends to be an alcoholic, son of a pair of cancer victims who died after he had cared for them for several years. The preacher takes him under his wing and offers to get him into a rehabilitation program. In the meantime, he arranges for D'Ray to stay with a good woman, Ms. Dorothy, who takes in strays in need of help. D'Ray's plan is to retrieve his money from the hotel room, and head out, but one of Ms. Dorothy's charges, Sparkle, is skeptical, and before he can leave town, he is arrested on suspicion of burglary. His record comes out, he is tried, convicted of murder, and sentenced to six years in the Louisiana Youth Authority facility. Before he leaves jail, he is visited by his mother, who says that as far as she is concerned, he is dead, and by Mr. Henry Earl, the father of Stanley, the boy he killed. To his surprise, Mr. Henry does not

ask him why he killed Stanley, but tells him about the boy, their life together, and Stanley's ambition to go to college and become the next Thurgood Marshall. After a humiliating strip search, D'Ray establishes his position by beating up a bully who has beaten and raped a smaller boy, but after that he lives from day to day, with only one visitor on each second Sunday, Mr. Henry, who comes faithfully, bringing him books and good things to eat and telling him about his life, his wife, Vanessa, who died, his mother, Mama Bea, and his sisters, Ida Mae and Big Sis. He encourages D'Ray to get his GED and to think about college. When D'Ray is released on his twenty-first birthday, Mr. Henry takes him to his Lake Providence home, where he installs him in Stanley's old room. D'Ray enrolls in a local college, but just before he is about to graduate, Mr. Henry has a stroke. At first D'Ray wants to give up, but the women in Mr. Henry's family, all of whom were originally suspicious of him, persuade him to finish college since that is the only way he can pay back for the harm he did to the family. Immediately after his graduation, D'Ray goes to the hospital and gives his diploma to Mr. Henry, who, though he cannot speak, sees him in cap and gown, shows that he understands, and dies. The novel is strangely disjointed, being very detailed and agonizingly real up to D'Ray's imprisonment, then, telling more than showing, skips through years with only a few scenes of Mr. Henry's visits until his release. This makes the boy's rehabilitation and turnaround less convincing than his earlier rage and resentment. While minor characters are adequate for their parts, the only developed ones are D'Ray and Mr. Henry, who is almost too forgiving to be plausible. ALA/YA.

LIFE IN THE FAT LANE (Bennett*, Cherie, Delacorte, 1998) Contemporary realistic physical-, psychological-, and sociological-problem novel set during two school years in Nashville, Tennessee, and later in Blooming Woods, Michigan. Lara Ardeche, 18, the narrator, is wonderfully happy. A beautiful, popular, blue-eyed blond, honors student, talented pianist, beauty pageant winner, she has loving, supportive parents. Her handsome father, Jim, is an advertising executive, and her gorgeous mother, Carol, owns a catering service. She has a cute younger brother, Scott; a good-looking, dark-haired boyfriend, Jett Anston, whom all the girls lust after; a very generous maternal grandfather; lots of friends—what more could any girl want? She even feels superior to, and somewhat sorry for, her best friend, Molly* Sheridan, because Molly is chubby, has a fat mother, and is derided by the kids for having a "mouth." Lara is a shoo-in for Homecoming Queen. About a month after winning, however, her life begins to change. She notices that her clothes are getting tight, and her scale tells her that she has gained weight. And so does her always observant mother, who assumes Lara is sneaking food. Lara blames the weight gain on her allergy medicine. Sure that losing weight is just a matter of willpower and exercise, she cuts back on food and steps up her workouts, to no avail. By Thanksgiving, she is up to 136 pounds, although she eats hardly anything. Molly and Jett assure her they love her despite her new appearance, but she is very worried about competing in the upcoming Miss Teen Tennessee Pageant and soon drops out. Her father looks at her with disgust, and her mother thinks the weight gain indicates she is a failure as a mother. Lara is increasingly miserable, drops piano, and becomes irritable

and angry at the world and herself. Then a specialist suggests that she may be suffering from a little-known, controversial disease called "Axell-Crowne's Syndrome," which afflicts teenagers, whereby the body uses decreasing amounts of food more and more efficiently. Jett cools toward her, and other friends drop away, but Molly remains loyal. Lara's parents, who have been having marital problems, move to Blooming Woods, Michigan, and Lara faces the additional problem of doing her senior year in a new school. The students in this affluent and appearance-conscious community reject her, since she now tops 200 pounds and wears size 22/24. She takes up her music again, playing the piano in the school orchestra and quartet, and makes friends with an overweight boy, Perry* Jameson, a talented saxophonist, and with some other students who are odds-outers like herself. Her piano teacher, fat Suzanne Silver, introduces her to other fat, plain, or alternative types. By book's end, her family has fallen apart, and she has contemplated suicide, but she confides to Molly that she appreciates her continued loyalty and, while sometimes bad things happen, life can be good anyway. She's not perfect, but she's okay anyway. The school scenes show graphically how young people are overly concerned with looks and how cruel they often are toward those who do not measure up to whatever the area's standards for appearance and popularity are. The book suggests that the blame for the current fixation on a slim, trim appearance and high popularity lies with the commercial arena and with parents, who want their children "perfect" in every way. The social commentary is heavy-handed, and the reality-programming scenes seem overdone, at least to the adult reader. Lara's angst goes on too long, and her shallowness becomes tedious, but teen girls, especially those with a weight or popularity problem, will relate. ALA/YA.

THE LIKES OF ME (Platt*, Randall Beth, Delacorte, 2000)   Realistic period and girl's growing-up novel that begins in a lumber camp in Washington State in 1911 and ends in Seattle in 1918. Caucasian Chinese, albino Cordy (Cordelia) Hankins, 7, who tells the story, is the daughter of widower Red Hankins, the responsible, aloof superintendent of a small lumber camp near Centner's Mills. Aware that she is considered a freak, Cordy lives a lonely, isolated existence, motherless, friendless, haphazardly schooled at home, expected to help around the office and otherwise as needed, but mostly to stay out of the way. A giant of a woman, six-feet-ten-inches tall and 350 pounds, applies for work as a cook, no-nonsense, commanding Fern Killingsworth, called "Babe." Soon Babe's feats of strength become legendary, as do her occasional "toots," bouts of excessive drinking with which Cordy especially must cope. Father marries Babe, and although neither parent spends time with Cordy, she knows they love and provide well for her. When she is fourteen, in 1918, Father hires a handsome, young, very graceful "boom man" to work logs, Squirl, 17, whose feats and escapades also become legendary. Warned by Father to stay away from him, Cordy falls in love with Squirl from a distance, completely unaware, because she is uninstructed, of the physical and emotional changes her body is experiencing that attract her to him. They have several conversations, in one of which he tells her about Cousin Sally's, a place in Luna Park in Seattle, where he says he has had terrifically good times. Out on the mountain one day, after he daringly shoots the log-rolling flume on a raft, they hug, kiss, and roll around passionately in the mud. Cordy begins to bleed, but does not realize she is menstruating, and her odd behavior causes Father, Babe, and then Cordy, too, to think she is pregnant. Father dismisses Squirl and arranges to send Cordy to a convent, but she runs away, leaving a suicide note behind. With great resource and daring, she makes her way to Cousin Sally's, which Cordy is unaware is a brothel, in Luna Park, a Seattle amusement park. Cousin Sally is the madam, elegant Sally Littlehood Burleson, Squirl's older half sister. Sally takes the girl in, informs her that she is not pregnant, and gives her a book on human physiology. Soon Sally and other Luna Park entertainers see possibilities in exploiting Cordy's appearance, especially her long white hair. They develop an act whereby as Cordelia, Daughter of the Orient, Seer of All Sights, whose assistant is Burleson (Squirl), she tells fortunes, gives away swatches of her hair for luck, and becomes a Seattle sensation. One of her promoters is Dr. Ridenour, who has a museum of human oddities. There Cordy finds a newspaper article with a photo of a huge, sideshow woman performer in Chicago some years earlier called "Giganta," who was accused of murdering her husband and for whom a reward of ten thousand dollars was posted. Cordy recognizes the woman as Babe, and when Squirl (now heavily in debt from dissolute living) discovers the article, he is determined to turn Babe in for the reward, marry Cordy, and take off with her for parts exotic. Cordy, however, has moral reservations and cannot bring herself to hurt Babe and Father by doing so. Squirl lures Babe to Seattle, and in a melodramatic, rushed conclusion, Dr. Ridenour's establishment burns, and Squirl is killed. It is discovered that Dr. Ridenour had committed the Chicago murder and put the blame on Babe. Cordy prepares to go home, and while she recognizes that Squirl was no good, as Father had implied, she will remember him as her first, exciting love. An amusing assortment of characters; a fast pace (after a slow beginning) with many twists, turns, coincidences, and humorous happenings; good details of logging and amusement park activities; some talk of World War I and the flu epidemic; and a staunch heroine who grows from a naive girl into a resourceful young woman with a better sense of self make for a page turner that comes to a sensationalistic but satisfying conclusion. ALA/YA.

LILLY MUSCOVITZ (*The Princess Diaries**) Mia Thermopolis's best friend since kindergarten, both of whose parents are psychoanalysts. Lilly is opinionated, bossy, and outspoken, inclined to try to make Mia over so she reaches "self-actualization" and to search for and espouse causes that she can showcase on her Saturday local-channel television show, *Lilly Tells It Like It Is*. One of her campaigns is against the Asians who run a deli and charge Asians five cents less than everyone else. After Mia tells her off, the two girls do not speak for a while, but when Michael, Lilly's brother, tutors Mia in algebra and takes over after Josh Richter humiliates Mia at the dance, the two girls become close friends again.

LIVESEY, MARGOT Born in Scotland; writer and teacher of writing. She grew up in the Scottish Highlands and received a B.A. in literature and philosophy at the University of York in England. For most of her twenties, she lived in Toronto, writing and managing a restaurant, and later moved to the United States, becoming a citizen in 2001. She has taught in numerous writing programs, among them the Iowa Writer's Workshop and the University of California–Irvine. Besides a collection of stories, she has published several novels, including *Criminals** (Knopf, 1996), a story, both amusing and touching, of misunderstandings and deliberate misleadings, all revolving around a baby found in a men's rest room in a Scottish town. Among her other novels are *Homework* (Viking, 1990), *The Missing World* (Knopf, 2000), and *Eva Moves the Furniture* (Holt, 2001). Livesey has received grants from the National Education Association and the Guggenheim Foundation.

LIZ KITCHELL (*What Child Is This?: A Christmas Story**) Bright, warm-hearted daughter of an affluent family. Liz takes pride in being a good student and is attracted to Tack* Knight, also a good student and well-liked classmate. Liz dislikes her father's tendency to surround himself with people but isolate himself from them as persons and from such significant life matters as poverty, which he attributes to laziness. Liz uses money of her own to grant a ski-weekend wish for a girl whose bell she finds on the Knights' restaurant Christmas tree. She represents the true spirit of Christmas.

LOGAN LABAUVE (*Meely LaBauve: A Novel**) The much-loved Daddy of Meely LaBauve, the protagonist. Although Logan is known in town as a "character" and is always a little to the left of the law, he is also regarded as helpful, generous, decent, and polite by those who, like the LaBauves, are at the bottom of the social ladder. His problems with the law stem from his drinking, which is extensive, and his "principles"; for example, he maintains that nowhere in the Constitution does it say that a person has to have a license plate or insurance on his car. The town police harass him regularly, partly for good reason and partly out of sheer meanness. Logan and Mr. Hebert, Joey's wealthy father, are foils.

LOGUE, MARY (1952–)   Poet, editor, mystery novelist. Among her books for adults are *Still Explosion: A Laura Malloy Mystery* (Seal Press, 1993), set in an abortion clinic, and *Halfway House: A Granddaughter's Biography* (Minnesota Historical Society, 1996), about Mae McNally Kirwin (1894–1961), who lived in Chokio, Minnesota. For young people she has written biographies of Elizabeth Barrett Browning, Gandhi, Helen Keller, and Walt Disney, and several mysteries, including *The Haunting of Hunter House* (Child's World, 1993) and *The Missing Statue of Minnehaha* (Child's World, 1993). More serious is her futuristic fantasy, *Dancing With an Alien** (Harper-Collins, 2000), set, like most of her other fiction, in the Twin Cities area.

LONDON BLOOD: FURTHER ADVENTURES OF THE AMERICAN AGENT ABROAD (Hall*, Robert Lee, St. Martin's Press, 1997)   Historical mystery set in 1759 during Benjamin Franklin's stay in London, the seventh in a series for adults starring the American diplomat, scientist, and writer. The narrator is Nicolas Handy, 14, Franklin's illegitimate son, whom, out of consideration for his wife, daughter, and older son, William, Franklin has not acknowledged but whom he has taken in and educated as his "assistant." Franklin has become an unofficial aid to John Fielding, the historical blind magistrate who organized the Bow Street Runners,

London's first police force, and who is known popularly as the "Blind Beak." The action starts with the discovery of the body of a highborn young lady, Hester Ward, in a foul alley with her heart cut out. Inquiry discovers that she was the niece of Silas Ward, arrogant marquess of Bathurst, a girl who was known to have wild tendencies and questionable friends. Further investigation reveals that she was not the first such victim, the earlier one being a prostitute named Tuesday Marrowbone from the house maintained by Mother Cockburn. Clues point to the involvement of strange, flamboyant Charles Ravenden, earl of Chalton and leader of a society of young rakes known as the "Dionysus Club," whose motto, from Rabelais, is *fay ce que vondras* (roughly translated, "do what you will"). Franklin is invited to attend a grand party to open Ravenden's temple to Dionysus at his country estate and asked, especially, to bring Nick, his "pretty boy." There they witness wild orgies, including rapes of both boys and young women, are taken by Ravenden into a cave at the rear of his phallic-shaped temple where they see a bloodstained altar, and are approached by Tom Elstree, one of Ravenden's followers, who is known to have loved Hester and who seems to want to tell them something, but who flees when Ravenden's servant appears. Scenes include Fielding's court, Mother Cockburn's whorehouse, Ward's grand house, fetid alleys and low taverns, and Franklin's comfortable lodgings where his landlady, Mrs. Margaret Stevenson, is finally persuaded to let him install a lightning rod. Action culminates back in the cave behind Ravenden's temple, where the young man, now clearly insane and believing he is Dionysus incarnate, tries to murder Franklin and is saved by Nick's quick action with the aid of Franklin's black servant, Peter, and a disaffected servant of Ravenden. This occurs during a terrible thunderstorm, which brings the temple down on its builder, who, of course, has not installed a lightning rod. Franklin proves that Hester was not killed by Elstree, a basically decent young man, as Ravenden told him he had after blacking out from drugged liquor, but by the leader of the Dionysus Club. Many other characters, some real, some fictional, appear, among them William Strahan, publisher; William, Franklin's older son, now studying law in London; Polly, Mrs. Stevenson's perky daughter; Pyecraft, journalist for low, sensational sheets known as "Jack Scratch"; Long John Enderby, brutal procurer or "twang"; and Birdy Prinsop, young prostitute visited by Nick, who treats with scorn his offer to find her legitimate work as a housemaid. The main interest, however, is in the fast action and the picture of London in the mid-eighteenth century, shown in both lavish and squalid detail. Booklist.

A LONG WAY FROM CHICAGO: A NOVEL IN STORIES (Peck*, Richard, Dial, 1998)   Humorous episodic, realistic novel replete with local color and period flavor, set in a small railroad town in Illinois, somewhere between Chicago and St. Louis, during the Great Depression. Narrator Joey Dowdel, 9, and his sister, Mary Alice, 7, travel by train to spend the month with their Grandma* Dowdel, who lives alone in a big house with a privy out back. Each of the episodes is the story of a month's visit, a month a year, and each adds to the characterization of Grandma, the strong-willed, clever, determined central figure, who always manages to get her way. Staunch Grandma, vivid details of town and time, and plenty of humor both slapstick and subtle have endeared this

book to readers of all ages. Previously the novel was a Newbery Honor book, listed in *Fanfare*, and cited for middle readers by the American Library Association. The sequel, which features Mary Alice, is *A Year Down Yonder**. For a longer entry, see *Dictionary, 1995–1999*. ALA/YA.

THE LOST YEARS OF MERLIN (Barron*, T. A., Philomel, 1996)   Fantasy novel filling in the childhood of Merlin, enchanter of the Arthurian tales, those "lost" years not treated in medieval poems and tales. After a brief third-person prologue, recounting the washing ashore of a woman and a little boy on an unfamiliar coast, which proves to be Gwynedd (Wales), and their rescue from a wild boar by the sudden appearance of a stag, action skips about five years to first-person narration by the boy, known as Emrys, now about twelve, who lives in a village not far from the coast with the woman, Branwen*, whom he refuses to believe is his mother. He can remember nothing before landing on the rocky shore, and she will give him no clue to his past, though she tells marvelous stories from several cultures, notably the Greek and Celtic, but also those of the Christian faith, in which she is a devout believer. As semioutcasts, they exist because of her ability to heal, which the villagers both employ and distrust. When a gang led by Dinatius, the blacksmith's boy, attacks Branwen and plans to burn her alive, Emrys uses powers he is not aware he possesses to save her by bringing a burning tree crashing down on Dinatius. Horrified at what he has done, Emrys dives into the flames to rescue him. When Emrys wakes he is in the convent at the Church of St. Peter, where Branwen is tending him. He discovers he is totally blind. His body heals, but he despairs until gradually he gains not his real sight again but a "second sight," by which he can distinguish enough to get around. His compulsion to find out who he is drives him to set off, despite Branwen's misgivings, back to the place where they first came to land. There he builds and launches a raft, and after days of thirst and near delirium, he is washed ashore on another coast, which he later discovers to be Fincayra, an island between the real world and the Otherworld. In a short time he learns that Fincayra is being destroyed by a terrible blight, that its King Stangmar has made a pact with the evil spirit, Rhita Gawr, that the giants have all been killed or have disappeared, and that the once-beautiful palace has been transformed into the Shrouded Castle, always spinning and therefore impregnable. He also has made two friends, a merlin he saves from two vicious rats and dubs "Trouble," and a leaf-draped girl named Rhia (Rhiannon), who lives in Druma Woods and understands the language of the trees. Although he is determined not to use his magic abilities, which he fears, he has the Galator, a token of great power given him by Branwen. Together, he and Rhia set off to try to rescue Fincayra from the evil that is overtaking it. Before long they are joined by Shim*, a dwarf who insists he is a giant, and Rhia is captured by goblins who take her to the Shrouded Castle. On their quest to find and save her, Emrys and Shim meet various helpful characters and overcome a number of dire threats. When, with the help of the merlin, they finally make their way into the Shrouded Castle, they are brought face to face with Stangmar, who is totally in the power of the evil Rhita Gawr. The king admits that the boy is his son and that he intends to kill him to make his power complete. Using some of his magic powers to save Rhia, Emrys

duels with his father. In the ensuing uproar, Rhita Gawr is destroyed, Shim returns to his true giant self and other giants emerge from hiding, the castle collapses, Emrys saves the Seven Treasures of Fincayra, and the land begins to blossom again. In a long author's note that precedes the narrative, Barron discusses the Merlin figure in ancient lore and modern retellings and explains why he chose to concentrate on these early years. The novel, however, echoes the stories by J. R. R. Tolkien and Lloyd Alexander far more in both event and tone than it does the Arthurian tradition. Events crowd upon each other at a pace that keeps the reader breathless, but characters and incidents are not always convincing. Because Emrys chooses not to explore and use his powers of magic, one loses sight of his connection with the enchanter of oral and literary tradition. Included is a very helpful map of Fincayra. ALA/YA.

LOVE AMONG THE WALNUTS (Ferris*, Jean, Harcourt, 1998)   Amusing, often funny novel of grasping relatives' duplicity and greed in the manner of Victorian melodrama. The action occurs in the countryside of probably the eastern United States and covers perhaps twenty-five years. Heading the very large cast is extremely rich Horatio* Alger Huntington-Ackerman, a self-made business mogul, who, despite his wealth, is increasingly unhappy with the world and rapidly becoming a recluse. His valet, Bentley, gives him tickets to the hottest new musical in town, where he falls instantly in love with and soon marries an ingenue actress, Mousey* Malone, called so for her tiny, squeaky voice. Idyllically happy, a baby on the way, they decide to move to the country, where they build their dream house, Eclipse, on a beautiful knoll next door to Walnut Manor, a somewhat rundown residence for mental patients. They are wonderfully happy with their handsome, bright son, Sandy* (Alexander), and with Bentley and his wife, Flossie, with the exception that one Thursday night a month Horatio's two greedy, lazy, whiny, younger brothers, Bart and Bernie, come to dinner. One evening when Sandy is a young man, the two arrive with a beautiful cake, of which Horatio, Mousey, and Flossie eat but not Sandy and Bentley. Sandy feeds a little of it to Attila the family chicken and puts the rest down the disposal, innocently destroying the evidence they realize would be of use when the eaters fall into comas from which they cannot be roused. Bart and Bernie demand a court hearing to declare Sandy incompetent to manage the estate and are obviously disappointed when Horatio's lawyers are appointed administrators. Since the court orders Sandy to have a doctor on hand, the sleepers are moved to Walnut Manor, where the resident physician, elderly Dr. Waldemar, seems capable and kind. Hired as live-in nurse is dazzlingly beautiful, blue-eyed, talkative Sunnie* Stone, with whom Sandy falls immediately in love but to whom, being shy, he cannot declare his affections. More untoward happenings occur before Bentley, who has been experimenting with cures, devises a liquid, which, although it looks terrible, awakens the sleepers. Soon thereafter, the house burns during the night, with fortunately no harm to anyone. Although Bart and Bernie are caught on the roof, obviously arsonists, police say they lack evidence for conviction. Bentley remembers a bottle of cheap port wine the two had brought one evening and gives it to police, who find it poisoned. Much of the central portion of the book focuses on the Manor residents,

a charming set of lovable oddballs and society rejects, whom Sunnie's loving ministrations return to excellent physical and mental health: Mr.* Moreland and his pal, L. Barlow Van Dyke, both business tycoons in their previous lives; Everett, who speaks in quotations; Boom-Boom, a split personality; and Louie the cat who loves Attila the chicken, among others. It also happens that Dr. Waldemar's employers, the Manor board of directors, have confined the residents, their own relatives, in Walnut so they can embezzle their money. With the help of Mr. Moreland and Van Dyke, Sandy has become a businessman in his own right and forces the board to repay the stolen money. He and the residents set up the Walnut Foundation, a nonprofit to which people tired of the world can come to acquire new vigor. The book ends with Opal*, the housekeeper, and Mr. Moreland getting married in a lovely outdoor wedding at which there are "no guests . . . [but] many attendants"; Bart and Bernie sitting in jail; and Sunnie and Sandy planning a honeymoon trip to Hawaii. Although at first it seems the book will merely regurgitate well-worn narrative material, the reader is most pleasantly surprised. The themes of the value to personal and group well-being of loving-kindness and caring are conveyed with skill and invention; the large cast consists of individualized, complementary, and affectionately handled characters; and the style is fast moving, engaging, and witty. ALA/YA.

LUBAR, DAVID (1954–)   Born in Morristown, New Jersey; magazine editor, computer programmer, designer of video games, writer for young people. His novel, *Hidden Talents** (Tor, 1999), is set in an alternative boarding school of last resort for youngsters who have been expelled from all other available schools. Far from grim, it is an entertaining fantasy in which the young people eventually outwit the adults and the few really vicious older boys. Among his other books are *The Wavering Werewolf* (Scholastic, 1997), *Monster Road* (Little Apple, 1999), *The Trouble with Heroes* (Tor, 2002), and *Wizards of the Game* (Philomel, 2003). He has also published two short story collections.

THE LUCKIEST GIRL IN THE WORLD
(Levenkron*, Steven, Scribner, 1997) Realistic psychological novel of a figure skater who, driven by the pressures of competition, becomes a self-mutilator, cutting herself with a small pair of scissors until she draws blood and her forearms are covered with scars. Bright, attractive Kate Roskova, 15, seems to have everything—talent, intelligence, a winning personality, and a chance at the junior championship. Although her coach, Ron, suspects something is wrong, her ambitious mother refuses to see the signs of trouble and berates her for her failure to concentrate enough to master the dangerous jumps consistently. When her fear is so great she thinks she will "space out," Katie secretly slices into her arm until the pain and blood bring her back to reality, and she is able to come smiling back onto the rink. At her exclusive private school, Westchester Academy, she does well academically but has few friends, her schedule so busy rushing from her home in New Rochelle, New York, to the ice rink in Hartford, Connecticut, and back that she has never learned to communicate with her peers. Only her English teacher, Jenny Moran, worries about her, but the school psychologist pooh-poohs her concern until one day, unable to control her terror, Katie slams her locker door on her hand repeat-

edly, fighting off anyone trying to help her. The school's headmaster is so afraid of alienating parents that he wants to expel Katie, but Jenny and the school nurse team up to point out that the school might be liable if they neglect her needs and eventually get her to a psychiatrist, Dr. Sandy Sherman. At first Katie is determined to tune him out, not even answering his questions, but gradually she finds relief in having someone who genuinely wants to help her. The rest of the book is a record, almost a case history, of her tentative steps toward recovery, with occasional setbacks. One devastating scene is when Sandy gets her divorced father and mother to come for a family counseling session that ends with both parents shouting recriminations and Katie in tears. An interesting development is the group therapy, where there are five other girls, one an overeater, one anorexic, one a continual runaway, one so alienated from her divorced parents that she is acting out in bizarre ways, and one other a "slasher." Although she resents being classed with these unattractive problem cases, for the first time Katie feels a connection to girls her own age. One day she skips school with the one boy in the academy that she knows spells trouble, and in the terrifying, drunken ride they are chased and stopped by the police. At the station, Katie, unable to face her mother, calls Jenny, who takes her home and is met by verbal abuse. After Ron drops her as a student, Katie thinks she may get some relief from the pressure, but her mother is furious and is soon making plans to take Katie out of school and move to Connecticut with a new coach. It is only when Katie slashes her arm, in front of her mother, that the truth finally dawns on the woman. Although there is no cure or final closure, the novel ends with the hope that Katie will recover and learn to lead a happy life. This is, frankly, a case history, if a composite one, but Katie is an attractive protagonist and her compulsion is made understandable and compelling. Her mother is somewhat overdrawn, but enough is told about her background to make her blind drive for her daughter's success plausible. ALA/YA.

LYNCH, CHRIS (1962–   )   Popular writer of eighteen novels involving family relationships, friendship, growing up, and sports for middle grade and adolescent boys. In *Gold Dust** (HarperCollins, 2000), an American Library Association selection for young adults, a Boston youth befriends a black boy from the Caribbean and eventually realizes that he has been selfishly using the boy to advance his own interests. More recently, Lynch has published a book of short stories about teenagers, *All the Old Haunts* (HarperCollins, 2001). For more information about Lynch, other titles, and title entries, see *Dictionary, 1990–1994* [*Shadow Boxer*] and *Dictionary, 1995–1999* [*Gypsy Davey*; *Iceman*].

M

MACK REESE (*God Bless the Child**) Local high school teacher and fisherman in a small town at the eastern tip of Long Island, New York, where Bailey Bender works in the bookstore, Livres of Grass. Divorced, Mack has a thirteen-year-old son, Will, whose mother has custody, but occasionally Mack takes the boy for a day, a situation trying to both of them since Will is miserable, resentful, and openly hostile, willing to go only where none of his friends will see him with Mack and demanding to control a program of events that his father can scarcely bear. When Mack's ex-wife finds a new boyfriend who wants to take her to Las Vegas, she decides Mack can have the boy temporarily and soon wants to make it permanent. While Will thinks about it, Mack is tense. The boy is a pain to have in his little house, but Mack really loves him and does not want to admit failure. When Will decides to stay, Mack is relieved, although it means changing his life, putting up with Will's foul mouth, sloppiness, and disrespect. Mack has already given up drinking. Will is scornful of Mack's Vietnam service, calling it "torching the villages and killing the babies," but when he steals money from Mack's wallet and runs away, he heads for the Vietnam memorial in Washington, D.C., where the police find him sleeping in the rain and call Mack to retrieve him. Mack leans on Bailey for emotional support, although she stays independent. In the end, Will seems to be coming around toward a companionable relationship with his father, and Bailey is welcoming Mack occasionally to her bed.

MAGDA (MAGDALENA) ORTEGA GREY (*The Tree of Red Stars**) Privileged, attractive, red-haired young Uruguayan woman, who becomes involved in the revolutionary group known as the Tupamaros, or Tupas. While she attends the university in Montevideo, she works as a secretary and translator for the United States Information Service. Sent to do some translating for an American official named Dan Mitrone, she overhears him describing how he has been teaching methods of torture to Uruguayan police, demonstrating them on beggars kidnapped in Montevideo. She discovers photographs of victims, among them Gabriela*, a beggar woman of whom Magda has been fond and has helped. This is a turning point in Magda's life. She casts in her lot with the Tupas.

MAKING UP MEGABOY (Walter*, Virginia, illus. Katrina Roeckelein, DK, 1998) Nontraditional novel set in recent times in a California city. It is made up of interviews, drawings, newspaper clippings, and other items related to the murder of a Korean liquor store proprietor by a middle school boy who has become obsessed by a comic book character he has invented. For a longer entry, see *Dictionary, 1995–1999.* ALA/YA.

THE MAN WHO ATE THE 747 (Sherwood*, Ben, Bantam, 2000) Lighthearted novel for adults of two men, one obsessed by records—the biggest, the longest, the greatest—the other obsessed by the need to impress a woman he loves by eating an entire 747 airplane. The main protagonist (and narrator of a brief introduction and afterword) is John J. (J.J.) Smith, who works as an authenticator for *The Book of Records*, traveling to far continents to verify claims of the tallest, the fastest, the oldest, the heaviest, and other superlatives. On a tip in a letter signed only "The Guy Who Knows," obviously from a child, he goes to Superior, Nebraska, where he finds the locals reluctant to part with much information, but the chief of police called "Shrimp," because he weighs only 114 pounds, finally gives him directions to the farm of Wally Chubb, into whose cornfield an aging 747 heading for a junkyard crashed and was abandoned. Because Wally has been hopelessly in love with Willa Wyatt, editor of the town weekly paper, since they were ten-

year-olds, it occurs to him that he might get her attention by eating the plane. His friend Nate Schoof, a mechanical genius, has rigged up a huge chopper-shredder into which they feed chunks of the plane and extract bucketfuls of ground-up metal, which Wally stirs into his milk and sprinkles on his cereal and consumes bit by bit, steadily working his way through the aircraft. J.J. visits the newspaper office, where Willa gives him the brush-off, but he is not discouraged. Instead, he is deeply smitten, a situation he knows is not good in his line of work where he travels excessively. He also finds The Guy Who Knows, Blake Wyatt, 10, a kid on a bicycle who happens to be Willa's little brother. Working all the angles, J.J. persuades Wally that with the publicity of a record he could hardly be ignored by Willa. He persuades some of the townspeople that having a record holder will revive Superior, which has been suffering the fate of many small towns in the midwest, gradual erosion of businesses and residents. After a tip to an Associated Press friend by J.J., the press and hucksters descend on the town and camp out in Wally's pasture. Willa is not impressed, but she cannot help being attracted to J.J., though she has sworn off men after one lover left her humiliated and heartbroken. She lets him ride with her as she delivers newspapers and even joins him in trying to break the record for tossing eggs without breaking them. His real trial comes when Blake climbs to the top of the water tower with a kite he has made, convinced that it will carry him all the way to Kansas and set a new record. With a storm coming, J.J. climbs after Blake, pulls him back when the wind catches his kite, and talks him down. Willa and J.J. spend one delightful night together, but in the morning, when it is announced that *The Book of Records* has decided not to certify the 747 consumption because it is too dangerous, she is furious at him for not warning her, the reporters all leave, and Wally punches him in the nose. J.J. leaves for an island in the Aegean where a man hopes to break the record for standing absolutely motionless (eighteen hours, five minutes, and fifty seconds). Willa goes to Wally, thanks him for his long love, and, as gently as possible, tells him that she cannot reciprocate and asks him to stop eating the airplane. He collapses and is taken to the hospital where Rose, a widow who has been in love with him for years, sits at his bedside. The whole town prays for Wally's recovery, and they go to his farm where they find J.J., returned from Greece, preparing to eat the rest of the plane to express his appreciation for Wally's devotion. In a great show of solidarity, they all take helpings of the metal grindings. Wally, who wakes from his coma to see the scene on television, is so moved that he turns to Rose and realizes that she is the one for him. J.J. quits *The Book of Records*, moves to Superior, and starts to write his own chronicle of achievements that cannot be measured but exhibit greatness and splendor, which he will call *The Book of Wonders*. Frequently quoted records (all genuine, although the story is fiction) give a sense of authenticity to this preposterous narrative, and details of the small Nebraska town and its people ring true. Many of the characters, though eccentric, are plausible, and the main ones are well developed. Altogether, it is a funny and touching book. Alex.

MANY STONES (Coman*, Carolyn, Front Street, 2000)   Realistic contemporary sociological- and personal-problem novel of a girl who must deal with the murder of her beloved older sister and her antag-onism toward her father. The narrator, Berry Morgan, 16, resents her take-charge father, Myles, a Washington, D.C., lobbyist, much preferring her more laid-back mother, especially since their divorce about four years ago and then the brutal murder in South Africa of her beloved older sister, Laura, while Laura was volunteering at a school for black children there. Myles turns up to manage a swimathon to raise money for a memorial and then peremptorily arranges for Berry to accompany him to dedicate it, further arousing resentments that continue throughout their almost two-week trip to South Africa. Berry sees the tremendous material differences between the lives of the blacks and her own circumstances and snaps at Myles for bringing her. She knows she is unreasonable but seems unable to stop herself. She learns from their black waiter, Phillip, how he lost two brothers, one to a gunshot, the other through diabolical torture, and yet he seems reconciled to the horror and forgiving toward the perpetrators. Since she knows her father is vulnerable on the matter of forgiveness, she forces him to discuss it. Her open antagonism, snide remarks, snubs, and passive resistance continue during the trip to Kruger Park, where she enjoys the wild animals but pulls away from sharing her pleasure with him or with anyone else. She meets Father Alan, whom she likes, at the school where Laura taught, listens to the memorial ceremony plans, and appreciates learning about Nelson Mandela when they visit Robben Island where Mandela was imprisoned for twenty-five years. All of these experiences make her feel heavy, however, weighed down and overburdened, as though she is lying beneath the stones that she has gathered and placed on her bedside table at home. The tension between father and daughter comes to a head while they are at Rocky End Bed and Breakfast in wine country. Myles, who enjoys flirting, is attracted to blond Suzanne, the proprietor, whose racist remarks disgust Berry so greatly that she challenges her father about them but which he casually accepts. She wonders whether they are sleeping together and refuses to accompany them on the trip to the winery. After they return, she attacks him about being her father at his "convenience," and he admits he does not try hard enough to take care of those he loves. His remark serves as a sort of catharsis. She weeps all over his high-fashion shirt but does not pursue the matter. At the ceremony, she makes the presentation, impressed by the children's heartfelt singing and the beautiful memorial vase created by a teacher. She points out that, like her, they have lost loved ones, and that the money for the memorial was raised out of Laura's love for them and their country. The novel ends, on a note of semireconciliation for Berry and her father. Since the plot is lean, Berry's feelings and reflections are forced to carry the book. The novel will appeal in particular to disaffected young people, but Berry's anger and hatred get tiresome, and it is sometimes hard to determine what she says and what words are only in her head and never voiced. Best is the picture of conditions in South Africa, and it is Berry's only real saving grace that she gains an understanding of the emptiness and hardships confronting the black people of that nation, an emptiness that is akin to her own. ALA/YA; Printz Honor.

MARCO PERIERA (*The Tree of Red Stars**)   Handsome young neighbor of Magda* (Magdalene) Ortega Grey, about five years older than she, who falls in love with her and whose affections she eventually returns. Marco becomes a political revolutionary of the Tupamaros (Tupas) movement, which includes many students and which opposes a military dictatorship in Uruguay. From his teens, he is idealistic and concerned with human rights. He wishes to study political science at the university in Montevideo and to help the poor and weak. His father, a retired army colonel, however, urges him to join the military. Marco does so reluctantly but secretly retains his contacts with the Tupas and helps Tupas who have been caught or people who are in great need like the beggar Gabriela*. When his covert activities become known, he is tortured and held in solitary confinement in a notorious prison for seven years. When he is released, he knows he does not have long to live.

MARCUS (*The Sand-Reckoner**)   Slave of Archimedes, the novel's main character. Although his name marks him as Roman, Marcus maintains he is Samnite, a tributary people of the Romans. At sixteen, he ran away during a battle in which the Romans were engaged and eventually ended up in a slave market, where Phidias, Archimedes's father and a mathematician, bought him to serve the household and later Archimedes when he went to Egypt to study. When King Hieron questions Marcus about his part in helping his brother, Gaius Valerius, escape, Marcus could have lied but tells the whole truth. Similarly, he could have lied later to the Roman commander about his remarks defending Hieron to the Roman commander but does not. Hence, he is condemned to death after he is turned over to the Romans. Because of his help in the Syracusan cause, Hieron gives Marcus the poison with which Marcus commits suicide. Marcus is a well-drawn, intriguing figure.

MARK BAILEY (*Nathan's Run**)   Alcoholic, abusive, ne'er-do-well uncle of Nathan Bailey, the boy of twelve who becomes a fugitive after he kills in self-defense his child-care supervisor (guard) at the Juvenile Detention Center. All his life Mark was resentful of Nathan's father, a successful lawyer and businessman, who was killed in an auto accident. When Nathan runs away in Mark's car to avoid Mark's abuse, Mark arranges for him to be punished by a term in the Juvenile Detention Center. Nathan, however, has been left money in trust by his paternal grandfather, which can come to Mark if Nathan dies. On the strength of this money, Mark enters into an unsavory business deal with gangster Mr. Slater. When the deal goes sour, Mr. Slater sends Lyle Pointer, the hit man, as an enforcer. Mark hires Ricky Harris, the detention home guard, to kill Nathan, but Nathan kills Ricky instead and runs. Eventually, Pointer murders Mark in horrible fashion.

MARON, MARGARET   Born in Greensboro and raised on a farm near Raleigh, North Carolina; highly acclaimed for her adult mystery novels; recipient of such honors as the Edgar Allan Poe, Agatha Christie, Anthony Boucher, and Macavity Awards. She is best known for two sets of books that draw on her North Carolina roots, the private eye procedures books featuring Sigrid Harald, the first of which was *One Coffee With* (Raven, 1981), and the amateur-sleuth novels involving Judge Deborah Knott, the first of which was *Bootlegger's Daughter* (Mysterious, 1992). In Up *Jumps the Devil** (Mysterious, 1996), a *Booklist* choice for young adults, Judge Knott helps solve several murders in her rural community. Other stories about Judge Knott include *Storm Track* (Mysterious, 2000) and *Uncommon Clay* (Mysterious, 2001). Maron has made her home in North Carolina with her artist husband.

MARTYRS' CROSSING (Wilentz*, Amy, Simon & Schuster, 2001)   Intense, wrenching novel published for adults of conflicts between Palestinians and Israelis at the beginning of the twenty-first century. The particular incident around which the action swirls starts when Marina Raad Hajimi, a young woman born and raised in the United States but Palestinian by family, marriage, and sympathy, arrives in the rain at a checkpoint between Ramallah and Jerusalem carrying her son, Ibrahim, 2 1/2, who is suffering a severe asthma attack that can be treated only at the hospital in Jerusalem. In the wake of various suicide bombings, the checkpoint has been closed to all Palestinians, and the crowd trying to get through is restive and angry. At the little checkpoint trailer, young Lieutenant Ari Doron is in charge, afraid that the situation will blow up and not happy to have the beautiful, distraught young woman begging him to make an exception for the gravely ill child. His humane instincts, however, drive him to attempt to get permission, and he is frustrated when he keeps being put on hold while the child gasps for air. Finally, although he has been explicitly told not to let the Hajimi child through, he agrees to let Marina take Ibrahim in the ambulance just arriving for one of the slightly injured soldiers, and he is appalled to see the little boy die before their eyes. Dreadful as this incident is, it is made far worse as it is exploited by the Palestinian side as "baby murder" and subjected to public relations "spin" by the Israeli side. Marina's husband, Hassan, a zealot for the Palestinian cause, is in jail as a suspected terrorist. Her father, George Raad, a cardiologist in

Cambridge, Massachusetts, is one of the old guard Palestinians, noted for his brilliant essays on the conflict. His childhood friend, Amr Ahmad, a leader who opposes the Authority and hopes to supplant the Chairman, seizes on the situation for his own advancement. On the Israeli side, Doron, who has always despised Palestinians, is deeply moved by the death and Marina's plight and is sleepless with shame and guilt at his part in it. He is summoned by Colonel Daniel Yizhar, head of public relations for the army, who tells him to forget his version of the occurrence and listen to the new one Yizhar is formulating, not entirely untrue but with various facts, like the time Marina and Ibrahim were in the checkpoint trailer reduced from an hour to fifteen minutes, altered to make the Israeli army look better. When Marina's father, ill himself and sincerely grieving for his delightful little grandson, arrives with his protégé, Philip, he refuses to play the part assigned him by Ahmed, and at the huge rally he speaks only the truth, or at least some of the truth, filling his old friend with consternation. Ahmed, however, plays his ace card, which he has negotiated, the release of Hassan from jail on the eve of Ramadan. Doron, in the meantime, is obsessed by his memories of Marina, and against orders and reason finds his way to her house, not to ask forgiveness but just to say he's sorry. She pushes him away, realizing that Hassan will kill him if he knows he is there, and, if someone else kills him, Hassan will be blamed and in either case will have to go into hiding. Two Palestinians who have been trailing Doron, a lawyer who was at the checkpoint and his nephew, kidnap him and try to kill him, but cannot bring themselves to do it and finally dump him, badly injured, near a mosque into which he stumbles, bloody and disoriented, during prayers. Whether good-hearted, naive Doron survives, is not told, but George Raad's heart gives out at last, and he dies in a Jerusalem hospital. Hassan goes into hiding. Marina, having lost her son, her husband, her father, and her belief in the cause she has devoted her life to, is about to return to Cambridge. The only survivors are the two utterly corrupt and cynical characters, Yizhar and Ahmed. Around this ironic incident is a wealth of detail about the cities, the beliefs, the history, the inevitable misunderstandings, the misery, and the persisting beauty of the area. The novel, though compelling, is dense and not easy or pleasant reading, with a sense of foreboding predominant. The title comes from the name of the checkpoint, Shuhada or Martyr Crossing. Booklist.

MARY, BLOODY MARY (Meyer*, Carolyn, Gulliver, 1999)   Historical novel of the girlhood of Mary Tudor (1516–1558), who ruled briefly as queen of England in the mid-sixteenth century. In a prologue, Mary, who tells the story, puts the blame for her sad early years and her mother's untimely death on Anne* Boleyn, the beautiful court lady who supplanted Mary's mother, Catherine* of Aragon, as the wife and queen of Henry* VIII. Mary says that Anne was a "witch" who "beguiled my father and seduced him," so that Henry rejected Catherine, declared Mary illegitimate, and ruined Mary's chances for a good marriage. Mary begins her actual story the year she is ten, just before she is betrothed to Francis I of France, and concludes it ten years later when Henry executes Anne and marries Lady Jane Seymour. Mary remembers her youth as isolated and lonely, lived in the country away from the activity of London and her parents, for both of whom she yearned, reared by her beloved governess

Lady Margaret Salisbury*, and well educated by tutors in Latin, Greek, and modern languages and in the noted philosophers. When her mother's partisans attempt to smuggle her to the continent, the plot is discovered, and she is pressured to renounce her claim to the throne and her legitimacy of birth. When Anne gives birth to Elizabeth (who later becomes Elizabeth I), Mary, no longer the princess of Wales and heiress presumptive, must change the baby and labor like a scullery maid. The increasingly unstable and mercurial Henry tires of Anne and takes up with Lady Jane, ostensibly because Anne has given him no male heir, and then executes Anne. After the marriage, Mary, although still regarded as illegitimate, regains her father's favor, and her circumstances improve as she concludes her story. Mary's account is less notable for the facts as for the picture of the social and political atmosphere as seen from the vantage of a young woman who is the age of most of her readers: her almost complete lack of friends; the highly structured social functions, all politically mandated and regulated; the many hours spent in study; the intrigues, of which she is aware from an early age and in which she participates for survival; her realization that she is important politically; and her understanding that she is both hated and admired. The book's title is ironic and ambiguous, a misnomer in context. As the author's historical note at the end explains, Mary becomes a bloody ruler because of her intense desire to restore Catholicism to England. In Mary's account, however, she prays frequently, but there is little sense of the religious fervor that motivates her later. Adjectives that might better describe her during this period are rejected, despised, unwanted, dispirited, useless. The sense of the period's political realities and the characterizations of the principals are strong. Another, quite different portayal of Anne Boleyn appears in *The Secret Diary of Anne Boleyn**. A family tree and an author's historical note are included but no bibliography of sources. ALA/YA.

MASSEY, SUJATA (1964–)   Born in Sussex, England; journalist, mystery novelist. With her father, from India, and her mother, from Germany, Massey came to the United States at the age of five and grew up in Philadelphia, Pennsylvania; Berkeley, California; and St. Paul, Minnesota. She is a 1986 graduate of Johns Hopkins University in Baltimore, Maryland, and has worked on the Baltimore *Evening Sun*. With her naval medical officer husband, she moved to Japan, where she taught English and studied Japanese. Her novel, *The Floating Girl** (HarperCollins, 2000), is one of a series starring Rei Shimura, an American Japanese antiques dealer who becomes involved in various mysteries. It was nominated for the 2000 Agatha Award for the Best Novel. Others in the series include *The Flower Master* (HarperCollins, 1999), which won the Macavity Award for the Best Novel; *The Bride's Kimona* (HarperCollins, 2001), nominated for the Agatha Award for Best Novel; and *The Samurai's Daughter* (HarperCollins, 2003). Like Rei, whose American upbringing keeps her somewhat alien in her ancestral land, Massey's mixed heritage makes it possible to blend into both Oriental and American cultures without ever entirely fitting.

MATCHECK, DIANE   Writer whose first novel, *The Sacrifice** (Farrar, 1998), is set in the eighteenth century in what is now Nebraska and Yellowstone Park. It is the story of a Native American Indian girl who is captured and escapes, becoming a sacrifice in a ritual later discontinued. Matcheck lives in Palo Alto, California.

MATT MORDEN (*What Child Is This?: A Christmas Story**)   Foster son of lower-middle-class, elderly, good-hearted Mr. and Mrs. Rowen. The Rowens have also taken in little Katie, of whom Matt has grown fond. Matt is a closed-off young man, who fears to allow himself to feel affection because he has been moved from home to home so many times. Matt knows he is smart and can be a good student but endures school, work, and the Rowens' home, even though everything is going well, because he simply wants to turn eighteen and decide for himself about life. At the same time, he likes the Rowens and dreads being moved to another place. Although he envies Tack* Knight for his close relationship with his father, he purposely holds himself aloof from the Knights, who offer friendship. His desire to please Katie, to help her hope for a truly big thing at Christmas, surprises even Matt himself. Later, when Katie is happily settled with Allison and her husband, he wonders which role he played, a shepherd or a wise man. He takes the little girl in his arms and swings her high in the air, realizing as he does so that he has never before done anything as beautiful as lift up someone he loved.

MAXWELL, ROBIN (1948–)   Born in Washington, D.C.; graduate of Tufts University with a B.A. She has been an occupational therapist and unit supervisor at a psychiatric hospital in New York, and, since 1981, a screenwriter and writer for television. Her first novel, *The Secret Diary of Anne Boleyn** (Arcade, 1997), arose from her long and intense interest in period drama and in England's Tudor era.

Chosen by the American Library Association for young adults, it is a biographical novel of Elizabeth I and her mother, Anne Boleyn, and overflows with fascinating details of the people at court and of the times. *The Queen's Bastard* (Arcade, 1999) concerns Arthur Dudley, presumed son of Elizabeth I, and *Virgin: A Novel* (Arcade, 2001) concerns an attempt to capture Elizabeth I after Henry VIII dies.

THE MAZE (Hobbs*, Will, Morrow, 1998) Contemporary adventure and boy's growing-up novel set in that part of the wilds of Utah's Canyonlands National Park called the "Maze." Rick Walker, 14, runs away from his Las Vegas, Nevada, detention home, eventually finding himself at a remote campsite in the rugged Canyonlands. He becomes involved in the project of a moody biologist, who is reintroducing condors into the wilds and is a hang glider specialist. He helps the biologist thwart two men out to steal Native American artifacts. In the process, Rick begins to deal with the knotty personal problems that landed him in detention. The action-filled plot, clearly delineated problems, gripping details of setting and avian life, and thrilling glider flights produce a top-notch adventure story. Earlier the novel was nominated for an Edgar Allan Poe Award. For a longer entry, see *Dictionary, 1995–1999*. ALA/YA.

MAZER, NORMA FOX (1931–) Born in New York City; for many years a popular writer, recipient of numerous awards, best known for her problem novels for adolescents, some written with her husband, Harry Mazer, also long popular with young readers. *When She Was Good** (Scholastic, 1997), selected by the New York Public Library and by the American Library Association for young adults, tells the unhappy story of two sisters, the older of whom abuses the younger. *Good Night, Maman* (Harcourt, 1999), departs from form, being a historical novel of a Jewish Parisian family during World War II. Mazer has made her home in Manhattan and Jamesville, New York. For more information about her, titles, and title entries, see *Dictionary, 1960–1984* [*A Figure of Speech*; *Saturday, the Twelfth of October*; *Taking Terri Mueller*]; *Dictionary, 1984–1989* [*After the Rain*]; and *Dictionary, 1995–1999* [*When She Was Good*].

MCDEVITT, JACK (JOHN CHARLES) (1935–)   Born in Philadelphia, Pennsylvania; theater director and teacher of English and history at several high schools. He received his B.A. from LaSalle College and his M.A.L.S. from Wesleyan University. A full-time writer since 1995, he is a highly acclaimed author of science fiction, for which he has received or been nominated for awards, including the Hugo and the Nebula. In addition to publishing numerous novels, he has contributed short stories to magazines. His first novel, *The Hercules Text* (Ace, 1986), involves competition with the Russians during the Cold War; *Ancient Shores* (HarperCollins, 1996) revolves around the discovery of a sea vessel; in *Deep Six* (HarperCollins, 2001) an interplanetary mission goes awry; and *Moonfall** (HarperPrism, 1998), chosen by *Booklist*, describes the near-destruction of the United States when a comet hits the Moon.

MCDONALD, JOYCE (1946–) Born in San Francisco, California; editor, publisher, professor of English, writer. McDonald received her B.A. degree in 1972 and her M.A. in 1974 from the University of Iowa, and her Ph.D. from Drew University in 1994. Through the late 1970s and 1980s, she worked in various editorial capacities, including her own company, McDonald Publishing Company/Shoe Tree Press, from 1984 to 1989. From 1990 to 1996, she taught English at Drew University in Madison, New Jersey. Her novels include *Mail Order Kid* (Putnam, 1988), about the resentment a fifth-grade boy feels when his family adopts a Korean six-year-old; *Comfort Creek* (Delacorte, 1996), in which a family falls on hard times; and *Swallowing Stones** (Delacorte, 1997), about guilt and redemption for a thoughtless act that causes a death. She has also published literary criticism and a picture book.

MCGOLPHIN, FINN (*The War in Georgia**)   Next-door neighbor to the Morgan family, the best neighbor ever, Shanta's grandmother says, although he is gruff talking and likes to tease the old woman into showing some temper. A large man, he comes at once, barefoot, when Shanta is sent for him to lift Uncle Louie from the bathtub, where the arthritic man has frozen. He thoughtfully wraps Louie in a bath towel, carries him to his bed, and gently settles him in, where he will spend the rest of his life. McGolphin rescues Ralph Edward Weathers, the preacher's pesky boy, who has been riding his bike past and taunting Shanta about her skinny legs. Mr. Walling, the strange, scary man across the street, grabs Ralph Edward and is making him remove his pants to show his own legs, when McGolphin ambles into the street with his hand out, introduces himself to Walling so the man must drop his hold on the boy, and then tells Ralph Edward to stop pestering and go home, which he does in a streak. In the culminating incident with the Walling men, Shanta hides under the magnolia tree while they hunt for her. She knows that when she does not answer her grandmother, the old woman will call McGolphin, and if she can get to him before the Wallings catch her, she will be safe. After the police have taken the two Walling men away and told McGolphin that they will bathe and dress Earl, take him to the hospital to be checked over, and then to a group home, Shanta pleads with McGolphin to tell them to call Earl by the name he prefers, Roy Rogers. He crosses the street again, talks to the policeman, and comes back to report that they are taking Roy Rogers to the ranch after a quick stop at the hospital. McGolphin lives alone, is unsentimental, but is always dependable in a crisis.

MCINTOSH, ALISTAIR (*Cloudy in the West**)   Dour, elderly, Scottish American sheep man of some means, who befriends Joey and Beau Shipman while they are on the run because they think that they killed Blair Meacham. McIntosh's herd of some two thousand sheep is capably managed by a clever, knowledgeable collie, Old Rustler. McIntosh loves the land and sings its praises, but he is also a shrewd businessman who feels certain that the terrain of west Texas would be better for sheep than for cattle, an idea that few entertained at that period in the history of Texas. McIntosh recognizes Miller Dawson* and reports him to the sheriff in Stockton, who sets a trap for the outlaw, captures, and hangs him. In his wagon McIntosh carries books that he shares with Joey and that whet the boy's appetite for reading, among them *Tom Sawyer*.

MCKILLIP,   PATRICIA   A(NNE) (1948–)   Born in Salem, Oregon; highly acclaimed author of science fiction and fantasy novels. McKillip was graduated from San Jose State University with a B.A. in 1971 and an M.A. in l973. Probably best known for her fantasy trilogy starting with *The Riddle-Master of Hed* (Atheneum, 1976), she earlier published well-received novels including *The House on Parchment Street* (Atheneum, 1973), with a setting based on an old house she lived in when her father was stationed in England, and *The Forgotten Beasts of Eld* (Atheneum, 1974), which won the World Fantasy Award. More recently, she has written a second trilogy that starts with *The Sorceress and the Cygnet* (Ace, 1991). *Winter Rose** (Ace, 1996) is a haunting novel of a family caught in a collision between everyday life and other worlds.

MCKINLEY, ROBIN (1952–)   Born in Warren, Ohio; editor, novelist. Her *Beauty* (Harper, 1978), a fictionalized retelling of the *Beauty and the Beast* folktale, was chosen as a Phoenix Award Honor Book in 1998. A second retelling of the same tale in a more complicated form, *Rose Daughter** (Greenwillow, 1997), was named to the American Library Association Young Adult list. Earlier biographical information and title entries appear in *Dictionary, 1960–1984* [*Beauty*; *The Blue Sword*]; *Dictionary, 1985–1989* [*The Hero and the Crown*; *The Outlaws of Sherwood*]; and *Dictionary, 1995–1999* [*Beauty*].

MCLAMORE, JAMES (*I Want to Buy a Vowel**)   Police chief in Waxahachie, Texas. When the outbreak of religious fervor hits the town, he remarks that "Satanism is not illegal in Texas," and when the local ministers protest that he arrest someone for crimes against God, he starts to say that God would have to come in and sign a complaint, but wisely refrains. When the stamp machine is stolen from the post office and he is asked whether he thinks Satanists are responsible, he says sarcastically, "Maybe they're planning a letter-writing rampage." This gets reported seriously in the newspaper and gives Kenlow Schindler the idea of writing anonymous letters. McLamore, on getting one of the letters, contacts the newspaper with one of his own invention, promising to forego any more Satanist activities, signed "Unidentified Teenager." This so enrages Kenlow that he decides to make a real statement with a pentagram in the warlock's house and ends by accidentally burning the house and starting a forest fire. McLamore is so disgusted with Reverend Schindler's exorcism in front of the jail that he says for five minutes it is freedom of religion; after that, he will call it loitering and issue a citation. By now fond of Alfredo, he has his Spanish-speaking sergeant bring the boy from his cell to watch the farce. A good, sensible officer of the law, he is almost defeated by the town's hysteria.

MCLAREN, CLEMENCE (1938–) Born in New Jersey; educated at Rutgers University (A.B.) and at the University of Hawaii at Manoa (Ed.D.); with her husband a teacher in various places abroad, including Greece and Honolulu, Hawaii, where they have made their home. In Greece, they lived on an island near Aegina, Achilles's home island. Their experiences in Greece nourished her love of the old stories of Troy and resulted in *Inside the Walls of Troy: A Novel of the Women Who Lived the Trojan War** (Atheneum, 1996), an American Library Association selection for young adults. Among her other books are *Waiting for Odysseus* (Atheneum, 2000) and *Aphrodite's Blessings: Love Stories from the Greek Myths* (Atheneum, 2002). She has also written *Dance for the Land* (Atheneum, 1999), about a half-Hawaiian girl whose lawyer father fights for native rights.

MCNEAL, LAURA RHOTON   Writer with her husband, Tom NcNeal*, of such popular novels for teenagers as *Crooked** (Knopf, 1999), chosen for young adults by the American Library Association. It concerns two teens who are harassed by two hoodlum brothers. They have also published *Zipped* (Knopf, 2003), about four high school sophomores whose lives are interwoven, and *The Dog Who Lost His Bob* (Morton Grove, 1996), in which a lost dog tells his story. A graduate of Brigham Young University, she received an M.A. in creative writing from Syracuse University. Before becoming a full-time writer, she taught in middle school and high school. She lives with her husband and son in Falbrook, California.

MCNEAL, TOM   Grew up in Orange County, California; author with his wife, Laura Rhoton McNeal*, of *Crooked** (Knopf, 1999), a tense novel about two young people who are harassed by two hoodlum brothers, which was cited by the American Library Association for young adults. With Laura, he has also published *Zipped* (Knopf, 2003), about four high school sophomores whose lives intertwine, and *The Dog Who Lost His Bob* (Morton Grove, 1996), in which a lost dog tells his story. Alone, he has also written many short stories and a novel, *Goodnight, Nebraska* (Random House, 1998). He received a Master's in Fine Arts from the University of California–Irvine and has taught creative writing at Stanford University. He and Laura live in Falbrook, California, with their son.

MEAD, ALICE (1952–)   Born in Portchester, New York; art teacher, writer. She received her B.A. from Bryn Mawr College in 1973, her M.Ed. from Southern Connecticut State University in 1975, and her B.A. in art education from the University of Southern Maine in 1985. In the 1970s and early 1980s, she taught art and preschool in Connecticut and Maine. Her first novel, *Crossing the Starlight Bridge* (Bradbury, 1994), deals with Native Americans. *Junebugs* (Farrar, 1997) is the first of several about life for African American youth in housing projects. *Adem's Cross** (Farrar, 1996) concerns the conflict between Serbs and Albanians in Kosovo. She has also edited a collection of ancient Wabanaki tales. A title entry for *Crossing the Starlight Bridge* appears in *Many Peoples, One Land* [no. 462].

MEELY LABAUVE: A NOVEL (Wells*, Ken, Random House, 2000)   Realistic period boy's growing-up novel set in southern Louisiana Cajun country for a few months in 1961, published for adults. Narrator Meely (Emile) LaBauve, 15, lives at the edge of Catahoula Bayou in a dilapidated house, with his hard-drinking, often absent father, Logan*. They live off the land, poaching game and fishing the bayou. Logan, who Meely says pretty much gave up when Momma and the new baby died in childbirth eight years earlier, sometimes appears with a little money from catching "gators" and occasionally with a loose woman. Sometimes, he is in jail, mostly for minor infractions. Meely enjoys the social life of school but is often truant, although Miz* Lirette, his teacher, urges him to attend regularly. Meely holds to his father's notion that school does not do much for anybody and devotes his attention to getting his next meal. He goes swimming sometimes with fat, scorned, not-bright Chickie Naquin, or with pleasant, popular Joey Hebert, the son of Francis Hebert, the owner of vast acres of cane fields and the richest man around. As does his father, Meely helps out neighbors, like the black Jackson family, with fish or a possum, and Cassie Jackson, the daughter, introduces Meely to the pleasures of sexual fondling. The main problem involves bully Junior Guidry, one of the eight children of the tough, low-down Guidrys. Junior heads a mini-mob of toughs and is often "whupped" at school for bullying, brawling, baiting, and general insolence. He especially dislikes Meely, who plays shortstop and often snags Junior's line drives. One day, having been razzed by Meely's team, Junior loses his cool, strikes out, and decides to take his disappointment out on Meely, who races into the schoolhouse for safety. The principal catches, whups, and suspends Junior, who mobilizes his mob to beat up Meely. They are interrupted in the act by Chilly (Chester) Cox, 19, a big black man and sometime boyfriend of Cassie, who trounces them thoroughly. Junior claims that Meely assaulted him, enlists the aid of Uncle, a mean, corrupt policeman, and Uncle's partner, equally mean and sadistic Sergeant Picou. Meely is jailed and threatened with reform school and various ugly acts like rape, since the cops take Junior's word over Meely's. Miz Lirette engages a good lawyer, speaks for Meely, and the truth eventually comes out. Junior's true character and behavior are disclosed through the testimony of Chickie and especially Joey, the Judge severely admonishes the cops and the Guidrys, and Miz Lirette takes Meely in to keep him from being sent to an orphanage. Near book's end, Logan turns up at Miz Lirette's just before leaving for Florida to work for a man who owns a gator farm. Meely is an attractive protagonist, self-sufficient, honest, respectful, well brought up in character by anyone's standards. He abides by the best principles his father, when home and in good form, has held up to him, justice, respect, loyalty, decency, and fairness—"a measure of a big dog ain't that he can bite the little ones"—and that advantages do not always make the boy. Especially strong is the setting, the physical side of bayou, woods, fields, wildlife, all of which Meely loves and nurtures his spirit, and the social side of segregation of blacks from whites, and discrimination based on color, money, and power. Meely tells his story in unschooled English mixed with Cajun dialect, a good smattering of off-color terms, and extensive dialogue that demands close attention because no quotation marks appear. After the plot problem is introduced, the action moves fast with plenty of excitement, some cliff-hangers, dramatic courtroom scenes, and a sprinkling of humor both of situation and of Meely's ironic and naive observations and conclusions. ALA/YA; NYPL.

MEMORIES OF SUMMER (White*, Ruth, Farrar, 2000)   Realistic period novel set in 1955, mostly in Flint, Michigan, about a family's efforts to cope with the schizophrenia of the elder daughter. Lyric Compton, 13, the narrator, and her sister, Summer, three years older, have always been close emotionally, to each other and to their coal miner father, Poppy, especially since their mother died when Summer was six. The girls have freedom and happiness in the southwestern Virginia hills, but are excited when Poppy decides to go take them to Flint, where his friend Henry assures him he will easily get a job in the General Motors plant. They are dismayed by the apartment Henry has found for them, but hope to get something better soon. When Poppy's last check does not come from the company in Virginia, he swallows his pride and goes to the local grocery store to ask for credit. To his relief, the manager is a woman named Gayle Stiltner from Buchanan County, Virginia, as they are, and they soon are comparing acquaintances and relatives. She gives them credit to tide them over until Poppy gets on at Chevrolet. Summer has always had some peculiarities, being afraid of electricity and of dogs, which she insists are wolves, and inclined to stare at the sky and whisper, but these have never been real problems until they come to Michigan. After the first day of school she refuses to go back, or even to get out of bed. Lyric, who goes to a different school, soon adjusts and even makes a friend in Yolanda from Texas, but she avoids letting anyone know where she lives or that her older sister is acting strange. One night Summer comes into the kitchen with deep scratches down her cheeks, saying the wolves did it. Poppy takes her to the emergency room, and she is kept in the hospital for three days, returning medicated like a zombie. Even when Poppy finds a real house for them, Summer's troubles continue. Most of her care falls on Lyric, since their father works the afternoon-evening shift. Sometimes the old, bright Summer comes through again, but often she is depressed, fearing she is fading away. She makes Lyric promise that she will write a book about her, so she will be kept alive. When Lyric, who has a fine voice, stays after school to audition for a part in *The Mikado*, Summer appears suddenly, her clothes and hair awry, making odd noises and announcing, "I am queen for a day." Lyric admits to her friends and her teacher that her sister is ill and takes Summer home, giving up her chance at a part in the production. Summer becomes more paranoid and starts lighting fires and cutting herself with sharp objects. After one of her frequent hospitalizations, they learn that she has been given shock treatments, which, considering her fear of electricity, cause a setback in her condition. Not wanting Lyric to miss out on friends and fun, Poppy tries to find occasional baby-sitters for Summer, so her sister won't be trapped as caregiver, but none of them works out. Finally, after she injures Lyric, who is trying to get her to the basement during a tornado watch, Poppy reluctantly admits Summer to the state hospital in Pontiac. Life goes on for Lyric and Poppy, but not without permanent scars. The pain and grief of mental illness for not only the victim but also the victim's family are vividly evoked, especially in this situation where everyone concerned is well intentioned and trying hard. The setting in the 1950s is not belabored, but makes some difference since treatment has changed and most state mental hospitals in Michigan have long been closed. Lyric's closeness to Summer when they are younger and her sadness, mixed with exasperation, ring true. ALA/YA.

MEMPHIS (*The Starlite Drive-in**) Charlie Memphis, the handsome, courteous drifter with whom Teal Benton, mother of Callie* Anne (Benton Dicksen), the narrator, falls in love. Although Memphis many times could take advantage of Callie Anne's romantic notions about him, he is always kind and respectful toward her, treating her as a father would. Teal and Memphis plan to run away as soon as Memphis can get together enough money, but Memphis mysteriously disappears before they do so. Claude Junior, Teal's husband and Memphis's employer, tells Teal and Callie Anne that Memphis ran off, taking with him three hundred dollars belonging to the theater, after he and Memphis have a terrible fistfight. In adulthood, Callie Anne learns what is most likely the truth about what happened to Memphis: that her father murdered the man and dumped his body in a pit near by.

MEYER, CAROLYN (1935–)   Born in Lewiston, Pennsylvania; graduate of Bucknell University; teacher and lecturer; author of books of fiction and nonfiction for middle graders and young adults. Many of these have received critical acclaim, among them, three recent American Library Association selections for young adults: *Gideon's People** (Harcourt, 1996), which contrasts the ways of life of two boys, one Amish and one Jewish; *Jubilee Journey** (Harcourt, 1997), set in 1996 in Texas among African Americans who have gathered for the seventy-fifth celebration of the Emancipation Proclamation, sequel to *White Lilacs* (Harcourt, 1993); and *Mary, Bloody Mary** (Gulliver, 1999), historical novel of the girlhood of Mary Tudor of England. More recently, she has published *Isabel: Jewel of Castilla* (Scholastic, 2000) and *Beware, Princess Elizabeth* (Harcourt, 2001). She has made her home in Albuquerque, New Mexico. For additional information about Meyer, titles, and a title entry, see *Dictionary, 1995–1999* [*Jubilee Journey*]; *This Land Is Our Land* [*Denny's Tapes*, no. 86; *White Lilacs*, no. 87; *Where the Broken Heart Still Beats*, no. 447]; and *Many Peoples, One Land* [*Jubilee Journey*, no. 81].

MIAH ROSELIND (*If You Come Softly**) Jeremiah Roselind, handsome, intelligent, African American youth, 15, who falls in love with his white classmate, Ellie* Eisen, and who is shot and killed by a policeman. Miah is proud of his scholastic ability and loves basketball (he is the best player at exclusive Percy Academy), his homeboys, of whom Carlton has a black father and a white mother, and his parents. He is proud of both his parents' achievements, although he wants to be respected for himself alone, and of having traveled widely and of meeting many famous and talented people. He keeps in mind what his father says about being proud of being black but hates the baggage that seems to go with being black, like teachers' assuming that he cannot achieve academically and having white people doubt his motives without cause. Although Ellie Eisen is a good character, Miah is the better drawn and more memorable figure. With respect to handling the racial aspect of the romance between the two young people, the author might usefully have explored Carlton's interracial home situation.

MICHAELS, WARREN (*Nathan's Run**) Police lieutenant in Brookfield, Virginia, who eventually apprehends Nathan Bailey, saving the boy's life from the lynchmob police out to get him as a cop killer. Michaels is a solid family man, a loving husband, father of two daughters, and, the reader learns as the book goes on, of a deceased son who would be about Nathan's age. He is a stern cop, tough but fair, a stickler for rules but humane. He deplores the vengeful attitudes of the county prosecutor, J. Daniel Petrelli*, and of the uniformed police involved in the case, both of whom he believes have jumped to conclusions for vested interests. Details of his inner searchings and his behavior individualize him and make him a round figure.

MICHAEL WEINSTEIN (*My Sister's Bones**) Surgeon father of anorexic Cassie* and of narrator Billie. A driven, demanding man, he remains in denial about Cassie's illness throughout the book. As Billie describes him, he has many irritating qualities. He is stingy with money; puts down his wife, Jane, over almost everything; and nags the girls about excelling in school and getting good SAT scores. Cassie has learned to stand up to him, even if it results in a yelling match, and Billie is learning to follow suit. Michael is a good provider, however, genuinely loves his family, and gives generously of his medical skills. He is a foil to Mr. Zefferelli, father of Tiffany*, Billie's best friend. Both are fathers whose behavior severely damages their families. If Cassie dies from her disease, it may be because Michael, who has disagreed with her psychiatrist over her treatment, insists that she leave the hospital and come home.

MIKAELSEN, BEN(JAMIN JOHN) (1952–) Born in Bolivia; author of adventure and problem novels for middle graders and teenagers. Cited by the American Library Association for young adults, *Petey** (Hyperion, 1998) is the affecting story of a boy born in 1920 with cerebral palsy, notable for its plucky hero and depiction of attitudes toward and treatment of such handicapped people throughout most of the twentieth century. Among his recent publications is *Touching Spirit Bear* (HarperCollins, 2001), in which a juvenile offender is sentenced according to Native American justice to a remote Alaskan Island. For more details about Mikaelsen, titles, and title entries, see *Dictionary, 1990–1994* [*Rescue Josh McGuire*] and *Dictionary, 1995–1999* [*Petey*].

MIKKO RIPANEN (*Necessary Roughness**) Good-looking, friendly Finnish-American, teenage son of the high school principal, Mr. Ripanen, in Iron River,

Minnesota, the town the Korean American Kim family move to. Mikko has seen Chan Kim, the narrator, practicing soccer in his yard. When the high school football team's regular kicker is hurt in an accident, Mikko suggests that Chan try out for the team. Mikko helps Chan learn about the game and coaches him in extra practices. He would like to date Young, but he understands why she refuses him. He takes her death hard and for a time blames Young's girlfriend, who was driving the car.

MILLS, DEANIE FRANCIS Journalist, writer of suspense novels, set mostly in Texas. She has been a columnist for the local newspaper in Snyder, Texas, and lives in Hermleigh, Texas. Her novel of a woman and her son kidnapped by a survivalist group, *Ordeal** (Dutton, 1997), is a fast-paced story of terror and growing desperation. Among her other novels are *Torch* (Signet, 1999), about an investigative reporter on the trail of a serial arsonist; *The Jigsaw Man* (Jove, 1997), in which a young woman suffers a recurrence of the horror of her mother's death that she witnessed years ago; *Tightrope* (Signet, 1999), about a woman released early from prison to become an FBI informant; and *Love Me Not* (Jove, 1995), about a forensic artist with hands broken in an assault.

MIND'S EYE (Fleischman*, Paul, Holt, 1999)   Unusual novel celebrating the power of the imagination. Written entirely in dialogue, although clearly not intended to be dramatized, it is set in recent times in a nursing home in Bismarck, North Dakota, where Courtney, 16, who through a riding accident is paralyzed from the waist down, shares a room with two elderly women, May, an Alzheimer's victim, and Elva, 88, a for-

mer high school teacher of English. Elva starts by quoting at length from *Snow-Bound*, pointing out that their condition, locked in during a heavy snowfall, is not so different from that of the family in John Greenleaf Whittier's poem. To all her overtures, Courtney, newly arrived from a hospital, answers in sulky monosyllables, revealing gradually that her parents are dead, that her stepfather, whom she loathes, is glad to be rid of her, that her friends find it creepy to visit her, that she does not like to read, that she knows no poems, and that she is not interested in learning any. Elva, whose eyesight is failing, persists in trying to interest Courtney in something outside her own condition, proposing that they take a trip together by imagination, using a 1910 copy of *Baedekker's Italy*, which she prefers to more modern editions because there are fewer pictures and more complete descriptions. At first Courtney is thoroughly bored and makes no effort to cooperate, but since the television has long been broken and someone has stolen her Walkman, she reluctantly starts reading aloud about Naples, where Elva proposes they start, accompanied in her mind by her late husband, Emmett, an artist who always longed to see Italy. As Courtney reads, haltingly, Elva fills in with romantic descriptions of what they are seeing, of what Emmett thinks of it, as they stand at the ship's rail, of how he quotes Walt Whitman and kisses her gently. Tracing a route on the map, Courtney guides them around Naples, her interest perking up only at the head of Medusa in the Museo Nazionale, with which she secretly identifies, both having, she thinks, the Evil Eye. The game, however, is taking hold of her, and when Elva is out of the room she continues to read and describe things to May. They go on to

Rome, which mostly bores her. On the way to Florence, she tires of Elva and Emmett, goes down the train corridor, finds a compartment almost empty, and meets Edward, who is blind. She describes the scenery to him, even taking him on side trips via *Baedekker's*. In Florence, at the Uffizi Gallery, Courtney's frustration erupts, and at the Botticelli painting, *The Birth of Venus*, she rebels, hating the perfection of female beauty now denied her, and turns her evil Medusa eye on the picture, starting a fire that consumes the whole museum. Elva is outraged, wrests the *Baedekker's* from her, and declares that the trip is over. Courtney weeps and begs to go back, and Elva finally sees the journey through Courtney's imagination. They decide to head for the mountains, and they walk back to the hotel arm in arm. The last chapter occurs some months later, after Elva's death. Courtney greets Muriel, her new roommate, a North Dakota housewife whose main interest has been soap operas. She explains that the television is broken, but that she spends most of her days taking her boyfriend, Edward, on a tour of the Italian mountains via *Baedekker's*. She claims the photograph of Emmett and his drawing of Elva are pictures of her parents. The Italian trip is interrupted a couple of times, once by one of Courtney's girlfriends who chatters about the high school drinking parties and is repulsed by Courtney's talk of bedsores and catheters, and once when the new night janitor proposes that he and Courtney go for a quick "gallop," a suggestion she rejects firmly. The novel remarkably characterizes Elva, Courtney, and May vividly, just through what they say, and also, through their descriptions, makes Emmett and Edward both real and appealing. Italy of 1910 is as delight-

ful for the reader as it is for Elva. ALA/YA.

MIRACLE'S BOYS (Woodson*, Jacqueline, Putnam, 2000)   Contemporary realistic sociological-problem novel of the family life of three Puerto Rican/African American brothers in New York's inner city. Miracle's boys are the orphaned sons of Milagro Bailey, which means Miracle, called "Mama," who died about two years before the story begins, and of Daddy, who died earlier of hypothermia after saving the life of a drowning woman. Earnest Lafayette, 12, tells of two fateful days that change his own life and those of chip-on-the-shoulder Charlie, 15, just returned from Rahway Home for Boys where he was sent for two years for robbing a candy store, and of intelligent, hardworking Ty'ree, who has forgone college in order to provide for himself and his brothers. Lafayette yearns for the Charlie he knew and loved before, the one who prayed even for stray animals and was a good student. He deplores the Newcharlie, as he calls him, who constantly puts Lafayette down, blames him for their mother's death, and revels in the adulation he receives from Aaron, his gangbanger chum, and other street kids. On Friday, after Newcharlie takes off with Aaron before Ty'ree returns from work, Ty'ree cooks a good chicken dinner, and then he and Lafayette leave for a movie, chatting and reminiscing about better days. Ty'ree is convinced that much of Charlie's hostility stems from feeling left out, especially since he was incarcerated at the time their mother died of insulin shock. At about five o'clock the following morning, Ty'ree gets a phone call from the police that they are holding Charlie at the station. The brothers find him badly bruised from a fight, tearful, and handcuffed. He has been caught in a stolen car. The situation is tense, since Charlie may be returned to Rahway, Lafayette sent to a foster home, and Ty'ree regarded as too young to remain their guardian. The policeman in charge is understanding, however, and says that Charlie innocently attended a party that turned out to be a gang initiation, was beaten as a test for entry, and then taken away in the stolen car. He releases Charlie to Ty'ree. Later, Lafayette goes to the park with friends, sees Aaron there unconcerned about Charlie, and returns thinking about his mother's admonitions to him to be good to his brothers. He finds Charlie nursing his wounds on their doorstep, tells him, for the first time, that emergency services had arrived but could not save their mother and that he had not just foolishly let her die. Charlie in turn confides that he had stuck up the store to get money so they could all go to Puerto Rico for a visit. The book ends with Charlie disavowing friendship with Aaron and the three brothers planning activities they can do together. The conclusion seems pat, abrupt, and cliché, if just what the reader hopes for. The memories and stories of life with Mama in the days they were all together, days better psychologically if not financially, are warm and ring true and put the reader firmly on the side of Miracle's three boys. ALA/YA.

MISS ELIZABETH CHANNING (*The Chatham School Affair**)   Beautiful young teacher whom headmaster Mr.* Arthur Griswald hires to teach art at the exclusive Chatham School for boys and who becomes the focus of scandal and tragedy. Miss Channing, as Henry Griswald, the narrator, always refers to her, lived in Africa with an uncle before she came to Massachusetts. Before that,

she traveled extensively with her father, a well-known travel writer. To Henry, and apparently many other people in the village, she projects an exotic and romantic air. Miss Channing is a kind and gentle person, who cares about her students and enjoys teaching them various art techniques. When she learns that Sarah* Doyle wishes to learn to read, she gladly assumes the responsibility of teaching her.

MISS JONETTA GOODE (*Only Twice I've Wished for Heaven**)   Woman of about sixty who befriends Tempestt Saville, whom she calls "Child," and other people on Thirty-fifth Street in Chicago of 1975, despite a background scorned by the preachers and soul savers. In 1932 when she was sixteen, she came from Annington County, Mississipi, with her older sister, Essie, to stay with their Aunt Ethel, a mean, self-righteous woman who underfeeds and overworks them, beating them for any infractions. Jonetta escapes out a window to the fire escape and wanders to Thirty-fifth Street, where she is picked up by Alfred Mayes, who talks of marrying her but soon has her established in his brothel. When she becomes pregnant enough to show, he turns her out into wintry streets, and she goes back to Aunt Ethel, who shuts her in a cold basement until she has the baby, whom she has named in her mind Chloe. Aunt Ethel takes the baby, who she says died but Jonetta suspects was smothered, and turns her out again. Hump (Herbert Porter) finds her in his alley near Thirty-fifth Street and cares for her through the winter. When Mayes hears that she is back, he comes, says he is truly sorry and has changed his ways, and persuades her to go off with him again. Three days later, he says one of his girls is sick, and he wants Jonetta to fill in for her. When she refuses, he attacks her, and she hits him over the head with a heavy candleholder and knocks him out. At first contemplating suicide, she has second thoughts, scoops up some of the money Mayes has hidden in a shoe box, and runs, ending up on the steps of O'Cala's, where she soon is working. She has been there ever since. Later, she finds her own sister, Essie, whom Aunt Ethel never let her see again, and Essie's daughter, Ruth, singing in the New Saved Choir of Reverend Mayes, whom she knows is a sham. Miss Jonetta is a strong, compassionate woman who deplores the crime of Thirty-fifth Street, although she admits to watering down the liquor she sells along with a variety of bread and necessities in her little store.

MISS ODETTA (*Imani All Mine**) Gossipy, often drunken or partially inebriated friend of the Dawson family, who lives next door and whose son, June Bug, about nineteen, sells drugs. She works at a hotel, where she says that the rich and famous stay, even one of the Rolling Stones. It is thought that her house, the Dawsons', and others in the neighborhood were shot up by dealers out to get June Bug in the incident in which little Imani is killed. When Mama, Tasha's mother, attacks her and pummels her with her fists after Mama learns that Imani has been shot, Miss Odetta insists that Mama be arrested. The policeman talks her out of the notion. Miss Odetta is a vivid, if not likable, figure.

MITCH (*Imani All Mine**)   Big, red-haired, freckle-faced white man, a postal worker, whom Tasha Dawson's Mama starts seeing because he is generous with money. He takes immediately to little Imani, and he also shows an interest in

Tasha that seems truly genuine. He encourages her to do well in school, because, he says, he wasn't much older than Tasha when he "screwed" his life up. He tells Tasha that after his father left his family for another woman, they were evicted from their house and had to go on welfare. Mitch became very unstable in his teens and was on drugs until he joined the army. He thinks that the street kids that lurk around the neighborhood just need male figures to take a solid interest in them. He shows himself to be a firm, kind support for Mama and Tasha when Imani is killed and weeps for Imani as much as they do.

MIZ ELDA KENDRIC (*The Last Sin Eater**)   The oldest woman in the valley in the Great Smoky Mountains where Cadi Forbes's family live. A widow, she sent the rest of her family out of the valley to keep them from getting caught up in the local hatreds led or inspired by the Brogan Kai clan. Brogan Kai hates her, even though he married her daughter, Iona. Miz Elda is the historian of the community and gradually tells Cadi and Fagan Kai, Brogan's son, the story of how Sim Gillivray came to be the sin eater. She also makes it possible for Cadi to find Sim and allows the girl to become friends with Bletsung* Macleod, thus giving the children more opportunity to hunt for the sin eater and to hear the man of God. Miz Elda gives Fagan the deed to her house, so that he and Cadi can use it as a center for their preaching, teaching, and baptizing.

MIZ LIRETTE (*Meely LaBauve: A Novel**) Teacher at the school Meely LaBauve attends. She urges Meely to stay in school, gives him a place to live, and secures him a lawyer, Alphonse Dorsey, who investigates well on Meely's behalf. He serves as an effective foil to the country prosecutor, who apparently for political reasons, or maybe out of meanness, overlooks Junior Guidry's reputation for bullying and accepts Junior's story of being bullied and assaulted by Meely, although Meely is smaller and known to cause trouble for no one. Meely enjoys living at Miz Lirette's house. Although modest, it is the most pleasant and best appointed he has ever known, and he does not have to hunt and fish for his supper.

MOE (*The Yokota Officers Club**) Mary Clare Mohoric Root, mother of Bernie and her five siblings, wife of Major Mason Patrick Root. As a young woman, Moe was a nurse in World War II, serving in North Africa and Italy. On their trip to Japan, when Bernie is six and seasick most of the way, Moe, pregnant with twins, entertains her with stories of the crowded troopship, sixteen nurses crammed into a tiny cabin with damp underwear hanging everywhere, stories that form a special bond between them not shared by her sister, Kit, or her father. Moe has a strong sense of what is right and decent and resents having to kowtow to LaRue Wingo, the wife of the squadron leader. When LaRue takes the stage at a welcome home party for the husbands and sings badly, Moe, already furious because her husband has insisted on firing their maid at LaRue's direction, marches up, seizes the microphone, and dedicates a song to Fumiko*, a rendition of *Somewhere over the Rainbow* far superior to anything LaRue has sung and received with wild applause. The whole incident gets Mace RIF'd (fired) early the next morning, sent to Idaho, with no chance of going to Staff and Command College, and never allowed to fly again. Although they

remain together through the next eight years, never staying at one post more than a year, Mace stops talking to Moe by the time they get to Okinawa, and she falls into deep depression.

MOLLIE MUNRO LAFFERTY (*Criminals**)   Sister of Ewan* Munro. She has begged him to come and rescue her from the terrible black birds that are threatening and other aspects of her troubled mental state. Mollie, an adopted child, has always been emotional, very different from her repressed, controlled brother, but they are close, and he responds to her plea, although he is troubled by the possibility of being accused of insider trading at his investment banking firm. When he turns up with a baby he found in a rest room, Mollie seems competent, totally under control, though she refuses to talk about her recently departed husband, Chae* Lafferty. In reality, she has fallen in love with the baby, whom she names Olivia, partly because she herself was an abandoned baby and partly because Chae, who had a vasectomy years ago, is unable to give her the child she desperately desires. When Ewan's inept attempts to report the baby are not successful, she contrives to thwart his efforts to reach the police or social services, and she sends him back to London on a plane, assuring him that she will go right to the police station with Olivia, a promise she has no intention of keeping. She is never able to explain to Ewan that her fury with Chae is not because he has found another woman, but because in his last novel he has "used" her, drawing on her intimate experiences for the main character, whom he names Maudie, even describing in detailed scenes their sex together. When Chae returns, drunk, despairing, and repentant, she takes him back, but it is clear that she is deteriorating mentally, and after she lets the baby fall to the stone floor, she goes to pieces completely and is hospitalized.

MOLLY SHERIDAN (*Life in the Fat Lane**)   Best friend of Lara Ardeche, the eighteen-year-old narrator and protagonist. Lara thinks of her as funny and brave, even though she patronizes her since Molly is plump and has a fat mother. Nor is Lara honest with Molly. She pretends to Molly that the Ardeches are a perfect family. Molly is a fine sidekick for Lara, always there, always loyal. Only at the end does Lara finally tell Molly the truth, but true to form, Molly accepts Lara as she is, the fat daughter of a fractured family, but still her friend.

MONICA ROBY (*Painting the Black**) Pretty, talented, assertive high school senior, who dares to stand up to Josh Daniels, reprimand him publicly for boorish behavior, and question his comments about literature in English class. These, among other instances in which Monica gets under Josh's skin, apparently provoke his attack on her. Monica becomes class valedictorian and Crown High School Student of the Year, among other honors, and receives a full scholarship to Stanford University. Although she is absent from school after the attack, she returns, to Ryan Ward's surprise, for commencement and delivers a speech that Ryan admires greatly. Monica is the stereotypical "modern girl" but advances the plot appropriately.

MONSTER (Myers*, Walter Dean, illus. Christopher Myers, HarperCollins, 1999) Gritty realistic present-day novel written mostly as a script for a movie, with portions in flashbacks to real happenings and monologues by the narrator as he goes through his trial for murder. African American Steve Harmon, 16, has been an active participant in Mr. Sawicki's high school film club until his arrest for allegedly acting as lookout for a drugstore robbery in Harlem in which the store owner, Alguinaldo Nesbitt, a black man originally from St. Kitts in the Caribbean Leeward Islands, was shot with his own gun. To get through the extreme pain of living in the Manhattan Detention Center, where he is constantly afraid of the other inmates and the guards and of being on trial for murder, Steve writes out the happenings as if he were scripting a movie. He names it *Monster! The Story of My Miserable Life* and further explains, "The incredible story of how one guy's life was turned around by a few events and how he might spend the rest of his life behind bars. Told as it actually happened!" In courtroom scenes, the prosecutor, Sandra Petrocelli, questions various witnesses, including Osvaldo Cruz, 14, a member of the Diablos gang, Bobo (Richard) Evans, 22, and James King, also in his early twenties, all of whom were in jail or prison, admit to being part of the holdup, and have agreed to cut a deal with the prosecution for a reduction in their sentences. The defense, Asa Briggs, the lead counsel for James King, and Kathy O'Brien, lawyer for Steve, question all three, trying to expose their motivations for testifying and to poke holes in their version of the events. Steve has supportive parents who attend the trial and a little brother, Jerry, whom he deeply loves. Mr. Sawicki testifies to his good character and intelligence. As the trial proceeds, Steve sees that O'Brien does not believe in his innocence and that his own father doubts it. He begins to doubt it himself. As the verdict is about to be read, Steve ends the film script with words to roll slowly down the screen announcing that it is the true story of his life and trial and adding, "It was not an episode that he expected. It was not the life or activity that he thought would fill every bit of his soul or change what life meant to him." King is sentenced to twenty-five years to life. Bobo is returned to prison. Osvaldo is evidently found not guilty, but soon is arrested for car theft and sent to the reformatory. Steve is found not guilty, but his life has changed. He continually films himself, sometimes walking toward where a camera is set up, sometimes in front of a mirror, sometimes getting Jerry to film him, trying different voices, trying to discover who he really is, and whether whatever O'Brien saw in him that made her turn away after the verdict is the real Steve Harmon, the monster he fears. The clever structure of the novel raises it above the usual story of an African American boy in trouble with the law and helps characterize the attorneys and the three chief prosecution witnesses, two thugs and a young Puerto Rican boy already hardened in street crime. It also shows Steve, bright, scared, and, in the end, self-doubting. The illustrations are photographs, some altered to enhance the effect. ALA/YA; Printz Winner.

MOONFALL (McDevitt*, Jack, Harper-Prism, 1998)   Adult futuristic science fiction novel set on Earth, the Moon, and spaceships in between for a little more than one week beginning on Monday, April 8, 2024. The novel postulates a disaster of such magnitude that it threatens the very existence of the United States and devastates the world. Charlie (Charles L.) Haskell, vice president of the United States, has flown to the Moon to preside at the ribbon-cutting ceremony of the new international Moonbase. During a solar eclipse, Tomiko Harrington, a young woman amateur astronomer in St. Louis, discovers an extremely large comet, bigger than the state of New Jersey, which is subsequently named after her. Previously hidden from view by the Sun's glare, Tomiko is deemed by scientists to be interstellar and predicted to demolish the Moon on Saturday night. An evacuation of Moonbase and other stations on the Moon is immediately ordered. Since there are not enough moonbuses and spaceships to get everyone out before impact, Charlie volunteers to be among the last to leave. He is seeking the presidential nomination and knows that being among the first to depart will doom his chances. The Moonbase chaplain, Mark Pinnacle, also stays, as does Evelyn Hampton, one of the Moonbase administrators, and several others. At almost the last minute, a ship is found, however, and they depart. Charlie performs heroically en route, even spacewalking to keep the vehicle flying. Harvard scientist Wes Feinberg predicts that there will be massive damage from the debris caused by the impact to the Moon. Soon mammoth tidal waves devastate both coasts, causing incredible damage and loss of life, power outages, shortages of food and other supplies, and looting. President Henry Kolladner is killed when his helicopter is struck by debris and crashes outside the White House, and Charlie is sworn in as president via radio on the returning spaceship. Then scientists discover that a huge moonrock, called "Possum," carved from the Moon (which is no longer in existence) by the impact, is hurtling at tremendous velocity toward the United States and will strike in the heartland of Kansas and Nebraska. Feinberg suggests that spaceships be attached to Possum to shove it slightly off course.

Among these, indeed the crucial vehicle, is a nuclear-powered Mars spaceship, piloted by Colonel Rachel Quinn. Despite troublesome obstacles, the mission is accomplished, and Possum is set into another orbit. An epilogue set a year later finds Charlie at a memorial ceremony for the many who gave their lives in the effort. Since the tremendous drain on national treasuries has forced world leaders into cooperation never previously dreamed of, Charlie sees this new communal spirit as a blessing gained from the comet. The novel is typical of its genre in its use of undeveloped, cliché characters (Charlie is the only dynamic one, and his change is minimal and predictable); heightened tension and action; and tendency to project ideas. These are, in a certain way, also this novel's strengths. The main characters, including Charlie, are ordinary, nonheroic types, who expectedly rise to the occasion in doing their jobs. The tense, tight situations excel in excitement and are vividly described. The settings, whether in space, on the Moon, or on Earth are easily visualized, and the political maneuvering and public attitudes are conveyed in various ways, including by a newsman following Charlie around and sending reports back to Earth, talk and call-in shows in progress, and scene switching, including showing militiamen preparing to shoot down spaceships in order to scuttle the Possum effort and the U.S. government. Culturally, African Americans and women have made great gains. President Kolladner, for example, is African American. This is an engrossing novel, but it is long and requires keeping track of rapidly changing settings and lots of characters. Booklist.

MORRIS, GERALD (PAUL) (1963–) Born in Riverside, Wisconsin; teacher of religious studies, pastor of the First Baptist Church of Wausau, Wisconsin. His first novel based on Arthurian legend, *The Squire's Tale* (Houghton, 1989), was well received and has been followed by two more, *The Squire, His Knight, & His Lady** (Houghton, 1999), retelling, with many additions, the ancient story of *Sir Gawain and the Green Knight*, and *The Savage Damsel and the Dwarf** (Houghton, 2000), basically the tale of Sir Gareth, the "Kitchen Knight." All these novels are meant for middle school and junior high school students, treating the stories with humor, using often comic dialogue, eschewing the high seriousness usually associated with the legends. A more recent novel, loosely based on the story of Sir Parsifal and his quest for the Holy Grail, is *Parsifal's Page* (Houghton, 2001).

MOUSEY MALONE (*Love Among the Walnuts**) Beautiful, dark-haired, musical-comedy actress, who becomes the wife of millionaire Horatio* Alger Huntington-Ackerman and mother of Sandy*. When Mousey, whose voice is very squeaky and cannot be heard beyond the second row in the theater, tells Horatio that her career is washed up because there are no parts for actresses who cannot project, he builds a theater with only two rows for her in their house. After she emerges from the coma into which she has fallen because she ate poisoned cake, her voice is low and pleasant, and she resumes her stage career.

MR. ARTHUR GRISWALD (*The Chatham School Affair**) Founder, headmaster, and guiding spirit of the Chatham School for the sons of well-to-do and influential families of New England. He is highly respected and regarded as an accomplished gentleman, a kind teacher and leader, who truly cares about his students and his teachers. He takes Henry, his son and the narrator, with him when he travels to the prison to visit Miss* Elizabeth Channing, and he makes the arrangements after her death. He hired her, creating the art position for her, because he was a friend of the uncle with whom she lived after her father's death. Eventually, the school is closed, since the benefactors refuse to support it any longer. Mr. Griswald is a sad figure, his life's dream gone because he was kind and generous to a young woman in need.

MR. JAP (JASPER) STANCIL (*Up Jumps the Devil**)   Old man, community eccentric, whose son, Dallas, is murdered and who is himself murdered a few weeks later. He grows a little corn and a few vegetables, signed over his land to Dallas years ago, before the IRS could take it for taxes, regains ownership of the land after Dallas's death, and makes a deal with Billy Wall to grow ornamental corn. He also gets religion after his son's death, paints a purple cross on his front door, and tacks about twenty pictures of Jesus on the walls of the house. After Allen* Stancil returns, Mr. Jap resumes his former life, loses his religious impulses, and drinks again. He intends to set Allen up to run his repair garage and fix up the old cars that litter his yard. Mr. Jap is murdered with a tire iron in his garage, a deed for which Billy and Allen are the prime suspects.

MR. JOHN BOARDMAN (*Sunshine Rider: The First Vegetarian Western**) Serious, highly respected owner and trail boss of the Circle Six outfit, with which Wylie Jackson sets out on a cattle drive from Odessa, Texas, to Wichita, Kansas. Mr. Boardman is the stepfather of ZeeZee, who later in the story shoots Roselle, the cattalo (half cow, half buffalo) in Wylie's

charge. Despite his reputation for being strict, Mr. Boardman seems indulgent toward Wylie, a matter explained late in the book when he reveals that he is Wylie's real father. He explains that he was a Confederate officer during the American Civil War. He and Clara Hampton, who has raised Wylie, met and fell in love but were unable to marry because Mr. Boardman was already married. Up to this time, Wylie has believed that his father was a cotton broker, who was killed at Vicksburg, and that Clara is his aunt.

MR. LELAND REED (*The Chatham School Affair**)   Teacher at the Chatham School for boys near Cape Cod, Massachusetts, who falls in love with the beautiful newcomer, Miss* Elizabeth Channing, art teacher, and whose wife, Mrs.* Abigail Reed uses their car as a weapon to kill Miss Channing but kills Sarah* Doyle instead. Mr. Reed came to Chatham School seven years before the action begins, hired to teach literature, a veteran of World War I, lame and scarred from his war experiences, and gray and bent beyond his age. As time passes and the romance causes tongues to wag, Mr. Reed wishes that he were rid of Miss Channing. He and Abigail have a daughter, Mary, who is taken away from him shortly after his wife's death and raised by the local physician, Dr. Craddock, who renames her Alice.

MR. MORELAND (*Love Among the Walnuts**)   One of the residents of Walnut Manor, considered, like the rest, to be mentally unhinged and committed by his relatives presumably for his well-being but in reality to get his money. He is weak and forgetful, a sad condition for a millionaire businessman. He, Boom-Boom, a split personality, Everett, who speaks in quotations, and churlish L. Barlow Van Dyke, also a millionaire, spend their time in endless card games. Later, having benefited greatly from Sunnie* Stone's insisting that the residents become more physically and intellectually active, he and L. Barlow become good friends and teach Sandy* Huntington-Ackerman about finance and investments through such games as Monopoly. At first, Mr. Moreland dislikes L. Barlow, calling him a cat molester, because when L. Barlow arrived at Walnut Manor, he appeared to call himself that. The residents are afraid that L. Barlow might molest Louie the cat. Later, they learn that L. Barlow, who could barely speak when he arrived, meant to say that he wished to be called Captain Lester. All along, Mr. Moreland thinks Opal* is beautiful, and at the end they get married in a lovely, simple, outdoor wedding.

MRS. ABIGAIL REED (*The Chatham School Affair**)   Wife of Mr.* Leland Reed, the Chatham School teacher who becomes romantically involved with Miss* Elizabeth Channing. By all accounts, Mrs. Reed is a faithful wife and a good mother to their little girl, Mary. Before marrying Mr. Reed, Mrs. Reed was dumped by an earlier love, and when talk gets around about Mr. Reed and Miss Channing, she becomes withdrawn and angry. She confides in Mrs. Griswald that she believes that the two are planning to do away with her and leave the village in the boat Mr. Reed has been constructing. She cites as evidence of possible murder the rope, knife, and bottle of arsenic she found in the shed where the boat is being built. Mrs. Griswald later reports what Mrs. Reed told her to the prosecuting attorney.

MRS. KNUDSON (*Necessary Roughness**) Friendly, kind, helpful landlady of the Korean American Kims, Abogee*, the father; O-Ma*, his wife; and Young* and Chan (the narrator), sixteen-year-old twins. When the Kims first arrive in Iron River, Minnesota, no one will rent to them. They go to the local Chamber of Commerce, where they are referred to Mrs. Knudson, who rents them the entire second floor and the attic and happily shares the kitchen with them. She teaches O-Ma to cook American dishes, attends functions at school to cheer for Chan and Young, and helps O-Ma develop the idea of selling football and local novelties at their store. The novelties become popular and bring in some needed cash for the Kims.

MRS. POOLE (*Imani All Mine**) Teacher of the parenting class that Tasha Dawson takes in school. At first, Tasha does not think much of the woman because she makes the girls pay attention and has bad breath. Tasha follows her instructions carefully and wishes that Mrs. Poole had given the lecture on shaken baby syndrome earlier, because she shook Imani out of frustration and worries that she may have hurt her. Mrs. Poole has four children of her own, and when Mama suggests that Mrs. Poole may not know what she is talking about, Tasha reminds her of that fact. Tasha develops a lot of respect for Mrs. Poole because she realizes that Mrs. Poole really cares about the girls in her class and their children.

MR. WAS (Hautman*, Pete, Simon & Schuster, 1996)   Involved time-travel fantasy in which a door in a house owned by a boy's deceased grandfather leads to fifty years in the past. Through a complex series of events, he meets friends in the past who later become his grandparents. For a longer entry, see *Dictionary, 1995–1999*. ALA/YA.

MURPHY, RITA Resident of Vermont where she lives with her husband and son. *Night Flying** (Delacorte, 2000), an American Library Association selection for young adults, tells of a family of Vermont women gifted with the ability to fly. She has also published *Black Angels* (Delacorte, 2001), in which Celli, 11, spends the summer with her black babysitter, and *Harmony* (Delacorte, 2002), about a Tennessee-mountain foundling with extrasensory perception.

THE MUSIC OF DOLPHINS (Hesse*, Karen, Scholastic, 1996) Novel about a girl who has lived with dolphins until captured and reeducated in a research laboratory at Boston College in recent years, possibly fantasy but treated realistically. As she develops in English and understanding of the human world, she realizes she must go back to the sea to preserve her sanity. For a longer entry, see *Dictionary, 1995–1999*. ALA/YA.

MYERS, WALTER DEAN (1937–) Born in Martinsburg, West Virginia; prominent author of novels and biography about African Americans. His basketball novel *Slam!* (Scholastic, 1996), was winner of a Coretta Scott King Award. More recently, it was named to the American Library Association Young Adult list. A more experimental style appears in *Monster** (HarperCollins, 1999). It is written as a script for a movie by the protagonist, as he awaits his trial for murder. For earlier biographical information and title entries, see *Dictionary, 1960–1984* [*Fast Sam, Cool Clyde, and Stuff*; *Hoops*]; *Dictionary, 1985–1989* [*Fallen Angels*; *Me, Mop, and the Moondance Kid*; *Motown and Didi*; *Scorpions*]; *Dictionary, 1990–1994* [*Somewhere in the Darkness*]; and *Dictionary, 1995–1999* [*The Glory Field*; *Slam!*].

MY FATHER'S SCAR: A NOVEL (Cart*, Michael, Simon & Schuster, 1996) Growing-up novel of a sensitive boy in the 1960s and early 1970s who suffers from his abusive, alcoholic father, Harold*, and from his own gradual realization that he is gay. The narrator, Andy Logan, is a fat little boy tormented by other youngsters because he is the smartest in the class and because they sense that he is afraid of them. The story alternates between Andy's first year in college and flashbacks to earlier periods, starting when he is eleven in an unidentified town, probably in California. His solace and sanctuary as a child is the room of his grandmother's Uncle* Charles Abbott, who lives in the top floor of her house, surrounded by his books. Although they are both brow beaten by fierce, grim-faced Grandma* Logan, Andy finds in Uncle Charles the first person who approves and appreciates the intellectual life. When Uncle Charles suddenly dies suddenly, Andy is desolated and further sickened by his grandmother's destruction of her uncle's books. Flashbacks re-create other miserable incidents. Grandma Logan tries to buy Andy friendship from Eddie Adams, one of his chief tormentors. With his pal, Billy Curtis, Eddie ditches Andy, then pelts him with popcorn and pours Coke on him from the movie theater balcony. In another scene, some months later, Andy's father, half drunk, rides him on the handlebars of his bike to find Billy and beat him up, it having come out that Billy waylays Andy daily after school and torments him. Predictably, Billy easily beats up Andy, but worse, Andy's father, disgusted, kicks his son into the gravel. This last humiliation starts Andy running, not at first in any effort to lose weight, but just to exhaust himself so he will not dwell on his misery. Although he does become wiry and fit, he still thinks of himself as a pale, clumsy fat boy. When he is a freshman in high school, he is commanded by Pastor Peterson to write the Easter pageant and cochair it with Evan* Adams, brother of Eddie and a senior whom Andy has admired from afar. Not only is Evan extremely good-looking, he is clever and unafraid of the pastor, a former marine he refers to as "Old Leatherlung." Their collaboration provides Andy rare companionship until, after one of Pastor Peterson's hellfire sermons on the sin of lust, in which he condemns homosexuality, Evan rises in church and calmly says, "That's not true." In the stunned silence he announces that he is gay. Not only is Evan forbidden to enter the church again, he is shunned at school. Since Evan is the star of the high school gymnastics team, Andy attends the meet, hoping his friend can redeem himself, only to see the judges deliberately rate him below far inferior contestants. On Good Friday, Eddie, having been egged on by Pastor Peterson, leads a gang threatening to castrate Evan. While Andy watches, aghast but afraid to intervene, they beat Evan until Patti Sheldon, daughter of the Sunday school superintendent, who has a crush on Evan, throws herself on his body and saves him from possible death. Eddie is sent away to some corrective institution, and Evan and his mother disappear, but he leaves with Patti a note for Andy in which he has written "I love you." Although he has finally admitted his homosexuality to himself, Andy keeps it carefully concealed until, in his senior year, the football coach asks him to tutor, for pay, one of the players who is failing two subjects. It turns out to be Billy Curtis, whom Andy had pretty much lost track of over the years. After several only moderately successful tutoring sessions, Billy suddenly kisses Andy

and embraces him, and Andy realizes that the strange looks Billy has been giving him reflect not suspicions but infatuation. For the rest of the year they meet frequently in an abandoned house where they have Andy's first consummated sexual experiences. When Andy announces to his parents that he is gay, they throw him out. Before Andy leaves for college on scholarship, he realizes that he and Billy are too different for their relationship to persist. At college he is lonely. One class he enjoys is The Art of the Novel taught by flamboyant Professor* Hawthorne, who invites him to Thanksgiving dinner at his lavish house, flirts shamelessly with him, but, when he responds, is furious and throws him out. Again humiliated and also scared of Hawthorne's retribution, Andy becomes almost sick from worry. Later, Sascha Stevenson, Hawthorne's graduate assistant, catches up with him on the track, points out that Hawthorne is a mean egotist, and admits that he himself is in love with Andy. Under Andy's pain and self-loathing is a sturdy survivor, highly intelligent, and ultimately likable. Other characters are well developed and convincing. Although many of the scenes are searing, they are believable. This is one of the best pictures in books for young people of the agony of growing up in a bigotted society for those with a different sexual orientation, the shame and loneliness, but also the joy of finding someone who understands. ALA/YA.

MY LOUISIANA SKY (Holt*, Kimberly Willis, Scholastic, 1996)   Novel, set in recent years, of a girl whose parents are both retarded and who has a chance to escape the responsibilities and embarrassment they entail by living with her aunt in Baton Rouge. Ultimately, she decides that home, with her parents, who are both good, if limited, people, is where her heart is. For a longer entry, see *Dictionary, 1995–1999.* ALA/YA.

MY SISTER'S BONES (Hanauer*, Cathi, Delacorte, 1996)   Realistic, contemporary sociological-problem, physical-problem, and girl's growing-up novel lasting from Thanksgiving to May. The Weinsteins—directive, controlling Michael*, a cardiac surgeon; his wife, peacemaking Jane, a second-grade teacher; and their daughters, Cassie*, 18, a good student with compulsive tendencies in her first year at Cornell University, and the narrator, Billie, 16—live in upscale West Berry, New Jersey, where they are nonpracticing Jews in a mixed-ethnic community. Billie gets the first hint that all is not well with her sister when Cassie calls home from college just before Thanksgiving, remarks that she has given away all her clothes, and appears unfocused mentally and excessively concerned about her classes. Home for the holiday, she refuses to eat and seems abstracted from events, and very thin. Cassie's physical and mental health are the most troubling of several matters that Billie copes with in this loosely plotted novel. She also faces her SAT exams, experiences increasingly intense sexual yearnings, finds life with her father often intolerable, especially concerning Cassie, and makes friends with Tiffany* Zefferelli, youngest daughter in the large Italian family near by. Since Michael is determined that both his girls enter what he feels are top-notch colleges, she is under pressure to do well on her SATs. One day while she is in the library preparing for a class demonstration, senior Vinnie DiNardio, the star wrestler lusted after by every girl in West Berry High, asks her out. Although Billie has come to the conclusion that Vinnie is not

the boy of her dreams, they make out in the bus on the way home from a wrestling meet. Stimulated by Southern Comfort and his blandishments, she gives him a "hand job" and then almost immediately blurts out that she wants to break up, leaving him confused and hurt. Later, more frightened for her sister than she cares to admit, she seeks out Dominick Zefferelli, Tiffany's good-looking, college-student brother, and initiates both oral and penetration sex with him, her first time for both. Billie envies Tiffany's outgoing manner, her often exhibitionist mannerisms and dress, and especially her warm, active, accepting family, seemingly the antithesis of Billie's own. Near the end, Billie discovers that the Zefferellis have unexpectedly and inexplicably moved away. Only later does she learn that they moved because Mr. Zefferelli is in some sort of trouble. Other than these general matters of Billie's growing up and into life, which are to be taken as typical of today's upper-middle-class teens, the thread that connects all these aspects is Cassie, who has been Billie's anchor as well as her prod from infancy. Early, Billie suspects that Cassie is suffering from anorexia. Michael refuses to believe that there is anything seriously wrong with Cassie. Not long after Cassie's college house director calls home with alarming accounts of Cassie's behavior, Cassie is taken to an exclusive mental hospital, where she makes erratic progress until Michael insists she come home. Billie observes Cassie's strong bony facial structure and feels certain Cassie "can get back the rest" again. The book ends inconclusively, as the two girls dream about a better future and Cassie "teeters" toward and into the house. The book excels in the detailed creation of home and teen life. The principal figures and the Weinstein and

Zefferelli families are obviously foiled stereotypes; the teenagers are obsessed with sex, clothes, and themselves; dialogue is sometimes raw with sexual terms and trashy with four-letter words; and the sex scenes are explicit. Except for Michael, the characters are likable, and even he has redeeming moments. Long and detailed, the book is memorable as a picture of a girl's attempt to cope with pressures of contemporary domestic existence. ALA/YA.

N

NAMIOKA, LENSEY (CHAO) (1929–) Born in Beijing, China; mathematician and novelist. Most of her novels are set in Asia or have characters of Oriental ancestry, among them *Ties That Bind, Ties That Break** (Delacorte, 1999), about a girl growing up in Nanjing, China, who is rejected for an arranged marriage because her feet are unbound. For earlier biographical information and title entries, see *Dictionary, 1960–1984* [*Village of the Vampire Cat*] and *Dictionary, 1990–1994* [*Yang the Youngest and His Terrible Ear*].

NANA (*The True Colors of Caitlynne Jackson**) Grandmother on their mother's side of Caitlynne Jackson, the narrator, and her younger sister, Cara. The girls set out on their bicycles to find her after their abusive mother abandons them. Nana takes them in with no hesitation, telling them that her home is their home, words that are very comforting to Caitlynne. Nana loves television game shows and soap operas, wears polyster clothes, and has set days on which she visits shut-ins and older people who need help. She tells the girls that she had some idea that Mom was abusive but was unaware to what extent.

NAPOLI, DONNA JO (1948–) Born in Miami, Florida; received her B.A. and Ph.D. from Harvard University; author of scholarly books and articles, poetry, and short stories and novels for children and young adults, mostly fantasies and improvisations on material from oral tradition. *Song of the Magdalene** (Scholastic, 1996), an American Library Association choice for young adults, describes the childhood and youth of the woman known as Mary Magdalene. *Stones in the Water** (Dutton, 1997), also an American Library Association selection for young adults, is a historical novel of World War II. *Sirena** (Scholastic, 1998), another American Library Association selection for young adults, improvises cleverly on stories from Greek mythology. Recent books include *Three Days* (Dutton, 2001), about a kidnapped girl in Italy, and *Daughter of Venice* (Delacorte, 2002), in which a noble girl sneaks out to explore the streets of sixteenth-century Venice. Napoli has made her home in Swarthmore, Pennsylvania. For more information, titles, and title entries, see *Dictionary, 1995–1999* [*Stones in the Water*; *Zel*].

NATHAN (*Archangel**). Gentler brother of Gabriel*, a good, loyal angel but without the driving force for justice and right that characterizes the archangel designate. Nathan acts as Gabriel's right-hand man and closest confidant. He is a worry to his brother, however, because he is obviously in love with Magdalena, a sweet angel from Monteverde, and angels are forbidden to marry because their offspring often are deformed. Although they strive against their attraction, Nathan and Magdalena can hardly stay apart when they are in the same hold. When it seems that Jovah may destroy the world, Gabriel decides he should not try to separate the two, and after the Gloria has been successfully sung and Windy Point is destroyed, he plans to have the two of them start a new hold in Jordana with a third of the angels from both Monteverde and the Eyrie*.

NATHAN'S RUN (Gilstrap*, John, HarperCollins, 1996)　Adult contemporary thriller with mystery-detective aspects set in Virginia, Pennsylvania, and New York State, beginning on July 4 and lasting about a week. By wit and luck, a frightened boy on the run evades authorities and a determined hit man and is eventually rescued by an understanding, high-minded police detective. Orphaned Nathan Bailey, 12, stabs to death in self-defense Ricky Harris, an abusive, utterly reprehensible child-care supervisor (guard) at the Juvenile Detention Center where Nathan is being held for stealing the car of his alcoholic, abusive guardian-

uncle, Mark* Bailey. Terrified, certain that no one will believe his account of what happened, Nathan hides in the house of a vacationing family. He hears himself, and other juvenile offenders, discussed unfavorably on a radio talk show hosted by voluble, acid-tongued, African American Denise Carpenter, who calls herself "The Bitch." Nathan dials her 800 number, hoping to set the record straight, and wins not only her sympathy but also that of millions of listeners across the nation. This pattern repeats—he flees again in a stolen red BMW to another empty house in Pennsylvania and again calls Denise, and then once more in a Honda stolen from a Pennsylvania vacationing family. In rural New York State, he is caught in a police roadblock and incarcerated. Lyle Pointer, a hit man for shady Mr. Slater, who wants Nathan dead to get the boy's inheritance, traces him, kills two deputies execution style trying to kill Nathan, and cleverly makes it seem that Nathan is the murderer. Nathan escapes again, evades police, and again calls Denise, because, although despairing, he still wants to get his story out to the world. While all this is going on, Police Lieutenant Warren Michaels* in Virginia has astutely spotted errors in police reports about Nathan and is reminded of his own dead son by photos of the fugitive. He is put off by the aggressive tendencies of the politically ambitious county prosecutor, J. Daniel Petrelli*, is repelled by the bloodthirsty, vengeful, lynch-mob attitudes of county and town police, and concludes from the dogged detective work of a couple of worthy subordinates that a hit man is involved. He luckily makes contact with Nathan by phone and persuades the boy to meet him at the obelisk in the town square not far from the apartment house where Nathan is now hiding, aided by an

African American boy, Billy Alexander. All elements come together in a grand and melodramatic climax. While media helicopters hover overhead, police converge from all directions, Pointer grabs the boy as a shield, and a police sniper kills the man with a shot to the head. The last time that the reader sees Nathan, he and Michaels are huddled together on the sidewalk, Michaels's arms wrapped tightly around the boy. Both "cried like babies on national television." This account of a smart and moral cop saving a wronged good kid in the face of tremendous odds from callous social workers, organized crime, unscrupulous politicians, and tough-guy cops bent on vengeance overflows with human interest and action. Information about why the guard tried to kill Nathan (hired to do so by Mark Bailey who is in trouble with Mr. Slater) and why Pointer is chasing the boy comes out gradually. On the one hand, this is a top-notch, consistently engrossing if often sensationalistic, thriller; on the other hand, it is an eloquent plea for examining certain social institutions with respect to whether they really serve those for whom they are commissioned to serve, especially children. ALA/YA.

NAYLOR, PHYLLIS REYNOLDS (1933–)   Born in Anderson, Indiana; educator, prolific full-time writer since 1960. Among her best-loved books are those in the series about motherless Alice McKinley, one of the more recent being *Outrageously Alice** (Atheneum, 1997). She makes her home in Bethesda, Maryland. Earlier biographical information and title entries appear in *Dictionary, 1960–1984* [*The Solomon System*]; *Dictionary, 1985–89* [*The Agony of Alice*; *The Keeper*; *Night Cry*]; and *Dictionary, 1990–1994* [*Reluctantly Alice*; *All But Alice*; *Shiloh*; *The Face in the Bessledorf Funeral Parlor*; *Witch Weed*].

NAZARIO, EDWARD (*Bodega Dreams**) The clever, always engaged lawyer of Willie Bodega, Bodega's trusted lieutenant and occasional savior, and, as it turns out, his betrayer. Nazario immediately takes an interest in Julio Mercado because he wishes to enlist him in the cause and thereby attract more young men like him. Julio says that he had seen Nazario around El Barrio, spreading Bodega's largess, but had not realized who he was. After Julio realizes that Nazario has set him up to help destroy Bodega, he remembers that when his apartment building burned, one that had been renovated by Bodega, Nazario had walked around during and after the fire reassuring people as though he and not Bodega were the owner, a clear hint, although Julio missed it at the time, that Nazario was positioning himself as the area's future kingpin.

NECESSARY ROUGHNESS (Lee*, Marie G., HarperCollins, 1996)   Contemporary novel of Korean American family life in a sports-story format set in the small town of Iron River, Minnesota. The Kim family—father Abogee*, mother O-Ma*, and daughter Young* and son Chan, twins of sixteen—are Korean Americans who immigrated when the children were three. Chan, the narrator, describes their experiences the year they pull up roots, sell their grocery store, and move from Los Angeles to Iron River to take over Abogee's brother, Bong's, failed convenience store, Froggie's 24-Hour Express. Chan immediately notes that the school is a "complete whiteout"; the Kims are the only nonwhites in this sleepy town of tall, northern-European-descended blonds, except for Jimmi Beargrease, a Native

American Indian classmate, who is not well thought of either, except for his ability at football. Used to being part of the "male establishment" in school, Chan gains partial acceptance through the help of his first and only real friend, Finnish American Mikko* Ripanen, also known as ALL-PRO from his T-shirt, quarterback son of the school principal. Not much of a student, Chan works hard at the game, endures what near-sadist Assistant Coach Kearny calls the "necessary roughness" of practices, and becomes the Miners' main kicker and all-around utility player. Football becomes the catalyst for solving the several problems that confront Chan and his family. The discrimination and bigotry they encounter as the only Orientals in town lessen as Chan contributes more and more to the success of the team and the town's sense of pride in itself, helping the team qualify for the state tournament and become state champs. The financial problems that plague the family are partly relieved through the friendship offered by their kind and generous landlady, Mrs.* Knudson, who with O-Ma comes up with the idea of selling town-booster novelties at the convenience store. Throughout, Chan yearns to be friends with his father, who strongly disapproves of football and Chan's new friends. When Coach Larson learns that Chan's father will not attend the football banquet at which Chan will receive his letter sweater, he visits Mr. Kim and persuades him to change his mind. Another catalyst for solving family problems and gaining them acceptance is, ironically, Young's death in a car accident just after the team wins the game that takes them to the state tournament. The town responds with many expressions of sympathy, gifts of food, and other offers of friendship, because Young has been a valuable member of the band and a loyal school supporter, in addition to being a top student. At the end, the Kims have experienced many instances of seemingly necessary roughness, but their lives together in this community will go on. Although characters and events offer few surprises, the plot moves well. Young's death, however, seems gratuitous, and the concluding scene, in which Chan places the winning trophy on her grave, oozes sentimentality. Projected well are the sense of small-town provincialism and the importance of football and school events to the town's sense of self. Football practices are especially well described, and instances of discrimination are not neglected. Strongest is the tension between generations in the Kim family, arising from conflict between the old-world, traditional perceptions and the pull the children feel toward American life. ALA/YA.

NELL HARRIS (*God Bless the Child**) Late-blooming high school girl in the small town at the eastern tip of Long Island where Bailey Bender works in the bookstore, Livres of Grass. At fourteen, Nell arrived at the store, begging to be hired, and the owner, Maude Thwait, put her to work where she flourished, becoming especially attracted to Bailey. At sixteen, she has begun to be conscious of clothes, weight, appearance, and boys, in particular Kevin Lonergan, football player from a year-round family at the lower end of the local social scale, as is Nell. When it becomes known that Bailey is the birth mother of Charlie Prinze, Nell's mother comes to the store and announces that her daughter will work there no more, and the girl avoids Bailey as if she is infectious, although she once remarked that she had talked to Charlie in a local music club and found him, unlike his friends, "nice." After that, when Bailey sees her occasionally around town, Nell studiously ignores her. At the beach hamburger stand where Bailey and Charlie find her working, she tries hard to pretend she knows neither of them. Later, after Eliot Prinze has killed himself and charges have been dropped against Charlie, he gives Nell a ride home, which both worries and thrills her, and he asks her to do him a favor, to drop in on Bailey some time. A couple of weeks later, she comes to the bookstore near closing time, and Bailey offers her a ride home. After a series of monosyllabic answers to questions, Nell is quiet until they reach her driveway, where she tells Bailey she is sorry for being so mean. While it is not a complete reconciliation, it is a first step.

NEST FREEMARK (*A Knight of the Word**)   Nineteen-year-old young woman of Hopewell, Illinois, who attends Northwestern University on a track scholarship and who assists the Lady of the Word (an ancient and powerful force for good) in persuading John Ross*, the lapsed Knight of the Word, to resume his responsibilities for making the world a better place. Although she has not used them in several years, Nest has magical powers passed along through the Freemark women, and also from her father, who was a demon in the service of the Void and whom Nest helped defeat. She has the power of Wraith, a ghost wolf created by her father out of dark magic to protect her while she grew. Now that her father is dead, the magic of Wraith is within her.

NEVER TRUST A DEAD MAN (Vande Velde*, Vivian, Harcourt, 1999)   Comic fantasy and murder-mystery thriller set once upon a time in a Wales-like land. Convicted kangaroo-court style, Selwyn,

17, is sealed inside the village burial vault along with the corpse of the man he is supposed to have killed. An irritable witch who calls herself Elswyth appears, and in exchange for Selwyn's working for her, she agrees to raise the dead man so that Selwyn can ask him who killed him. The ceremony goes awry, with increasingly comic results, and the end product is plenty of just plain good fun. The book earlier was a *School Library Journal* choice. For a longer entry, see *Dictionary, 1995–1999*. ALA/YA.

NICHOLSON, JOY   Native of Palos Verdes, California, the setting of her first novel, *The Tribes of Palos Verdes* * (St. Martin's, 1997). Chosen by the American Library Association for young adults, the novel is a starkly realistic, no-holds-barred look behind the elegant facade of family and community life in an upscale coastal California community as seen from the perspective of a fourteen-year-old girl.

NICK THOMAS (*At All Costs**) Safety engineer at a hazardous-materials site at the time of an explosion in Newark, Arkansas, in 1983. When the book opens in 1997, he is working for the Environmental Protection Agency. He receives a phone call from a mysterious "Mr. Fox," really tycoon Harry Sinclair, prompting him to investigate the official records on the Newark case. Never having thought that Jake* and Carolyn (Donovan) Brighton were guilty of the deed, he feels exhilarated at the opportunity to set the record straight and joins them in seeking evidence to prove their innocence. He sticks with them throughout the rest of the novel, although Wiggins*, FBI Deputy Director Peter Frankel's man, threatens his family. Nick's downloading the computer files, however, gives Frankel the tip he needs to locate the Brightons but also tips Jake off as to who really was responsible for the bombing. He then gets the idea of taking his suspicions to FBI Special Agent Irene* Rivers personally.

NIGHT FLYING (Murphy*, Rita, Delacorte, 2000) Contemporary fantasy, girl's growing-up, and family novel in which flying is a metaphor for determining one's direction in life. The intelligent narrator, Georgia, almost sixteen, is the sixth generation of Hansen women, all of whom have been able to fly unaided. Her mother, Maeve, her two aunts, Eva and Suki, and Grandmother Myra also have the gift, each having been allowed to fly solo upon reaching her sixteenth birthday. They and Georgia all live together in a large rambling old Victorian house painted blue near Hawthorne in rural Vermont by Lake Champlain. Grandmother Myra strictly enforces rules she says are traditional: They will eat no meat because it will render them unfit for flying; no men will be allowed in the house; no flying will be done during daylight; and all will use the Hansen name. The women live well, if they chafe under Grandmother Myra's iron hand, on a legacy from Georgia's great-grandfather, Harold, who invented the flusher apparatus inside the toilet tank known as the "Cooney Clasp." Georgia's small contact with the outside world occurs in school, which she finds boring; during her weekly Saturday night visits with Alice, her age, and Alice's midwife mother, Grace, down the road; and when she goes shopping for the family on Saturdays. One Sunday in October, Aunt Carmen* flies in, and after overhearing an argument between Carmen and Grandmother Myra, Georgia is so angry she runs to the nearby cliff and takes off, flying on her own before she has been initiated to do so as Grandmother has commanded. On her return, she eavesdrops on another conversation in which she learns that Carmen has discovered that the family will specifies that each of the aunts owns part of the property. She learns that Carmen is deeding some of her acreage to Georgia. Preparations proceed during the week for her birthday party and initiation. At the party on Thursday, each aunt gives her a fine gift, and Grandmother presides over the ritual of initiation, during which, among other questions, Grandmother asks her whether she has ever flown alone. Although she is tempted to lie, Georgia suddenly realizes that she has a right to a life of her own, unburdened by Grandmother's desire for power over the lives of her family, and answers in the affirmative—alone and, in addition, in daylight. She has broken two rules. Grandmother huffs off when the rest of the women vote unanimously that Georgia is a woman fully entitled to fly. Georgia now learns the truth, that Carmen, not Maeve, is her mother, that Carmen was banished when Georgia was born illegitimately, and that Maeve, although constantly put down by Grandmother, has raised her with love and compassion as her own. Georgia flies first with Maeve and then all alone, a young woman in her own right. Georgia has freed them all from Grandmother's abuse of power and authority, freed them from the weight of family secrets, and freed herself to determine, with the love of all her family, the direction of her future. Elements recall the story of Georgie in Jane Langton's *The Fledgling*, but the carefully worked out gothic aspects, skillfully delineated characters, minimalistic style, economically depicted setting, and controlled tone make for a gripping, unsensationalized mystery in the context of a convincing girl's growing-up story. ALA/YA.

NIGHT HOOPS (Deuker*, Carl, Houghton Mifflin, 2000) Rousing sports novel with boy's growing-up aspects set near Seattle, Washington, in recent years. Narrator Nick Abbott, 15, is crazy about basketball. He faces four main problems: making the Bothell High team in his sophomore year and also overcoming low academic achievement so that he remains eligible; getting Dad to pay attention to his playing instead of disparaging his older brother, Scott, who wants to switch from basketball to playing the trumpet; adjusting to the breakup of his parents' marriage; and competition from Trent Dawson, Nick's age, the youngest in the ne'er-do-well, mother-headed family who have just moved in across the street. Trent is a terrific competitor and an extraordinarily mean and dirty player, but one whom the coach needs desperately to sew up the championship this year. So that Scott can practice more, Dad installs a court in the Abbott backyard, tearing up Mom's rose garden to do it. Not long afterward, the tension between him and Mom becomes so great over the pressure he is putting on Scott that Dad moves out of the house for good. Although Scott avoids the court and spends his extra time practicing music with his girlfriend, Katya Ushakov, a clarinetist, Nick burns up the court as much as he can. One day at school playing touch football with the guys, among them Trent, he loses control and pushes Trent into a drainage ditch next to the field. On the way home, he is attacked by Trent and Trent's older brother, Zack, a tough often in trouble with the law. The two boys hold Nick down in a ditch, almost drowning him. He is rescued by Luke Jackman, a big black youth with whom Nick soon becomes close friends both on and off the court. All three—Nick, Trent, and Luke—try out and make the team. Nick is a skilled point guard, and because he wants to excel and win Dad's approval, he strives to elevate his point count and steal the show. His friendship with Luke cools when Luke points out that Nick is selfish and puts himself ahead of the team. Because of Luke, however, Nick's grades improve, and then Coach O'Leary asks Nick to keep Trent in line for the good of the team. The two practice long and hard in Nick's backyard, even at night, and all seems well until Zack gets into big trouble. He is accused by Katya's brother, Mike, an eyewitness, of having clubbed to death some roosters and chickens near a popular hiking trail. Then Mike is shot so seriously that he must undergo an operation to save his life. Zack runs, and Trent seems lost to the team. After Nick talks to him about the importance of the final game, Trent plays, and Bothell wins after a valiant struggle, a true team in that they all kept their eyes on the prize together. Questions remain: Will Trent take off to find and be with his brother? And does not Nick have a legal and moral obligation to report to the police what Trent has told him, that Trent took part in killing the birds, despite Zack's assertion to the contrary, and that he knew that Zack intended to shoot Mike? Moral issues receive more emphasis than in most sports stories. A page turner all the way, the book's greatest strength comes from the vivid and exciting court scenes, live action at its very best. ALA/YA.

NIKOLAI DELPHIKI (*Ender's Shadow**) Greek boy two years older than Bean who enters the Battle School of the International Fleet in the same group. Although very bright, Nikolai is not on the same level as Bean, yet he is attracted to the younger boy and becomes his first, almost his only, friend in the school. Bean helps Nikolai with his schoolwork, but Nikolai helps Bean in more subtle social ways. At one point, he admits to one of the officers that he fantasizes that Bean is his younger brother, mostly because of his appearance, but it is not until after the war that they learn that this is true. Because Nikolai's mother is unable to bear children, her eggs have been taken, fertilized with her husband's sperm, and frozen. The only child produced is Nikolai; the other fertilized eggs were stolen by the half brother of Nikolai's father who experimented with gene-altering on them until his secret nursery of one-year-olds was about to be discovered and he destroyed all the babies except Bean, who escaped and hid in a toilet tank. In the end, Nikolai's parents welcome Bean as their second son.

NILSSON, JENNY LIND   Wife of Garrison Keillor*, who collaborated with him on the novel, *The Sandy Bottom Orchestra** (Hyperion, 1996), a story of a musical girl in a small Wisconsin town, who learns to appreciate her unconventional parents. The appeal of the book lies largely in the gentle satire of small Midwestern town life, much in the vein of Keillor's radio show, *Prairie Home Companion*.

NINE KILLER (*People of the Mist**) War chief of Flat Pearl Village, who works with The Panther* to solve the mystery of the murder of Red Knot. Nine Killer is nondescript in appearance, short and bandy legged, but he is also regarded as exceptionally brave and loyal. He earned his name by sneaking into an enemy village and killing the chief and eight warriors single-handedly. As War Chief, he has

responsibility for the safety of the village, but he also faithfully fulfills his role as father figure for his sister's children, the custom among these matrilineal people.

NIXON, JOAN LOWERY (1927–2003) Born in Los Angeles, California; was graduated from the University of Southern California and received an elementary teaching certificate from California State College; had been a teacher, creative writing instructor, and author of more than one hundred books of nonfiction and fiction for children and young people. An acknowledged leader in mystery and suspense novels for young readers, she four times won the Edgar Allan Poe Award for Best Juvenile Mystery. She also wrote historical and period fiction for a young audience. Cited by the American Library Association for young adults, *The Haunting** (Delacorte, 1998) revolves around a pre–Civil War mansion in Louisiana. Recent publications include *Caesar's Story, 1759* (Delacorte, 2000), a short historical novel of a slave boy; *Ghost Town: Seven Ghostly Stories* (Delacorte, 2000) and *Gus & Gerty and the Lucky Charms* (SeaStar, 2001), a chapter book. Nixon lived in Houston, Texas. For earlier biographical information, titles, and title entries, see *Dictionary, 1960–1984* [*The Kidnapping of Christina Lattimore; The Mysterious Red Tape Gang; The Seance*]; *Dictionary, 1985-1989* [*The Ghosts of Now; The Other Side of Dark*]; *Dictionary, 1990–1994* [*The Name of the Game Was Murder; The Weekend Was Murder*]; and *Dictionary, 1995–1999* [*Shadowmaker; Spirit Seeker*].

NOBODY ELSE HAS TO KNOW (Tomey*, Ingrid, Delacorte, 1999)   Realistic contemporary grandfather–grandson sociological- and personal-problem novel set for about one school year in Lemon Lake, Michigan. Fatherless Webb (Webber) Freegy, 15, a so-so student, promises to become the best runner ever in Spratling High School, having just run in practice sixteen hundred meters in four minutes, thirty seconds. When Grampa* Freegy picks him up after school, Webb is delighted to share the news with the seventy-five-year-old man, who he knows loves him dearly and has been a fine substitute father for him since his own father died rescuing a drowning man when Webb was eight. As they joyride in the country, he asks Grampa to let him drive, and Grampa agrees, but Webb drifts off, hits, and seriously injures a young girl on her bike. Webb awakens in the hospital three days later, his right leg severely broken, but he has no memory of the accident. Just before Officer Clark comes to interview him, Grampa shows up, tells Webb that the little girl, Taffy Putnam, is in critical condition in the hospital in Ann Arbor, and that he, Grampa, is responsible, of course, since he was driving. Webb's recovery is slow and difficult. Maxie Gallagher, whom he thinks extremely attractive, pays him particular attention, and the two begin a romantic relationship. Determined that his athletic career has not ended, Webb starts therapy at the local clinic and tries to have as normal a life as possible. At a party, when the band plays the song that was on the car radio at the time of the accident, his memory of those events returns. He goes home, wakes Grampa, tells him that he knows what really happened, and asks Grampa if he lied to the police. Grampa replies that if Webb really had hit the girl, does Webb think that Grampa would let him take the blame? Besides, nobody else has to know what really happened. The remainder of the novel describes how Webb deals with his guilt, deteriorates in personality and in health, and decides what he must do. At the clinic, fat, disapproving, often disagreeable Dylis Clark, a classmate who is a hospital aide, says she was Taffy Putnam's baby-sitter and keeps him aware of Taffy's lack of progress. One day in March, increasingly dispirited, he goes to the lake where his father lost his life, reviews those events and the ones involving the accident, and concludes that he must tell the truth. He goes to Dylis's house and tells Dylis and her father what really happened. Officer Clark says that Grampa's deposition still stands, that at this point no one is going to jail—there was no reckless driving, no speeding, no drinking. Webb realizes he has told the truth, but telling the truth has not mattered. He asks Grampa to tell the truth to Officer Clark, then realizes that throughout Webb's life Grampa has tried to make up for having been a poor husband and bad father by being the best grandfather he can to Webb. Taking the blame for Webb in this instance is for Grampa a redeeming act of love. Webb realizes he cannot take this away from Grampa—he will not push Grampa to change his deposition—but he will tell his story to all those involved. That is the best he can do. Grampa, erratic, loving, an inveterate storyteller and fibber, is a charming figure, the book's most memorable character. The novel explores the concept of truth in a limited way, and the conclusion is curiously neither intellectually nor emotionally satisfying. There are indications that Webb may grow to become a responsible man with good values. He observes, for instance, that Maxie is an airhead, a "Barbie," while ugly, scorned Dylis has the courage of her convictions. ALA/YA.

NO CONDITION IS PERMANENT

(Kessler*, Cristina, Philomel, 2000) Contemporary realistic girl's growing-up novel set for about six months in an oceanside fishing village in western Africa. Shy, introverted Jodie Nichols, 14, the narrator, despairs when her divorced mother, Valeria, a university anthropologist, excitedly announces that she has received funding to continue the fieldwork she began in Bukama, Sierra Leone, sixteen years earlier, and that they will be leaving San Diego, California, in a month. Jodie is upset at leaving her friends and school to live in a remote village without running water and electricity, a place where she does not know the language, Krio. She and Valeria arrive in Bukama after a hard 220-mile, nine-hour ride from the airport at the capital of Freeport via an overcrowded dilapidated truck-bus, called "No Condition Is Permanent." Jodie is exhausted by the ride and low spirited but pleased that Valeria is happier than she has ever seen her. Valeria sympathizes with her discomfort and also reminds her that no condition is permanent. They are welcomed heartily by the villagers, many of whom remember Valeria. Jodie is aghast to see that all the Mende women are topless and somewhat put off at sharing a little palm-frond-thatched hut with her mother and four other people. Valeria has already told her about the constant need to look out for snakes in the hut and also in the latrine. Jodie is soon friends with an outgoing village girl, Khadi*, and likes the singing, dancing, drumming, and the friendliness and neighborliness of the people. She wears the typical women's wraparound garment, the lapa, with a T-shirt on top, and works alongside Khadi at the Mende woman's everyday duties. Slowly, Jodie realizes that she is happy in the village. The book's major problem arises over Jodie's wondering where Khadi disappears long hours at a time and then hearing about the Sande, the Secret Society of women and girls. The Sande custom of the Mende women, Valeria warns her, is strictly taboo, forbidden for outsiders to have anything to do with. Since Khadi spends more and more time with the women in their meetings, Jodie feels lonely, abandoned, and angry, but when she asks Khadi about it, Khadi says Jodie can have no part of it since she is not Mende. Valeria tells Jodie that the Sande trains girls to be wives and mothers and circumcises them on initiation. When Valeria explains the perils of circumcision, possible sterility and even death from infection, Jodie decides to try to save her friend. Although Khadi tells her that what happens is none of her business, Jodie traces the women to their gathering place among the trees and spies on them. Things come to a head when Khadi spots Jodie watching, and, fearing for Jodie's life, screams, alerting Jodie to run. Valeria grabs passports, money, and her notes, and they return immediately to San Diego. In an epilogue set eight months later, Jodie receives a letter from Khadi, saying that people praise Jodie's good deeds while she lived among them. She also says that, while she herself is a member of the Sande, no daughters of hers will ever be cut. Jodie sees that no condition is permanent and that change may be gradual. Jodie's whiny attitude, hardheadedness, and willful disobedience turn the reader off, not just at first, but also later when she breaks her promises to Valeria to stay away from the women's rituals. The message is clear: the ways of other people, even though the outsider may think them wrong, are to be respected. As part of her research, Valeria has discussed Sande with the women of the village, planted ideas among them about the dangers of cutting, and is willing to let time take its course. Jodie's attempts at change, though well meaning, have only caused trouble. ALA/YA.

NOLAN, HAN (1956–)   Born in Birmingham, Alabama; raised near New York City; graduate of the University of North Carolina–Greensboro and Ohio State University; teacher of dance and author of novels for young adults. *Dancing on the Edge** (Harcourt, 1997), an American Library Association choice for young adults, describes a girl's descent into mental illness. Recently, Nolan published *Born Blue* (Harcourt, 2001), in which an emotionally disturbed, orphaned teen tries to make a good life through her remarkable singing voice. For more information about Nolan, titles, and a title entry, see *Dictionary, 1995–1999* [*Dancing on the Edge*].

NORY RYAN'S SONG (Giff*, Patricia Reilly, Delacorte, 2000)   Historical novel lasting about six months during the Irish potato famine that began in 1845, a story of tremendous hardship and cruelty, and also of loving family life, devotion, resource, and neighborliness. On the coast of Maidin Bay, within walking distance of Galway, live the motherless Ryan family, Nory (Nora), 12, the narrator, the third daughter of the four children, who also include Maggie, Celia, and little Patch, and old, wise Granda. Da is away fishing, hoping to bring home enough coins to pay rent. Their grasping, cold English landlord, Lord Cunningham, thinks the Irish and their hovels are "filthy" and wants to drive them all out, tumble (tear down) their homes, and run sheep where they now live. This year the potatoes turn black and are inedible, and people are being put

out of their homes by Devlin, tax collector for the lord, and their houses are being destroyed. Nory and her friend Sean Red Mallon poach for fish in the lord's stream and gather mussels and limpets, but everyone grows steadily weaker and thinner, especially little Patch. Nory borrows a coin from old Anna* Donnelly, the area healer, to help neighbors with their rent, loses it, and then feels obligated to care for the old woman whom she fears a little and does not like because Anna could not save Nory's mother in childbirth. The eldest sister, Maggie, marries and leaves for America, for Brooklyn, New York, which Nory thinks has streets of diamonds. Staunch, loyal Celia manages with what little food they have, an occasional egg, mussels, and a hen, and then she and Granda leave for Galway to search for Da, whose return is overdue. Nory is resourceful: with help from Sean Red, she raids birds' nests in the cliff, and since she is a poor knitter, Anna helps her finish a shawl that she takes to town and sells. She is robbed of her meager purchases on the way home. The Mallon family secures tickets to America, one of which they offer to Nory or Patch, and the choice is simple for Nory—Patch must leave. When she and Anna are almost starved, a man arrives from Galway. Da has sent passage for her to America. At first she refuses to leave, since she knows Anna needs her, but Anna persuades her to join her family. After arranging for help for Anna, Nory leaves, promising to send money to Anna. Spring rains have come, and with them hope for a good harvest and a better life ahead. Characters are broadly drawn, and the plot is linear and straightforward. Language is simple and unadorned, consisting mostly of dialogue. The simplicity of story and style are the book's strongest features. They heighten the impact much as does the seeming simplicity of a folk tale. Scenes linger: Lord Cunningham on horseback trying to drive the children from the stream where they are poaching fish to stay alive; Celia's offering to work as a housemaid for Lord Cunningham and being ridiculed as filthy and ignorant; and Devlin's taking the Ryans' pig and chicken to send them to England—such scenes dramatize the intense poverty of these coastal Irish and the cruelty of the English toward them. An endnote indicates that the story is based on the author's own family history. ALA/YA.

NO STRANGE FIRE (Wojtasik*, Ted, Herald, 1996)   Mystery novel set in the farming region of Big Valley in central Pennsylvania among the White Top Amish. During the night before the first Sunday in December 1992, six White Top Amish barns burn, all by arson. One person is severely injured and dies later, little Eli Yoder, 10. The entire Amish community is alarmed and shocked, and even more so when the black car belonging to Jacob Hostetler, 19, the errant Hostetler son, is found abandoned near by, and Jacob is missing. Sergeant Henry Stuter of the Pennsylvania State Police, who is known and respected among the Amish, and FBI Special Agent Michael Tate have been put on the case, the latter because of possible civil rights violations. The plot structure is demanding. The story is told in real time; that is, it follows the events of the first week after the fire. It also looks back and describes events of the months leading up to the fires, in almost alternating chapters. The chapters set earlier mostly follow quiet, intelligent Jacob, and to some extent his twin brother, Esle*, beginning the previous March. Jacob is increasingly unhappy among the Amish and has taken a job in town. Faced with the prospect in the fall of baptism and initiation into the community, in May he leaves home, quits his job, and moves to Lewistown. He has already shown an affinity for the *englischer* (non-Amish) way of life. He becomes buddies with Jimmy Smith, who lives in the same apartment building, and Jimmy's sister, Jessica, both drinking-drugging types, and develops a sexual relationship with Jessica. Although the Smiths often denounce the Amish, Jacob relies on them to show him englischer ways. He buys a black Grand Prix, parties increasingly heavily every weekend and some nights in between, and soon hates and then quits his job at a local chicken factory. His family misses him and calls to keep in contact, most importantly his grandfather, Abraham C., who is also an Amish bishop. Jacob has discovered that the Smiths' father is an excommunicated Amish man and that Jessica has had an abortion. On the fateful Saturday night, furious with Jessica, disillusioned, hung over, he leaves in his car, abandons it near the Yoders, breaks his ankle in the dark, and takes refuge from a panther in a cave, where he is later found. It comes out that Jimmy and Jessica have used flares that were found in Jacob's car to set the barns afire, a deed done out of pure vindictiveness. Happy and relieved to be back, Jacob has a greater appreciation for the values and aspirations of his people, and the reader is left with the hope that he will become a leader among them. The raising of a new barn for the Yoders suggests a better future for them all. Abraham C. is strongly drawn and memorable. Jacob seems slow to realize the stupidity of his new way of life, despite the quiet, low-key support of his new friend, Paul Virgilia, a Pennsylvania State University student and the only decent person Jacob associates with away from home. The similarities to the stories of Jacob and Esau and the prodigal son are overly obvious. The police are dogged, patient, considerate, and skillful. Best are the many vivid scenes of Amish life, the daily work, Eli's laying out and funeral, Sunday services, baptism, and courting, among others. As Abraham C. notes, Jacob's struggle is really that of the Amish people. Although fiction, the book was motivated by actual fires among the Amish. Booklist.

NYE, NAOMI SHIHAB (1952–) Born in St. Louis, Missouri; writer best known for her poetry for adults and her poetry anthologies and translations for young readers; resident of San Antonio, Texas. *Habibi** (Simon & Schuster, 1997), about a Palestinian American family in Jerusalem based on her own experiences, was chosen by the American Library Association for young adults. Recent publications include *Come with Me: Poems for a Journey* (Greenwillow, 2000) and *19 Varieties of Gazelle: Poems of the Middle East* (Greenwillow, 2002). For more information about Nye, titles, and a title entry, see *Dictionary, 1995–1999* [*Habibi*].

O

ODOM, MEL   Prolific and popular author of novels of fantasy and science fiction, many of them spin-off books "for hire" for such television series as *Buffy the Vampire Slayer*, *Star Trek*, *Angel*, and *Sabrina the Teenage Witch*. On his own part, he has written *The Rover** (Tom Doherty, 2001), a long, entertaining, and fast-moving otherworld adventure fantasy for adults, featuring a reluctant hero, numerous human and mythical characters, and Tolkienesque incidents and conflicts. It was chosen by *Booklist* for young adults. He has also published *Lethal Interface* (Roc, 1997), a critically acclaimed police procedures and science fiction novel. Odom lives in Oklahoma.

OFF THE FACE OF THE EARTH (Harmetz*, Aljean, Scribner, 1997) Psychological thriller about a boy abducted recently from a shopping mall in the Los Angeles suburb of Sherwood, and of the efforts, mainly of his mother, to rescue him. Sent to his room for destroying a game of Clue he has been playing with his mother, Drew, and his brother, Kiley, 5,

David Greene, 8, expressed the anger that has seethed in him since his parents' divorce by dropping out his window and heading for the Sherwood Galleria, the shopping mall where he often buys baseball cards. His idea is to stay long enough to worry his mother, then call her or preferably his father, Chuck, to come get him. When, unable to reach either of his parents, he is approached by a young man offering to trade cards, he is at first wary, but, scared at the idea of staying in the mall after dark, he eventually is tricked by the offer to drop him off at a friend's house. Called by Drew, the police think that probably his father has taken him, and they send out a pickup order. Chuck, a high school teacher, who has gone for the weekend with his new wife, Tiffani, to a bed and breakfast in Santa Maria, is dragged from a hot tub by the local police. After being stopped and questioned twice, he arrives at Drew's house, concerned but not much practical help. In the next few days, Drew's mother, Ruth Miller, moves in with her three labrador retrievers, to whom she has given the devotion she has never really felt for her daughter. The case is turned over to Detective Sergeant Angus West, who at first despises it but gets caught up in it, partly because he feels guilt for having once stopped too soon in a search when he might have saved a girl's life. The young man who calls himself Denver has taken David to a third-rate motel named the Royal, where he alternately plays good daddy-bad daddy, feeding the boy junk food and playing ball with him but inexplicitly turning into a rage and slapping him viciously. He dyes David's hair black, cuts it short, and buys him new clothes, first nicking him and squeezing a few drops of the boy's blood onto his discarded underpants. He coaches David on his new identity as Andy Ellis, who lives on a farm in Iowa with a brown dog named Scooter. When he goes out, he handcuffs David to the bed frame. Once, when David, left alone, shouts and screams for help, Denver returns and chokes him so he is unable to speak clearly again. Having found a bag with David's clothes stashed in a hedge near where a mentally ill homeless man named Trout hangs out, the police pick him up, tape a rambling confession, and schedule a press conference. West, convinced that Trout is not their man, argues with his superior and is suspended for five days. Angered at the stupidity of the department and increasingly admiring of Drew, West joins forces with her, and they map out a strategy. Since Drew knows that David spends all his money on baseball cards, they start canvasing the shops, with Drew's executive ability recruiting her many friends and neighbors to assist them. Tentatively, Chuck suggests that Tiffani may be able to help with her computer knowledge. Biting off her angry response, Drew welcomes Tiffani, who turns out to be not the bimbo she seems, but a

savvy young person, though of a different generation from Drew and Chuck. Their first clues are found at baseball card stores, where David, who clings secretly to his own identity, has been bundling cards from the Kansas City Royals and players whose name is David with packets of mustard (for Colonel Mustard in the game of Clue) and catsup (for Miss Scarlet), and hiding them in the stores Denver frequents with him. Although many of his clues are thrown away, a few survive to give Drew and West some hope that they are really from him. Tiffani's work gives them lists of Royal motels, arcades, lunch counters, and other places, all organized by size and distance from Sherwood, and both Drew and West cling to the hope that David is still alive, although they know the unspoken truth that the more time passes, the less likely it is. For David, things have become worse. Denver sinks further into madness, stops eating or stops feeding David, and is increasingly hostile. The young man at the desk of the Royal Motel is persuaded, for considerable cash, to remember that the maid might have heard a child in a certain room, now empty and scrubbed clean with ammonia by Denver, and that his car might have had a New Mexico license plate. In the computer printouts of child victims that Tiffani has come up with, Drew finds a record of the skeleton found in northwestern New Mexico of a boy abducted in Orange County, California, and she gets in touch with his mother. The picture of the child shocks her by its similarity to David. She and West set out on what they fear is a wild goose chase to that part of New Mexico, taking Brisket, the one of Ruth Miller's dogs best at tracking. By now, David knows that he must take chances, and at one of the restaurants where they stop he runs to a young woman with a baby, but since he cannot talk, she believes Denver's glib explanation and lets him lead the boy away. Back in the car, he handcuffs David's wrists together as they drive into the remote mountains where Denver grew up. In the final scene, he leads David through brush to a spot he has preselected for the execution and is about to stab him when Brisket catches up, jumps against the knife, which cuts the dog's ear and gives the boy a chance to run, as his mother is shouting for him to do, while West shoots Denver. Although the end might be a little too pat in its timing, the tension building throughout the novel leads inevitably to the conclusion. Characterization is strong. It is clear why the marriage fell apart. Drew is efficient, angry, and undaunted, while Chuck is ineffectual, intellectual, and inclined to shy away from practical action. David's various attempts to leave a trail all too often go astray, but they are clever, the work of a child who inherits his parents' brain power and his mother's drive. Booklist.

O'LEARY, PATRICK (1952–)   Advertising creative director and novelist of fantasy and science fiction, who lives with his wife and children in Detroit, Michigan. His first novel, *Door Number Three* (Tor, 1995), won high praise and was named a Best Book of 1995 by *Publisher's Weekly*. Science fiction, it concerns a young woman from space who has been left on earth by an alien race. Although the detail is undisciplined, *The Gift** (Tor, 1997), a *Booklist* selection, is an engrossing other-world, good-versus-evil fantasy in the manner of J. R. R. Tolkien. *The Impossible Bird* (Tor, 2002) returns to science fiction with events built around alien abduction.

O-MA KIM (*Necessary Roughness**) Mother of Chan, the narrator, and Young* and wife of Abogee*, Korean Americans, who settle in Iron River, Minnesota, where they encounter ethnic discrimination. After they arrived in California and he was unable to find a job as a chemist, she opened a grocery store that became very successful. Because Abogee loaned money to his ne'er-do-well brother, Bong, Abogee decides they must move to Minnesota and take over Bong's failed business. O-Ma is typically uncomplaining and supportive and believes in the same general values with respect to Korean versus American life as Abogee does. She learns to cook American food, however, does not mind sharing the house and kitchen with Mrs.* Knudson, and readily goes to school events to show support for her children and her American friends. She and Mrs. Knudson enjoy figuring out what novelties will be most popular with customers in Abogee's convenience store.

ONLY TWICE I'VE WISHED FOR HEAVEN (Trice*, Dawn Turner, Crown, 1996)   Novel of a girl's growing up and interacting with an older woman in Chicago of the mid-1970s, but even more about the upscale Lakeland community for elite African Americans and adjacent rundown, crime-ridden Thirty-fifth Street, separated only by a high, ivy-covered fence. When her family moves to Lakeland from their little home on the far south side, Tempestt Rosa Saville, 11, is unhappy and unable to fit into the regimented life and social cliques of her new school, where most of the girls are scornful of her red hair. Her mother also dislikes the artificiality of Lakeland, but her father, who has become a teacher, is striving to be upwardly mobile. When unkempt Valerie Nicholae, appears in class, Tempestt spots her as a potential friend, but Valerie's attendance is irregular.

Squirming through a hole under the fence, Tempestt explores Thirty-fifth Street, fascinated by the noise and the action, and especially by a very tall, black street preacher named Alfred* Mayes. He spots her and, his performance over, starts talking seductively to her until she is dragged away and into a little store, O'Cala's Food and Drug, below street level. Her rescuer is Miss* Jonetta Goode, proprietor, who has had experience with Mayes previously. After he leaves, she tells Hump (Herbert Porter), one of the old men sitting around a checkers game, to take Tempestt, whom she calls "Child," back to the fence and see that she gets through safely. Although Miss Jonetta has told her to stay on her own side of the fence, Tempestt is fascinated by the life of Thirty-fifth Street and returns, soon using a small gate hidden in the ivy pointed out by Valerie. In chapters alternately narrated by Tempestt (Child) and Miss Jonetta, the story of their developing relationship and of Miss Jonetta's past is revealed. Originally from Mississippi, she was picked up by Alfred Mayes on Thirty-fifth Street when she was sixteen and forced to work in his brothel. Eventually, she escaped from him and started working at O'Cala's, where she has been ever since. Having lost her own baby shortly after its birth, she has a tender spot for children, as well as for many of the good-hearted near-derelicts on the street, and she keeps an eye out for Tempestt, making sure she always gets back safely to Lakeland. At O'Cala's, Tempestt gets to know many of the customers, especially four older men who play checkers there most afternoons: Hump, who is epileptic; Judd, owner of the rib joint down the street, who occasionally plays the piano with amazing skill; Mr. Chittey, who took over the building when O'Cala abandoned it;

and Fat Daddy (Rooster Tucker), who owns a pool hall and knows the ins and outs of everything on the street. Valerie, Tempestt discovers, lives with her brother, John, who is one of the Lakeland janitors, although her mother stays on Thirty-fifth street in the projects, where she is one of Reverend Mayes's New Saveds, and picks up her daughter most afternoons. On the night of the biggest social event of the Lakeland year, the debutante ball, to which the younger teenagers also are invited as Young Debs, Tempestt's parents allow her to ask Valerie to spend the night. Tempestt is disturbed by the way Valerie, possibly in her sleep, kisses her. When she describes it to Miss Jonetta, the older woman is concerned, knowing it was a kiss that demonstrated some sexual experience, and she asks Tempestt to bring Valerie to O'Cala's the next day, when they are going to have a wedding for Hump and Retha Mae Richardson, another Thirty-fifth Street resident. In the meantime, she gets Fat Daddy to investigate, and he finds what she suspected, that Valerie's mother, to finance her drug habit, has been selling her daughter to men, not for actual intercourse but to pose nearly naked while they masturbate. Hunting for Valerie, Tempestt goes to find her in the projects. The door unlatched, she comes in on a scene she does not understand. Valerie, in horror at being discovered, rushes out and leaps from the twelfth-floor balcony, pursued by Reverend Mayes, who was her client. Miss Jonetta, who suspects something bad is going on, has followed Tempestt and knows as well as the girl does that it is suicide, not murder, but she does not try to contradict the people below who swear they saw Mayes push Valerie. Because she was a Lakeland child, the newspapers and city officials make much of her death and determine to convict him and wipe out Thirty-fifth Street. Displaced, with no compensation, all Tempestt's friends disperse, and her own father, disgusted at the attitude that kept other Lakeland people from Valerie's funeral, moves the family to California. The hypocrisy of city officials and Lakeland's upper-class blacks is contrasted to the crime, drug dealing, and deterioration of Thirty-fifth Street and shown to be just as bad. Alex.

OPAL (*Love Among the Walnuts**) Housekeeper and jill-of-all-work at Walnut Manor, through whose efforts the place keeps going until Sunnie* Stone gets the residents to take an active role in maintaining it. Opal does all the cooking, saws off broken tree limbs, patches walls with mortar, skates up and down corridors dusting them with mops affixed to her feet and patching chips in the paint as she goes—anything that needs to be done. She has also acquired a nursing degree by correspondence school. Along with Sandy* Huntington-Ackerman, she stands up to Bart and Bernie, the avaricious, scheming younger brothers of Horatio* Alger Huntington-Ackerman, Sandy's father. She marries Mr.* Moreland in a lovely, modest, outdoor wedding at the end of the book. At first presented as a slapstick comedy figure and eccentric, she seems more normal as the novel progresses.

OPEN SEASON (Box*, C. J., Putnam, 2001)   Mystery-detective novel published for adults set in recent years in the Bighorn Mountains of Wyoming about six hours' drive from Cheyenne. Joe Pickett, the new state Game Warden for the Saddlestring District in Twelve Sleep County, has two passions in life, his family (pregnant wife, Marybeth, and two daughters, Sheridan*, 7, and Lucy, 2) and his job.

When he discovers the body of "white-trash" mountain guide and hunting outfitter Ote Keely sprawled dead over the woodpile in the backyard of Joe's government-provided house, still holding a small cooler containing a few animal droppings, Joe has no idea that it will almost cost him his job and his wife Marybeth's and daughter Sheridan's lives. Joe gathers a few droppings to send to headquarters and helps Sheriff O. R. "Bud" Barnum, law enforcement veteran who is running for reelection, complete the on-site investigation. Joe then organizes an expedition to search for Ote's two companions, who have not been seen for some time, starting at their camp in the mountains. Accompanying Joe are rookie Deputy McLanahan and Wacey* Hedeman, state Game Warden in the next district, who is also running for sheriff. At the camp, Wacey seriously wounds Clyde Lidyard as he comes out of a tent before they discover two other men dead in their tents. Everyone assumes Lidyard, known to be mentally unbalanced, killed them, and the case is closed. Joe has reservations, however, and pursues clues, prompted by several strange occurrences. Lidyard's trailer burns down right after Joe searches it and finds remnants of animal parts in the freezer. Vern* Dunvegan, the former Game Warden of the area, who mentored Joe and helped get him this job, offers Joe a position with his company, InterWest Resources, which is building a pipeline to California, at a salary three times Joe's current twenty-six thousand dollars. Two old mountain men ask Joe if he has heard anything about an endangered species being found. Ote's widow mentions that Ote had found an animal with a name that started with M that Ote said Joe would be pleased to know about. Joe thinks immediately of the extinct Miller's weasel. He explores the remote area behind the outfitters' camp and discovers "killing fields." Numerous animals and burrows have been deliberately destroyed, among them, he is sure, Miller's weasels. Joe is then strangely threatened with the loss of his job. Unknown to Joe and Marybeth, Sheridan and Lucy have found in the woodpile where Ote's body lay three small furry animals, which they keep secret, feed, and regard as their very special playmates. Then Marybeth is shot by a backyard intruder, and Sheridan runs for the hills and hides, while the intruder searches vainly for her, and, she realizes, for the animals. Joe returns home in time to take Marybeth to the hospital, but she loses their baby. Eventually, it is discovered that Wacey and Vern are the murderers, having been caught in a picture by Lidyard, an avid photographer, at the killing fields intent on eradicating the few surviving weasels so that the Saddlestring is not restricted from development. Wacey's motive is power—once elected sheriff of the county he has the control he desires—and Vern wishes his company to prosper so that he will be regarded as a big shot entrepreneur. A spellbinding story from the rifle shot on the first page to the weasel kits born in safety at the end, the novel combines the personal and the public convincingly in a symbolic way—private well-being cannot be separated from the ecological. The setting is almost a character in its own right, an integral part of the plot because of the environmental protection elements. Joe is an engaging protagonist—an honest, decent, hardworking, family-loving man, not too bright but doggedly determined. Booklist.

ORDEAL (Mills*, Deanie Francis, Dutton, 1997)   Novel of suspense dealing with the Armageddon Army, a terrorist group in Texas led by a charismatic sociopath in the late 1990s. Wren Cameron, mother of Daniel, 15, and Zoe*, 12, is horrified and terrified when a man from her past, Jeremiah Hunter, whom she helped to convict of bank robbery sixteen years earlier, reappears. With a couple of his thugs he abducts both her and Daniel and takes them to a compound in southwest Texas or New Mexico where he has a new group in many ways like the environmental community she joined as a naive teenager, but this one much more militant and threatening, led by men he met in prison. As she and Daniel are held in a windowless concrete cell for several days, she tries to tell him about her background, that she was Lizzie Montgmery, a rebellious adolescent, when she met Hunter and fell under his spell, in love and idealistic about the professed goals of his group. When she saw him shoot one of the members in cold blood, her growing disillusionment crystallized, and she contacted the FBI, whose agent, Steve Austin*, promised that in a raid on the compound no one would be hurt. In fact, the well-armed community is alerted and fires first, and in the resulting melee many are killed, even children. Lizzie escapes through a tunnel, wanders for a period with her memory blacked out, and eventually meets Harry Cameron (Cam*), a mild-mannered defense attorney, whom she marries, using the name "Wren." Daniel, who has been rebellious and resentful of his parents' authority, is furious at what he sees as lies she has told for his entire life and refuses to listen to her whole story. At first Wren cannot understand why Hunter has kidnapped them, surely not for revenge, since she never appeared in court and he does not know about her betrayal. Then she realizes he wants her expertise with explosives, which, as a chemistry teacher, she has kept current. When they are released from the cell, they are at first kept under guard, which is gradually relaxed as Wren appears compliant, and Daniel, deliberately wooed by Hunter, becomes an avid follower. After some time, by carefully stealing supplies, Wren escapes across the desertlike terrain and eludes the intense search for several days, only to be recaptured just when it appears she will reach freedom. Hunter disciplines her in front of the whole community by beating her brutally with his fists until Daniel protests and is backed by Big John, the munitions keeper, who helps to nurse her and even obtains an antibiotic for her infected feet. Apparently chastened, Wren tries to fit into the community and find out what is being planned. She deliberately seduces Hunter, whose ego is so great he does not doubt that she is again in love with him. He jettisons his current girlfriend and insists that Wren move into his trailer, the most lavish living space in the compound. When the plan is revealed, the reason for her abduction becomes clear. Hunter is plotting to blow up the northern part of the Leatherwood building in which Buck Leatherwood, a very wealthy antigun activist, will be giving a speech. As this diversion occurs, Hunter and his men will rob the bank in the southern part of the building, gathering great wealth. He needs the explosion to be specific enough to destroy Leatherwood and the auditorium where he speaks without wrecking the structure enough to harm the bank. Wren plans carefully to make one small explosion occur, partially shielded from the speaker's platform, while the other bombs, hidden in potted plants and supposed by Hunter to be timed a few seconds later to destroy all the guards and police, are actually disabled. Her plan

works but Hunter gets away with Daniel, drops in on Cam and Zoe, shoots Cam when he finds that Wren is not there, and takes off with Daniel as a hostage to a cabin in the mountains. Wren escapes and takes a bus to Dallas, where she visits her father, whom she has not seen for eighteen years, and gets his car and his financial help. She figures out where Hunter has taken Daniel, stalks them, and when she finally has the opportunity, shoots and kills Hunter. Cam recovers, Wren builds on her reunion with her father, her mother having died some years earlier, and the family members, all admitting some faults, are together again. The novel makes the militia mentality believable and keeps a relentless pace throughout, with several appealing and memorable characters trapped in events beyond their control. An element of otherworldly direction that Wren presumably gets from her long-dead Cherokee grandmother can be taken at face value or attributed to the stress and fear of her attempted escape. Booklist.

ORLEANNA PRICE (*The Poisonwood Bible: A Novel**)   Mother of four girls, wife of Nathan, a fundamentalist Baptist preacher who takes the family to Africa to minister unto the heathen. As a girl in Mississippi, Orleanna was not especially religious, but she attended a revival meeting with friends and almost before she knew it was married to the young, redhaired preacher. Very shortly, he was called into the army where he served for three months on Corregidor before being wounded and sent home, the only one of his company to survive, a circumstance that shamed him and drove him, ever afterward, to try to prove himself by saving souls. Although he is embarrassed by sex and accuses his wife of wantonness, they have three babies in less than two years. As she says in her memories, "I cannot believe any woman on earth has ever made more babies out of less coition." From then on until their second year in the Congo, she is so overworked and cowed by his righteousness that she does not protest his treatment of her or their daughters. When the baby, Ruth* May, becomes desperately ill with malaria, she works day and night nursing her, paying no attention to her husband's pronouncements that the Lord will provide. After Ruth May, finally recovered from the illness, is bitten by a snake whose venom kills in minutes, Orleanna simply walks away from Nathan, followed by the three surviving girls who dare not stay behind. When she finally gets back to the United States, she ends up on Sanderling Island in Georgia, where she devotes herself to gardening. Years later, Adah* tells her that Leah* has learned of Nathan's death. Still trying to baptize children, he was blamed for a group of youngsters killed by crocodiles, chased into an old tower, and burned alive. Orleanna answers, "Adah, what can it possibly mean to me now?"

THE ORNAMENT TREE (Thesman*, Jean, Houghton, 1996) Historical novel set in Seattle, Washington, in 1918. Orphan Bonnie Shaster comes to live with a relative who runs an upscale boardinghouse and meets there a young man blinded in World War I. The ways this spirited girl affects the lives in the house as well as the difficulties of independent women of the period are the main focuses. For a longer entry, see *Dictionary, 1995–1999*. ALA/YA.

THE OTHER ONES (Thesman*, Jean, Viking, 1999) Fantasy set in the ordinary world of Bayhead, Washington,

north of Seattle, in the late 1990s, about extraordinary people. Bridget Raynes, the narrator, has always known she is different but has tried to deny and conceal her own nature in the hope that she will fit in with her schoolmates and neighbors. As a high school sophomore, however, she is an outsider, with only one real friend, fat Mitzie Coburn, a sweet girl who is also ostracized by the popular crowd. Bridget longs to be closer to her next-door neighbor, Jordan O'Neal, with whom she often feeds the quail at the edge of the woods behind their yards. Because she cannot only see tree spirits and xiii, the threshold guardian assigned to her, and can also read minds, she knows that Jordan is troubled since the death of his dog, Mikey, and worried about his alcoholic father, who seems to have left him with no money. Only two adults in her life are helpful, her Aunt Cait, her father's older sister, who is commonly called a witch, and Miss Ireland, the art teacher, who is very encouraging. Her chief tormentors are Mrs. Munson, her English teacher, and Woody McCready, a bully whom Mrs. Munson and the other school authorities always forgive because he has "emotional problems." Appearing sometimes as a frog, sometimes as a white parrot, occasionally as a small dragon, sometimes as a tiny elf boy, xiii is sarcastic, scornful of Bridget's stammer, her clumsiness, and her unwillingness to admit she is special, and he warns her that trouble is coming. This forecast seems tied to a new girl at school, Althea Peale, whose unusual clothes and strange manner make her the butt of Woody's meanness. She is living in a condemned house at the top of a ridge, an area subject to mudslides into Puget Sound that have carried away other houses. Bridget's parents are less than helpful. Her mother tells her to stop sulking and to learn to get along, while her father, more sympathetic, is careless, not realizing or forgetting what she needs. She pictures them all on a runaway bus with no driver, careening down a steep hill. On Saturdays Bridget works at the family nursery that her father runs. Also working there is Greg Thompson, a red-haired, green-eyed junior and the best artist in the school, whom she gradually comes to see as one of the Others, a group that includes Cait and Miss Ireland. Her own art project, a four-panel painting of the seasons, is completed except for fall, for which she cannot decide what bird to paint on the fence. One day she sees a peregrine falcon, and, knowing it is just right for her painting, she stares at it, trying to remember every detail. Suddenly it fades, and there is Althea. Bridget realizes that Althea and her parents are shape-changers, probably the falcons whose nest was swept away by the last mudslide. Bridget's conflicts come to a head at the art show, where Greg wins first place, as expected, and she wins third. Then Woody bursts in with a gang, making loud scornful comments, deriding her falcon and pulling a real, dried falcon foot from his pocket, saying he cut it off a bird flopping around on the beach. Knowing that the bird was her brother, for whom she has been searching, Althea seems about to faint. In fury, Bridget uses her powers to dig the claws into Woody's palm until blood spurts out. Greg pulls out the claw pretending to be just helpful, but one of Woody's friends bumps him on his rib cracked by an earlier kick from Woody. Althea disappears. Cait and Miss Ireland look reproachfully at Bridget, saddened that she has used her power this way. That night Bridget finally agrees to go with xiii to the meeting in the forest, where she meets all the Other Ones, including Greg, and is initiated into the cir-

cle, not at all like the witches' covens of story but a loving group at peace with each other and with nature. When it is over, Bridget goes to Jordan's house, finds him very ill, but takes him to the house on the ridge, where Althea and her parents wait. She asks them to take him "as far as the wind's gate and then let him go." She sees him, as a fourth falcon, fly high to where Mikey runs joyously between constellations. As she turns, the ground shifts, and she just escapes the mudslide that takes the house and part of the cliff down into the sound. If a reader does not pry too hard into questions like what happens to Jordan's body, the sensitive story is moving, with convincing characters and good school scenes. Since Greg has asked Bridget out and given her a first kiss, her social life seems assured, even if she is "different," and she seems to have gained enough confidence to find her own way of coping with Woody, Mrs. Munson, and her parents. ALA/YA.

THE OTHER SHEPARDS (Griffin*, Adele, Hyperion, 1998) Realistic problem novel with fantasy aspects set in the Manhattan section of New York City, about the time of publication. Intelligent, responsible Holland Shepard, 13, the narrator, describes the effect on her and her younger sister, Geneva, of the obsession their parents feel toward their much-older brother and sister, who were killed in an auto accident. A blond, lively, all-knowing young woman, who says her name is Annie, appears one day, a personage whom no one else sees but with whom Holland and Geneva have adventures that help them develop higher self-esteem and bring their parents to a greater appreciation of these remaining children. The plot moves sensitively, a surreal quality enhances the atmosphere of intense family trauma, and the reader is left to decide whether Annie really exists. Previously, the book was cited by the American Library Association for younger readers and by School Library Journal. For a longer entry, see *Dictionary, 1995–1999*. ALA/YA.

OUGHTON, JERRIE (1937–) Born in Atlanta, Georgia; teacher, reteller of Navajo legends in picture-book form, novelist for young adults. Her *The War in Georgia** (Houghton, 1997) is a compelling story of an untraditional but loving group of relatives who contrast with an abusive family that moves in across the street. More conventional but well handled is *Perfect Family** (Houghton, 2000), about a teenage pregnancy. For earlier biographical material and a title entry, see *Dictionary, 1995–1999* [*Music from a Place Called Half Moon*].

OUTRAGEOUSLY ALICE (Naylor*, Phyllis Reynolds, Atheneum, 1997) Ninth in a series of amusing present-day novels about Alice McKinley of Silver Spring, Maryland, which started with *The Agony of Alice*. In this sequel, Alice, the narrator, is thirteen, in eighth grade, and determined to make changes in her boring life. Most of the things she tries backfire. She agrees to be a bridesmaid for Crystal Harkins, one of her brother Lester's former girlfriends, a role for which she is chosen because a younger girl is needed to pair up with the groom's younger brother, and she discovers that attending the bridal shower and being part of the wedding party are social events she is not prepared for and does not enjoy. With her longtime friend Pamela, she experiments with makeup, using so much green eyeshadow that everyone in school stares. For Halloween, she dresses like a tart, but when, in the dark closet of the haunted house constructed in the school gym, someone seizes and French-kisses her, she is shocked. Later, when she discovers it is her old boyfriend, Patrick, just playing a joke, she is not amused. With Pamela, she dyes her hair with green mousse and wears it to school in spikes, then is humiliated when her father sends Lester to pick her up and bring her home. Her relationship with Pamela changes after Pamela's parents decide to get a divorce and she sees how vulnerable her ever-confident friend actually is. Her father, cleaning out the rain gutters, has a fall, and in a panic Alice calls her former English teacher, Miss Summers, whom he sometimes dates. Miss Summers comes at once and helps Alice get her father to the hospital. He has a concussion, but is not seriously injured, and Miss Summers's aid in caring for him seems to bring them closer, much to Alice's satisfaction. As in the other Alice books, ordinary events of a young adolescent girl's life are made interesting by the protagonist's strong, lively character, with a warm and amusing relationship to her father and her older brother. The series is unusually well sustained. For details about *The Agony of Alice*, see *Dictionary, 1985–1989*. For details about *Alice in Rapture, Sort Of* and *All But Alice*, see *Dictionary, 1990–1994*. ALA/YA.

P

PAINTING THE BLACK (Deuker*, Carl, Houghton, 1997) Exciting, thought-provoking sports novel set in Seattle, Washington, in recent years. Until star prep school pitcher Josh Daniels, 17, moves in across the street during the summer, the narrator, Ryan Ward, also seventeen, has not picked up a baseball in the five years since he broke his ankle. Catching for Josh proves so enjoyable that Ryan's abandoned dreams of being a star himself are revived, and he and Josh spend many hours together, throwing, catching, and working out. While Ryan lacks self-confidence and has no plans for college or anything else in particular, Josh confidently expects to be courted by major league scouts. He also encourages Ryan to try out for the Crown Hill High School team in the spring. When in mid-August Josh puts baseball on hold in favor of football, Ryan feels alone and neglected. He notices that Josh collects friends just to be the center of attention. Josh is certain, for example, that he can win the affections even of Monica* Roby, one of the prettiest and smartest girls in school, if he wants to. Ryan continues to be conflicted in his feelings about Josh, at first not wanting him to win the quarterback position and then, when Josh does well, feeling proud of him. Ryan sees, too, that although Josh says Ryan is his best friend, he readily breaks promises to him and even stands him up to go out with the football guys or a girl. Since Ryan cannot count on Josh, he looks forward to baseball season and starts to work out regularly and vigorously on his own. Enjoying some sense of success at that, he also applies himself to his studies, where he earns top grades. After Christmas, to Ryan's delight, Josh initiates baseball practice again. Ryan is a good deal better now because of his workouts during the fall and advice he has received from his Grandpa* Kevin Ward. Josh so manipulates matters that only Ryan is able to catch his best ball, a slider, and Ryan becomes backup catcher. He blossoms in the position, demonstrating good control of the fielders, hitting well in a pinch, and handling the other pitchers capably. One night, after practice, as Ryan comes late out of the locker room, he notices two young men approach the portable classroom where Monica regularly practices the piano. Curious, he follows them and bursts in when he sees them assaulting her, possibly preventing a rape. Although they are masked, he recognizes one of them as Josh and so informs Josh the next day. Josh downplays the incident, saying it was just a joke. At first, Ryan lies, saying he has no idea who attacked Monica, but later, realizing that Josh is not in the least sorry, Ryan tells what he knows. When Josh is suspended, students blame Ryan for telling, except for Chris Selin, another catcher, who says that it is Josh who has let the team and the school down. The team loses badly in the big game, but Josh, who wins the team's Most Valuable Player Award, is drafted by the Colorado Rockies. Ryan's family says they are proud of his courage, and Grandpa Kevin says Ryan should be magnanimous and congratulate Josh. Ryan does so, and Josh accepts graciously. Ryan enrolls for summer school in university-level classes at the local community college and proudly puts his mortar board and the team's Most Inspirational Player trophy on his dresser. Best are the tense, convincing game scenes, wealth of information about sports, and the troubling moral question the book poses. The author puts it this way on the book flap: "Some [athletes] inevitably begin to think of themselves as being outside or above regular rules. I wanted to write the story of such an athlete without either demonizing him or excusing him." The book's title comes from a baseball term for skillfully passing the ball over the edge of the plate to trip up the batter. ALA/YA.

THE PANTHER (*People of the Mist**) Very old man believed to be a witch or sorcerer who lives on an island near Chesapeake Bay and who is persuaded to come to Three Myrtle and Flat Pearl villages to discover who killed Red Knot, the granddaughter of the Flat Pearl Weroansqua (chief). The Panther refuses to tell anything about himself, except to say that he did a lot of things in his life that he is thoroughly ashamed of. Near the book's end, however, when warriors from the south attack, The Panther reveals that he is of their Sky Rider Clan, that his real name is Eight Rocks, and that he is their rightful ruler. He commands them not to attack. Earlier, Copper Thunder, the frightening and ambitious man to whom Red Knot was promised, recognizes The Panther as once a dreaded war chief of the western villages who committed many atrocities. The Panther then reveals to the village that Copper Thunder and his mother had once been The Panther's slaves, taken in war. This revelation ruins Copper Thunder's plans to build a small empire by assimilating the villages in the region, since, knowing that he was once a slave, the people refuse to follow him. The main reason that The Panther agrees to help find Red Knot's killer is to atone for his misdeeds.

PASTWATCH: THE REDEMPTION OF CHRISTOPHER COLUMBUS (Card*, Orson Scott, Tor, 1996) Historical-fiction fantasy for adults based on the idea that people in the future can transform history by traveling back to a decisive point and changing what happens, thereby wiping out everything that has occurred since and starting events into a new pattern. In the far future, Tagiri, a woman from Africa in a study group called "Pastwatch," takes up slavery as her special subject, in particular the enslavement of the people of what became

Central and South America by the Spanish conquerors. Tagiri's daughter, Diko, starting as a child of eleven or twelve, zeroes in on Columbus as the key figure and discovers the moment when he decides to sail west. A vision he assumes to be the Trinity appears to him on the beach where he has been shipwrecked on a voyage to Flanders, a vision that directs him to sail west to the Orient, rather than east as he has long planned. To the scholars of Pastwatch, it is clear that this vision is actually an intervention from some time in the future, determined to deflect Columbus from a crusade that will destroy Arabic learning and change the course of European history. They also realize that if this were possible once, it will be possible again, and they may be able to avert the terrible cruelty of the Spanish conquest in the New World and the resulting disaster, centuries later, of global warming and, in a matter of decades, the eventual starvation of the remaining population. Three people are chosen to make this backward journey: Diko; her lover Hunahpu Matamoro, a Pastwatcher from the Caribbean islands; and Kemal Akyazi, an Arab who has discovered Noah and Atlantis in the Red Sea and is zealously Islamic, hoping to thwart the Christianization of the Western world. The Pastwatch scenes are alternated with those from the life of Columbus, starting with his boyhood as the son of a weaver in Genova, through his determination to become a rich gentleman, his early seafaring, his vision on the beach, his long years of persuading the court of Spain to sanction his voyage west, and the revisionist history that the three from Pastwatch are able to create for him. Each one has his own job: Kemal sinks two of the three ships of the Columbus expedition, the other having run aground through clumsy seamanship of its captain, and dies as he wishes, a martyr for Islam. Hunahpu impersonates one of the Maya gods from Xibalba, whom he calls "One-Hunahpu," and commands the warring peoples to give up human sacrifice and slavery and to develop bronze and iron smelting and a culture that will rival the strongest in Europe. Diko, an imposing, tall, very black woman, goes to the Taino village of Ankuash in Haiti, where she denies that she has special powers but, because she seems to know so much, is called "Sees-in-the-Dark." There she teaches Chipa, 10, a very bright girl, Spanish, and sends her to the camp of Columbus, where the sailors are trying to force the Tainos to build new ships for them. As interpreter, Chipa invites Columbus to Ankuash, where Diko teaches him the true meaning of Christianity, as if he has discovered it himself, and where, when his men mutiny, he and those faithful to him flee. The plan works as the Pastwatch scholars have hoped. The culture developed in Central and South America rivals that of Europe, but it is peaceful, devoted to trade, and treats even dark-skinned people, including women, as equals. All this is not without sacrifice. Tagiri, all her colleagues, and the people of her time have to agree to oblivion, to be wiped out as if they had never existed. Diko and Hunahpu, although they meet once later, have to agree to forego their love rather than reveal their true roles. Kemal is tortured and murdered by the Spaniards. Columbus never gives up his great devotion to God, but he has lost his first wife, Felipa, loses the possibility of really knowing his son, Diego, loses his longtime mistress, Beatrice, and any possible closeness to their son, Fernando. The novel is long and dense, with many scenes and characters, both historical and fictional, and complex reasoning, as well as a wealth of detail about life in Genova, in the courts of Iberia, at sea, and in the lands and among the different peoples of the New World. The basic premise is ingenious and cleverly worked out. The book lacks, however, a central character with whom a reader can identify, though Columbus and Diko come near to serving this purpose. ALA/YA.

PATERSON, KATHERINE (WOMEL-DORF) (1932–) Born in Tsing-Tsiang, China; one of the most acclaimed writers for young people of the late twentieth century. Her novel, *Jip His Story** (Lodestar, 1996), which won the Scott O'Dell Award for Historical Fiction, has since been named to the American Library Association Young Adult list. For earlier biographical information and title entries, see *Dictionary, 1960–1984* [*Bridge to Terebithia*; *The Great Gilly Hopkins*; *The Master Puppeteer*; *Of Nightingales That Weep*]; *Dictionary, 1985–1989* [*Come Sing, Jimmy Jo*; *Park's Quest*]; *Dictionary, 1990–1994* [*Flip-Flop Girl*; *Lyddie*; *Of Nightingales That Weep*], and *Dictionary, 1995–1999* [*Flip-Flop Girl*; *Jip His Story*].

PAULSEN, GARY (1939–) For more than thirty years a popular and highly honored writer of 140 books of fiction and nonfiction for mostly middle grade and early adolescent readers, many in series, most on outdoor themes and topics, and some illustrated by his wife, painter Ruth Wright Paulsen. He was born in Minneapolis, Minnesota, and educated at Bemidji State University in Minnesota and the University of Colorado–Boulder. He lives in New Mexico and on a boat on the Pacific Ocean. *The Schernoff Discoveries** (Delacorte, 1997) is a hilarious episodic novel of two schoolboys. It was cited by the American

Library Association for young adults. Among his historical novels is *Soldier's Heart: A Novel of the Civil War** (Delacorte, 1998), about a real Minnesota boy in the Union army, which has been cited for young adults by both the New York Public Library and the American Library Association. Another historical fiction is *Sarny: A Life Remembered* (Delacorte, 1997), concerning the young black slave girl introduced in *Nightjohn* (Delacorte, 1993). Other titles include *The Transall Saga* (Delacorte, 1998), a futuristic fantasy; *Brian's Return* (Delacorte, 1999), which completes the story begun in *Hatchet* (Delacorte, 1997); *Guts: The True Stories behind Hatchet and the Brian Books* (Delacorte, 2001); and *How Angel Peterson Got His Name* (Wendy Lamb, 2003), incidents based on Paulsen's youth. For more information about Paulsen, titles, and title entries, see *Dictionary, 1985–1989* [*Dogsong*; *Hatchet*]; *Dictionary, 1990–1994* [*The Cookcamp*; *Nightjohn*; *The Voyage of the "Frog"*; *The Winter Room*]; and *Dictionary, 1995–1999* [*Soldier's Heart*].

PAY IT FORWARD (Hyde*, Catherine Ryan, Simon & Schuster, 1999) Fantasy set in the near future, in which a boy's assignment for his social studies class, a plan to change the world, actually takes hold and makes a difference for many people. In Atascadero, California, early in the 1990s, Trevor McKinney, 12, responds with enthusiasm to an extra-credit assignment by his new teacher, Reuben St. Clair: Think of an idea for world change, and put it into action. A direct, honest boy, Trevor comes up with a simple plan, which he calls "Paying Forward." He will do nice things for three people, not little courtesies but each one a thing important to someone, and when those people offer to pay him back, he will tell them instead to pay forward by doing nice things for three other people, who in turn will pay forward to three other people. His quick brain calculates the mathematics involved and realizes that this could spread over the whole world population. His first three acts seem to him to be total busts. He gives money from his paper route to Jerry Busconi, a homeless man, for new clothes, takes him home for a bath, and is pleased when he gets a job, but the first payday Jerry falls off the wagon and ends up in jail. Trevor is more hopeful about helping his arthritic neighbor, Mrs. Greenberg, fix up the garden she loves, but she dies before she has had time to pay forward, he thinks. His third idea is to help his teacher, Mr. St. Clair, a black man who had half his face blown off and his left arm badly injured in Vietnam, and his single mother, Arlene, both of whom he can see are lonely, by getting them together and possibly eventually married. Although Trevor never knows it, Jerry, released from jail and living in a park, talks a desperate young woman out of throwing herself off the Golden Gate Bridge. Mrs. Greenberg, knowing she has not long to live, has wasted no time in changing her will, leaving her life insurance not to her ungrateful son but to Matt and Terri, two young people who work at the local supermarket, and to the nice lady at the North County Cat Shelter. Matt invests most of his share in a Honda 250, resisting the urge to buy a bigger motorcycle, and by racing into the middle of a gang in an alley is able to save Sidney G., a thug about to be murdered. Although it seems unlikely that cynical Sidney will pay anything forward, he spares a gang member he is about to kill and extracts a promise to pay that bit of compassion forward. And so on. With Arlene and Reuben

it goes more slowly. Arlene thinks Reuben, higher socially and educationally, looks down on her, while he cannot believe that any woman can be interested in a man with half his face gone. Things seem to be gradually working out for them, and Reuben has actually given Arlene a ring when Trevor's father, Ricky, turns up after more than a year with no communication. Although they were never married, Arlene feels responsible for her son's father and takes him in, only to discover that he is using her again and sleeping with another woman. The Movement, as it has come to be called, reaches the attention of an investigative reporter, Chris Chandler, firing his imagination, and he manages to trace it back to Trevor and Reuben's assignment. His resulting story documents how gang warfare has lessened and crime rates have dropped, and a television program spreads the word. Reuben and Arlene, however, are both too proud and afraid of rejection to get together again. Then the White House invites all three of them to meet President Clinton, and they fly to Washington, D.C., where Arlene and Reuben become engaged, much to Trevor's delight. After a tour of the city and a meeting with the president, they are just about to enter the limousine for the airport when Trevor sees an older man and a boy, a homosexual couple, set upon by thugs as they leave a club. He dashes into the fray and is fatally knifed. The reaction is worldwide. Although Arlene is pregnant and does not know whether the baby is Ricky's or Reuben's, she and Reuben get married. Later, when Ricky turns up, down and out again, and demands to see his child, they show him the beautiful, dark-skinned baby girl, clearly Reuben's. Realizing he has never paid anything forward, Reuben gives Ricky a check for two thousand dollars, half his checking account. Being futuristic, the novel qualifies as fantasy, but whether it is by other criteria is up to the reader to decide. Obviously, it *could* happen, without magic or otherworldly intervention, and it has enough tough-edged scenes to keep the outcome in doubt. It is saved from total sentimentality by a light touch and by the character of Trevor, a bright, open, very appealing kid. ALA/YA.

PECK, RICHARD (1934–   )   Born in Decatur, Illinois; educated at Exeter University in England and at DePauw University and Southern Illinois University; teacher; resident of New York City. Highly popular and much-acclaimed writer of two dozen novels mostly for middle school readers and young adults, Peck has received many awards, including the Margaret A. Edwards Award for the body of his work, the Edgar Allan Poe Award, and the Newbery Award for *A Year Down Yonder** (Dial, 2000), which is also an American Library Association choice for young adults. The sequel to the Newbery Honor book, *A Long Way from Chicago: A Novel in Stories** (Dial, 1998), it continues the story of the Dowdel family as Mary Alice spends a year during the Great Depression with the unflappable Grandma Dowdel. Peck has also published *Strays Like Us** (Dial, 1998), another American Library Association selection for young adults, in which a girl feels like a stray until she discovers other outsiders like herself. For additional information about Peck, titles, and title entries, see *Dictionary, 1960–1984* [*Are You in the House Alone?*; *Dreamland Lake*]; *Dictionary, 1985–1989* [*Blossom Culp and the Sleep of Death*; *Princess Ashley*; *Remembering the Good Times*]; *Dictionary, 1990–1994* [*Bel-Air Bambi and the Mall Rats*]; and *Dictionary, 1995–1999* [*A Long Way from Chicago*].

PELLEGRINO, CHARLES R. (1953–   ) Born in New York City; received a B.A. and an M.S. from Long Island University and a Ph.D. from Victoria University, Wellington, New Zealand. Best known for his books of nonfiction, he has also published science fiction. A working scientist in paleobiology, astronomy, and similar areas, he has designed rocket and nuclear projects; has been affiliated with presitigious institutions, including Brookhaven National Laboratory on Long Island, New York, and the Princeton Space Studies Institute; has taught at Hofstra University, among others; and has been extensively involved in the Titanic project. *Dust** (Avon, 1998), a New York Public Library selection, concerns a plague of black mites that create devastation and pandemonium throughout the earth. In *Flying to Valhalla* (Morrow, 1993), a husband-and-wife science team set out to ensure that another galactic system will not destroy Earth. Its sequel is *The Killing Star* (Morrow, 1995), written with George Zebrowski. With Zebrowski, Pellegrino has also published *Star Trek: The Next Generation #50: Dyson Sphere* (Pocket Books, 1999). His theories about cloning dinosaurs from amber were the basis for Michael Crichton's* Jurassic Park books. He received the Isaac Asimov Memorial Award for science writing and lives in New York City.

PENMAN, SHARON KAY   Lawyer, historian, novelist. Best known for her biographical novel about Richard III and the War of the Roses, *The Sunne in Splendor* (Holt, 1982) and her massive trilogy set in the thirteenth century, *Here Be Dragons* (Holt, 1985), *Falls the Shadow* (Holt, 1988), and *The Reckoning* (Holt, 1991), she has also published two historical mysteries, *The Queen's Man: A*

Medieval Mystery* (Holt, 1998), set in the later years of Eleanor of Aquitaine when Richard I has been captured on his return from the Crusades, and its sequel, *Cruel as the Grave* (Holt, 1998). A second long historical-biographical trilogy about Eleanor and Henry Plantagenet starts with *When Christ and His Saints Slept* (Holt, 1995) and *Time & Chance* (Putnam, 2002).

PENNEBAKER, RUTH   Journalist, novelist. Her story of the girls in a home for unwed mothers, *Don't Think Twice** (Holt, 1996), has been praised for its compassion and emotional realism. Pennebaker has written about her own struggle with breast cancer in the *Dallas Morning News*, an experience reflected in *Both Sides Now* (Holt, 2000), in which a girl reevaluates her life as her mother dies of breast cancer. Another well-received novel is *Conditions of Love* (Holt, 1999), about a girl's adjustment to her father's death and to discovering his faults. Pennebaker has also written two humorous books for expectant mothers. She lives in Austin, Texas.

PEOPLE OF THE MIST (Gear*, Kathleen O'Neal, and W. Michael Gear*, Forge, 1997)   Adult historical-romance and mystery-detective novel set about 1300 A.D. on Chesapeake Bay, involving prehistoric Native American Algonquian Indians and based on the authors' archaeological investigations, one in their First North Americans series. When Red Knot, 14, of Flat Pearl Village, learns that her Weroansqua (chief) grandmother, Hunting Hawk, has promised her for political reasons to much-older Copper Thunder, the warring Great Taqua (chief) of another village, the girl runs away at night to join her lover, High Fox, of Three Myrtle Village to the south. The next day, she is found murdered, and the hunt for her killer occupies the remainder of the narrative in murder-mystery fashion like the stories involving such sleuths as Hercule Poirot or Columbo. High Fox, who is the not well-respected son of Black Spike, the Weroance (chief) of Three Myrtle Village, asks a girl of the village who loves him for assistance, since he knows he is under suspicion. Daring, intelligent Sun Conch, 14, contacts reclusive The Panther*, the old man reputed to be a witch or sorcerer who lives alone on a nearby island, and offers to serve him in return for his help. Although he does not entirely believe High Fox's alibi, The Panther agrees to accompany the girl to Three Myrtle Village, which is about to defend itself from an attack by Flat Pearl Village led by the renowned warrior, Nine* Killer. Persuading the combatants to make a truce, The Panther enlists the help of Nine Killer, and together with Sun Conch they return to Flat Pearl. They investigate the crime scene, reenact the murder as best they can, interview villagers, and in detective-story style conclude with a list of suspects: High Fox, to keep Red Knot from being given to another man; Flat Willow, who also loved Red Knot, to keep her from running off with High Fox; Copper Thunder, to prevent Red Knot's affair with High Fox from endangering the alliance between the two clans and end his chances of assimilating Flat Pearl; Hunting Hawk, to keep the alliance from jeopardizing the autonomy of her clan; and even Red Knot's mother, Shell Comb, to keep Red Knot from marrying Copper Thunder, whom she herself loves. After they have applied deductive reasoning, The Panther unmasks the killer at a large public gathering in Flat Pearl Village about ten days after the murder. Black Spike, High Fox's father, who earlier was not a suspect, admits that he killed Red Knot because she was his daughter by Shell Comb and, hence, the sister of High Fox, a fact that neither young person knew. Black Spike then leaps into the fire in the middle of the plaza and commits suicide. Later, Shell Comb admits to The Panther that it was really she who killed Red Knot but allowed Black Spike to take the blame. The Panther forces her to agree to let Nine Killer, a good and worthy man, become the next Weroance of Flat Pearl Village. Adding spice to this mixture is a small mystery introduced about half way through the book concerning the identity and purposes of The Panther himself. Plot and characters are formulaic, but the story moves fast and holds the attention to the very end. Best are the details of the way of life, beliefs, attitudes, and worldview of these people, which are skillfully worked into the narrative without didacticism. Booklist.

PERFECT FAMILY (Oughton*, Jerrie, Houghton Mifflin, 2000)   Novel of a girl whose unmarried pregnancy in Lily, North Carolina, of the 1950s shocks her family, changes her life, but ultimately strengthens rather than destroys it. Although her older sister, Evelyn Sue, 20, runs off with friends to California hoping to find James Dean, the family of Welcome Marie O'Neal, 15, keeps up the pretense of being perfect, meaning conventional in every respect. Her older brother, Julian, with his wife, Wysteria, and their two children, lives up to the ideal, as does Welcome until she meets Nicholas Canton. Newly arrived in town, handsome, muscular, self-assured Nicholas is "not our kind of people," according to Welcome's mother, and that only adds to his allure for Welcome. She has had only one boyfriend, Randy Newsome, red-haired, shorter than she is, and comfortable to be with, but not exciting like Nicholas. Over the late summer, Nicholas starts a determined campaign to win over Welcome's parents, going to their church every Sunday and talking politely to them when he comes to sit on the porch, the only evening dates she is allowed, until by October, when he comes home briefly from football practice at college in Raleigh and asks her to a square dance accompanied by his parents, they agree to let her go. Halfway through the evening, he leaves her to join a group of men drinking in the parking lot and, when she hunts him down, decides they will leave, drives her to a remote area, starts to make love, and passes out. Furious, she tugs him into the passenger seat, and, although she is too young for a license and has driven very little, manages to get them back to his house where she leaves him slumped in his car and marches home down the middle of the dark streets. Disillusioned, Evelyn Sue returns from California planning to go to beauty school. Welcome waits in vain for Nicholas to apologize, then hears that he is going with a blonde. When Randy, who is now at North Carolina State in Raleigh, asks her to the big Clemson game the next weekend, her parents agree if she gets back by midnight. After the game, they drive to a park and, pretending to herself that he is Nicholas, she encourages him to make love to her. By Christmas, she knows she is pregnant and confides in Evelyn Sue, who scrapes up money for an illegal abortion, but the sleazy place horrifies her, and she does not go through with it. She tells her parents that Nicholas is not the father and that she does not know who is, not wanting to involve Randy and destroy his college career, and also feeling that it was more her fault than his. Her parents send her to Virginia Beach to stay with her mother's sister, Aunt Lacey, and her husband, Uncle Mac Hall. On the bus she sits with an African American woman named Hattie Mercer, who is making an annual pilgrimage to the grave of her son, Adam, who was killed about ten years before in an automobile crash. Hattie is the first person who hugs Welcome and is willing to talk about the baby and give her advice. Her aunt and uncle are kind, but both work, and the winter is lonesome for Welcome, who does the housework and cooking to pay her way. In March, her father has a stroke, and they drive her to Lily to see him before he dies. She wears a long, full coat at the funeral so her condition is not apparent, and her aunt drives her back to Virginia Beach immediately. Hattie sends her a box of clothes and a Mother Goose book for the baby. When he is born, Welcome names him Adam and is delighted, but as she sees, in the next few weeks, how exhausting his care is and begins to realize how unprepared she is to support him and also how much Aunt Lacey, who could never have children, covets him, she makes the difficult decision to let her aunt and uncle adopt him. The book ends with an announcement, dated 1968, of Welcome's graduation from medical school, with a special note to Adam from "your best buddy, Welcome." Except for this unlikely culmination, the entire novel is predictable, and while Welcome is an appealing protagonist, the same story has been told in any number of other novels for young adults. Not enough is made of her parents' rigid conformity and her mother's fear of what people will say. Young people in the twenty-first century may not appreciate the sense of disaster that unmarried pregnancy once meant. ALA/YA.

THE PERKS OF BEING A WALLFLOWER (Chbosky*, Stephen, Pocket Books, 1999)   Boy's growing-up novel in the form of letters to an unnamed recipient from a troubled boy in his first year of high school in what appears to be Pittsburgh, Pennsylvania, in the late twentieth century. Even before his friend Michael killed himself while they were in middle school, Charlie was given to spells of weeping and is a worry to his family and teachers. In an effort to participate and become more connected, as he has been advised, he goes to a football game and says hello to a senior from his shop class named Patrick, who introduces him to Sam, the girl he is with, and they invite him to sit with them. Charlie learns that they are stepbrother and stepsister. In the next months, they take him under their wings, introducing him into their crowd, letting him go to parties with them, and trying to teach him how to act normal. When Charlie confesses that he has sex dreams about Sam, she tells him kindly that she is too old for him. He also learns that well-adjusted Patrick is openly gay and that Brad, the star quarterback, is secretly homosexual and in love with Patrick. Charlie is also befriended by Bill, his Advanced English teacher, who recognizes that he is far more intelligent than the average student and supplies him with extra books to read and to write about. From the letters, one learns about Charlie's family: His older brother is a football player at Penn State. His sister is pretty and popular, and at one point discovers she is pregnant and has Charlie accompany her to an abortion clinic. When her current boyfriend hits her in the face, she accepts it, but Charlie, who has witnessed it, tells Bill, and inadvertently triggers a family crisis. She tells Charlie that she hates him for it. Charlie is fond of his parents, but the relative he really loved, the only one who hugged him, was Aunt Helen, who lived with them when he was young and was killed in an automobile crash when he was seven. He knows that she had been sexually molested by a family friend when she was a child, and no one believed her or took any action. When Brad's father finds his son and Patrick together, he kicks Patrick out and beats Brad, who then turns against his former friend. For a while, Charlie accompanies Patrick everywhere, listening to his woes, even going with him to parks where he waits while Patrick picks up men, disappears for a while, then returns, no happier. When Brad calls Patrick, "faggot," in front of a group of his friends, Patrick slugs him, and soon the fight is joined by four of Brad's buddies. Charlie jumps in, fighting as his brother taught him with no restraint, scratching, gouging, bashing, and so astonishes and frightens the participants that the fight stops. During the year, Charlie tries marijuana, takes out a girl for the first time, experiences LSD when someone slips it into his drink (and decides to stay away from it forever), attends family reunions, and goes to the *Rocky Horror Picture Show* where his friends act out the parts in front of the screen, all with the detachment of a spectator. When Sam is about to leave for a summer session at college, she initiates sex with him, and, unable to participate although he has loved her all year, he has a severe flashback to times with his Aunt Helen, memories he has repressed. He ends up in a mental hospital for two months, where he manages to work through many problems and decides that it is all right to be as he is, without blaming his aunt or anyone else. The premise that these are letters to someone he does not know is strained, but Charlie's voice is

so frank and intelligent and funny that it carries the story and endears him to the reader. It also makes possible the unlikely idea that a group of high school seniors would adopt such a freakish boy and put up with his frequent tears and odd behavior. Perhaps because he stands on the sidelines and watches, his comments characterize a number of minor figures sharply, as well as his family members and his crowd at high school. ALA/YA.

PERROTTA, TOM (1961–)   Born in Summit, New Jersey; educator, novelist and short story writer. He received his B.A. from Yale University in 1983 and his M.A. from Syracuse University in 1988. From 1988 to 1993, he was a lecturer at Yale and from 1994 to 1998 a preceptor at Harvard University. His highly ironic and amusing second novel, *Election** (Putnam, 1998), deals with a campaign for high school president, meaningless in itself, that profoundly changes several lives. An earlier novel, *The Wishbones* (Putnam, 1997), is about a musician who, at thirty-one, still lives with his parents and dreams of being a rock star. *Joe College* (St. Martin's, 2000), a novel both comic and serious, features a junior at Yale who drives a lunch truck during school breaks. Perrotta has also published a book of short stories, *Bad Haircut: Stories of the Seventies* (Bridge Works, 1994).

PERRY JAMESON (*Life in the Fat Lane**) A high school senior at Blooming Woods High School, which Lara Ardeche, the protagonist and narrator, also attends. Perry is scorned and teased by most of the students as fat and gay and has friends only among the other unpopular and odds-out kids. He is a talented saxophone player and admires Lara's piano playing. Both are in the school orchestra. He apparently can accept being called fat, but he takes pains to assure Lara he is not gay. He invites Lara to attend a party with him, but she refuses because she has accepted an invitation to a birthday party in a jazz club. To her surprise, this was the party to which he had invited her. Since he likes her as she is and they have common interests, they may become more than friends.

PETERS, JULIE ANNE (1952–) Born in Jamestown, New York; received her B.A. from the University of Denver, her B.S. from Metropolitan State College of Denver, and her M.B.A. from the University of Colorado–Denver; has been an elementary teacher, research assistant, computer programmer, systems designer, and special needs educational assistant. She is the author of nine books for middle graders and young adults, has contributed to periodicals for young people and adults, and lives in Lakewood, Colorado. Her first novel, an easy-to-read chapter book whose title explains its content, *The Stinky Sneakers Contest* (Little, Brown, 1992), gained attention for its good humor and exploration of friendship. The Snob Squad books, for a somewhat older audience, amusingly describe how a group of outsider sixth-grade girls deal with issues that confront them, like bullies, a school theft, and family problems: *Revenge of the Snob Squad* (Little, Brown, 1998), *Romance of the Snob Squad* (Little, Brown, 1999), and *A Snitch in the Snob Squad* (Little, Brown, 2001). Her most critically praised book has been *Define "Normal"** (Little, Brown, 2000), about an unlikely friendship, which was chosen by the American Library Association for young adults.

PETEY (Mikaelsen*, Ben, Hyperion, 1998)   Realistic sociological-problem novel set in Montana during most of the twentieth century. Petey Corbin, is born in 1920 with cerebral palsy and a deformed body. He is made a ward of the state and committed to Warm Springs Insane Asylum, where he is placed with the other "idiots" and given only minimal custodial care, a circumstance that continues when he is moved to other institutions. Through the help of several astute attendants, Petey eventually makes a few friends and with a wheelchair is able to leave the institution for brief periods. For the most part, however, Petey is lonely, isolated, and friendless, and his intellect is never developed. The novel excels in creating its plucky protagonist and depicts graphically how handicapped people have been treated, their basic humanity denied, even in presumably enlightened times. Previously, the novel received the Spur Award. For a longer entry, see *Dictionary, 1995–1999*. ALA/YA.

PETRELLI, J. DANIEL (*Nathan's Run**) Politically ambitious prosecutor in the county in which Warren Michaels* is a police lieutenant. Petrelli is presented stereotypically—obnoxious, disrespectful to law enforcement officers, and determined to make political hay from the death of Ricky Harris, the child-care supervisor (guard) at the Juvenile Detention Center, whom Nathan Bailey is accused of killing. Petrelli has little interest in learning the truth about Nathan and openly courts the media, making rash statements that assume Nathan is guilty.

PHILBRICK, W. RODMAN (1951–) Born in Boston, Massachusetts; longshoreman, boat builder, writer. His first book for young people, *Freak the Mighty* (Blue Sky Press, 1993), was republished in l997 by Scholastic as *The Mighty* and made into a film. It was followed by a sequel, *Max the Mighty* (Scholastic, 1998). His science-fantasy novel, *The Last Book in the Universe** (Scholastic, 2000), is a look, ultimately hopeful, into a grim future of the planet. With his wife, Lynn Harnett, he wrote *Abduction* (Scholastic, 1998) and two groups of novels, The House on Cherry Street series, which starts with *The Haunting* (Scholastic, 1997), and the Visitors series, starting with *Strange Invaders* (Scholastic, 1997). He has also written two novels for adults, *Brothers and Sisters* (Dutton, 1993) and *Dark Matter* (Xlibris, 2000), under his own name, ten mysteries using the name W. R. Philbrick, and four using the name William R. Danz.

PHUONG (*Bull Catcher**)   Ngo Huynh Phuong, Phuong being his first name. He is a Vietnamese American high school student, who becomes a star pitcher for the Shipley (Wisconsin) High School baseball team, while Bull Larsen, who tells the story, is playing on it. Phuong's father is a doctor, new to the Shipley clinic. As soon as Jeff* Hanson, Bull's classmate and fellow lover of baseball, sees Phuong, he thinks that Phuong's tall frame and long, strong arms spell great pitcher and sets about courting him for his pickup team. By their junior year, Phuong has become a notable presence on the mound and has earned the nickname of "Nolan Ryan Phuong." Phuong decides not to play ball his senior year. Moved by stories and pictures of his father's current work in establishing and upgrading clinics in Vietnam, he opts to graduate in January and go directly to the University of Chicago to study medicine. When Jeff remarks that the game never meant much to Phuong, Phuong answers, "Not the game. But you guys did. A lot."

PICK (*A Knight of the Word**)   A small crotchety forest and woods creature six inches high made of twigs, hair, and moss, called a "sylvan." More than 150 years old, Pick's main task is to look after Sinnissippi Park near Rock River in Hopewell, Illinois, where Nest* Freemark lives. Guarding the park against feeders (cannibal creatures who lure children to the park and devour them) and other beings in service to the evil Void, an ancient force for chaos, is a big job, and generations of Freemark women before Nest have helped him. Pick leads Nest to the tatterdamalion Ariel, who tells Nest that the Lady of the Word wishes her to go to Seattle to order John Ross* to resume his tasks as Knight of the Word. Although a serious creature in essence, Pick provides occasional comic relief.

PLAINSONG   (Haruf*, Kent, Knopf, 1999)   Quiet, moving novel for adults of a family and several of their acquaintances in Holt, Colorado, in the last part of the twentieth century, how their lives intertwine, and how they survive emotional trauma with fortitude. Action centers on Tom Guthrie, teacher at the local high school, and his sons, Ike, 10, and Bobby, 9, serious little boys who stick together and seldom ask or expect sympathy. They worry that their mother, Ella, seems to be ill, lying in her darkened room, not rising to dress or eat. Tom has his own troubles at school, mostly concerned with Russell Beckman, who has done no work in his American History class and will not graduate if he does not pass. The principal wants to avoid trouble by passing the boy anyway, to get rid of him, but Tom cannot bring himself to compromise his principles so blatantly. At school his friend and fellow teacher is Maggie Jones, a tall, competent woman who lives with her aging father. Ike and Bobby, who ride their morning paper route on their bikes, both have horses that they care for diligently. After their mother moves out, they ride their bikes to see her in the little rented house, and take her perfume and bubble bath they have bought with some of their newspaper money, which makes her cry. One Saturday, they go with their father to the cattle ranch of the McPheron brothers, Raymond and Harold, aging bachelors, to help him sort the pregnant cows from the ones that didn't "stick," where they watch from the corral fence and then help drive the cows into the chute. To their surprise, Raymond gives them each ten dollars and assures them that they can come back any time. When a high school student, Victoria Roubideaux, gets pregnant and is thrown out by her mother, she comes to Maggie, who lets her sleep on the sofa, but her old father is confused and scares her. Since it is apparent that the old man will not accept Victoria, the teacher drives to the McPheron ranch and proposes that they take Victoria in. The brothers are dumbfounded. After they think it over, however, they agree and give her the room where their parents slept, explaining that their bedrooms are upstairs. After some days Victoria tearfully tells Maggie that they are kind enough but they do not talk, and she does not understand what is wrong. Maggie corners Harold in the grocery store and explains that they better start some conversation. Since they seldom talk even to each other, the McPherons are baffled, but they determinedly start that evening, explaining to Victoria about market reports and futures sales and other subjects that they think up each day and discuss with her in the evening. She keeps the house cleaner than it has been in years, but they worry that

she might not be happy and decide she needs some diversion. They settle on driving her to Phillips and buying a crib. Ike and Bobby spend Christmas with their mother in Denver, where she has gone to live with her sister, but they are not comfortable with their aunt. Tom spends a night with a girl from the school office, but is more interested in Maggie, with whom he starts a regular affair. One day at school, Dwayne, the father of Victoria's baby, shows up and takes her to Denver, where he has been staying. After one wild party with his friends, she has had enough, and gets a bus back to Holt. The McPherons take her in again. Russell Beckman and his redneck parents continue to give Tom trouble and eventually the boy and a friend intercept Ike and Bobby on their way home from a movie, drive them out into the country, strip them and leave them to walk home some five miles in the dark. Tom is furious, rushes to the Beckman house, tries to attack Russell and is beaten up by his father. Ike and Bobby, alone too much, go to the apartment of Mrs. Stearns, one of their newspaper clients who has been nice to them and has given them a key, so they can come see her without making her get up. They find her dead. Riding together on Bobby's horse, Ike's having died, they head out to the McPheron ranch, the other place where people have been nice to them and invited them to return. They miss the turnoff, and riding in the dark, have to backtrack, getting there after the McPherons and Victoria are all asleep. She gives them supper and makes a bed for them on the floor while Raymond calls Tom. In the end, Victoria has a baby girl, and the two old men are delighted. When Dwayne shows up, demanding that Victoria return to him in Denver and she refuses, they manhandle him off their land. Tom and Maggie are seeing each other regularly. Ella stays in Denver, recovering gradually from her depression. The Beckmans have hired a lawyer, but Tom is not much worried. They all seem to have weathered their own storms and moved on. The tone of the novel is quiet, all the strong emotion modulated as befits the landscape, with deep love unspoken but not unfelt. ALA/YA; Alex; Booklist.

PLATT, RANDALL BETH (1948–) Born in Seattle, Washington; attended Portland State University and Oregon State University; worked in data processing, as a private secretary, and as membership coordinator for the Tacoma, Washington, YMCA before becoming a freelance writer in 1983. She has written several novels for adults, including *The Four Arrows Fe-As-Ko* (Catbird, 1991), *Out of a Forest Clearing: An Environmental Fable* (John Daniel, 1991), and *Seashore Stables* (Cora Verlag, 1992). Her first book for young people, *Honor Bright* (Delacorte, 1997), concerns a girl in conflict with her mother during World War II. *The Likes of Me** (Delacorte, 2000), a selection for teenagers of the American Library Association, is a lively story about an albino girl who learns that she can have a good life despite her handicap. Platt lives in the Puget Sound area.

PLAYING WITHOUT THE BALL (Wallace*, Rich, Knopf, 2000) Sports and boy's growing-up novel, set in Sturbridge, Pennsylvania, in the late 1990s. Jay McLeod, 17, is living in a room over Shorty's Bar, where he works as a cook and dishwasher, since his feckless father has gone to California, his alcoholic mother having left the family some eight years earlier. Although Jay is in his last year of high school, his interests are al-

most entirely on two things: basketball and girls. A good, but not spectacular, player and a hard worker, Jay thinks he has a chance for the varsity team, but the coach passes him by for a sophomore, since he prefers to be seen as building a young team rather than possibly failing with experienced players. Unable to drop basketball, Jay plays now and then at the YMCA, but when he learns that Alan Murray, a boy who was cut from the high school team at the same time as Jay, is heading a team for Sturbridge Methodist in a church league, he joins up, even though he has not been near a church since nursery school and being on the team means attending service and taking part in the youth group. His shunning of both liquor and drugs has nothing to do with religion or even his working underage in a bar, but, instead, a lot to do with his perception of the failure of both his parents. Chief among the girls in Jay's life is Spit (Sarita) whose band, Elyit, plays in Shorty's bar frequently. Although he knows she drinks too much, uses drugs, and sleeps around, he really admires her spirit, her creativity, and her quirky humor, and he knows she likes him. Another is Julie, a tennis player at Scranton University, who comes into the kitchen to ice her elbow one night and returns now and then to make out with him in the alley behind the bar. There are also Dana, who plays sometimes at the YMCA, but whose ambition is focused on high jumping, for which she has been awarded a scholarship for the next year; Beth, who plays with him for Sturbridge Methodist, but is interested in a player from one of the Catholic teams; and Brenda, a waitress from the diner across the street from Shorty's. Except for Dana and Beth, they have all shared Jay's bed occasionally, but while the sex attracts him, it does not drive away his essential loneliness. In the church league, Methodist is doing well until Brian Kaipo, a really good player, quits the high school team in disgust at the coach and joins the St. Joseph Bishops. In the end the tournament comes down to these two teams, and to the surprise of everyone, including themselves, Methodist wins. Jay, feeling more confident than he did before, has arranged a real date with Julie and had a talk with Spit, in which they agree that sex is not a good idea for them and they will do better to be good friends. He has also picked up an application for Weston Community College, where Brian, whom he really likes despite their rivalry, plans to go the next year. Essentially, the novel is a story of Jay's finding himself through basketball, despite his dysfunctional family and the general neglect of Shorty, who is supposedly his guardian. Basketball, both pickup games and tournament finals, are described in detail with an intensity that gives even a nonsports fan insight into Jay's fascination and helps to reveal his independent personality and solid character. ALA/YA.

PLUMMER, LOUISE   Author of novels for young adults, sensitive and well received. *A Dance for Three** (Delacorte, 2000), is a story of teenage pregnancy and mental illness, set in Salt Lake City, Utah. For earlier biographical information and title entries, see *Dictionary, 1990–1994* [*My Name is Sus5an Smith. The 5 is Silent*] and *Dictionary, 1995–1999* [*The Unlikely Romance of Kate Bjorkman*].

PLUM-UCCI, CAROL   From Brigantine Island, just north of Atlantic City, New Jersey; journalist, writer. She is a graduate of Purdue University and has received numerous awards and citations, including the Kneale Award in Journalistic Excellence in Feature Writing. For fifteen years she was a staff writer for the Miss America Organization in Atlantic City. Her first novel, *The Body of Christopher Creed** (Harcourt, 2000), is an open-ended mystery concerning the disappearance of an unlikable high school boy who may be a suicide victim or perhaps chose a method to escape his unhappy home for more promising prospects elsewhere. Plum-Ucci makes her home in Ocean City, New Jersey.

THE POISONWOOD BIBLE: A NOVEL
(Kingsolver*, Barbara, HarperCollins, 1998)   Long, compelling, detailed novel published for adults of a missionary family from Bethlehem, Georgia, who go to a Congo village in 1959, and of their lives for more than three decades thereafter. Evangelical Baptist Minister Nathan Price, arrogant and zealous, takes his wife and four daughters to the village of Kilanga on the Kwilu River, certain that he will bring the word of God to the heathen and win their unquestioning gratitude. The family is totally unprepared for what they find. Almost nothing they bring with them is suitable, and Nathan is unwilling to listen to advice. Since he knows no French or any of the local languages and there are no other whites in Kilanga, it takes a long time for him to learn that the villagers are unwilling to be baptized in the river, because a crocodile there ate a child recently. His other misunderstandings are equally disastrous. When he learns a few words of Congolese, he ends each sermon with a loud cry of "Tata Jesus is *bangala!*" not realizing that the word means something precious and dear as he thinks but also, with the slightly different pronunciation he uses, the poisonwood tree. The schoolteacher, Anatole Ngemba, the only educated villager, trans-

lates his sermons as he speaks and sometimes tries to warn him about mishaps ahead, but Nathan charges on blindly, contemptuous not only of the Africans but also of his own wife and daughters. The novel is divided into seven books, most of which start with the recollections of his wife, Orleanna*, years later when she lives on Sanderling Island, Georgia. The rest is narrated in turn by his four daughters, Rachel*, almost sixteen when they arrive in Kilanga, the twins, Leah* and Adah*, 14 1/2, and Ruth* May, 5. All the girls fear their father, with good reason, since he is quick to punish them with a strap or "The Verse," which they dread even more: a requirement that they write out one hundred Bible verses, starting where he indicates and ending, always, on a verse that condemns whatever sin he has observed in them. Although at first Leah tries desperately to please him, even she becomes disillusioned and is the first to openly defy him. During their two years in Kilanga, the Prices, and usually the whole village, suffer a series of misfortunes: flood, drought, famine, even an army of ants that drives all the people into the river and eats everything in the village. For a while the Mission League sends them a very small stipend, but as the political situation changes, that also is cut off. Nathan alienates the village headman, Tata Nda, and wins the enmity of the priest of traditions, Tata Kuvudundu, bringing on their first true disaster. This "witch doctor," as Nathan calls him, leaves a green mamba snake in their chicken house, and it kills Ruth May. Orleanna, without a word to any of them, carries out everything they own, piling it in front of the house for the villagers to take, and starts walking in the sudden rain on the almost impassable road toward Leopoldville. Dismayed, but unwilling to be left behind, the three girls follow her. They never see their father again. The last quarter of the novel tells what happened to each family member in the next thirty years. In some ways this is a letdown, since the dramatic action is all in the earlier parts, but the novel is really about Africa and the insults it has suffered not only from Christianity but also from the greed, politics, and misunderstandings of Portugal, Belgium, the United States, and even Cuba. The Price family members all suffer lasting harm from their experience, but the four living women all manage to transcend their trauma and reconstruct their lives, damaged but undefeated. Booklist.

PORTER, CONNIE (ROSE) (1959–   ) African American writer born in New York City; raised with seven siblings near Buffalo, New York, the setting of her second adult novel, *Imani All Mine* (Houghton Mifflin, 1999), which was selected for the Alex list, by *Booklist*, and by the American Library Association for young adults. It concerns an inner-city, single-parent girl who struggles to raise her baby girl. Porter's first novel, also for adults, *All-Bright Court* (Houghton Mifflin, 1991), is about southern blacks who move North in search of better lives. Between these two books she wrote a series of historical novels in the American Girls series. She attended Louisana State University and taught English and creative writing at Emerson College in Boston, Massachusetts, and Southern Illinois University–Carbondale. She has made her home in Virginia.

PORTER, TRACEY   Teacher, poet, writer. She is a graduate of Georgetown University and the University of London, and has published poems in various magazines and anthologies. Her first novel, intended for middle school youngsters like those she teaches English to in Santa Monica, California, is *Treasures in the Dust** (HarperCollins/Joanna Cotler, 1997), concerning how the lives of two young Oklahoma girls are changed by the drought of the Dust Bowl of the 1930s and how their friendship persists. She has since written *A Dance of Sisters* (Joanna Cotler, 2002), about two sisters in ballet school after the death of their mother. Porter lives in Los Angeles.

POURNELLE, JERRY (EUGENE) (1933–)   Born in Shreveport, Louisiana; attended the University of Iowa and received his B.S., M.S., and Ph.D. from the University of Washington; has lived in Studio City, California; is considered a leading writer of science fiction; and was nominated for the Hugo Award and Nebula Award. Among other positions, he has been an aviation psychologist and systems engineer for Boeing Corporation; a systems scientist for North American Aviation; a professor of history and political science at Pepperdine University; and, from 1969, a freelance writer, lecturer, and consultant. Individually and with other writers, chiefly Larry Nivens, he has published for adults more than thirty books of science fiction, edited twenty more, mainly with John F. Carr, and written several nonfiction books on such topics as computers, nuclear survival, and the space age. He published his first novel in 1972, *A Spaceship for the King* (DAW), about a planet's attempts to join a galactic empire. He collaborated with Charles Sheffield* in initiating the Jupiter series with *Higher Education** (Tor, 1996), a boy's growing-up and adventure novel set against the background of a mining operation in

space, which was chosen by *Booklist* for young adults.

POWELL, RANDY (1956–)   Born in Seattle, Washington; teacher in an alternative school for junior high and high school dropouts from 1984 to 1988, technical writer for Boeing Corporation, and writer since 1988. He is a graduate of the University of Washington, with an M.A. in 1984. The protagonists of all his novels are caught at fragile moments when they are trying to decide on their life's direction; all are open ended, dealing with neglect and rejection. His *Tribute to Another Dead Rock Star** (Farrar, 1999) is about a teenager trying to decide whether to spend a year in Europe, which means abandoning his retarded half brother, or stay with the boy's father and rigid Christian stepmother, with whom he feuds continually. Among his other novels are *The Whistling Toilets* (Farrar, 1996), *Dean Duffy* (Farrar, 1995), and *Is Kissing a Girl Who Smokes Like Licking an Ashtray?* (Farrar, 1992). All Powell's books deal with sports, but not as their major focus.

POWER (Hogan*, Linda, Norton, 1998) Adult contemporary realistic novel set among Native American Taiga Indians in the Kili Swamp region of southern Florida, a little inland from the Gulf of Mexico. The narrator, Omishto, 16, is one of only thirty of the Taiga Panther Clan remaining. She is a small, thin, intelligent, quiet girl, and as her name indicates, watchful. She enjoys the company of Ama Eaton, a sort of cousin of her mother and a recluse who lives back from the highway in a faded blue tumbledown shack. Omishto sees a sharp contrast between her mother's Christian beliefs and liking for modern ways and the old beliefs and nature ways of Ama. She also feels safe with Ama, since her mother's current husband threatens her both physically and sexually. The plot starts after a tremendous and excitingly described hurricane sweeps the area, taking down even the huge centuries-old tree called "Methuselah." Ama dreams of a golden panther, the animal which was, according to Taiga belief, the first being in the world and the ancestor of the Taiga. Ama gathers supplies to search for a deer wounded in the storm and takes Omishto with her. Omishto soon realizes that Ama is really hunting a panther; the deer is just the bait she knows the cat will follow. She finds it, the cat kills the deer, and then Ama shoots the cat, a grayish, ragged creature. As she does so, Omishto tells Ama that she has really killed herself. Both know that the shooting will be reported, because Florida panthers are on the endangered list. The sheriff, his deputy, and a wildlife man arrive and take Ama away, even though they cannot find the panther's carcass or the rifle. Environmental protesters are loudly active at Ama's trial, and some clan elders speak, but Ama is acquitted because the evidence is inconclusive. Ama takes Omishto with her when she goes to the old people, as the traditional Taiga are called, to face a traditional trial because she did not take the slain panther to the clan according to clan law. When Omishto is questioned, she does not tell about the sorry condition of the panther, realizing that a parallel exists between the animal and the tribe. Ama is banished for four years, and Omishto runs away from home. She moves into Ama's empty house. Annie Hide, the healer and peacemaker of the clan, tells her that the old ones were wrong about Ama. She learns that Janie Soto, another old one, had surreptitiously taken the panther's carcass and thus helped to acquit Ama in the white court. Ama's shooting the panther was a kind of sacrifice for the life of the tribe, and a kind of redemption for herself. Omishto calls her sister, Donna, to come with a truck to pick up Ama's chickens and goats and leaves to join the old ones above Kili Swamp. She will learn to be a leader among them as independent, stubborn Ama had refused to be. Although they sometimes impede the plot, which is not strong, Omishto's musings about beliefs and her memories of the old tales contribute a mystical flavor and texture. The novel excels in its depiction of physical place and of the traditional ways and beliefs, which are almost blatantly contrasted with those of the whites. Omishto sees the terrible irony between the whites' destruction of the land and pollution of the waters through building, farming, and sugarcane growing, crimes, as she sees them, that go unpunished, while Ama's slaying the panther, according to white law, demands punishment. Some scenes are very vivid: the courtroom activities, Ama's trial before the old ones, and, especially, the hurricane's power and destruction, which foreshadows the turbulent events to come. The style is poetic, lyrical, and highly visual. Booklist.

THE PRINCESS DIARIES (Cabot*, Meg, HarperCollins, 2000)   Present-day romantic comedy set for about three weeks in Greenwich Village, New York City. Mia Thermopolis, 14, writes copiously in her diary about problems mostly typical for her years. She bemoans being five-feet-nine-inches tall and flat chested; having "triangular" hair; and not being able to get the attention of handsome, super-smart senior, Josh Richter. She especially deplores her single-parent, painter mother Helen's dating Mia's algebra teacher at Alfred Einstein High School, Mr. G [sic] (Gianini), whose class she is flunking. She also frets about being put down by snotty Lana Weinberger, who is going with Josh, and being bossed and psychoanalyzed by her best friend, Lilly* Muscovitz, whose father and mother are psychoanalysts. One problem is on the way to being solved when Lilly's brother, Michael, a senior and truly nice, offers to tutor her in math. A really big problem arises when her father, Phillipe Renaldo, informs her that he is the ruling prince of Genovia, a country of fifty thousand people nestled between France and Italy, and that she is his heir, Amelia Mignonette Grimaldi Thermopolis Renaldo, and will henceforth live in Genovia. Mia is terribly upset, refuses to entertain the idea of leaving New York, and carries on until a compromise is reached: she will finish high school at Albert Einstein. Also upsetting is the news that her father's mother, imperious Grandmère*, is to give her "princess lessons," training in how to behave as royalty. When Grandmère has her "redone" to fit Grandmère's idea of how a princess should look, Mia, who has informed no one about her new status, suddenly becomes assertive and tells Lilly off when Lilly remarks that she looks like snippy, too-fashionable Lana. Mia's circle widens when she becomes friends with shunned Tina Hakim Baba, an overweight Arab girl, daughter of a sheikh. When Mia's picture appears on the front page of the *New York Post*, she suddenly becomes very popular; even Lana wants to be friends. When reporters hound her, she tells her father she wants to quit being a princess. He tells her she cannot, that she cannot stop being what she is. Then to Mia's delight, Josh drops Lana and invites her to the Cultural Diversity Dance. The dream bubble bursts when he drinks too much at the predance dinner, she discovers that he has informed the media that she will be at the dance, and, to top matters off, he kisses her as they enter the school in front of all the cameras. Embarrassed and angry, she tells him off, too. Things turn out all right, however, because Michael, who has no date, spends the evening with her. She stays the night with the Muscovitzes, all animosities aside, and has a grand time. Mia's whininess and teenaged egocentrism are relieved by the abundant humor, which comes from situations as well as from the central irony: Mia wants to escape what is almost every girl's fairytale dream—to be a real-life princess. The diaries are too detailed to be believable as such, but the author excels in creating the teen scene, freaky friends, backbiting, gossip, talk of boys that are "hot" and those that aren't, and the like. Mia is idealistic, responsible, loving, loyal—she has many fine qualities. Her voice is bubbly and filled with such expressions as "like," "sucky," and "jerky." Much of the book's appeal to young readers lies in its real-seeming picture of teen life and its predictability. ALA/YA.

PROFESSOR HAWTHORNE (*My Father's Scar: A Novel**)   Highly popular and flamboyant university professor of literature whose class Andy Logan has been allowed to enter because he is a gifted student. He conducts his class with dramatic flair and scorn for the students, whose names he never bothers to learn. Andy comes to his attention when he supplies a definition of culpability for a girl whom the professor is hectoring and is able to quote lines to show he gets the reference when Hawthorne sneeringly calls him Lochinvar. Still, Andy is dazzled when Hawthorne invites him to Thanksgiving dinner and cannot understand the professor's graduate assistant, Sashcha Stevenson, who advises him to refuse. At Hawthorne's lavish house, he shows off for Andy and plies him with wine, but when the boy interprets it as a gay invitation, he is incensed and throws him out with threats of reprisals. Stevenson later explains to Andy that Hawthorne is a monster who lives for adulation and sucks up approval greedily but wants to give nothing back. He also points out that Andy will not be expelled but will get an A plus, since the last thing Professor Hawthorne wants is to have any sort of scandal mar his shining career.

Q

QUALEY, MARSHA (RICHARDSON)
(1953–)   Born in Austin, Minnesota;
writer of novels set in the upper Midwest.
Her mystery, *Close to a Killer** (Delacorte,
1999), a novel of a beauty salon owned
and staffed by women who learned the
trade in prison, was named to the New
York Public Library list of outstanding
books of the year for young adults. Along
with her earlier mystery, *Thin Ice** (Delacorte, 1997), it was also added to the
American Library Association Young
Adult list. For earlier biographical information and title entries, see *Dictionary,
1900–1994* [*Revolutions of the Heart*] and
Dictionary, 1995–1999 [*Come in from the
Cold*; *Thin Ice*].

QUARLES, HEATHER   Author of *A
Door Near Here** (Delacorte, 1998), a
novel of a dysfunctional family in which
the divorced father has remarried and
sends money for an Episcopal church
school (which they loathe) for his three
children, but will have nothing to do with
their much younger half sister, whose paternity is unknown. Determined to keep

their mother's alcoholism secret so authorities will not send the child to foster
parents, the three teenagers make one
mistake after another but remain devoted
to the little girl.

***THE QUEEN'S MAN: A MEDIEVAL
MYSTERY*** (Penman*, Sharon Kay, Holt,
1996)   Historical mystery set in England in the late twelfth century, when
Richard the Lion Hearted has disappeared while returning from a crusade
and his mother, Queen Eleanor, juggles
the intrigues of those who are dedicated
to his kingship and of the faction hoping
to wrest it away for his brother, John.
Young Justin, having recently learned of
his parentage and confronted his father,
the bishop of Chester, only to be rejected,
is riding near Winchester, thinking of trying to become a scribe in London, since
his father did see that he was educated,
when he interrupts an attack on a goldsmith, Gervase Fitz Randolph, by two
men. Before the man dies, he entrusts to
Justin a letter that he says must get to the
queen. Only because one of Eleanor's

ladies, Claudine de Loudun, finds him attractive, Justin is able to get an audience with the queen. The letter is a copy of one from the emperor of the Holy Roman Empire to Philip, king of France, both enemies of Richard, telling of his capture and imprisonment in Austria. Eleanor, impressed by his candor and good sense, enlists Justin in her service to find the killers of Fitz Randolph, since that may tell her how much Philip, and also her son John, are involved. Back in Winchester, Justin calls at the Fitz Randolph home and soon discovers that several there have motives for the slaying. The goldsmith's son, Thomas, wants to join the Benedictine order, a move his father had vehemently opposed. Jonet, his daughter, wants to wed Miles, a journeyman in his shop, although her father was set to find her a highborn husband. His brother, Guy, who acted as his business manager, has come up short in the accounts. The undersheriff, Luke de Marston, is in love with Fitz Randolph's mistress, Aldith Talbot. When he returns to London to tell the queen that he sees no way to solve the crime, she sends him off again, saying that he is the only one who saw the murderers, and she needs to know whether they were in the pay of the French king. In the rest of the story, a host of colorful characters aid or hinder Justin as he makes various discoveries and suffers attacks, with court intrigue and street brutality multiplying the complexities of the situation. It is soon apparent that the actual killer was a cutthroat known as Gilbert the Fleming, but apprehending him is difficult. With the help of a young woman named Nell, who manages the alehouse where Justin finds a room, Luke, Justin, and a police sergeant named Jonas finally are able to trap him. In the denouement, it is revealed that the goldsmith's slaying was a mistake. Gilbert and his giant henchman, Samson, were paid to kill another man. Justin reports this to Eleanor, who is relieved that her son John was not involved. She offers Justin a permanent position in her service. Although in an author's note Penman says that the goldsmith and his murder are fictional, as are Justin and his father, the copy of the letter from the Holy Roman emperor to the French king and Eleanor's obtaining a copy of it is historical, as are many of the minor characters and incidents. The characterization of Eleanor, who had been queen of both France and England and was a power in European politics even in her old age, is vivid. There is a wealth of action, not likely perhaps but plausible given the Machiavellian nature of the court in that era. ALA/YA

QUEEN'S OWN FOOL (Yolen*, Jane, and Robert Harris, Philomel, 2000)   Historical novel about Mary, queen of Scots, set in France and Scotland from 1559 to 1568. The narrator, Nicola Ambruzzi, 11, comes to Rheims as part of the Troupe Brufort, traveling entertainers led by her Uncle Armand, who has reluctantly taken her on after the death of her parents in Italy. Through sheer chance, they are summoned to the palace of the cardinal of Lorraine, where the king and queen are guests, because the old king has just died and the young queen wants at least a little gaiety to celebrate the ascension to the throne of her husband, now King Francis. Used only to rough street audiences, Troupe Brufort makes little impression on the nobles until Nicola slips on the slick floor and somersaults under a table, crawls to the end, and reappears as if it is part of the act. Her frank explanation amuses the queen and king, but so infuriates her uncle that as soon as they are out of the big hall he beats her with his cane, and she runs down the corridor to escape, finally coming out into a small garden. There Queen Mary finds her and recognizes something of her own childhood spirit in Nicola, such a refreshing change from the courtiers that she literally buys the girl from Uncle Armand to be her fool, or jester, to entertain with witty remarks but mostly to tell her the truth and to "remind her that she is mortal." In the weeks that follow, Nicola meets the four Marys, young Scottish women who were brought to France to be companions to the young queen but have been kept for years away from her in a convent; the cardinal and Duke de Guise, the queen's uncles; Madam Jacqueline, the stern governess who teaches her, with much use of her stick, court protocol and how to read; and many other figures from history. When King Francis, who has never been well, dies, the dowager Queen Catherine declares herself regent, demands that Queen Mary return her jewels to the royal treasury and strips her of any power in France. Although her uncles want to marry her posthaste to someone with power on the Continent, she decides to go to Scotland, where she has been queen since she was an infant. During the next eight years, Nicola stays with Queen Mary through her marriage to Henry Lord Darnley, a handsome but weak and dissolute man; is actually present at his death, which is engineered by the earl of Bothwell; is witness to the disasters of Mary's marriage to Bothwell; and accompanies her to her imprisonment at Lochleven, the grim Douglas castle on a tiny island in the lake. During this period her one real friend is Davie Riccio, a crippled Italian minstrel who gains great power in the country and is murdered. Later, Nicola's affections turn to Davie's brother, Joseph, a less-skilled musician but also steadier and not so ambitious. Having aided Mary's escape from Lochleven, Nicola accompanies her on a fruitless quest to arouse her followers, and finally leaves, at the queen's request, for France with Joseph, while the queen heads for England to throw herself on the mercy of Elizabeth I, her cousin. Throughout, the queen is shown to be beautiful, kind, and beset by self-serving advisers who treat her alternately as a frivolous child or a wicked schemer. Her story is dramatic enough to hold a reader's attention, and the point of view of the fool adds fresh interest. Many historical personages play roles in the novel, including La Renaudie, the Huguenot, and John Knox, the wintry-souled Protestant leader. The queen's fool, La Jariniere, a pet name for Nicola, was a real person, but little is recorded about her. It is known that she got back to France when Mary went to England, but the "house filled with the laughter of children" and the school for jesters she starts with Joseph are fictional additions. ALA/YA.

QUIÑONEZ, ERNESTO (1966–) Born in Ecuador; attended City College of New York, where he studied creative writing; teacher of bilingual fourth graders in the New York City public schools; writer. His first novel, *Bodega Dreams** (Vintage, 2000), which was named to the New York Public Library list for teens, seems strongly autobiographical. It is an intense and descriptive story of life for young Latinos in Spanish Harlem in the mid-1980s.

R

RABBI JUDAH HIRSCH (*Snow in August**)   The rabbi who serves the rundown synagogue near the home of Michael Devlin, the protagonist. Some of the book's best scenes are those in which the rabbi teaches Michael Yiddish and Michael gives the rabbi lessons in English and baseball. The rabbi's wife, Leah, died in a Nazi camp in Poland, and he himself just managed to survive, walking from Prague to Greece, where he took a ship to the Dominican Republic. He is experiencing a crisis of faith, and when Kate* Devlin, Michael's mother, asks him if he believes in God, he replies that he believes in sin and evil. He tells Michael the legend of the Golem*, a tale so powerfully imaginative and similar to Michael's dreams of Captain Marvel–type heroics that the boy seizes on it to confront the evil of Frankie McCarthy and the Falcons gang. The rabbi sometimes seems very old, much beyond his age, which is thirty-nine, and at other times not much older than Michael.

RACHEL (*Archangel**)   Twenty-five, slave of wealthy Lord Jethro in Semorrah since the nomadic Edori group who adopted her as a child were attacked by Jansai five years earlier and she was sold into slavery. Originally, she was the daughter of a hill farmer, but their village was destroyed when she was a young child, and she was lost and starving when the Edori found her. She had a lover among them, Simon, who was captured in the same raid she was. When she learns from the oracle, Josiah, that Simon has been dead for two years, she is distraught, not because of his death but because he was a suffering slave for three years. Although Rachel dislikes the angels and is angry much of the time, she is kind to servants and the poor, and even to Leah, the repressed wife of Raphael*. She distrusts her own love for Gabriel*, since she has lost everything she cared about and fears to make herself vulnerable again. Her "height-sickness" makes her physically ill, but when she thinks the only way to save Gabriel and Samaria is by her suicide, she boldly steps off the cliff at Windy Point, where she is a captive. Throughout her stay at the Eyrie*, she has never sung in public, and there is considerable apprehension among the angels that she may not have the voice essential for the Gloria, but she chooses Hagar's Mass, the most difficult, and performs perfectly. In the end, she finds Hagar's cabin in the Corinni Mountains, which has not been used for many generations, and settles herself there where no angel can fly, knowing that Gabriel will come and trudge up the long path to find her. Her pride, which was all she had during her years as a slave, is one reason Gabriel admires her, and his pride eventually bows before hers.

RACHEL PRICE (*The Poisonwood Bible: A Novel**)   Eldest and prettiest of the four daughters of Nathan, the evangelical preacher who takes his family to Africa to run a mission. Very blond, with striking blue eyes and long, almost white hair, Rachel is vain and shallow and not nearly as intelligent as her younger sisters, and she resents their being considered gifted. In some ways, Congolese village life is hardest on her, because she longs for American teenage life, for nice clothes, Cokes, and movies, and never makes any friends in Kilanga. When the chief, Tata Nda, suddenly decides to make her one of his numerous wives, she is horrified and falls in with her mother's plan to pretend she is engaged to the pilot, Eeben Axelroot, who flies in occasional supplies and whom her sisters have discovered is a diamond smuggler and engaged in the plot to murder Patrice Lumumba, the only elected president of free Congo. After the terrible journey from Kilanga, she throws herself at him, although she knows he is a despicable man, and is soon his mistress, pretending to be his wife in Johannesburg, South Africa. Later she throws him over for an attaché in the foreign service, whom she eventually dumps for an older man who dies, leaving her the Equatorial Hotel. This she runs as a luxurious stopping point from Brazzaville in French Congo for white adventurers of all sorts going to other parts of Africa. She never gets over her fear and contempt for the black African. Her conversation is full of malapropisms: "like a putative from the law," "Thyroid Mary," "the transition to wifehood and adulteration." Although she never developed an understanding or love of Africa and longed to get back to the Georgia of her early teen years, she knows she would never fit in and concentrates on having fun and making money.

RADIX (*The Good Children**)   William Radix the Third, son of a wealthy and powerful lawyer in Philadelphia. His father was past fifty when his only son was born and decided then that the boy would become a lawyer. Precocious, Radix finished prep school early, and his mother, afraid he would be corrupted by college at that age, took him to Europe, where he fell in love with music and especially art. After law school, he persuades his father that he needs to be on his own for a while, before going into the family firm. His father arranges with Mr. Martens to take him into his firm for five years, but even before that time, his father's illness calls him home to Philadelphia. He admits that he has never been camping before knowing the McNairs, and Liz realizes that he has had a lonely life and is greatly attracted to their family feeling. His family's money is tied up with his being part of the firm, so he cannot help Kevin directly with financing his computer program, but he introduces him to some friends who do. When Liz is still in high school, he realizes that she is a talented violinist and arranges for her and soon Brian, also, to have lessons from Mr. Kimmelman. Radix at first seems attracted to Amy, but is always amused by Liz, who as a skinny eleven-year-old challenges him when he shows up in running shorts and asks whether this is "billable time." His description of the Alhambra inspires Liz's story, which a teacher sends in and which wins third prize in a contest. Liz is disgusted to realize that she copied, but Radix insists that it is quite different, a transformation, and he tries to persuade her she should be a writer. He complains that she is awfully bossy, but by the time she enlists his help to rescue Brian from the mental hospital, it is clear that he is committed to her, even at risk of breaking the law. When his father dies, it is probable that he will return to Oregon, giving up his family wealth that will go to a foundation if he is not in the firm.

RAE JEAN WILSON (*Kinship**) Mother of Pert and Jimmy Wilson. A single parent, she enjoys life for the most part in Happy Trails trailer park in Kinship, Georgia, although times for the Wilsons are very hard. She has taken classes to become a veterinarian's assistant and runs the trailer park in which the Wilsons stay, in return for living rent free in their small trailer. She is a pretty, pink-skinned blond, a lover of iced tea, and a devout Roman Catholic. Every Sunday, she and her mother, Gram Wilma Winder, hire a taxi to take the family to Troy to worship at the Roman Catholic Church there, because the Wilsons are the only practicing Catholics in Kinship. She can be diplomatic, as when she persuades the home economics teacher that Pert really does know the four food groups; resourceful, as when she engineers an engagement party for Jimmy and his girl; and stubborn, as when she refuses to leave with James* William.

RAILBORN SKINNER (*Downsiders**) Boy of fourteen who lives in Downside and is a companion of Talon* Angler and Gutta in learning adult ways. He is the son of a hunter, and, hence, has the surname Skinner, and is much more traditional in his thinking than the rebellious, adventurous Talon. An ambitious boy, he sees an opportunity to elevate himself by denouncing Talon to Downside authorities for bringing Lindsay Matthias, a Topsider, into Downside. The reader loses all sympathy for him at this point, but later he redeems himself when he takes Gutta, injured seriously in the great explosion, to the hospital. In doing so, he knows he can never return, except as a faller, to Downside.

RANDLE, KRISTEN D(OWNEY) (1952–) Born in Kansas City, Missouri; educated at Brigham Young University (B.A.); taught at Brigham Young University and at high schools in Utah; held various positions in the music industry. The author of several novels for young adults, she was highly praised by critics for *The Only Alien on the Planet* (Scholastic, 1995), in which two young people attempt to help an emotionally disturbed teenager. *Breaking Rank** (Morrow, 1999), recommended by the American Library Association for young adults, concerns a teenage boy and girl who dare to defy the dictates of their social peers. Randle lives in Utah with her husband and four children. She and her husband manage a recording studio.

RAPHAEL (*Archangel**) Corrupt archangel who has lost faith in Jovah and who wants to continue in his position of wealth and power when his twenty-year term is up. During this time he has brought many destructive policies to

Samaria, favoring the wealthy, encouraging slavery, and indulging in drugs and licentious behavior. His appearance is striking, all black and gold, and he has a gorgeous singing voice, though not as good as that of Gabriel*. He admits to Rachel* that he did away with the woman designated by Jovah to be his angelica, substituting an angel-seeker, one of the women who want to have children by an angel in the hope thereby to gain entry to an angel hold. Because he knows she is the angelica-designate for Gabriel, he has three times tried to destroy Rachel, the first by attacking her village when she was a young child, again when she was about twenty by encouraging slave-raiders to attack her Edori band, and, finally, by kidnapping her and imprisoning her in a tower at Windy Point, his hold. At the great gathering for the Gloria, he has led his heretic followers to Mount Galo, where he defies Jovah to strike them, as has been predicted if the Gloria is delayed. Not only are all of them destroyed, but so are his wife, Leah, and all the others at Windy Point.

RATS SAW GOD (Thomas*, Rob, Simon & Schuster, 1996)   Realistic psychological- and personal-problem and boy's growing-up novel set in San Diego, California, in recent years. High school senior and narrator Steve York is caught in school high on drugs and sent to the counselor, who orders him to produce one hundred typewritten pages of any literary form to satisfy graduation requirements. Steve writes about his life in Houston, Texas, beginning with his parents' divorce; his life in school, especially with iconoclastic Doug Chappell who organizes the Grace Order of Dadaists, or GOD, a group of iconoclasts; his love for Dub Varner; and his move to San Diego to live with

his mother. The novel is a late-twentieth-century slice of home and school life, occasionally sexually explicit, sometimes funny, often poignant, and always engaging. Earlier the book was cited by *School Library Journal*. For a longer entry, see *Dictionary, 1995–1999*. ALA/YA.

THE REAPPEARANCE OF SAM WEBBER (Fuqua*, Jonathan Scott, Bancroft, 1998)   Boy's growing-up novel set in Baltimore, Maryland, about the time of publication, following one troubled year after the disappearance of his father. At first, when Sam Webber's father, known as Big Sam, vanishes, his son, the narrator known as "Little Sam," 11, is sure he has been kidnapped, although his old car is found at Dulles Airport in Washington, D.C. It soon becomes clear to the reader, as it must be to Sam's mother, Maxine, that Big Sam has deliberately deserted his wife and son, and eventually Sam (who has now dropped the "Little") realizes this must be so, but not before he suffers a number of traumatic experiences. When their savings run out, he and his mother are helped to move from upscale Roger's Forge neighborhood to a ramshackle apartment in Charles Village by Ditch* and Junie Gordon, owners of the flower shop where Maxine works. Sam starts at Robert Poole Middle School in the Hampden neighborhood, where everything is threatening. One of Sam's biggest troubles is that his father, a large, confident man, was convinced that his son could not cope in an ordinary neighborhood, and he tried to buffer Sam from the world around him, picking him up each day from school and continually warning him that he is not tough enough to survive among other boys. At first this seems to be true. At Robert Poole, Sam is targeted by big, fat Newt Novacek, a bully who attacks him in the rest room and ambushes him on his way home. The African American janitor at the school, Greely* Clemons, intervenes and soon becomes Sam's friend and protector, so important to Sam that he insists on inviting him to Christmas dinner at the Gordons' house, although both Maxine and Junie have some qualms about how Ditch might treat him. To Sam's dismay, his mother starts to go out with Howard Ivanesavich, the man who delivers clay pots to the flower shop. Gradually, Howard builds a relationship with Sam, mostly based on their mutual love of certain comic books, but after a while Maxine decides that Howard is not for her, and he recedes from being a boyfriend to just a friend of the family. Over the winter, Sam, who works part time at the flower shop, begins to see the charm of this neighborhood and feel more confident. When Newt Novacek waylays him and starts a fight, Sam rams his head into the bully's stomach and, to his own surprise, wins the fight. In the winter and spring, Sam has three disillusioning experiences. He and his mother are mugged on the way home one evening, and though he faints briefly, he gets a good look at the mugger and is able to give a detailed description to the police that helps them catch the man. On his birthday, he overhears Maxine and Junie discussing whether Big Sam is in Florida, as they think likely, a conversation that makes Sam face up to his father's disappearance being desertion. Greely, who often eats at the Little Tavern in Charles Village while Sam has a Coke, decides the boy should get some athletic skills and starts to throw a football with him in the park. When he collapses from a heart attack, Sam runs for help, thinking the old man has been shot. In the hospital, Greely insists on confessing to the boy that years

ago he deserted his wife and children, a guilt-ridden memory that has made him especially interested in helping Sam. The revelation temporarily shatters Sam's devotion to the old man, but he begins to see that like his father, Greely was both bad and good, and that he can forgive both of them. This "reappearance" of the real Sam Webber is a healing event for young Sam, the realization that his father, whom he idolized, had been a bully and a thug, was probably manic-depressive or at least somewhat bipolar, and, though truly loving, was unable to face reality. In the end, an older Cuban man whom Sam has met in the next block and questioned, naively, about his colostomy bag, dies and leaves Sam his dog, Pepe, and enough money to buy food for it. Young Sam grows up in the year to appreciate his new neighborhood, where people were so good to them after the mugging, and his new "family" of people who really care for each other. Sam is drawn as a sensitive, artistic boy, and the year described by him in a believable voice is one of both fear and beauty, with sensory images and telling detail. Alex; Booklist.

REBEL: A TIBETAN ODYSSEY (Whitesel*, Cheryl Aylward, HarperCollins, 2000)   Historical novel set in Tibet in the very early days of the twentieth century. In his traditional village of Chu Lungba, Thunder, 14, whose real name is Dorje, lives with his parents, his brother, Joker, 7, his sister, Dolma, the infant Razim, and his Second Aku (or uncle), Tendruk. Although strong, obedient, and a hard worker, Thunder is criticized for questioning the way things are done and asking for reasons, and hushed severely when he says he would like to see the world outside Tibet. Caught in a storm while he straggles behind his uncle and brother to watch some traders, Thunder is nearly killed. He is rescued and treated by a fringle, a Caucasian foreigner, who even gives him a small vial of medicine to soothe his burning throat. When he returns home and this story is forced out of him, his parents are shocked and the whole village turns against him for having concourse with a fringle. To save him from possible physical assault, his father sends him off with Aku Tendrun to Tharpa Dok, the gompa or monastery where First Aku Gyalo is an important monk. When they arrive after a several days' journey, Gyalo is not there, having led a search for the new tulku, or reincarnation of the founder of the monastery, the ninth tulku having died several years before. Tendrun tells him to go, as Zangpo, the servant boy at Gyalo's house insists, to the gompa kitchen until First Aku returns. Tendrun admits that he aroused the villagers and persuaded his brother to send Thunder away so that the boy would not be able to inherit the land that Second Aku wants for himself. For several months, Thunder works as the lowliest of the kitchen boys, who are the most despised group at the gompa. Several times he befriends Seventh Hand, a crippled boy largely ostracized by the group. All the kitchen boys, especially Seventh Hand, fear Pounder, captain of the dub dubs, or gompa soldiers, a bully who brutalized him and damaged his legs. After many weeks, Gyalo, having returned from his search, comes to the kitchen, claims Thunder, and has him formally admitted to the gompa as his student. Although Gyalo is kind, life in his house is not easy because Zang-po resents Thunder's position and does all he can to harass and discredit him. He even shows Thunder a hidden box containing gul-gyan, necklaces that make up a woman's dowry and

are used to pay her funeral expenses, which he says Gyalo stole instead of turning in to the gompa. After the new tulku, a five-year-old, arrives, one of the senior monks tells Thunder to return a necklace of turquoise prayer beads that the child dropped. He is waylaid by Pounder, who tries to steal the beads and, when Thunder dodges, crashes through a balcony wall to the stone floor below. Although Thunder feels guilty about this, he is afraid to confess to his uncle. Because the new tulku, named Samjam*, is homesick, Thunder is chosen to be his companion. When Gyalo learns about Pounder, he is furious that Thunder has not told him and insists that his nephew must mentor the bully, now paralyzed, and try to change his heart. Thunder resents the "must" from one who stole the gul-gyan, and when Samjam begs him for an adventure outside the gompa, he impulsively agrees. With the help of Seventh Hand, he sneaks the little tulku out, and they have a glorious day. Resting, they see a group of foreigners, evidently a surveying party, attacked and wiped out by a group of mounted Tibetans. The three boys are captured by a foreign soldier and imprisoned, but the officer, who speaks a little Tibetan, understands their protest that they are monks and that it is the foreigners who are troublemakers, and he lets them go. They spend the night outside, huddled together for warmth, and the next day trudge back to the gompa. Thunder goes to Gyalo's house, tries to confess, and finds his uncle is so glad he is back and safe that he wants no explanations. Thunder shows him the necklace he stole from his uncle's hoard. Gyalo explains that he has collected the gul-gyan as insurance for Samjam, knowing that their way of life is threatened and that the valuable beads may ensure his escape. Admitting that he was wrong, he gives them all to Thunder to save for the little tulku or to give away, some of them, to Seventh Hand and possibly his sister, Dolma, and even Zang-po. Their understanding is interrupted by the arrival of Thunder's father, come to tell Gyalo that their brother, Tendruk, has been killed by an avalanche, and to take Thunder home again, the village having relented. Faced with the choice, Thunder realizes that he has changed too much to return, that his life has taken a different path and is now bound up in the gompa and his obligations there. An afterword briefly tells the history of Tibet in the twentieth century, and an author's note explains sources, gives an interesting-looking bibliography and a glossary of Tibetan terms. Thunder's realization at the end may come too abruptly, but his characterization is good and several of the minor figures are also well realized. The picture of Tibet during the period, both in the village and the gompa, is compelling. NYPL.

REEF OF DEATH (Zindel*, Paul, Harper-Collins, 1998) Hyperbolic, action-filled contemporary thriller set for a few days off Australia's Great Barrier Reef. At his home in San Francisco, PC McPhee, 17, called PC because he is addicted to computer games, receives a phone call from his adventurous Uncle Cliff, telling him to fly immediately to Cairns, Australia. Cliff says he needs PC's help in assisting an Aboriginal girl, Maruul, 16, in finding a sacred tribal treasure and determining what happened to her brother, Arnhem, 17. PC leaves immediately with only essentials and his cherished laptop, Ratboy. On his arrival, tall, tanned Cliff informs PC that Maruul and her brother were diving for the treasure when a huge fish, maybe a shark, attacked Arnhem.

The two had been chosen as arukas (seekers) by their Arnhem Land tribe to find the treasure. The tribe needs the treasure to buy food and hire lawyers to fight the politicians and business interests who are trying to appropriate their land. Uncle Cliff takes PC and Maruul out from Cape Tribulation in his thirty-six-foot tour boat, *Sea Quest*, to the Reef mooring platform. The next morning, they hear a high-pitched drilling sound that appears to emanate from a nearby Malaysian freighter, *Anemone*. The sound is like that Maruul heard earlier when her brother disappeared, but Cliff says drilling is not allowed in this area. As they explore the ledge, savage eels and a huge black monster fish attack. PC and Maruul get away, but Cliff is killed, his body disfigured and dismembered. Afraid to report Cliff's death to the Coast Guard lest PC be sent home, they decide to consult an old Aboriginal Maruul knows, Wally Wallygong, a lively, idea-filled man, who says sailors report that terrible experiments are being conducted on the *Anemone*. He says he'll help them, especially since a renegade shaman (holy man) from Maruul's tribe appears to be on the ship. The rest of the novel describes their valiant efforts to protect the treasure, which turns out to be a tall wall of opal, from being blasted away and extracted from the water by a German woman scientist, Dr. Ecenbarger, who runs the *Anemone*; to avoid becoming subjects for horrible experiments she conducts there, involving, among other matters, training fish to kill in response to the drilling sound; and to get at least some of the opal for Maruul's tribe. The three have frightening experiences on board ship and in the area pools, but they manage to get enough pieces of opal to help the tribe. PC uses Ratboy to download the ship's files for evidence of evildoing and later employs its batteries to foil the devious doctor, whose body is shredded to bits by the monster fish, and to blow up the ship. Sensationalized and melodramatic, the novel reads like a horror comic book without the illustrations. The plot overflows with fighting, torture, death, and violence. The outcome is predictable, but the way to the end is never dull, at least for those readers who like their thrills thick, heavy, and obvious. ALA/YA.

REVEREND RAYMOND BEELSON (*Armageddon Summer**)   Leader of the Believers, a millennialist sect convinced that the world will be destroyed by fire on July 27, 2000, except for the dozen-dozen faithful who will be saved at the top of Mount Weeupcut in western Massachusetts. A tall, charismatic man, Beelson has what an FBI report calls a "checkered past," but he is not pictured as a charlatan nor as a person in religion to make money, but as a man genuinely convinced of his revelation. When he finds Jed* Hoskins using a laptop computer on the mountain at night, he talks gently, persuading the boy of his sincerity if not the truth of his beliefs. Later, when Jed has broken his promise not to use the laptop, modern technology having been banned from the campground, and goes to confess and warn Beelson of the trouble brewing in the world outside, he briefly shows his fear and loneliness, then asks the boy to pray with him. The last person to arrive at the campground, the 144th, is Beelson's son who has not spoken to him in years. A nurse, the young man is instrumental in saving Marina Marlow's little brother, Leo, who has become ill in the uncongenial environment. He later tells Jed that he broke with his father to take care of his brother, who was dying of AIDS. In the end, Beelson dies in the fire consuming the camp hall, trying to quiet the crowd and bring order in the chaos.

REYNOLDS, MARJORIE (1944–) Born in Indiana; graduate with a journalism degree of Indiana University; has been regional advertising director of Ceneplex Odeon and an associate at a movie advertising agency. Her first novel, selected by the American Library Association for young adults, *The Starlite Drive-in** (Morrow, 1997), came out to high critical acclaim. Set in a small town in central Indiana, it is a taut murder-mystery and girl's growing-up story. Reynolds has also published *The Civil Wars of Jonah Moran: A Novel* (Morrow, 1999), in which a girl has mixed emotions when her brother is accused of arson. Writer of books for adults as well as young people, Reynolds has made her home on Mercer Island, Washington.

RINALDI, ANN (1934–)   Born in New York City; columnist and feature writer for Somerset and Trenton, New Jersey, newspapers; prolific writer best known for her historical novels for young adults; resident of New Jersey. Her son's participation in reenactments of the American Revolution during the U.S. bicentennial stimulated her interest in American history and resulted in twenty-four novels, among them *Hang a Thousand Trees with Ribbons: The Story of Phillis Wheatley** (Harcourt, 1996), a selection of the American Library Association for young adults; *An Acquaintance with Darkness** (Gulliver, 1997), about the beginning of medical research in the United States, also an American Library Association choice; and *Cast Two Shadows: The American Revolution in the South** (Harcourt, 1998), in which a girl becomes involved in home-front war events, a selection of the New York Public Library for teenagers. Other titles include *Girl in Blue* (Scholastic, 2001), about a Michigan girl who enlists in the Union army, and *Numbering All the Bones* (Hyperion, 2002), about cleaning up Andersonville Prison after the Civil War. Although Rinaldi's books have been criticized as formulaic in plot and stereotypical in characters, they convey a good sense of their times and are consistently interesting.

RITTER, JOHN H. Raised in San Diego County, California, the son of a sportswriter; attended the University of California–San Diego; resident of San Diego; writer and lecturer. His first novel, *Choosing Up Sides** (Putnam, 1998), cited by the American Library Association for young adults, tells of a left-handed Ohio boy whose desire to play baseball brings him into conflict with his Baptist preacher father. Earlier, the book received the International Reading Association Award. Other titles include *Over the Wall* (Philomel, 2000) and *The Boy Who Saved Baseball* (Philomel, 2003), both baseball stories. For more information about Ritter, see *Dictionary, 1995–1999* [*Choosing Up Sides*].

RIVER, CROSS MY HEART (Clarke*, Breena, Little, Brown, 1999) Adult period novel treating one year of family and community life and a girl's growing up among African Americans in the Georgetown area of Washington, D.C., beginning in 1928. Focusing almost exclusively on female activities and attitudes, the book opens with a terrible tragedy. Late on a hot afternoon in July, seven "colored" (a term of the time) girls, all friends and neighbors, stroll to the Potomac River for a cooling swim, among them tall, assertive, athletic Johnnie Mae Bynum, 12, and her shy, plump little sister, Clara, 6. Engrossed in their swimming, the girls fail to notice that Clara has slipped off the log on which she has been sitting. Late that night, her lifeless body is found, and her parents, normally stalwart Alice and laid-back Willie, and indeed the entire community are in shock. Johnnie Mae lies in a near-coma for several days. Aunt Ina Carson, Alice's widowed and childless seamstress cousin, takes care of Johnnie Mae until she recovers and extends help and comfort throughout the book. Among others who figure in the Bynums' lives are Miss Ann-Martha Pendel, the laundress for whom Johnnie Mae (and formerly Clara, too) works; Ella Bromsen, the black community healer; Miss Clementine Chichester, who gathers books for the Mt. Zion Community Center; and Miss Gladys Perryman, an elegantly dressed and coifed beautician. Providing some unity is Johnnie Mae's relationship with Pearl Miller, who, new in school, is very shy, awkward, and inarticulate. Pearl reminds Johnnie Mae so strongly of Clara that she is sure Pearl is Clara's ghost or "haint," as Johnnie Mae puts it. The more Johnnie Mae tries to get Pearl to admit to being Clara, the more Pearl pulls away and retreats into herself. She does so poorly in school that her teacher, Miss Boston, decides something must be done. One of the most memorable episodes is that in which Miss Boston asks Alice and Johnnie Mae to accompany her on a visit to Hattie (Pearl's mother) to try to help Pearl. Hattie explains the Pearl is still reacting to the (historical) burnings in Tulsa, Oklahoma, and the theft of their property there that precipitated their move. Another memorable episode involves Johnnie Mae's persuading Pearl to go with her at night to swim in the whites-only pool, where Johnnie Mae is caught by the white policeman. Book's end finds the family welcoming baby Calvin and enjoying the pre–Labor Day Mt. Zion Church picnic with their friends. The book creates a rich picture of working-class blacks of the period, many of whom were, like the Bynums, immigrants from North Carolina, seeking opportunities the farming area could not offer. Events are based on conversations with people who lived in Georgetown during the time, including the author's parents. Readers can almost make their way around the town, sense the cultural biases, and anticipate the changes that will soon come with the advent of electricity, for example. Although plot is almost nonexistent and characters are types, the book is a rich glimpse of the time and place. Some language common to the era, like coloreds and the "n" word, may offend some readers. Alex.

RIVERS, FRANCINE (1947–) Highly popular writer of historical and inspirational romances with a religious slant. She was born in Berkeley, California, and received her B.A. from the University of Nebraska and her teaching credentials from California State University–Hayward. She has held a wide variety of positions, and since 1977 has been a freelance writer. The author of more than twenty novels, the early ones of which were historical romances some critics and reviewers called "steamy," she became a born-again Christian in 1986 and turned to writing religious historical romances. Chosen by *Booklist*, *The Last Sin Eater** (Tyndale House, 1998), about how dedication to Jesus saves a nineteenth-century Great Smoky Mountains community, exemplifies her more recent work and exhibits her ability to tell a good story. She

won the Rita Award for best inspirational romance for her novel *Sarina* (Jove, 1983) and was inducted into the Romance Writers of America Hall of Fame, among other awards and honors. She and her husband live in California and have three grown children.

ROBERT DEGRAAF (*An Acquaintance with Darkness**) Nonhistorical medical student and assistant to Uncle* Valentine Bransby, the uncle and guardian of Emily Bransby Pigbush, the protagonist and narrator, and a much-loved and respected physician. Robert is a foil for the scapegrace Johnny* Surratt, the historical figure involved in the assassination of President Lincoln. Robert is about twenty, crippled from a wound he received at Fredericksburg during the Civil War, dedicated to his work, and intensely loyal to Uncle Valentine. Although at first he denies that Uncle Valentine snatches bodies and robs graves, he eventually admits to Emily that her uncle does indeed gain bodies for medical reserach by such illegal means. Two episodes of importance involving him are those in which he plans to get bodies from a steamboat explosion and helps bring a body from the local Almshouse.

ROSE DAUGHTER (McKinley*, Robin, Greenwillow, 1997) Like her earlier novel, *Beauty* (Harper, 1978), a retelling in fictional form of the folktale, *Beauty and the Beast*. This novel does not follow the most familiar version of the tale as closely as her earlier work, and it is more complex, both in characterization, especially of the two elder sisters, and in the explanations for the beast's enchantment and the way it is finally broken. Beauty is the youngest of three daughters of a wealthy merchant whose wife, a beautiful, reckless, party-loving woman, is killed in a riding accident when Beauty is only five. After that she is raised by a series of nursemaids and governesses and finds her solace by disappearing into the garden where working with the flowers brings her peace and happiness. She is plagued, however, by a recurring dream in which she walks down a long dark corridor, lit by a few candles, knowing that a monster is waiting for her at its end. Her eldest sister, Lionheart, is beautiful, brave, loud, and athletic; the second, Jeweltongue, is also beautiful and acidly clever. Both are engaged to wealthy nobles and are planning an elaborate double wedding when news of their father's business failure becomes public. Both noble swains break off the engagements, the servants depart, and creditors claim all the valuables in the house. Among her father's papers, Beauty finds a will and a lawyer's letter, saying that a rural dwelling, Rose Cottage, had been left to their family, and since the old woman who lived there had disappeared seven years ago, they could claim it if they wished. With their father weak and wandering in his wits, they join a traders' convoy going in the direction of the cottage many weeks away. They find the cottage has been long empty but is not in great disrepair. The girls do essential rough carpentry, and in the nearest village, Longchance, trade their horses and wagon for a goat named Lydia, some chickens, and fresh vegetables. Each of the girls develops a special skill: Lionheart teaches herself to cook expertly; Jeweltongue sews and soon has commissions to make clothes for the local gentry; and Beauty minds the garden, where she finds that the thorny plants are roses, flowers almost unknown in the city and thought to be grown only by magicians. She also discovers that some enchantment, from a long-ago greenwitch, she supposes, keeps animals out of the garden. Lionheart disappears and returns in man's clothes with her hair chopped short, having become the squire's new stable hand, sure of advancement because she alone can ride the wild new colt belonging to Jack Trueword, his eldest son. Their father, whose health and mind gradually improve, begins writing busily and secretly, and also gets occasional jobs keeping books for local businesses. When one of the traders, stopping by on another trip, brings a letter saying that one of their father's ships, thought to be lost, has reached port, he feels obligated to return to the city to use whatever is of value to further pay his creditors. The older girls tell him to bring them nothing, but Beauty, seeing how sad this makes him, suggests jokingly that he bring her a rose. As in the folktale, he loses his way on the return trip, finds himself in a marvelous palace, waited on by invisible servants, spends the night, and, leaving, plucks a rose from the garden to take to Beauty. Suddenly confronted by a terrifying beast, he stammers out his excuse and is told he must send his youngest daughter back to pay for his theft. Although he intends to say farewell to the girls, then return and die rather than sacrifice Beauty, he falls ill after reaching Rose Cottage, and while he is semidelirious, she leaves for the Beast's palace. There she finds the long corridor of her dream, with the Beast waiting at the end, not a monster but a creature who gradually inspires her pity and then her love. She spends her days in his glass house, where the roses seem to have died, but where she finds some shoots alive and is able to coax them into new growth and bloom. She does not, as in the tale, leave the palace to visit her home, but in her dreams she sees what is going on in Longchance and Rose Cottage. Jewel-tongue, spurning the squire's son Jack, falls in love with the baker, Mr. White-hand. Lionheart is in love with Aubrey Trueword, Jack's much superior younger brother, but dares not admit it, fearing Jack's revenge. In a long and complicated denouement, the Beast is revealed to have been a powerful sorcerer, intent on finding the true meaning of the universe and thereby attracting the enmity of a wicked enchanter, who enspelled him in the palace. The simple greenwitch, owner of Rose Cottage and his friend, had an adopted daughter who ran away and became the mother of the three girls. Beauty, by bringing new life to the roses and attracting living things to the once-barren palace, has broken the spell. She has the opportunity to restore the Beast to his former grandeur, but instead chooses a simple life at Rose Cottage where he can paint, a talent he perfected in his solitude, and she can grow the roses they both love. Although he does not change from his beast shape to a handsome prince, they love each other as they are. Inevitably, this novel must be compared to *Beauty*. In many ways it is stronger and deeper. The final solution of the pair living at Rose Cottage while Jeweltongue and her father, who has become a poet, go to live with Mr. Whitehand in Longchance, and Lion-heart marries Aubrey, who becomes a horse coper, is more satisfying than the sudden transformation of the earlier novel. The final portion, however, is unnecessarily complex and abstract, with intellectual concepts that detract from the simple love story. ALA/YA.

ROSS, JOHN (*A Knight of the Word*) Nondescript-appearing, slightly lame, soft-spoken, well-educated man of forty-three who worked for the Lady of the Word for fifteen years before deciding that he was no longer worthy to serve. The mission of a Knight of the Word is to change the course of history for good ends. After Ross failed to complete a mission successfully and a number of children were killed, he tried to renounce his position by going to the glen in Wales where the Lady resides, but she never received him or even spoke to him, to his great disappointment. For several years, he drifted, then accepted a position working for Simon* Lawrence's homeless shelter, Fresh Start, in Seattle, Washington, where he is when the book begins. He still possesses magical powers, however, embodied in the rune-covered staff he always carries. He is told what his tasks are in dreams sent to him by the Lady.

ROTTMAN, S(USAN) L(YNN) (1970–   ) Born in Albany, Georgia; English teacher, swimming coach, novelist. A graduate of Colorado State University, she has taught in both Oklahoma, where her first novel, *Hero** (Peachtree, 1997), was set, and in Colorado, where she now resides. *Rough Waters* (Peachtree, 1998), a tale of a white-water rafting trip in which a boy who has been scorned by his divorced father for his lack of macho courage ends up saving both his father and his half brother, was named an American Library Association selection for reluctant readers. More subtle psychology appears in *Head above Water** (Peachtree, 1999), about a high school girl who must divide her attention between her swimming ambitions and her responsibility to care for her older brother, who has Down's syndrome.

THE ROVER (Odom*, Mel, Tom Doherty, 2001)   Picaresque fantasy-adventure novel published for adults set in a time of sailing ships in a mythical world of goblins, elves, trolls, and some humans. The story's protagonist is a "dweller," little people similar to dwarves but symmetrical and to elves but less slender, halflings who inhabit dark, hidden places. The story's basic pattern involves the hero who engages in a series of adventures during which he proves heroic despite himself. Wick (Edgewick) Lamplighter, 70, three feet four, likes being a librarian because he can steal away to explore old romantic storybooks in out-of-the-way stacks. He is a Third Level Librarian in the Vault of All Known Knowledge, a huge, isolated library that safeguards important treasures and all the books believed to exist, placed there for safekeeping since Lord Kharrion and his goblin hordes almost obliterated all the world's knowledge. Grandmagister Frollo sends Wick on an errand to deliver a box to the Customs House at the seaport city of Greydawn Moors. Wick helps a tall man attacked by revenants of Kharrion's goblins escape to a ship and is promptly shanghaied by pirate dwarves. He soon learns that their ship is one of several commissioned to patrol the coast against marauding goblins who wish to destroy the library. Although at first Wick is regarded with suspicion by the crew because he can read and is too little to be of much use, he saves the ship from a flaming Embyr, a fiery female creature, by reciting from his reading the story of how she became an Embyr. For his bravery, he is commissioned a "proper pirate." When they are attacked by a goblin ship, Wick gives himself to the goblins to save his mates, another deeply heroic act. This pattern repeats for each of Wick's major adventures. He is despised as useless, but because of his ability to read and his unselfish, if reluctant, heroism, he saves the group. The goblins sell Wick in the slave

market at Hanged Elf's Point, where he eventually falls into the hands of a mysterious, sly, clever man dressed in black named Brant. Brant is the master thief of a group bent on acquiring whatever treasure they can find and then sailing to safety on the Blood Soaked Sea. They have fallen afoul of the ruler of the area and, hence, are being ruthlessly pursued by bloodthirsty Purple Cloaks through the Forest of Fangs and Shadows. Throughout, Wick steals moments to record his adventures and illustrate them in a book he fashions of found materials. While the thieves rummage in an underground burial crypt, Wick finds four books that he takes as his share of the loot. His adventures with the thieves also include a long episode inside a rumbling volcano in the Broken Forge Mountains, where he and Sonne, a human woman thief, search for a way through a rock slide. They encounter the terrible Shenghrack, King of the Dragons, whom Wick slays by recalling from his reading that dragons often hide their hearts in the form of a beautiful gem in their treasure troves. He finds the gem, the dragon is slain, the thieves help themselves to his horde, and all get away as the volcano collapses. At story's end, Wick is back in the library and promoted to Second Level Librarian. The author seems to thoroughly enjoy blatantly borrowing from such fantasy masters as J. R. R. Tolkien, sometimes even poking fun at himself for doing it. For example, he points out that Wick enjoys sitting in front of the fire, reading, and smoking his pipe, as though he were a relative of Tolkien's hobbits. Action abounds; Wick, always referred to by the author as the "little librarian," becomes more confident, resolute, and stalwart; names of people and places are deliciously mouth filling; the history is intriguing; the tone is sprightly and engaging; and the message, if any other than pure pleasure, is that books are to be cherished for themselves as well as for their possible practical value. Booklist.

RULES OF THE ROAD (Bauer*, Joan, Putnam, 1998)   Present-day career novel of a girl who is dedicated to her job selling shoes in Chicago and, after becoming chauffeur to the shoe company president, attends a stockholder's meeting in Dallas, Texas, speaks up for her boss, and gains enough confidence to confront her drunken father and insist that he reform or leave her life. For a longer entry, see *Dictionary, 1995–1999.* ALA/YA; NYPL.

RUN FOR YOUR LIFE (Levy*, Marilyn, Houghton, 1996)   Realistic novel of contemporary family and community life set in Oakland, California, based on real people and incidents. Kisha Clark, 13, the narrator, lives on welfare with her mother, unemployed father, and younger brother in a tiny apartment in an almost completely African American, poverty-, drug-, and violence-ridden housing project. After Darren Hayes, a young, black social worker reopens the local community center and picks Kisha to help him organize a girls' track team, prospects open for a better life for all of them. Although the problems the girls face are the expected ones, especially in encountering prejudice, there is enough tension to hold the interest, and Kisha is a likable figure. Darren is round and appealing and serves as a credible example for the girls to emulate. For a longer entry, see *Many Peoples, One Land* [no. 71]. ALA/YA.

RUNNING OUT OF TIME (Haddix*, Margaret Peterson, Simon & Schuster, 1995)   Mystery of a tourist attraction, exhibiting an 1840s town, whose residents believe they have reverted to a better, simpler time and are not aware that they are part of a diabolical experiment. One girl in her early teens escapes to the modern world, different from anything she has known, and ultimately is able to expose the hoax. For a longer entry, see *Dictionary, 1995–1999.* ALA/YA.

RUTH MAY PRICE (*The Poisonwood Bible: A Novel**)   Youngest of the family that goes to the Congo with their evangelical preacher father and also in some ways the one who fits in best. She is the first to make any friends and to understand some of the language, and to the surprise of her sisters soon has a group of children playing Mother May I? She becomes a favorite of Nelson, the orphan boy who sleeps in their chicken house, carries water from the river, and helps with the cooking. Ruth May's grasp of theology is strange and confused, but she has a clear idea of her father as a person to avoid if possible. Somewhat spoiled, she hides her bitter-tasting quinine pills and comes down with severe malaria, through which her mother nurses her tirelessly. When she recovers, she is subdued, possibly slightly brain-damaged. Not long afterward, the green mamba snake that Nelson drives out of the chicken house bites her, killing her almost instantly. In the end, her aging mother returns to Africa, hoping to place a marker on her grave, but the political situation there makes it impossible to get to Kilanga.

RYAN, PAM MUÑOZ   Born in Bakersfield, California, the area of the San Joaquin Valley in which her novel, *Esperanza Rising** (Scholastic, 2000), an American Library Association choice for young adults, is placed. About Mexican immigrants who come to the United States during the Great Depression and meet back-breaking labor, prejudice, and exploitation, the story is based on the experiences of Ryan's maternal grandmother, Esperanza Ortega. Ryan has been a public school teacher and administrator and has written twenty picture books and novels for younger readers, many of them concept books or highly illustrated narrative informational books. Although her shorter books are praised and some have won awards, most highly regarded, in addition to *Esperanza Rising*, is the historical novel *Riding Freedom* (Scholastic, 1998), about Charlotte Parkhurst, the woman who lived disguised as a man and became a stage-coach driver in California. Ryan lives in Leucadia, California.

S

SACHAR, LOUIS (1954–)   Born in East Meadow, New York; received his undergraduate degree from the University of California–Berkeley and his law degree from the University of California–San Francisco; attorney and, since 1977, a writer, very popular for his humorous Wayside School and Marvin Redpost sets of novels. His most highly acclaimed and best-known novel is *Holes** (Farrar, 1998), an often ironically funny book about a boy who is convicted, although innocent, of stealing a pair of sneakers and sent to a terribly cruel correctional facilty in the very hot Texas desert, where he discovers a surprising treasure. The book received several prestigious honors, among them, the Newbery Award and the *Boston Globe–Horn Book* Award. It was also selected by the American Library Association for young adults. For more information about Sachar, titles, and a title entry, see *Dictionary, 1995–1999* [*Holes*].

THE SACRIFICE (Matcheck*, Diane, Farrar, 1998)   Novel of the painful coming of age of a Native American Indian girl in the mid-eighteenth century in what is now the Montana–Wyoming–Nebraska area. The protagonist, 15, is known among her Apsaalooka (commonly called Crow) people as Weak-one-who-does-not-last, because when she was born her twin brother was thought to be the fulfillment of a dream that one twin would be among the greatest Apsaalooka ever to live, while the other would die young. Her brother, called Born-great, was showered with praise and gifts and even when young wore a sacred owl–shaped stone as an amulet, while she was seldom noticed or was pushed aside. Before they were four years old, enraged, she broke a wing from the owl stone, and when, not long after, he was killed by a Cheyenne ambush, she was convinced that she was responsible for his death. Because her mother died at her birth, she never learned women's work in the camp and her father, Chews-the-bear, refuses to let her go with hunters and war parties, although she is better at both riding and shooting than most of the boys her age. After he is killed by a raiding band of

Headcutters, or Lakota, she tries at the council to claim the right to join the band going to avenge him, but she is silenced, although she is offered a home in the lodge of Broken Branch, medicine man and father of her only friend, Grasshopper, a boy with a withered left arm and one short leg. Determined to follow the band and join it later, she waits until the village is asleep, takes Bull, her ugly but strong gelding, and rides after them. By the next day she has lost their trail and soon wanders into the Land of Boiling Waters, now Yellowstone National Park. There, in about two months, she finds the fabled obsidian cliff, is badly burned when she falls into a scalding pool, loses Bull and with him her supplies and her bow, learns to cook in the hot water, and, most importantly, kills a grizzly bear with her knife, more by courage and accident than by skill. With tremendous effort, she butchers and skins the bear, dries some of the meat, tans the hide, and makes a necklace of its claws. When she is almost ready to return triumphantly to her village, she spots a band of Pawnee. Trying to steal their horses, including Bull, whom they must have found, she is captured and taken to their village, where, after a ceremony she does not understand, she is put into the charge of a boy named Wolfstar, who keeps her with him always, but does not harm her. At first she is distant and angry, pretending she does not understand any Pawnee, though she knows a little, but gradually she picks up the language. Wolfstar's mother, Hercorn-says-so, is kind, and his father, Two-voices, treats her as someone special, but there is some mystery she does not understand. Wolfstar, who calls her Danger-with-snarled-hair, tells her that he is really adopted, but has become the keeper of the sacred bundle, without

which his people will die out, and she tells him the story of her birth and her brother, Born-great. Before she realizes it, she has fallen in love with the boy, and she gives him her grizzly-claw necklace, while he retrieves her grizzly robe for her. When she tries to persuade him that she would be a good wife, he turns away, and soon all the villagers avert their eyes and avoid speaking to her. From their attitude and bits she overhears, she realizes that her death will be a sacrifice to Morning Star. As the ceremony reaches its climax, Wolfstar whispers to her to run, and she careens through the entrance tunnel, her wrists tied together, into a tremendous rain. Wolfstar has tethered Bull in a wash, with full saddlebags, and as she leaps down, her wrist tether breaks. Wolfstar tumbles after her, an arrow through his back. She heaves him onto the horse, climbs up after him, and rides until she dares stop to try to remove the arrow and staunch the blood. Although she is unable to save him, he declares his love before he dies, and she carries him to the great bluff she remembers from the trip after her capture. At its top, after a slight hesitation, she leaves the grizzly-claw necklace on him, covers him with her grizzly robe, and piles stones over his body. Briefly, she contemplates suicide, then turns back toward her Apsaalooka village, intending to call herself Grizzly-fire and to take up the offer of a home from Broken Branch. An author's note at the end identifies the burial place as Scotts Bluff and discusses the Pawnee Morning Star sacrifice, which died out in the early nineteenth century. Just what her life will be among her own people is not foretold, although the author's note says that while rare, Apsaalooka women warriors were not unknown. The action in the book always stays within possibility, with a good pace and believable psychology, as Weak-one moves from anger and resentment to Grizzlyfire, with understanding and love. ALA/YA.

SAFE AT SECOND (Johnson*, Scott, Philomel, 1999)   Boy's growing-up story with a sports background set in recent years in a small town in New York State. Hard decisions face proud Todd, star high school pitcher, and his loyal sidekick, Paulie, 16, the narrator, when Todd loses an eye, ending what was a promising career in baseball and forcing each boy to sort out what he feels is truly important in life. The two boys are overly obvious foils, and the ending is predictable if satisfactory, but the sports scenes are exciting and convincing, and the two boys mature credibly. Previously the book was selected by *School Library Journal*. For a longer entry, see *Dictionary, 1995–1999*. ALA/YA.

SALISBURY (*Mary, Bloody Mary**) Lady Margaret, countess of Salisbury, governess and surrogate mother of Mary Tudor, daughter of Henry* VIII of England. Salisbury (as Mary always refers to her) is plain, long-nosed, and gentle. Salisbury genuinely loves Mary, and throughout the novel she not only looks out for the girl's physical, emotional, and intellectual needs, she also tries to advance Mary's efforts to defend her mother and retain her own claim to the throne. Salisbury is imprisoned and executed for treason.

SALISBURY, GRAHAM (1944–) Born in Philadelphia, Pennsylvania; received his undergraduate degree from California State University and his M.F.A. from Vermont College; resident of Oregon. Descended from some of the first missionaries in the Hawaiian Islands and raised in Oahu and Hawaii, he often writes novels involving mixed-ethnic boys in the islands. Among these is the American Library Association selection for young adults, *Jungle Dogs** (Delacorte, 1998), a sociological-problem novel of a boy whose brother leads a school gang. He has also published *Under the Blood-Red Sun* (Delacorte, 1994), a substantial historical novel of the Japanese attack on Pearl Harbor; *Lord of the Deep* (Delacorte, 2001), about a boy who works on his stepfather's deep sea fishing boat; and *Island Boyz* (Wendy Lamb, 2002), short stories. For more information about Salisbury, titles, and title entries, see *Dictionary, 1995–1999* [*Under the Blood-Red Sun*] and *Many Peoples, One Land* [*Jungle Dogs*, no. 228; *Under the Blood-Red Sun*, no. 229].

SAL PAVY (*Shakespeare's Scribe**) Salathiel Pavy, a new apprentice in the Lord Chamberlain's Men, William Shakespeare's* theater company. Widge and his apprentice friend, Sam, immediately notice that Sal is two faced and deceitful. He is always respectful and agreeable with the owners of the company but is arrogant and rude to the other boys. Sam concludes that Sal is really a girl and arranges for them to spy on Sal in the bathhouse. To their surprise, Sal is indeed a boy, but he bears deep, livid scars on his back that shock them. Widge learns that Sal had been in the Children of the Chapel choir at St. Paul's Cathedral but was forced into service with the Children of the Chapel theater company, which he hated. Every time he ran away he was beaten, the source of the scars, until he gave in. Then, to his credit, he decided to become the best actor he could be. Sal is both a sympathetic and despicable figure.

SAM (*Kissing Doorknobs**)   The tall, handsome, high school boy in the class of Allan Jacobson, high school science teacher. Sam is being treated for Obsessive-Compulsive Disorder. He explains to Tara that his main fear is germs, gives her some information about the disorder, and describes his progress toward health. He and Tara enjoy each other's company. He jokes about her compulsion for kissing doorknobs and brings her a gift of a crystal knob. When his pet parrot dies, he relapses, and Tara tries to encourage him as he did her.

SAM DEGHEYN (*Hotel Paradise**) Sheriff of La Porte, to whom Emma Graham is devoted and follows around as a sort of surrogate for her dead father. A kind, decent man, he is concerned that the twelve-year-old is neglected, particularly when he finds that she has spent several winter days alone in the eighty-some-room hotel with only her great-aunt, Aurora Paradise, who never leaves her fourth-floor rooms. He also fondly accepts her help in checking the parking meters and often joins her in the Rainbow Cafe, where she has a Cherry Coke while he eats, usually chili. Although Emma admits that she knows little about sex, she can tell there is something "funny" about the sheriff's marriage, and she puzzles about his bantering relationship with Maud Chadwick, waitress at the cafe, not realizing that her presence is a cover for them when Maud skips lunch to walk the parking meters with her and the sheriff or they eat together while she has her Coke. Emma is not the only one to find the sheriff attractive; she especially dislikes having Rae-Jane Davidow refer to him as "Sam" and intimate that they are close friends. The sheriff, however, politely and tactfully keeps Rae-Jane and his other admirers at a distance. In the end, he is sure Emma knows something about the murder and, when she refuses to tell, walks away coldly, effectively ending their long, chummy friendship.

SAMJAM (*Rebel: A Tibetan Odyssey**) The new tulku, or reincarnation of the founder of Tharpa Dok gompa or monastery, a five-year-old boy sought out by a group of monks, who looked for one born at the right time and under auspicious conditions and then brought him to the gompa to be their spiritual leader. Homesick, he begs Thunder, the older boy chosen to be his friend, to take him back to his ama (his mother), who will miss her "little radish." He later tells Thunder that home is where he fed the chickens himself and had his own pony, until the monks came and asked him many questions and showed him strings of beads and prayer wheels and had him choose among them, saying that if he picked well he could keep the pretty things. He learned he chose things that belonged to the last tulku, and since the other signs pointed to him, he must be the new incarnation. Having a younger child, a daughter, often sick, his mother has sent him off with directions to pray for his little sister, a heavy obligation for a five-year-old. Obviously a very bright little boy with a strange mixture of adult understanding and childishness, Samjam often surprises Thunder by his responses. He is mostly delighted with the games and diversions that Thunder thinks up for him. When they go on the adventure he has begged for, he is appalled to see the skirmish between the mounted Tibetans and the foreign surveyors, and he runs into the middle of the conflict commanding them to stop. He tells Thunder, who rescues him, that he thought, being tulku, he could make a difference.

SANDI WATKINS (*Bull Catcher**) Big girl on campus at Shipley (Wisconsin) High School, which Bull Larsen, Jeff* Hanson, and Billy* Collins also attend. Sandi is very pretty, at least in Bull's eyes, involved in many school activities, a good student, and a cheerleader who participates at the baseball games the boys play in. Bull has had a crush on Sandi since childhood, a matter about which Jeff teases him, and despite repeated rejections calls her frequently to ask her to go out. When she starts going with Billy, Bull is more angry with her than he is with Billy. When Bull is named to the National Honor Society and Sandi is not, despite her many activities and good scholastic record, she complains loudly to the principal, so loudly her words carry into the hallway, calling Bull a "brainless jock." She tells Bull that, if he really cared about her, he would refuse to accept the honor. He tells her off, realizing finally how selfish she really is.

THE SAND-RECKONER (Bradshaw*, Gillian, Forge, 2000)   Adult historical and biographical novel set in ancient Syracuse, Sicily, for one year beginning in 264 B.C., during the First Punic War, strong in characterizations and in the sense of the times and the conflicting Greek and Roman cultures. Archimedes, 23, a historical figure generally regarded as one of the world's greatest mathematicians, has just returned from Egypt where he has been studying at King Ptolemy's Museum and has attracted widespread attention for his mathematical genius and for inventing a time- and labor-saving water pump. Often forgetful, abstracted, and impractical about mundane matters,

he has been cared for by his faithful but enigmatic slave, Marcus*, about thirty. The two arrive home as Archimedes's father, Phidias, a mathematician and astronomer, lies dying of jaundice, and as Syracuse is at war with the Romans. Archimedes is soon in the employ of generous, clever, astute King Hieron of Syracuse to make war machines called "catapults," which are larger and more powerful than the ones currently employed. The catapults prove very effective, and the much-impressed king urges Archimedes to make good his assertion that with the proper equipment he can move anything, even a huge warship. Having done so, Archimedes becomes well-known in Syracuse also, and his household, consisting of his mother, sister, and several slaves, need no longer worry about money. Although Archimedes's catapults have earned him fame and the assurance of much fortune, he longs to return to pure mathematics, and much of the novel revolves around the king's efforts to ensure that Archimedes does not return to Egypt and his beloved studies there but remains in the king's employ. The king is particularly determined as the war with Rome grows hotter. While Archimedes is at the book's center and commands attention mostly for his intellect and the king is admirable for his dedication to his city, his generosity, and his cleverness at outwitting the Romans, the book's emotional focus is on Marcus, Archimedes's slave. Although Marcus's name appears to mark him as Roman, the man waffles about his background but never hesitates to express his appreciation for Syracuse. Nor does he stint on working for the family while his master is occupied on Hieron's tasks and oblivious to almost everything else. Marcus's Roman background, however, comes out when, during an attack in which the

Romans are soundly trounced thanks to Archimedes's catapults, Marcus spots his brother, Gaius Valerius, whom he has not seen in many years, among the Roman captives. Marcus enables his brother to escape, is found out, and is imprisoned. He interprets for Hieron in a parley with the Romans, and thus Marcus incurs the hatred of the Roman commander. In a prisoner exchange, Marcus is also returned to the Romans. Archimedes learns much later from Gaius that Marcus committed suicide the night before he was to be executed by flogging. Too late, Archimedes is aware of the loyalty, dedication, and basic goodness of the man he had since childhood taken for granted. The plot consists of a skillful mixture of action, intrigue, romance, and mystery. Even minor characters stand out, for example, Philyra, Archimedes's pretty sister, who alone in the house realizes Marcus's worth; and Gelon, the king's little son, who pops in and out of the story, exhibiting a child's interest in and appreciation of the inventor's talent. One of the book's finest features is its portrayal of the conflicting values of the two warring cultures. The scenes in which the catapults are employed show vividly how much carnage they produced and why those ancient war machines were so greatly feared. A valuable and interesting historical note concludes the book. Alex.

THE SANDY BOTTOM ORCHESTRA (Keillor*, Garrison, and Jenny Lind Nilsson*, Hyperion, 1996)   Novel of family and small-town life, set in Sandy Bottom, Wisconsin, in the late 1990s. What starts as a rather ordinary story of a young teenage girl's angst—eccentric parents, defecting best friend, unspectacular physical appearance, stultifying prospects for summer entertainment—

slides effortlessly into a charmingly ironic picture of a family with three distinctive personalities and a town of offbeat characters described with unsentimental affection. Rachel Green, 13, fears that everyone in town will think she is as strange as her mother, Ingrid, who plays the piano expertly but spends most of her energy writing scathing letters to the editor about the mayor and the school board, or her father, Norman, who happily manages a dairy and more happily spends his leisure time conducting classical recordings in his den. Although Rachel loves music and plays the violin with skill, she knows that in Sandy Bottom these qualities make her a nerd. Two major worries dominate Rachel's early summer. She finds a communication from Interlochen Center for the Arts in Michigan, evidently in answer to a letter from her mother, saying that there is an opening for a freshman violinist and enclosing an application for a scholarship. She fears her parents are going to split up and send her off to boarding school. She is more immediately concerned because her father, who is in charge of the annual Fourth of July celebration, engages the Dairyland Symphony Orchestra for the occasion, an unheard-of insertion of culture into the town festivities. Worse yet, the conductor backs out, and Norman decides to conduct the concert himself. Rachel's music teacher in Oshkosh recommends her for the orchestra along with a cellist, Scott Miller, 16. Delighted to be chosen, especially since Scott begins to pay attention to her, Rachel is at the same time apprehensive that she will be witness to her father's humiliation. The plot moves gently to the expected finish: Norman wins over the initially scornful musicians, and, when the youthful pianist engaged to solo in the Mozart concerto has a nervous breakdown, Ingrid agrees to fill in, a role she secretly wanted all the time. On Independence Day, Ingrid plays flawlessly, and the unprecedented concert is a grand success, mostly because it ends with Tchaikovsky's *1812 Overture*, complete with cannons imported to the lot across the park, followed by fireworks. Rachel's personal life is looking up, too. Scott takes her to a drive-in movie, her first date, and she will play three more summer concerts with the Dairyland Orchestra. She realizes that she does not depend on her erstwhile best friend, Carol, as much as she did, and she decides that since the choice is left up to her, she will go to Interlochen where she will get better musical training than in Sandy Bottom. The events themselves are plausible, but the charm of the novel is in the descriptions that echo the gentle satire of Keillor's *Prairie Home Companion* show and the wry comments of independent, perceptive Rachel. Characterizations are strong of both parents and of many of the townspeople and other musicians. ALA/YA.

SANDY   HUNTINGTON-ACKERMAN (*Love Among the Walnuts**)   Alexander, son of Horatio* Alger Huntington-Ackerman, a business tycoon, and Mousey* Malone, former actress. He grows up content in the country, homeschooled, and loved by his parents, Bentley, his father's valet, and Flossie, Bentley's wife. Sandy is the main male character in the book, responsible for keeping the family going with the help of Bentley and Sunnie* Stone, the nurse, after his parents fall into comas. He discovers that the board of directors have been stealing Walnut Manor funds, forces the embezzlers to pay back the money, and then helps

create the Walnut Foundation for social improvement. He marries Sunnie, whom he has loved for many months but was too shy to tell her so.

SARAH DOYLE (*The Chatham School Affair**)   Pretty serving girl of fifteen who works for the family of Mr.* Arthur Griswald. An Irish immigrant, she was working for a Boston family when Mr. Griswald engaged her. Young Henry Griswald, her age, is somewhat attracted to her and she to him, but his romantic delusions about Miss* Emily Channing, as well as the difference in their social positions, stand in the way. Later, Henry wonders briefly what life might have been like for them if the Chatham School Affair had not occurred. He admires, as does the rest of his family and Miss Channing, Sarah's desire to get an education, and in particular her desire to elevate her status.

SASQUATCH (Smith*, Roland, Hyperion, 1998)   Father–son mystery and adventure story with fantasy aspects set for a few weeks in recent years in Portland, Oregon, and on the slopes of Mount Saint Helens. Successful realtor and landlord, Bill Hickock, the father of Dylan, 14, the narrator, has always been somewhat erratic, but when he comes back from a hunting trip to Mount Saint Helens without a deer and with his clothes torn and face and hands scratched from a fall on the mountain, both Dylan and his Mom are alarmed. Later, he takes Dylan to a meeting of B.F.I. (Bigfoot International), where they view what the photographer says are pictures of Big Foot, astonishing shots of a creature like the one Dad prefers to call by its Native American name of Sasquatch and says he saw when he fell and got scratched up. Dad reads up on Big Foot and on cryptozoology, the science of creatures thought but not proved to exist. He takes Dylan to another B.F.I. meeting, where self-important Dr. Theodore Flagg, a world authority on Big Foot, is organizing an expedition to "harvest" one, that is, bring one back dead or alive. An old man with a limp stands up during the meeting and objects, saying that Big Foot should just be left alone. Privately agreeing with the old man, Buckley Johnson, a former field biologist, Dad contacts him and discovers that Buck*, as he prefers to be called, is being watched. Dad joins Flagg's expedition to the mountain at the suggestion of Buck as a way of foiling Flagg, and Buck will leave on his own to help Dad. Directly after Dad departs, a man calling himself FBI Special Agent Steven Crow turns up asking for Dad and warns Dylan away from Buck. Dylan, however, gets Buck to take him along to the mountain. They carry with them a radio that Dad swiped from Flagg's equipment with which they can monitor the activities of the Flagg group. Against the backdrop of the rumbling, quaking, ash-spewing mountain, adventures follow thick and fast. Buck's cabin is filled with a terrible stench when they arrive, which later Dylan identifies as Sasquatch odor; Dylan discovers that the trail outside the cabin has Sasquatch footprints; Crow arrives, looking for Buck, who, he says, years ago hijacked a plane for still unrecovered ransom money; and Dylan, snooping in the cabin, opens Buck's "Pandora's box" locker and discovers that it is the entrance to an extensive network of caverns inside the mountain that form a Sasquatch lair. Dylan gets lost in the lair but is found by Buck with the help of a Sasquatch, one of several with whom over the years Buck has formed a friendship of sorts. The mountain explodes, and Dylan finds Dad unconscious.

He is helped by a Sasquatch who carries Dad to the highway where a helicopter picks Dad and Dylan up and takes Dad to the hospital. Buck later gives Dylan the deed to the cabin and returns the ransom money to Crow. Dylan keeps quiet about the Sasquatch. Although the plot will not hold up under scrutiny, the thrills, conflict, and sympathy for the Sasquatch offset any shortcomings. Dad proves to be less erratic and bumbling than first presented, or perhaps Dylan gains greater respect and understanding for him; and Buck, though sympathetic and a "good guy," has a surprisingly checkered background. Details about Sasquatch (a word that in the book has the same form for both singular and plural) and similar "cryptids" provide texture. ALA/YA.

THE SAVAGE DAMSEL AND THE DWARF (Morris*, Gerald, Houghton Mifflin, 2000)   Third in a series of fictionalized retellings of Arthurian tales, following *The Squire's Tale* and *The Squire, His Knight, & His Lady*. This is the story of Sir Gareth, who has been working as a kitchen drudge, known as "Beaumains," because he took a vow to find his brothers, Sir Gawain and Sir Gaheris, who have left court and not returned, and he does not want to show his face as a failure. In Castle Perle in Cornwall, Lynet, 16, tires of being cooped up while the Knight of the Red Lands lays siege to the castle, declaring he will fight any knight who challenges him until beautiful Lyonesse, Lynet's older sister and heiress to her father's lands, agrees to marry him. Lynet slips out with her horse at night and starts for Camelot, hoping to persuade one of the knights of the Round Table to become Lyonesse's champion. To get through her first difficulty, the Red Knight's camp, Lynet is aided by a figure from the Seelie

Court, elfland, who returns several times during her journey. Not long after that, she meets a dwarf named Roger, who joins her and leads her, disguised as a mute boy, to the Knight's Sabbath, a secret resting place for knights-errant, where she is disabused of her illusions about the gentility of knights. Since her father was fighting against King Arthur when he was killed, she does not want to give her name, but at Camelot no knights are willing to undertake a quest to champion a nameless girl except Beaumains, the kitchen servant. Lynet refuses his help and, when he comes anyway, insults him at every opportunity. As they travel toward Cornwall, Beaumains takes on six thieves who have set upon a young knight, killing some and scaring away two, defeats two knights who are guarding a ford, then a Knight of the Black Woods and his three brothers, killing some and sending others off to Camelot. In the last contest, Beaumains is wounded, and Lynet tends him with herbs given her by Robin of Seelie Court, whom she recognizes as the figure that helped her on the first night of her journey. Through these various adventures, Lynet's scorn turns to love, and when they reach Castle Perle, she is dismayed that the sight of Lyonesse in a window, carefully displaying her profile, turns Beaumains to instant adoration. When he beheads the Red Knight and declares his devotion to Lyonesse, she thanks him prettily and sends him away, saying she cannot marry any lowborn knight, even if he is a good fighter. Bored by life in the castle after her travels, Lynet goes out one night, meets Terrence, a figure from elfland who has acted as squire to Sir Gawain. He takes her to the Other World and introduces her to Morgan Le Fay, who teaches her some sorcery. When she returns, she learns that she has been

away a fortnight and finds that her uncle has captured Roger and intends to torture him to discover who Beaumains really is. Trying to rescue him, Lynet is imprisoned, and to win her release Roger admits that the kitchen knight is actually Sir Gareth, Arthur's nephew. Lyonesse changes her tune. Before the end, Roger is revealed to be Sir Gaheris, under a spell that is broken by his love for Lynet; a forester living nearby is shown to be Sir Lancelot; and Sir Gawain turns up soon after. Lyonesse plans a fancy wedding with Gareth, but Gaheris and Lynet have a quiet ceremony before heading north, where he will administer the family lands for Gawain. Lynet is a spirited young woman, hence the title, and the action is fast paced, but the retelling has none of the high seriousness of the Arthurian tale, opting instead for a flippant tone full of middle school insult and humor. ALA/YA.

SAYING IT OUT LOUD (Abelove*, Joan, DK Ink, 1999)   Realistic novel of a girl's coping with the terminal cancer and death of her mother set in the town of Roseville, New York, for about three weeks in November 1961. Only-child Mindy, 16, a high school senior and the narrator, has been very close to her pretty, gentle, loving mother. When the book opens, she is visiting her mother, who has a brain tumor, in her hospital room and notices that the normally vibrant woman is unusually tired. Mindy returns home with her distant, commanding father, who visits his wife in the hospital every day but otherwise seems undisturbed about the illness. When he informs her that the surgeon will operate on her mother soon and that a biopsy will then be performed, Mindy has trouble accepting the idea that the lemon-size tumor, which turns out to be the size of a grapefruit, may be cancerous, as it is eventually diagnosed. She reflects on the things she and her mother enjoyed together, among them reading Dr. Seuss books and those by James Thurber, shopping, and combing their hair and applying makeup, standing in front of the mirror like the mother and daughter in the painting of Madame Lebrun and her daughter. Mindy experiences the range of emotions that those who are about to lose a loved one often do, including anger at her mother for depriving her of her love and comfort and activities they would do together, like filling out college applications. She denies that her mother is really so sick and is angry at the unfairness of life. Mindy's greatest support comes from her longtime friend, Gail, and Gail's life-loving, sometimes silly little brother, Andrew, 7, who, among other things, shows Mindy the story he wrote for school, entitled "The Three Told Sloth." A new boy in Mindy's school, Bobby, provides support, too. They go to a movie, *Spartacus*, which Bobby enjoys explaining thematically, and for a ride, during which Mindy shares the bad news of her mother's impending death and he gently consoles her. After her mother dies, neighbors and friends pay their respects, and several help about the house, Mindy notes, putting items in the wrong places, for instance, refilling her mother's M & Ms dish with nuts, all matters that she understands but finds disturbing. Having already begun to fill out college applications, she decides that she must go on with her life, try to live as normally as possible, be content with herself, accept her father as he is, and take comfort in the friends who love her. The book offers nothing new in coming to terms with death, but unlike many novels on terminal illness and death, it is neither sentimental nor didactic. It is perhaps too coincidental that Gail's father died eight

years earlier and that Bobby's best friend in New York City was sick with cancer for months before he died. ALA/YA.

THE SCHERNOFF DISCOVERIES
(Paulsen*, Gary, Delacorte, 1997) Humorous, occasionally hilarious, episodic novel of friendship with school-story aspects, which takes place in the 1950s in a rural area of Minnesota. The unnamed narrator (probably the author) and his best (and only) friend, Harold Schernoff, both fourteen, see themselves as outcasts. The narrator describes himself as a skinny, nerdy-looking, not-too-bright kid from a ne'er-do-well family, who manages to get through his classes with Harold's help. He describes Harold as a science genius, who wears ties and tight suits, slicks his hair with grease, has thick glasses, carries lots of ballpoint pens, and speaks in scientific jargon. Each of the seven episodes constitutes a self-contained adventure, some of which stem from Harold's current science interest. Having learned about electrons and wishing to somehow harness human electrons, Harold links together a ballpoint pen cartridge and a metal paper clip, wets them, and inserts them into an electrical outlet. He terrifies his science teacher and classmates by almost electrocuting himself and coating the entire left side of his head with dark blue ink. Since both boys yearn for feminine companionship, Harold suggests taking Home Economics in order to meet some girls. Although the narrator does miserably with cooking, Harold succeeds phenomenally, explaining his success as "it's simply chemistry." When girls react positively to them, as the two had hoped, but the football players taunt and bully them unmercifully, Harold retaliates by presenting the team with two enormous, decorated cakes that he has

baked and laced with forty-three boxes of chocolate-flavored laxative. Harold courageously asks beautiful Arlene to go to the movies with him and, when she accepts, studies up on technique by reading romance novels and a "book with a plain cover and no author's name." He both pleases and perplexes her by utilizing "Sir Walter Raleigh methods" and then angers her by naively employing romantic suggestions from the plain-covered book. Deciding they should do research on gravity, Harold suggests they learn to ski. While the narrator manages a drastic downhill swoop, Harold barely survives a tremendous fall. They take jobs setting pins at the local bowling alley, a demanding enterprise. Disasters follow when Harold prevails on the narrator to teach him to fish, but good fortune ensues for both when Harold decides that they can make money by retrieving balls golfers have lost and selling them to the local golf pro. With the more than sixty dollars they make, they buy a junky old 1934 Dodge sedan and succeed in driving it eight miles before it blows up. On that note the novel ends, but in an afterword the narrator informs the reader that Harold became a famous scientist, while he himself grew up to raise dogs and tell stories. The appeal of the novel lies in the outrageous incidents—lively, action filled, funny, and unexpected, but still the kind of thing two odds-out boys, one of them an innovative thinker, might engage in. The extensive detail with which the escapades are drawn adds to the humor, the dialogue is often very funny, and the writer's sympathetic, perceptive look into the early teen male mind adds to the entertainment. ALA/YA.

SCHMIDT, GARY D. (1957–   )   Born in New York; professor of English, biographer. Schmidt received his B.A. in 1979 from Gordon College and both his M.A. in 1981 and Ph.D. in 1985 from the University of Illinois at Champaign–Urbana. Since 1985 he has been a professor of English at Calvin College in Grand Rapids, Michigan, where he makes his home. For adults he has written books on Robert McCloskey, Hugh Lofting, Katherine Paterson, and Robert Lawson, and for children biographies of William Bradford and Robert Frost. His novel, *The Sin Eater* (Lodestar, 1996), is about a boy who, after the death of his mother, goes to stay with grandparents in New England and manages to come to terms with that death and the subsequent suicide of his father. More recent novels are *Anson's Way* (Houghton Mifflin, 1999), about eighteenth-century Ireland; *Mara's Stories: Glimmers in the Darkness* (Holt, 2001), set in a World War II concentration camp; and *Straw into Gold* (Clarion, 2001), a fantasy based on *Rumplestiltskin*.

SCHWARTZ, VIRGINIA FRANCES (1950–   )   Born in Stoney Creek, Ontario; registered nurse, elementary school teacher. She received her B.A. from Waterloo Lutheran University (now Wilfrid Laurier University) and her M.S. from Pace University. She worked in nursing in both New York and Canada and since 1988 has taught elementary school, specializing in teaching writing. *Send One Angel Down* (Holiday, 2000) is a biographical novel of a slave girl based on the story told by her cousin, as an old man, to the Federal Writers Project during the Depression. Her other novels are *If I Just Had Two Wings* (Stoddart Kids, 2001), a story of the Underground Railroad, and *Messenger* (Holiday, 2002), about Croatian immigrants in the coal mining country of Canada between the two world wars.

THE SECRET DIARY OF ANNE BO-LEYN (Maxwell*, Robin, Arcade, 1997) Adult biographical novel of two of Britain's most fascinating women, Anne* Boleyn (1507–1536), second wife of Henry* VIII (1491–1547), and Anne's daughter by Henry, Queen Elizabeth* I (1533–1603). Elizabeth's story, in third-person, linear narrative, covers a few months very early in her reign, while Anne's appears in irregularly inserted diary entries, as written by Anne, beginning in January 1522 and ending with her beheading at Henry's order in May 1536. Strong-willed, tart-tongued, red-haired Elizabeth, 25, is urged to make a foreign marriage by her councillors. She refuses, however, asserting that she has a husband, the "Kingdom of England." One day, old Lady Matilda Sommerville, once lady-in-waiting to Elizabeth's mother, presents Elizabeth with a diary of claret-colored leather, which she says was written by Anne and intended for Elizabeth's eyes only. Elizabeth devours it every spare moment that she has, fascinated by the historical events described and especially by the character and sentiments of the mother she never knew. From the diaries, Elizabeth also clarifies her conception of the queen's role and of the advisability of marrying. Elizabeth learns that Anne, beautiful, black-haired second daughter of Thomas Boleyn, a minor but ambitious noble, returns to Henry's court from France as a maid of honor. Henry's current wife is Katherine* of Aragon. For six years, Henry pledges his love to Anne, who inflames his passion by coquetry, and promises to marry her and make her queen. Henry is determined to put aside Katherine, asserting that their marriage is incestuous because Katherine was the widow of Henry's older brother, Arthur. In attempting to have their marriage an-nulled, Henry comes up against the Roman Catholic Church and the most powerful men of his time. Years of political maneuvering ensue, during which Anne provides Henry with books with Reformation thinking that embolden his resolve. She also inflames his desire for her by refusing to share his bed until they are married. Thomas Cromwell, Henry's chief minister, proposes that Henry be made head of the Church of England, declare his marriage invalid, and put Katherine aside. Anne marries Henry and is crowned queen. Soon Henry is unfaithful to her with Jane Seymour, and when Anne gives birth to Elizabeth instead of the promised son, and then miscarries two times, Henry has her beheaded on trumped-up charges of adultery, including incest with her beloved brother, George. Reading the diaries, Elizabeth admires the courage with which Anne and Henry changed English political and religious history. She decides to follow Henry's example of ruling absolutely in order to secure her throne. She also decides never to marry, since to do so would mean that, like her mother, she would relinquish control of her very person to her husband. The novel projects fascinating views of the times from the woman's perspective of the ways of the upper classes of sixteenth-century England—the political intrigues, treacheries, self-indulgent lifestyle, posturing, revelries. A host of other historical figures parade across the pages—Archbishop Thomas Cranmer, Lord Chancellor Thomas More, Thomas Cardinal Wolsey, Lady Katherine Ashley, to name some. Foremost of all, the book draws a complicated, candid, detailed, often sexually frank picture of two women and the man who connected them and determined the course of their lives, one the woman Henry married, in her case, for worse, and the other the daughter he fathered and to whom he bequeathed the intelligence, vigor, and determination to become a great sovereign in her own right. A demanding, mature account, the novel would be more easily apprehended if accompanied by a genealogical table and chronology. ALA/YA.

SECRET REALMS (Cool*, Tom, Tor, 1998)   Futuristic fantasy of an experimental computer-designed world, in which fourteen seventeen-year-olds have been kept from infancy and trained in endless battles until they are super warriors, unaware of the actual world around them. The program, called "Standing Whirlwind," is run by what they know as System, but actually is controlled by Director Chang, the Chinese dictator who is about to engage in a war with Japan, once again an imperial power. The brilliant protagonist, Trickster, has begun to suspect the truth, partly from clues he has intuited from Dreamer, the most poetic of the group. Since each young person is enclosed by his own invisible barrier, they have never been able to touch, and their communication by speech is closely monitored by System. Each has a number of avatars, which can be directed to move and perform various tasks, and a private realm, a virtual space designed differently by each. To these they can retreat between battles, knowing the others can enter only with their permission. Since the Standing Whirlwind group is usually divided into two or more groups, which vie for success, there is inevitable rivalry. Trickster is closest to Cat and Dreamer, while his chief antagonist is Snake. Clued by Dreamer's vision, Trickster discovers the differences in the sexes, which are concealed by their virtual appearances, and eventually realizes that they are kept in a large cage on Batan Island near the Philippines. As war in the actual world heats up, the aircraft carrier USS *Abraham Lincoln* heads for the Pacific area of Batan, as does a typhoon and the Japanese submarine *Uzushio*. These all coincide with the decision of Trickster and his tribe to break out of their cage and opt for freedom, even though it means pain and actual death for some. In the end, mostly through electronic messages and orders that Trickster generates, the Japanese emperor and his staff are killed; the *Lincoln* has been sunk, with the admiral and many hands aboard; Director Chang is left hanging in the cage formerly occupied by Standing Whirlwind; the one American to engage with Trickster, Lieutenant Commander Mike McCullough, is allowed to go ashore on Batan, waiting for rescue; and the remaining four teenagers, Trickster, Dreamer, Sly, and Crush, take the *Uzushio* and head for deep waters, knowing they have supplies for five or six years. The idea of children raised and trained in continual mock battles specifically to lead in some future cataclysmic confrontation has been the premise of previous science fantasy novels, for instance, *Ender's Game* (T. Doherty, 1985). *Secret Realms* depends largely on its jargon and technical terms, many referring to computer generation, to give it a sense of authenticity, even when the reader does not understand much of the language. Of the fourteen members of the Standing Whirlwind tribe, ten are male, ten are Chinese, or at least Oriental, including Trickster and Dreamer, two are dark skinned, and two are Caucasian. Trickster's discovery of their condition and of the sensual pleasure of touching, as well as the sexual arousal that he and Cat, the dark-skinned female he loves most, enjoy, is the most engrossing part of the novel. Although there is some discussion between Trickster and McCullough about whether the destruction of a thousand to save a million is a morally defensible choice, fast-paced action is predominant. NYPL.

SEEDFOLKS (Fleischman*, Paul, illus. Judy Pedersen, HarperCollins, 1997) Novel of how the development of a garden by a contemporary Cleveland, Ohio, neighborhood not only transforms a trash-filled lot into a place of beauty and useful production but also changes the lives of people in the surrounding buildings. For a longer entry, see *Dictionary, 1995–1999*. ALA/YA.

SELIM BEY (*Forgotten Fire**)   Dignified, well-dressed, historical Turkish governor who lives in the house that once belonged to the Kenderians and for whom the Armenian boy protagonist, Vahan Kenderian, works as a stable boy during the Armenian Holocaust. Selim Bey is called the "butcher of Armenians" for killing thousands of Armenians, some by ordering horseshoes to be nailed to their feet. Ironically, he is very kind to Vahan, ordering that Vahan be given additional food and blankets. When, however, Vahan informs him of the brutal treatment of the girl, younger than Vahan, who is repeatedly raped by several soldiers every night for a week until she dies, Selim Bey says casually that she was brought to the stable for the soldiers to use.

SEND ONE ANGEL DOWN (Schwartz*, Virginia Frances, Holiday, 2000)   Biographical novel of a slave girl in the South from 1846 to 1860, told by her cousin, Abram, who as an old man in 1930 related it to the Federal Writers' Project. Abram is six years old when his Aunt Charity gives birth to Eliza, her first born and there-

fore, by Master Turner's promise, a child who will not be sold off as any subsequent babies will be. Abram is the "running boy" for Granny, who manages the breeding cabins and helps with the deliveries. Eliza, named after Abram's mother who died at his birth, is almost immediately turned over to the boy, who carries her everywhere strapped to his chest, enraptured by her blue-eyed beauty and her light, almost white skin, the legacy from Master Turner, her father. When Eliza is two and Master has decreed that Charity must stop nursing her, Abram takes her to the outskirts of the big house and shows her to the new nanny, Miss Layotte, a young Creole slave bought to care for the two Turner girls, Abigail, 7, and Emma, 2. As he hopes, Miss Layotte agrees that if he brings her up each evening to play with the girls, she will secretly set aside a few mouthfuls of food daily for Eliza so she will get more than the other slaves, who eat grits mixed up in a trough. When Eliza is five, she is in charge of keeping the babies clean and safe, and Abram, now eleven, is sent to pick cotton in the fields. When they are young, the Turner girls like to have Eliza come play with them, usually pretending she is their servant for tea parties, and she is pleased with the arrangement, even when Abigail is imperious and demanding, since she gets something extra to eat and Miss Layotte teaches her how to be a nanny and a house slave. As they grow older, however, Abigail and even Emma, who has always been kinder, begin to wonder about Eliza's light skin and blue eyes, and they banish her from their yard. A year later, some young men courting Abigail see Eliza and are struck by her beauty. When Abigail points out that she is a slave, one man blurts out, "That's why your daddy is so uncommon rich! He fathers his own slaves!" That evening the overseer tells all the slaves that any who go near the big house will be whipped, and Eliza is to start picking cotton in the fields. Some months later, Miss Layotte, who has become Abram's girlfriend, warns them that Master Turner plans to sell Eliza at the next auction. Abram sneaks through the night to the church of Father Johnson, known secretly as an abolitionist who will help runaways. He advises Abram that there is no way to hide Eliza or to send her by the Underground Railway, since she will be closely watched, but that perhaps they can collect enough money to buy her. Every slave gives what he can from secret hoards, a few cents, a quarter, even a silver dollar saved for a wedding, and Father Johnson sends a Mr. Lloyd to pick up what he has collected and bid at the auction. On the morning of the auction, Abram and Charity sneak away and hide among the tobacco plants at the edge of Pott's field, where the platform stands. The first bidder is a man called Swedelander, well known for his drunken uncouthness and cruelty. Mr. Lloyd's raising bid is rejected, since he is local and known to own no slaves, but when an abolitionist from New York outbids Swedelander, his money is accepted because the local sheriff fears trouble from antislavery groups in the north. Though Master Turner objects and Miss Abigail is furious, the New York man immediately frees Eliza and turns toward his carriage. When Eliza asks what she should do, he says there must be some freed slaves in town, but she rightly realizes that if she stays in the area she will be hunted down and Swedelander will claim her without opposition from the white community. Since the crowd has all left, Charity rises up from the edge of the field and challenges the New York man to take Eliza home to be nanny to his own children, and, reluctantly, he agrees. The story, a variation on a familiar plot, gets its power from the authentic source and the wealth of detail about life on the plantation, whose location is never mentioned. Abram is a stronger character than Eliza, a boy devoted to Eliza, and a young man, known on the place as an expert drummer probably destined to marry Miss Layotte, taking great risk to help his younger cousin. ALA/YA.

SENNA, DANZY (1970–   )   Born in Boston, Massachusetts; educated at Stanford University and the University of California–Irvine, from which she received a Master's of Fine Arts in creative writing. She has been a researcher and reporter for *Newsweek* and a contributing editor to *American Benefactor*, both in New York City. Her first novel, *Caucasia** (Riverhead, 1998), which concerns the problems a biracial family meets during the turbulent activism of the 1970s, was named to the Alex list for young adults and was selected as a Book-of-the-Month Club alternate. It was followed by *From Caucasia with Love* (Bloomsbury, 2000). African American, Senna seems to write from personal knowledge and experience about race in current America.

THE SERPENT'S SHADOW (Lackey*, Mercedes, Daw, 2001)   Fantasy novel of mystery, magic, and suspense published for adults, set in Edwardian London. Maya Witherspoon, 25, newly certified Doctor of Medicine and Surgery, has already surmounted several obstacles to starting a practice in London: she is a woman, she is a foreigner, and she is a Eurasian. Her father was a British doctor, her mother a high-caste Brahmin. After their deaths, in both of which she suspects the use of magic, she fled from India, hoping to escape the powers of her aunt, her mother's twin sister Shivani, who has become a priestess of Kali Durga and practices black arts. Maya herself is something of a mage, though untrained, since her mother, an adept, refused to teach her the arts of Hindu magicians, saying that if she has any talent she must follow the arts of her father's people. In London, Maya has set up a small house containing her office, where she lives with her Hindu servant and friend, Gupta, and his family, and an assortment of animals that were her mother's pets: a peacock, a pair of mongooses, an owl, a parrot, a falcon, and a small Hanuman monkey. She has also used what magic she can summon and cobble together to set up protections around the house, knowing that she may not be free of her aunt's threat. This magic, however inexpert, attracts the attention of a group of British magicians known as the "Elemental Masters," some devoted to fire, some to air, some to water, but none to earth, since Earth Masters usually live in the country and are often women, not accepted into their exclusive club. One of the Water Masters, Peter Scott, a former ship's captain, is assigned to investigate, since only he is able to fit into the lower-class neighborhood where the magic seems to be centered without attracting undue notice. To his astonishment, he discovers Maya has more power than he anticipated, and he offers to train her as far as his powers go, then perhaps find her an Earth Master to teach her further. Since Maya's only real friend outside of her household is a young medical student, Amelia Drew, who works with her at the Fleet Charity Clinic, she is lonely and easily attracted to Peter. Inevitably this leads to romance and eventually marriage, but not before they have to deal with a variety of difficulties, including the animosity of Lord Alderscroft, the Fire Master who heads the council. More dangerous is Shivani, who has come to London to get revenge on the English, whom she hates, and to capture and extract the magic from Maya to increase her own power. Their various encounters culminate when she drugs Maya, abducts her spirit, and holds it in an underground temple of evil until Peter, with Gupta and another Water Master, Lord Peter Almsley, led by a pickpocket girl whom Maya has cured of tuberculosis, find and storm the stronghold of Shivani and her followers. Getting to this point takes nearly four hundred pages with long descriptions of magical practices, suffragette marches and arrests, conditions in hospitals of the day, and other problems of society, interesting in themselves but sometimes belabored to tedium. This novel is one of a series about the Elemental Masters. Booklist.

SHADOW SPINNER (Fletcher*, Susan, Atheneum, 1998) Realistic mystery novel with fantasy aspects that is set in an ancient Persia-like kingdom and cleverly improvises on the tale of Scheherazade. Crippled Marjan, 13, the narrator, accompanies her foster mother to the Sultan's palace to sell jewels and fine cloth to the harem ladies. To pass the time, Marjan tells stories to the children, is overheard, and is taken to the Sultan's current consort, Shahrazad, who is running out of tales to entertain the Sultan. Scheming, intrigue, treachery, a couple of puzzling mysteries, a brave, intelligent heroine, and a convincingly evoked setting combine for a top-notch suspense story that also explores the power of narrative to change and enrich lives. Earlier, the novel was cited by the American Library Association for younger readers and also by *School Library Journal*. For a longer entry, see *Dictionary, 1995–1999*. ALA/YA.

SHAKESPEARE'S SCRIBE (Blackwood*, Gary, Dutton, 2000)   Realistic mystery, boy's growing-up, and historical novel set in London and the English countryside in the spring and summer of 1602, the year that the Black Death begins to spread, sequel to *The Shakespeare Stealer**. Orphaned Widge, 15, the narrator, enjoys his apprenticeship with the Lord Chamberlain's Men, the acting company for whom William Shakespeare* writes and acts. Just as they are about to open in a new production of *Richard III*, Queen Elizabeth I bans all public gatherings because of the dreaded bubonic plague, the Black Death. Shakespeare decides the company should go on the road, be "gypsy players," and head north, eventually to Yorkshire. Widge hopes that he can find information about his origins there. Sander, also an apprentice, remains in London to help Mr. Pope, another member of the company, with the orphans he has taken in. The company hires a new boy, Sal* (Salathiel) Pavy, in Sander's place, blond, good-looking, and charming with the adults but arrogant and rude to the other boys. During the trip, Widge proves he has some medical knowledge, among other instances setting and splinting Will's broken arm. He also takes dictation from Will for a new comedy, eventually called *All's Well That Ends Well*, which Will has promised the queen. Widge writes the lines down in a kind of shorthand, charactery, which he learned from a previous master, and then transcribes them. He also occasionally helps Will compose, coming up with an expression that aptly fills Will's need for an answer to fit all questions: "Oh, Lord, sir."

Untoward happenings occur along the way. Their wagons are burned, another company usurps their name, and their handbills are stolen. In York, when Widge visits the orphanage where he lived as a child, an attendant gives him a crucifix that she says belonged to his deceased mother. In an alehouse, a man of about thirty-five says he recognizes the crucifix and identifies himself as Widge's father, Jamie Redshaw. Widge is overjoyed when Jamie decides to accompany the players. Problems soon transpire, however. Sal is competent as a player, so much so that he preempts Widge's parts, and the company finds that someone has emptied its treasury. When Sal says it was Jamie, Widge sets out to learn the truth. In an alehouse, he finds Jamie in the company of a peculiar one-eyed man, who turns out to be Nick, the dishonest apprentice of the first book. Nick is responsible for burning the wagons, stealing the money, and other skullduggery. Sal is right about Jamie, however. He also has been stealing small sums and finally admits to Widge that he made up the story about being Widge's father. Widge returns to London to help Mr. Pope and Sander with the orphans and finds Sander dying of the plague in a pesthouse. The company prepares to perform *All's Well*, with Sal as Helena, when Widge, who feels the part is rightfully his, challenges Sal to an acting competition and wins handily. Mr. Armin, the company's main leader and Widge's mentor, praises him for his playing of Helena. Widge's response is the line he made up for Will, "Oh, Lord, sir." Although Widge has failed to learn who he is in the literal sense, he has discovered that he has vast moral and practical resources and that heritage is less important than using one's abilities. The details of how the company manages on the road are fascinating, the brief glimpses of the growing plague and its effects on society are worked well into the plot, and Widge's growing sense that he can indeed trust the company to recognize his ability, reward him for good work, and sympathize with his personal problems are good features. An author's note indicates that all the people in the company, with the exception of Jamie and Widge, are historical. ALA/YA.

THE SHAKESPEARE STEALER (Blackwood*, Gary, Dutton, 1998) Picaresque historical novel set in Yorkshire and London, England, in 1601. The master of orphaned Widge, 14, the narrator, orders Widge to infiltrate the Lord Chamberlain's Men, William Shakespeare's* theater company at the Globe Theatre and copy Shakespeare's new play, *The Tragedy of Hamlet, Prince of Denmark*. Widge eventually joins the company as an apprentice and finds himself in the midst of exciting intrigue. The book excels in depicting life in the theater, London, and environs, and real historical figures associated with the theater, in addition to telling a first-rate story. Previously, the book was cited by the American Library Association for younger readers and by *School Library Journal*. The sequel is *Shakespeare's Scribe*. For a longer entry, see *Dictionary, 1995–1999*. ALA/YA.

SHAKESPEARE, WILLIAM (*King of Shadows*; *Shakespeare's Scribe*; *The Shakespeare Stealer*)   Historical English playwright and actor. He becomes a surrogate father to Nat Field in the fantasy section of *King of Shadows*. Nat describes Will as not tall, with receding hair and a high forehead, though young. Nat thinks that otherwise Will does not look like the modern pictures of him. His face has lots of laugh lines, and he wears his beard thick. When Will learns that Nat's mother died of cancer when Nat was very young and that Nat's father committed suicide for love of her, he gives Nat a handwritten copy of Sonnet 116 ("Let me not to the marriage of true minds"), saying "love does not vanish with death." Nat puts the paper under his pillow and is disappointed at not finding it when he awakens in the twentieth-century dimension. Later, Arby gives him a paperback copy of Shakespeare's sonnets containing the poem. In the other two novels, Shakespeare is less personally involved with the boys, the emphasis being more on his roles as playwright and actor.

SHEFFIELD, CHARLES (1935–) Born in Hull, England; received his B.A., M.A., and Ph.D. (physics) from St. John's College, Cambridge; immigrated to the United States in 1971; highly praised for his science fiction, for which he has received both the Hugo Award and the Nebula Award. He has been chief scientist for Earth Satellite Corporation since 1971 and a freelance writer since 1978, mostly for adults. He lives in Silver Spring, Maryland. His books appear in several sets: novels of science fiction and horror; a series built around the hero Behrooz Wolf; the Heritage Universe series; and for young people, the Jupiter series. Of these, the first, *Higher Education** (Tor, 1996), was written with Jerry Pournelle*. It was chosen by *Booklist* for young adults. Others in the Jupiter set include *Putting up Roots* (Tor, 1997) and *The Cyborg from Earth* (Tor, 1998).

SHERIDAN PICKETT (*Open Season**) Quick-thinking, courageous daughter, 7, of Joe Pickett, the protagonist. She and her sister, Lucy, discover three little animals in the backyard woodpile where Ote

Keely died and smuggle food to them, determined to keep them a secret. They are not aware that the creatures are thought to be extinct Miller's weasels and, hence, extremely valuable. Wacey* Hedeman threatens Sheridan on several occasions not to let anyone know about the weasels. He hopes to capture the animals and destroy them, so that their presence does not impede the building of a pipeline and hasten the death of the little town of which he wants to be sheriff. After Wacey shoots her mother, Marybeth, Sheridan runs into the hills that surround the house and hides. Later, her little group of weasels has kits, a secret that she and her father share.

SHERIFF (*Dangerous Skies**)   The sheriff of the area in which Buck Smith, the narrator, lives. The law officer charged with finding out who killed Jorge* Rodriguez, Sheriff steadfastly refuses to believe Tunes* Smith's story, to accept what Buck tells him must have happened, and to consider Jumbo* Rawlin the prime suspect. At first, Sheriff praises Buck for sticking to details and giving a clear, understandable account of finding Jorge's body. When he learns that Buck has withheld information, he discounts what Buck has told him. Thus, Buck's attempts to help Tunes cast further suspicion on her. Mostly, however, Sheriff takes Jumbo's part because Jumbo is wealthy, powerful, and white and Tunes is the daughter of a poor, black farm manager. Sheriff illustrates how even the judicial system is prejudiced.

SHERWOOD, BEN   Television producer, writer of both fiction and nonfiction. A graduate of Harvard University and Oxford University, Sherwood has been senior producer of the *NBC Nightly News* and has written for the *New York Times*, the *Washington Post*, the *Los Angeles Times*, and other periodicals. His quirky novel, *The Man Who Ate the 747** (Bantam, 2000), has been widely popular. Sherwood has made his home in New York City.

SHIM (*The Lost Years of Merlin**) Pint-size companion to Emrys and Rhia whom they first meet when they feast on honey of wild bees and Emrys grabs and pulls what he thinks is a piece of honeycomb but what turns out to be the nose of a dwarflike creature. After a brief altercation, he tells them his name is Shim, and he tumbles with them into the crystal cave of the Grand Elusha, a menacing creature in the shape of a spider. After their escape and Rhia's capture by goblins, Shim sticks with Emrys to help find her, because she has been kind to him. He is a figure of fun in much of the adventure, being greedy for sweets, self-important, and usually fearful, and he speaks in a strange pattern: "I don't mean to hurts you. Really, truly, honestly." At the crucial moment in the Shrouded Castle, however, he leaps willingly into the Cauldron of Death to save Emrys, thereby destroying it and initiating the collapse of the castle. Moreover, his brave act restores him to his true shape of a giant, and he joins with other giants who appear and dance in the hall to cause the walls of the castle to crumble.

SHINN, SHARON (1957–)   Born in Wichita, Kansas; professional photographer, editor, novelist. She received her B.S. from Northwestern University. Her long, complex fantasy, using names and some ideas from the Old Testament, *Archangel** (Ace, 1996), has been followed by two other books set in Samaria, *Jovah's Angel* (Ace, 1997) and *The Alleluia Files* (Penguin, 1999). More recent are *Wrapt in Crystal* (Ace, 2000), about the backwater world of Semay where a serial killer stalks the planet's priestesses, and *Heart of Gold* (Ace, 2000), a cross-racial romance set on a planet where a blue-skinned matriarchy vies with golden-skinned people.

SHOUP, BARBARA (1947–) Born in Hammond, Indiana; educator, writer. Her young adult novel, *Stranded in Harmony** (Hyperion, 1997), is about a boy who, feeling suffocated by his small town, becomes involved with an older woman. For earlier biographical information and a title entry, see *Dictionary, 1995–1999* [*Wish You Were Here*].

SHUSTERMAN, NEAL (1962–) Born in New York City; graduate in psychology and drama from the University of California–Irvine; playwright, screenwriter, and author of more than twenty novels and collections of short stories mostly for young adults and mostly thrillers and suspense novels. He lives in Dove Canyon, California. Several books have won awards or citations, chiefly from the American Library Association, International Reading Association, and New York Public Library. Shusterman's first novel, *The Shadow Club* (Little, Brown, 1988) concerns a group of junior high youngsters who play tricks on their rivals. Its sequel is *The Shadow Club Rising* (Dutton, 2002). *Scorpion Shards* (Forge, 1995), which tells of six teenagers who try to stop beasts they think threaten the world, is the first of a trilogy, also including *The Thief of Souls* (Tor, 1999) and *Shattered Sky* (Tor, 2002). *The Dark Side of Nowhere** (Little, Brown, 1997), a science fiction thriller about a boy who discovers that his family are space aliens, was selected by American Library Association for young adults. *Downsiders** (Simon & Schuster, 1999), also cited by American

Library Association for young adults, is a tense, imaginative fantasy that postulates a civilization called "Downside" beneath New York City. Hailed for the high-interest value of his work, Shusterman has also written for television and film.

SILENT TO THE BONE (Konigsburg*, E. L., Atheneum, 2000) Contemporary realistic mystery novel with psychological- and sociological-problem, friendship, and family-life aspects set in Epiphany, New York. The book opens with a startling scene—a 911 emergency call on the afternoon of November 25, in which British au pair Vivian Shawcurt screams that baby Nikki (Nicole) Zamborska won't wake up, that she is breathing strangely, and that "he," meaning Nikki's half brother, tall, red-haired Branwell Zamborska, 13, dropped her. During the next month, little Nikki slowly recovers in the hospital, and Branwell is held in the Clarion County Juvenile Behavioral Center without charge, pending the outcome of Nikki's condition. He is completely mute, unable to speak, and dispirited—silent to the bone. His father, Dr. Stefan Zamborska, a university research scientist, asks Branwell's best friend since nursery school, Connor* Kane, the narrator, to visit Branwell to try to get him to speak. Every day Connor faithfully does so, and with skill and patience gradually gets Branwell, who Connor says is "screaming inside," to describe what happened in the Zamborska house that afternoon. Connor devises a flash card system of words to which Branwell responds by blinking his eyes. Thus, Branwell initiates the investigation that eventually clears him and indicates that Vivian did what she accused Branwell of. Connor's partner in sleuthing is his older half sister, Margaret Kane, 27, owner of a computer service company.

She enlists the help of their university registrar father, from whom she has been somewhat estranged since he divorced her mother and married Connor's mother, and the tension between father and daughter lessens. Among others, Connor interviews Yolanda, the cleaning woman, who reports that Vivian smoked in the house against the rules, and Morris Ditmer, local pizza delivery boy, who admits that he and Vivian had a sexual relationship, carried on in the house. When Connor and Margaret interview Vivian, she slyly awakens Connor's sexual interest in her, leading Connor to explore what happened between Branwell and Vivian when Vivian first came to the Zamborskas. In somewhat the same way, Vivian induced Branwell to do her bidding with Nikki so that she could meet Morris. This caused Branwell such great guilt that when she dropped the baby on the fateful day, he became completely mute. Eventually, Morris tells the truth, the British au pair agency agrees to see that Vivian never gets another such position, Nikki recovers, and Branwell is exonerated. Although the reader early suspects that Vivian's tale simply substitutes Branwell for herslf as the culprit, the way in which Connor and Margaret ferret out the truth cleverly holds the interest. The details of family life add texture to the story as well as complicate the mystery. A stereotypical villain, Vivian has no redeeming qualities, Morris slowly realizes he has been used, and Connor and Margaret are worthy, the real protagonists. If the reader accepts the premise that Branwell cannot write, the puzzle is totally intriguing. ALA/YA.

SIMON (*Anna of Byzantium**) Wise and learned slave, a mere "runt" of a man, who teaches Anna, crown princess of Byzantium, her sister, Maria, and their many cousins who live at court, and tries to instruct John, Anna's younger brother, who becomes emperor. Simon is gentle, respectful, and unassuming and tries to mold Anna's character as well as her mind. For example, he tells her stories from Greek mythology that carry morals, urging her to detect the lessons and let them affect her thinking and behavior. One of these concerns Daedalus and Icarus, through which Simon cautions her not to think too highly of herself, to be careful not to "fly too close to the sun." He also tells her the myth of the Atreid family, because he does not want her to incur blood guilt by killing her brother. In fact, he betrays the plot of Anna and her mother, Irene, to poison John. When John decrees, however, that the pages that Anna had written for the *Alexiad*, her account of the deeds of her father, Emperor Alexius, be destroyed, Simon courageously preserves them. After Simon dies, Sophia and Malik bring the pages to Anna, who subsequently completes the book. Simon and Sophia are the two most attractive characters in the novel, loyal, loving, and faithful.

SIMON LAWRENCE (*A Knight of the Word**) Highly respected founder and operator of the Seattle, Washington, downtown homeless shelter known as Fresh Start and the accompanying alternative school, Pass/Go. For his amazing work in this metropolis, sometimes called the "Emerald City," Simon has become known as the "Wizard of Oz." Although he has been remarkably successful after starting from scratch, Simon is sometimes dispirited because the problem of homelessness is so widespread and acute. The investigative reporter Andrew Wren has come to Seattle to find something wrong with Simon's operation, and after the matter of the suspected embezzlement is cleared up, returns to New York to write an article praising Simon's work. Simon is completely dedicated to his cause, a selfless man justly admired.

THE SIN EATER (Schmidt*, Gary D., Lodestar, 1996) Contemporary boy's growing-up novel about a year in which Cole Hallett, 11, moves in with his grandparents near Albion, New Hampshire, and comes to terms with his mother's death from cancer and, eventually, his father's suicide. For two years Cole and his father, a jazz trombonist, have lived together in Pennsylvania, but at the end of the school year Dad decides to move to the New Hampshire farm of his father-in-law, Hiram Emerson, so Cole can be near his roots. For the boy, this is ideal. He has always summered at the farm, loves his cantankerous grandfather and his energetic little grandmother, Livia, and enjoys the rural life. He soon makes two good friends, Will Hurd, the minister's son, and Peter Gealy, from one of the old families in the area. The three go fishing and roam the woods, about which Will knows all the secrets. For Cole's father, however, the change is not good. He opts to stay in the hired man's room above the kitchen, where he becomes increasingly reclusive, playing low, moaning music on his trombone, eventually not even coming down for meals. Through the summer and fall, Cole takes part in all the activities of the area, clearing out the Emerson family burial ground with his grandmother and puzzling over three unmarked stones that stand separated from the others, attending the Portsmouth County Fair, where Livia wins the overall Best in Show ribbon for her apple pie, and most of all listening to the stories his grandparents tell of his ancestors and other early timers. In particular, he is interested in stories of the Sin Eater, a Thomas Gealy, who came from Wales to escape the obligation to knead the sins of individuals or the community into bread dough, bake it, and eat it, thereby freeing the sinner from the guilt of his transgressions. His profession followed him to New Hampshire, however, and he began absorbing people's miseries and faults as he had in Wales. Cole finds bits of the story in various parts of the area: the foundation of a burned house in the woods where he and Peter go camping, a picture in Mrs. Dowdle's parlor, a letter kept by Peter Gealy's family, and an inscription, "Who Are We To Judge," on the back of one of the unmarked gravestones in the Emerson cemetery. When he and Will research the role of Civil War paid substitutes for a local history school project, he learns of Ephraim Cottrell, who substituted for some local man and was killed at Antietam. Ephraim's remains were returned to Albion and buried; the next day his wife died by suicide and was not allowed to be buried in hallowed ground. The church records show that Ephraim was disinterred the next day. Cole realizes that the two other unmarked stones in the Emerson burying ground must be for Ephraim and his wife. After finding the family Bible, he pieces the rest of the story together. His ancestor, Hieroymous Emerson, a well-to-do sawmill owner, paid Ephraim to take his place, and after Ephraim's death and his wife's suicide, adopted their little son, Erastus, Grandpa's grandfather. He also had the bodies buried on his ground, but because of the history, he and Erastus hated each other until Thomas Gealy, the Sin Eater, sat between them and made peace. After becoming more and more isolated from his son and in-laws, Cole's father shoots himself on Christmas eve. Through the rest of the winter, Cole is emotionally numb. In still icy early spring, Miss Cottrell, old-maid descendant in the family of Ephraim, gets lost in the hills near town. The boys join the men scouring the woods and find her, with a broken leg, at the bottom of Cobb's Hill, where, according to one of Hiram's stories, Erastus slid one Sunday morning and broke his leg. Miss Cottrell confirms the rest of the Sin Eater story, how he taught the Emerson household to love. Cole is finally able to give up the hate he has been nursing at his father for leaving and to remember him as he was before his mother's death, fun loving, full of interest in life. The connections between Cole's plight and that of his ancestors are tenuous and somewhat strained, but pictures of life in rural New Hampshire are wonderfully evocative. The woods, the farm, the small town, the school, the church—all come alive in sharp sensory detail. With the possible exception of Will Hurd, who is almost too good to be true, both major and many minor characters, living and dead, are believable and interesting. ALA/YA.

SIRENA (Napoli*, Donna Jo, Scholastic, 1998)   Romantic fantasy novel set in the Aegean Sea during the Trojan War, which improvises cleverly and convincingly on stories from Greek mythology. The narrator, Sirena, 17, a mermaid, leaves the company of her sisters because she no longer wishes to aid them in luring sailors to their deaths with seductive songs. She swims to the uninhabited island of Lemnos, where she observes a sailor whose fellows sail away leaving him behind. This is Philoctetes, who has been bitten by a serpent of the goddess Hera. He unwittingly incurred the goddess's disfavor because he was a friend of Heracles, whom Hera hated. Sirena brings food for the man and tends his wound, nursing him to health. The two fall in love, mate, and enjoy ten mostly blissful years together. Sirena believes Philoctetes truly loves her since she did not use her songs to enthrall him, and he devotedly and delightedly shares with her relics of a past human civilization he finds on the island and stories of the gods and human doings. She worries, however, because she knows he misses his old life and companions, and, since she was granted immortality when they mated, she knows that he is aging while she is not. A ship puts in one day, bearing Odysseus and Neoptolemus, fellow Greeks who wish Philoctetes to return with them to Troy in order to defeat the Trojans by slaying Paris, prince of Troy. It has been foretold that Paris cannot be slain except by the arrows of Heracles, items Philoctetes possesses. Although Sirena attempts to dissuade him, he feels compelled by honor and duty to join them. He says he will return to her and sails off, leaving her alone on the island and aware that she will probably never see him again. She knows that by using her magical songs she could keep him but chooses not do so. She too reponds to the call of honor. The linear plot is uncomplicated in structure and substance but not in thematic elements, which tackle universal human matters that are examined in the Homeric epics: the obligations of duty, love, honor, and war; the nature of immortals and of humans; and the relationships between the two orders. Sirena and Philoctetes are both sympathetically drawn, and information about the gods and mythological events are skillfully worked into the base narrative. The style is lyrical and moving, especially in the early part of the book, and evokes the sounds and sense of the winds, seas, waves, and the purity of the elements and helps to establish Sirena's character, but also because of the descriptive aspect, lessening the credibility of the first-person narration. Visual imagery is strong and widespread, and the book projects a pleasing elegance worthy of events of a long-ago and far-off time. ALA/YA.

THE SKIN I'M IN (Flake*, Sharon G., Hyperion, 1998)   Mostly psychological-problem novel of an African American seventh grader with low self-esteem in an unidentified big U.S. city. Maleeka Madison, 13, has some external problems: her father died four years ago; her mother, who fell apart at his death, is still in fragile emotional condition; and they have very little money. Her most important problem, however, is her self-perception as a loser, because, though she is very bright, she is also very dark and is constantly teased about her appearance, harassment usually instigated by her classmate, John-John McIntrye. She is also bullied and exploited by Charlese, an older girl now in seventh grade for the third time, who deliberately humiliates her and, in exchange for Maleeka's doing her homework, brings some of her cast-off fancy clothes to school each day so Maleeka can change out of the ill-fitting garments her mother makes. By keeping a low profile, Maleeka is able to bear all this until the arrival of the new English teacher, Miss Saunders, an advertising agency executive trying her hand at teaching for a change. Miss Saunders is not only very tall, she also has a disfiguring birthmark on one side of her face. When she directs her concern on Maleeka, it makes the girl's life worse, since the other students resent the special attention. After Maleeka gets in a fight in the hall, Miss Saunders arranges that she work in

the school office, free, after school each day, a job she at first despises, then begins to like. There she observes how the other teachers resent Miss Saunders for her successful career, her new ideas, and her different relationship to the students. In a series of incidents, Charlese threatens and dominates Maleeka, teaming up with her sidekicks, the twins, Raina and Raise, to lead her on and then humiliate her. This culminates in a midnight venture into the school, which Charlese insists Maleeka join to vandalize Miss Saunders's room. Charlese finds some foreign paper money in one of the drawers, piles it on the desk, holds out her cigarette lighter, and demands that Maleeka start a fire. When Maleeka refuses, Charlese threatens her physically until she complies. A breeze catches the flames, and the window curtains blaze up. They all flee, but the janitor recognizes Maleeka. She is suspended from school and restricted by her mother. Sent to the store, partly to embarrass her further because all the neighbors know the story, she is joined by John-John, who is suddenly jumped and beaten by a gang of older boys. She grabs a branch from a nearby bush and swings at the boys. They turn from John-John and attack her, but suddenly the neighbors, who have been watching passively, are there with brooms, bats, and shovels, led by Caleb Assam, a boy from her school, wading in and driving off the big boys. In the midst of all her trauma, a letter arrives saying that Maleeka has won a writing contest with a one-hundred-dollar prize. It will not go far, however, to pay for the two-thousand-dollar damages. Although Charlese offers to help pay and then reneges, Maleeka does not tell on her until they meet in Miss Saunders's room and Charlese is so verbally abusive that Maleeka flares up, screaming that she may be black but she is not as ugly inside as Charlese, that she would never force someone to burn a teacher's room and lie about it as she and the twins are doing. With the truth out, Charlese disappears, sent by her older party girl sister with whom she lives to her grandparents in Alabama; the twins are suspended; Caleb declares his love for Maleeka in a poem; and she realizes that even John-John is glad she came out of the trouble all right. Although the story is predictable, the ending is contrived, and most of the characters are one dimensional, Maleeka's problems catch the interest and sympathy of a reader. School scenes, which dominate the book, show an institution on the verge of chaos, with kids mouthing off at teachers, threatening and bullying each other, casually destroying property, and covering rest room and hall walls with graffiti. All the students and most of the teachers seem to be African Americans. ALA/YA.

SKURZYNSKI, GLORIA (JEAN FLISTER) (1930–   )   Born in Duquesne, Pennsylvania; author of many different kinds of books for young people. Her *Virtual War** (Simon & Schuster, 1997) is a futuristic fantasy in which young people are bred and trained to compete in a computer-based battle among the few remaining peoples on earth. Diving into the past, she wrote *Spider's Voice** (Simon & Schuster, 1999), a biographical novel of the twelfth-century French lovers, Abelard and Eloise. For earlier biographical information and title entries, see *Dictionary, 1960–1984* [*What Happened in Hamlin*], *Dictionary, 1985–1989* [*Trapped in Slickrock Canyon*], and *Dictionary, 1995–1999* [*Wolf Stalker*].

SLAM! (Myers*, Walter Dean, Scholastic, 1996)   Basketball novel set recently in the Harlem section of New York City, in which a resentful African American boy comes to terms with his place in a mostly white school and his discovery that his best friend is dealing drugs. For a longer entry, see *Dictionary, 1995–1999*. ALA/YA.

SMITH, DIANE   A Montana naturalist who writes about science and the environment from her home. Her first novel, *Letters from Yellowstone** (Viking, 1999), published for adults, was chosen by *Booklist* for young adult readers. A period story told entirely in letters, it describes a botanical expedition to Yellowstone National Park in the summer of 1898.

SMITH, ROLAND (1951–   )   Born in Portland, Oregon; received his B.A. from Portland State University; research biologist and author. He is best known for his twelve nonfiction books for middle grade readers illustrated with his own photographs, several of which have received prestigious awards for science and social studies. Of his novels for young readers, *Sasquatch** (Hyperion, 1998), a father–son adventure story involving the Sasquatch on Mount Saint Helens, was selected by the American Library Association for young adults. Earlier, he published *Thunder Cave* (Hyperion, 1995), about a boy who travels to Kenya to find his father; *Jaguar* (Hyperion, 1997), which takes the same boy to the Amazon; and, more recently, *The Last Lobo* (Hyperion, 1999), which is set in Hopi land in Arizona. In *Zach's Lie* (Hyperion, 2001), a family flees to Nevada to escape a drug cartel. Smith lives in Wilsonville, Oregon.

SNOW IN AUGUST (Hamill*, Pete, Little, Brown, 1997)   Adult realistic period novel about religious and racial discrimination with fantasy and boy's growing-up elements set from December 1946 to August 1947. Crazy about Captain Marvel comics and swashbuckling deeds, Irish-Catholic Michael Devlin, 11, awakens early one snowy Saturday morning late in December. As he trudges through the deep drifts in his mixed-ethnic, deteriorating neighborhood in Brooklyn, New York, toward Sacred Heart Church for his duties as altar boy for Father* Heaney, he encounters Rabbi* Judah Hirsch. He is a little afraid of the rabbi with his long black beard and heavy, dark tweed coat who is new to America and the neighborhood. This chance meeting between the earnest, conscientious boy and the rabbi initiates a mutually satisfying friendship. The rabbi helps the boy discover the joy of words, books, and school achievement, tells him fascinating stories about his native Prague, and teaches him Yiddish. Michael instructs the rabbi in the mysteries of baseball and the English language, both of which the Rabbi feels are important to being an American. For weeks, Michael spends most Tuesday and Thursday afternoons with his new friend, thrilling to his stories, especially the one about the legendary Golem*, the huge man created years ago from clay to defend the Jews. The two attend a baseball game at Ebbets Field, cheer for Jacky Robinson, and hear jeers directed against him, the first black player in the major league. Michael's association with the rabbi also introduces him to local prejudice against Jews, first, with his pals Sonny and Jimmy, who spout anti-Semitic gossip, and second, and most significantly, with Frankie McCarthy, an older boy who belongs to a gang of local toughs, the Falcons. Frankie viciously beats Mr. G [*sic*], the Jewish owner of the nearby candy store. Michael faces a dilemma: whether to tell the police he witnessed the incident. He shares his dilemma with the rabbi, who says that not telling about a crime is as bad as the crime itself. More incidents follow, among them swastikas painted on the synagogue wall, "Jew lover" painted on the roof door of the Devlin flat, and a severe assault against Michael that lands him in the hospital. Michael and his mother, Kate*, are attacked by five Falcons, Kate is almost raped, and the rabbi is beaten and left for dead in the gutter. When Michael hears that Frankie has a gun, Michael visits Rabbi Hirsch in the hospital, asks him for the secret name of God, and with meticulous care fashions the Golem and brings him to life with the sacred word. In the midst of a tremendous, unseasonable snowstorm, the Golem and the boy, invisible, march to the pool room where Frankie hangs out, and, now visible, the Golem attacks the Falcons, especially Frankie, but not before Michael tells Frankie that he did not squeal but truly wishes that he had. The snow stops suddenly, and the pair, again invisible, go to the hospital, the Golem picks up Rabbi Hirsch, and the three return to the synagogue, on the way passing the pool room in front of which stands an ambulance. The conclusion is puzzling: Did this episode really happen, or did Michael imagine it, acting out in his mind what he would have liked to have happen? The main characters are strongly drawn, especially the dynamic Michael and the distinctive rabbi. Period details re-create the times vividly, but some dialogue and expressions seem more late than mid-twentieth century. It is also unclear whether Michael merely imagines himself in the stories Rabbi Hirsch tells or whether he actually goes back in time to the earlier era. The antidiscrimination message becomes heavy, but the book has many funny scenes, as when the Rabbi strives to master idioms and poses questions about baseball terms and jargon. Alex; Booklist.

SOLDIER'S HEART: A NOVEL OF THE CIVIL WAR (Paulsen*, Gary, Delacorte, 1998)   Historical novel of a Minnesota farm boy in the American Civil War, based on the experiences of an actual figure. In June 1861, Charley Goddard, 15, lies about his age and joins the Minnesota Volunteers. After Bull Run and Gettysburg, only forty-seven of the one thousand Minnesota men are left standing. Sorely wounded, Charley returns home, broken in body and spirit, old at twenty-one. The real Charley Goddard died at twenty-three of "soldier's heart," what today is called "posttraumatic stress disorder." This short novel's lean, laconic style, vividly drawn scenes, and gallant-spirited hero make the war very personal. Previously, the book won the Jefferson Cup Award for Historical Fiction. For a longer entry, see *Dictionary, 1995–1999*. ALA/YA; NYPL.

SOMEONE LIKE YOU (Dessen*, Sarah, Viking, 1998)   Novel set in an unidentified American town about a high school friendship of two girls who support each other through difficulties, one with a pregnancy and the other with an unsuitable boyfriend who becomes abusive. A secondary plot involves their relationships with their mothers. For a longer entry, see *Dictionary, 1995–1999*. ALA/YA.

SOMEONE TO LOVE (Lantz*, Francess L., Avon, 1997)   Epistolary novel of modern family life in which the projected adoption of a newborn brings to a crisis the relationship between a fifteen-year-old girl and her parents. In a long letter to her yet-to-be-born sibling, with entries from September to February, Sara Dewherst, the narrator, records her life at Laguna Verde High and her conflicts with her parents, whom she views as conventional, materialistic, and controlling. She and her close high school friends, especially Marc, who is an articulate activist, are vegetarians devoted to PETA (People for the Ethical Treatment of Animals) and other social causes. When her parents, Marty and Jeanette, who run an upscale restaurant called "The Wharf," find that their best friends have a new baby acquired through an open adoption, the idea begins to percolate with them and soon they are in contact with Iris Boone, 18, from Indio, who is almost six months pregnant and planning to give up the baby. They meet in a park and discuss the possibility in a stiff, stilted way, but Sara is able to talk to Iris privately and learn more about her. Iris is from a large, dysfunctional family, left home when the responsibilty for her younger siblings became overpowering, and now lives in a blue-collar town about twenty miles away with her boyfriend, Eddie, who wants nothing to do with the baby. In the next months, although her parents have forbidden her to talk to the prospective mother alone, afraid she will either be contaminated or will somehow disrupt the prospects for adoption, Sara makes frequent contact with Iris and greatly admires her spirit and her skill at making jewelry and imaginative clothes. She even finds occasion to get Iris to their house, so she can see the expensive crib and toys her parents have already acquired. When Marc invites Sara to a pro-choice concert in Los Angeles, she impulsively suggests that Iris and Eddie go with them, but both Marc and Eddie back out. Secretly, because Sara has not been given permission, the girls take the train and have a fine time until some anti-choice demonstrators start a riot and they have difficulty escaping uninjured. In the meantime, Sara gets to know Cody, a quiet, outdoorsish boy, because she has learned that he is adopted and wonders how he feels about contact with his birth mother. Without telling him the reason for her interest, she questions him and gets some perspective on adoption, which he thinks was great for him, even though he looked up his birth mother and went to see her. Sara and Cody take a long hike at Howorth Ranch, a beautiful area Cody obsessively wants to save from development. Sara goes with her parents and Iris to an obstetrician and to a birthing class, but she is infuriated by their attitude, treating Iris as their property and even giving her an allowance so she can buy a used van, but still wanting to keep an emotional distance from her. The relationship reaches a climax when Iris shows up one night when Sara is alone, having been beaten by Eddie and needing a place to stay. Sara gets her to her bed, but when her parents come home they erupt in anger. Iris overhears them and, saying she will make other arrangements for the baby, walks out. Marty, infuriated, says they don't want another teenager, they don't even want the one they have. Sara slams out, joins Iris in her van, and persuades her to drive to Los Angeles, where they will get an apartment together and Iris can start selling her jewelry. The trip is a disaster from the start. The van breaks down, and they hitchhike into the city, spend the night in Union Station, get a dismal third-rate apartment, and have no luck at the stores where Sara tries to place the jewelry on consignment. Although Sara is too young, Iris gets a job at a hamburger stand but, after a few ten-hour days, faints at the job and is fired.

They quarrel, and Iris says she will call Eddie to come and get her, but before she does she goes into labor. Sara calls an ambulance, gets her to a hospital, and helps her through her contractions, but she realizes that she cannot handle this alone and calls her parents. By the time they arrive, the doctor has decided Iris needs a cesarean section, and the Dewhersts wait together for the birth of the baby, a boy whom they call Skyler. A letter from Iris says she has moved back to Indio and started junior college. Although Cody and Sara have a falling out over her using him as a research source on adoption, they run into each other when she is walking Skyler in a stroller, he adores the baby, and their future looks rosy. The novel is obviously written to explain one aspect of adoption with characters drawn to fill roles. The parents, especially, are types, as are Marc, the ego-driven activist; Cody, the genuine nature lover; Eddie, the wild, drugging, motorcycling batterer; and even Sara, the naive but good-hearted teenager. Despite pedestrian style, there is some interest in what will happen to Iris, the most interesting character. ALA/YA.

SONG IN THE SILENCE: THE TALE OF LANEN KAELAR (Kerner*, Elizabeth, Tor, 1997)   Adult fantasy of adventure and romance set once upon a time in the mythical land of Kolmar, involving magic, dragons, and the fight between good and evil. Tall, strong, plain Lanen Kaelar, the main narrator, has never been away from the farm of her birth in the northern part of Kolmar. Her mother, Maran Vena, left home shortly after Lanen's birth; her father, Hadron, is a cold, remote man; and her dearest friend and surrogate father is her father's steward, Jamie*. When she is twenty-three and Hadron dies, she accompanies Jamie to the horse fair in the city of Illara and, once the horse selling is finished, continues to the Dragon Isle off the coast to the southwest, having had a deep desire to go there ever since she heard a passing bard sing of the True Kindred who live there. While in Illara, she learns from Jamie that Jamie knew her mother before she married Hadron. Maran was living with a merchant, Marik of Gundar, who leagued himself with Berys, the Demonlord, for special powers in return for which Marik pledged his first child. Lanen also meets handsome, light-haired Bors of Trissen, a merchant who she learns later is really Marik and whose ship is soon to sail for the Dragon Isle to harvest lansip, leaves from a tree that can heal and bring back youth. Lanen travels downriver on a riverboat, and at the coast embarks upon Marik's ship, and twelve days' sailing later arrives at the Isle. The True Kindred emphasize law and order, and their rules for Gedri (humans) on the island are strict. Gedri are especially never to cross the Boundary that separates the very southeastern area from the rest of the island where the Kindred live. Yearning to see one of the True Kindred, Lanen goes by night to the Boundary, where she meets the Guardian, a large, gentle, silver Dragon named Akhor. She addresses him as brother, unlike most Gedri who despise the Kindred and call them Dragons, a disparaging term. The two soon fall in love, and much of the book concerns their romance, which is not viewed with favor by the True Kindred because it violates the natural order of things, and, in particular, because Akhor is their king. The True Kindred gather in Council and, although both Akhor and Lanen speak valiantly on their own behalf, sentiment runs against them. Marik changes matters completely and abruptly, however, when he steals across the

Boundary, seizes the Kindred's gold and most valuable gems, and, having determined that Lanen is really his daughter, prepares to dedicate her in death to the Demonlord. A mighty struggle ensues between Marik and the Kindred. Things so fall out that Akhor is slain, but as he dies, the Kindred part of him is burned away by his internal Dragon fire, and he is revived as a man, Varien. Lanen is injured but recovers, and at the end both return to Lanen's farm, are married, and prepare for a life together. The central part of the novel, which deals with the romance, is tedious, and the book seems derivative of other mythical world and dragon novels. The many struggles, however, and the details about the ways, history, hopes, and ethical standards of the True Kindred, all of which are supported by high diction, are skillfully worked out. Jamie is a strong figure who carries the first part of the novel. The geography of Kolmar and of the Dragon Isle is another good element, but the book outruns itself and would have benefited from cutting. Its nearly five hundred pages may challenge some teens, while true fantasy fans will find the length, detail, and abundant conversation much to their liking. The sequel is *The Lesser Kindred*. ALA/YA.

SONG OF THE MAGDALENE (Napoli*, Donna Jo, Scholastic, 1996)   Period novel set in Palestine in the first century of the Christian era, telling of the childhood and early youth of the woman known as Mary Magdalene. Miriam, 10, the narrator, lives in a pious household in the village of Magdala just west of the Sea of Galilee with her widower father, a wealthy trader, their housekeeper, Hannah, and Hannah's son, Abraham, 13, frail, crippled, palsied since birth, and considered an idiot. In the countryside one day, Miriam suffers a sudden, unexplained fit. Sure that she is somehow impure, she tells no one what happened. Abraham teaches her to read the sacred texts and the canticles, always in private. When she is close to twelve, she has another fit, alone with Abraham at home in front of the fireplace. He now knows why she is so often unhappy and assures her that despite her malady she is a good person and valued. The special relationship they enjoy ripens into romantic love. A chance encounter with a Roman foot soldier in the marketplace during which she is almost propositioned impresses on her the need to be more circumspect, to spend less time by herself and with Abraham, and to veil herself, dress modestly, and behave according to Jewish custom. She finds comfort in going to the women's house after her periods and to the house of prayer, where the Levites sing, but one day she forgets herself and sings alone, something that women never do, horrifying everyone present. Judith, her father's new wife, mothers her emotionally and intellectually and helps her adjust to expectations. When Abraham falls ill of what will be a terminal fever, Miriam nurses him day and night and becomes pregnant by him. They are sure the baby will be a son, and Abraham names him Isaac. Abraham dies before the baby is born, leaving Miriam with a second secret, again alone and isolated. She suffers another fit when she is accosted and raped by a village carpenter, who justifies the act by asserting she is wanton, and the baby boy is born dead. Despised generally now, she is sent to live with her mother's brother in Dor, stays there for two years, and leaves after she has another fit and is considered possessed. She travels south along the Jordan River, sees the preacher Jochanan the Baptist, who emphasizes

love and acceptance, but she decides not to join his followers. For six months she lives quietly in caves near the Dead Sea, until she encounters a Roman woman, Lucia, who hopes that a Galilean healer named Joshua can cure her ill daughter. On the way north to Capernaum, Miriam pays her respects at the graves of her mother, Abraham, and Isaac, and is stoned by the village women. She runs toward the house of prayer, where she suffers her seventh and last fit. She is rescued by Joshua, a small, thin, ugly man who has come to heal in Magdala. He assures everyone that she has no devils within her. The book's last short paragraph informs the reader that Miriam joins Joshua's company, carrying an alabaster jar of ointment to minister to beggars and the infirm. She also carries a song in her heart, "for there were many souls to heal." Occasionally the dialogue is stilted and sentimentality creeps in, but Miriam's plight is made credible and sympathetic. The emphasis is always on Miriam's feelings and situation, but a strong if limited sense of a woman's life comes through—male supremacy, women's duties, the assumption that nonconforming or unfortunate women are prostitutes, being forced into prostitution to exist, hatred of the Romans—the period is painted in broad strokes. ALA/YA.

SONS OF LIBERTY (Griffin*, Adele, Hyperion, 1997)   Realistic family novel of contemporary home life and sociological-problem novel set in the small town of Sheffield, Connecticut. Rock Hinkle, 14, from whose vantage point most events are seen, loves history and is deeply involved in collecting information for and writing a paper about the American Revolution. His brother, Cliff, 16, a good student with ambitions for college, spends his spare time preparing architectural drawings. Both deeply love their increasingly shy mother, Katherine, who lives in fear of her loud-mouthed, bullying husband, George. The boys resentfully call their father "Cowboy George," for his belligerent attitude. They are more and more rebellious about what they term the "Interruptions," the times when he wakes them up at night to punish them for what is usually a minor infraction or involve them in some project. Down the street lives Liza Vincent, a tiny, flamboyant, strong-minded girl Rock's age, who is beaten and abused by her stepfather to the extent that she sometimes cannot attend school. Liza asks the boys' help in running away to New Haven, where she has the address of one Seamus Barnes, a school dropout, who invited her to join him. They discover that Seamus's place has been raided and shut down by police as a hangout for runaways and druggies, and Liza elects to head for San Diego. The boys return to Sheffield, where they tell the family and authorities that Liza will soon come home. Later, in another rage, George destroys Rock's essay and index cards, berates their little sister, Brontie, for wetting her bed, and punishes her by taking away her beloved doll, Wynona. What Liza has done inspires Cliff to make arrangements for them to go to Arizona to live with Katherine's sister, Louise. Rock, who has all along compared what is happening to his family with the American Revolution, sees their situation as a battle, Cliff as the general, and their father as the enemy. One rainy night, Dad awakens them again, ranting about the leaking roof, which they had earlier repaired in another nighttime work detail, and insists they help him fix it. Rock soon learns that Cliff has removed shingles in order to get

their father up on the roof so that he, Rock, Brontie, and their mother can leave. At first Rock drags his feet, feeling that by leaving he is betraying his father, but when Cliff says their father is not letting them function as a real family, the logic of Cliff's words and a "thousand memories" of good times with his brother lure him. He gets into the car, thinking that "a revolution is a strange and complicated thing." Characters are one dimensional, events proceed much as anticipated, and the reader is left to ponder what has happened to Liza, what options are open to the Hinkle family, and what extended meaning this bleak account of two severely dysfunctional families is intended to convey. ALA/YA.

SOTO, GARY (1952–)   Born in Fresno, California; raised in the San Joaquin Valley where he worked as a farm laborer when he was a child; graduate with a B.A. from California State University–Fresno and with an M.F.A. from the University of California–Irvine; teacher, lecturer, and poet in residence at several universities; full-time writer since 1993. One of the most highly regarded of contemporary Hispanic American writers, the versatile Soto has published poetry, novels, plays, and short stories for adults, young adults, and children that reflect with wit, understanding, and compassion the Hispanic experience in central California. For his more than fifty published works and several films he has received numerous awards, prizes, and fellowships. *Buried Onions** (Harcourt, 1997), an American Library Association choice for young adults, is typical of his concern for the plight of young urban Hispanics. Although this book is serious and often bleak, many of Soto's works are more upbeat and even humorous. Recent titles include *If the Shoe Fits* (Putnam, 2002), a picture book, and *Fearless Fernie* (Putnam, 2002), poems. For other titles by Soto, see *This Land Is Our Land* [*Baseball in April and Other Stories*, no. 376; *The Cat's Meow*, no. 377; *Neighborhood Odes*, 409a; *Pieces of the Heart*, no. 378; *The Skirt*, no. 379; *Taking Sides*, no. 380; *Who Will Know Us?*, no. 409b] and *Many Peoples, One Land* [*Big Bushy Mustache*, no. 355; *Boys at Work*, no. 356; *Canto familiar*, no. 411; *Chato's Kitchen*, no. 358; *Crazy Weekend*, no. 359; *Jesse*, no. 360; *Junior College*, no. 412; *New and Selected Poems*, no. 413; *Off and Running*, no. 361; *The Old Man and the Door*, no. 362; *Petty Crimes*, no. 361.

SOUTHGATE, MARTHA Born in Cleveland, Ohio; received a B.A. from Smith College and an M.F.A. from Goddard College; reporter, editor, and writer of the African American experience. Selected by the American Library Association for young adults, *Another Way to Dance** (Delacorte, 1996) is a career novel of an African American girl chosen for the summer program at the School of American ballet. Southgate has also published *The Fall of Rome* (Scribner, 2002), a complex adult novel about two teachers in a prestigious white Connecticut private school, one white, one black. Southgate has contributed to periodicals and has made her home in Brooklyn, New York.

SPARKS, NICHOLAS (1965–) Born in Omaha, Nebraska; author of several best-selling novels, some of which have been made into movies. In his early childhood, he lived in Minnesota, Los Angeles, and Grand Island, Nebraska, until settling, at the age of eight, in Fair Oaks, California, where he was graduated valedictorian from high school in 1984. He at-tended the University of Notre Dame on a track scholarship, graduating in 1989. After a variety of short-lived jobs, he moved to North Carolina and wrote *The Notebook* (Warner, 1995), which was on the *New York Times* bestseller list for fifty-six weeks, followed by another bestseller, *Message in a Bottle* (Warner, 1998). Other novels include *A Walk to Remember** (Warner, 1999), named by *Booklist* for young adulta; *The Rescue* (Warner, 2000); and *A Bend in the Road* (Warner, 2001).

SPEAK (Anderson*, Laurie Halse, Farrar, 1999) Psychological-problem novel of a ninth-grade girl who has been raped at a party and, unable to tell anyone, suffers severe depression and becomes unable to speak. It is also a scathing picture of social life in a modern high school, this one in Syracuse, New York. For a longer entry, see *Dictionary, 1995–1999*. ALA/YA; Printz Honor.

SPIDER'S VOICE (Skurzynski*, Gloria, Atheneum, 1999) Biographical novel of the twelfth-century French lovers, Abelard and Eloise, as witnessed by a mute peasant boy who becomes the servant of Abelard and friend of both. The narrator, Aran, born mute with his tongue attached to the floor of his mouth, is thought by his father to be an idiot, but his mother sees that he has intelligence, and she teaches him what she can, including spinning, though his chief job is to watch the sheep. After her death, Aran spins the wool into fine thread and goes from their home village of Les Andelys in Normandy to Paris with his brutal brother, Eustace, to sell it. Eustace gets drunk, is robbed, and to recoup his losses sells Aran to Galien of Laon, a man who deals in freaks. To produce a "human spi-der," Galien has him fitted with a metal carapace that will keep his body from growing but allow his legs and arms to lengthen, producing a monstrosity to amuse nobles and court ladies. Badly burned by the blacksmith, Aran suffers terribly, but is kindly treated by Flore, the grotesquely ugly woman who cares for the freaks until they are sold. To the astonishment of all, a group of students led by their teacher, Abelard, storm Galien's stronghold and steal Aran to be a servant for the famous lecturer, who needs the utter discretion of one unable to tell of his love trysts with beautiful Eloise, to whom he is tutor. Called "Spider," although his carapace is cut off, Aran listens to his master's lectures and discussions with his students and absorbs all the learning he can. When Eloise's uncle, Canon Fulbert, learns of their lovemaking and Eloise tells Abelard she is with child, they flee to his family home in Brittany, where his sister, Denise, welcomes them. Eloise and Aran are happy through the summer, but Abelard is restless, needing the stimulus of his audience of students. Trying to find an interest for him, Eloise suggests that he teach Aran to read, and he starts, but soon decides to return to Paris, leaving Aran behind as a servant for Eloise, who tries to continue the lessons but is distracted by cares of the household. Just before Christmas, she gives birth to a boy, Peter Astrolabe, and Abelard returns briefly, but is soon gone again. He returns for Easter, as he has promised, with a new idea: he will marry Eloise, thereby making peace with Fulbert. She refuses, saying scholars are not supposed to marry and it will bring disaster. Abelard insists, and they agree to be married secretly, pleasing no one, not even Fulbert, who cannot brag about his famous relative. Afraid that in his fury he will harm Eloise, Abelard takes her to a nearby nunnery, an act that further enrages Fulbert, who thinks he might be planning to have their marriage annulled. Aran sleeps at the foot of the stairs to warn him, but is seized and gagged, while Fulbert's men castrate Abelard. Afterward, in horrible pain, Abelard, knife in hand, lunges at the boy and cuts the cord that binds his tongue to the floor of his mouth. Why he takes that action at the moment is never clear; later he cannot remember having done it. Aran stumbles off and eventually finds his way back to his father's hut, where he again watches the sheep and spins, but now secretly tries to make his freed tongue form words. When he leaves his drunken father and returns to Paris, he learns that Abelard is being tried for heresy and is put under house arrest. From that time on, Aran's life is attached to Abelard, who hardly notices that the boy now speaks and sends him to stay at Rambouillet, the estate of Marcel DuChesne, one of his former students. Still mute, since he does not trust his own voice, Aran spends months playing chess with Marcel and waiting for a summons from Abelard. In the winter, a holy hermit arrives, and Marcel's shallow wife demands a miracle. Among the hermit's straggly band of followers, Aran finds Flore, ill and emaciated, with a lovely three-year-old daughter. To get aid for her, Aran allows a "miracle" to be performed on him, and shouts out, "Praise Jesus!" As a reward, Aran asks that Flore be brought into his tiny room, washed, given a warm garment, and put in his bed, while the little girl, Joie, becomes a favorite in the house. As Flore gets healthier, he manages to get her to be a supervisor in the kitchen, knowing she is an excellent cook. Although she is grateful, Flore devastates Aran by telling him that he will never be a true man because the burns he received when Galien had him fitted with the cage essentially castrated him. Traveling between Abelard and Eloise, who is now a mother superior of a nunnery, Aran carries letters and sees that copies are made so the world will know of their great love. After Flore dies, he comes to terms with his own condition and makes sure that Eloise will see that Joie, who loves him like the father she has never known, will have an education and be assured some freedom in life. Although they share a great passion, Abelard is shown to be self-centered, a far less admirable person than Eloise. The pictures of life in Paris of the twelfth century and in the peasant huts and on the rich estates are compelling, and while Aran's injuries paralleling Abelard's may be too pat, he is an appealing character. An author's note tells what in the novel is fiction and gives references to more information about the famous lovers. ALA/YA.

SPINELLI, JERRY (1941–)   Born in Norristown, Pennsylvania; received an A.B. from Gettysburg College and an M.A. from Johns Hopkins University, and did further work at Temple University; popular writer of more than twenty humorous novels of school, family, and community life mostly for middle graders. Best known for the brash, lively *Maniac Magee* (Little, Brown, 1990), which won the Newbery Medal and other awards and citations, he has also published *Crash** (Knopf, 1996), about the friendship between a football hero and a Quaker boy, and *Stargirl** (Knopf, 2000), about a flamboyant, nonconformist girl who shakes up her high school. Both books are American Library Association choices for young adults. Among his recent publications is *Loser* (Joanna Cotler, 2002), about a boy who thinks he is one. For more in-formation about Spinelli, titles, and title entries, see *Dictionary, 1990–1994* [*Maniac Magee*] and *Dictionary, 1995–1999* [*Crash*; *Wringer*].

THE SPIRIT WINDOW (Sweeney*, Joyce, Delacorte, 1998)   Realistic novel of family life set one summer in recent years on Turtle Island off the east coast of southern Florida. The Gates family—pretty, self-assured Miranda, 15; her often contentious and superior-acting father, Richard, a successful psychiatrist; and his second wife much his junior, beautiful, golden-haired Ariel—travel from Cincinnati, Ohio, to Florida to spend the summer with Richard's wealthy mother, Lila, from whom he has been estranged for ten years. About eighty, flamboyant, lively Lila lives on a remote part of Turtle Island in a big, well-appointed house surrounded by woods and wetlands teeming with wildlife. Miranda soon learns that her grandmother is a nature activist, determined to preserve the environment on her part of the island and involved in environmental groups. Miranda meets Lila's good-looking gardener, Adam Fitzgerald, about eighteen, who lives in the gardener's shed, a half-Cherokee, half-Irish American young man of whom Lila is very fond and who seems devoted to her. He and Miranda meet inauspiciously, since he startles her as she strolls in the woods and frightens her. As a result, bad blood begins between Adam and Richard and persists throughout the book. Adam and Miranda spend her first day in town, on errands, and on the beach, and a low-key romance begins. Richard spends the day with an old school chum, sharp-dressing, smooth-talking real estate developer Skip Wilson, star athlete and Richard's hero in high school. Miranda learns that Richard signed a paper promising Skip that when he inherits the property he will sign it over to Skip who wants it for a shopping mall. Three weeks later, Lila suffers a heart attack and dies. The formalities over, Lila's lawyer plays a videotape in which Lila specifies that substantial sums of money go to Miranda and Richard, but the house and estate go to Adam, because he respects her wishes about the land. Richard is furious and accuses Adam of undue influence. Skip encourages Richard in this attitude and suggests that they hire a detective to investigate Adam in order to blackmail him into signing the estate over to Richard. Adam is frightened, explaining to Miranda that he had been in jail briefly in Tennessee for hitting his drunken, abusive father and then jumped bail and came to Florida. Ariel is upset because of Richard's intense anger and desire to please Skip and leaves him. Richard and Adam get into an argument, Adam strikes him, and Richard presses charges. Before visiting Adam in jail, Miranda tells Richard that he has won. He now has the information that he needs to get the property away from Adam, but she also points out that in the process he has ironically lost everyone dear to him, almost including her. Later, after a walk in the marsh to the place where he had proposed to her deceased mother, Richard drops the charges against Adam and sends Skip packing. Richard and Miranda prepare to return to Ohio. Miranda and Adam may some day be sweethearts, and Richard will try to make up with Ariel. The title comes from an episode on a hill in the woods where Miranda, as she and Adam commemorate Lila's life in a kind of Native American ceremony, sees Lila's spirit face in a window in a short fantasy sequence, an obscure scene. The conclusion is rushed, with proud, strong-willed Richard changing very abruptly. Skip is a transparently greedy, manipulative figure; Lila is strongly drawn and credible; Miranda gains praise for her strength, perception, and courage; and Adam, although the Native American part seems forced and convenient, is decent and sympathetic. Descriptions of the area and its wildlife, in particular the birds, are vivid and dramatic, and the family life, if turbulent, seems believable. ALA/YA.

SPRINGER, NANCY (1948–) Born in Montclair, New Jersey; educator, writer. Her novel, *I Am Mordred: A Tale from Camelot** (Philomel, 1998), is a new look at the pivotal character of the King Arthur stories. For earlier biographical information and title entries, see *Dictionary, 1995–1999* [*Looking for Jamie Bridger; Toughing It*].

THE SQUIRE, HIS KNIGHT, & HIS LADY (Morris*, Gerald, Houghton, 1999) Second in a series of lightly humorous retellings of Arthurian tales, following *The Squire's Tale* (Houghton, 1998). This novel is basically the story of *Sir Gawain and the Green Knight*, with the focus on his squire, Terrence, and the girl they rescue and take with them on their quest, Eileen, niece of the wicked marquis of Alva. In its outline, it follows the action of the medieval poem. At the great Christmas feast at Camelot, a strange knight appears and challenges anyone there to a contest: he will bare his neck for a blow from his mighty war ax, and if he survives, the one who dealt the blow must come, one year from that day, to receive a similar blow from the Green Knight at his chapel. Although Arthur is willing to take up the challenge himself, Gawain intervenes, pointing out that Arthur is essential to the realm and insisting on wielding the blow in his stead. With his mighty cut from the ax, the Green Knight's head falls off. The man, obviously from faeryland, picks up the head and walks off. For a year Gawain and Terrence hunt for the Green Chapel, coming to the castle of Sir Bercilak just before Christmas, and there being entertained, with the assurance that the Green Chapel is not far off. In the contest, which is more psychological than physical, Gawain learns of his own character flaw and escapes humbled. This novel adds numerous adventures, including a visit to the Other World, where Terrence finally gets to know his father, Ganscotter the Enchanter, and Gawain sees his long-dead little sister, Elaine, and marries Ganscotter's daughter, Lorie. Purists will regret the change in tone from Arthurian tale, this novel being comic in much of its dialogue and events. Eileen is more an independent late-twentieth-century type of girl than any from tales of the period. The action, however, is fast paced, never faltering, and should keep the intended audience of middle school readers amused and spellbound. ALA/YA.

STANLEY, DIANE (1943–)   Born in Abilene, Texas; educated at Trinity University, San Antonio (B.A.), Edinburgh College of Art, and Johns Hopkins University (M.A.). She has been art director of children's books for G. P. Putnam's Sons, illustrator, and writer. She is the author of more than two dozen mostly self-illustrated books for children, the most acclaimed of which are the several picture-book biographies of such figures as Peter the Great and Elizabeth I. *A Time Apart** (Morrow, 1999) is her first novel. Cited for young adults by the American Library Association, it tells of an American girl who reluctantly goes to live with her anthropologist father in England while he is working on an Iron Age proj-

ect. The book was inspired by an actual Iron Age project in 1978, which was the focus of a BBC documentary and which Stanley's mother, also a writer, had intended to write about. Recent publications include *The Mysterious Matter of I. M. Fine* (HarperCollins, 2001), in which two girls search for the author of horror novels, and two time-travel picture books, *Roughing It on the Oregon Trail* (HarperCollins, 2000) and *Joining the Boston Tea Party* (HarperCollins, 2001).

STAPLES, SUZANNE FISHER (1945–) Born in Philadelphia, Pennsylvania; graduate of Cedar Crest College with a B.A.; journalist, news editor, correspondent, and foreign editor; writer of novels mostly for young adults. Her best-known book is her first, *Shabanu* (Knopf, 1989), about the nomads of Pakistan, which, among other citations, was a Newbery Honor Book. Chosen by the American Library Association for young adults is *Dangerous Skies** (Farrar, 1996), set among the fisherfolk and farmers of Chesapeake Bay and involving racial prejudice. More recently, she has published *Shiva's Fire* (Farrar, 2000), about a talented girl dancer in India, and *The Green Dog: A Mostly True Story* (Farrar, 2003), for younger readers. Staples has made her home in Chattanooga, Tennessee. For additional information about her, titles, and a title entry, see *Dictionary, 1990–1994* [*Shabanu*].

STARDUST (Gaiman*, Neil, Avon, 1999) Otherworld fantasy of magic and wonders published for adults, which begins in the sleepy village of Wall in mid-nineteenth-century England at the beginning of Queen Victoria's reign. To the east is the high gray rock wall from which the town's name came six hundred years earlier. In the wall is a gap beyond which lies a large green meadow. Two townsmen stand constant guard at the gap to keep visitors out and townspeople in, except for every ninth year on May Day, when a fair comes to the meadow and townspeople intermingle with foreigners and fairy folk who revel there. On one such day, earnest, somewhat simple young Dunstan Thorne, 17, yearning for his Heart's Desire, enters the meadow, and while savoring the wonders of the varied merchandise there, encounters a beautiful young woman with curly black hair and cat ears. She is in bondage to a witch and must remain a slave until the moon loses her daughter and two Mondays join in one week. Dunstan returns home, soon marries, and nine months after his encounter with the cat-eared girl a basket containing a baby boy appears at the gap. Attached to the baby's blanket is a sliver of parchment bearing the name Tristan Thorne. These events set the stage for Tristan's entry into the Land of Faerie two Fair Days later in search of the falling star that he and his lady love have seen and that he rashly promises to bring to her. His journey, in true fairy-tale fashion is long, arduous, and fraught with dangers and surprises as he becomes entangled with a startling assortment of otherworld beings, among them, the star, Yvaine, an irritable creature because she broke her leg in the fall; Tristan's mother; a lion and a unicorn (of nursery rhyme fame) who rampage around; and numerous other animate creatures and inanimate objects that have life, like talking trees and helpful clouds. As in the typical old tale, Tristan succeeds through pluck, luck, his own innate goodness, and, of course, the fairy blood from his mother. At the end, all mixups are straightened out, and all loose threads tied up neatly. Tristan marries, not the lady in Wall he loved, but Yvaine. They go to Stormhold high on a mountain, where with Tristan's mother, now freed from her bondage to the witch, they rule in peace and prosperity for many years. The moon has lost her daughter, Yvaine, to Tristan, and two Mondays join in one week when Tristan's old sweetheart weds the man of her choice, wealthy old Mr. Monday. Characters are flat, either good or bad, as is true of the traditional form; the plot holds up well except in the middle where too many characters and too many undeveloped episodes tend to become confusing; and the style is frequently humorous and witty with plays on words and substance and usually projects the intimate storytelling quality of the told story, warm, inviting, and charming, truly the best part of this sophisticated book. Material is drawn from a variety of oral traditions, nursery rhyme, folktale, and hero tale. In an afternote, the author acknowledges his debt to such masters of the literary tale as C. S. Lewis. Alex; Booklist.

STARGIRL (Spinelli*, Jerry, Knopf, 2000) Realistic novel of school life and friendship set in the late twentieth century, revolving around social discrimination, the demands of popularity, and first love. Shy, introverted Leo Borlock, 16, the narrator, looks back from fifteen years later at his junior year in Mica (Arizona) Area High School when homeschooled Susan Caraway, 15, who calls herself "Stargirl," enrolls and takes the school by storm. An extreme noncomformist, she has long sandy-colored hair and freckles, wears ankle-length, ruffled dresses, and carries a ukulele slung over her shoulder, which she plays at a moment's notice and also serenades students on their birthdays. She immediately arouses the enmity of tart-tongued, big woman on campus Hillari Kimble. Leo's best friend, talkative

Kevin Quinlan, wants to interview Stargirl on *Hot Seat*, the school television cable show of which he is host and Leo is producer/director, but Leo persuades him to hold off until second semester. Curious, Leo shadows Stargirl to learn why she is as she is, to no avail except to discover that she likes the desert, is completely at home by herself, and enjoys performing random acts of kindness both in school and in the community. She delights the handful of home fans by performing an impromptu act at a Mica Electrons' home football game, stimulating an attendance of more than one thousand at the next game and an invitation to join the cheerleading squad. Her antics make school inviting, and students eagerly look forward to what new entertainment she will provide but still regard her as alien. Kevin says they must consult Archie* (Archibald Hapwood Brubaker), a retired paleontologist, who says he knows Stargirl well and implies she has qualities they should welcome. By Christmas she is the most popular, and the most hated, girl in school and the center of a lunch bunch. Among deeds that arouse dislike, she leads cheers for the opponents at basketball games to acknowledge their efforts, too. During the *Hot Seat* interview, she cleverly lampoons the show's name and then becomes the target of taunting, antagonistic, and derisive questions and comments from the show's jury, to such an extent that the faculty adviser literally pulls the plug on the show, and it is never aired. Stargirl is kicked off the cheerleading squad, but Leo still associates with her. The students now derisively call him "Starboy." The two find themselves in a happy, low-key, first-love relationship. At the same time, they become more and more isolated from the other students. Leo discusses this with Archie, who tells him that he

must decide whose affections he wants, Stargirl's or the students'. When Leo explains to Stargirl that she must not be so different, she tries to please him by reverting to the Susan she once was. Although she looks and behaves like every other girl in school, she still makes no friends. The really big disappointment for her occurs when she wins the state high school oratorical contest and envisions a big, joyous reception from the students on her return from Phoenix, but only Leo and three other people cheer her. She becomes Stargirl again and attends the Ocotillo Ball, the big school bash, with another odds-out girl riding in a bicycle sidecar. She provides a good time for everyone but the Stargirl haters, and Hillari is so angry she slaps her in front of the group, to which Stargirl responds with a kiss to Hillari's cheek. Then Stargirl gets into her sidecar and mysteriously disappears from Mica. Leo tells Archie that his year with Stargirl feels like a dream. Short, pithy sentences, a saucy, brash tone, fast pace, humor of situation and dialogue, and near-comic-book scenes and characters present a vivid satire of school life, where winning is all and being part of a large coterie of rubber stampers and look-alike, behave-alike clones is what matters. Leo represents those who cannot muster the courage to identify their convictions, let alone stand up for them. ALA/YA.

THE STARLITE DRIVE-IN (Reynolds*, Marjorie, Morrow, 1997)   Girl's growing-up and mystery novel published for adults and set for six hot summer months in 1956 near the central Indiana town of Jessup. Excavations in the early 1990s around the old Starlite Theater grounds reveal human bones and artifacts. When the sheriff asks narrator Callie* Anne Benton Dicksen, 49, if she can identify them, since her deceased father had once managed the theater, Callie Anne recalls disturbing events from the summer she was twelve. An only child, romantically inclined, Callie Anne loves to sit beside her father, Claude Junior Benton, in the theater projection booth and knows scenes and dialogue by heart for hundreds of movies. She loses interest in them, however, when tall, good-looking, polite drifter Charlie Memphis* is hired to help out, and soon develops a crush on him. She even becomes a little jealous when he seems attracted to her beautiful mother, tall, auburn-haired, anxiety-ridden Teal. Teal is unhappy in her marriage, since Claude Junior is a rigid, demanding man, who frequently belittles her and Callie Anne. The first intimation that Memphis might not be "just a drifter" occurs when he helps the conscientious, fifteen-year-old high school student who sells tickets, Virgil, foil two robbers, almost beating one of them to death. But Memphis is kind and generous and wins Teal's confidence enough to induce her to leave the house for ever-lengthening periods, and Callie Anne realizes they are in love. She often spies on them, observes them embrace and kiss passionately, and overhears them talk about running away. After Claude Junior complains that money is missing, Callie searches Memphis's room and finds a clipping that suggests that he may have killed a man. When a detective inquires about Billy Watson, a mentally challenged man whom Teal has befriended and who is missing, Claude Junior becomes even more suspicious of Memphis. Callie Anne is caught in a dilemma: if Memphis is indeed a murderer, Dad may be in danger, but if she informs Dad about the contents of the clipping, she betrays her mother. A little later, Claude Junior observes Memphis coming from the house one night, and the two men have a terrible fistfight. The next morning, Claude Junior announces that Memphis is gone, having taken three hundred of the theater's money with him. After Memphis's departure, Claude Junior becomes more irascible, and when he forces Teal to have sex with him and then strikes her, she takes the money she has saved and Callie Anne and goes to live with her sister. Some weeks pass before Claude Junior amends his behavior and tongue enough that Teal decides to live with him again. He takes a job at the new Dodge plant in Jessup and moves the family there. About twenty years after they leave the theater, Claude Junior dies of cancer, a long illness through which Teal nurses him. Back at the frame story, Callie Anne recognizes certain items from the excavation as belonging to Memphis but does not identify them as such. She does convey her suspicions about Memphis's end to her mother, only to hear Teal adamantly deny that Memphis is dead and assert that the remains must be Billy's. She pathetically clings to her belief that Memphis will some day return. Callie Anne is sure Claude Junior killed Memphis after the terrible fight. The brooding, excessively hot weather, the strong local color and sense of the claustrophobic life imposed by the business and Teal's anxiety attacks, the smoldering eroticism, and the importance of family and suppressing family secrets recall the southern regional fiction genre. Characters are carefully foiled, gradually revealed, and round, and the author realizes the moment well. Although Callie oddly has few compunctions about listening in on intimate moments and is too fortuitously on the spot, her voice is convincingly impressionistic, her budding romance with Virgil is sweetly believable, and her growing awareness of her sexuality plausible, as are Memphis's tenderness and love for Teal. Published for adults and, as noted on the book flap, reminiscent of *The Bridges of Madison County* (Warner, 1992), the book explores human passion without melodrama or sentimentality. ALA/YA.

STEALING FREEDOM (Carbone*, Elisa, Knopf, 1998)   Historical novel, beginning in 1853 and lasting about four years, of slavery and an actual girl's flight to freedom in Dresden, Ontario, from Unity, Maryland, via the Underground Railroad. Events are based on letters, land records, newspaper accounts, and similar primary sources. Spunky, resourceful Ann Maria Weems, 11, her sensible mother, Arabella, her older sister, Catharine, and three brothers, all slaves, and their freeman father, earnest, responsible John, work long, hard hours on the farm and in the tavern and house of Master Charles Price. John has been trying to buy the freedom of his family, but Master Charles keeps raising the price. When Master Charles, who is brutal, often drunk, and debt ridden, sells off the brothers to Alabama, John contacts the Vigilance Committee in New York City, a collaboration of Quakers and other Abolitionists with worldwide contacts, who raise money to buy slaves from the owners and then set them free. Jacob Bigelow, a Washington City (Washington, D.C.) attorney, arrives with funds to buy Arabella and the girls, but Master Charles refuses to sell Ann, claiming that his wife needs her. Ann continues to drudge in the kitchen, and after the Prices move to Rockville, where Charles becomes a prosperous slave dealer, she also must feed the slaves confined in the cellar and take care of little Sarah, the mistress's niece who has come to live with them. She becomes acquainted through church with several young slaves, among them Alfred, who works for the local doctor, and a sweet, quiet romance begins. Since Master Charles persists in refusing to sell Ann, Mr. Bigelow has her kidnapped and taken to his house, where she is hidden for several months. Disguised as a stable boy, she is transported to a Dr. H. in New York City, and eventually travels with a Reverend Freeman by train to Niagara Falls and into Canada, not without incident because she is almost apprehended as they cross the border. In Dresden in western Ontario, she joins her Aunt Mimi and Uncle William, who had fled there several years before and now own a farm. Although she yearns for her family and for Alfred, she is able to go to school, make friends, and live otherwise happily. At the very end, Alfred joins her, having run away from his owner. For the most part, the plot is predictable, and the characters are one-dimensional types. Life on the farm and service in the house are presented in vivid detail, as is the bustling activity on the streets of New York City and Washington City, including the Capitol area. Family gatherings, the fair, and occasional celebrations provide some relief for the unrelenting labor, and the few times when the slaves trick the masters offer some ironic humor. Although the book duplicates other such stories, the author's endnote indicating that Ann and her family and most of the characters really lived and that most events are based on historical fact lend strength and conviction to events. The passages in which Ann is kidnapped and taken to Mr. Bigelow are taut with suspense. ALA/YA.

STEFANIE WINSLOW (*A Knight of the Word**)   Young woman who, along with her lover, John Ross*, works for

Simon* Lawrence at the homeless project called "Fresh Start" in Seattle, Washington. Stefanie is early described as tall, slim, and lithe, beautiful in an "exotic" way with a "dazzling" smile, and very black hair. She is a truly bewitching woman—a stereotypically evil being. When readers reflect on this description, they realize they have early been alerted as to Stefanie's real role, an instrument of the Void. She is behind all the disasters at Fresh Start, which she simply wishes to destroy because Fresh Start is an instrument for good. She is the anonymous person who gives erroneous information to Andrew Wren in an effort to destroy both Simon Lawrence and John Ross. She reveals her true demonic nature when she shapechanges into a huge, monstrous hyena-like creature.

STONES IN THE WATER (Napoli*, Donna Jo, Dutton, 1997) Historical novel, with survival and growing-up aspects, of Italian boys kidnapped and enslaved by the Germans during World War II. The war seems remote to fun-loving Roberto, 13, and his friends in Venice, Italy, until German soldiers round them up and herd them onto a train, destination unknown. There follow months of cold, starvation, brutality, and unending labor building airfields and working on other German war efforts. One of Roberto's main problems is protecting Samuele, his Jewish friend, who adopts the name Enzo. After Enzo dies, Roberto runs away to the Black Sea where he falls in with an Italian deserter, with whom he eventually arrives in Italy and joins the partisans. The book's force lies in its graphic account of the kidnapping and the horrible servitude, during which most of the boys die. Earlier the book was cited by the American Library Association for middle grades. For a longer entry, see *Dictionary, 1995–1999*. ALA/YA.

STRANDED IN HARMONY (Shoup*, Barbara, Hyperion, 1997) Boy's growing-up novel set in Harmony, Indiana, in the late twentieth century. In his last year of high school, Lucas Cantrell, the narrator, feels stifled—unable to communicate with his parents, tired of football, overwhelmed by the demands of Sara, his longtime girlfriend, and deeply afraid that he will fall into the small-town rut of his father and many of his friends. His one relief is visiting and helping care for Ronnie Dale, a bedridden cousin of his mother, who lives in a small, isolated cabin. There he meets Allie Bowen, a young woman some twenty to twenty-five years his senior, who has taken a small house nearby. As Allie visits Ronnie Dale and talks with him, he improves, and Lucas hopes he can continue to live without being sent to a nursing home, a move Lucas's father favors. Lucas also enjoys talking to Allie, especially about the 1960s, a period he is writing about for a term paper. At the same time, Lucas is increasingly annoyed with Sara's dependence on him and with his younger sister, Dawn, who is going with his best friend, Bill Finney, and who reports his every move to Sara. When Sara, spending the night with Dawn, comes into his room naked, she and Lucas have sex without using a condom, and Lucas becomes convinced that she is pregnant. Knowing that he will marry her if she is, he realizes that while he loves her, he is not in love with her, and he feels trapped and outraged. His anger works well on the football field, where he moves from a mediocre player to a top performer, and he is offered a full sports scholarship to small Manchester College. His father, an avid fan, is delighted, but Lucas sees the offer as another cord binding him to a life he wishes to escape. When he finally asks Sara, she says she is not pregnant, but she is furious, seeing that the idea of marrying her has made him surly and unapproachable, and she breaks up with him. Confused, he goes to see Allie, tells her the story, breaks down and weeps, and gets understanding comfort. She then confesses that she has done bad things, that in the 1960s she joined a friend setting a bomb to protest the Vietnam War, a bomb that malfunctioned and killed a woman and a child. She spent twelve years in prison and came to Harmony with a changed name, trying to get a new start. Lucas takes her to a cave he and Bill have explored and, unlike Sara, she sees the beauty and wonder of it. Before the last game of the season, his father asks him for the first time if he really wants to go to Manchester, and when he admits, with guilt, that he does not, his father is surprisingly understanding. Lucas avoids the party after the game, but later that night a frantic phone call from Dawn says Ronnie Dale is in the emergency room. Lucas rushes there, finds that his old friend is dead of a heart attack caused by fear when Sara and her new boyfriend, along with Dawn and Bill, all of whom have been drinking, scare him for the fun of it. The death is a catalyst for several changes: Bill, who has been estranged, apologizes and becomes a friend again. Allie decides it is time to move on. Lucas finds he can look forward with hope and enthusiasm once more. A brief final episode is set one year later in his room at the state university when he receives a call from Allie, just checking, as she has promised, to see how he is. The actual events of the novel are not as important as the evocation of Lucas's emotional state, his feeling of helplessness

and desperation at the way his future seems predetermined. The other characters are two dimensional. Lucas's parents are loving if conventional. Sara is a sweet girl, though unable to see Lucas's need for freedom. Ronnie Dale is probably responsible for his own condition. Allie is strong despite her past. Even Harmony, which is suffocating Lucas, is a pleasant town. ALA/YA.

STRAUSS, DARIN Grew up in New York City; educator, editor, novelist. Strauss is a graduate of Tufts University and attended a creative writing program at New York University. He has been senior publicist for Penguin/Putnam/Dutton Publishers and taught at New York University. His first novel, *Chang and Eng** (Dutton, 2000), is about the original Siamese twins, a work of fiction based solidly on what is known of their lives. He followed this with another biographical novel, *The Real McCoy* (Dutton, 2002), about a fighter and flim-flam artist, set in 1900. Strauss lives in Brooklyn, New York.

STRAYS LIKE US (Peck*, Richard, Dial, 1998) Realistic psychological- and sociological-problem novel set in a small Missouri town in recent years. Fatherless Molly Moberly, 15, the narrator, comes to live with her great-aunt on her mother's side, capable, strong-minded, articulate Aunt Fay Moberly, because her mother, Debbie, is in the hospital for drug addiction. For the first time in her life, Molly has a home and a room of her own, but since she has no family of her own, she feels like a stray and counts the days until Debbie comes for her. She willingly helps her busy aunt, a gray-haired, bespectacled practical nurse, widely respected in town for her professional skills, neighborliness, and good sense. Also new in town and living with his grandparents is scrawny, splay-eared, outgoing Will* McKinney, Molly's age, who persuades her to walk to school with him when they start junior high and are among the few new kids. Aunt Fay spends a lot of time helping Will's grandmother, Wilma McKinney, whose husband is senile and who just manages on Social Security. A wealthy patient is old, snappish Edith Voorhees, three times widowed and a longtime friend of Aunt Fay. Molly soon notices that while everybody knows everybody in this town, there also seem to be community secrets, things that no one talks about. She also discovers that there are other outsiders like herself and Will. One is vicious Rocky Roberts, who also lives with his grandmother, a "hip" waitress. Tracy* Pringle may be a stray; she lives with her wealthy mother in a big house near Mrs. Voorhees's mansion, dresses in fine clothes, and is being homeschooled by her mother. One secret Molly learns is that someone else is living with the McKinneys. It turns out to be Will's very ill father, a patient of Aunt Fay. When he dies and the news that he died of AIDS gets out, the kids in school want nothing to do with Will. Another big secret, the biggest of all, concerns Molly herself. Since Debbie is now in jail for selling drugs, Aunt Fay insists that Molly accompany her to visit Mrs. Voorhees. Molly learns that the old woman is her grandmother, Debbie's mother. Because Aunt Fay's house is ramshackle and Molly's few clothes are poor, the two women arrange for Mrs. Voorhees to assume financial obligations for Molly. One year after she arrived, Molly still loves her mother but is happy to stay with Aunt Fay, whose house has become home. Sturdy and self-reliant, a survivor type, Molly adjusts as expected. She never wallows in self-pity but tells enough about her longings to gain the sympathy of the reader. Her counterpart is Will, who faces similar needs and adjustments. The book's main strengths are the economical and credible characterization of Aunt Fay and the picture of the ingrown small town, which is just beginning to accept new family patterns. That Aunt Fay resembles the grandmother of Peck's *A Long Way from Chicago** and Newbery-winning *A Year Down Yonder** does not diminish Aunt Fay as a positive influence on Molly and the most memorable figure in the novel. ALA/YA.

STUCK IN NEUTRAL (Trueman*, Terry, HarperCollins, 2000)   Contemporary realistic problem novel set in Seattle, Washington, about a victim of cerebral palsy, especially intriguing for two aspects: the boy's relationship with his father and the contrast between the boy's view of himself and that of others concerning him. Narrator Shawn McDaniel, 14, who has been diagnosed as "profoundly developmentally disabled," feels "stuck in neutral." He says that people seem to pity him because he can do nothing for himself, think he is stupid, are sure that he comprehends nothing in life, and is in great pain, especially when he has seizures, which occur several times a day. Although Shawn cannot alter his circumstances, he sees the world quite differently. He knows he loves his family—mother, Lindy; older sister, Cindy; older brother, Paul; and father, Sydney* E. McDaniel. He longs for a girlfriend and appreciates the physical, natural, and intellectual worlds around him insofar as his limited mobility allows. He takes special pride in his ability to recall every conversation he has ever heard. He enjoys the bits of food, often junk, that Paul slips to him, and is grateful to Cindy for teaching him to read. He regrets, however, being the reason that his father divorced his mother, since it is apparent to everyone that Sydney could no longer tolerate the circumstances under which his son, and the rest of the family as well, were forced to live, and simply opted out. Although Sydney supports them financially, he has pretty much left them to cope as they can. He has focused on his career, become a well-known radio personality, and won a Pulitzer Prize for a poem he wrote about Shawn, portions of which introduce each chapter. The book's central problem revolves around Shawn's suspicion that his father is planning to kill him, a perception increased by his father's championing on a television talk show the man who confessed to killing his son, who had cerebral palsy, and a conversation he overheard between Paul and Cindy that Sydney might indeed do that. The evening that Shawn's mother and siblings are away on a sports trip, Sydney turns up, dismisses Shawn's caregiver, and sits talking to Shawn, all the time fingering the pillow he holds in his lap—at which point the book ends, leaving Shawn and the reader to ponder what might happen next. Shawn's description of his life is amazingly compelling and acceptable, even during the seizures, in which there are wondrous miracles. The book thus becomes a nondidactic commentary not only on the morality of euthanasia but also on whether any human being can, even with sophisticated modern methods, determine the extent to which another feels pain and distress. Whether one agrees with Sydney, one feels sympathy and a kind of admiration for him. Although short, this powerful novel grabs and holds both emotions and intellect. The novel is based on the author's experiences with and reflections about his own son, who has cerebral palsy and has been diagnosed as profoundly developmentally disabled. ALA/YA; Printz Honor.

SUNDAY YOU LEARN HOW TO BOX (Wright*, Bil, Simon & Schuster, 2000) Realistic, episodic novel of family life and a boy's growing up, published for adults. African American Louis Bowman starts his story in 1968 when he is eight and first meets Ben Stamps, who will soon be his stepfather, and concludes it about seven years later. A strong, controlling woman, Mom (Jeanette Stamps) manages a department at Saks Fifth Avenue where Ben is a shipping clerk. Mom hopes that by marrying Ben she can achieve her dream of moving out of the Stratfield Projects in Connecticut into a real house. Louis knows that she is proud of his academic success and tries hard to please her by doing such household chores as scrubbing and mopping floors; shopping for her liquor, cigarettes, and groceries; and helping with his new little half sister, Lorelle. Since he has no friends in the neighborhood and is often beaten up, Mom suggests that Ben teach Louis the manly art of boxing so that he can protect himself, a sport he fears and detests. Boxing becomes a metaphor for life in the Stamps household. Mom and Ben spar with words and sometimes blows. For Louis, life with Ben is full of verbal as well as physical blows, since the man often belittles Louis, accuses him of a smart mouth, says Jeanette coddles the boy, and complains that Louis acts like a faggot. Mom has other opponents to box with, too—a racist society, poverty, her sexual needs, and even snoopy neighbors. In addition, Louis's white teacher insists on calling him Louie and likens him to the pygmies in their unit on Africa. An additional opponent for Louis appears in the form of an unwanted Christmas bike when Louis is twelve, a machine he is unable to master. Louis becomes acquainted with Ray Anthony Robinson, a fancy-dressing neighbor youth a few years older, who sticks up for him on occasion and for whom Louis has increasing admiration and awe. Among other events, Louis visits his Grandaddy (Mom's father) in Harlem; is almost raped by enigmatic Ed MacMillan, an older man he meets on the train to Harlem; goes to church on occasion, which he likes; and lies and dissembles to keep Mom and Ben out of his life as much as possible. Pressures accumulate, his grades decline, and the school recommends he attend an outpatient mental health treatment center, which he does faithfully, appreciating in particular a black Jamaican woman therapist, Dr. Davis. After Ben dies of a heart attack when Louis is fourteen, his feelings of isolation increase. Louis yearns, even lusts, for Ray Anthony, whose walk he finds especially attractive but who, Mom says, minces around in "pimp pants." When a girl from a hoodlum bunch from neighboring Creighton Heights who wants sex with Ray Anthony is disappointed with his performance, she comes to Ray Anthony's house with some hoods to beat him up. Louis joins the fray on Ray Anthony's behalf, biting his friend hard in the shoulder to keep him from killing one of the assailants. Released by the police, Ray Anthony comes home, walks across the courtyard, and puts his hand on Louis's shoulder. At last for Louis, all is right with the world. This novel of a boy's trying to make sense of chaotic circumstances and identify his sexuality is sometimes funny, sometimes serious, sometimes poignant, sometimes repulsive, sometimes as confused as Louis is, but always provocative.

Although the story lacks cohesion, it is easy to feel sympathy for Louis, growing up gay, small, shy, black, smart, and poor when these qualities get him little but scorn. Mom is strongly drawn, the most vivid figure, and trash and sex talk add to the setting. Despite cliché problems and characters, this is an impressive if flawed first novel. Booklist.

SUNNIE STONE (*Love Among the Walnuts**)   Dazzlingly beautiful, silvery-blond, blue-eyed young woman, fresh out of nurse's training, engaged by Sandy* Huntington-Ackerman to care for his father, Horatio*; his mother, Mousey* Malone; and Bentley's wife, Flossie, while they are in comas. Sunnie is consistently optimistic, loving, capable, outgoing, and talkative, with opinions on just about everything that comes up. She helps the residents of Walnut Manor regain their strength of mind and body by reading to them from such classics as *The Wind in the Willows* and *Treasure Island* and by getting them involved in such activities as making snowmen and helping about the Manor. At the end, she and Sandy plan their honeymoon to Hawaii, a trip that is her idea. She is the most consistently interesting figure in the book and the first to note that something is not right about the Manor. She asserts that a place that charges the fees that Walnut Manor does should not have to save money by turning off the heat to the swimming pool and keeping a cow and chickens. It turns out that her suspicions are correct; the board of directors has been embezzling funds.

SUNSHINE RIDER: THE FIRST VEGE-TARIAN WESTERN (Hardman*, Ric Lynden, Delacorte, 1998)   Fast-moving, picaresque, incident-filled, tall-tale western set from 1881 to 1884. Although he hesitates to leave his beloved Aunt Clara Hampton, the schoolteacher who has raised him, and pretty Alice Beck, orphan Wylie Jackson, 17, the narrator, is elated to have been chosen to accompany Mr.* John Boardman's Circle Six trail drive from Odessa, Texas, to Wichita, Kansas, as *coosie segundo* (second cook) to Chauncey* Potter. He promises Alice that along the way he will deliver her pet cattalo, a creature half cow, half buffalo named Roselle, to Alice's cousin in Enid, Oklahoma. Wylie becomes involved with an extraordinary assortment of colorful figures, pops in and out of predicaments, gains a vocation, and learns some surprising things about himself, including his real identity. In the first of many adventures and escapades, which follow in profusion, he fears that he will be embarrassed if the Circle Six cowboys discover that he has in his possession Alice's drawers, an item she gave him to keep Roselle from straying. He steals a Circle Six horse and lights out; falls in with the OHO herd, which soon comes down with anthrax; encounters an Oklahoma sodbuster posse with whom he pretends to be Axel Beane, a doctor; falls in with Cherokee Tim-ooleh, the medicine man for the Indian nations; travels for a while with slick confidence man Dr. Majul Majul, a Sikh Hindu from the Punjab, also known as Dr. Dad Budge Burns, Specialist; is almost hanged for murder in the town of Cleo Springs; helps an army doctor, Izard McNally, save the life of very ill Cory Bigler, a farmer's daughter; starts to study medicine with Dr. McNally; and nearly proposes to Cory before he leaves for medical school in Chicago. He almost kills Mr. Boardman's stepson, ZeeZee, because he thinks ZeeZee shot and killed Roselle (whose life, unbeknownst to Wylie is

saved by Dr. McNally) but is rescued by Mr. Boardman, who reveals in an astonishing interview that he is Wylie's father and Aunt Clara is his mother. Wylie never does deliver Roselle to Enid, Oklahoma, but keeps her on Mr. Boardman's ranch. This is but a brief summary of the mix-ups, upsets, and complications that propel the plot. The title refers to Wylie's becoming a vegetarian—he hates the idea of the cattle they are driving being slaughtered—and also to his delight at seeing himself on horseback, his shadow long, slender, and imposing in the lowering sun. The last chapter sees Wylie in later life, a prominent physician and married to Alice Beck, addressing a class of graduating medical students. In this parody of old-time westerns, various devices produce humor: exotic characters, puns, irony, literal misunderstandings, spoofs like the song *The Vegetable Hymn of the Republic*, the crazy names, and the recipes that head each chapter. Some aspects seem more typical of late-twentieth-century thinking than the mid-nineteenth, for example, Wylie's becoming a vegetarian and Dr. Majul's coming to the United States as a missionary to save cattle from becoming human food. The book's greatest strength is that it is jolly good fun from start to finish. ALA/YA.

SWALLOWING STONES (McDonald*, Joyce, Delacorte, 1997) Novel of an accidental shooting in contemporary Briarwood, New Jersey, that kills a man, devastates two families, and causes two young people, through their suffering and guilt, to mature and face their responsibilities. At his all-day seventeenth birthday party on July 4, Michael MacKenzie shows his best friend, Joe Sadowski, the .45–70 Winchester rifle his grandfather has given him and cannot resist firing one shot into the air, a shot not heard above the loud music and firecrackers. Then, eluding his beautiful girlfriend, Darcy Kelly, he ducks into the garage to make out with Amy* Ruggerio, a "babe" Joe has brought as a birthday present. Across town, Jenna Ward, 15, having just stepped outside to call her father for lunch, sees him crouching on the roof where he is fixing a leak and watches, unbelieving, as he flops over and crashes to her feet, a bullet through his head. When he hears the news, Michael knows immediately what has happened, but he tries to deny it to himself. On Joe's advice to get rid of the gun, he buys a length of PVC pipe, inserts the rifle, seals the ends, and buries it in a three-foot trench under the woodpile. For the rest of the summer, he suffers fear and guilt, barely able to perform at his lifeguard job at the city pool, breaking up with Darcy, and haunting the area around the Ward house, often sitting for long periods on the steps of the church across the street. Frequently, he finds himself going to the small house where Amy lives with her grandfather. They play Scrabble or some other game and, even when they are alone, Michael does not make a pass at her or even touch her. Jenna, who has had a strained relationship with her mother, feels numbed by her father's death, unable to grieve and equally unable to enjoy any of her usual summer pastimes. When her boyfriend, Jason, returns from Maine, she is plagued by panic attacks whenever they are together. At a movie she escapes to the rest room, where Amy Ruggerio, whom she hardly knows, saves her from fainting. Frequently, she sees a boy sitting on the church steps and eventually recognizes him as the pool lifeguard, a boy she does not know but learns is Michael

MacKenzie. After the police narrow the source of the shot to a four-block area, Michael gets increasingly tense. He tells them that he loaned the gun to Joe, and that it was stolen from Joe's car, a story his friend backs up, but their friendship falls to pieces after Joe is arrested and grilled. Jenna finally realizes that her panic with Jason is caused by her suppressed guilt for having stayed on the phone with him instead of calling her father to lunch as soon as her mother asked her to do so. When she confesses, she learns that her mother also feels guilty for not calling her husband herself instead of nagging Jenna to hang up and do it. Their shared realization that neither is at fault brings them closer than they have been before. In the middle of the night, Jenna gets up and goes to the "ghost tree," an ancient sycamore where her father took her one memorable night. The same night, Michael digs up the gun, determined to take it to the police and confess, but first he goes to the ghost tree where he finds Jenna asleep. He waits quietly for her to wake, wanting to confess to her before turning himself in. Told in sections alternating between the points of view of Michael and Jenna, the novel does a good job of building the increasing tension. Both the main characters develop from essentially shallow, self-centered teenagers to more compassionate, responsible young adults. Secondary characters—Joe, a troublemaker easy for police and public to suspect; Andrea, Jenna's supportive best friend; Josh, Michael's younger brother, who sees the whole episode as an exciting story; Michael's worried parents; Jenna's brittly correct mother—all are well developed. The title comes from a story about a girl who suffocated by drawing a stone in her mouth into her windpipe, but could have survived if she had swallowed the stone. ALA/YA.

SWEENEY, JOYCE (1955–) Born in Dayton, Ohio; graduate of Wright State University; teacher of creative writing; author of poems, articles, and novels for young adults; resident of Coral Springs, Florida. Her novels often revolve around family relationships, like *The Spirit Window** (Delacorte, 1998), recommended by the American Library Association for young adults, in which a young girl helps her father accept the terms of his estranged, deceased mother's will. More recently, Sweeney has published *Players* (Winslow, 2000), which focuses on the bad blood between two high school basketball players. A longer entry with more information about Sweeney, titles, and a title entry appears in *Dictionary, 1995–1999* [*Shadow*].

SYDNEY E. MCDANIEL (*Stuck in Neutral**) Father of the narrator, Shawn, and his siblings, Cindy and Paul, and ex-husband of Lindy, whom he divorced because he could no longer tolerate having a son who is profoundly developmentally disabled from cerebral palsy. Sydney supports his family, however, and drops in occasionally. As the novel progresses, it appears that he is attempting to come to a decision about whether Shawn should continue to live, considering both Shawn's best interests and those of society. Is it reasonable (and cost effective) to attempt to educate the uneducable, for example? Is it right to allow Shawn to live in pain? He assumes Shawn cannot learn and is in pain, especially during seizures, both of which conclusions are at odds with what Shawn says. Is it right to allow someone as defenseless as Shawn to live? Shawn describes how furious his father is when he drives away a crow he is afraid is going to peck Shawn's eyes. While Shawn is "stuck in neutral," as it were, so is his father, who seems to feel that it is his responsibility as Shawn's father to do something to help Shawn and society as well. Sydney is a complex figure.

T

TACK KNIGHT (*What Child Is This?: A Christmas Story**) Thomas Knight, son of a community-spirited restaurateur. Tack (which comes from his initials T.K.) is a good student, well liked by his classmates, and employed as a waiter at his father's River Wind Inn, where his broad grin and pleasant ways have endeared him to patrons. He is a leader in the youth group at church that implements the Christmas tree project for distributing gifts to needy children and tries to get Matt* Morden involved in math team at school, because Matt is good at math. When Tack complains to his father about Matt's aloofness and occasional surliness, his father reminds him that regardless of the way Matt behaves toward Tack, he expects Tack to be kind and continue to try to involve Matt, simply because it is the right thing to do.

TALON ANGLER (*Downsiders**) Downsider boy of fourteen who is romantically attracted to Lindsay Matthias, a Topsider girl. Believing that the fates intended him to survive being executed, he chooses to devote himself to his people and accepts the position of Most-Beloved, the Downsiders' leader. He dresses in the fashion of Downsider youth, with his dense hair long but shaved about his ears and his tidy clothes made up of hundreds of tiny patches sewn together from scraps of salvaged materials. Bold and adventuresome, he yearns to learn more about Topside, and it is this rebellious nature that eventually saves Downside and is the reason that Talon must choose between his love for his people and his affection for Lindsay. Talon's surname is Angler because his father is a fisherman, and his first name comes because a bat clawed his cheek when he was a baby.

TANGERINE (Bloor*, Edward, Harcourt, 1997) Sports novel of a present-day dysfunctional family in which a middle school soccer player finally proves that his high school football hero brother is a sociopath. Also involved are central Florida citrus growing and prejudice against Hispanics. For a longer entry, see *Dictionary, 1995–1999*. ALA/YA.

TELLER, ASTRO (1970–) Born Eric Teller; expert in artificial intelligence. Grandson of nuclear physicist Edward Teller, he received his Ph.D. from Carnegie-Mellon University and is chief executive officer of Sandbox Advanced Development. His novel, *Exegesis** (Vintage, 1997), a study in what it means to be human, is about an artificial intelligence developed by a girl for her graduate thesis that becomes independent. It has been translated into Danish, Dutch, German, Japanese, Italian, and Greek.

TENDERNESS (Cormier*, Robert, Delacorte, 1997) Grim realistic contemporary novel of a sociopath and a runaway girl who bring about their mutual destruction. Both characters crave what they call "tenderness," though their definitions are different. Lori (Lorelei) Granston, 15, wants someone to treat her gently and lovingly, not with the lust and naked desire she usually inspires in men. As she says in her first-person sections, she is technically still a virgin, though she has engaged in sexual activity short of intercourse, usually in return for money. She runs away from the Massachusetts town where she has been living with her fond but alcoholic mother and her mother's latest man, Gary, because he has begun to paw her and brush against her as they pass in the hallway. On the way to Wicksburg, where they once lived, she hitches a ride, lets the driver kiss and feel her up until he climaxes, then lifts his wallet. While it is not the first time she has stolen, it is the first time from an individual, not a store. At about the same time, Eric Poole turns eighteen and must be released from the juvenile facility where he has been incarcerated since he murdered his mother and stepfather three years earlier as well as two girls that his arresting officer, Lieutenant Jake Proctor, suspects but cannot prove and one that even the officer knows nothing about. To Eric, tenderness means the feeling he gets as his victim slumps into death and he strokes the smooth skin and long hair, always dark. Very clever at fooling people and enlisting their sympathy with well-practiced smiles, one he calls "The Charm" and the other a wan, wistful look, he manipulates the press and many in authority, but not Proctor, who knows he is a psychopath and is determined to trap him. Lori sees Eric on a news broadcast and is taken in by the wistful look. Moreover, she recognizes him from an incident just after her twelfth birthday when, walking along railroad tracks, she saw him enter a woods with a girl and emerge alone. Because he spoke to her kindly and understood her hurt that her mother had forgotten her birthday, she has always been half in love with him and her fascination returns when she learns he will be living in Wicksburg with his aunt. As she admits, Lori has an obsessive personality, and now she turns her attention to Eric, waiting for hours outside his aunt's house with the television crews and angry neighbors, all hoping for a glimpse of the murderer. He stays inside, sneaking out only once to get his driver's license and buy a used van with some of his parents' insurance money his aunt has set aside for him. Finally, the local interest subsides, and he plans to leave. The same night Lori decides to go home to her mother, but walks one last time to the house where Eric is staying, gets caught in the rain and chased by a dog, breaks into the van, and falls asleep in the back. She wakes to find the vehicle in motion with Eric behind the wheel. On discovering her, he knows immediately that he will have to kill her, but, afraid he is being followed, has to be careful. Besides, he is hoping to meet Maria Valdez, a girl he saw and had illicit correspondence with at the facility, who fits his criteria for a "tenderness" victim, while blond Lori does not. For the next couple of days they travel together, each trying to understand the other. Eric, especially, finds Lori baffling, childlike yet seemingly aware of his hidden desires. He buys her new clothes and is amused by her delight in outfits he plans she will not live long enough to wear. When they spend a night together, in separate motel beds, and he starts to make his move to smother her with a pillow, she wakes, realizes what he plans, and, insisting that she loves him, tells him to go ahead. Confused, he desists, but still feels she will have to die. The next night, after he has made a date to meet Maria at a carnival, Lori urges him to go ahead, wanting him to be happy. When, from the top of the Ferris wheel she sees police converging on the grove where he has led Maria, she frantically gets the operator to let her off and runs to warn him before he makes his incriminating move. Eric realizes that he has been set up by Maria and Lieutenant Proctor, but still plans to kill Lori. After the canoe they rent overturns, however, he tries desperately but unsuccessfully to save her and ends up in a prison cell for the one crime he did not do. Although the pace and tension keep the novel interesting, it is more sensational than believable. Even the plot does not hold up to close examination. The last scene is of Eric in prison, but there is nothing in Lori's death that could not have been the accident he insists it is. The characters are not totally convincing. Such an emotionless monster (as Proctor labels Eric) is unlikely to accept Lori's love and to reform, as he seems to in the end. Lori is an even more ambiguous figure, bright enough to understand what Eric did to the girl by the railroad tracks, what he plans for Maria, and what he will undoubtedly do to her, yet willing to help him, perhaps as much of a sociopath as he is. The structure, which alternates between the two main characters with occasional short passages from Proctor's point of view, is illogical, since the only first-person narration is by Lori, who is dead at the novel's end. ALA/YA.

THE TERRORIST (Cooney*, Caroline B., Scholastic, 1997)   Thriller novel set about the time of publication during the school year the Williams family, Americans, are in London, England. Since outgoing, budding entrepreneur Billy Williams, 11, is well liked by everyone in the London International Academy and in his neighborhood, why would anyone walk up to him in the London subway, hand him a package, detonate the bomb inside it, and blow him to bits? This is the question that his older sister, Laura, 16, her parents, and Mr. Evans of Scotland Yard ponder. Throughout much of the book, Thomas, the father, Nicole, the mother, and Laura grapple with denial, grief, and the need to try to comprehend how anyone could do such a terrible thing. Laura, who becomes the central figure in the novel, has paid little attention to domestic and international politics, finding current events class an utter bore and has paid only necessary attention to her schoolmates. Many of the parents of this exclusive school for the children of wealthy and influential diplomats, executives, and expatriates have now withdrawn their children. Laura only gradually becomes aware that the ones that remain have been staunchly sympathetic, although she wonders whether any of them could have been involved, since she now sees that anti-Americanism is rampant. Jehran, a small, strikingly beautiful Middle Eastern student Laura's age, holds a slumber party at her large, richly but sparsely appointed mansion guarded by uniformed soldiers. During the evening, Jehran confides to Laura that her much older brother has arranged for her to marry a man almost sixty who already has several wives. She says that the man is after her fortune and that if she refuses, she will be executed. She asks that Laura secure for her Billy's passport so that she can leave the country and gives Laura money for tickets. The rest of the novel involves Laura's activities in getting the passport from her home and buying tickets to New York for both of them and a return one for herself, and providing cover by giving the impression that she is going on a class trip to Scotland. All comes unraveled when a fellow student, a lover of television cop shows, thinks Laura is behaving suspiciously and follows her, even securing copies of the tickets to New York. Other students wonder why she does not appear when the group is ready to leave for Scotland, put together their suspicions and information, and call Mr. Evans. The plane at Heathrow Airport is held up, and Laura and Jehran are detained, but when authorities arrive at Jehran's home, the place is empty. Laura decides Jehran engineered Billy's death, but no proof is found. Laura's conclusion seems appropriate for Laura but simplistic in entirety, and it is peculiar that Mr. Evans, who previously had turned up occasionally, keeping an eye on Laura, had not tumbled to what was going on. The grieving and shock that the family experience ring true, and the minimalistic style works suitably. Laura is intelligent, courageous, and likable, a well-drawn and credible character. ALA/YA.

THAT SUMMER (Dessen*, Sarah, Orchard Books, 1996)   Girl's growing-up novel, set in Haven McPhail's fifteenth summer in the 1990s, a season when her divorced father marries Lorna Queen, weather girl at the local television station, and her wildly popular older sister, Ashley, 21, marries boring, conventional Lewis Warsher. In an unidentified eastern town, the narrator, Haven, has a summer job at Little Feet, a shoe store for children, in the Lakeview Mall. Her main preoccupation besides the two weddings, which dominate family life, is her height, nearly six feet and so sudden that her joints do not seem to have caught up with her growth and she feels all knees and elbows. At her weekly dinner with her father, she runs into Sumner Lee, the only one of Ashley's ex-boyfriends she really liked, and recalls a wonderful week the summer she was ten when the family and Sumner stayed at Virginia Beach where her father, sports anchor for the local television station, was covering a golf tournament. She keeps running into Sumner, who is taking a break from college, working at a variety of jobs, including being a security guard at the mall and dancing with older women at the senior center. He has always been exuberant and unpredictable, full of laughter, and Haven remembers his tenure as Ashley's boyfriend as the only time her older sister was really nice to her. She also remembers watching from her window the Halloween night when Ashley broke up with him and sent him away, as she has so many other boyfriends. With Ashley's wedding approaching, problems in the family increase and mostly exclude Haven. Since Ashley has always been her father's favorite, she avoids making derogatory comments about Lorna, whom their mother acidly calls "the Weather Pet," except to agree that she is dumb. Plans for her own wedding are orchestrated by their neighbor, Lydia Catrell, a widow who has befriended their mother and wants her to go on a European tour as soon as the wedding is out of the way. Tensions build for Haven and culminate on the day of the rehearsal dinner, when at the mall sale a woman angrily throws a rejected sneaker and hits Haven in the face. Suddenly furious, Haven follows her and retaliates by throwing the shoe at her. As the woman screams about suing for assault, Haven runs off and hides, as she used to when she was a child, under the slide at the neighborhood park. Eventually she emerges, walks home, naps, has a confrontation with Ashley, refusing to back down for the first time in their history, ignores her mother's conciliatory intervention, and waits for her father to take her to their weekly meal, but when he honks she stays on the porch, willing him to come to the door for her, until he drives away. After wandering around town for a while, she goes to the senior center, watches Sumner charm the older women in his genuine, good-hearted way, until the last dance, when he insists that she be his partner, even though she protests that she cannot dance. With her eyes closed, she is able to follow his lead, and when the music ends, the old people in a circle watching applaud. Sundenly she feels graceful, fitting into her new height. As Sumner drives her home, she tries to explain to him the pain of the last few years and, when he doesn't seem to understand, jumps out of the car and runs into the woods. There she gets lost, encounters a beautiful, tall local girl named Gwendolyn Rogers, who has become a nationally recognized model and suffered a nervous breakdown. When Ashley finally finds her and Haven accuses her of dumping Sum-

ner, the only boy worth her time, Ashley tells her that she broke up with Sumner because she caught him with another girl and has chosen dull Lewis because she knows he will not be unfaithful. At the wedding, Haven walks confidently, aware that she has understood her father, made peace with her sister, broken the invisible tether that seemed to bind her to her mother, and relegated the memory of the summer at Virginia Beach with Sumner to a proper perspective. Two subplots run through the novel, the story of Gwendolyn Rogers, who keeps turning up in a more and more distraught condition, and that of Casey Melvin, Haven's longtime best friend, who returns from 4-H camp wild and in love with a boy she met there. Both are contrived to illustrate Haven's difference. Characters of the main figures in the story are well developed, especially that of Haven, and her realization that she has to give up her illusions about perfect past times is a natural outcome of the various incidents of the summer. Ashley's choice of safe Lewis, sublimating her own lively personality, is not shown as the potential time bomb that experience leads a reader to fear, but since events are seen through Haven's eyes, that is not a major problem. Haven is a sharp-eyed observer, and her ironic comments provide humor. ALA/YA.

THESMAN, JEAN   Author of both mass-market series novels and more highly commended young adult novels. Her *The Ornament Tree** (Houghton Mifflin, 1996) won the Jefferson Cup for Historical Fiction and more recently was named to the American Library Association Young Adult list. *The Other Ones** (Viking, 1999), a fantasy of extraordinary people living in the ordinary world, was also named to the American Library Association Young Adult list. For earlier biographical information and title entries, see *Dictionary, 1990–1994* [*Rachel Chance*; *The Rain Catchers*; *When the Road Ends*] and *Dictionary, 1995–1999* [*The Ornament Tree*].

THE THIEF (Turner*, Megan Whalen, Greenwillow, 1996)   Lively adventure, mystery, and fantasy novel set in Sounis, a land that resembles ancient Greece. In jail for theft, Gen, about eighteen, is brought to the palace where the king's scholar, the magus, persuades him to join a quest to locate and steal Hamiathes's Gift, a fabled stone that entitles the holder to the throne of Eddis, a neighboring country. An unusual set of traveling companions, unexpected happenings along the way, the recovery of the stone fraught with peril, plot twists galore, and a surprising conclusion produce a top-notch adventure story. The story continues in *The Queen of Attolia*. Previously, the novel was elected to the Newbery Honor and *Fanfare* lists and was cited by the American Library Association for middle readers. For a longer, more detailed entry, see *Dictionary, 1995–1999*. ALA/YA.

THIN ICE (Qualey*, Marsha, Delacorte, 1997)   Contemporary mystery novel of a girl's search to find out what has happened to her brother, whose disappearance has been attributed to a snowmobile accident on a river. Her insistence that he is still alive is vindicated when she runs into him in Chicago and comes to understand his need to get away. For a longer entry, see *Dictionary, 1995–1999*. ALA/YA.

THOMAS, ROB (1966?–   )   Attended the University of Texas–Austin, and has made his home in Austin; writer of screenplays and novels for young adults. His first novel, published before he was thirty, *Rats Saw GOD** (Simon & Schuster, 1996), came out to critical acclaim. A high school senior tells in late-twentieth-century style and candor of his relationships in school and with his parents. The novel was cited by the American Library Association for young adults. Recent titles include *Doing Time: Notes from the Undergrad* (Simon & Schuster, 1997), short stories; *Satellite Down* (Simon & Schuster, 1998), about a student reporter for a news show; and *Green Thumb* (Simon & Schuster, 1999), about a research team in a Brazilian rain forest. For additional information about Thomas and a title entry, see *Dictionary, 1995–1999* [*Rats Saw GOD*].

TIES THAT BIND, TIES THAT BREAK (Namioka*, Lensey, Delacorte, 1999) Girl's growing-up novel set mostly in Nanjing, China, starting in 1925. Tao Ailin is the third daughter in her branch of the Tao family, being the favorite of Grandmother, who rules the compound, and of her father. She has had much more freedom than most girls in well-to-do families like hers and is allowed to play with her younger brother and develop her intelligence more than either of her much-older sisters were. When she is five, Mrs. Liu, a family friend and neighbor, comes with her son, Liu Hanwei, 7, to propose a marriage contract between the two children, but is horrified to see that Ailin's feet have not yet been bound. Grandmother decrees that the binding should start. Having seen Second Sister's feet naked, deformed from binding and smelly from the tightly covering cloths, Ailin protests, and for a while the subject is dropped. Later, when her amah and her mother come, hold her down, bend her toes under and bind them in that position, she becomes hysterical, tears at the cloth strips, and is so impassioned that her father, a forward-thinking man, arrives, surveys the situation, and says that Ailin need not have her feet bound. The Lius break off the marriage contract. After four years in the family school, where the children mostly recite passages from the classics by rote, Ailin's father enrolls her in the MacIntosh School, a "public" school run by missionaries. There she loves her English teacher, Miss Gilbertson, and makes a friend, Zhang Xueyan, a lively girl with unbound feet who says she does not want to get married but to be a doctor. At school Ailin is called "Eileen" and praised for her very good English pronunciation. Two years later, she is called home from school by the death of her Grandmother, which leaves Big Uncle, her father's only brother, in charge of the family compound. Big Uncle, a bad-tempered man with two cowed wives, hates and fears all modern ways, complains of the expense of Ailin's schooling and argues with her father about the prospects for the government of Sun Yat-sen. One day outside the school, Lin Hanwei, who attends a school just down the street, comes up to her and makes friendly conversation. When Ailin's father, who has been suffering from tuberculosis, dies, Big Uncle announces that she will stop school, but after she protests that her tuition is paid until the semester's end, he lets her continue, and during the next summer Miss Gilbertson tutors her privately in English. In the fall, Big Uncle tells Ailin that he has arranged for her to be sold as a concubine to a man who has two wives but no sons. When she confesses, in tears, to Miss Gilbertson, her teacher arranges for her to become an amah to the Warners, a missionary family with two children. Big Uncle is furious, her mother is appalled, and Little Brother is sad, but she soon fits into the Warner family and the foreign way of life, al-

though the Chinese servants, especially the houseboy, resent her. After about two years, not always easy, the Warner parents go off to a retreat, leaving Ailin in charge of the children. When Billy becomes ill and the houseboy has no idea who their doctor is, Ailin takes a rickshaw to her family home, but her mother is visiting Second Sister. Not wanting to face Big Uncle, Ailin goes to her sister's home, where the gatekeeper bangs the gate in her face. As a last resort, she goes to Miss Gilbertson, who knows and summons the American doctor. The Warners are grateful, and later, when they are to return to America on a sabbatical leave, they ask Ailin to go with them. Before she leaves, she returns to her family's home to say good-bye to her mother. She also gives Big Uncle all the money she has saved in her three years with the Warners, suggesting that it may help with the expenses of Little Brother's schooling. At the ship, before they sail, Xueyan shows up to say good-bye and to give her the money bag that has been returned by Big Uncle. During the trip, the Warners are in second-class accomodations, and Ailin is in third class, a difference that causes some embarrassment. She meets a young man named James Chew from San Francisco, where his father owns a restaurant, and they become good friends. Ailin is amazed that in San Francisco the Warners cannot afford servants and is also surprised that Mrs. Warner is such a bad cook. Although she herself has done little cooking, she soon takes over the kitchen and, in Chinatown to get supplies, meets James Chew again. By the time the Warners return to China, Ailin has decided to stay in San Francisco, marry James, and help him run the restaurant he expects to start. All this is enclosed in a brief frame story of her meeting with Liu Hanwei, who comes to their restaurant on his way back to Nanjing, after studying in Illinois for three years. He asks her sadly why she ran away to that American family. After reviewing mentally her whole story, she tells him she is happy to be standing on her own two big feet. Although the basic story has been told many times before, this novel does a good job of capturing Ailin's frustration at the plight of Chinese women and the density of the missionary mind, for instance, the Warners' objection to her teaching the children to paint Chinese characters because it is a "heathen language." At the end is a long note on the Chinese tradition of foot binding. ALA/YA.

TIFFANY ZEFFERELLI (*My Sister's Bones**) New girl in school and best friend of Billie Weinstein. Tiffany loves flashy clothes and lots of makeup and is an indifferent student. Her family is loud and seemingly happy, busy with one another and friends. Billie never learns what Mr. Zefferelli does for a living, but whatever it is, it lands him in trouble, apparently with gangsters, and the family leaves town abruptly. Billie has a crush on Tiffany's college-student brother, Dominick, and initiates sex with him. Tiffany is a foil to both Cassie*, Billie's anorexic older sister, and Billie.

A TIME APART (Stanley*, Diane, Morrow, 1999) Realistic psychological-problem novel in a family-life context set in Houston, Texas, and in and near London, England, one summer in recent years. Worried, angry Ginny (Virginia) Dorris, 13, flies from Houston to London to stay with her father, Hugh, an anthropology professor whom she barely knows, while her mother, Rena, is in the hospital with breast cancer. Ginny is met at the airport, not by her father, but by the head of the Anthro-

pology Department, crusty, peremptory, condescending Maurice Everett, who is directing a project to re-create an Iron Age village. He drives her to the secluded, remote area of which Hugh is site director. Ginny is appalled at the muddy village and at having to live without such amenities as a toothbrush or shampoo or comfortable beds. Of the fourteen people in the village, some are graduate students and three are children, but all are volunteers who have agreed to participate for a year. All have assigned responsibilities; Hugh's is to be the village smith, a demanding and only partially successful effort. Ginny helps Mark, the potter, whose pots always break because the clay is unsuitable, and then, although reluctantly, she takes care of Daisy, 5, the child of the Fieldings. Ginny helps Daisy fix up a small play roundhouse on the edge of the village, and when Daisy finds the clay on the bank of the nearby river good for molding toys and makes some pots that turn out well when fired, Mark's pot problem is solved. Corey Donnelly, 17, whose sister is also in the village, is helpful and pleasant, but he thinks her father disdains him because he is working class. Ginny gathers that Hugh is respected but not liked, and indeed he seems isolated and always engrossed in his work. When an August mail brings a box of schoolbooks—meaning Ginny will not leave for home before school starts—she runs away to London, where she is helped by Corey's "punk goddess" girlfriend to get on a plane for home. To her surprise, Hugh takes the adjoining seat. In Houston, Rena explains that the cancer has spread and that she needs more time to recover. Ginny returns to London with Hugh, who tells her about his family, a cold, undemonstrative group from whom he never received or learned to show affection. Ginny stays to celebrate Winter Solstice, then leaves with an amulet

Hugh has fashioned especially for her, more comfortable with him than she has ever been. The plot is weak and marred by too many flashbacks. Except for the scenes in which Ginny runs away, the story ambles along focusing on Ginny's sullen, resentful attitude. The setting is the book's main appeal—the group's attempts to replicate life in an Iron Age village based on research. The contrast between ancient and modern life is vivid and clear. Of the characters, Daisy steals the show, small, vulnerable, aware she is in the way. She attaches herself firmly to Ginny, her new "lovey-dovey" (nanny). Ginny has found new strengths—she is inventive and good with her hands—and knows that Hugh is proud of her. She also knows that he is, as her mother has said, kind, generous, and loving but unable to convey his feelings. The book concludes with a detailed and fascinating explanation of the book's genesis. ALA/YA.

TIMELINE (Crichton*, Michael, Knopf, 1999) Hefty adult techno-thriller novel that combines time travel, quantum theory physics, history, and archaeology set in New Mexico and southern France. An autopsy performed on the body of an ITC Research engineer found on the Navajo Reservation raises troubling questions about what has caused his death, why he carries what appears to be a computer-generated floor plan of a monastery in southern France, and why ITC is eager to hush up the whole matter. ITC Research is the brainchild of Robert Doniger, 38, brilliant physicist and billionaire from two earlier very successful scientific start-up companies. Arrogant, self-engrossed, and indefatigable, he employs some two hundred physicists engaged in supersecret research at the main ITC facility at Black Rock in New Mexico. In the first of many scene switches, the novel moves from Doniger and his associates to an archaeological site along the Dordogne River in southern France involving in particular the Monastery of Sainte-Mère but also including a mill and two castles. The site is being studied by highly regarded Edward Johnston, Regius Professor of History at Yale; his associate, Assistant Professor Andre Marék; and some Yale graduate students, among them diffident Christopher Hughes, who is interested in mills; Kate Erickson, an architecture student; and David Stern, a physicist who happens to be in the region. Puzzled by questions posed to him by a French investigative reporter and by the attitude of Doniger's attorney, Johnston returns to New Mexico. Then Elsie Kastner, team linguist and graphologist, discovers a puzzling cry for help in Johnston's handwriting on a medieval parchment in old ink, and the main team is summoned back to Black Rock. There they discover something of what Doniger is working on: sending people back into time. Marék, Stern, Kate, and Chris are asked to go back to medieval France to bring Johnston home. Stern is suspicious about the ability of the machines to transport them safely there and back and refuses to go, but the others do. Almost upon arrival, they are set upon viciously by apparently marauding knights and scatter variously. They have arrived on April 7, 1357, during an especially critical period in the Hundred Years War between the English and French, who vie for the Dordogne region. A superabundance of close encounters, nick-of-time escapes, and seemingly impossible difficulties follow, during which Kate, Marék, and Chris try to connect with one another and with Johnston in order to embark on a teleporting machine back to New Mexico before they are killed and their allotted thirty-seven hours for the whole expedition are used up. At the very last moment, Marék decides to stay in the Middle Ages, which he has spent his life studying and loves, while the others return. Back in New Mexico, the team learns that ITC has surreptitiously acquired large land parcels in remote areas of the world surrounding archaeological sites, the objective being to develop theme parks complete with hotels, restaurants, and the like, and to teleport tourists back in time to experience the original sites. The novel is clever in concept but overburdened with content and incident. The cast contains a studied, large mix of flat, barely differentiated characters. There are too many highly detailed incidents; too many details of history, science, and technology baldly inserted into the narrative; and too many television conventions like lengthy chases and unexpected falls into empty space. The narrative and the fore- and afternotes convey a good sense of the brutality, violence, inhumanity, and technology (not as primitive as most would believe) of the period. A few questions remain unanswered, but Crichton fans and techno-thriller buffs will persist to the startling conclusion. Booklist.

TOMEY, INGRID (1943–   )   Born in Port Huron, Michigan; a graduate of Michigan State University with a B.A., of Oakland University with an M.A., and of the University of Michigan with an M.F.A.; resident of West Bloomfield, Michigan. She has been an instructor for the Michigan Literacy Program, has published poems and novels, mainly for a juvenile audience, and has contributed to popular magazines. *Grandfather's Day* (Boyds Mills, 1992) concerns a depressed widower grandfather who moves in with his family. In *Savage Carrot* (Scribner,

1993), a girl connects with her deceased father's mentally disabled brother, and in *The Queen of Dreamland* (Scribner, 1993), a girl has conflicting feelings after she discovers her birth mother. *Nobody Else Has to Know** (Delacorte, 1999), an American Library Association selection for young adults, concerns a grandfather and grandson who face hard decisions after an auto accident.

TORN THREAD (Isaacs*, Anne, Scholastic, 2000)   Historical novel of the Jewish Holocaust in Poland and Czechoslovakia from June 1943 to May 1945, based on the childhood experiences of Eva Buchbinder Koplowicz, the author's mother-in-law. Eva, 12, her older sister, Rachel, 14, and their widower Papa have been living in cramped attic quarters in the Jewish ghetto in Bedzin, Poland. Rachel is caught in a roundup by German soldiers and shipped for slave labor to a factory in Parschnitz (present-day Porici), Czechoslovakia, which makes uniforms and blankets for German soldiers. Soon Papa somehow arranges for Eva to join her, so that Eva will not also be caught and perhaps shipped elsewhere and so that she can look after Rachel, who is frail. Eva puts on all the clothes she can find, stuffs her pockets with photographs, prayer books, and similar family items, and is transported in an extremely crowded, filthy railroad car to Parschnitz. Along the way, as she does throughout the book, she consoles herself by thinking of earlier, better days and by praying. Arrived, with other girls she is forced to march on a dirt road under a hot sun to the camp. She is assigned to a barracks, where almost miraculously she encounters Rachel. The camp inspectors are brutal, and the camp commander, Frau Hawlik, confiscates whatever she wishes of the girls' possessions and cruelly eats candy in front of them. A tall, blond girl, Kayla* Rubenstein, 17, grabs and hides Eva's bundles, so that they will not be stolen by guards or by other Jews. The workday lasts from 5:15 in the morning to long after dark, and rations are sparse and become more so as the war goes on. Eva has the good fortune of being assigned to the flax spinning room, where her coworker is a kind Czech girl and the supervisor is German Herr Schmidt, a devout Christian who allows the girls to read their prayer books and Torah and treats them kindly. Rachel works in the washing room and is increasingly feverish and sickly. Items, especially food, are often stolen by other workers, and no one can be trusted except their very closest friends. As the months pass, Eva begins to look far older than her years, wrinkled, gray, and emaciated. Rumors are rampant—that the Germans have rounded up all the Jews in Bedzin and shipped them to Auschwitz, and that the Russians are defeating the Germans on the eastern front. Eva often wonders why God lets them suffer this way, and whether God even cares about them. Her worst personal time is when her hair gets caught in the flax machine and she almost dies from the scalp wound. Her biggest problem throughout, however, is caring for Rachel, who falls very ill of typhus. After the Russians arrive in the spring of 1945, the slave laborers are fed healthy food and their injuries and illnesses treated by good doctors so that by the end of May, Rachel is on the mend. In an epilogue the reader learns that, back in Bedzin, they discover that Papa is dead, and that later both emigrate to Canada. Eva married there, and her son, Samuel, became the author's husband. Additional family details appear in the afterword. Although the book is much like other Holocaust narratives, the two girls are well drawn and admirable, especially the plucky, determined Eva, and the terrible living conditions and brutality of the camp are vividly depicted. The author is especially good at conveying the sense of the tedium and desolation of their lives. The title probably comes from the thread and pieces of material that Eva picks up and knits into garments for Rachel and the other always cold prisoners and thus earns bits of much-needed food. ALA/YA.

TO SAY NOTHING OF THE DOG, OR, HOW WE FOUND THE BISHOP'S BIRD STUMP AT LAST (Willis*, Connie, Bantam, 1997)   Adult farcical comedy-of-errors science fiction novel involving time travel set at Oxford University in England in 2057 and in 1888, as well as a few other places and periods in between. Wealthy, imperious Lady Schrapnel decides to rebuild Coventry Cathedral as it was before the Germans bombed it in World War II, move it to Oxford, and furnish it with artifacts of the early twentieth century. She enlists Oxford time-travel experts to "drop" through the time "net" to get what she needs. Among these is narrator Ned Henry, a young man whose task is to recover the bishop's bird stump, a cast-iron footed pedestal urn for flowers. When Ned develops a bad case of time lag, he is sent for much-needed rest back to Victorian England in 1888, since that period is regarded as particularly peaceful and orderly. Ironically, he immediately becomes involved with a large number of eccentric Victorians and in matters unexpectedly and often humorously related to the cathedral's reconstruction that culminate in the recovery of the bird stump. On arriving in the 1888 period, he falls in with Terence St. Trewes, a chattering, somewhat bumbling Oxford student, who behaves much like the rabbit in *Alice's Adventures in Wonderland* (one of many literary allusions in the novel). Terence is accompanied by a black bulldog named Cyril, who is apparently the dog of the title. With Professor Peddick, an absent-minded history don who is crazy about fishing, Ned and Terence take Cyril and paddle down the Thames, finally after some mishaps arriving at the home of Colonel and Mrs. Mering, stereotypically pretentious upper-class Victorians. Like the professor, the colonel is addicted to fishing, and Mrs. Mering is heavily immersed in spiritism and seances. Ned's task now is to return to their rattle-headed, beautiful daughter, Tossie, her beloved cat, Princess Arjamund, which he does with the help of another twenty-first-century time traveler, Verity Brown, with whom by book's end he is in love. Ned and Verity also seek Tossie's diary, since Tossie is the great-great-great-great-grandmother of Lady Scharpnel, who needs the diary for information about her building project. Ned and Verity must also prevent Tossie and Terence from marrying, since that would, of course, upset the composition of succeeding generations. Entanglements, twists, and humorous turns along with many trips between time periods occur before all is straightened out at the end. The bishop's bird stump is located, as well as numerous other artifacts. Tossie runs off with the butler, which outrages her mother; and the book ends with the cathedral's consecration. Although the time-travel method discovered by the Oxford crew has produced many funny incongruities, it has also been shown to be of immense value for museums and historians in locating and bringing into the twenty-first century priceless artifacts long thought to be irrecoverable. There are many long, discursive discussions about historical events and personages; literary quotations and allusions abound; details about drops, nets, time lags, and incongruities are worked out in sufficient detail to be intriguing if not totally convincing; and the sensible, caring Ned and Verity grow more engaging and appealing as the book progresses. The humor makes use of various devices—mistaken identities, sudden disappearances and reappearances, literal misunderstandings, trivia taken seriously, slapstick, patter, insults, wordplay, quotations from literary works that are distorted or are out of place, and satire on literary forms and works and on history—in addition to the eccentricized figures. Plot motivations get lost in the shuffle of characters and the long conversations, but science fiction devotees are bound to enjoy the time-travel aspects. Alex; ALA/YA.

TRACY PRINGLE (*Strays Like Us**) Poor-little-rich-girl type who becomes acquainted with Molly Moberly through the public library. The Pringles live in a big, well-appointed house in the wealthy part of town. One night Aunt Fay is called to the Pringle house, where she and Molly discover that Tracy has been terribly burned. Strangely, Tracy's mother does not want an ambulance called or the authorities notified, but Aunt Fay absolutely insists. Later, it comes out that Tracy was the arsonist who set the junior high school on fire, although Molly and the reader never learn why she wanted to burn the place. Tracy's family situation is also shrouded in secrecy.

TRAPPED BETWEEN THE LASH AND THE GUN (Whitmore*, Arvella, Dial, 1999) Time-slip fantasy of an African American boy from a modern city who is drawn back into slavery times, suffers many of the horrors, and returns chastened and newly appreciative of his family. Jordan Henning Scott, 12, resents the idea that his mother is planning to move to the "honkey" suburb of Springdale, expecting him, along with his younger sister, Tachelle, to move with her. He really wants to go to see his father, about whose whereabouts his mother is deliberately vague, and expects to earn money for a ticket by joining the Cobra gang, where younger members get paid for delivering drugs and other illegal activities. To join the Cobras, he must come up with money, supposedly to buy a gun. He steals his grandfather's treasure, an old gold watch owned by Jordan's great-great-great-great-grandfather, that has an etching on the cover of Hilltop, the Henning plantation on which he was a slave. As he hurries to the pawnshop, he goes through a street underpass and comes out in a strange, swampy place where a little black boy is hunting for his master's watch. Stopped by paddyrollers, slave catchers, the boy hides Jordan, shows his pass to be off the plantation, and says his name is Uriah Henning from Hilltop. They let him go, and Jordan, no longer carrying his grandfather's watch, follows him. No one believes any of the story Jordan tells, so he is sent to the slave quarters where he is lodged in a shack with Uriah's family. From that point on, the story is like almost every other slave tale. He is forced to work in the cotton fields, with only a little corn cake for breakfast and lunch. When Uriah's mother, Clara, tries to help him, she is hauled away and whipped. Jordan himself is whipped, but really given only a couple of lashes after which the black overseer's helper tells him to scream when the whip hits the ground. Hunting for the watch, which Master Hennings realizes

he did not lose in the swamp, Jordan hides under the bed and hears the man's wife insist that they sell at least three slaves, including Jordan and Clara, against whom she is vindictive. At the slave auction, a red-haired man tries to buy Clara but is outbid, so he buys Jordan instead. He turns out to be with the Underground Railroad and is ready to send Clara's husband, Seth, and all the children north, but Uriah has been taken into the house by Master Hennings to be his personal servant, and the others are waiting for someone to persuade him to join them. The job falls to Jordan, who has a hard time because being a house servant is a big step up from a field hand and also because Uriah thinks the master is favoring him because he is his father. Finally, the idea of being able to go to school in Canada tips the balance, and they both go off to the red-haired man's barn. He gives Jordan his freedom papers, and leads them both to a wagon of hay, into which they burrow with Seth and the other children. Under the hay, Jordan feels a cold round thing under Uriah's nightshirt and realizes that it is the watch, which the master has entrusted to the boy for safekeeping. Immediately, Jordan finds himself back in the city, and he runs to Grandpa's house, where he returns the watch. From his grandfather he learns that Uriah Henning found freedom papers made out to Jordan Henning, and he changed his name. On the way home, Jordan is waylaid by King, the leader of the Cobras, and other gang members. Since he does not have the money and says he wants to leave the gang, they start to beat him up. He feels a terrible pain and hears a shot. He wakes in the hospital to learn that King shot at him, killed a rival gang member, and is in jail charged with murder. His mother admits that Jordan's father is in prison. Jordan is relieved to be going to Springdale with his mother and sister. The novel is aimed at a middle school or junior high school reader, with a resulting simplification of situations in both time periods. The bulk of the story has been told many times before, the travel in time being the only new element. An author's note adds the interesting information that she had no idea of any African American blood in her family until after the book was accepted for publication, when a distant cousin wrote her that her great-grandmother was an ex-slave. ALA/YA.

TRAVIS BRIGHTON (*At All Costs**) Thirteen-year-old son of Jake* and Carolyn Brighton (real name Donovan). Travis has grown resentful and angry in particular at his father, because the family has moved so many times. He hates living in dumpy places and being the new kid at school who is always picked on. When the Brightons leave Phoenix, South Carolina, hurriedly for a hideout in the West Virginia mountains, he learns why they move so often. Travis is a brave boy, going alone inside a restaurant to call Harry Sinclair for help and running inside the hazardous-materials depot to warn his parents that a policeman has arrived. The most gripping scenes involving Travis are those when he becomes sick in the car while the family and Nick* Thomas are fleeing from the depot and when Wiggins* tries to kill him when he lies helpless, suffering from hazardous-materials poisoning. He sticks up for his parents, firmly telling the attorney general of the United States that they never did anything wrong.

TREASURES IN THE DUST (Porter*, Tracey, HarperCollins, 1997) Novel of the friendship of two girls in the Oklahoma Dust Bowl of the 1930s. In alternating first-person, present-tense chapters, Annie May Weightman and Violet Cobble, both about eleven, tell about the storms that darken the sky and blow dust through the cracks to cover the tables, hang suspended in the air, and bring on lung disease in humans and animals. As dust piles up around their houses and outbuildings, both farm families try to cope. In Annie's family, where she has only one sibling, older brother Liam, life is hard enough, but it is much worse for the Cobbles, who lose all their chickens and eventually their only cow, and who have four children and an aging blind relative, Aunt Miracle, living with them. Their land will grow no crops, not even hay, and although they would like to head west to pick crops in California, as have many of the farm families in Cimarron County, they know that Aunt Miracle could not stand the trip. Although best friends, the girls are very different. Tall, red-haired Violet is imaginative, loving to act out scenes from romance and dreaming of taking dancing lessons and having an acting career. Annie, a much more practical sort, is mostly interested in finding arrowheads that have been uncovered by the shifting sands and hoping to become an archeologist. When she finds an especially fine obsidian arrowhead, almost as long as her hand, she consults the town librarian, Mr. Coates, who admires it, suggests that he take it to his college professor friend who is an expert on Indian artifacts, and insists on giving her a receipt for it. Both girls are looking forward to the coming year at Garlington School with their teacher, Miss Littlewood, but before school starts, Violet's mother decides she must keep the girl at home to help her with the twins, lively four-year-old boys, the baby, Joseph, and Aunt Miracle, whose lungs have been damaged by the dust. Violet reads and talks to the old woman, who says the girl is like her, "mindfull," meaning she has a head full of ideas and stories. At school, Annie, who is far ahead of the other sixth graders, is asked to help by tutoring three slow readers. Aunt Miracle dies, and after a brief service at the windblown graveside, the Cobble family packs up and heads west. The rest of Violet's chapters are letters that she writes to Annie and saves up until she can buy a stamp. These tell of the difficulties of the trip and the disappointments of California, where there are too many workers for the jobs, farmers and orchard owners cheat them, and local residents look at them with scorn. Eventually, Mr. Cobble leaves his family and rides the rails to Los Angeles, where he and a friend find work at a slaughterhouse and earn enough money to head back to Oklahoma. In the meantime, Annie has become involved with a project with Mr. Coates to start a local museum, mostly of curiosities but with some real treasures, like her black arrowhead, which has been identified as being Comanche, from two hundred years before when they lived in the Panhandle and hunted buffalo. In the end, the Cobbles have returned to Cimarron County and so has the rain, and the girls are able to resume their friendship. Although the Okie Depression tale has been told many times, notably in John Steinbeck's *The Grapes of Wrath*, this novel is aimed at young teens who may not have read any of the more mature versions. The sensory details of the dust storms and the disillusionment in California are well handled. The whole story is oversimplified but not falsified. Both girls and their families, however, talk more like educated people in the 1990s than in the dialect of Oklahoma farmers of the 1930s. ALA/YA.

THE TREE OF RED STARS (Bridal*, Tessa, Milkweed, 1997)   Substantial, thought-provoking, historical novel published for adults set mostly in Montevideo, Uruguay, in the late 1950s and 1960s about life and culture among the affluent and student activism against political repression. In a prologue set in the late 1970s, Magda* (Magdalena) Ortega Grey, the narrator, returns to her native Uruguay from Europe, where she has been shuttling for seven years between Paris and London in efforts to secure the release of Marco* Periera, her close friend from childhood and an army colonel who has been imprisoned in solitary confinement and tortured for aiding the revolutionary group known as the Tupamaros, Tupas for short. The early chapters have few political undertones, describing mainly domestic adventures with Emilia, who is Magda's age, in their privileged neighborhood—teas, overheard conversations between the women about the men in their lives, school, and observations from their perches in the branches of the old poinsettia tree outside Magda's house, from which the novel takes its title. They are somewhat aware of larger events— a new friend in the neighborhood is Jewish Cora* Allenberg, whose family are refugees; they overhear a conversation between Emilia's mother and a neighbor woman about fighting and hiding guns and learn later that both have connections to the Tupas; and they steal out to hear a speech by historical Che Guevera, during which a riot ensues and Magda is almost raped by a policeman. Magda has become aware of Marco as a potential sweetheart and knows that he is highly concerned about justice and equality; helps the poor, among them a neighborhood beggar named Gabriela*; and has ties with the Tupas, although, pressured by his father, he joins the army. While she is attracted to Marco, Magda has a small romance with a friend of Marco, Jaime* Betancourt, which continues while she and Emilia are exchange students in the United States. Magda becomes involved with the Tupas in earnest when she takes college classes and encounters Cora's husband, Ramiro, a Tupa who enlists her in spying in her secretarial and translator's job with the United States Information Service. She learns that the United States has been giving aid to the government to repress the revolutionary movement. In particular, she learns of sophisticated methods of torture the Americans have been teaching the police. Many terrible events ensue, among them that Emilia is tortured and Magda herself is picked up and imprisoned, released, she later learns, through the intervention of Marco, who is now a double agent, soon also to be exposed as such, imprisoned, and tortured for seven years. Magda is persuaded to seek safety in Europe and help from human rights and governmental agencies for Marco and others like him. In the epilogue, she and Marco meet joyfully, but both know that they will have little time together since Marco has been released from prison because he is dying. Based on actual events and people, a story of friendship and growing up as well as political intrigue, the novel is rich in detail and substantial in concept, and Magda's gradual understanding of the political and economic arena and the part she might play in helping the unfortunate and righting wrongs is completely convincing. American influence on Uruguay culturally, economically, and politically is not glossed over, nor is anti-American senti-

ment. Although the book is serious for the most part, some amusing scenes occur, as when Caramba, the parrot, invades the ladies' fashionable tea parties. The imprisonment scenes are ghastly. Summarizing this multifaceted book is difficult; reading it explores issues of compassion, ethics, and human rights. Booklist.

THE TRIBES OF PALOS VERDES (Nicholson*, Joy, St. Martin's, 1997) Adult realistic novel replete with scathing social commentary of family, school, and community life in the exclusive oceanside neighborhood of Palos Verdes, California, for about two years in the late 1970s or the 1980s. To advance his career, Phil Mason, handsome "heart surgeon to the stars," one of whom is Elizabeth Taylor, moves his family from Michigan to Palos Verdes. Although his work goes well, his family encounters numerous difficulties that tear them apart. In revenge for his womanizing, Sandy, once a svelte, beautiful model, eats herself into a size sixteen, earning the intense disdain of her new neighbors and the rude remarks of the neighborhood young people. The dearest friend—indeed the only friend—of their daughter, intelligent, plain, outspoken Medina, 14, the narrator, is her good-looking, affable, outgoing twin, Jim, who is immediately accepted. Since the girls at school disparage Medina at every turn, and the neighborhood youth, who are divided into cliques by looks, social scale, ethnicity, and wealth, also exclude her, she decides to become adept at surfing, only to discover that the sport is considered reserved for boys. She works hard at it, however, studying moves and waves, until she gains reluctant acceptance from the ultracool Bayboys. Although they admire her spunk and prowess, they make cutting remarks about her appearance, and when it gets around that she had sex with a maker of surfboards more than twice her age, they jibe about her morals. Her marriage disintegrated, Sandy fashions Jim into a substitute husband. While Medina is accepted into the Mentally Gifted Minors (the "brainbox") in school, Jim seems satisfied being a mediocre student. He gradually spends more and more time with the lowest rung of surfers, known as the "bottomfeeders," some of whom deal drugs. He gets stoned frequently and pops pills until he is heavily in debt to them. Phil acquires a live-in girlfriend, Ava Adare, and moves with her into a beautiful new house in another part of the subdivision. Ava's bright, ambitious son, Adrian, 17, meets Medina on the beach, and the two become sweethearts. Jim gets into serious trouble from drugs and liquor, commits arson, and is sent to a mental hospital where he kills himself. Phil sells the house, gives Medina the proceeds, and sends her to an exclusive girls' school. Sandy dies from a massive heart attack, and Phil marries another woman, having already shed Ava. In many short, rapidly moving vignettes, the book presents sordid views of the Palos Verdes community—self-engrossed, shallow, a complex of "tribes" attempting to outdo one another, whose out-of-control children ape the ways of their elders and are as vicious, murderous, and self-destructive in their way as the gangs of inner-city youth whom they despise. ALA/YA.

TRIBUTE TO ANOTHER DEAD ROCK STAR (Powell*, Randy, Farrar, 1999) Realistic novel of a clever but troubled boy whose mother was a rock star, suffocated three years earlier by her own vomit after an overdose of drugs. The narrator, Grady Grennan, 15, has been invited to speak briefly at a concert in tribute to his mother, Debbie, although her own mother, Rena, refuses to attend and has gone off for the weekend with her new husband, Shorty Pettibone. They leave Grady at a radio station, where he is interviewed and makes a point of saying hello to his half brother, Louie. Afterward he goes to spend the weekend with Vickie and Mitch, the nearest to a father Grady has known, with whom his mother lived for three years on Lopez Island and who is father to Debbie's other son, retarded Louie, 12. When Grady was seven, Debbie left, taking him to Rena. Mitch has since married Vickie, an uptight, proper, church-obsessed woman, and had three children with her. Although Grady and Vickie are mutually antagonistic, Grady saw a lot of his half brother when he lived with Rena in Seattle, but after she married and took Grady with her to live with Shorty in Red Fish, his visits have been rare and filled with conflict. Vickie thinks the only way to handle Louie is with strict structure and firm discipline. Although Grady admits that Louie is unpredictable and sometimes difficult, he wants to give the boy more freedom and an opportunity to express himself. This visit is complicated by several factors. Louie wants to go to the tribute, too, especially since the band will be his favorite, Tantrum, and Grady will ride in a limousine. He also wants to try a skateboard, like Grady. More seriously, they all know that Rena and Shorty are planning to sell out in Red Fish, buy a motor home, and cruise around for at least a year. There is a vague plan that Grady might study overseas during that time, but he is not sure he wants to spend that long without Louie, and he realistically sees that he cannot take his brother along. Grady arrives with his skateboard, which Vickie loathes, and they begin verbal sparring immediately. Grady sees that in Louie's room, all the Tantrum posters have been replaced by those of a Christian rock group. He also learns that Vickie has told Louie that she is his real mother, that Debbie was just his "bio" mother. When the limousine comes for Grady, Louie is left behind. Grady spends some time with Mindy Connor, his mother's manager, and meets again some people who played with Debbie. At the tribute, he comes up to the microphone still not knowing what he will say. After a few seconds' hesitation, he says he is not sure he knew his mother, that she was better at making music than at mothering, but that they had some good times together and he wishes her other son, Louie, could be there, too. Afterward, he gets the limousine driver to take him to the top of the parking structure, where Debbie was on her last night, and looks out at the water, realizing how alone she was. Then he hops on his skateboard, which he has with him always, and rides down the spiral ramp all seven levels, takes the elevator up, and does it again. Both Mitch and Vickie invite him to live with them next year, and he is pretty sure he will. Grady is a very bright kid, not intimidated by Vickie and not always patient with Louie, who is often hard to be with, but genuinely fond of him. Vickie is a very convincing control freak, but she is also a good enough person to admit it and to promise to try to get along with Grady. Since both Grady and Louie have inherited a lot of money from Debbie, his decision to forego the study year in Europe is not based on the cost but on his realization that he needs family and roots or he will end up alone, like his mother. There is no guarantee that the arrangement will work, but Grady is smart and honest enough to get along, and his reporting of the situation is funny and often touching. ALA/YA.

TRICE, DAWN TURNER   Journalist, author of novels about the African American experience. She makes her home in Chicago, where she is an editor at the *Chicago Tribune*. Her highly acclaimed novel, *Only Twice I've Wished for Heaven** (Crown, 1997), is about a friendship between a middle-class girl and an old woman who runs a small liquor and convenience store, an ex-prostitute, but even more about a period when upward mobility among African Americans split the community in the city. A more recent novel, *An Eighth of August* (Crown, 2000), is set in a small Illinois town at a festival celebrating the signing of the Emancipation Proclamation.

TROUBLE (*The Lost Years of Merlin**) Small hawk or merlin that Emrys saves from an attack of two large, vicious rats when he first arrives in Fincayra. After that the bird follows Emrys and Rhia, usually riding with a painful grip on the boy's shoulder. At first Emrys resents this and tries to rid himself of his passenger, but Trouble attacks what they think is a rare alleah bird but which turns out to be an evil shifting wraith, and they realize his value. Several other times he is instrumental in advancing their quest, in particular after the Domnu has made Emrys and Shim* tiny and he carries them to the Shrouded Castle and dives through a window opening. Finally, in the scene when Emrys confronts King Stangmar, Trouble escapes from the goblin that holds him and dives at the evil Rhita Gawr, destroying his power and driving him from Fincayra but being killed in the struggle. Emrys, who has never been comfortable with that name, takes his true name, Merlin, from the bird.

TROUT SUMMER (Conly*, Jane Leslie, Holt, 1995)   Adventure novel of two young teenage siblings who spend a summer in the 1990s at a rundown Pennsylvania cabin on a fast-moving river, and their encounters with an eccentric old man who claims he is a ranger. Action centers on their gradually growing friendship and eventual effort to save him from a disastrous canoe journey. For a longer entry, see *Dictionary, 1995–1999*. ALA/YA.

TROY, JUDY (1951–   )   Born in Chicago, Illinois; English professor, editor, novelist. She is a graduate of the University of Illinois–Chicago, with an M.A. from Indiana University. Since 1991 she has taught at Auburn University and from 1991 to 1996 was fiction editor for *Crazyhorse*, a literary periodical published there. Her collection of short stories, *Mourning Doves* (Scribner, 1993), was widely acclaimed and became the basis for her first novel, *West of Venus* (Random, 1997), which elaborates on some of the small-town characters in the stories. In another small-town setting, *From the Black Hills** (Random, 1999) follows the almost devastating effect on a teenage boy after his father kills his receptionist and disappears. The novel has been praised for its strong sense of the western South Dakota landscape.

THE TRUE COLORS OF CAITLYNNE JACKSON (Williams*, Carol Lynch, Delacorte, 1997)   Contemporary realistic novel of child abuse and mental illness set in central Florida. Caitlynne Jackson, 12, the narrator, and her half sister, Cara, 11, fear their obese, erratic, easily angered single-parent Mom, Virginia, an aspiring novelist. Their little house, which sits alone beside a lake, is filthy most of the time, and food often runs low. Caitlynne's best friend, Kathy, refuses to visit, because she once saw Mrs. Jackson strike Caitlynne with her fist and scream at her. In fact, Mom strikes the girls and screams at them frequently. Cara has friends, but she is slight physically and emotionally brittle. School, where Caitlynne excels at art, is their refuge. A big, strong girl, she loves to play ball with the boys, who welcome her, especially Brandon Hill, who lives near by. Brandon's family is well off, with a big house, roaming yard, and a pool. While life is precarious for the girls at best, the really bad days start when Brandon invites Caitlynne to the end-of-the-school-year dance. On the night of the dance, however, Mom suddenly refuses to let Caitlynne go. Brandon, who is a truly understanding boy, has some idea of what is going on. He comforts Caitlynne as they sit later by the side of the lake in the moonlight. The next day, Mom angrily stuffs the refrigerator and cupboards with food, puts some money in the honey jar, and announces that she is leaving. Although Caitlynne begs her not to go, she drives off. Caitlynne wants to call Nana*, Mom's mother, but Cara is afraid to, since Mom has been on the outs with Nana for some time. Although they miss Mom and wonder what will happen to them, they are happy. Brandon visits every day, is sworn to secrecy, and says he will watch out for them. They tell no one about their predicament, for fear that they will be taken away and placed in separate foster homes. A visit to replenish the food supply takes most of the forty-three dollars Mom left, and they discuss alternatives— get jobs, go to Nana, go to Cara's father's mother in Idaho. To pass the time, they play ball with the neighborhood kids, go to the library, chat with Brandon, and daydream of good times. Just before leaving on vacation at the end of July, Brandon and his mother bring over food that the Hills have not used, a most welcome addition to the girls' rapidly dwindling stores, and Brandon kisses Caitlynne a sweet good-bye. After a terrifying storm hits, Caitlynne decides they will bike the forty-five miles to Nana's house in New Smyrna, Florida. They start early in the morning with a little food and a few essentials and pedal over the hot, country roads, worrying whether they can make it, and if they do, whether Nana will take them in. They arrive not without incident at Nana's and live happily there until the end of August, when Mom comes and angrily insists they return with her. A big argument ensues, during which Mom strikes Caitlynne repeatedly, police are called, and Mom is taken away to a hospital. The novel ends inconclusively; the girls are waiting to see what will happen next to Mom and them. Events seem contrived to show what life can be like with a mentally ill parent. Good features include the loving relationship between the sisters and the pleasing little romance between Caitlynne and Brandon. As it happens, one of the books the girls know is Cynthia Voigt's* *Homecoming*, a novel about four children who are also abandoned by their mother and undertake a long journey to reach their grandmother. Ironically, *The True Colors of Caitlynne Jackson* pales in comparison, but readers who are reluctant to tackle the earlier, longer book might find this one more accessible—the only advantage it offers over its predecessor. ALA/YA.

TRUEMAN, TERRY (1947–   )   Born in Birmingham, Alabama; raised in Seattle, Washington; graduate of the University of Washington with a B.A. and of Eastern Washington University with an M.S. in developmental psychology; attended the Washington State University Ph.D. program; received an M.F.A. in cre-

ative writing from Eastern Washington University. He has been a teacher; therapist; and counselor in secondary schools in Australia, Washington, and Honduras; a substance-abuse specialist; a film, video, and media critic in Spokane, Washington; and a poet, novelist, and nonfiction writer. After publishing several books of well-received poems, at the age of forty-eight he embarked on fiction with *Stuck in Neutral** (HarperCollins, 2000), a highly acclaimed book that won many honors in the United States and abroad, including being named a Michael L. Printz Honor Book and an American Library Association choice for young adults. Based on Trueman's own son, the book tells of a boy born with cerebral palsy, who sees a great contrast between the way he views himself and the way others regard him and who worries that his father may be planning to do away with him. The book has been lauded for its delicate treatment of the ethical problem of euthanasia as well as the clarity and compassion with which it tackles attitudes toward the handicapped.

TUNES   SMITH (*Dangerous   Skies**) Best friend and classmate of narrator Buck Smith, 12. A bright, pretty black girl, also twelve, she lives alone with her widower father, Kneebone*, but has practically been raised by Buck's mother and grandmother. As she has grown older, Tunes has become more mysterious in her ways, often disappearing for many hours, and increasingly quiet. Very intelligent, although she tries to hide it, she easily makes the honor roll in school, but her ability is not acknowledged as it would be if she were white. In fact, so good is an exam she turns in that Miz Timmons, her English teacher, accuses her of copying. She tells Buck about how Jumbo* Rawlin has been sexually molesting her for more than a year, forcing her to submit or he would see that her father lost the little bit of land he owns. She also informs Buck that it is common for black women to be subjected to such abuse from the area white men. Buck insists that she tell her story—he mistakenly has faith in the judicial system—but she is certain that Jumbo's story will prevail, and her fears prove correct. During the arrest, she is treated shamefully, with no regard for her dignity and sensibilities. After the trial, she goes to live with relatives in another state.

TURNER, MEGAN WHALEN (1965–   ) Born in Fort Sill, Oklahoma; graduate of the University of Chicago; writer of fiction for middle graders and teens. *The Thief** (Greenwillow, 1996), an American Library Association choice for young adults, is a humorous fantasy novel, generous with adventure and action, set in an ancient Greece-like land. Its sequel is *The Queen of Attolia* (Greenwillow, 2000). For more information about Turner, titles, and a title entry, see *Dictionary, 1995–1999* [*The Thief*].

TWO SUNS IN THE SKY (Bat-Ami*, Miriam, Front Street, 1999)   Historical novel centering on a young, tormented romance between an American Catholic girl of Oswego, New York, and a Jewish boy from Croatia at the Oswego Emergency Refugee Shelter in 1944 and 1945. Chris (Christine) Cook, 15, is curious about the refugees about to be housed at old Fort Ontario, but her very traditional father forbids her to go near them, saying they are dirty scum who will use up all the American food and cigarettes. Still, Chris goes secretly to see them arrive and immediately notices a boy with dark, curly hair holding a younger girl by the hand.

Seeing that the child is looking longingly at her bike, Chris gets two boys to boost her up and another to lift her bike, which she hands over the fence to the Jewish boy, with signs to return it later. A few days after this, Chris and her cousin sneak into the camp through a hole under the fence, and she meets Tikvah, who eventually introduces her to Adam Bornstein, 17, and their romance begins. Adam, his mother, and his sister, Mira, are originally from Zagreb, Yugoslavia, but, with their father and brother, Villi, all disguised as Christians, made their way to Rome, where Adam attended school. After the fall of Italy, his father and Villi returned to Yugoslavia to try to find Adam's grandmother, but after months of waiting with no word, his mother applied to be sent to the camp in Oswego. Caught in political red tape, it turns out to be the only refugee camp in the country. After a period of quarantine, the children and teenagers are allowed to attend local schools, so the contacts between Chris and Adam can be more open. At Thanksgiving, Chris persuades her mother to invite the Bornsteins to dinner, which starts out pretty well, with all the relatives behaving. Then her father suggests playing Ten Bible Questions, insisting on using questions from the Missal, thinking Adam might know the Old Testament but not this. He makes Chris ask the questions, and soon all the relatives are eliminated, leaving only Mr. Cook and Adam, who was well taught in a Catholic school and is very bright. As the contest heats up, Adam forfeits rather than beat Mr. Cook, thereby forcing Mr. Cook to forfeit, too, or look small. After that, the romance continues, secret from Chris's father, both delighting Chris and tormenting her, since her conscience bothers her, especially after at confession the priest tells her to avoid the occasion of sin. The Bornsteins get word from Villi that they have not been able to find his grandmother, and that their father has died on the way. The death of Roosevelt saddens them all, and Chris decides to be more open about seeing Adam. When she defies her father and refuses to say she will never see Adam again, he beats her with a strap. The next day, Chris persuades Adam to go to New York with her, where they eat in an automat and go up to the top of the Empire State Building. After they return, Adam gives her the cross he wore in Italy, when he pretended to be a Christian. To protect her from her father, Adam insists that they do not see each other again. When the war ends, the officials do not know what to do with the refugees. After hearings, it is decided that those who want to can immigrate officially to the United States, leaving and reentering at Niagara Falls. Adam's mother wants to go to New York, since she has trained as a hairdresser and thinks she can get a job, perhaps start a shop there. Before they leave, Chris goes to the camp, and she and Adam kiss but do not say good-bye. The information about the camp is factual, and Chris's struggles with her conscience ring true. Her father is a bigot and in some ways a caricature, but he is shown to genuinely want to protect her, and he beats her more in frustration at not knowing what to do than in anger. Religion is shown to cause far more problems than it solves. ALA/YA.

U

ULUB AND UBUB WOODS (*Hotel Paradise**)   Brothers in their fifties or sixties who sit every day on the bench outside Britten's store, often with Mr. Root, who seems to understand them. When Emma Graham learns that they used to work for the Devereaus and she questions them about the drowning of Mary-Evelyn, she has difficulty with their speech, but with Mr. Root's help soon finds that they not only know something, they are eager to tell it. Ulub, whose real name is Alonzo, worked for the Devereau women forty years ago, when he was a teenager. He and his brother, whose real name may be Bob, each have old trucks, and they are more than willing to take Emma and Mr. Root as far as the road now goes around Spirit Lake, then walk through the overgrown trail to the house. They find it unlocked, still full of pictures, clothes, and other items, as if the women who left so long ago were expecting to return. Ulub, with Ubub's help, acts out a scene he saw through the window, of the three aunts stiffly eating dinner while Mary-Evelyn is forced for punishment to play the piano for them. He also tells them that he saw the three women and the girl with a lantern go to the boathouse in the night. He obviously thinks that they put Mary-Evelyn into a leaky boat and pushed it out into the lake, essentially murdering her. Afterward, Emma realizes that Ulub could not have seen clearly at night and that the women might have been hunting for the unhappy girl who had run away. Ulub shows them a heart he carved into a tree not far from the house with his initials, AL, on it, probably not daring to add Mary-Evelyn's.

UNCLE CHARLES ABBOTT (*My Father's Scar**)   Gentle, bookish uncle of Andy Logan's grandmother, who lives in the top floor of her house and suffers her bullying with mild sarcasm and an occasional subversive action to annoy her, as when he talks Latin with his friend, Horace Biddle. To Andy, he offers understanding and a place to read, the first person who has ever respected his interest in books. He also provides Andy's first glimpse into the meaning of love, as he and his friend Mr. Biddle, whom he introduces as the town historian, converse about their younger days. Although Andy does not fully realize it, they appear to have had a homosexual relationship, whether latent or overt; what he does realize is that they have real love for each other, lasting into their old age.

UNCLE VALENTINE BRANSBY (*An Acquaintance with Darkness**) Nonhistorical physician and medical scientist who is presented as the third physician (name unknown to history) who attended President Lincoln the night he was shot. In the novel, Uncle Valentine is the uncle of the protagonist, Emily Bransby Pigbush. Emily reports that he is a University of Edinburgh–trained doctor, a polished gentleman who knows the Lincolns and other important and influential people in Washington, D.C. He is much loved by his patients, whom he helps to the best of his ability whether or not they can pay. He has long taken a special interest in Emily and has arranged for her to be educated at one of Washington's best schools for young ladies. He needs bodies for his studies and is involved in body snatching and grave robbing. He tries hard to prevent Dr. Mudd, the historical physician who helped John Wilkes Booth, from being imprisoned as a conspirator, gets lawyers for the historical Surratts, and tries unsuccessfully to keep authorities from hanging Mary Surratt, also historical. Although almost a paragon of too many virtues, he is a likable figure.

UNCLE ZENO MCBRIDE (*Jim the Boy**) Oldest of the three tall, lean, rock-solid McBride brothers of Aliceville, North Carolina, who together with their widowed sister, Cissy, raise her son, Jim Glass. Uncle Zeno is a religious man, concerned, like his brothers, that Jim grow up to be a God-fearing, kind, sensible, moral man. Uncle Zeno spends more time with Jim than the others, because Jim and Cissy live in his house. He tells Jim stories about the boy's father, presenting Jim, Sr., as a good man who loved Cissy very much and who enjoyed and was good at hunting. On the ride up the mountain to Amos* Glass's house, Uncle Zeno tells Jim about how his grandfather had fallen afoul of the law and was sent to prison for nine years.

UP JUMPS THE DEVIL (Maron*, Margaret, Mysterious, 1996) Contemporary adult realistic mystery-detective novel, fourth in the set featuring thirtysomething Deborah Knott, district court judge in mostly rural Colleton County, North Carolina. Astute, observant, and reliable narrator, Judge Knott describes three murders that rock the close-knit community from mid-October through Thanksgiving. She returns to her home in Dobbs from subbing for another judge to learn that Dallas Stancil, an old friend of Kezzie, her father, has been shot to death. Soon Dallas's third wife, trashy Cherry Lou, and her equally trashy son-in-law, Tig Wentworth, are charged with the killing, presumably over Dallas's land, for which Dallas supposedly was offered one hundred thousand dollars by a developer. Soon colorful Mr.* Jap (Jasper) Stancil, Dallas's father who stood to inherit Dallas's land, is found murdered with a tire iron and lying in blood in his garage, the safe open and rifled. Later, Dick Sutterly, an eager developer who has had many business contacts in the region, is found dead in his car, shot with a small-bore gun. There is no shortage of likely suspects for amateur detective Deborah and law officers to explore. Young Billy

Wall owed Mr. Jap money. Mr. Jap's nephew, Allen* Stancil, long absent from the community, turns up unexpectedly. As the only blood kin, he stands to inherit the old man's property. Merrilee Yadkin Grimes, a niece by marriage, has been looking out for Mr. Jap for years and possibly might gain, although Deborah later learns Mr. Jap had not yet signed the will intended to leave property to Merrilee. Adam* Knott, one of Deborah's eleven older brothers, who has come home from California, having fallen on hard times, was seen hunting with a small-bore gun. Before the truth comes out and a surprising villain is identified, Deborah interacts with law enforcement officers, many members of the community, and her own large and often rowdy family for a highly engrossing, if formulaic, mystery. More memorably, however, the novel offers a sharply executed portrait of an ingrown community whose roots go back through bootleg days and whose values are changing as the built environment evolves from modest rural homesteads to shopping malls and housing developments. The reader sees Deborah as a strong figure in the courtroom handling typical cases and in her personal life with Allen to whom late in her teens she was briefly married and with Kidd Chapin, the wildlife officer with whom she is in love. Courtroom and police procedures contribute a good deal of attraction. Family scenes include a hoedown, reminiscences about bootleg days and stock car races, and Kezzie's getting the family together to think about the possibilities for the family from the sale of family land. The tone is mostly straightforward, but occasionally the writer strikes a nostalgic note for the bygone era when family, neighbors, and respect for the open land were supreme. An assortment of colorful figures peoples the book, in addition to Deborah, strong yet surprisingly vulnerable. Booklist.

UTLEY, DEAN (*Killer.app**) Ruthless head of SJR DataSystems, a cyberworld company with taps into most of the legitimate and illegal enterprises in Chicago and throughout much of the country. Utley is a megalomaniac, determined to control everything. He is also smooth talking, very intelligent, and without conscience. In building his company, he has deliberately sought employees who have been in trouble with the law, especially young computer hackers like Howie Borke, knowing that their fascination with programming is great enough to overcome any scruples they might feel. He also has some honest workers like Sheryl Birch, whom he usually can control because they do not suspect anything, or if they do, he has so much information about them and their families that he can find a weakness and use it against them. His plot to kill the president is relatively simple: one of his right-hand men, Glen Jaffee, gets a job in the kitchen of the restaurant where the president, the first lady, and the vice president will eat, and poisons the sour cream in the salad dressing with salmanella. They will all be very sick, but the hospital records will be changed temporarily to delete information about the president's severe allergy to antibiotics, so that while the others recover, he will not. The vice president is in on the scheme and can be controlled by Utley. A sociopath, Utley loves to gloat over people he is manipulating. He lives in a lavish apartment where he raises amaryllis, a connection to the death of Detective Frieswyk that leads to the final confrontation in which both Utley and Max Black are killed.

V

VANDE VELDE, VIVIAN (1951–) Born in New York City; attended the State University of New York–Brockport and Rochester Business Institute; author of more than a dozen amusing parody and thriller novels. She lives in Rochester, New York. In *Ghost of a Hanged Man** (Marshall Cavendish, 1998), an American Library Association choice for young adults, a notorious outlaw rises from the dead to take vengeance for his conviction and hanging. *There's a Dead Person Following My Sister Around* (Harcourt, 1999) is about children from a present-day family who become involved with ghosts from Underground Railroad times. A comic mystery-thriller, *Never Trust a Dead Man** (Harcourt, 1999), also chosen by American Library Association for young adults, revolves around a youth who is entombed with the body of the man he is supposed to have murdered. For additional information about Vande Velde, titles, and a title entry, see *Dictionary, 1995–1999* [*Never Trust a Dead Man*].

VANESSA (*Criminals**) Beautiful red-haired young lady from an investment company rival to Ewan* Munro's, with whom Ewan is hopelessly in love. Since he is naive socially, he does not realize that while she likes him, she has no romantic interest in him, and in a moment of relative intimacy he has mentioned a merger on which he has been working. While she has no desire to pump him, she does give this information to her brother, who is in financial straits, thinking he will make a small investment that no one will notice. His greed and that of his partner turn this into a major buy that has come to the attention of the regulatory authorities. Vanessa, who has been in New York, calls Ewan in Milan, urging him to admit to nothing. His very straitlaced conscience balks at this, but he realizes that he could ruin not only himself but also Vanessa by confessing, so he holds out as being unable to remember any discussion of the merger until several other things in his life converge, and he decides to make a clean breast of it all. The investigator, who has suspected the truth all along, lets him off with a warning. Vanessa, who has explained to him that their relationship is platonic, leaves her firm "for personal reasons" and goes to New York to rejoin her lover.

VERN DUNVEGAN (*Open Season**) Longtime state Game Warden in the Saddlestring part of the Bighorn Mountains in Wyoming, well known and much liked because he was inclined to wink at infractions of the law. A power broker, he uses these "favors" to advance his entrepreneurial interests. His defense, in trying to eradicate the Miller's weasels is that he is looking out for the welfare of the town, which he says is dying. To some extent this is true, but at the same time he lines his pockets and destroys the environment with the pipeline he is building. He exemplifies the conflict between "progress" and preservation of the environment, jobs or weasels. Vern helped Joe Pickett, the protagonist, get his state Game Warden position and, even though he does not now work for the state, Vern calls the shots in Cheyenne. He offers Joe a job with the company he is now with, hoping that Joe will then drop the investigation, but later, when Joe fears that he will lose his state job, Vern withdraws the offer, saying that Joe waited too long to accept it. What he really means is that he is punishing Joe for continuing to investigate the murder case. Vern is the book's major villain.

VIRTUAL WAR (Skurzynski*, Gloria, Simon & Schuster, 1997)   Science fiction novel set in the year 2080, when the world has become so contaminated that most of the population has died out and the remaining live in a few domed cities with communications between them only through a small elite group, known as the "Supreme Councils." In a city set in what was Wyoming, Corgan, 14, has been bred and raised to be the champion of the Western Hemisphere Federation in its war with the other two remaining groups, the Eurasian Alliance and the Pan Pacific Coalition, to gain possession of Hiva, a group of islands once known as the Marquesas, where contamination has somehow disappeared. He is kept in a Box, a small, sterile compartment with an attached Clean Room, most of his contact with the outer world through Mendor, his virtual caretaker, who is alternatingly the Stern Father Figure and the Mother Comforter. Mendor can order up virtual pets for Corgan, virtual environments in which Corgan can exercise or rest, and even virtual opponents, but he has never been out of his box or seen a real person. The war is to be fought in virtual reality by three-person teams. Corgan is team leader for the Western Hemisphere Federation, bred and trained for his incredibly quick reactions and his innate sense of time, down to the hundredths of seconds. Fewer than three weeks before the scheduled start of the war, he is introduced to the two other team members, Sharla, 14, cryptanalyst, and Brig, 10, strategist. Sharla is blond, beautiful, brilliant, impulsive, and willful. By the age of eight she learned how to get out of her box and explore the city. She has a far better grasp on reality than naive Corgan, and soon has reprogrammed the codes so Corgan can leave his box secretly at night and meet her in person. This first contact with a real girl so excites and thrills him that when she brings Brig on a subsequent night, Corgan deeply resents the younger boy, even though Brig is a mutant, very small with spindly, deformed arms and legs and a large head. One night Sharla takes them to see, through a window, the Supreme Council, six ordinary-looking men and women, not the mysterious, faceless beings he has seen in the virtual world. Brig wants to go to the

Mutant Pen, where the genetic mistakes are dumped and where he spent the first six years of his life until he was discovered to be brilliant. One day, after a night when they are almost caught, Corgan is bullied by Mendor into betraying Sharla. In his shame and grief, he loses some of his incredible manual sensitivity on which winning the war will depend. A few nights later, they get to the Mutant Pen, where stunted, helpless creatures are lying in cribs or propelling themselves awkwardly across the floor. Corgan is filled with pity and for the first time realizes that if his genetic engineering had gone wrong, as it had for these, he, too, would be a Mutant. Brig proposes a plan to ask for a reward if they win the war: permission to live on the Isles of Hiva. Spurred by the possibility, Corgan tries even harder as they practice manipulating virtual people, about the size of his hands, through a battlefield, the purpose of which is to reach the top of a certain hill, the team achieving this goal with the most men winning. He cannot touch them without destroying them. He must control them by electromagnetic contact within five hundred microns of each image. All this goes on in the midst of what appears to be real carnage and suffering. Brig, who has a view of the whole battlefield, communicates strategy to Corgan, and Sharla intercepts actions by changing trajectory codes of artillery and jamming codes of the other teams. The night before the war, Sharla proposes to Corgan that she may be able to change, as if by mistake, the distance between his hands and his troops, thereby giving them an advantage, but he is shocked, having taken seriously his pledge to fight with honor, and he makes her promise not to cheat. The war itself, which lasts eight hours without break, is a grueling experience, with all three players feeling the torments of the virtual troops as if they were real. Their team wins by a margin of seven hundredths of a second. Corgan is devastated to learn from Sharla that the promise of life on Hiva was an incentive to manipulate him to greater effort, and that both Sharla and Brig have negotiated for other rewards. Brig has insisted that the Mutants, whom the Council has been planning to put to sleep, be allowed to live and that he be allowed to work with them to make their lives better. Sharla has requested that an automated DNA sequencing machine in Nebraska be decontaminated and she be in charge of decoding human DNA, thereby making grotesque Mutants no longer a frequent result of experimentation. Since getting the machine will take six months, she agrees to go to Hiva with Corgan for that period. There Corgan works with genetics researchers recombining genes to counteract plague viruses. Just as her plane leaves to take her back to the domed city in Wyoming, she lets Corgan know that she may have "tweaked" the statistics on the war games, tricking him after all. The ingenious story is fast paced and holds the interest, though just why a war must be fought for the islands and how the three groups can be held to their agreement is not entirely clear. Corgan is too innocent to be a completely compelling hero, and amoral Sharla proves to be too self-centered to be likable. The most interesting character is little Brig, stronger psychologically than either of the others. ALA/YA.

THE VOICE ON THE RADIO (Cooney*, Caroline B., Delacorte, 1996) Contemporary personal-problem, sociological-problem, and growing-up novel with mystery-story aspects, set in Connecticut, Massachusetts, and New Jersey, about Janie* Johnson, 16, who was kidnapped when she was three. Tall, handsome, personable Reeve Shields, a freshman at Hills College in Boston, earns a coveted spot as a deejay on the college radio station, WSCK. Struck by sudden stage fright and unable to think of anything to say that might appeal to his unseen audience, he launches into a story based on the real-life experiences of his red-headed, next-door girlfriend in Connecticut, Janie Johnson. Throughout the first half of the novel, he tells in snippets to pique his listeners' curiosity how Janie discovered that, then known as Jennie Spring, she was kidnapped when she was three, located her real family in New Jersey with his help, and chose to continue living with her current parents, the Johnsons, in Connecticut. Listeners gobble up the well-embroidered story, and he becomes a celebrity over night. The station is delighted with his success and pushes him to contribute more "janies." Reeve starts to confront the morality of his actions when he receives a phone call one night from Brian* Spring, 13, Janie's younger brother. Brian, Janie, and Jodie Spring, 18, their sister, have come to Boston so that Jodie can visit colleges in preparation for entering the next fall. In their hotel room, they turn on the radio, hear Reeve's voice, and are aghast to hear him telling Janie's story. That same night a woman on the station's call-in line says that she is Hannah, which was the name of the kidnapper. Janie is devastated by Reeve's betrayal and repeatedly rejects his apologies. Brian, who has the coolest head, insists that they tell no one what happened. Reeve is horrified to realize that he has, as he comes to think of it, raped Janie in a certain way. He worries about what will happen if the caller is really that Hannah, examines the values that led him to exploit Janie, and does not like the venal side he sees in himself. Reeve continues to

apologize to Janie, and at Thanksgiving the two keep up a pretense and go out together, but their relationship stays cold. Janie visits the Spring family, and since she is obviously still upset, Jodie tells their Spring mother the story. Her mother advises Janie to forgive Reeve in order to heal her anger and soothe her hurt. Realizing how weak and soft he really is, at the end Janie prepares to forgive him so that he can make another start in life. Janie is maturing, coming out of the little-girl, romantic mode she has been in and is beginning to see that people have bad sides as well as good. Janie realizes for the first time that she loves both sets of parents and also that she loves her Spring siblings, who steadfastly support her throughout this ordeal. The details of what happened to Janie when she was a child come out gradually, giving the story the force of a mystery. The main emphasis, however, is on Reeve's action, its effect on Janie and on him, and the tawdry sensationalism that radio talk shows foster for commercial gain. The narrative switches quickly and often from Reeve to Janie and back again and explores their innermost thoughts as well as describing the action and situations. Another good aspect of the book is that it explores how losing a child has made the Springs overly protective of their children, smothering them to the point of rebellion. The style is contemporary, some humor relieves the seriousness, and ending on the note of forgiveness seems appropriate. ALA/YA.

VOIGT, CYNTHIA (1942–)   Born in Boston, Massachusetts; received her B.A. from Smith College; teacher of high school English and department chair; author for more than twenty years for middle graders and adolescents of family novels, mysteries, school stories, problem novels, and adventure novels. Although her other books have been well received and she is considered one of the premier contemporary novelists for young people, she is best known for her books in the Tillerman Family series, of which *Dicey's Song* (Atheneum, 1982) received the Newbery Medal. *Elske** (Atheneum, 1999) is a historical-adventure romance in the Kingdom series begun with *Jackaroo* (Atheneum, 1985) and an American Library Association choice for young adults. A recent title is *Bad Girls in Love* (Atheneum, 2002), another in her amusing Bad Girls series. For more information about Voigt, titles, and title entries, see *Dictionary, 1960–1984* [*The Callendar Papers*; *Dicey's Song*; *A Solitary Blue*]; *Dictionary, 1985–1990* [*Building Blocks*; *Come A Stranger*; *Izzy, Willy-Nilly*; *Sons from Afar*]; *Dictionary, 1990–1994* [*Seventeen against the Dealer*; *When She Hollers*]; and *Dictionary, 1995–1999* [*Bad Girls*; *When She Hollers*].

VOLSKY, PAULA   Contemporary fantasy novelist, born and raised in Fanwood, New Jersey. After receiving her degree in English literature at Vassar College, she completed her M.A. in Shakespearean studies at the University of Birmingham, England. While working for the U.S. Bureau of Housing and Urban Development, she completed her first novel, *The Curse of the Witch-Queen* (Ballantine, 1982). Soon after, she turned to full-time writing and has published almost a dozen more novels of mythical otherworlds, magic, and sorcery for adults. The Sorcerer trilogy, which revolves around Lady Veran who is forced to marry an old and very powerful magician, includes *The Sorcerer's Lady* (Ace, 1986), *The Sorcerer's Heir* (Ace, 1988), and *The Sorcerer's Curse* (Ace, 1989). A *Booklist* selection, *The Gates of Twilight** (Bantam, 1996), set in a land that resembles India under British rule, is notable for its strongly drawn main characters, in particular the native women, and for its credible depiction of a fantasy land. Other more recent publications include *The White Tribunal* (Bantam, 1997) and *The Grand Ellipse* (Bantam, 2000). Volsky lives in Washington, D.C.

W

WACEY HEDEMAN (*Open Season**) State Game Warden in the district adjoining that of Joe Pickett, the protagonist. Once a rodeo cowboy, Wacey has an oily charm that draws people to him and claims their confidence. Underneath, however, he schemes for influence and control. He and Vern* Dunvegan murdered the three outfitters because the men discovered that Vern and Wacey had killed the colony of Miller's weasels. Wacey also threatens little Sheridan* Pickett, even hinting at kidnapping and raping her and murdering her family if she tells anyone about the three little animals in her backyard. When Sheriff Barnum hears that Wacey is accompanying Joe on the hunt for the missing outfitters, he is shocked, perhaps because Wacey is running against Barnum for sheriff but also perhaps because he knows that Wacey is not to be trusted.

A WALK TO REMEMBER (Sparks*, Nicholas, Warner, 1999) Boy's growing-up novel set in 1958 in Beaufort, North Carolina, about how through his relationship with a dying girl he is changed from a thoughtless, lighthearted kid to a deeply moved young man. Pressured by his father, Worth Carter, a congressman who spends very little time in their small town and whom his son scarcely knows, Landon Carter, 16, the narrator, runs for student-body president and, to his surprise, wins. Since there are few duties, this is not much of a problem until it is time for the homecoming dance, where an appearance by everyone on the student council is mandatory. Having been dumped by his girlfriend, Angela Clark, Landon looks at the possibilities and calls all the likely girls, finding they already have dates. At last, in desperation, he asks Jamie Sullivan, whom he has known forever and has never considered dating. Jamie, whose mother died at her birth and who has been raised by her father, the Reverend Hegbert Sullivan of the Southern Baptist Church, is not only out of the mainstream in appearance, dressed in the same plaid skirt and brown sweater every day and wearing her hair in a tight bun, she is forever doing good works, carrying her Bible with her everywhere, offering to pray for people, and attributing whatever happens to God's plan. Moreover, she has always merited Landon's scorn by being unfailingly cheerful. To complicate matters, Jamie has been chosen to be the angel in the annual Christmas play, a schmaltzy piece written by her father, and Landon finds himself coerced into the male lead. At the dance, Angela, who is with an older fellow named Lew, has been drinking and vomits all over the restroom, while Lew disappears. Jamie insists on helping, getting Landon to clean up the mess and take Angela home in his father's car, where she gets sick again. In the next weeks, he suffers the derision of his friends because he walks Jamie home from play practices, her father not wanting her out alone after dark, and then takes on the job of collecting all the cans she has put into local establishments for donations to the orphans' Christmas. When he discovers how little there is, he supplements it with most of his savings, pretending it all came in the cans. The play, in which he is a father helped out by an angel to find the perfect gift for his little daughter, depends partly on Landon's line when the angel appears and he says, "You're beautiful!" In rehearsals, he has never managed the line with any conviction, but on the night of the play, when he turns onstage to see Jamie in her diaphanous costume, with a bit of makeup and her hair flowing down around her shoulders, his voice echoes his true amazement, and the play is a big success. At the orphan home on Christmas Eve, he helps Jamie distribute the gifts, far more than the children usually get, then quietly gives her the new brown sweater he has purchased for her. To his astonishment, she gives him her Bible, which she has already told him she carries because it was her mother's. She has also told him

that what she wants most in her future is to be married with all her friends filling the church. The next week he gets his first chaste kiss from Jamie and admits to himself, and even to his mother, that he is in love. At his mother's instigation he takes Jamie to a fancy waterfront restaurant on New Year's Eve, having received her father's reluctant permission and orders to get her home by ten o'clock. A few days later, she tells him what she has known since August, that she is very ill with leukemia. In the next weeks, she gets weaker, and, since she very much wants to die at home and not in a hospital, Landon's mother prevails upon her husband to provide expensive equipment and nursing help, despite his personal dislike of the minister. As Jamie gets weaker, they read the Bible together, but Landon feels unable to help her until he suddenly realizes what he should do. Both just seventeen, they are married by Reverend Sullivan in the Baptist church with everyone they know, all their classmates who regret their snide remarks and all their parents who are appalled at such illness in one so young. Although she arrives in a wheelchair, Jamie is able to walk up the aisle supported by her father to where Landon waits, with his father as his best man. The novel's sentimentality is relieved partly by Landon's uninhibited comments about the townspeople, especially the minister and the drama teacher, but on the whole it is a tearjerker. Jamie is never entirely believable, and Landon's parents and his high school friends are stereotypes. The last sentence, spoken forty years after the story's events, "I now believe, by the way, that miracles can happen," seems to be intended to refer to Landon's change and his reconciliation with his father, not to Jamie's recovery, although her death does not occur in the narrative. Booklist.

WALLACE, RICH (1957–)   Born in Hackensack, New Jersey; journalist, novelist. He received his B.A. from Montclair State College (now University) in 1980 and worked as a sports reporter and in editorial positions on newspapers in New Jersey until 1989. His novel, *Wrestling Sturbridge** (Knopf, 1996), is as much about a small town obsessed by its high school wrestling team as it is about the sport itself. *Playing Without the Ball** (Knopf, 2000) has a slightly older protagonist, a basketball player, struggling to come to terms with his disrupted family. His books have been praised for their well-developed characters. Wallace lives in Honesdale, Pennsylvania.

WALTER, VIRGINIA   Librarian and information services professor at the University of California–Los Angeles. She received her Ph.D. and her M.P.A. from the University of Southern Califonia, and her M.L.S. in library science from the University of California–Berkeley. She has published many monographs, chapters in professional books, reviews, and articles in library publications. She has lived in both Los Angeles and Venice, California. The Ameican Library Association, which earlier cited her unusually structured novel, *Making Up Megaboy** (DK, 1998), as a Notable Book for Children, has added it to their list of Best Books for Young Adults. For earlier biographical information and a title entry, see *Dictionary, 1995–1999* [*Making Up Megaboy*].

THE WANDERER (Creech*, Sharon, illus. David Diaz, HarperCollins, 2000) Realistic sea-adventure and growing-up novel with family-story aspects set mostly on the North Atlantic from Connecticut to England in recent years. Sophie, 13, who keeps a log of their journey, has recently moved with her adoptive parents from coastal Virginia to a sleepy Kentucky town on the Ohio River. In love with the sea, she is delighted to join her mother's three brothers and their two sons on a sailing trip across the ocean to visit their father and grandfather, Bompie, who is ill in England. The crew includes Dock, a carpenter, who owns the boat and whose typical response is "yep"; Stew, a recently fired insurance salesman, who is a stickler for protocol and order; and Mo, a computer "number-cruncher" who once dreamed of becoming an artist; and Stew's and Mo's sons, respectively, serious, studious Brian, like his father a control freak, and charming, impulsive, smart Cody, who, like Sophie, writes in his "dog-log" occasionally, portions that flesh out Sophie's account. All meet in Connecticut to refurbish Dock's forty-five-foot boat and sail for Nova Scotia to continue their work at Grand Manan Island in the Bay of Fundy. Sophie insists on taking her turn at all tasks, not just cooking and cleaning, and once underway is the only one brave enough to be hoisted aloft in the bosun's chair. Each member of the crew is responsible for teaching the others something special. Dock teaches how to read charts; Brian teaches points of sail (sailing terms); Stew teaches using the sextant; Mo teaches radio code; Cody offers to teach juggling, which elicits the disparaging comment of "doofus" from Mo but which brings the others great pleasure; and Sophie surprises everyone by telling stories Bompie told. Everyone wonders how she knows them, since she has never met Bompie. The adventures are typical of sea stories, problems with equipment, spotting sea creatures, dealing with short tempers, ignoring bickering, and learning to accommodate to their different personalities and tight quarters. They complete the trip to Ireland and drive by car to Bompie's house outside London. Two mysteries keep this book from being just another sea adventure. One concerns Rosalie, a mystery woman with whom Dock has been in love, who turns up at their destination, and who leaves for Spain, to which Dock heads after the book ends. The other, more detailed mystery concerns Sophie herself. How was she orphaned and how does she know so much about Bompie? After they arrive, she reveals that Bompie had written many letters to her from England about his childhood and youth along the Ohio River where she now lives. The stories are vibrant and lively as she repeats them to the crew and later to Bompie. She also tells the one about "The Wave" that she says killed Bompie's parents when he was a small boy, but which it is pointed out to her gently is really her own story. At the end, the family has grown closer and has come to appreciate each person's unique talents and peculiar quirks. Why the uncles will not tell the boys about Sophie's orphan background is never made clear, and the letters seem an overly clever way out of why Sophie knows so much about Bompie. The descriptions of the sea, the best part of the book, are magnificent—clear, vivid, sensory, lyrical—altogether beautiful, as is the book itself with the distinctive typography and Diaz's strong but judicious woodcutlike black-and-white drawings. *The Wanderer* (boat) is obviously symbolic. Everyone on it is in some way a wanderer, especially Sophie, who wins herself an extended family, but everyone else in his way also finds a new home or means of fulfillment, even Mo who draws as they sail along. ALA/YA.

THE WAR IN GEORGIA (Oughton*, Jerrie, Houghton, 1997)   Novel of family love and neighborhood life in Atlanta, Georgia, during World War II. Shanta Morgan, the narrator, is thirteen in 1945 when what she thinks of as their own war develops and comes to a crisis. She lives with her father's mother, Grandmorgan, her Uncle Louie Morgan, his wife, Louray, and their five-year-old daughter, Honey, on Clay Street in a very nonpretentious part of the city, her own parents having been dead for more than ten years. Although Honey is much younger, Shanta thinks of her as a best friend, while Louray works and Uncle Louie, who is badly crippled by rheumatoid arthritis that affects most of his body but leaves his hands free, repairs watches. Together, Shanta and Honey explore the recently vacated house across the street, even the spooky basement, then watch the new people move in, noting that there are three girls and one boy, and that a tall man, evidently the father, is brutally abusive when the boy drops and breaks a lamp. About this time Louie has a bad setback, with further paralysis that makes him permanently bedridden. Louray, an extremely pretty but angry woman, comes home furious one day, accuses Grandmorgan of being hostile, Louie of being worthless, and Shanta of teaching Honey to swear, then takes the little girl and departs, leaving the three behind, each believing the rift is his fault. Soon Shanta gets to know the youngest girl across the street, Dennie Walling, about her age, and the boy, Earl, who insists he is Roy Rogers. Dennie explains that Earl has a steel plate in his head and that he is really twenty-one with the mind of a five-year-old. Almost every night one or more of the magicians, whom Louie knew when he was learning stage tricks before his arthritis, comes to visit, cheering him up and sometimes surreptitiously leaving five or ten dollar bills to help out the meager income from a long-dead grandfather's pension. The two elements of conflict on Clay Street erupt to open war just as World War II is winding down. Dennie, the other girls, and their mother drive away in a great hurry. One night Shanta from high in the mimosa tree sees Mr. Walling sidling down her driveway and peering in at the window, where the visiting nurse is bathing Uncle Louie. Not sure what to do about it, she follows secretly and hears what sounds like a dog howling, a sound she has heard before. Sneaking around the back of the Walling house, she hears the howling coming from the cellar. She creeps down the outdoor cellar stairs and finds Earl shirtless and barefoot chained to the wall amid empty beer bottles, mud, and vomit. To her horror, a man she has identified as Dennie's uncle stomps into the cellar, taunts Earl, and slaps him before he sees Shanta. She leaps up the steps, races across backyards, turns her ankle badly, and hides under the circle of branches made by the magnolia tree, while the man and Mr. Walling hunt for her. She hears her grandmother call her but dares not answer. Grandmorgan dials Finn McGolphin*, her next-door neighbor, who comes into the street and bellows for Shanta. She hops and staggers to him, and he carries her home and calls the police. The other conflict is resolved after Louray arrives, demanding child support, although she and Honey are living in her mother's fancy house across town, and then sues for an annulment. Since Louie cannot get to court, Grandmorgan goes, walking much farther than she is accustomed and arriving home exhausted and footsore but triumphant, since the judge has listened to her and granted the annulment on the condition that Honey be brought to spend one weekend a month with her father. She also brings a note from Honey, who has learned to print, to

Shanta, which says, "Tell my daddy I love him." Just exactly what the Walling men intend to do to Earl is mercifully not spelled out, although they have been arrested and he has been taken away, nor can she discuss it with Dennie, since the rest of the family moves away without speaking to anyone. Shanta's main concern, throughout, is whether she, Grandmorgan, and Louie are a family. Grandmorgan assures her that they are, that a family is any group bound together by love, the urgency to survive, a good cry now and then, and "always a good laugh." She has provided a good laugh herself now and then, topping a dressmaker's dummy with a face and hat and standing her next to Louie's bed to greet and, for a moment, fool the magicians, and fastening a quarter to the floor under Louie's bed with glue, so when he deliberately spills some change and they try to pick it up for him they will be baffled. Framed by a brief prologue and epilogue, the narrative is in the present tense, as if, years later, Shanta is reliving the summer in her mind as it happened. ALA/YA.

THE WATCHER (Howe*, James, Atheneum, 1997)   Novel of a summer in recent times on a resort island, presumably Fire Island on the New York coast, where the lives of four young people intersect and affect each other in unpredictable ways. The primary character, Margaret, 13, who is unnamed until nearly the end, is an abused child, held captive by her brutish father, whom she refers to as "the beast." During their unprecedented vacation on the island, she has learned to get her mother, whom she refers to as "the enchanted doll," almost unconscious by playing sad opera music. She then takes the key that locks her in, sneaks past her snoring father, and goes to the beach on the far side of the island, where she sits on the steps and watches, never going down to the sand or speaking to anyone. The other three are the lifeguard, Chris Powell, 18, disaffected with himself and his family, and the Saltaire children, Evan, 14, and Callie, 7, summer visitors. Margaret watches these three, making up stories about them in which Evan and Callie are a prince and princess and Chris is an angel who rescues her from the beast. Actually, Chris is at loose ends, often hungover from island parties, uncertain what to do with his life except that he does not want to go to college, as his mother wishes, or to live with his father, an alcoholic who drinks to forget that he neglected to watch his first child, little Michael, who drowned in a swimming pool before Chris was born. Evan, who is solicitous of his little sister and genuinely fond of her, is worried about his parents' change from a spontaneous, fun-loving couple to tense, unhappy people, about Callie's assumption that they are getting a divorce, which will separate her from Evan, and about the nightmares she suffers as a result. Almost lost in her fantasy world, Margaret goes to the house where the Saltaires are staying and steals Callie's picture of the family, a shawl Evan once gave his mother, and a kite he and Callie have flown on the beach. She then takes a family snapshot from her mother's purse, cuts her own picture from it, and inserts it into the Saltaire family picture. Evan, whose mother has repeatedly urged him to join the other boys on the beach, finally responds to an invitation from Shane, who has been temporarily deserted by the others, to bicycle to Fair Harbor, where he tries to introduce Evan to the thrill of shoplifting. Although Evan very much wants sunglasses like those Chris wears, he is unable to bring himself to pocket them, and rides home, humili-

ated by his lack of nerve and Shane's scorn. The separate plots join and culminate on the day Chris, disgusted with himself and the unlikelihood that he will save anyone and somehow repair his father's self-esteem, quits and packs his belongings, planning to leave on the two o'clock ferry. The same day, the Saltaires discover that Callie's picture is missing, along with the shawl and the kite. Assuming that Shane has taken them for kicks, Evan bravely sets out to get them back, only to find the house deserted. Wandering on, deflated, he sees Chris, whom he has hero-worshiped all summer, but does not accost him. As he passes the house where the "sad music" plays, he glimpses his kite in the crawl space under the porch, pulls it out carefully, and then peers in the window. There he sees a burly man holding a girl's head under water in the kitchen sink, then grabbing her hair, pulling her head up as she chokes and gasps, then plunging it back under water. Aghast, Evan races off to get help. Just as Margaret is about to lose consciousness, Evan returns with Chris, who orders the man to stop and holds Margaret until she stops shaking. At first bullying and blustering in the face of Chris's calm accusing look, the man suddenly switches to a placating attitude, pretending he was just teaching his little girl to breathe under water, although actually he has found the picture and is punishing his daughter. Suddenly, Margaret's mother, who has come to the bedroom door unnoticed, locks herself back in and turns up the music full volume. The man throws himself at the door and is trying to break it down when a policeman charges up, demanding to know what is going on. Margaret is able to say, for the first time, "My father hurts me." The assumptions at the book's end are that Margaret will now be free of the abuse, that Evan's parents will somehow solve their differences and be happy again, and that Chris, having finally saved a drowning victim, can get on with his own life. While none of these holds up as certainties under hard-eyed scrutiny, the book has set an accepting mood, with its long passages in Margaret's dream kingdom set in italics, and the stories Callie tells her little friend about how she is Harriet the Spy. The book's structure also gives a feeling of unreality as the actual stories are revealed only gradually with side paths that might be imaginary or might be interpretations of a mentality slightly off balance. ALA/YA; NYPL.

THE WATERBORN (Keyes*, J. Gregory, Ballantine, 1996)   Long adult fantasy-adventure and rites-of-passage novel set in a mythological world of humans and half humans, talking swords, ghosts, wraiths, strange beasts, and gods of nature, deserts, and mountains. A long sprawling River races through the area and is personified in the emperor of the powerful land of Nhol, a region that resembles ancient Egypt. The chapters alternately tell two stories that come together at the end. Each concerns a young person on a quest that involves violence and killing, tested loyalty, twists and turns, and a smash-bang conclusion. Pretty, dark-haired, dark-eyed Hezhi, 10, daughter of the emperor of Nhol and, hence, also a bearer of the River blood, is determined to find her beloved cousin, D'en, who has mysteriously disappeared in the flooded underreaches of the Palace. Unsuccessful, she is increasingly fearful that, since her River power is growing and will soon become evident, she will be killed by the priests or banished to the palace lower reaches. She prays that a hero comes to her aid and then dreams of a light-skinned, brown-haired youth. No weak maiden, however, Hezhi spends many months in the royal library investigating the descriptions and diagrams of the palace water ducts and sewers and learning about the palace power structure, knowledge that will be eventually vital to her survival. She is aided in her searches by her faithful half-human, half-giant servant, Tsem, about twenty, and also by the royal librarian, Ghan, a crotchety fellow who admires her spunk and intelligence. Concurrently, Perkar Bar Karku, 15, of a clan far to the west beyond the desert at the base of the forested mountains, newly initiated into manhood and given his sword, joins a group headed by the local king and including, among others, Ngangata, a primitive man, to travel into the mountains to request land from the king of the forest. Perkar also wishes to kill the River, which periodically devours the beautiful goddess who lives in the river and with whom Perkar has fallen in love. The group endures many problems from the elements, local hazards, their own folly, and various human and nonhuman beings, and fail to secure land. Aided by sensible, brave Ngangata and his own talking sword, Harka, Perkar makes his way downriver to Nhol, to which he has been drawn by dreams of a beautiful girl calling him. How the two groups join and evade the priests who are determined to kill Hezhi, Tsem, and Ghan, and then Perkar and Ngangata as well, makes for hurried but tense action. After the rushed conclusion, Hezhi and Perkar agree that some day they may travel westward together to Perkar's homeland. The mysticism is strained and sometimes overwhelming, the chapter shifts are disconcerting because the chapters are lengthy cliff-hangers, and the writing is often self-indulgent. The protagonists are worthy, however, and by book's middle the reader is engrossed in their plights. The various folklore beliefs add interest and depth, and the endpaper maps advance the narrative. Only those young adults who are devoted to the genre, are persevering, and can handle long, sometimes slow-moving stories will stick with this book. Booklist.

WEAVER, WILL(IAM WELLER) (1950–) Born in Park Rapids, Minnesota; attended Saint Cloud State University and received his B.A. and M.A. from the University of Minnesota and Stanford University, respectively. After farming for several years, he joined the faculty in English and creative writing at Bemidji (Minnesota) State University. He first published books for adults, among them the novel *Red Earth, White Earth* (Simon & Schuster, 1986) and a collection of short stories, *A Gravestone Made of Wheat* (Simon & Schuster, 1989), before writing fiction for young adults. His three books about Billy Baggs, a Minnesota farm boy who has attracted attention for his pitching, were all American Library Association selections for young adults: *Striking Out* (HarperCollins, 1993), *Farm Team* (HarperCollins, 1995), and *Hard Ball** (HarperCollins, 1998). The latter shows Billy having to deal with both his irascible father as well as his arch rival on the baseball field and for the affections of the same girl. More recently, Weaver has published *Memory Boy* (HarperCollins, 2001), a wilderness survival story. He lives in Bemidji.

WELLS, KEN A native of the Cajun bayou country in southern Louisiana of which he writes in his first novel, *Meely LaBauve: A Novel** (Random House, 2000), a lighthearted, exciting boy's growing-up story and the introduction to his Catahoula Trilogy. Published for adults, *Meely LaBauve* was both a New York Public Library and an American Library Association selection for young adults. The other two books in the set are *Junior's Leg* (Random House, 2001), which focuses on the bully who was Meely's antagonist in the first book, and *Logan's Storm* (Random House, 2002), about Meely's father's escape to Florida. For twenty years Wells has been a writer and editor for the *Wall Street Journal*. A college dropout, he got his start as a writer working for a weekly paper in Houma, Louisiana, while still helping with his family's snake-collecting business. He has also edited *Floating Off the Page: The Best Stories from the Wall Street Journal's Middle Column* (Free Press, 2002). He lives in New York City.

WELTER, JOHN Born in Texas, grew up in Oklahoma, Colorado, Kansas, and Missouri; journalist, novelist. He is a graduate of the University of Missouri–Kansas City, and has been a reporter for newspapers in the Midwest and the Southeast. His humor column for the *Chapel Hill Herald* is nationally distributed for Universal Press Syndicate. Welter's novels are all humorous but have underlying concerns with serious issues. Among them is the very funny *I Want to Buy a Vowel** (Algonquin, 1966), about a naive illegal immigrant from Guatemala whose plight stirs up and divides a small Texas town. Earlier novels are *Begin to Exit Here: A Novel of the Wayward Press* (Algonquin, 1992) and *Night of the Avenging Blowfish: A Novel of Covert Operations, Love, and Luncheon Meat* (Algonquin, 1994). Welter makes his home in Carrboro, North Carolina.

WERLIN, NANCY (1961–) Born in Salem, Massachusetts; software technical writer and novelist for young adults. Her mystery, *The Killer's Cousin** (Delacorte,

1998), won an Edgar Allan Poe Award and, more recently, was cited to the American Library Association Young Adult list and added to the New York Public Library list of the best books for young adults. For earlier biographical information and a title entry, see *Dictionary, 1995–1999* [*The Killer's Cousin*].

WERSBA, BARBARA (1932–) Born in Chicago, Illinois; actress, novelist. She was graduated from Bard College and for fifteen years was a professional stage and television actress. She is the author of many books for young people, including *Whistle Me Home** (Holt, 1997), a novel set in Sag Harbor, New York, where she makes her home. Earlier biographical information and title entries appear in *Dictionary, 1960–1984* [*The Dream Watcher*; *Tunes for a Small Harmonica*].

WHAT CHILD IS THIS?: A CHRISTMAS STORY (Cooney*, Caroline B., Delacorte, 1997)   Realistic novel of family life set in a small Vermont town during late December about the time of publication. Events are seen from the viewpoint of (but not related by) four main characters: Liz* Kitchell, 16, daughter of one of the most affluent but uninvolved families in town; her classmates, Tack* Knight, 16, son of a prominent, community-spirited restaurateur, and Matt* Morden, 16, foster son of a lower-middle-class, good-hearted, elderly couple, Mr. and Mrs. Rowen; and Katie, 8, his small, diffident foster sister. The straightforward plot is quickly summarized. When Mr. Pollard, the social worker to whom Matt and Katie are assigned, takes from his "ratty old briefcase" a stack of white paper bells and informs Matt and Katie that the bells will be hung on Christmas trees in area restaurants with the children's names on

them and their wishes for presents so that patrons can play Santa Claus and grant them anonymously, Matt, characteristically cynical, asks for a laptop computer. Katie, however, expresses her heart's real desire and asks for a family. After discussion, Pollard changes her request to a radio and a Christmas-story tape. Later Matt, feeling unusually big brotherly toward the little girl, fills out another bell with her first request and hangs it along with the other one on the tree in Knights' restaurant, the River Wind Inn, where he works evenings. Mr. Kitchell sees the request on the tree, deems it evil to fool a child this way, and rips up the bell. Matt observes and feels extremely guilty for raising Katie's now-doomed hopes. On Christmas Eve, Katie begs to go to the pageant at the church near by. Matt, still guilt ridden, walks her there through the snow, and during the service, tells her about the bell. Outwardly pretending she has known all along that the wish could not be granted but inwardly crushed with disappointment, she leaves the service ostensibly for a drink of water, sneaks outside, and wanders through the night and harsh weather until, tired and cold, she lies down on a dark porch. When she does not return, Matt looks for her, realizes that she has left the church, and informs the Kitchells and the Knights, who call 911 and mobilize the congregation into a search party. Liz finds Katie and helps take her to the emergency room. Liz's older sister, Allison, and her husband, Daniel, whose baby girl, also named Katie, died recently, set in motion procedures to adopt the child. When everyone gathers at the Kitchell's upscale house for a reunion a year later, Matt realizes that he has learned a lesson: Christmas offers a chance, he took it with Katie, and he now dares to have hope about life in general. The story's sentimentality, obvious moral lessons, trite plot, and tipped-hand conclusion are relieved by the universal belief in the goodness of life and the very detailed reporting of the innermost feelings of, in particular, Liz and the two foster children. If the Kitchell parents are somewhat too callous and self-centered and the Knights and Tack are somewhat too noble and loving, they suit the story and enable events to turn out the way every reader hopes they will. ALA/YA.

WHAT GIRLS LEARN (Cook*, Karin, Pantheon, 1997)   Novel of the lingering death of a girl's mother, intertwined with problems of a new stepfather and the introduction of sexual knowledge, all of which are part of her growing up. It is set mostly on Long Island, New York, in the 1980s. Although the mother's death dominates the novel, much of it is amusing, with telling details. For a longer entry, see *Dictionary, 1995–1999*. Alex; ALA/YA; Booklist; NYPL.

WHAT'S IN A NAME? (Wittlinger*, Ellen, Simon & Shuster, 2000)   Contemporary school, friendship, and growing-up novel set in a small oceanside town in Massachusetts. Against the tumultuous background of a community's trying to determine whether the town should remain Cold Harbor, which the longtime residents wish, or become Folly Bay, which the newer inhabitants propose as more enticing and elegant, a matter eventually taken to a vote, ten Scrub High School students grapple with class and identity problems of their own. In as many interlocking chapters and in the first person, five girls and five boys, some new residents, some native, some temporary, describe personal matters, like dating and sexual orientation, and other issues that have broader significance for teens in voices that are clear and sometimes startling. Georgie Pinkus, whose only real friend is the owner of the dog-grooming parlor over which she and her mother live, acquires a gentle, understanding boyfriend in Ricardo from Brazil, in whom Christine Muser, her coeditor of the school literary magazine, *The Pickle*, has been somewhat interested. O'Neill Sayers, whose favorite class is English with gay Mr. Tompkins, addresses his identity problem by coming out as gay, causing more than a bit of a stir in the school and embarrassing his older brother, Quincy. Quincy, popular jock and an unusually caring and sensitive youth, is the boyfriend of Gretchen Carstenson, the daughter of the leader of the Folly Bay effort. Gretchen is the most popular girl in school (at least until the Folly Bay matter), champion of causes, and chair or president of almost every club and committee in school. After the Folly Bay vote goes down badly, she refuses to help her demanding mother mount another fight and is determined to find out who she really is as a person in her own right. Christine Muser, who has long had a crush on O'Neill and has not been able to figure out why he has not returned her interest, helps him make public a controversial poem about his gay gender orientation and in the process loses Ricardo to Georgie. Ricardo is pleased that, among other virtues, Georgie knows he speaks Portuguese and not Spanish. After his brother's coming-out poem, Quincy is regarded in his family as the conventional, reliable son and isn't sure he likes it. Newcomer Adam Russell is impressed by the self-assurance of outsider Nadia Kazerinko, whose family emigrated from Russia seven years earlier. African American Shaquanda Nichols, among several

Scrub Harbor students who are bused from the inner city because they have academic potential, chooses African American Nelson Coleridge, from the "haves" side of town, to tutor her in calculus and resents his patronizing attitude. The students are too studied a mix, and the story needed a bigger bed to allow for more character development, but the concerns voiced and the interlocking episodes offer a serious, sometimes humorous, often poignant story of small-community life and work together like a puzzle. They demand close reading for important details of plot and character and give a vivid picture of Scrub High and probably a good many other secondary schools, too. The community identity problem brings out social, economic, and ethnic distinctions and strongly counterpoints similar aspects within the school. ALA/YA.

WHELAN, GLORIA (1923–   )   Born in Detroit, Michigan; received both B.A. and an M.S.W. from the University of Michigan; author of novels for middle graders and young adults and of fiction and poetry for adults. She lives in the northern part of Michigan's Lower Peninsula, where many of her more than two dozen books are set. One of these is *The Secret Keeper* (Knopf, 1990), which was nominated for the Edgar Allan Poe Award. *Homeless Bird** (HarperCollins, 2000), however, is set in India, a much-praised novel about the trials and eventual triumph of a widow in her teens. It was cited by the American Library Association for young adults. Recent titles include *The Wanigan: A Life on the River* (Knopf, 2002) and *Are There Bears in Starvation Lake?* (Golden, 2002). For more information about Whelan, titles, and a title entry, see *Dictionary, 1990–1994* [*The Secret Keeper*].

WHEN JEFF COMES HOME (Atkins*, Catherine, Penguin Putnam, 1999) Intense psychological novel of a boy's agonized efforts to readjust when his kidnapper releases him after more than two years of isolation and abuse. Abducted from a highway rest stop near Fresno while the family is on vacation, presumably in the 1990s, Jeff Hart, 14, seems to have disappeared off the face of the earth until, two and a half years later, he is let off near his home in Wayne, northern California, by Ray Slaight, the man who took him. His whole family is strange to Jeff: his father, Ken, his stepmother, Connie, his sister, Charlotte, now in high school, and his brother Brian, almost eleven. Although pressed by Ken and later by Dave Stephens, the FBI man who has followed the case, Jeff finds it impossible to tell them what really happened, instead insisting that he was not molested. He is equally terrified that Ray will return and that his family and friends will discover that he has been a catamite, unwilling but cooperative because it was the only way to save his life. Jeff has always been Ken's favorite child, to the exclusion of the other two, and his father is baffled and hurt by his new attitude. When the whole family goes to San Francisco so that Jeff can look at mug shots, Ray is apprehended in the lobby of their hotel. Jeff picks him out in a police lineup, but he can see that Stephens and others think he may have had an agreement to meet Ray. The reporters who shout questions at him every time he appears appall him. Vin Perini, who was his best friend, comes to see him, obviously full of goodwill, but he cannot help asking Jeff whether the man molested him. Jeff denies it, and Vin relaxes, suggesting that he come over every day for lunch until the new semester starts, when Jeff will return to school.

Before that, the police discover Ray's room and reveal to reporters that they have found nude pictures of Jeff. Vin feels betrayed and accuses Jeff of lying. The first day of school is torture, starting with gym class, where the boys avoid him and call him faggot. Charlotte stands by him, and, after some hesitation, so does Vin, but Jeff leaves and is determined not to go back. Ken reports that Ray has been saying that Jeff came with him willingly, that the boy had been hitchhiking when he picked him up, and as a runaway was unwilling to go home. He also says that Ray is about to make bail. Jeff finally finds himself able to admit that Ray raped him and agrees to go back to San Francisco and tell Stephens the entire story. The novel is strongest in evoking Jeff's humiliation and his reasons for denial. Most devastating to him is his realization that, along with his cruelty and deviant behavior, Ray really loved him, and, besides his fear of the man and revulsion at his actions, on one level he returned that affection. What actually happened to him is not reported in lurid detail, but enough is shown in the italicized memories interjected into the action to give a good idea of the abuse—physical, sexual, and psychological—that he endured. Ken's preference for Jeff and the effect it has on his siblings is made clear, but what it will mean in the family's future is not pursued. The stepmother has no real part in the story beyond being a teacher and generally supportive. ALA/YA.

WHEN KAMBIA ELAINE FLEW IN FROM NEPTUNE (Williams*, Lori Aurelia, Simon & Schuster, 2000)   Sober, contemporary, sometimes humorous realistic novel of an African American girl's growing up and family life in a household of women in a troubled black neighborhood known as the "Bottom" in Houston,

Texas: hardworking Mama (Vera) Dubois, a single mother, grocery store stock clerk; beautiful Tia, 15; and Shayla, 12, who aspires to become a writer. Shayla describes three problems that increasingly occupy her thoughts. She worries about Tia who has run away from home because Mama objects to her becoming romantically involved with Doo-witty (Dwight) Jackson, a young man eight years Tia's senior thought to be mentally challenged. Shayla wonders why Kambia Elaine, the new girl next door who is Shayla's age, daughter of a prostitute, tells outlandish stories, gets thinner and thinner, has bruises on her thighs and legs, and wears bloodstained panties that she says the Wallpaper Wolves in her house have caused. Shayla's third concern is whether her mother will take back Mr. Anderson Fox, Shayla's father who abandoned the family when Shayla was little. One day, with Mama and Grandma Augustine (Mama's mother) at a special service for women in the Tabernacle of the Blessed Redeemer, Shayla mistakenly enters a side room, and surprises Tia and Doo-witty kissing. Shayla does not tell Mama, but she visits Tia almost every afternoon in her quarters at the Tabernacle. She also learns that Doo-witty is a talented painter and has done murals at the Tabernacle and for public places. On the way to school one morning with Shayla, Kambia collapses, blood gushing from between her legs. Since Kambia insists that Shayla not summon her mother, Shayla runs the couple of blocks to the Tabernacle for Tia, who administers first aid. Shayla calls 911 and also Mama. At the hospital, Kambia undergoes a lifesaving operation, Mama becomes reconciled with Tia and later with Doo-witty, and Shayla learns what the reader has suspected, that Kambia is being raped and molested by her mother's boyfriends.

Mama has regained some of her zest for life because of Mr. Anderson Fox, then learns that he has been stepping out on her. At story's end, he moves out to be with his new wife and their coming baby. Although Shayla has resented him, she heeds her mother's advice and wishes him well, realizing that to do anything else would be more harmful to her than to him. Story buildup is subtle, strong women dominate the cast, and foils Shayla and Kambia are especially well drawn and memorable. Grandma Augustine is an eccentric yet credible and likable figure whose old-fashioned, well-meaning ways add welcome humor to what would otherwise be a story almost too terrible to bear. Shayla learns that there are times when it is best to break one's word for the common good and also that some lies are acceptable. Why the Dubois women have not heard of Doo-witty's painting talent before is not clear. The style is intimate and conversational and employs natural-sounding street slang and occasional trash talk. A companion novel is *Shayla's Double Brown Baby Blues*. ALA/YA.

WHEN SHE WAS GOOD (Mazer*, Norma Fox, Scholastic, 1997)   Contemporary sociological-problem novel of domestic abuse set in New York State. After her ugly, obese older sister dies, Em, 17, looks back on their life together both with their parents and especially on their own after their widower father marries again. She realizes that although she always tried to be the good person her mother admonished her to be, she could never satisfy her sister, who was physically, psychologically, and verbally abusive. This is a serious, sometimes horrifying look at what can happen to children of dysfunctional families. For a more detailed entry, see *Dictionary, 1995–1999*. ALA/YA; NYPL.

WHEN ZACHARY BEAVER CAME TO TOWN (Holt*, Kimberly Willis, Holt, 1999)   Amusing, gentle novel of how a small Texas town in the Vietnam War period reacts when The Fattest Boy in the World is evidently abandoned by his freak-show manager and left alone in his house trailer. As they come to understand his plight, local boys provide him with experiences he otherwise could never have. For a longer entry, see *Dictionary, 1995–1999*. ALA/YA.

WHIRLIGIG (Fleischman*, Paul, Holt, 1998)   Contemporary novel of the rehabilitation of a teenager whose drunk driving has killed a girl in the Chicago area. Through the construction of whirligigs, each bearing her picture, at the four corners of the country, as her mother has requested, he achieves peace and perspective and affects positively a number of lives. For a longer entry, see *Dictionary, 1995–1999*. ALA/YA.

WHISTLE ME HOME (Wersba*, Barbara, Holt, 1997)   Contemporary novel of young love and a girl's painful maturing when it becomes apparent that the object of her affections will never become her physical lover. Noli (Noelle) Brown, 17, starts her junior year at Peterson High in Sag Harbor, Long Island, at odds with her mother, close to her friend, Tracy, and still a virgin. In English class the first day she meets TJ Baker, the most beautiful boy she has ever seen, a boy with a face like an angel and the body of a Greek god. To her astonishment, he selects her from all the girls swooning over him and soon they are constant companions, enjoying old movies, flea markets, vegetarian food, book sales, and just walking on the beach. Although their relationship seems wonderful, a few things puzzle her. He makes no attempt to paw her, like other boys she has known, and kisses her gently, without passion. When she suggests that they go to the Halloween dance as Ingrid Bergman and Humphrey Bogart, cross-dressing, he is angry and upset, and insists on alternative costumes. On New Year's Day in New York, they go to an old movie in Greenwich Village, though he is reluctant, and a wildly obvious gay man greets TJ by name and is persistent, until the boy hits him and they run to a restaurant. Mulling it all over, Noli realizes that TJ has always selected their clothes to look alike, so she now dresses more like a boy than a girl. It is not until March that the truth comes out. Noli's parents have gone away for the weekend, and she sees the opportunity to seduce TJ. In front of the fire, they both strip, and she is enthralled by the beauty of his body, but she realizes that he is not aroused, and she says what she has guessed but never admitted, "You're gay, aren't you?" He begins to sob, saying how much he has wanted to change and admitting that he used to pick up older men until he was arrested, before his family moved to Long Island. At first she is sympathetic and understanding, but when he closes up, reluctant to discuss it with her further, she becomes angry, calls him a faggot and a queer, and he leaves. For a while Noli tries to drown her grief in vodka, which she has been secretly using for a long time. After she arrives at school drunk, she is confronted by her parents and the school psychologist, and is required to go to Alcoholics Anonymous meetings for teens, of which she is initially scornful but gradually accepting. Tracy tells her that TJ has found a new friend, a boy named Walker Lewis, who goes to a prep school in East Hampton. Since they are both athletic, no one suspects that the two boys are gay. More than once TJ writes her, saying that he still loves her and would like to be friends, but she cannot bring herself to try that. In May she gets a call regarding Alice, the poodle puppy TJ gave her and she lost on Easter Sunday, and after she retrieves and washes the dog she is surprised that her mother, who had her earlier dog euthanized and whom she has long thought to be cold and without emotion, is so delighted to see the puppy again. By the end of the summer, Noli has begun to make peace with her mother, has talked to TJ and explained that, because she loves him deeply, she cannot switch gears and be just friends, and is beginning to look ahead. The entire novel is in the present tense, which helps give it a feel of immediacy, and Noli is well characterized as a girl with lots of faults but strong spirit. TJ's character is not so successful. He is sensitive, intelligent, and sweet, as well as beautiful and a good athlete, and although he is obviously troubled, he seems too idealized. Although Noli's complete rejection of him is meant to show her courage and maturity, it leaves a question of whether it is fair to him and a good solution for her, whether switching gears might not be possible and better for both of them, at least until he leaves for college after their next school year. The novel tackles a big and important subject, but is not completely satisfying. ALA/YA.

WHITE, RUTH (1942–)   Born in Whitewood, Virginia; teacher, librarian, novelist. Her *Memories of Summer** (Farrar, 2000) is set mostly in Flint, Michigan, in the 1950s, a sensitive novel about the protagonist's mentally ill sister. Her earlier novel, *Bell Prater's Boy** (Farrar, 1996), was an honor book for both the *Boston Globe–Horn Book* Award and the Newbery Medal. It has also been named to the

American Library Association Young Adult list. For earlier biographical information and a title entry, see *Dictionary, 1995–1999* [*Belle Prater's Boy*].

WHITESEL, CHERYL AYLWARD

Born in Rochester, New York. She earned a speech degree from Northwestern University and a J.D. from Tulane University Law School. She and her family moved to Asia in 1985 and lived there for twelve years. One result is her first novel, *Rebel: A Tibetan Odyssey** (HarperCollins, 2000). She lives in Western Springs, Illinois, near Chicago.

WHITMORE, ARVELLA (1933–)

Dramatist, educator, historical novelist. She attended Christian College (now Columbia College) and Washburn University, and received her M.A. in speech and theater from the University of Iowa. She was head of the Speech and Drama Department at Marymount College, Salina, Kansas, and is the former director of Twig Theater, a touring theater troupe performing in Minneapolis, for which she also wrote plays. Her time-slip fantasy, *Trapped between the Lash and the Gun** (Dial, 1999), takes an African American boy involved with a street gang back to pre–Civil War days, giving a strong picture of plantation life for the slaves. Her earlier novels are *You're a Real Hero, Amanda* (Houghton, 1985), about a girl and her pet rooster in 1931, and *The Bread Winner* (Houghton, 1990), in which a girl saves her family from financial ruin during the Depression by baking and selling bread. Whitmore lives in Minneapolis.

WIGGINS (*At All Costs**)

Clyde Dalton, brutal psychopathic hit man and perpetrator of dirty deeds for Peter Frankel, deputy director of the FBI. On behalf of Frankel, Wiggins threatens to release to the media evidence that Senator Clayton Albricht is a pedophile, a false assertion but one that will nevertheless ruin him, the senator knows. Wiggins also tries to induce Carolyn Brighton to hang herself in her cell. He says that if she does not, he will kill her son, Travis*. Carolyn recognizes him as the unknown gunman in camouflage who shot at her and Jake Brighton when they were fleeing from the hazardous-materials depot inferno. Wiggins is caught trying to kill Travis, after he has killed a little girl in the hospital in order to get to Travis, but escapes. He then tries to induce Melissa Thomas, Nick's* wife, to hang herself on pain of harming her children. He is overcome in a brutal fight and later is murdered by Thorne.

WILDSIDE (*Wildside**)

A fantasy world much like the United States. The entrance to wildside lies behind bales of hay in the barn on the ranch belonging to Charlie Newell. Charlie's mother and his now-deceased Uncle Max had once lived there but after they formed attachments in tameside, or present-day United States, they remained in tameside. When Uncle Max suddenly disappeared, no one knew what happened to him. Charlie finds his bones in wildside, where he had been killed by animals. Wildside is an alternate Earth but without humans and with wildlife long extinct in tameside. It is quiet, unspoiled, and, except for the danger always posed by the animals, a comforting, inviting place. At one point, Charlie says the entrance is much like a wardrobe, apparently an allusion to the C. S. Lewis Narnia books, where the entrance to the land of Narnia lies through the back of a closet.

WILDSIDE (Gould*, Steven, Tor, 1996)

Thrilling, action-filled science fiction

novel for adults set one recent summer on a ranch in southern Texas. Right after he and four close classmates have been graduated from high school, narrator Charlie Newell, 18, invites Joey Maloney and his girl, Vietnamese American Marie Nguyen, and Rick Bockrath and his girl, Clara Prentice, to the ranch near the Brazos River that Charlie has inherited from his Uncle Max. Swearing them to secrecy, Charlie shows them his sixteen cages of passenger pigeons, birds extinct since 1914. After clandestinely selling the birds to several institutions, among them the San Diego Zoo and the National Zoo, for twenty-five thousand dollars each, Charlie persuades his friends to join him in an enterprise to exploit for gold an area they come to call "wildside." Wildside* is reached through a tunnel that Charlie has discovered, the entrance to which lies at the back of the barn. Wildside is much like the "tameside" in geography, the Brazos clearly running through it, but without humans, technology, and environmental degradation, and contains many species extinct on the tameside, like saber-toothed tigers, huge wolves, and mammoths. Marie and Charlie already have pilots' licenses, Charlie often copiloting with his commercial pilot father on commuter hops, and the others soon take lessons and become accredited flyers. Forming Wildside Investments Corporation, they buy planes and equipment and build hangars and lookouts, all the time on guard with guns against the danger posed by the wild creatures and the possibility of someone in tameside finding out. Charlie has enlisted the services of Luis Cervantes, a young, able lawyer, in setting up bank accounts so that money will be hard to trace and he will be able to meet his payroll with his friends and other obligations. A large portion of the book describes the ways in which they outfit wildside without disturbing the environment or angering the creatures. All goes well, and they recover at great cost in labor the potential for more than two million dollars in gold from the Colorado Mountains. The possibility for trouble has always been present since Joey is too fond of the bottle and might let word of wildside slip; since Rick, who comes out as homosexual, might tell his lover about wildside; or that Clara might talk, being angry at Rick. Real trouble, however, comes when federal authorities trace the pigeon money and arrive with soldiers, helicopters, and weapons and deliberately set out to intimidate the young people. Charlie races for the tunnel and throws the switch to close the connecting door just in time. The authorities insist on instant surrender, declaring that the young people are endangering security, although Charlie reminds them that no laws have been broken. Charlie's father staunchly defends his son, especially after being apprised of the young people's activities in wildside. Matters accelerate to a climax of high tension, with gate stormings, the youths' making incriminating videotapes of the authorities' behavior, and laborious preparations for alternate exits. Luis phones a judge, some other lawyers, and the media, but all are arrested anyway except Charlie, who escapes into wildside. On coming out ostensibly for his last time, the others having been released for lack of evidence, Charlie blows up the gate so no unscrupulous person can enter wildside. Charlie, however, has cleverly set the gate on a timer and retained a controller to it, and next spring, he and Clara return to wildside for good. An epilogue finds them raising a family, reclaiming deserts, and training others in similar ecological tasks. The first part of the book is slow with details of technology and setting. Allusion to the Waco incident is obvious, wildside is credibly and fascinatingly established, and the young people are so sympathetically depicted that one is both relieved that they come out of the ordeal safely and sad that wildside could not continue for all of them as it was. ALA/YA.

WILENTZ, AMY (1954–)   Journalist, novelist. She was Jerusalem correspondent for *The New Yorker* magazine from 1995 to 1997, experience echoed in her novel, *Martyrs' Crossing** (Simon & Schuster, 2001), which involves characters on both sides of the Israeli-Palestinian conflict. She is also author of *The Rainy Season: Haiti Since Duvalier* (Simon & Schuster, 1989), for which she won the PEN/Martha Albrand Prize for nonfiction and the Whiting Writers Award and was a nominee for the National Book Critics Circle Award in 1990. She has also written for *The Nation*, the *New Republic*, and the *New York Times*. She lives in New York City.

WILHELM, KATE (KATIE GERTRUDE) (1928–)   Born in Toledo, Ohio; prolific novelist. After a series of unrelated jobs—model, telephone operator, sales clerk, insurance underwriter—she became a full-time writer in 1956, and for much of the period since has averaged a novel a year. Originally known as an author of science fiction and fantasy, she is married to Damon Knight, a well-known science fiction author, and won both the Hugo Award and the Juniper Award for *Where Late the Sweet Birds Sang* (Harper, 1976), in which a post-Holocaust community of clones struggles to preserve civilization. She later turned to mystery, producing two series, one about lawyer Barbara Holloway, with more than five courtroom novels including *No Defense* (St. Martin's, 2000), and one known as the Constance and Charlie books, including *The Casebook of Constance and Charlie* (St. Martin's, 2000). In a rather different vein is *The Good Children** (St. Martin's, 2000), about four children who manage to conceal their widowed mother's death so they will not be split up and sent to foster homes. Wilhelm attended high school in Louisville, Kentucky, and makes her home in Eugene, Oregon.

WILLIAMS, CAROL LYNCH   Author of several problem and growing-up novels for middle graders and teenagers. Two involve the Florida Orton family: *Kelly and Me* (Delacorte, 1993) and *Adeline Street* (Delacorte, 1995). Chosen by the American Library Association for young adults, *The True Colors of Caitlynne Jackson** (Delacorte, 1997), also set in Florida, concerns child abuse, mental illness, and child abandonment in a mother-headed family. More recently, Williams has published *Christmas in Heaven* (Putnam, 2000), which revolves around the granddaughter of a born-again preacher, and *A Mother to Embarrass Me* (Delacorte, 2002), which tells of a girl who is embarrassed by her mother's pregnancy. Williams makes her home in Mapleton, Utah, with her husband and four daughters.

WILLIAMS, LORI AURELIA   Born in Houston, Texas; received an M.A. in English from the University of Texas–Austin, where she won awards and scholarships for creative writing. African American, she grew up in a neighborhood much like that of Shayla Dubois in *When Kambia Elaine Flew in from Neptune** (Simon & Schuster, 2000), the moving account of a household of African American women doing their best to stay afloat under troubling circumstances. Her first novel, the book was selected for young adults by the American Library Association. A companion book is *Shayla's Double Brown Baby Blues* (Simon & Schuster, 2001). She lives in Austin, Texas.

WILLIS, CONNIE (1945–) Born in Denver, Colorado; graduate of the University of Northern Colorado (B.A.); elementary school teacher; since 1969 a freelance writer. She has won several Hugo and Nebula awards and is praised for her twelve cleverly constructed, witty science fiction novels, novelettes, and short stories. These range widely in tone and substance, including horror, fantasy, romance, slapstick comedy, and time travel. Typical is the comic *To Say Nothing of the Dog, Or, How We Found the Bishop's Bird Stump at Last** (Bantam, 1997). Wealthy English eccentric Lady Schrapnel decides to rebuild Coventry Cathedral as it was before it was bombed in World War II, an endeavor that necessitates considerable time travel. Published for adults, it was chosen for the Alex list and by the American Library Association for teenagers. Other titles include *Lincoln's Dreams* (Bantam, 1988); *Doomsday Book* (Bantam, 1992), which time-travels back to the fourteenth century; *Remake* (Ziesing, 1994), set in the Hollywood of the future; and *Passage* (Bantam, 2001), a medical thriller. Willis has collaborated on several books with novelist Cynthia DeFelice and published collections of science fiction stories.

WILL MCKINNEY (*Strays Like Us**) Willis Eugene McKinney, 12, the next-door neighbor of the narrator, Molly Moberly, and her best friend. Half orphaned, he comes to live (dropped off at, Molly says) with his grandparents, the townspeople are led to believe because his father is in prison, although another story is that his father is a traveling man. Later, Molly learns that since the McKinneys are renters, they are afraid that the landlord will evict them if the news gets out that Will's father has AIDS. Will and Molly meet early in the book, when both are perched in trees in their respective yards and he initiates a conversation. The book ends the same way, about a year later, only this time Molly is no longer cool toward him and appreciates his light-hearted attitude and friendliness. He goes out for softball in the spring, and when he hurts his leg sliding into third, trouble starts because the other boys have learned that his father had AIDS and are afraid of contacting his blood. Coach Allen suggests he stay home, but Will decides he no longer wants to be on the team and quits. Like Molly, whose counterpart he is, Will is proud, sturdy, and likable.

WILSON, DIANE LEE Historical novelist. An accomplished horsewoman, Wilson is the author of two novels with exotic settings, both concerned with horse-loving characters. The first, *I Rode a Horse of Milk White Jade** (Orchard, 1998), is set among the nomadic people in Mongolia at the time of Genghis Khan, with a cameo appearance by Marco Polo. Another is *To Ride God's Own Stallion* (DK, 2000), concerned with palace intrigue in Nineveh, seat of the Assyrian Kingdom. Wilson lives in Escondido, California.

THE WINDOW (Dorris*, Michael, Hyperion, 1997) Contemporary sociological- and personal-problem, girl's growing-up novel, and family-life novel set in Tacoma, Washington, and Louisville, Kentucky. When Rayona Taylor, 11, the narrator, is unable to continue living with her alcoholic Native American mother, Elgin, her

African American/white father, sends her to stay with his mother, Rayona's great-aunt, and Rayona's great-grandmother, in Louisville, white relatives whom she has never met. As she learns about her father's family, she grows to love them and they her, and she is able to return to her mother with a broadened perspective on life. While the plot seems curiously truncated, the story is a satisfactory introduction to the triracial Rayona of *A Yellow Raft in Blue Water*, the novel to which this book is a companion. For a more detailed entry, see *Dictionary, 1995–1999*. ALA/YA.

THE WINDOW (Ingold*, Jeanette, Harcourt, 1996)   Contemporary physical- and psychological-problem novel with family-life, time-travel, fantasy, and school-story aspects. Narrator Mandy, 15, blinded in the auto accident that killed her mother, goes to live with her great-aunt and two great-uncles on their Texas farm. She gradually learns to cope with her disability and gains information about the events that led up to the tragic accident through voices she hears outside the window of her attic bedroom and her relationships with her newly found relatives. The fantasy elements work satisfactorily, and Mandy grows convincingly in knowledge of family and self. For a longer, more detailed entry, see *Dictionary, 1995–1999*. ALA/YA.

WINTER ROSE (McKillip*, Patricia A., Ace, 1996)   Strange, compelling fantasy novel set in a preindustrial village in which, by love and determination, a girl is able to render an old curse inoperable. Unlike her beautiful, calm, capable older sister, Laurel, Rois Melior is wildly unpredictable, inclined to roam the woods, forget the time, and return, her dark hair in tangles and her arms full of flowers or healing herbs. One particular spot she loves is a well, hidden among vines and rose briars, where she first sees Corbet Lynn, who seems to emerge from the water and the light. A little later, all the village is talking about him, of how he has come back to the once-lavish house his grandfather, much-hated Nial Lynn, owned and is trying to rebuild it from near ruin. The older people remember the curse Nial laid on his son, Tearle, but they all remember it differently, some saying the house would go to the wood, not to his son, some saying that each son is destined to kill his father. As nearest neighbors to Lynn Hall, the Melior family welcome Corbet, and he frequently spends his evenings with them, watching Laurel and her lover, Perrin, who are to be married in the spring, and watched by Rois, who has fallen in love with him. She becomes obsessed with the curse, trying to find the truth of it by interviewing all the oldest people and learning much about the family—that Nial and Tearle lived in two small rooms blocked off from the rest of the house, that Nial was cruel to the boy, whose mother died young, and that the child seemed to crave a family but was never able to fit into village life—but she is unable to pin down the facts of the curse. Either Corbet himself does not know or he is unwilling to say; he has a way of politely not answering even direct questions put to him. As autumn approaches, Rois sees Corbet's eyes more and more on Laurel and her sister's gradual response. Perrin, a hardworking, practical farmer whose romantic ability seems limited to playing the flute, at first does not notice, then seems to deny to himself that there is any attraction between the two. Though deeply hurt, Rois is more worried about Laurel than jealous, and not until winter has set in do the girls admit to each other what they feel. Several times, in dreamlike sequences, Rois seems to follow Corbet into another world, perhaps elfland, which he struggles to leave but where he is held by a beautiful, cruel woman figure. In one fierce winter storm, Rois finds her way to Lynn Hall and into the other world, only to wake, almost frozen, before the fireplace of the empty house with a dead body beside her. Though no one can identify the man, Rois knows it is Corbet's father. Corbet himself is missing. As winter closes in, Laurel spends most of her time staring out the window at the frozen landscape, eating almost nothing and paying no attention to Perrin or her father, who is frantic with worry, since that is how her mother died, staring at winter, unable, he thinks, to hold out until spring. Each time Rois visits the other world, it becomes more real and she becomes more desperate to save Corbet, if possible, but at least Laurel from the fate of a mortal in that strange land. Among other inhabitants of that place, she sees Nial and Tearle and her own mother, who, she realizes, fell in love with a spirit in the wood when Rois was a baby and finally left our world for the other. In a last attempt to save Laurel, Rois offers herself to the other world if her sister is released from the spell and in a harrowing encounter holds fast to Corbet in a series of shapes until at last he has broken free of the other world spell. When Rois wakes at home, Laurel, who is so weakened that she is bedridden, is for the first time hungry. In the next weeks, she gains strength and with it interest in Perrin, who gratefully forgives her for rejecting him, and they again plan a spring wedding. As warmer weather returns, they hear hammering from Lynn Hall and know that Corbet has come back. Just how much he remembers is unclear, but he now is definitely human, relieved that Laurel and Perrin are together again, and possibly willing to turn his attention to Rois. Her free-spirited affinity for the woods is explained possibly by her father's inability to discipline the daughter who looks so like her mother or possibly because her actual father was the spirit from the wood her mother loved. Although the Melior farm, the village, the ruin of Lynn Hall, and even the wood are well realized, the other world is harder to believe, more dependent on atmosphere than any sense of reality. Good, solid Perrin is in many ways more convincing than handsome Corbet. Booklist.

WITTLINGER, ELLEN (1948–) Born in Belleville, Illinois; educated at Millikin University and the University of Iowa; children's librarian and writer of poetry, plays, short stories, and young adult novels, for which she is best known. She lives in Swampscott, Massachusetts. In *Hard Love** (Simon & Schuster, 1999), putting out his own literary magazine and becoming friends with a bright Puerto Rican American girl helps a boy of sixteen deal with tough times. It was a Printz Honor Book and was cited by the American Library Association for young adults and by *School Library Journal*. Recent titles include *What's in a Name** (Simon & Schuster, 2000), also an American Library Association book for young adults, in which ten high school students explore problems of personal identity; *Razzle* (Simon & Schuster, 2001), about an eccentric girl; and *The Long Night of Leo and Bree* (Simon & Schuster, 2002), about family problems, murder, and kidnapping. For additional information about Wittlinger, titles, and a title entry, see *Dictionary, 1995–1999* [*Hard Love*].

WOJTASIK, TED   Born in Wallingford, Connecticut; received an M.F.A. from Columbia University and a Ph.D.

from the University of South Carolina. He has taught English at a private school in Connecticut and on the university level, worked as a researcher in the archives of the National Geographic Society, and published short stories in various journals. He lived and worked among the Pennsylvania White Top Amish, the most conservative Amish, for many months in order to depict their way of life and attitudes faithfully for *No Strange Fire** (Herald, 1996), an engrossing mystery. It was a *Booklist* choice for young adults. He lives in Columbia, South Carolina.

THE WOMAN IN THE WALL (Kindl*, Patrice, Houghton, 1997)   Strange fantasy of an extremely shy girl who disappears for seven years into hidden rooms and passageways she has built in her family's very large old house. As a young child, Anna Newland is able to fade into the background at will, and since she is unusually small, she is often overlooked by people outside her immediate family—her mother, Elaine, her older sister, Andrea, and her younger sister, Kirsty. Her father, also a shy person, disappeared years ago in the Library of Congress book stacks and has not been heard from since. When Anna is seven, her mother decides that she must go to school, but a visit from the school psychologist so terrifies the girl that she hides and begins to build an intricate series of passageways and secret rooms so cleverly constructed that no one notices that the main rooms of the house are a little smaller than they should be. Not only is Anna skilled at any construction project, she also is an expert seamstress. For the next several years she keeps the house in repair by working at night and often makes beautiful outfits for her sisters and cooks treats that she leaves where they will find them. Occasionally,

she allows Kirsty to glimpse her, but her mother and Andrea almost forget she ever existed. She keeps track of what goes on in the house through a series of peepholes cleverly concealed and watches Andrea turn into a beauty, the center of an adoring crowd who wander through the house at all hours. After Anna's twelfth birthday, she begins to grow and to notice new and terrifying changes in her body. At first she decides that she is dying until she notices similar changes beginning in Kirsty and realizes that it is just puberty. Her size, however, presents new problems; she has difficulty getting through her narrow passageways. Her life changes forever when she notices a note, folded over and over and wedged into a crack in the molding leading to one of her little rooms. It says, "Dear A, I love you. Sincerely yours, F." With trepidation, she answers, starting a correspondence through the crack that soon consumes all her attention. Although after the first few exchanges she realizes that F is writing to Andrea, she continues to answer his notes. Since F is a smart boy, though too plump and young to attract glamorous Andrea, he figures out what is happening and squeezes into one of Anna's rooms, soon followed by Kirsty, who is delighted to see Anna again, having begun to think that this sister was someone she imagined. They confirm the impending change she has been suspecting and dreading. Her mother is about to marry F's father, Frank Albright, and move the family to Chicago, abandoning the house and exposing her refuge to sale. Although Anna is distraught, F, whose real name is Francis, and Kirsty work out a plan to reintroduce her to the real world. They decide she shall appear at Andrea's Halloween costume party. While Anna is terrified, she is so in love with Francis by now that she agrees, hoping to prove to him how brave she is. She makes a gorgeous black cat costume for Kirsty, and for herself a costume as a poisonous green Luna moth. When she looks in the mirror, she is astonished at the beautiful creature. Still, she expects just to appear, ask a boy to dance as she has promised Francis, and then retreat. The boy she approaches, Foster Addams, turns out to be entranced by her and, worse, is Andrea's current infatuation. When Andrea recognizes her almost forgotten sister, she becomes hysterical. Mr. Albright tries to throw Anna out, assuming she is a party crasher. The misunderstanding develops into a wild chase, Anna fleeing through the house with the others in hot pursuit until she collapses and the truth comes out. Mr. Albright, a take-charge sort of man, sends the party-goers home, gets a semicoherent explanation from Anna's mother, and starts making plans for a private tutor to help Anna catch up academically when they move from Bitter Creek to Chicago. This highly implausible plot is slow to convince, but Anna's matter-of-fact first-person narrative gradually becomes believable, even her incredible construction and sewing skills. The hidden passageways and cozy little room she inhabits have a seductive charm. Francis, a boy who appreciates Anna's wide interests and unusual life, and Kirsty, a feisty, no-nonsense twelve-year-old, are just the characters to help her emerge. Although the whole story can be taken as symbolic, especially the moth costume, the novel does not rely on metaphoric meaning for its interest. ALA/YA.

WOODSON, JACQUELINE (1964–   ) African American writer born in Columbus, Ohio; received her B.A. in English from Adelphi University and studied further at New School for Social Research; teacher of creative writing; popular and acclaimed writer of more than a dozen novels for middle graders and young adults about the African American experience. *If You Come Softly** (Putnam, 1998), an American Library Association choice for young adults, concerns a romance between a white girl and a black boy. *Miracle's Boys** (Putnam, 2000), also an American Library Association selection for young adults, is about three orphaned Puerto Rican/African American brothers in New York's inner city. More recent is *Hush* (Putnam, 2002), a girl's coming-of-age novel. For more information about Woodson and a title entry, see *Dictionary, 1995–1999* [*I Hadn't Meant to Tell You This*]. For other title entries, see *This Land Is Our Land* [*The Dear One*, no. 174; *Last Summer with Maizon*, no. 175] and *Many Peoples, One Land* [*From the Notebooks of Melanin Sun*, no. 139; *I Hadn't Meant to Tell You This*, no. 140].

WRESTLING STURBRIDGE (Wallace*, Rich, Knopf, 1996)   Sports novel set recently in Sturbridge, Pennsylvania, a small town obsessed by its only claim to fame, an award-winning high school wrestling team. Of the four thousand residents, most of the men work in the local cinder-block factory, with about four hundred of them members of the Wrestling Boosters Association. In their senior year, Benny, the narrator, and his three friends, Al, Hatcher, and Digit, are all skilled wrestlers, sure to be among the top in the state. Their main problem is that both Al and Benny are in the 135 lb. weight class, so they must vie for opportunity to appear at meets, and Benny's problem is that Al is a little better than he is, perhaps the best high school wrestler in Pennyslvania. Digit, who is lighter, dominates the 130 class, and Hatcher is strong at 140. The friendship, which has been close since junior high, begins to fray under the competition. Al, whose mother died recently, is close to his father but inclined to stupid practical jokes. Hatcher, whose father is the local bank president, is a slightly arrogant swaggerer. Digit is the brightest of the four, perceiving Benny's resentment of the coach's assumption that his role is as a workout partner for Al and also Benny's ambivalent attachment to Kim Chavez, an attractive junior who runs competitively. While Benny knows Kim is sensible, understanding, and evidently attracted to him, he is leery of getting too close and is preoccupied with his wrestling ambitions. He is also attracted to a girl named Jody Mullins, who works at a gas station on the edge of town. As the season progresses, Benny gets fewer chances to perform at meets and becomes determined to beat Al at the wrestle-offs, where it is decided who will represent the school in each weight class. Just before the league meet, the only event left before the state tournament, Al and two other boys, all a little drunk, are apprehended sneaking into the school and urinating into the radiators, a trick that creates an unbearable stench in the classroom the next morning. Although the coach protests, Al is suspended for three days and cannot participate in the league meet. Benny defeats his first two opponents easily, then fights Arnie Kiefer of Laurelton, an almost unbeaten opponent who defeated him a year before. When Benny pins him in thirty-seven seconds, the crowd goes wild, and he is awarded the Most Outstanding Wrestler trophy. Al is the only one uncomplimentary, saying, "Kiefer sucks." Benny realizes with surprise that, since they will wrestle-off for position the next Wednesday, Al is scared. In an unprecedented move, the wrestle-off is held in the main gym with a large crowd in attendance, most of them probably rooting for Al, since he is likely to be best in the state and bring further glory to the town. Driven by anger and desire to achieve, Benny puts on the best performance of his career and almost beats Al, losing 8–7 in the hardest competition either of them has experienced. Benny's father, choked up and obviously proud of him, gives him twenty dollars to take Kim out to dinner. Walking alone in the woods later, Benny realizes that he has exorcised the demon that has been driving him all year, that he is happy, and that he will eventually escape from Sturbridge and its claustrophobic obsession. The matches and the milieu of the gym and the locker room are well described, but the more important emphasis is on the town itself and what its focus on sports does to the young people. Several subthemes are touched on but not belabored: the relationship of Benny's mother and Hatcher's father, for whom she used to work, which might have been an affair; Benny's discovery that Jody has a child, whose father is a less-than-satisfactory parent; his own father's strange recreation of occasionally breaking into one of the summer cabins on the lakeshore and stealing minor items; his grandmother's bigotry and prejudice against Puerto Ricans and Catholics; and the hypocrisy of Reverend Fletcher of the church his family attends, an attitude that once drove Benny to punch him out at a sports day for little kids, an incident well-known in the small town. Although the novel is not long, it draws a good picture of the confusions and ambivalences of boys at Benny's age and develops his growth of understanding in a convincing way. ALA/YA.

WRIGHT, BIL African American playwright, poet, and fiction writer born in the Bronx, New York; graduate of New York University with an acting major; received his M.F.A. in playwriting from Brooklyn College. He has worked at The Door, a walk-in center for adolescents; taught English at New York's Housing Works, a service organization for men and women with HIV; has been a director of a special performing arts program at the Martin Luther King Center for Social Change; and has taught English composition and literature at Brooklyn College and Long Island University and acting at Marymount Manhattan College. His plays have been produced variously, published, and received acclaim, as have his poems and short stories. His first novel, published for adults, *Sunday You Learn How to Box** (Simon & Schuster, 2000), of a boy's growing up black and gay in the projects of a Connecticut town, was selected by *Booklist* for young adults. He lives in New York City.

Y

A YEAR DOWN YONDER (Peck*, Richard, Dial, 2000)   Amusing, realistic, episodic girl's growing-up and period novel set for one school year in a small Illinois town, sequel to *A Long Way from Chicago*. In 1937, the nation is deep in the Great Depression, and Dad is out of a job. The Dowdels live in a room too small to accommodate narrator Mary Alice, 15, who reluctantly leaves Chicago to stay with Grandma* Dowdel in her Illinois "hick town," as Mary Alice calls it. No-nonsense Grandma meets Mary Alice at the Wabash Railroad Station and promptly marches her off to the high school, which has been in session for two weeks. Each of the seven chapters is a self-contained episode, in which events take surprising turns when Grandma takes charge. Mary Alice's school seatmate, big, dirty, mean-spirited Mildred Burdick, daughter of the town's ne'er-do-wells, takes Mary Alice for a rich kid and demands a dollar. Grandma notes that Mildred's horse is stolen (the Burdicks are notorious horse thieves), cuts it loose, and lets Mildred cope with her runaway horse.

The dollar is forgotten. At Halloween, Grandma booby-traps her privy with a ground wire. She trips up a potential trickster upon whom she dumps glue and who turns out to be the son of the high school principal, Mr. Fluke. At the annual Armistice Day turkey shoot, Grandma dishes up the traditional burgoo stew, demanding that her customers pay in accordance with what she thinks each can afford and giving the proceeds to Mrs. Abernathy, whose son was gassed in World War I. In December, Grandma traps and shoots foxes to sell to the fur broker for money for Christmas gifts—shoes for Mary Alice, a Lane Bryant dress for herself, and a round-trip ticket for Mary Alice to visit her parents in Chicago. In February, snooty Mrs. L. J. Weidenbach, the banker's wife, asks Grandma to make tarts for the annual Daughters of the American Revolution George Washington Tea. To Mrs. Weidenbach's consternation, Grandma invites two town women, Mrs. Effie Wilcox and aged Aunt Mae Griswold. Aunt Mae announces that Mrs. Weidenbach does not have the Early

American lineage she claims but is in reality a Burdick. In March, Grandma takes in a boarder, Arnold Green, a painter. While he is painting a nude of postmistress Maxine Patch in his attic room, Grandma's resident snake drops down on her, Maxine flees from the house, unclothed, of course, and races through town, screaming. Grandma grabs her trusty Winchester and shoots the snake dead. After a tornado brings the school year to a roaring conclusion, Mary Alice wants to remain with Grandma, partly because she has enjoyed her year and mostly because she is sweet on Royce McNabb, also a newcomer and the handsomest boy in town, but Grandma sends her home. In the epilogue set in 1945, Mary Alice, now a cub reporter for a Chicago paper, returns to Grandma's house to marry Royce. The people of the town, from the old and the infirm whom Grandma champions to the upper crust that she lays low for their snobbery, and the social patterns with women's cliques, paralleled by those of the high school girls, are depicted with humor and underlying seriousness. References to the period abound, like Kate Smith, the Works Progress Administration, and Philco radios. Some scenes, like the snake one, are pure slapstick, but much of the humor derives from character revelation, the small-town social system and mores, and clever turns of phrase. Mary Alice grows up as expected, but the inimitable old woman steals the show, always the winner in whatever situation confronts her. She makes the book tops in reading entertainment. ALA/YA.

YEP, LAURENCE (MICHAEL) (1948–) Born in San Francisco, California; author of many different kinds of books for young people, most of them about the Chinese American experience. His novel, *The Cook's Family** (Putnam, 1998), was listed by the New York Public Library as one of the best books for young adults for the year. For a title entry, see *Many Peoples, One Land* [no. 238]. For biographical information and other title entries, see *Dictionary, 1960–1984* [*Child of the Owl; Dragonwings*]; *Dictionary, 1990–1994* [*The Star Fisher; Dragon's Gate*] and *Dictionary, 1995–1999* [Dragonwings].

THE YOKOTA OFFICERS CLUB (Bird*, Sarah, Knopf, 2001)   Novel of the family of an air force officer on Okinawa in the 1960s and the eldest daughter's realization of her part in the strains and bitterness she has seen but not understood. As Bernie (Bernadette) Root, 18, leaves the University of New Mexico, where her family deposited her nine months before, and flies on a military transport through a storm to Okinawa, where her father, Major Mason Patrick Root, is now stationed, she mentally reviews the many moves from one post to another since they left Japan eight years before. Just what caused his sudden transfer to stateside bases, mostly in the West, all lacking prestige and opportunity to fly, she does not know, but she suffered as the new girl in schools from Idaho to Texas, shy and self-conscious, while her sister Kit (Eileen), one year her junior, was always immediately popular, admired for her blond hair and blue eyes and winning ways. With the twins, Buzz (Frances Xavier) and Abner (Bryan Patrick), now 12, Bosco (Mary Colleen), 10, and Bob (Joseph Anthony), 7 or 8, all crammed into a station wagon with their unsympathetic father driving madly, their mother, Moe* (Mohoric) dosed them all with phenobarbital, doled out bologna sandwiches, and passed around the potty chair. Their four years in

Japan, their longest stay in any station, stand out for Bernie as the happiest, especially because of Fumiko*, the maid in their off-base house, who strangely has never been mentioned since they left Yokota base. In Okinawa, she finds they live on base, where they all are expected to be representatives of the United States, and their infractions (failing to mow the lawn, dressing unconventionally, drinking, smoking pot) can get their father RIF'd (fired). Bernie is astonished at the disorganization in the family. Her mother is almost a zombie, sleeping half the day, wandering around in her nightgown. Kit disappears frequently with groups of friends, to go to a cave in the northern part of the island where they smoke opium. The twins run wild, pummeling each other and pummel Bob, who mostly watches television and quotes, verbatim, every cartoon he has ever seen. Bosco, who has a photographic memory and seems to know what is going on more than anyone else, worries. Mace, their father, is seldom around, mostly ignoring the children when he is not snapping his fingers and giving military orders, and not speaking, Bernie notices, to Moe. When he suddenly goes off on a TDA (Temporary Duty Assignment), destination undisclosed, Moe snaps to, gets the twins to cut the grass and fix the sagging screens, orders the others to clean the house, and generally takes charge. Kit has seen announcements of a dance contest, the prize being an all-expense-paid trip to Japan to perform with Bobby* Moses on his tour of military bases, and she is confident that she will win, although she has no sense of rhythm. Partly to thwart her sister and partly because she really loves to dance, Bernie also auditions and to her sister's amazement, she wins. Bobby Moses is a grossly overweight comedian, a poor-man's Bob Hope,

who assures Moe he is gay, so that she won't worry about her daughter, although Bernie soon finds out this is not true. Their tour gets a so-so reception, better with enlisted men than with officers. Their last stop is the Yokota Officers Club, which Bernie remembers from various occasions when her father was stationed there. Because the act is bombing, Bernie suddenly drops her persona as Zelda, dumb straightman for Bobby, and announces that she is the daughter of Major Mason Root of the Thirty-eighty-first Reconnaissance Squadron, the "Bong Bunnies," who flew out of Yokota a decade earlier. To her surprise, her father's reputation is still alive, and the young flyers go mad, forming a conga line as she dances with real zest, a wild party suddenly interrupted by a typhoon alert alarm. Against regulations, the young officers get her on a weather observation plane and take her to her family in Okinawa. The main force of the novel is its picture of life for military dependents and the way it has all but destroyed the Root marriage and would have made the children's lives unbearable had it not been for Moe's strong sense of independence and self-worth. Many characters are well portrayed and settings are vividly realized. The incident that Bernie discovers got them RIF'd from Yokota is predictable but heart wrenching. Booklist.

YOLEN, JANE (HYATT) (1939–) Born in New York City; prolific author, editor, lecturer, songwriter. With Bruce Coville*, she wrote *Armageddon Summer** (Harcourt, 1998), a realistic novel of an apocalyptic sect preparing for the end of the world as they know it, and with the Scottish writer, Robert J. Harris, she wrote *Queen's Own Fool** (Philomel, 2000), a historical novel concerned with Mary, queen of Scots. She lives in Hatfield, Massachusetts, and spends summers in St. Andrews, Scotland. For earlier biographical information and a title entry, see *Dictionary, 1985-1989* [*Heart's Blood*].

YOUNG, KAREN ROMANO (1959–   ) Born in Ithaca, New York; writer of both fiction and nonfiction for young people. She received her B.S. in education from Syracuse University in 1981 and worked during the early 1980s as writer and editor for *Scholastic News*. With Marlane Barron, she has coauthored a series of educational books intended for parents of three-to-seven-year-olds. Her first novel for young adults is *The Beetle and Me: A Love Story** (Greenwillow, 1999), an amusing tale of a girl who is determined to repair and restore an ancient VW Beetle, despite her family's attempts to discourage her. Another novel is *Video* (Greenwillow, 1999), about a boy who secretly videotapes a classmate for his spring term project and finds that she has an older man stalking her. Young lives in Bethel, Connecticut.

YOUNG KIM (*Necessary Roughness**) Pretty, intelligent daughter of Abogee* and O-Ma* Kim and sixteen-year-old twin sister of Chan, the narrator, Korean Americans. Young is an obedient daughter, who, although she is very attracted to Mikko* Ripanen, a Finnish American teenager, defers to her parents' wishes and does not date him. A good student, especially in music and mathematics, she is well liked by teachers and by the other high school students, after the initial bias against Asians is overcome in the community. She joins the school band, and Chan can often hear her flute above the other instruments when the band plays at football games. She dies when the car in which she is riding, driven by her best friend, Donna, swerves to miss a deer and crashes. The entire town mourns her death. Ironically, losing her makes Abogee value Chan more, although he earlier had compared his son unfavorably with his daughter, because Young stayed closer to traditional values and behavior. As a parting gesture of love, Chan places her flute in her casket.

Z

ZETTEL, SARAH (1965–) Born in Sacramento, California; received a B.A. in communications from the University of Michigan; acclaimed for her novels of science fiction; has been a technical writer specializing in software systems instructional manuals; lives in Ypsilanti, Michigan. She received the Locus Award for best first novel of the year for *Reclamation* (Aspect/Warner, 1996), about a group in an interplanetary colonial system who hunt for humankind's original home. Her second book, *Fool's War* (Aspect/Warner, 1997), deals with a threat from artificial intelligence to control humans. *Kingdom of Cages** (Warner, 2001), a science fiction novel about an interplanetary system of human habitation in danger of collapse, was selected by *Booklist* for teen readers. Her most recent novel is *A Sorcerer's Treason* (Tor, 2002), in which a lighthouse keeper rescues a sailor who comes from a magical world.

ZINDEL, PAUL (1936–2003) Born on Staten Island, New York; received his B.S. and M.S. from Wagner College; dramatist and author for adults and young people. He published more than three dozen books mostly for young adults but also for juveniles, many of which have received acclaim, as well as plays for stage, screen, and television. Celebrated for his "alienation" books of the 1960s and 1970s, in recent years he turned to horror-thriller and grotesquerie fiction, which overexploit the sensationalistic. Examples are *Reef of Death** (HarperCollins, 1998), chosen for young adults by the American Library Association, which concerns the search for a sacred Aboriginal treasure off the Great Barrier Reef, and *Rats* (Hyperion, 1999), about giant rats who attack residents on Staten Island. Zindel also recently published a series of novels featuring the boy detective, P. C. Hawke, among them, *The Square Root of Murder* (Hyperion, 2002) and *The Scream Museum* (Hyperion, 2001). He lived in Montague, New Jersey. For more information about Zindel and a title entry, see *Dictionary, 1960–1984* [*The Pigman*].

ZOE CAMERON (*Ordeal**)   Twelve-year-old daughter of Wren and Cam*, a level-headed, intelligent girl who has driven her older brother, Daniel, to fury by getting good grades, keeping her room neat, and generally doing all the things he has been criticized for not doing. After Wren and Daniel are kidnapped, Zoe displays remarkable strength to support her father, only breaking down briefly, then rallying to keep him from going to pieces. When Hunter arrives with Daniel and shoots Cam, she is horrified, but she calls for help, stanches his bleeding, and stays with him in the hospital, even taking her mother's call and relaying information to Steve Austin* as she is asked. At the same time, she is typical of her age, bickering with her brother and complaining when she feels slighted.

List of
Books by Awards

The following novels have been cited for the awards indicated and appear in this dictionary. Nonfiction books and collections of short stories are not included.

Alex Award for Top Ten Adult Books for Young Adults

At All Costs
Caucasia
Chang and Eng
Election
Ender's Shadow
Getting In
Imani All Mine
Last Days of Summer
The Man Who Ate the 747
Only Twice I've Wished for Heaven

Plainsong
The Reappearance of Sam Webber
River, Cross My Heart
The Sand-Reckoner
Snow in August
Stardust
To Say Nothing of the Dog, Or, How We Found the Bishop's Bird Stump at Last
What Girls Learn

American Library Association Best Books for Young Adults

An Acquaintance with Darkness
Adem's Cross
The Adventures of Blue Avenger
Among the Hidden
Anna of Byzantium
Another Kind of Monday
Another Way to Dance

Aria of the Sea
Armageddon Summer
Bad
The Beetle and Me: A Love Story
Belle Prater's Boy
Beyond the Western Sea: Book One: The Escape from Home

Blood and Chocolate
The Body of Christopher Creed
The Boxer
Breaking Rank
Bud, Not Buddy
Bull Catcher
Buried Onions
Chasing Redbird
Choosing Up Sides
Close to a Killer
Cloudy in the West
Crash
Crooked
Crossing Jordan
The Cuckoo's Child
A Dance for Three
Dancer
Dancing on the Edge
Dancing with an Alien
Dangerous Skies
Danger Zone
The Dark Side of Nowhere
Dave at Night
Define "Normal"
Don't Think Twice
Don't You Dare Read This, Mrs.
    Dunphrey
The Door in the Lake
A Door Near Here
Downsiders
Dreamland
Dust Devils
Ella Enchanted
Elske
Ender's Shadow
Esperanza Rising
The Exchange Student
The Falcon
Far North
Fever 1793
Firegold
Flyers
Forged by Fire
Forgotten Fire
The Ghost in the Tokaido Inn

Ghost of a Hanged Man
Gideon's People
A Girl Named Disaster
The Girls
The Girl Who Loved Tom Gordon
Go and Come Back
Gold Dust
Habibi
Hang a Thousand Trees with Ribbons:
    The Story of Phillis Wheatley
Hard Ball
Hard Love
Harley Like a Person
The Haunting
Head Above Water
Heaven
Hero
Heroes
Hidden Talents
Holding Up the Earth
Holes
Homeless Bird
Hope Was Here
I Am Mordred: A Tale from Camelot
If You Come Softly
Imani All Mine
Inside the Walls of Troy: A Novel of the
    Women Who Lived the Trojan War
I Rode a Horse of Milk White Jade
The Iron Ring
I Want to Buy a Vowel
Jason's Gold
Jip His Story
Johnny Voodoo
Joy School
Jubilee Journey
Jungle Dogs
Just Ella
Keeping the Moon
The Killer's Cousin
King of Shadows
Kinship
Kissing Doorknobs
The Last Book in the Universe
Leaving Fishers

A Life for a Life

Life in the Fat Lane

The Likes of Me

A Long Way from Chicago: A Novel in Stories

The Lost Years of Merlin

Love Among the Walnuts

The Luckiest Girl in the World

Making Up Megaboy

Many Stones

Mary, Bloody Mary

The Maze

Meely LaBauve: A Novel

Memories of Summer

Mind's Eye

Miracle's Boys

Monster

Mr. Was

The Music of Dolphins

My Father's Scar: A Novel

My Louisiana Sky

My Sister's Bones

Nathan's Run

Necessary Roughness

Never Trust a Dead Man

Night Flying

Night Hoops

Nobody Else Has to Know

No Condition Is Permanent

Nory Ryan's Song

The Ornament Tree

The Other Ones

The Other Shepards

Outrageously Alice

Painting the Black

Pastwatch: The Redemption of Christopher Columbus

Pay It Forward

Perfect Family

The Perks of Being a Wallflower

Petey

Plainsong

Playing Without the Ball

The Princess Diaries

The Queen's Man: A Medieval Mystery

Queen's Own Fool

Rats Saw GOD

Reef of Death

Rose Daughter

Rules of the Road

Run for Your Life

Running Out of Time

The Sacrifice

Safe at Second

The Sandy Bottom Orchestra

Sasquatch

The Savage Damsel and the Dwarf

Saying It Out Loud

The Schernoff Discoveries

The Secret Diary of Anne Boleyn

Seedfolks

Send One Angel Down

Shadow Spinner

Shakespeare's Scribe

The Shakespeare Stealer

Silent to the Bone

The Sin Eater

Sirena

The Skin I'm In

Slam!

Soldier's Heart: A Novel of the Civil War

Someone Like You

Someone to Love

Song In the Silence: The Tale of Lanen Kaelar

Song of the Magdalene

Sons of Liberty

Speak

Spider's Voice

The Spirit Window

The Squire, His Knight, & His Lady

Stargirl

The Starlite Drive-in

Stealing Freedom

Stones in the Water

Stranded in Harmony

Strays Like Us

Stuck in Neutral

Sunshine Rider: The First Vegetarian Western

Swallowing Stones
Tangerine
Tenderness
The Terrorist
That Summer
The Thief
Thin Ice
Ties That Bind, Ties That Break
A Time Apart
Torn Thread
To Say Nothing of the Dog, Or, How We
    Found the Bishop's Bird Stump at Last
Trapped Between the Lash and the Gun
Treasures in the Dust
The Tribes of Palos Verdes
Tribute to Another Dead Rock Star
Trout Summer
The True Colors of Caitlynne Jackson
Two Suns in the Sky
Virtual War

The Voice on the Radio
The Wanderer
The War in Georgia
The Watcher
What Child Is This?: A Christmas Story
What Girls Learn
What's in a Name?
When Jeff Comes Home
When Kambia Elaine Flew in from
    Neptune
When She Was Good
When Zachary Beaver Came to Town
Whirligig
Whistle Me Home
Wildside
The Window (Dorris)
The Window (Ingold)
The Woman in the Wall
Wrestling Sturbridge
A Year Down Yonder

Booklist Adult Books for Young Adults

Airframe
Alice's Tulips
All Loves Excelling
Archangel
Bombingham: A Novel
The Chatham School Affair
Chinhominey's Secret
Criminals
Election
Ender's Shadow
Exegesis
Farewell, I'm Bound to Leave You
The Floating Girl
From the Black Hills
The Gates of Twilight
Getting In
The Gift
The Girl Who Loved Tom Gordon
God Bless the Child
Heartlight
Higher Education

Hotel Paradise
How All This Started
Imani All Mine
I Want to Buy a Vowel
Jim the Boy
Killer.app
Kingdom of Cages
The Last Day
The Last Sin Eater
Letters from Yellowstone
London Blood: Further Adventures of the
    American Agent Abroad
Martyrs' Crossing
Moonfall
No Strange Fire
Off the Face of the Earth
Open Season
Ordeal
People of the Mist
Plainsong
The Poisonwood Bible: A Novel

Power
The Reappearance of Sam Webber
The Rover
The Serpent's Shadow
Snow in August
Stardust
Sunday You Learn How to Box
Timeline

The Tree of Red Stars
Up Jumps the Devil
A Walk to Remember
The Waterborn
What Girls Learn
Winter Rose
The Yokota Officers Club

New York Public Library Books for the Teen Age

Bodega Dreams
Cast Two Shadows: The American
    Revolution in the South
Close to a Killer
The Cook's Family
Dreamland
Dust
Fever 1793
Forgotten Fire
The Good Children
How All This Started

I Am Mordred: A Tale from Camelot
The Killer's Cousin
A Knight of the Word
Meely LaBauve: A Novel
Rebel: A Tibetan Odyssey
Rules of the Road
Secret Realms
Soldier's Heart: A Novel of the Civil War
The Watcher
What Girls Learn
When She Was Good

Michael L. Printz Award for Excellence in Young Adult Literature Honor Books

The Body of Christopher Creed
Hard Love
Many Stones

Speak
Stuck in Neutral

Michael L. Printz Award for Excellence in Young Adult Literature Winner

Monster

Index

Names and titles in CAPITAL LETTERS refer to the main entries of the dictionary, and page numbers in *italics* refer to the location of the main entries in the dictionary.

assaults: boy blamed for not preventing, 143; gay boy by brother's gang, 95, 236; rancher of boy's father, 142. *See also* attacks

assertiveness: developing, 173; girl develops, 352

assignments: extracredit, 265; to sink Columbus's ships, 264; social studies class, 265

Assistant Coach Kearny, 242

Assistant Deputy Secretary of the Civil Service, 113

assistants: Ben Franklin's, 209; botanical, woman, 197

asteroid, mining on, 146

asthma, 214

astronomers: Japanese, 192; Phidias, 304

AT ALL COSTS, *24*, 120

Atascadero, California, late twentieth century, 265

Atenar, 185

Athens, Theseus, king of, 158

Athira, young queen, 105, 185

athletes: girl, runner, 243; high school wrestlers, 400; letterman, Cribs gang member, 42. *See also* specific sports

athletic scholarship: for fencing, 115; girl's ambition, 167

athletic skills, encouraged, 289

ATKINS, CATHERINE, *25*, 388

Atlanta, Georgia: late twentieth century, 195; mid-twentieth century, 381

Atlantic Ocean: boy and uncle view for first time, 169; boy expelled into, rescued, 84; Connecticut to England in sailboat, late twentieth century, 380

Atlas missile launch site, 148

ATM cards, mother's, 82

Atreid family, 320

atrocities: against Armenians, 108; against Jews, 359

attaché, foreign service, 286

attacks: of bear, 122; boy by mare, 142; on Edori by Jansai, 285; by furious boyfriend, 85; on goldsmith, 282; in middle school restroom, 289; by pimp, 228; push down on escalator, 107; by savage eels and monster fish, 291; on street gang by Golem, 325; uncle suffers some sort of , 55. *See also* assaults; battles; conflicts; fights; rivalry

attendants, several hospital helpful to handicapped boy, 272

attics: farmhouse, with special attic window, 396; Jewish family confined to, 357

Attila the chicken, 207

Attorney General of the United States, 361

attorneys: defense, 48, 230; defense, mild-mannered, 257; doubts client's innocence, 230; saves boy, 221; Washington City (Washington, D.C.), 339. *See also* lawyers

Aubrey Truword, 296

auditions: for ballet company summer programs, 72; dance, 404; interrupted by mentally ill sister, 222

Aunt Cait, 259

Aunt Carmen Hansen, 244

Aunt Chancy, 100

Aunt Charity, 313

Aunt Clara Hampton, 345

Aunt Dot Lee, 51

Aunt Ethel, 227

Aunt Fay Moberly, 341, 359

Aunt Helen, 271

Auntie Annie, syndicated newspaper columnist, 6

Aunt Ina Carson, 293

Aunt Jessie Taylor, 54

Aunt Lacey Hall, 270

Aunt Mae Griswold, 402

Aunt Mimi, 339

Aunt Miracle, 361

Aunt Nicole Pandolfi, 29

aunts: called witch, 259; capable, strong-minded, articulate, 341; deceased, remembered with love, 271; dies of insulin shock, 54; eccentric, 177; great, girl lives with, 341, 396; great, tyrannical, 152; great, wild in youth, 31; helpful to bereaved family, 293; helps mentally ill girl, 72; inexperienced, well meaning, 68; loved by El Barrio boss, 34; mean, self-righteous, 227; mechanic and garage owner, 30; mother figure, 150; oddball, red-haired, 54; offers home in Baton Rouge, 236; practical nurse, 341; priestess of black arts, 315; schoolteacher, 345; sexually molested when a child, 271; smothers baby, 227; surrogate mother for boy, 345; three grim looking, 152; two, 244; unkind, 370

bankers: investment, 65, 95; wife is snooty, 402

bank robberies, by environmental community, 25. *See also* bandits; robbers; thieves

bankruptcy, forced by brother's vote, 115

Banks, Charlie, 193

Banner, Mike, 138

bans: on all public gatherings, queen issues, 316; on finishing paintings for play, 136; of ill from entering village, 103; from school property, 135

baptisms: of chicks, 169; as Fisher cult member, 196; of Great Smoky Mountains girl, 194; of many in community, 195; resisted because of crocodiles, 276

Baptist minister, father, 58

bargains: doctor to treat acne with payer anonymous, 6; five years on own before joining family firm, 286; to teach retarded boy to swim, 138; VW Beetle if girl repairs it, 30. *See also* agreements; truce

Barli, 105

bar mitzvah: ballplayer helps boy prepare for, 193; boy prepares for, 118

Barn, The, 26

Barnette, Jake, 117

barns: burn, arson, 250; entrance to wildside, 392, 393; red-haired man's hiding place for slaves, 360

Barnum, P. T., 52

Barons, 12

BARRETT, TRACY, 15, *28*

Barrie Dupre, 59

BARRON T(HOMAS) A(RCHIBALD), *28*, 205

Bartram family, 197

Baryshnikov, Mikhail, 18

baseball: boy gives rabbi lessons in game, 285, 325; boy good at, enjoys, 58; boy loves, good at, 134; boys love, 169; boys rivals at, 221; siblings crazy about, 153

baseball cards, 252

baseball card stores, 253

baseball game, boy and rabbi attend together, 325

baseball glove and bat, birthday gifts, 169

baseball player: first black, 325; girl's favorite, 122; major league, New York Giants, rookie third baseman, 193; Red Sox, 125; rowdy, rude, 262; star shortstop, 167

Baseball in April and Other Stories, 331

baseball novels, 44, 262, 302

basket, with baby boy inside, 336

basketball: 74; African American boy loves the sport, 156; boy crazy about, 245; boy dislikes, 245; court built on Mom's rose garden, 245; player especially mean and dirty, 245; practices in backyard at night, 245; player quits high school team in disgust at coach, 276

basketball novels, 245, 324

Basques, writings about, 195

bastard, Mordred told he is Arthur's, 155

BAT-AMI, MIRIAM, *29*, 368

Batan Island, 312

bat boy, Jewish boy travels with team as, 193

bathing, Isabo Indians enjoy every day, 123

Baton Rouge, Louisana, 137, 236

Bator the cat, 160

bats, attack people in Caribbean, 86

battles: between evil human and True Kindred (Dragons), 328; good versus evil, 328; supposedly simulated, actual, 93; various, symbolic, 38; Vietnam War, 37. *See also* attacks; conflicts; fights; wars; war novels

Battle School of International Space Fleet, 2, 92, 93, 245

BAUER, CAT, *29*, 135

BAUER, JOAN, *29*, 150, 298

Baxter, Allison, 114

Bayan the white mare, 160

bayboys, surfers, 363

Bayhead, Washington, late twentieth century, 259

Bay of Fundy, 380

Beach, Alfred Ely, 52, 83

Bean (*Ender's Shadow*), 92, 93, 245

Bean (*The Last Book in the Universe*), 191

Bean Columba, 135

Bean Trees, The, 183

Beargrease, Jimmi, 241

Bearkeeper's Daughter, The, 40

bears: cub, caught by Gypsies, 5; huge old, attacks, 122

Beast, 295

beast, terrifying, 295

beatings: of boy, severe, 325; boy of Jewish owner of candy store, 325; by boyfriend, 327; of bully raping smaller boy, 200;

boxing: 38; metaphor for life in boy's home, 343; parents decide boy needs to learn, 343
"boxing clubs," 39
boxing lessons: boy detests, 343; for girl, eleven, 41
Boxing Masters, New York Athletic Club, 39
boyfriends: abusive, 70, 85, 326; African American mother's is white, 157; girl acquires from Brazil, 387; good-looking college student, 237; lumpish, 120; mother is comforting, 158; mother's, rape her daughter, 389; "nice-boy" type, 18; red-haired white man, 228; sister's ex, 351; star high school wrestler, 237; unsuitable, 326; very handsome, 201; weak, self-promoting, 376
Boyfriend School, The, 32
BOYLAN, JAMES FINNEY, *40,* 114
Boy Regis, 173
boys: abducted by older boys, stripped, left to walk five miles home in dark, 274; abused, runaway, 240; academically very successful, 343; accused of dropping baby sister, proved innocent, 319; accused of killing chickens, 245; acrobat, 182; actor, malicious, 182; actors, in Shakespeare's theater, 182; adjustment after return home painful, 81; adopted by judge, 116; African American aids runaway white boy, 241; African American wantonly shot to death by white boy, 37; altar, 325; Amish, decides to leave home, 118; with amputated leg, 166; angry at parents' divorce, 252; Armenian refugee, 108; attractive protagonist, morally upright, good values, 221; avid cult follower, 258; beaten in gang initiation, 227; beaten often by father, 32; beaten up by toughs, 245; beautiful, 390; becomes a vegetarian, 345; big, tough, 38; brave, resilient, 361; bright, ambitious, 364; bright, open, 267; brilliant, 92; called destructive and vicious, 145; caught high on drugs in school, 288; with cerebral palsy, lonely, isolated, 272; with cerebral palsy, ward of state, 272; charming, impulsive, smart, 380; Chelan, seven feet tall, very thin, silvery-gray, 96; chip-on-the-shoulderish, 226; clever but troubled, 364; coach asks boy to keep rival player in line, 245; coach orders rivals to spend a week together, 134; comes out as gay, 387;

compulsively neat, 170; computer-games addict, 291; conventional, reliable son, 387; convicted of murder, 243; convicted of theft of sneakers, innocent, 148; crazy about basketball, 245; crazy about Captain Marvel comics, 325; crippled from birth, 328; deals drugs, 228; decent, unpretentious, 115; describes mother's last moments, 227; detests boxing, 343; dies in fire, 93; direct, honest, 265; disaffected, 383; distorts truth to save friend, 74; drinks too much before big dance, 280; drops out to support family, 184; earnest, conscientious, 325; egocentric, callous, 262; enjoys classical music, 125; entrepreneur in Dawson City with brothers, 166; errant Amish, 250; evidently abandoned in Texas town, 390; expelled from school, 146; expelled into Atlantic Ocean, 84; farm, Minnesota, in American Civil War, 326; fat, sensitive, 235; father pressures to excel at sports and studies, 134; fears germs, 186; five-year-old, new tulku, 303; gang member, gifted, 42; gay, 235, 236, 344, 391; given to spells of weeping, 270; good basketball player, coach needs, 245; good-looking, outgoing, accepted, 363; good student, 348; grades decline and seems distressed, 344; Grampa lets him drive, 247; gritty, tough survivor, 166; guileless, 9; half orphan, small town, 168; handicapped, appreciates natural and intellectual worlds, 342; handicapped, fears father plans to kill him, 343; handicapped, longs for girlfriend, 342; handicapped, with cerebral palsy, 342; handsome, new in town, 403; has cerebral palsy, 347; has fine, true singing voice, 125; has Obsessive-Compulsive Disorder, 186; high school, iconoclast, 288; incarcerated in detention home for car theft, 240; injured when wagon overturns, 118; innocent, jailed, exonerated, 221; innovative thinker, 310; intelligent, enterprising, compassionate, 107; inventive in helping mute boy, 319; Italian kidnapped and enslaved by Germans, 340; leads gang called Falcons, 325; lonely, isolated, friendless, 272; lost, helped by Sasquatch, 307; in love with goddess of River, 384; loves history, 329; mean, dirty basketball player,

245; mechanical genius, 81; mediocre student, 364; miserable, resentful, hostile, 210; missing for two years, 80; mob beats up, 221; model, plays prank on town, 162; model, protected, 8; morally conflicted, 58; must take monthly shots, 74; naive, 374; nearly illiterate, surly, 145; neighbor, fancy dresser, 344; never loses hope, 108; new, across the street, 245; new in school, 309; new in town, alluring, 269; newly initiated into manhood, 384; obedient but inquisitive, 289; with Obsessive Compulsive Disorder, relapses, 186; often beaten up, 343; often truant from school, 221; older forgoes college to care for younger brothers, 226; ordered to steal Shakespeare's new play, *Hamlet*, 317; passionate about baseball, 125; physically abused by father, 129; popular jock, 387; prays even for stray animals, 226; precocious, 286; pretends to be deaf and dumb, 108; pretends to be doctor, 345; rapes girl, later appears at school, 157; rebellious, iconoclastic, bored, 74; recalls every conversation, 342; red-haired artist, 260; resentful, 324; returns from detention facility angry, mean, 226; returns to age of twelve, 81; rivals for starting pitcher, 134; rivals over girl, 134; science genius, 309; scrawny, splay-eared, 342; sealed alive in burial vault, 243; searches for promised spell, 119; seeming tough, actually responsible and loving, 38; sentenced to death, 84; serious, stoic, 273; shy, introverted, 336; simple, earnest, 336; skeptic, 166; skinny, nerdy, 309; sloppy, disrespectful, 210; small but quick, 39, 143; small, handicapped, 19; sneaks away to Mount Saint Helens, 307; son of school principal, 224, 402; space alien, has misgivings about destroying humanity, 75; spunky, sympathetic protagonist, 117; studious, control freak, 380; suffers from guilt over accident, 247; sympathetic to doomed cattle, becomes vegetarian, 345; teaches girl to read sacred texts, 329; teaches rabbi English and baseball, 325; teenage, rebellious, 48; think of selves as outcasts, 309; thought to be a girl, 302; thought dead, 75; three brothers, slaves, sold to Alabama, 339; tough, often whipped in school, 221; trained in swordplay and acting, 116; troubled, 270; two-faced, deceitful, 302; unlikable, 35; uses drugs, 364; waiter at father's restaurant, 348; wants to be basketball hero, steal the show, 245; wants father's attention for basketball, 245; in wheelchair from polio, 169; white lives with Indian friend's sister, 87; working class, feels looked down upon, 355; works hard to help mother in house and with errands, 343. *See also* children

Boys at Work, 331

Boy Who Saved Baseball, The, 293

Brad (*Leaving Fishers*), 196

Brad (*The Perks of Being a Wallflower*), 270

Braddock, Pennsylvania, late twentieth century, 17

BRADLEY, MARION ZIMMER, *40*, 139

BRADSHAW, GILLIAN, *40*, 304

Brae family, 104

Brahman, father-in-law is, 149

"brainbox," Mentally Gifted Minors, 364

brain damage, slight, 298

brains: half undeveloped, 3; metal obstruction found in boy's, 80

Bramble Farm, 9

Brandon Hill, 366

Branko, 72

Bransby, Uncle Valentine, 371

Bransby family, 2, 170, 294, 371

Brant, sly man dressed in black, 297

Branwell Zamborska, 61, 319

BRANWEN, *41*, 205

Brashear, John, 17

BRAVERMAN, *41*, 151

Brazil, father takes darker sister to, 50

Brazilian boy, in United States, 387

Brazos River, 393

BREAKING RANK, *41*, 287

Bread Winner, The, 392

Breck Hunter, 102, 192

Brenda, 275

breeder, licensed private, 96

breeding facilities, for endangered species, 96,

Brian, 380

Briana, 121

Brian Brae, 104

Brian Green, 49

59; grows close to son, 393; handsome, charming con man, 184; handsome surgeon, 363; hard-drinking, often absent, 221; hardscrabble, penny-pinching, irascible, 134; harsh toward son, 118; has AIDS, 395; has alcoholism, 203; has heart attack, 185; has "principles," 204; head custodian, 71; high school science teacher, African American, 37; hill farmer, 19; history teacher, 252; ill, 127; impractical, ineffective, 252; Indian and white, now friends, 169; insurance agent, 109; jailed for helping Palestinian refugee, 132; jazz trombonist, 321; Jewish, died in search for grandmother, 369; killed by stray bullet, 346; killed in accident, 127; killed in Lakota raid, 300; killed in riot, 23; lawyer, 79, 134; leaves for Florida, 221; likely murderer, 223; lived with an alcoholic, died, 78; lumber camp superintendent, 202; maintenance man, 67; man says he is boy's, lies, 316; marries again, 202, 329; master of slaves, 313; mathematician and astronomer, 304; melts away, 72; merchant, wealthy, 294; murdered by bandits, 93; murderer, serving life sentence, 199; murder suspect, 269; ne'er-do-well, 165; nonbeliever, 23; not speaking to mother, 404; oil man, 101; operates movie theater, 338; opposes boy's pitching with left hand, calls it hand of Devil, 58; Palestinian doctor, 132; papermaker, 116; perhaps in Rome, 7; physically abusive, 32; poet, gray bearded, 166; police officer, 6, 247; preacher, 218; presumed, famous musician and band leader, 44; prince of Genovia, 280; in prison, 361; proper private school headmaster, 55; proud, independent Indian chief, 87; proud, independent rancher, 87; psychiatrist, 333; punk hooligan, 65, 178; radio personality and Pulitzer Prize poet, 343; reappears after more than a year, 266; recants of duplicitous behavior, 334; reclusive, 321; refuses to let girl go with hunters, 300; rejecting, 282; remote, 51, 355; rescued by Sasquatch, 307; rides rails to find work, 362; RIFd (fired), sent to Idaho, 229; of rock star's retarded son, 364; roofer, abandons family, 76; rude, self-important, 115; sailmaker, 21; saved from hanging by ghost of dead wife, 117; scribe, 149; sheriff, 117; shuns responsibility for baby, 326; single parent, 156, 168, 202, 212, 221, 249; sometimes in jail, 221; step, abusive, 330; step, dies of heart attack, 344; step, shipping clerk at Saks Fifth avenue, 343; step, threatening to girl both sexually and physically, 279; step, tries to humiliate boy, 344; step, verbally and physically abusive, 343; stingy, nagging, 224; stunned by wife's death, 104; structural steel-stress engineer, 126; suddenly reappears, 184; suicide, 183; Sunday School Superintendent, 236; surgeon, 224, 237; surrogate, farm steward, 327; surrogate, grandfather, 128, 247; surrogate, Shakespeare is for boy, 183; takes darker sister to Brazil, 50; teacher, furious at treatment of sons, is also beaten up, 274; tea merchant, 116; television sportscaster, 351; traditional, bigoted, 368; traditional Korean attitudes, 242; transferred when fantasy closes, 196; unaware of child, 65; uninvolved, 172; university research scientist, 319; unsympathetic, 403; village smith, 355; villain, most interesting character, 185; verbally abusive, 330, 338; very ill, 342; wants older son to be basketball star, 245; Washington lobbyist, 212; weak, wandering in wits, 295; wealthy, powerful lawyer, 286; whereabouts unknown by son, 360; white professor, 17; white, takes black son for personal servant, 360; widower, farm manager, African American, 73; widower, marries again, 202; widower trader, 328; wishes to return to homeland of Palestine, 132; womanizer, 363

father–son novels: 58, 134, 306, 329, 342, 343

Fatmira, 4

Fattest Boy in the World, 390

Favorite Tales of Edgar Allan Poe, 54, 137

fay ce que vondras, motto of club, 204

FBI: agents, 23, 25, 48, 257; deputy director, 392; director, ruthless, 24; files, read by artificial intelligence, 97; investigating self-aware computer program, 97; in kidnapping case, 388; Special Agent Irene Rivers, 159; Special Agent Michael Tate, 250; Special Agent Steven Crow, 44, 307; Ten Most Wanted List, 24

gender orientation: boy comes out as gay, 387; boy identifies his straight, 135

gene altering, 246; experiment, illegal, 92

General Motors plant, 222

generational tension, Korean American, 242

gene replacement, for leukemia, 191

genetically improved people, 191

genetic engineering, gone wrong, 375

genetic experiment, Eden Project, 181

genetic material, for endangered species, 97

genetic researchers: on Hiva, 375; on Pandora, 181

Geneva Shepard, 260

Gene Walenski, 42

geniuses: computer, 179; mathematical, forgetful, impractical, abstracted, 304; mechanical, 211; science, boy, 309

genocide, Armenian by Turks, 108

Genova, 264

George Boleyn, 16

George Bird Grinnell, ed., *Forest and Stream*, 198

George Hinkle, 330

George Read, 214

Georgetown area, Washington, D.C., early twentieth century, 293

George Washington Tea, 402

Georgia
—mid-twentieth century: Atlanta, 381; Kinship, 184
—late twentieth century: Atlanta, 72

Georgia Hansen, 49, 244

Georgie Pinkus, 387

German people, in United States, 148

Germany, origin of Thulist Movement, 140

germs, boy fears, 186

gers, huts, rounded, felt-covered, 160

Gervase Fitz Randolph, 282

GETTING IN, 40, *114*

Gettysburg and Bull Run, mid-nineteenth century, 326

Ghan, 384

ghetto, Jewish, 357

Ghost Canoe, 147

GHOST IN THE TOKAIDO INN, THE, 116, 150

Ghostlight, 40

ghost novels: of hanged man and of dead wife, 117; haunted plantation; 137; in an inn, 116

GHOST OF A HANGED MAN, 117, 373

ghosts: of dead wife saves husband, 117; girl orders to depart, 138; girl thinks new girl is of dead sister, 293; of grandfather, 138; of hanged man who kills those who convicted him, 117; "laid" by rural ceremony, 101; of overseer, 137; seen in inn, 116; sinks into floor, 116; tries to kill sheriff, 117. *See also* spirits; visions

Ghosts of Now, The, 246

ghost stories, 100; girl tells, 116

Ghost Town, 246

"ghost tree," sycamore, 346

giants: emerge from hiding, 206; killed or disappeared, 206; reappearing, 318

GIDEON'S PEOPLE, 117, 161, 223

Gideon Stoltzfuss, 117, 161

GIFF, PATRICIA REILLY, *118,* 249

GIFT, THE, 119, 254

Gifted and Talented Class, 107

Gift of Magic, origin of, 119

gifts: Bible, 379; at birth, of being obedient, 90; boys take their ill mother, 274; for dead wife, 55; for girl, stolen, 55; grizzly claw necklace, to Pawnee boy, 301; new brown sweater, 379; perfume and bubble bath, 274; puppy, 155; shop, 152; from retired school principal, 6; $2,000, 6

Giganta, the sideshow woman, 202

Gigi McCloy, 72

Gilbert the Fleming, 283

Gilda Bender, 124

Gillian Sporer, 71

Gillivray, Sim, 195, 228

GILMORE, KATE, 96, *120*

GILSTRAP, JOHN, 24, *120*, 240

Gina Styan, 146

GINGER, *120,* 172

Ginger Sumerell, 101

Ginny Dorris, 355

Giovanna Ferrante, 96

Girard, Stephen, 103

girlfriends: dependent on boyfriend, 78; father acquires, 364; father's crazy, 110; former, brother's, 261; former, drunk and sick at dance, 379; really half sister, 136; supportive, 78

Girl in Blue, 293

Girl in the Plastic Cage, The, 199

GIRL NAMED DISASTER, A, 101, *121*
GIRLS, THE, *121*, 189

girls: abused, impregnated by German consul, 108; acidly clever, 295; actions symbolize spirit of Christmas, 203; active in school, 76; African American, suspected of murder, 74; African American/Native American/ Caucasian, 395; albino, considered a freak, 202; angry, disobeys and flies, 244; anorexic, 50; approaching puberty, fears banishment, 384; arsonist, 359; assertive, 125, 330, 355; beautiful, patronizing, 201; beautiful blond, honors student, pianist, and beauty pageant winner, 201; becomes healer, 329; becomes preacher, 195; becomes very popular, then is hated, 337; believes she caused aunt's death, 54; believes she caused cousin's death, 54; betrothed to King Francis I of France, 215; big, dirty, mean high school, 402; big, strong, tough, 153; big-girl-on-campus in high school, 304, 336; on bike, struck by car, 247; biracial, African American/Caucasian, 50; birdlike, 78; birth-damaged, 3; black, caught by white policeman, 294; black, introduces white boy to sexual fondling, 221; black, swim in whites-only pool, 294; bossy, psychoanalyzes friends, 280; boys are rivals for, 134; brave, loyal, literate, 91; brave, loud, athletic, 295; called bossy, 287; in charge of home, 76; childlike yet knowing, 350; Chinese, allowed to develop intelligence, 353; chooses to live with single-parent mother, 387; clarinetist, 245; clique leader, manipulative, cruel, 121; collapses on way to school, 389; compulsive obsessive, 50; considered fast and easy, 14, 346; considered possessed, 329; courageous, intelligent, 351; crippled, 315; cynical, 3; cynical, angry, beautiful, 78; daughter of papermaker, 116; declared illegitimate by father, 215; despised, leaves village, 329; determined that brother becomes star pitcher, 153; develop greater self-esteem, 260; disorganized, 82; disoriented, 48; drunk and on drugs, 125; embarrassed by eccentric parents, 305; especially defiant, sixteen, 27; especially willful and stubborn, 91; excluded from sleepover, 121; extremely noncon-

forming, 336; extremely small, 398; extremely thin, 237; failing algebra, 280; fashion conscious, 96; fast runners, 67; fat Arab, 280; feels abandoned by friend, 248; feels isolated, restricted, 244; feels she has lost parents' love, 194; feisty, 101; finds comfort and self-esteem in baby, 157; find three furry little animals in woodpile, 257; first girl baseball player on boy's team, 45; flees to California and father, 51; flirts with Clan gang member, 42; fluent in Norther and Souther languages, 91; foster, 315; four months old, 65; frank, resilient, 151; gets thinner and thinner, 389; gifted, thought retarded, 3; gifted, tomboy, 195; given to good works, 378; goes up in bosun's chair, 380; gypsy, 117; half orphan, 27; half-orphaned African American, 74; has bruises on legs, 389; has fits, thought possessed by devils, 329; heir to throne of European principality, 280; hides in hills from intruder, 257; hired, for German immigrant pioneers, 148; homeschooled, 336, 342, 359; ignoring former idol, 243; ill, life saved, 345; illegitimate, 244; illiterate, 179; imaginative, dramatic, 361; inarticulate, awkward, 54; independent, 90, 101; independent, quiet African American, 367; initially hostile, 79; intelligent, prickly, 17; intelligent but perceived as a loser, 323; invisible adviser, 194; Irish, thinks streets in Brooklyn made of diamonds, 249; Jewish, aged by conditions in slave-labor camp, 358; Jewish, caught in roundup by German soldiers, 357; Jewish, declines in health in slave-labor camp, 358; Jewish, new in neighborhood, 362; Jewish prisoner, hides other prisoners' possessions for safekeeping, 358; Jewish sisters, emigrate to Canada, 358; Jewish slave laborer, frail, 357; joins Joshua's followers, 329; judged mentally gifted, 364; kept from school to help at home, 361; kidnapped at three, 43, 165; late-blooming, 242; level-headed, intelligent, 407; likes desert and doing kind deeds, 337; little, runs away on Christmas Eve, 286; lively, fun loving, 9; lively, wants to be a doctor, 354; lonely, isolated, 202; loses weight rapidly, 50; lost in wilds, 122; in love with sea, 380; loves girls (*continued*): movies, knows lines by heart, 338; manipulative, selfish, 304; marginalized, 337, 341; matures after brother's death, 350; mentally ill, 72, 153, 165; Middle Eastern, 351; more modern than medieval, 335; most popular in school, 387; mute, frail, 185; naked in boat, pretends to be Death Maiden, 91; new in school, 75, 196, 201, 293, 336, 402; nine, held by police during Civil Rights protests, 37; nonconforming, disappears, 337; no one else sees but protagonists, 194, 260; obese, abusive, 390; at odds, become friends, 76; often disappears, 153; outgoing, 125; outgoing, slightly wild, yearns for father, 184; outsider or "stray," 341; personable, "normal," 76; pious, 79; plagued by fears, 185; plain, outspoken, odds out, 363; popular, good student, 203; popular outsider, for a time, 337; practical, interested in archaeology, 361; practical, thoughtful, 95; proud of privilege, snobbish, 93; raven-haired, nurses boy, 166; reflects on good days with mother, 309; rejected from baseball team because is a girl, 153; rejected in new school, very fat, 201; responsible for boy's death, 351; responsible for family, 80; responsible for household, 70; runaway from family rules, 389; runner, 243; rushed off to high school, 402; searches for information about palace structure, 384; self-assured, pretty, 333; serving, Irish immigrant, 306; severely burned, 359; sharp-eyed, ironic observer, 352; shy, 398; shy, bookish, 137; shy, introverted, 248; six, drowns, 293; slapped by school leader at ball, 337; slave, literate and learned in Latin and Greek, 133; slave, smuggled to Canada, 339; small, diffident, 386; small, emotionally bitter, 366; snotty, 280; socially preoccupied, 81; softball player, 45; spies on Secret Society, 248; spirited, 259; spunky, 363; spunky, independent, 74; spunky, intelligent, 384; spunky, resourceful slave, 339; stable, sensible, 48; stammers, 259; stands up to Union soldiers, 137; stoned by village women, 329; storyteller, 315; sturdy, sensible, 22; suddenly assertive, 280; suddenly popular, 280; surly antagonistic toward father, 212; suspected

of stealing ruby, proved innocent, 116; Taiga Indian, joins elders of tribe, 279; tall, assertive, athletic, 293; tall, strong, athletic, 72; tattooed, unconventional in dress, 76; teenage, sulky, 225; tells outlandish stories, 389; ten, emissary to Columbus, 264; thinks of self as "vessel of sins," 194; thought immature and strange, by siblings, 54; tortured, in Uruguay, 363; tough, experienced, 36; tough, world-weary, 186; troublemaker in school, 76; unaware of developing sexuality, 202; understands language of trees, 206; unfailingly cheerful, 379; unwed mother, 79; unwed mother, determinedly cheerful, 79; vain, shallow, beautiful, 286; veils self, 329; very dark skinned, 323; Victorian, rattle-headed beauty, 359; visionary, 158; wealthy, homeschooled, 342; wears blood-stained panties, 389; whiny, self-absorbed, 280; whiny, willfully disobedient, 248; with wild tendencies, 204; worried, angry, flies to London to be with father, 35; yearns for father, 184. *See also* children

Girls' Rehabilitation Center, 27

GIRL WHO LOVED TOM GORDON, THE, 122, 183

Git Out the horse, 60

Glass, Ethan, 22, 81, 94, 179

Glass family, 1, 13, 168, 371

Gleick, William, 198

Glen Jaffee, 179, 372

Glenn Newlin, 78, 109

Globe Theatre, 182, 317, 372

Gloria, 240, 288

Gloria festival, 19

Gloria Wells, 96

Glory Field, The, 235

glove, metallic, elbow-length, is really BB gun, 75

glue, dumped on Halloween trickster, 402

goal, of quest, fortune, 17

GO AND COME BACK, 1, 123

"go and come back," traditional Isabo Indian parting words to friends, 123

go-betweens, between Abelard and Eloise, 333

goblins, 206, 297, 318, 365. *See also* dwarfs; dwellers

GOCHALLA XUNDUNISSE, 113, *123*

Green family, 305

Greengage Orchard, 185

Greengard Orchards, 104

Green Hornet, The, 193

Green Knight, 334

Green Mile, The, 183

Green Thumb, 353

Greenwar, 128

Greenwich Village, New York City, late twentieth century, 136, 279, 391

greenwitches, 296

Greg Thompson, 260

Grennan, Grady, 364

Gretchen Carstenson, 387

Greydawn Moors, seaport city, 297

Grey family, 63, 112, 164, 213, 362

Grey King, The, 63

GRIFFIN, ADELE, *130,* 260, 329

grillmen: for diner, 41; tall, skinny, 151

GRIMES, MARTHA, *130,* 152

Grinnell, George Bird, ed., *Forest and Stream,* 198

Griswald family, 55, 227, 232, 306

grizzly bear, killed by girl, 301

Grizzly fire, 301

grizzly robe, boy retrieves for girl, 301

grocery store manager, 222

Grolier's Encyclopedia, 97

GROOMS, ANTHONY, 37, *131*

Grooms, Tony M., 131

grotesque woman, ill, with beautiful daughter, 332

group homes, 59. *See also* homes

group therapy, 208

Growing Season, 49

Growing Up in Colonial America, 28

growing-up novels, boy's, by age: eight, 343; ten, 168; eleven, 235, 288, 321, 324; twelve, 60, 125, 148, 193; thirteen, 58, 270, 340; fourteen, 74, 134, 217; fifteen, 141, 156, 221, 245, 316; sixteen, 135, 145, 302, 378; seventeen, 99, 275; eighteen, 44, 109, 288, 340; eighteen to nineteen, 142; nineteen, 45. *See also* coming-of-age novels

growing-up novels, girl's, by age: five on, 353; seven, 202; eleven, 254, 395; twelve, 93, 171, 249, 293, 337, 366, 387, 389; thirteen, 54, 104, 149, 355, 380; fourteen, 18, 135, 140, 147, 181, 248, 279, 351; fifteen, 138, 156,

184, 300, 396, 402; sixteen, 150, 237, 244, 375; seventeen, 390; eighteen, 403. *See also* coming-of-age novels

growing-up novels: boy, in teens, 87, 199; boy and girl, 66, 384; boys', one twelve, and one sixteen, 117; five boys, five girls, 387; girl's, in teens, 177, 363; girl's, preteen, 68. *See also* coming-of-age novels

Gruber, Solly, 76

G. T. Stoop, 41, 150

Guadalcanal, 143, 193

Guaranteed Security Associates, 25

Guardian Angel Man, 95

Guardian Dragon, 328

guardians: abusive, alcoholic uncle, 214, 240; arrogant, 204; neglectful, 276; uncle of girl, 3. *See also* wards

guardianship, transferred to sympathetic lawyer, 127

guardian spirits, sarcastic, scornful, 259

guards: armed, at Armageddon camp, 23; boy is skilled point, 245; bribed, 39; detention home abusive, 272; detention home, hired to kill boy, 214; detention home, killed, 214; security, school, sinister, 75, 129; stabbed to death, 240

Guatemala: 162; immigrant boy from, 9

Gudger, Dave, 100

Guerric, 91

Guests, 83

Guevara, Che, 63, 362

guide, mountain, found dead, 256

Guidry family, 221, 229

guilt: boy suffers for accident, 247; brings on panic attack, 346; driving boy to recklessness, 100; girl feels for death of aunt and cousin, 54; girl feels for father's death, 346; for surviving fatal accidents, 14

guitars, homeless Guatemalan's, 162

gul-gyan, dowry necklaces, 290

Gull the white puppy, 155

gummies, old persons, 191

Gung-Fu, art of self-defense, 52

gunpowder, just coming into use, 91

guns: BB, in form of glove, 75; boy hears boy gang leader has, 325; carried to avenge girl, 143; hidden, 362; hidden under woodpile, 346; loaded Winchester, Grandma keeps, 128; mentally ill girl acquires, 153; murder

Raymond McPheron, 274

Raymond Nelson, 110

Raymond Providence, 101

Raynes family, 259

Rayon Taylor, 395

Ray Slaight, 388

Razim, 289

Razzle, 397

readers: girl and gas station manager, 168; self-taught, Siamese twin Eng, 53

Read, George, 214

reading: ability useful, earns acclamation, 297; African American girl and white girl enjoy, 67; Brahman teaches widow, 149; self-taught, 92; wide, especially poetry, 3; widow teaches rickshaw boy, 149

reading and writing, American girl teaches Mende girl, 179

"Reading Works," 28

readjustment, agonizing after kidnapping, 388

real estate: developers, 371; developers, scheming, 334; developers, smooth-talking, sharp-dressing, 333

Real Fresh Dairy, 151

realistic novels: death of mother, 387; dysfunctional family 81; gritty, 230; ironic, 89; period, 222; psychological, 69, 84, 196, 208, 236, 388, 390; sociological, 196, 349; surviving under oppression, 4. *See also* particular types, e.g., adventure novels; problem novels

realizations, girl to be sacrificed, 301

Real McCoy, The, *341*

REAPPEARANCE OF SAM WEBBER, THE, 111, *288*

reappearances: father who abandoned family, 39; shy girl into family, 399

Rear-View Mirrors, 106

Rebecca Randolph, 148

REBEL, 289, 392

Rebels, American Civil War, sympathizers with, 2

rebellion against overlords, 113

receipts, clue to killer, 59

reception, joyous, girl expects, doesn't receive, 337

recipes: head each chapter, 345; for nonweeping meringue, 6

recital chambers, in Eyrie, 20

recklessness, brings on disasters, 99

Reckoning, The, 267

Reclamation, 406

recluses: mother, 338; old Indian keeps nature ways, 278; Taiga Indian woman in woods, 278; wealthy, 206; woman in mountains, 33. *See also* hermits

reconciliations: boy and father, 379; effected between father and gardener, 334; foreseen for boy's two peoples, 105; girl and Muscovitz family, 280; with girlfriend, 100; husband and wife, contemplated, 334; mother and daughter, 195, 389; started, 243

records: biggest, longest, greatest, 211; frequently quoted, 212; for standing motionless, 212; for tossing eggs, 211

recovery, of stolen Arabian pony, 87

recruits: commandeered by soldiers, 160; for jobs in space, 146; tough, black, for space job, 146

Redbird, 54

Redbird Trail, The, 54

Red Earth, White Earth, 385

redemptions: boy saves girl and thus performs act of, 287; of Grampa for unsatisfactory past life, 247; Grampa's attempt at, 128; too sudden, 142

Red Fish, Washington, 364

red-haired persons: African American girl, 254; aunt, 54; boy, fifteen, 38; boy, seventeen, 73; boy, thirteen, 319; Elizabeth I of England, 311; girl, classmate of boy, twelve, 125; girl, college student, 22; girl, fifteen, 29; girl, sixteen, kidnapped, 165; girl, new in clique, 121; girl, twenty, 153; kidnapped girl, 376; mother, 338; mother's boyfriend, 157, 228; schoolgirl, 66; short boyfriend, 269; son of innkeeper, becomes king-consort, 91; Uruguayan girl, 210; young lady, 373

Red-Haired Beverly, 125

Red Hankins, 202

red herrings, bloody underpants, 253

Red Knot, 263, 268

Red Mountains, home of semi-nomadic Dalriadans, 104, 185

Redshaw, Jamie, 316

Red Sox, baseball players, 125

secrets: Achilles's vulnerability lies in heel, 159; about airmen's missions, told to child, 111; community, 342; Corvette, kept from wife, 172; from father, mix-up on SAT exam, 115; girl learns family, 244; good deeds, 6; information regarding Sasquatch, 307; paternity of son, 57; rooms and passageways inside walls, 398; sex with brother's wife, 115; sister will read poem from bridge, 4; from son, loss of company, 115; swimming lessons not from sister, 139; told to impress sister's friends, 111; visits to refugee camp, 368

sects: millennialist, 292. *See also* cults

security employees, 179

security guards, mall, 351

seductions: girl of boyfriend, 269; for information, 258; by minister, 80; planned, 391; unsuccessful, 155. *See also* molestations; rapes

SEEDFOLKS, 106, *313*

Seelie Court, 308

Sees Behind Trees, 83

Sees-in-the Dark, name for woman, 264

Seikei, 116

Seikko Hattori, 106

seizures: boy has several times every day, 342; boy suffers, 81; grand mal, 191

self-esteem: enhanced, 80, 171, 177; girl finds in baby, 157; girls' elevated, 260; girl's raised, 55; increased, 289; improved, 136; low, 323; raised, 262. *See also* self-identity

self-identity: boy clings to, 253. *See also* self-esteem

self-mutilation: girl scratches face, 222; girl slashes face, 70; ice skater, 208

self-sacrifice: alien, to save girl from life of servitude, 73; dwarf in Cauldron of Death, 318; to save world, attempted, 20

SELIM BEY, 19, 108, *313*

selling child, attempted, 178

Selwyn, 243

Semorrah, wicked city, 19, 285

Senator from Illinois, chairman of Senate Judiciary Committee, 24

SEND ONE ANGEL DOWN, 310, *313*

Senegalese man, stripper in Japan, 106

senior centers, dance at, 352

SENNA, DANZY, 50, *314*

Sensitive (psychic), young woman, 140

sensory experiences, created by mindprobe needles, 191

sensual pleasure of touching, discovered, 312

sentences: community service, 42; lenient, 67; six months, 39; six years at Louisiana Youth Authority facility, 200

Sephonie, 104

sequels, to *Cinderella*, 90, 174

Serbs, in Kosovo, 4

Sergeant Henry Stuter, 250

Sergeant Picou, corrupt policeman, 221

series books

—Adventures of the American Agent Abroad: *LONDON BLOOD: FURTHER ADVENTURES OF THE AMERICAN AGENT ABROAD*, 204

—Alice McKinley: *OUTRAGEOUSLY ALICE*, *261*

—Arthurian Tales Fictionalized: *THE SAVAGE DAMSEL AND THE DWARF*, 307; *THE SQUIRE, HIS KNIGHT, & HIS LADY*, 334

—Billy Baggs: *HARD BALL*, 134

—Elemental Masters: *THE SERPENT'S SHADOW*, 314

—Princess Diaries: *THE PRINCESS DIARIES*, *279*

—Rei Shimura: *THE FLOATING GIRL*, *106*

sermons: attack institutionalized religions, 192; charismatic, near Sea of Galilee, 192; translated by African teacher as spoken, 277

SERPENT'S SHADOW, THE, 190, *314*

servants: African American slave to spoiled white girl, 133; Armenian refugee boy, to doctor, 108; at dance school, 21; of flamboyant noble, 205; fleeing girl works as, 91; half human, half giant, faithful, 384; loyal, 93; mute peasant boy, 331; of noble, disaffected, 205; only friend of princess, 174; resents bosses nephew, 290. *See also* cooks; cleaning women; housekeepers; maids

Service, Robert, fictionalized, 166

serving girl, Irish immigrant, 306

sessions, discussion on timely topics at girls' detention center, 27

Seth, slave woman's husband, 360

setups, by girl and police, 350

Seventeen Against the Dealer, 377

from poem by character, 18; ways of Indians worked into narration skillfully, engrossing, 269

style, structure: alternating chapters, in present and past times, 250; alternating chapters tell two stories (eventually united), 384; alternating scenes of history and fantasy, 264; asides and editorial comments, 7; case histories, essentially, 86, 209; confusing, several narrators supplement main one, 184; demanding, 250; diaries, too detailed to be credible as such, 280; diary entries, inserted into linear narrative, 311; disjointed, 200; dreamlike sequences, 397; entirely dialogue, 225; episode per month, 402; episodes, seven, self-contained, 402; epistolary, 10, 270; excessive flashbacks interrupt action, 355; fantasy aspects in realistic novel, 260; film script, 230, 231; flashbacks, 73, 142, 230, 235, 362; flashbacks, life with lost girl's family, 123; flashbacks, story told partially in, 24; flashbacks, to year protagonist is eleven, 37; foreshadowing, shots of death to come, 158; frame narrative, awaiting death of grandmother, 100; frame story, meeting with childhood fiancé, 354; illogical, 350; interviews, drawings, newspaper clippings, 211; italicized memories, 389; journal entries, 80, 99; letters, 271; long flashbacks in writing, 15; many quick scene switches, 357; motifs repeat and provide unity, 148; much scene switching, 232; occasional monologues, 230; opening disclaimer, 98; outer and layered inner stories, 119; quest pattern, 159; references to factual information, 333; seven books, each a flashback, 277; self-contained episodes, 402; short, fast-moving vignettes, 364; short, snappy chapters, 77; story told by old woman to granddaughter, 161; story told in retrospect, 338; story within a story, 138, 148, 169, 195; told in e-mails, 97; voiced words and thought ideas hard to separate, 213

style, symbolism: battles, 38; boxing is metaphor for home life, 343; Christian on sword, 116; night-blooming flowers, 3; obvious, barn raising, 250; obvious, boat, 381; obvious, homeless bird, 150; obvious, labored, 94; obvious, steel strengthened by fire, 108; parallel between diminishing tribe and ragged old panther, 279; parallel between human and animal dogs, 173

style, theme: books are to be cherished for themselves, 298; change for better is gradual, 248; children's social services examined, 241; complex reasoning, 265; concept of truth, 247; conclusion morally slanted, 75; contemporary excess, emphasis on looks, 201; cooperation, hard work, dedication to common good, vital, 182; courage and perseverance, will to survive, 123; didactic intent, concerning Arab–Israeli relations, 132; didactic novel, Jews and Amish contrasted, 118; didactic novel, relationships between parents and children; 118; dilemma well described, 58; effect on family of mental illness well depicted, 154; evil wasteful, 120; family love and caring for one another, 184; fictionalized religious treatise, 195; futility of hatred and revenge, 120; generational conflict, Korean American, 242; goodness of life, 387; good picture of treatment of persons handicapped with cerebral palsy, 272; heavy-handed social comment, 201; irony of actual white ways as compared to projected beliefs, 279; issues of compassion, ethics, human rights, 363; least likely succeed, 297; live up to high moral principles, 222; message obvious, 118; morality of euthanasia, 343; moral question of attitudes toward athletics and of athlete, 263; neighborliness and family love, 249; neighborliness and true concern, 184; overly obvious, 55; private and public well-being interrelated, 257; power of story, 315; purpose of life, 161; racial superiority and cult mentality, 75; respect for nature, 198; respect for other cultures, 248; social, economic, ethnic distinctions, 388; social and religious commentary, 193; social comment, deploring gap between rich and poor, 146; social comment, examines services to children, 241; social comment, much, about poor school, 146; social comment, scathing, 363; social comment, subtle, 207; social commentary about exploiting rural area for development, 372;

Talk Before You Sleep, 32

Tallahassee, Florida, 67

tall-tale novel, Western, 344

TALON ANGLER, 52, 83, 84, 287, 348

Tam, 181

Tamar, king, 161

Tammy Warren, 89

Tameside, synonym for present-day United States, 393

Tammany Hall, 83

Tam Sinclair, 86

TANGERINE, 34, 348

Tangerine County, Florida, 348

TaNeece, 59

tanks, Serb, threaten village, 5

Tao Ailin, 353

Tao family, 353

tapes, comforting, 78

Taran Wanderer, 8

Tara Sullivan, 78, 185, 303

tarts, for Daughters of American Revolution George Washington Tea, 402

Tasha Dawson, 157, 228, 234

Tashian family, 108

Tata Kuvudundu, 277

Tata Nda, 277, 286

Tate, Michael, 250

tatterdamalion: named Ariel, 273; small force for good, 187

tattoos, face, elaborate, 195

Tatum family, 9

taunts: "janitor's daughter," 71; by loud sex with mother, 38

tavern, slaves work in, 339

Tavyan, the merchant, 91

Taw the horse, 60

tax collector, English among Irish, 249

taxes, raised prohibitively, 12

Tayla, 21

Taylor, 172

Taylor, Billy, 44

Taylor family (Chasing Redbird), 54

Taylor family (The Window), 395

T-Backs, T-Shirts, COAT, and Suit, 188

Tchaikovsky's 1812 Overture, 306

TDA (Temporary Duty Assignment), 404

tea, Daughters of American Revolution, 402

teachers: advanced-English, befriends weird boy, 270; African American, 2; African American, disfigured, 265; African village, 195, 276; aid to slave escape, 169; algebra, dating student's mother, 280; art, 227; at exclusive boys' school, 233; beautiful new art, 55; biology, 146; blamed and tried for deaths, 56; boy's aunt, 345; college of agriculture, 198; deceptive, 92; dedicated, 89; dies in prison, 56; dismissed, 82; engages a good lawyer for boy, 221; English, 142; English, new, 323; of English, gay, 387; falsely accused, 82; flower arranging, 106; former English, 261; high school, 124, 210; high school English, 208, 225; high school history, 89, 252, 273; high school science, 186, 303; infuriated at boy's insults, 145; likens black student to African pygmies, 343; literature, at exclusive boys' school, 233; missionary school, 354; mother, second grade, 237; odd assortment, 145; of parenting class, 157, 234; religion, 82; religion, interested in plight of refugees, 174; romance of, private school for boys, 55; second grade, 57; takes in homeless boy, 221; takes special interest in impoverished, wrongly accused boy, 228; tall, competent woman, 273; testifies for boy in murder trial, 230; Vietnam veteran, 265; visits home to try to help new girl, 293; white, racist, 343. See also headmasters; instructor; mentors; tutors

teaching: boy to drive, 6; reading to mute boy, 332; socially inept boy to act normal, 270

Teal Benton, 223, 338

Teal Trust, 181

teams, three person, for virtual war, 374

tear gas, shot at Kosovo schoolchildren, 4

Tearle Lynn, 396

technology: banned, 23; scorned, 166

Teen Angels Series, 31

teeth, capped in stainless steel, 134; injured by foul ball, 134

Tel Aviv University, 102

telekinesis, exhibited by Trash, 145

teleporting machines, 356

television: anchor, respected, 192; broken, 225; commentators, 124; investigative reporter for, 7; network, 192; show, Lilly Tells It Like It Is, 203; stations, 351; trash program, 85

Teller, 119

ABOUT THE AUTHORS

ALETHEA K. HELBIG is Professor of English Language and Literature at Eastern Michigan University. With Agnes Regan Perkins, she has authored such books as *Dictionary of American Children's Fiction, 1995–1999: Books of Recognized Merit* (2002), *Dictionary of American Children's Fiction, 1990–1994: Books of Recognized Merit* (1996), *Dictionary of American Children's Fiction, 1985–1989: Books of Recognized Merit* (1993), and *Dictionary of American Children's Fiction, 1960–1984: Books of Recognized Merit* (1986), all available from Greenwood Press.

AGNES REGAN PERKINS is Professor Emerita of English Language and Literature at Eastern Michigan University. With Alethea K. Helbig, she has authored such books as *Dictionary of American Children's Fiction, 1995–1999: Books of Recognized Merit* (2002), *Dictionary of American Children's Fiction, 1990–1994: Books of Recognized Merit* (1996), *Dictionary of American Children's Fiction, 1985–1989: Books of Recognized Merit* (1993), and *Dictionary of American Children's Fiction, 1960–1984: Books of Recognized Merit* (1986), all available from Greenwood Press.